FIX BAYONETS!
A ROYAL WELCH FUSILIER AT WAR,
1796-1815

BOOKS WRITTEN OR EDITED BY DONALD E. GRAVES

Century of Service: The History of the South Alberta Light Horse
Robin Brass Studio, 2005

More Fighting for Canada: Five Battles, 1760-1944
Robin Brass Studio, 2004

Another Place, Another Time: A U-boat Officer's Wartime Album
(with Werner Hirschmann) Robin Brass Studio, 2004

In Peril on the Sea: The Royal Canadian Navy and the Battle of the Atlantic
Canadian Naval Memorial Trust & Robin Brass Studio, 2003

C.P. Stacey. *Quebec 1759: The Siege and the Battle*
Edited and with new material by Donald E. Graves. Robin Brass Studio, 2002

Guns Across the River: The Battle of the Windmill, 1838
Friends of Windmill Point & Robin Brass Studio, 2001

Fighting for Canada: Seven Battles, 1758-1945
Robin Brass Studio, 2000

Field of Glory: The Battle of Crysler's Farm, 1813
Robin Brass Studio, 1999

J.Mackay Hitsman. *The Incredible War of 1812: A Military History*
Updated by Donald E. Graves. Robin Brass Studio, 1999

South Albertas: A Canadian Regiment at War
South Alberta Regiment Veterans Association & Robin Brass Studio, 1998, 2004

Where Right and Glory Lead! The Battle of Lundy's Lane, 1814
Robin Brass Studio, 1997

Soldiers of 1814: American Enlisted Men's Memoirs of the Niagara Campaign
Old Fort Niagara Press, 1996

Redcoats and Grey Jackets: The Battle of Chippawa, 1814
Dundurn Press, 1994

*Merry Hearts Make Light Days: The War of 1812 Journal of
Lieutenant John Le Couteur, 104th Foot*
Carleton University Press, 1993

Normandy 1944: The Canadian Summer
(with W.J. McAndrew and M.J. Whitby.) Art Global, 1993

"The Rocket's Red Glare:" Sir William Congreve and His Weapon System
Museum Restoration Service, 1989

**Major Thomas Pearson, 23rd Regiment of Foot,
Royal Welch Fusiliers, 1810**

Thomas Pearson sat for this miniature (signed in Halifax, Nova Scotia,
in 1811 by the artist Robert Field) shortly before he sailed for Portugal
in October 1810. Aged 29, Pearson had recently married Ann Eliza Coffin
of New Brunswick and this portrait was probably done because he was
leaving his bride for an active theatre of war. Compared with the 1805
portrait on page xxii, Pearson appears to have softened somewhat in the
intervening years but this may be a temporary aberration attributable to
his recent marriage. He would shortly be back at work doing what he did
best – killing Frenchmen – and about six months after sitting for this
portrait would win promotion for his part in the battle of Albuera, the
bloodiest engagement of the Peninsular War. (Courtesy, Royal Ontario
Museum (980.277), Toronto, Canada)

Donald E. Graves

Fix Bayonets!

A ROYAL WELCH FUSILIER AT WAR, 1796–1815

Being the Life and Times of
Lieutenant-General Sir Thomas Pearson, CB, KCH
1781–1847

Foreword by
Major-General J. P. Riley, DSO

Maps and diagrams by
Christopher Johnson

ROBIN BRASS STUDIO | SPELLMOUNT
Toronto | *Stroud*

ISBN-13: 978-1-896941-27-1

ISBN-10: 1-896941-27-3

First published 2006 by Robin Brass Studio Inc.
www.rbstudiobooks.com

First published in the UK in 2007
by Spellmount Limited
The Mill, Brimscombe Port
Stroud, Gloucestershire. GL5 2QG

Tel: 01453 883300
Fax: 01453 883233
www.spellmount.com

Printed and bound in Canada by Friesens, Altona, Manitoba

Library and Archives Canada Cataloguing in Publication

Graves, Donald E. (Donald Edward)
    Fix bayonets! : a Royal Welch Fusilier at war, 1796-1815 / Donald E. Graves.

Includes bibliographical references and index.
ISBN 978-1-896941-27-1 (bound)

    1. Pearson, Thomas, 1781-1847. 2. Great Britain. Army. Royal Welch Fusiliers
– Biography. 3. Great Britain. Army – Officers – Biography. 4. Napoleonic Wars,
1800-1815 – Personal narratives, British. 5. Canada – History – War of 1812 – Personal
narratives, British. I. Title.

U55.P43G73 2006   355'.0092   C2006-904195-4

British Library Cataloguing in Publication Data
A catalogue record for this book is available from the British Library.

To

Lieutenant-Colonel Harry ("Brig") Young,
Indian Army, 1917-1995
who, like the subject of this book,
fought for the Empire on several continents,
and was just as irascible.
Good soldier, good friend, good neighbour –
and sorely missed.

CONTENTS

MAPS AND TACTICAL DIAGRAMS

FOREWORD

BY MAJOR-GENERAL J.P. RILEY, DSO

As the last Colonel of the Royal Welch Fusiliers, and the current Chairman of the Regimental Trustees, I am honoured to write the foreword to this biography of such an eminent Royal Welchman. I am also delighted to do so from a personal point of view, since there is much in this book which is of interest to the general reader and student of history as well as to the regimental enthusiast. Thomas Pearson's career spanned the whole of the French Revolutionary and Napoleonic Wars, that titanic, worldwide struggle from which the British Empire emerged victorious. Pearson was present at some of the major continental actions of the war and was wounded several times. He fought at Albuhera, one of the bloodiest days in the history of the British army, but it is his contribution to the war in Canada for which he will best be remembered. That war is little studied on this side of the Atlantic since it was and is overshadowed by events in Spain and central Europe. At the time, it was fought on a shoestring but with considerable skill and daring. The courage of those involved, fighting a determined and capable enemy in far larger numbers, ensured that Canada survives to this day as an independent country.

Pearson the soldier is relatively easy to define, therefore. Pearson the man, however, is far more difficult, since he left no diaries or memoirs and precious little correspondence. Donald Graves has had to do some painstaking research to show us Pearson's character. Pearson seems to me to be an example of all that has typified the Royal Welch Fusiliers throughout its history: courage, honesty, fortitude, good humour in adversity, an absolute refusal to be beaten, and an insistence of the highest standards of professional conduct. He may not have won many popularity contests, but this would not have worried him for a second. What mattered to him was that he had been true to his country, his regiment and his family.

I commend this excellent, well researched and very readable book, and on behalf of all Royal Welchmen I thank Donald Graves for his labours.

MAJOR-GENERAL J. P. RILEY, DSO
Caernarfon, Wales

INTRODUCTION

Not far from where these words were written is the village of Pakenham, Ontario, Canada. It is a pleasant place, thankfully not yet overtaken by urban sprawl and distinguished by a particularly fine five-arch stone bridge spanning the nearby Mississippi River (the real Mississippi, not that pale American imitation). Most of the people who live in this scenic little community are aware that their village is named after an obscure British general, but not much more. For those who take an interest in such matters, Pakenham is just one of those places in Canada bearing the names of British soldiers and statesmen of the early 19th century – other examples being Brockville, Colborne, Drummondville, Kemptville, Maitland, Picton and, inevitably, Wellington.

Lieutenant-General Sir Edward Pakenham is the same officer, of course, who was the Duke of Wellington's brother-in-law and a very good soldier who was killed in action at New Orleans on 8 January 1815. He was also a contemporary of Thomas Pearson, whose life and times form the subject of this book, as the two served and fought together in Nova Scotia, Martinique and Spain between 1808 and 1811. Unlike Pakenham, however, no place in Canada bears Thomas Pearson's name. This is perhaps understandable as he was not well known in his time, but also unfortunate because Pearson played a major role in successfully defending Canada against foreign invasion during the War of 1812.

It was Thomas Pearson's participation in that conflict that brought him to my attention. I wrote a book about the 1813 battle of Crysler's Farm and discovered he had an important part in that engagement. I wrote a book about the 1814 battle of Chippawa and there he was, fighting hard, as he was when I wrote on the vicious battle of Lundy's Lane, and as he is in the research I have done and continue to do on the 1814 siege of Fort Erie. As far as I know, Thomas Pearson is the only British officer who fought in all four of these engagements, the largest and bloodiest military actions to take place in the northern theatre of the War of 1812 – and not only that, he was wounded in two of them.

This was enough for the man to warrant my notice but Thomas Pearson possessed certain personal traits that I found of interest. Many of those who knew Pearson in his lifetime characterized him as a first-class professional officer, a fine leader and trainer of troops, and a hard-biting combat soldier. But they also described him as a bad-tempered martinet who had no patience for foolish, dishonest, indolent, sycophantic or incompetent persons – and absolutely no compunction in telling them so, regardless of their station in life. That Pearson should allegedly exhibit these latter characteristics intrigued me because, like him, I have been the victim of similar slanders on the part of the uninformed (and my wife is not far from top on the list of detractors). It was therefore not only with empathy but considerable sympathy that I decided to find out more about this sometimes-maligned soldier and, ultimately, to write this book which has preoccupied me, intermittently, for nearly seven years.

It turned out to be a difficult task. Thomas Pearson never left a diary, journal or memoir, and such surviving correspondence concerning him or written by him is official correspondence that is short on personal details. Even worse, repeated searches have failed to turn up major documents concerning his military career, which one would expect to find in the War Office records, and even information pertaining to his childhood in Somerset is notably scarce. The reader should therefore take warning that sometimes the "life" aspect of this book is dimmed for long periods in favour of the "times" aspect.

But what interesting times they were! Thomas Pearson was about 12 when the Great War with France (as it was popularly known in Britain until 1914) broke out in 1793 and he was about 33 when it ended. He spent 19 years of his life, and his best years, fighting the enemies of Britain – not only the French but also the Danes, Dutch and Americans – on three continents.

Pearson was an officer in the 23rd Foot, or Royal Welch Fusiliers. This superb regiment was always his first and greatest love and his story cannot be separated from that of his unit. If one could ask Pearson to define himself, the answer would quickly come back that he was a Welch Fusilier, a British officer, a husband, a father and a son of Somerset – in that order. In an active military career that spanned nearly half a century, Pearson served 28 years with the "Old Welch" and commanded the regiment for 13 of those years. He was the model of a regimental officer and possibly one of his greatest regrets was that he was not with the Fusiliers from 1811 to 1815 when they added new laurels, including Waterloo, to their illustrious record. The fact that during those years he was instrumental in defending British North America against foreign aggression would not have meant nearly as much to him.

What follows, therefore, is the story of a soldier and of his regiment when he served with it, the battles they fought, and the times in which it all happened.

DONALD E. GRAVES
"Maple Cottage"
Valley of the Mississippi, Upper Canada

ACKNOWLEDGEMENTS

This book has had a lengthy gestation period and the longer an author works on a project, the more people he must acknowledge for rendering him assistance. In the case of *Fix Bayonets!,* it is my pleasant duty to thank a truly international cast who came to my aid and I only pray that I have not overlooked anyone – if I have, please forgive me.

Beginning with Britain, Thomas Pearson's birthplace, there are those in Somerset who assisted, foremost being that indefatigable detective, Rosalind Wilkinson, and, next, Linda Pearson (no relation), formerly of the Somerset County Archives. Desmond Brown and Reginald Greenow of Bath were helpful in locating the site of Pearson's grave and the City of Bath Public Library provided information on his later years.

Moving around the island, Sir Christopher and Lady Prevost furnished copies of family correspondence that had a bearing on Pearson while John Cook gave me a copy of a rare French cavalry manual and Yvonne Steward made several trips on my behalf to the National Archives in Kew and Family Records Centre in London. Lieutenant-Colonel (Retd.) Tony Broughton, FINS, rendered yeoman service by providing rare pictures and information on French military officers while Anthony Dawson contributed information on artillery matters and John Dangerfield did the same for uniforms of the period. I am grateful to the British Museum for permission to quote from Additional Mss. 37425, f65, *Général de division* La Tour-Maubourg's report on the battle of Albuera. Major Kenneth Gray of the Royal Greenjackets Museum in Winchester generously provided illustrations from that institution's collection and I am also most grateful to Mr. G.C. Streatfield, Curator, and the Trustees of the Gloucester Museum for permission to reproduce the painting "Alexandria, 1801" from the regimental history of The Gloucestershire Regiment. It is interesting to note that the original of this painting was lost in the retreat from Burma in 1942.

It is only fitting that I render particular thanks to Thomas Pearson's regiment, The Royal Welch Fusiliers. I am indebted to Lieutenant-Colonel (Retd.) P.A. Crocker, former Curator of The Regimental Museum in Caernarfon Castle, Gwynedd, Wales, and his successor, Brian Owen, and their staff who have patiently answered many inquiries and have been unflinching in their assistance. Lieutenant-Colonel (Retd.) Richard Sinnett of Llanfrynach, Wales, put at my disposal rare items from his own research into the history of his regiment and carefully read the entire manuscript. Finally, Major-General J.P. Riley, DSO, agreed to write the foreword which graces this book.

Moving around the globe, in Spain I received much aid – and considerable translation help – from Luis Sorando and Juan Patron Sandoval. In Portugal, I must signal my gratitude to João Centano for material from his forthcoming book on the Portuguese army of the Peninsular War. In France I have to thank J.-P. Loriot for solving the French artillery problem and Alain Chappet who located rare published sources, while in Germany Michael Taenzer provided equally rare German-language material. Robert Burnham, Don Hickey, Kevin Kiley, Howie Muir and Steven Smith of the United States were very helpful in locating published and unpublished sources and Bob, Don, Kevin and Howie made helpful comments on early drafts of the book. Tomislaw Paciorek of Poznan in Poland came up with an obscure Polish memoir while, on the far side of the world from me, Allan Wood of Australia provided information from his personal collection of British Army Lists.

Here in Canada I must thank many who laboured on my behalf, provided material or made helpful suggestions: Dennis Carter-Edwards of Cornwall; Miriam Wallis of the Halifax Defence Complex Library; René Chartrand, Dr. Faye Kert and David McCracken of Ottawa-Hull; Robert Malcomson of St. Catharines; Dr. Carl Benn and Stewart Sutherland of Toronto; Bob Foley of the Haunted Press in Niagara Falls; and Guy St. Denis of London. I must make special mention of Richard Feltoe, Paul Kelly and Chris Wattie of the modern re-enactment unit of the Incorporated Militia Battalion of Upper Canada, centred in Toronto, who contributed much information, most of it irreverent. As always, the staff of the Directorate of History and Heritage, Department of National Defence, in Ottawa were obliging and in particular I have to thank Majors Paul Lansey, CD, and James McKillip, CD, Captain (Retd.) F.S. Gannon, CD, Warrant Officer Carl Kletke, CD, Dr. Ken Reynolds, Madeleine Lafleur-Lemire and Michael Whitby. Locally, Doctors David Atack and Chris Parsons contributed useful (if frightening) information on medical practices, both in the early 19th and early 21st centuries.

I must express my particular gratitude to two fellow students of Albuera who saved me untold hours of labour and some very embarrassing errors. The first is Mark Thompson of England, author of *The Fatal Hill: The Allied Campaign under Beresford in Southern Spain in 1811* (the groundbreaking study of the battle of Albuera), who was unstinting in his help. Next there is Guy Dempsey of New York, who has been working for many years on what will eventually be the definitive study of that bloody engagement, tentatively titled "Glorious Field of Grief," which will see print next year. Guy generously gave me material from French archives as well as much other excellent information. Mark and Guy are among the few persons alive who have read through every page of the copious literature produced by the controversies over the battle which were waged in print in the 1830s and 1840s – and possibly the only persons who fully understand their intricacies. Our lengthy electronic conversations, which have proved useful in proving or disproving my theories about the battle, have been both enjoyable and educational.

There are others who merit special notice. In that respect I must particularly thank Randal Gray of London, author of the Pearson entry in the *Oxford Dictionary of National Biography,* who provided much information about the man, including a copy of his will, and who edited the entire manuscript in draft. Lieutenant-Colonel (Retd.) Brian Reid, CD, Royal Canadian Artillery, and Major John Grodzinski, CD, Royal Military College of Canada, also read the manuscript and made some brutal but, unfortunately, accurate criticisms which wounded me deeply as I am the soul of sensitivity. And, as always, much credit must go to Christopher Johnson, the best military cartographer in the business, whose work enhances this book.

I must not forget the little ones at home. George the gentleman cat, now sadly gone to his reward, beamed down on me contentedly for many of the years it took to write this book from his favourite perch on the shelf above my keyboard. In contrast, the best that can be said about the other creature, Ned, is that he caused no trouble as he spent most of those years either sleeping or eating, remaining throughout the same fat, cunning and wretched little beast he has been since I mistakenly acquired him.

And, finally, there is the lovely Dianne, who, besides her many inestimable qualities, including being fluent in French and German, possesses the most important quality of all – patience. Without her, this book could not have been written.

D.E.G.

A NOTE TO THE READER

In this book, "Welch" will be used in all matters pertaining to the 23rd Foot, or Royal Welch Fusiliers, and "Welsh" for all matters pertaining to that people who reside in the west of Britain. Although during the time Pearson served with the 23rd Foot, its official title was the Royal Welsh Fuzileers, the regiment used "Welch" in all but official documents, and after more than a century and a half of effort was ultimately able to get the older spelling restored. For this reason the regiment will be called the Royal Welch Fusiliers below, except where a different form is used in quoted passages.

In an effort to retain period flavour, I have used foreign-language rank and unit titles – and in some cases, words of command – in this book. Most are similar to their English equivalents and should cause no confusion but where they are not, I have provided translations in footnotes. There are some exceptions. The King's German Legion seems to have been comfortable with either English or German rank and unit titles and that is sometimes the case below. While I have used the original foreign language unit titles, I have opted to use the English language numbering system – thus it is 51st *Ligne*, not 51e *Ligne* – a concession to make things a bit more comfortable for the English reader.

As is my custom, when it comes to the two period armies that spoke English and had a similar unit numbering system, I have used numerals for British regiments and words for the American, and thus it is the 23rd Foot but the Twenty-Fifth Infantry Regiment. I should add that a British battalion and an American infantry regiment were very similar in strength, 400-800 men. On the other hand, a French regiment, which normally consisted of three battalions, was considerably larger than its American counterpart.

During the period of this book, different armies used a variety of terms – brigades, companies, divisions, etc. – to indicate what is generally now called a battery, or a unit of artillery with between four and eight pieces. To lessen the confusion I have used the modern term battery throughout except in the case of the Royal Horse Artillery because, being an ex-gunner, it is too ingrained in me to call a Royal Horse Artillery troop a battery, although the two terms mean the same thing in period context. I have therefore retained troop for the RHA and battery for everyone else.

With reference to place names in Spain and Portugal, I have generally followed those used by Charles Oman in his *History of the Peninsular War* for the names of major cities, towns and battles and thus it is Corunna, not Coruna,

Coruñna or Coruña. For the names of smaller communities I have taken the advice of my Spanish correspondents.

I have retained standard British and American measurement throughout as Napoleon's ultimate defeat meant that the horrors of the metric system have yet to be inflicted on the greater part of the English-speaking world – Canada being a protesting exception. The reader should note, however, that the French pound of the time was 1.1 to the British pound and thus a French 8-pdr. gun fired a solid shot that weighed 8.8 British pounds, making it almost the equivalent of a British 9-pdr. gun.

In Britain during the Napoleonic period, the system of currency differed from that in use today. It was based on the pound sterling, denominated by the £ symbol, with £1 equalling 20 shillings and 1 shilling (s.) equalling 12 pence (d.). Sums were written as pounds, shillings and pence and thus £5.1s.6d or £5.1.6. was 5 pounds, 1 shilling and six pence. A guinea, often used to price valuable items, was 1 pound and 1 shilling and thus 45 guineas was £47.5.0. Between 1793 and 1815 the value of the pound sterling fluctuated between $3.62 and $4.90 American but the average over the period was US$4.37.

D.E.G.

The Major

Thomas Pearson was promoted to major in December 1804 at the age of 24. He marked the occasion by having a new portrait painted in which he wore two epaulettes, the distinction for his new rank. The artist is unknown but the work appears to be in the style of John Hoppner, a well known portrait painter of the period. Of the three extent portaits of Thomas Pearson in his younger years, this one provides the most insight into the man, who was exactly what he appears to be – a tough, go-ahead, no-nonsense infantryman who would cheerfully and expeditiously dispatch His Britannic Majesty's enemies at any time in any place.

(Courtesy, Royal Welch Fusiliers)

PROLOGUE

SPAIN, 16 MAY 1811

The messenger reached the major just after the French cavalry had been repulsed. He had watched the green-uniformed dragoons charging down on Harvey's Portuguese brigade to the left in a very determined manner and had wondered whether they would hold. He need not have worried as the Johnnies had stood firm as Englishmen before putting a fine fusilier volley into the French, who wheeled quickly and rode away. When the smoke cleared, the wreckage – dead and broken men and horses – was visible lying out on the slope. The major noted with idle curiosity that some of the Frenchmen scattered about wore yellow facings on their coats and recalled that the 20th *Dragons* were supposed to have that colour so they must have carried out the attack – or was it the 26th or 27th *Dragons* that had yellow? It didn't matter because what was important was that these *crapauds* were no longer a threat and that was a good thing because the major was a firm believer that the best French dragoon was a dead one. He put the matter out of his mind, wiped his face with a handkerchief he took from under his hat and looked at his watch.

Nearly an hour had passed since the division had advanced across open fields and up the slope of the hill, all the while under heavy fire from the enemy artillery on the high ground to their front. The French gunners had concentrated on the infantry brigades to his left, which was bad luck for them but good luck for his light infantry companies on the right flank, and their casualties had been mercifully light. If only he knew what was happening with the Fusilier Brigade? Through the smoke and the rain, he had caught the occasional sight of that formation's three sets of Colours farther up the slope and, although it was hard to judge, he thought they had moved forward against the massed French columns, which were sometimes visible during a break in the haze and smoke. But the Colours also seemed to be drawing closer together, which meant the brigade was taking casualties. He could see nothing else, had no information and he damned and double-damned the confusion, the smoke, the rain and the Frogs.

The major glanced at his six companies formed in square around him. The green plumes on their shakos identified the men in the ranks as light infantry and he noted that they were not shifting or wavering, nor could he hear any anxious high-pitched voices – signs of unsteadiness. The men seemed to be in fine fettle and that at least was good thing because this battle was far from over. The major never had any doubts, of course, about his company from the Old Welch or the two from the Royals, which he had positioned on the side of the square facing the enemy, but he did not know the three companies from Kemmis's brigade posted on the opposite side. They appeared, however, to be bearing up well and he made a note to think about switching the companies around to give the Fusiliers a rest. He also contemplated ordering his company commanders to check their men's ammunition and flints but stopped the thought as his officers knew their jobs and it was not necessary.

Standing as tall as he could, the major strained to look about. On the hill in front he could see occasional muzzle flashes from the French artillery. This fire was being returned in fine style by Lefebvre's horse gunners and the German artillery out to his right although he noted that they spared the occasional round for the masses of French cavalry visible on the ridge line to the south.

But where was the allied cavalry? He decided they had run off and cursed all horsemen for damned prancing puppies who were never around when you needed them. Not that it mattered as they were generally useless in a hard fight and this was certainly a hard fight – he had seen nothing like it since Alexandria ten years before and he reckoned that whatever was taking place up ahead, it was a bloody business. In any case, Harvey's Portuguese had just demonstrated what well-trained infantry could do against cavalry so the major did not concern himself about the missing horsemen. He pulled out his watch again. One minute had gone by.

At this point the messenger arrived. An excited young officer, he began to babble until a cold stare from the major brought him to his senses and he slowed down and spoke clearly. His message was that Colonel Blakeney had been wounded while leading the brigade and could the major please come and assume command of the formation. Although he had guessed that the casualties in the fighting on the hill were heavy, the major was somewhat startled to learn this information. If Blakeney was down, that meant Myers, the commander of the Fusilier Brigade, and his own commanding officer, Henry Ellis, were also down because they ranked Blakeney. This was a sobering thought and it might indicate that things were not going at all well. The major did not hesitate, however, but calling to him his senior captain, Jack Hill of the 23rd Foot, he turned over command of the light infantry companies.

And then he followed the messenger up the hill into the smoke and confusion ......

LEARNING THE TRADE, 1796–1810

Royal Welch Fusiliers, 1800
Although some of the uniform details in this late 19th-century artist's creation
are incorrect, it represents the full dress uniform of the 23rd Foot about the time
Pearson joined the regiment in early 1797. Of interest is the bearskin headdress
worn by fusilier regiments. Note that the officer is using his left hand to return
the soldier's salute – prior to the First World War soldiers saluted with their free
hand, not necessarily their right hand. (From Rowland Broughton-Mainwaring,
Historical Records of the Royal Welch Fusiliers, 1888)

Officer in daily uniform, 1797

For daily dress in garrison, young Lieutenant Pearson would have a worn a
uniform similar to this officer of the 1st Regiment of Guards. Note the gorget
and sash, the insignia of a commissioned officer. (Sketch from life by Robert
Ker-Porter contained in David Roberts, *Military Instructions: Including Each
Particular Motion of the Manual and Platoon Exercise*, 1798)

CHAPTER ONE

"DREADFUL TIMES ARE APPROACHING."

THE PARSON'S LAD, KING GEORGE'S ARMY AND THE GREAT WAR WITH FRANCE, 1781–1797

When I was younger, gossips would say,
When I grew older, I'd be a soldier
Rattles and toys I threw them away
Except for a drum and a sabre.
When I was older, as up I grew,
I went to see a grand review,
Colours flying set me dying,
To embark on a life so new.

Roll, me merry drums, march away.
A soldier's glory lives in story,
His laurels are green when his locks are grey,
Then hurrah for the life of a soldier![1]

Thomas Pearson, the officer who assumed command of his brigade in the middle of a bloody battle in the rain on a Spanish hillside, was born in the year 1781. His father, the Reverend Thomas Horner Pearson, was the rector of St. Peter's Church in Podimore Milton, a small village about two miles northeast of Ilchester in Somerset. Young Tom Pearson was thus a son of Somerset and also of the church, his grandfather being the Reverend Robert Pearson, a graduate of Oxford who for most of his life was the rector of St. Bartholomew's Church in Crewkerne, 15 miles southwest of Ilchester. In 1747 Robert Pearson had married Edith Horner, the daughter of a wealthy and prominent east Somerset family, and Thomas Horner Pearson, their eldest son, followed in his father's footsteps, attending Oxford, from which he was

7

graduated with an M.A. in 1776, and assuming his duties at Podimore Milton that same year. He remained there until 1785 when he took over a larger parish at St. Barnabas Church at Queen Camel, five miles east of Ilchester, and there he served until his death in 1832 at the age of 81.

Beyond the fact that he grew up in the green and rolling hills of east Somerset, little is known about Thomas Pearson's childhood. His early years were spent in two small villages of less than 200 souls in well-wooded and rich farm country inhabited by a rural population with a slow, drawling way of speaking which has caused many a visitor to conclude they also think slowly – a big mistake. The major influence on young Tom's childhood would undoubtedly been his father's calling, and the life of Reverend Pearson revolved around the Church of England year with its "Moveable and Immoveable Feasts" and "Vigils, Fasts and Days of Abstinence": Lent, Advent Sunday, Good Friday, Easter Sunday, Ascension Day, Whitsunday, Trinity Sunday and the Nativity or Christmas Day. Since the head of the Church of England was the sovereign, there were also "Certain Solemn Days" on which special prayers were offered, including the day "kept in Memory of the Papists Conspiracy" (5 November or Guy Fawkes Day); that "kept in Memory of Martyrdom of King Charles I" (30

Saint Barnabas Church, Queen Camel, Somerset
In 1785 Thomas Pearson's father, the Reverend Thomas Horner Pearson, took over the parish of Saint Barnabas at Queen Camel, where he served 47 years until his death in 1832. As a child, Thomas Pearson's life would have revolved around his father's church duties. (Photograph by Rosalind Wilkinson)

January); that "kept in Memory of the Birth and Return of King Charles II" (29 May); and, finally, 25 October or "the Day on which His Majesty King George III began his Happy Reign."[2] Tom Pearson's early life was therefore an organized one, marked by respect for the established order and its traditions.

It would also have been influenced by service to others. Moving through a year marked by ecclesiastical signposts, Reverend Pearson tended his flock, solemnizing matrimony, baptizing the newborn, "churching" their mothers after childbirth, confirming children in the faith, visiting the sick, praying for and with them, and burying the dead. A marvellous insight into the life of a rural parson in late 18th-century England – and thus a glimpse into the childhood of Tom Pearson – can be found in the diary of Parson James Woodforde of Weston Longville in Norfolk. Originally from Somerset, Woodforde was a contemporary of Tom's father, although he was somewhat older, a bachelor and less wealthy. Many of Woodforde's experiences, recorded in detail in the diary he kept for 45 years, would have been similar to those of Reverend Pearson. Besides conducting the annual cycle of worship, country parsons like Woodforde and Pearson carried out other Christian activities such as providing a free dinner and a few coins to the poor of the parish on Christmas Day, dispensing charity in the

Old Vicarage, Queen Camel, Somerset
This was possibly Thomas Pearson's childhood home. When he was four years of age, his father, the Reverend Thomas Horner Pearson, moved from Podimore Milton to Queen Camel, and Thomas may have lived in this house until he joined the army. (Photograph by Rosalind Wilkinson)

form of a meal, clothing or small amounts of money to those who came daily to the doors of their rectories, presenting the village children with a penny on St. Valentine's Day, sometimes conducting the "singers" or church choir, teaching at Sunday and other parish schools, officiating at local events and fairs, and consulting with the parish burgesses or wardens on its financial affairs and the physical upkeep of the church. Parsons also spent much time resolving disputes – between persons, within families and within the congregation.

Both Reverend Pearson and Reverend Woodforde would have been familiar with the intrusion of the law into their religious duties, particularly as it concerned relations between the sexes. In an effort to reduce the number of illegitimate children, who too often ended up as wards of the parish and inmates of the local "House of Industry" or poorhouse, the law of England in the 18th century stated that if an unmarried woman with child named its father under oath, he had either to marry her or face imprisonment – basically a choice between two forms of captivity – and if the woman refused to name the father, she could be publicly shamed in church. Such legal provisions led to some interesting entries in Woodforde's diary:

> One Sarah Gore, came to me this morning and brought me an instrument from the Court of Wells, to perform publick Pennance next Sunday at C[astle]. Cary Church, for having a child [out of wedlock], which I am to administer to her publickly next Sunday after divine Service.[3] ....

> I married Tom Burge of Ansford to Charity Andrews of C[astle]. Cary by License this morning. The Parish of Cary made him marry her, and he came handbolted [handcuffed] to Church for fear of running away. ......[4]

> Rode to Ringland this Morning and married one Robert Astick and Elizabeth Howlett by Licence, Mr. Carter being from home, and the Man being in Custody, it was a long time before he could be prevailed on to marry her when in the Church Yard; and at the Altar behaved very unbecoming. It is a cruel thing that any Person should be compelled by Law to marry. I recd. of the Officers for marrying them 0. 10. 6.[5]

At other times in rural parishes, the law might be broken in church itself:

> I read prayers and preached at Cary Church and whilst I was preaching one Thos Speed of Gallhampton came into the Church, called the Singers a

Pack of Whoresbirds and gave me a nod or two in the pulpit. The Constable Roger Coles Sent [for and] took him into custody after will have him before a Magistrate's tomorrow.[6]

The household of a man of the faith could be strict. Woodforde, although he loved playing cards, would not do so on certain holy days and he would do no work, not even shave, on Sundays – although he would drink wine. But the clergy of the Church of England also led active social lives as they were men of standing in their communities and, unlike the clergy of other Protestant faiths, were not barred from many popular pursuits. Parson Woodforde drank, played cards, danced, hunted rabbits with his beloved greyhounds and attended a variety of social activities – and Parson Pearson would probably have done much the same. Country parsons had much to do with the prominent local landowner or "lord of the manor" in whose "patronage" the minister's church was situated and who was often its prime benefactor. When the Reverend Pearson was at St. Andrew in Podimore Milton, the squire was Thomas Horner, probably a kinsman through his mother, and their relations would have been close. At Preston Longville, Parson Woodforde was a welcome visitor at the house of his patron, a Mr. John Coustance, who, along with other members of the parish gentry, was a frequent dinner guest at the rectory. On such occasions Parson Woodforde, a dedicated trencherman, always made a special effort:

> I gave them for dinner, a Couple of Chickens boiled and a Tongue, A Leg of Mutton boiled and Capers and Batter Pudding for the first Course, Second, a couple of Ducks rosted and green Peas, some Artichokes, Tarts and Blancmange. After dinner, Almonds and Raisins, Oranges and Strawberries. Mountain and Port Wines. Peas and Strawberries the first gathered this year by me.[7]

An important annual event for country clergy was "tithe-audit day," which usually took place early in the year. On this day the burgesses or elders of the parish, almost all prominent farmers, came to pay the tithes or fees that constituted the major part of a parson's income and in return he would usually stage a "frolic" – a splendid dinner complete with copious amounts of alcohol. Parson Woodforde was particularly proud of his hospitality on such occasions:

This being the Day for my Tithe Auditt, the … Farmers paid me their Tithes. …… I gave them for Dinner, some Salt Fish, a Leg of Mutton boiled and Capers, a Knuckle of Veal, a Piggs Face, a fine Surloin of Beef rosted, and plenty of plumb Puddings. …… I dined with the Farmers in the great Parlour, Nancy dined bye herself in the Study. Wine drank 6 Bottles. Rum drank 5 Bottles besides Quantities of strong Beer and Ale.[8]

Note that Woodforde's niece and housekeeper, Nancy, withdrew on such occasions – the Reverend Mrs. Pearson and her family would have done the same during her husband's "frolics" at Podimore Milton and Queen Camel. Farmers being farmers (and farmers never change), some parsons found the annual "frolic" a bit wearisome:

> The punch goes round, and they are dull
> And lumpish still as ever;
> Like barrels with their bellies full,
> They only weigh the heavier.
>
> One talks of mildew and of frost,
> And one of storms of hail,
> And one of pigs that he has lost
> By maggots at the tail.
>
> Quoth one, "A rarer man than you
> In pulpit none shall hear;
> But ye methinks, to tell you true,
> You sell it plaguy dear."[9]

Country parsons spent much time and energy on gardening, both for pleasure and food. They were usually involved in agriculture not only because of their rural parishes but also because their emoluments often included agricultural land which they could farm themselves or, more likely, lease to others. There were vicarage farms at both Podimore Milton and Queen Camel and the Reverend Pearson also owned property in a number of rural Somerset villages, including a manor house and farm at Thorne Coffin, four miles southeast of Ilchester. Young Tom Pearson therefore grew up in a household that was involved in the rural community in which it was situated and which served that community.

His Majesty King George III (1738-1820)
On the throne for six decades, George III was a popular monarch known to his subjects as "Farmer George" because of his enthusiasm for agriculture. A devoted family man, his later years were blighted by recurring bouts of madness (now known to have been porphyria) and troubles with his many sons. George III was king when the Great War with France began in 1793 but a regency was needed after 1811. (Author's collection)

He also grew up in good times. Tom was just three years old in 1784, the year William Pitt became prime minister of Britain and set about repairing the nation's economy, damaged by the costs of the American Revolutionary War which had ended the year before in the loss of most of Britain's North American colonies. Pitt pared government expenditure, including defence expenditure, to the bone, balanced the budget and promoted measures that increased overseas trade. British exporters, including those in the increasingly industrialized Midlands, having lost much of the former American market, found new markets for their goods in the Indies and other places. Although the private enclosure of land formerly held in common was beginning to hurt the small farmer, most rural areas in southern England bore an air of prosperity, which was often remarked on by visitors from Europe, who noted the contrast between the well-fed farm families of England and the downtrodden peasants on the other side of the Channel. Agriculture was a national passion: genial King George III took an avid interest in it, hence his nickname "Farmer George." By now in the third decade of his reign, the king was popular among all classes but the same could not be said of his nine sons, who, with the exception of Frederick who showed a keen interest in military matters, were reckless, profligate and irresponsible. This was particularly true of George, Prince of Wales, heir to the throne and an overweight, overdressed ninny.

As parents, Reverend and Mrs. Pearson were more fortunate than their King. Tom was the eldest boy in the family but the Pearsons also had three younger sons, Charles, Robert and George, and two daughters, Anne and Frances. As Reverend Pearson was a steward of the Old Grammar School in Crewkerne, founded in 1449 and attached to St. Bartholomew's Church in that town, it is likely that young Tom received his education at that institution, which boasted Captain Thomas Masterman Hardy, RN (the "kiss me, Hardy" of Nelson and Trafalgar fame) among its more prominent ex-pupils. Given that the major influences on his childhood years were a respect for tradition, loyalty to the established social order and community service, the church would have been a natural career choice for Tom and it would be entirely reasonable to assume that the Reverend Pearson wished his eldest son to follow in the footsteps of his father and grandfather. If this was so, the reverend was to be disappointed because Tom Pearson was destined for a different calling.

For there had been another influence on his childhood and it had begun in July 1789 when Tom was about eight years old. In rural Norfolk, Parson Woodforde noted its beginning in his diary entry for 24 July: "Very great Rebellion in France by the Papers."[10] From that time until early 1793, three and a half years, Woodforde made only fleeting references to the tumultuous events taking place across the Channel, but on 26 January 1793 he sorrowfully recorded that King Louis XVI of France was "inhumanly and unjustly beheaded on Monday last by his cruel, blood-thirsty Subjects."[11] "Dreadful times," predicted the good parson with fatal accuracy, "are approaching to all Europe." On 1 February 1793, when Tom Pearson was 12, France declared war on Britain, initiating a conflict that would last, with short intermissions, for more than 22 years. War was therefore the other major influence on young Tom Pearson and thus it came about that, in 1796, at the age of 15, the parson's lad from rural Somerset applied for an officer's commission in the army of His Britannic Majesty King George III.

In the 1790s that army was neither a happy nor an efficient service. Its famous victories under Marlborough and Wolfe were distant memories and its reputation had been tarnished by defeat in the recent American War which had ended in 1783. It had sullenly returned from that conflict to its garrisons in Britain only to suffer financial cutbacks that reduced its already weak numbers. The simple truth was that, although Britons gloried in their army's past achievements, they did not really much like it because it was frequently used as a police force to quell civil disturbances and because, there being few barracks in which to house it, the unruly behaviour of soldiers billeted in taverns and inns was a constant annoyance. Parliament, which had a long memory, had never forgotten the mid-17th century military dictatorship of Oliver Cromwell and ensured that there were legislative checks to keep the army under control

– both its existence and its funding were subject to annual votes. Civilian scorn for the army led one literary redcoat to ask

> Why that despis'd but useful race of men,
> Whose youth, whose manhood, even to grey old age,
> Is spent to serve their country and their kind,
> Shall meet with such contempt from every age
> And rank of men, that even a beggar's child
> Is taught to scorn a common soldier's name.[12]

If the soldier was an object of disdain and ridicule to the average Briton, his officer was even more so, particularly if he had purchased his commission. The institution of purchase, almost unique to the British army, permitted an officer to buy his initial commission and then, if he had the funds, to gain advancement by paying his way up the ladder as far as the rank of lieutenant-colonel. The system had originated in the late 17th century to ensure that only men of substance (and therefore more likely to be loyal to the Crown) became officers in the King's army. It had a major advantage in that it saved the government the cost of pensions as, when an officer wished to leave the service, the sale price of his commission could be converted into an annuity. The system, however, had always been subject to abuses and the worst of these probably occurred from 1783 to 1795 when commissions were sold fast and furious, resulting in boys of 11 commanding regiments while qualified and veteran officers who could not afford their next step in rank had to obey them. There was more than a little truth in the broadside verse that proclaimed,

> By Dear Mama's Petition,
> And Good Papa's Purse,
> Jacky gets a Commission,
> And likewise a Nurse.[13]

Defenders of the system pointed out that it allowed young men of talent to rise fast, and there was some truth in this as many officers, who will appear below, were promoted very swiftly. Lowry Cole was a lieutenant-colonel at 21; Arthur Wesley, later Arthur Wellesley and later still, the Duke of Wellington, reached the same rank at 24; Edward Pakenham was a major at 17; Phineas Riall purchased an ensign's commission in the spring of 1794 and celebrated Christmas that year as a major; while Henry Ellis, who would be Pearson's commanding officer for many years, was commissioned an ensign at the age of six (although he did not serve) and a captain at the age of 14! These men proved to be very good officers but all too many of those who purchased their commissions were utterly useless and some were not even men – it is said that in the late 1780s a young lady held a captaincy in the dragoons and although she did not serve with her regiment, "was probably not much less fit for service than some who actually did duty."[14] The problem of unprofessional and incompetent officers was exacerbated in the early years of the war with France by a rush to raise new units, and commissions were granted by the hundreds to men who would prove to be nothing but a burden on the service.

It was even more difficult to obtain soldiers. At the outbreak of war in 1793 the strength of the army was just 38,945 infantry and cavalry and perhaps 5,500 "ordnance troops" of the Royal Artillery and Royal Engineers, administered by the Master General of Ordnance, not the commander-in-chief of the army. On the other hand, there had been no commander-in-chief since 1783 and when

"John Bull Going to the Wars," 1793
This cartoon by James Gillray lampoons the entry of Britain into the war with France in 1793. There was unwarranted confidence in the nation that it would all be over soon but the conflict was to last, with some pauses, for 22 years. It would take the British army nearly a decade of defeats before it acquired the professionalism necessary to beat its French opponent. (Author's collection)

Europe in 1792 – Major States Only

the appointment was filled in 1793 by Field Marshal Lord Jeffery Amherst, a good soldier three decades before but now a doddering old shell, he managed to create such mischief that it took his successor years to rectify the damage. Intensive recruiting more than tripled the size of the cavalry and infantry establishments to 129,262 by 1795. Unfortunately, this increase was almost totally absorbed by the heavy casualties suffered in the West Indies so that when Thomas Pearson joined in late 1796, the army's actual strength was not much greater than it had been in 1793.

Amherst had neither the wish nor the will to correct the army's other great fault – its lack of uniform training. The British soldier's extensive campaign experience in the boundless woods and wilds of North America during the 18th century had given rise to an "American" tactical school of thought which emphasized looser formations, rapid movement and the deployment of light infantry. The suggestions made by officers of this school to reorganize the army were opposed by the officers of the "German" school who followed the precepts of Frederick the Great, whose reputation as a military commander remained untarnished in the 1790s. The "Germans" emphasized tightly controlled infantry that fought in formations that could defend themselves against cavalry (which was not a factor in North America), and the use of disciplined firepower to defeat enemy infantry. It was not that the British army lacked an established tactical system. The *Rules and Regulations for the Formation, Field-Exercise, and Movements of His Majesty's Forces* compiled by Major-General David Dundas – a good, if somewhat complex text derived from the Prussian tactical system – had been made the authorized manual in 1792. The problem was that very few commanding officers saw fit to use it and many trained their units as they pleased.

The state of the British army at the outbreak of war with France has been accurately summed up by then Captain Henry Bunbury as being "lax in its discipline, entirely without system, and very weak in numbers." Each commanding officer of a regiment managed "according to his own notions, or neglected it altogether," and there was "no uniformity of drill or movement." Thus, Bunbury concluded, "professional pride was rare; professional knowledge still more so."[15]

These weaknesses in the army became apparent after France declared war on Britain in February 1793. This was not a war that Prime Minister Pitt wanted and he had tried to avoid it for four years by following a policy of appeasement toward the successive governments across the Channel. From the beginning of the French revolution in July 1789, however, those governments, month by month and year by year, became increasingly more radical just as the condition of the nation they governed became progressively worse. By 1792 France was bankrupt, starving and on the verge of anarchy and its leaders came to regard war as their best course to quell internal dissent by focusing it on external dangers. They therefore tried to provoke a war with other European powers but when these states proved as unaggressive as Britain, the French government solved its problem by simply declaring war on Austria and Prussia in 1792 and on Britain about six months later.

France was in no condition to wage war. The old royal army had been nearly destroyed by the revolution, which caused the loss of most of its experienced, but aristocratic officers, although there were enough trained soldiers and officers left to form a cadre for the thousands of willing volunteers who flocked to the colours when the government, proclaiming "*la patrie en danger!*", invaded the Austrian possessions in the Netherlands in the summer of 1792. That invasion was foiled but half-hearted Austrian and Prussian offensives were coun-

Grenadier, French infantry of the line, 1794

In the early 1790s, the French army was suffering from the loss of much of its aristocratic officer corps as a result of the revolution, but a new generation of capable leaders from humbler backgrounds turned it into a powerful, mobile and flexible fighting force superior to its European opponents. This soldier of the grenadier, or elite company, of a line infantry regiment is singularly well equipped and uniformed for the period. More often, French soldiers at the beginning of the Great War were short of everything including arms and ammunition. (Drawing by Edouard Detaille from *L'Armée française,* 1888)

tered by French armies which lacked almost everything except enthusiasm and numbers. The coming of war, however, permitted French leaders to introduce measures that would have been unthinkable just a few months before and in swift succession France declared itself a republic, executed its former king and created Committees of Public Safety to crush internal protest. Over the next two years, these committees executed an estimated 40,000 persons, most of them innocent, and they were particularly vigilant towards senior army officers: between 1793 and 1795 no fewer than 57 French generals were executed by government order while 299 others were arrested or cashiered.

Unwillingly forced into war, Pitt tried to turn it to Britain's advantage by using the power of the Royal Navy to conduct operations against his enemy's overseas possessions. A French invasion of Holland, however, brought an appeal for assistance from that nation and in May 1793 a small British expeditionary force was dispatched as part of an allied effort to defend Holland against French aggression. Frederick, Duke of York, the second and best of the king's sons, was appointed to command this force and it was gradually increased to a strength of nearly 10,000 by drafts of raw recruits whom one officer thought "totally unfit for service" being "mostly either old men or quite boys, extremely weak and short."[16] Pitt also entered into diplomatic negotiations that led to the creation of what would later be called the First Coalition against France consisting of Austria, Britain, Holland and Spain and a number of lesser nations. Powerful on paper, this alliance proved to be weak in reality as none of the major partners would agree on an overall strategy and there was much mutual antagonism and suspicion between Austria and Prussia. Nonetheless, by the summer of 1793 there were 100,000 allied troops in Holland under Austrian command.

Early operations went in favour of the coalition but it was gradually forced back on the defensive by the republican armies. The allied generals, following the tenets of 18th-century warfare with its emphasis on supplies, sieges and gradual and regulated movement, proved no match for the French generals, who, making a virtue of necessity, abandoned conventional supply systems to live off the land and were thus able to move swiftly and concentrate more rapidly at the crucial point. They also harnessed the raw enthusiasm of their half-trained levies to create a tactical system that involved harassing their opponents' line with hordes of skirmishers, (who could not be trusted to fight in line in any case), until the enemy was so unsettled that a vigorous attack by mass columns composed of soldiers not trained enough to fight in any other formation, achieved a breakthrough and gained a victory. Another factor that became apparent was that, while the loss of aristocratic officers had deprived the French army of experienced leadership, it had also created opportunities for able men of humbler backgrounds who now came to the fore. At the lower level, lack of trained leadership was partially solved by amalgamating the pre-revolutionary regular units with the new volunteer units to form *demi-brigades* which had a leavening of experience. These early campaigns proved an effective training ground for a generation of French officers who created an army that emphasized mobility, flexibility and aggression at both the operational and tactical levels. The allies were simply no match for its fervour and, in two years of desultory campaigning, were driven out of Holland, the British army being evacuated from German territory in April 1795. Holland, Prussia and Spain now made peace, leaving only Austria and Britain as the remaining major partners in the First Coalition.

Although it had fought bravely on occasion, the overall performance of the British army on the continent in 1793-1795 was abysmal. The Duke of York proved to be no field commander and his presence in that ill-fated campaign is now best remembered by the vivid but entirely inaccurate nursery rhyme coined at the time:

The grand old Duke of York,
He had ten thousand men;
He marched them up to the top of the hill,
And he marched them down again.

Major-General James Craig, who served as the duke's adjutant-general in Holland, was scathing about the army's performance. It was Craig's belief that it was

the most undisciplined, the most ignorant, the worst-provided army that ever took the field is equally certain; but we are not to blame for it … there is not a young man in the army that cares one farthing whether his command-ing officer, his brigadier, or the commander-in-chief himself approves of his conduct or not. His promotion depends not on their smiles or frowns – his friends can give him a thousand pounds … and in a fortnight he becomes a captain. Out of the fifteen regiments of cavalry and twenty-six regiments of infantry which we have here, twenty-one are literally commanded by boys or idiots – I have had the curiosity to count them over …… We have no discipline … we don't know how to post a picquet or instruct a sentinel in his duty, and as to moving, God forbid that we should attempt it within three miles of an enemy![17]

Another officer was critical of the army's staff work – and its discipline, which had collapsed on several occasions:

Every department of the staff was more or less deficient, particularly the commissariat and medical branches. The regimental officers in those days were, as well as their men, hard drinkers; and the latter, under a loose disci-pline, were much addicted to marauding, and to acts of licentious violence, which made them detested by the people of the country. Some of the cavalry, dashing fellows in a fight, picqued themselves on being "rough and ready"; to which it might justly have been added "drunken and disorderly."[18]

Lieutenant-Colonel Arthur Wesley, who would go on to greater fame, com-manded the 33rd Foot in Holland and concluded that the best thing to be said about his experience was that it showed him "what one ought not to do and that is always something."[19]

At sea, Britain was more successful. Shortly after the outbreak of war the Royal Navy had implemented a blockade of French ports, crippling French maritime commerce, and had occupied Toulon, the major French naval base in the Mediterranean. The French navy had been adversely affected by the revolution to a greater extent than the French army because it lost not only its aristocratic officers but many specialist ratings such as gunners who were taken from it for land service. The result was that the Royal Navy was successful in almost every major naval engagement of the first three years of the war, sinking or capturing 33 French ships of the line, and maritime superiority allowed Pitt to implement his strategy of overseas expeditions against French colonies. Between 1794 and 1796, the greater part of the British army was engaged in a series of "island hopping" campaigns in the West Indies. Unfortunately, its losses from disease were catastrophic and it has been estimated that in those years of war, the army lost no fewer than 80,000 men killed or crippled by yellow fever in the tropical islands. It was with good reason that the survivors of the garrisons in the sugar islands mournfully sang:

> Cut off from the land that bore us,
> Betrayed by the land we find,
> When the brightest have gone before us,
> And the dullest remain behind.
>
> So stand to your glasses steady,
> 'Tis all we have left to prize,
> Quaff a cup to the dead already,
> And one to the next who dies.[20]

The expansion of her overseas possessions, however, extended Britain's economic base and permitted her not only to wage war for more than two decades but also to financially support her allies to do the same.

The contrast between the performance of the army and navy in the opening years of the conflict was striking. On the whole, Britons much preferred the Royal Navy, the wooden wall that constituted the nation's first line of defence and which excited the respect and admiration of the average person – as long as they did not have to serve in its crowded lower decks. Civilians who scorned soldiers for their rowdy behaviour were willing to overlook the exuberance of sailors on shore and the financial and manufacturing sectors were fully aware

The press
In this Thomas Rowlandson cartoon, a woman faints after her husband is dragged off by a naval press gang. Unlike the army, which largely relied on voluntary enlistment, the Royal Navy partly used forcible conscription or impressment to obtain sailors for the fleet. The navy, however, was skilled at turning unwilling recruits into useful members of the service – one way or another. (Author's collection)

that their prosperity depended on the control of the sea. From the beginning of the war in 1793 to its conclusion in 1815, although it experienced occasional problems, the Royal Navy never faltered and lived up to a well-established reputation for ruthless efficiency. The difference in performance between the two services was so great that one admiral, only half in jest, suggested the army be disbanded and the Royal Marines expanded to take over its functions.

Although naval service was long and arduous, and its manpower maintained by the unpopular institution of impressment or forced conscription, if a man was lucky there were financial advantages. The officers and sailors of a British warship that captured an enemy warship in battle received "head money," a cash bonus of £5 per head for every member of the crew of the enemy ship before the action started, the total being divided evenly among all officers and seamen. Considering that an ordinary seaman in 1793 earned about £10.11.6 per year, this was an incentive to do as much battle as possible. Even more attractive was the possibility of the prize money that might be awarded for the capture of a merchant vessel. The proceeds from the sale of the ship and its cargo, whether sold on the open market or purchased by the government, were shared according to a formula that heavily favoured senior officers, with the captain getting a three-eighths share of the total and the able and ordinary seamen and marines having all to split a quarter share. Some enterprising captains made fortunes, particularly in the early years of the war, and all naval officers and seamen dreamed of a prize such as that made by the crews of the four frigates that took two Spanish vessels laden with gold and silver in 1799. The prize money assessed was £600,000, the highest award ever made, with each captain receiving £40,173.18.0, each lieutenant £5,091.7.3 and each individual seaman and marine £182.0.9, an amount equivalent to more than a dozen times their annual pay. The relative stature of soldiers and sailors in the eyes of the public was aptly summed up in the doggerel sung by the prostitutes of one British port who, to a woman, were experts at instantly assessing a man's wealth:

> Sailors they get all the money,
> Soldiers they get none but brass;
> I do love a jolly sailor,
> Soldiers they may kiss my arse
> Oh! my little rolling sailor,
> Oh! my little rolling he;
> I do love a jolly sailor,
> Soldiers may be damned for me.[21]

In comparison to the navy, which went from strength to strength, the British army reached its nadir in early 1795 when the Dutch campaign ended. Its eventual salvation began that year, however, when the Duke of York took over the duties of commander-in-chief in place of the incompetent and nearly senile Amherst. Although a poor field commander, York proved to be an excellent administrator who introduced badly needed reforms, which few dared to oppose as he was backed by the authority of the King. It took time but he gradually cleaned up the mess left by his predecessor and began to turn an amateurish and dispirited service into a professional fighting force. He introduced strict measures to curb the abuses of the purchase system, forcing officers to serve a certain period in every rank before purchasing promotion, and he made officers subject to confidential reports on their performance. York disbanded the many weak regiments raised in the early years of the war and distributed their personnel into long-established units, getting rid of inadequate officers as he did so. He used his considerable powers of patronage to ensure that poor but deserving officers, unable to gain promotion by purchase, were promoted on their ability and he gradually restricted the purchase system so that, by 1809, it was estimated that only 20% of promotions were obtained by purchase, 70% by seniority and 10% by the duke's patronage. He vetted all applications for commissions and made himself personally available to officers who had legitimate complaints. He tightened the discipline of both officers and men, improved the army's clothing, weaponry and rations and tried, as best he could, to improve its pay and housing. He founded two institutions for officer education that eventually evolved into the Royal Military College and the Staff College, and he created the Duke of York's School for the education of the orphans of soldiers who died on active service.

Above all, the Duke of York improved the army's training. Less than a month after he took up his appointment, he issued a general order directing that, without exception, all regiments were to use Dundas's 1792 *Regulations* to train and that two days in each week were to be devoted to battalion drill and two to brigade drill, which was to be supervised by a general officer who was to "take out the whole and make perform such Movements, Manoevures or other Exercises as he may think proper."[22] York made frequent inspections to see that these orders were carried out and he ensured that the half-yearly inspections

The Duke of York (1763-1827)
The second son of King George III, Frederick Augustus, the Duke of York, had early demonstrated an interest in a military career. Although he did not prove successful as a field commander in the Low Countries in 1793-1795 and Holland in 1799, York's genius lay in administration. In 1795 he was appointed commander-in-chief of the army and instituted much-needed reforms, which, although they took nearly a decade to be accomplished, turned the army into a professional service which rarely suffered defeat in the later years of the Great War. Known as "the soldier's friend," York did his best to improve the pay and living conditions of the enlisted men. When he died in 1827, he was universally mourned. (Print after portrait by William Beechey)

were conducted thoroughly and rigorously. He also paid some attention to the need for light infantry training and authorized translations of foreign manuals relating to this subject for the benefit of the army. Many of York's reforms would take years to be completely realized but, working 12 to 15 hours a day in the War Office in London – commonly called the "Horse Guards" from its proximity to the barracks of that regiment – he laboured hard to create an army that could defeat a formidable opponent whose capabilities he knew from personal experience.

The Duke had been engaged in this important work for just over a year when a letter landed on his desk from one Thomas Pearson, a parson's lad from Somerset, who wished to purchase a commission in the army.

In 1796, an applicant wishing to become an officer in the British army by purchase had to meet five requirements. He had to have the money to do so, be no younger than 16 years, be literate, be a "gentleman" (often defined by his literacy) and be recommended by an officer of field grade (major and above). The applicant's first step was to select a regiment and, as the army had been decimated by disease in the West Indies, there were many openings available which, by regulation, were advertised in the *London Gazette*. Often, the applicant had a connection through family or patronage to an officer in a particular unit whom they would approach to recommend the applicant. This appears to have been the case with Thomas Pearson as his father chose to purchase him a second lieutenant's commission in the 23rd Foot, a fusilier regiment, which cost £55 more than the equivalent rank in an ordinary line infantry regiment. This indicates a partiality and a possible connection but, unfortunately, we do not have the evidence that might clarify it.[23] There is the additional consideration, however, that there were many vacancies in the 23rd as the regiment had recently been nearly destroyed by disease in the West Indies and it may have been that Reverend Pearson was able to obtain his eldest son's commission at a price lower than that fixed by order.[24]

Once the regiment was selected, and it was the 23rd Foot for Tom Pearson, his father would have contacted the regimental agent, Greenwood and Cox of Craig's Court, London. After the purchase price, £460, had been lodged with them, Greenwood & Cox would supply the applicant with the two required forms. The first was a letter to be sent to the Duke of York certifying that the applicant was "willing to abide, in the fullest sense of the word, by the prescribed rules and regulations."[25] The second was a letter to be signed by an officer of field grade certifying that the applicant was "in every respect quali-fied to serve" as an officer.[26] The agent's efforts were not free of charge and this added an additional £4.7.6 to the price of the commission. If the applicant was approved, the agent then transferred the sum deposited with him to the Crown or to an individual if it was a private sale, and in due course the new officer would be gazetted (his commission officially announced). Thomas Pearson was gazetted a second lieutenant in the 23rd Foot on 2 October 1796 and his commission, an impressive piece of parchment signed by the King's hand, was sent to him shortly afterward.

The business arrangements having been concluded, now came the time-consuming and expensive business of equipping young Tom for his new pro-fession. More likely, as it appears that there was never any serious doubt that his application would be accepted, this process began some time before his of-ficial appointment. A period military guide for new officers by Thomas Simes advised that, before embarking on their careers, they furnish themselves with

A full suit of [full uniform] cloth[e]s; 2 frock suits [daily and service uni-forms], 2 hats, 2 cockades; 1 pair of leather gloves; sash, and gorget; fuzee [necessary for a fusilier officer] or espontoon [for a plain infantry officer]; sword, sword-knot and belt; ... 1 pair of black [spatterdashes or knee-length gaiters], and tops; 1 pair [of short spatterdashes]; 1 pair of garters; 1 pair of boots, (all regimentals); a case of pistols; a blue surtout coat; a Portugal cloak; 6 white waistcoats; 12 white, and 2 black stocks; 18 pairs of stock-ings; 10 handkerchiefs; 1 pair of leather breeches; 6 pair of shoes; 24 shirts; 8 towels; 3 pair of sheets; 3 pillow cases; 6 linen night caps, and 2 yarn; a field bedstead; and a painted canvas bag to hold it; bed-curtains, quilt, three blankets, bolster, pillow, 1 mattrass, and a pailace [palliase]. Those articles should be carried in a leather valise; a travelling lettercase, to contain pens, ink, paper, wax, and wafers; a case of instruments for drawing, and Muller's Works on Fortification, etc. It is also essential that he should have a watch that he may mark the hour exactly when he sends any report, or what he may have discovered that is of consequence.[27]

Reverend Pearson, his purse already thinner by £464.7.6 or more, would have looked askance at such a lengthy list and suggested some restraint, which is, after all, a Christian virtue. With the possible exception, however, of Muller's texts, the field bed and its accoutrements, and the suggested number of "small clothes" such as stocks, waistcoats, shirts and stockings, most of the articles listed by Simes were actually necessary. While economy could be exercised with some things, such items as uniforms, hats, belts, boots, weapons, sash, gorget, sword and sword knot were required by regulation, and of these the most expensive were the full dress uniform with its gold lace, the two daily uniforms and the headgear. Unless young Tom was lucky enough to procure these items from a former officer of his regiment, which would be doubtful as the 23rd Foot had been in the West Indies for the previous two years, the uniforms would have to be made by a tailor, either in the nearest large town, probably Bath in Somerset, or more likely in London, which would require expensive trips to that city for fittings. Not only would he need the cocked hat, "encircled with a crimson and gold cord; rosettes or tufts of the same brought to the end of the brims," but there was also the officer's pattern fur cap, the hallmark of a fusilier, manufactured of the best bearskin or some more costly fur dyed black and which, with its brass regimental plate, attendant cords and fittings, was in a league of its own when it came to expense.[28]

As the parcels, chests and boxes containing these things, undoubtedly fascinating to Tom's younger brothers, began to pile up in the front hall or the parlour of the rectory at Queen Camel, the bills began to pile up on the parson's desk. When all was said and bought, his expenses for the uniforms, clothing and other items his son required would have probably been between £75 and £100. Combined with the price of the lad's commission, the total cost to Reverend Pearson to send his eldest son off to serve King and Country could not have been much less than £550. And this was just the start because army officers were not really expected to live on their pay, which, for young Second Lieutenant Pearson, was £66.18.3 a year – indeed the officers of the army had not received a raise in pay for nearly a century. They needed financial support from their families and the amount of this support varied, of course, according to the wealth of the family but even such a professional and no-nonsense soldier as Sir John Moore calculated that an officer should have a private income of between £50 and £100 per year. Although Parson Pearson's annual income was probably between £400 and £500 per year and he owned extensive property and was moderately wealthy, this was still a heavy burden and he had three other sons for whom provision had yet to be made.

Like many another newly-hatched young officer, Tom Pearson probably tried on his finery in front of the mirror and his reaction would perhaps have been similar to that of Lieutenant George Bell, a near contemporary:

I now mounted my uniform for the first time, and when full dressed was ashamed to appear in the streets. I fancied all the people would be laughing at the raw Ensign, with his cocked hat and feather, jack boots, white breeches, sword, and belt; then the sword was always getting between my legs, trying to trip me up as I went cautiously along, not daring to look at any one. I thought myself the most observed of observers, being just brand-new out of the tailor's shop.[29]

Hopefully, the good people of Queen Camel were more impressed by the military splendour of the reverend's eldest son.

It was soon time – probably none too soon for Thomas but all too soon for his family – to leave home and report to his regiment. Parents being what they are, there is a good chance that the mother of the aspiring young hero added a few articles not on Simes's list, such as a flannel shirt for warmth in the winter, various items of food lovingly prepared, and a goodly supply of homemade medicines (Parson Woodforde always swore by "the rhubarb"). His father, if he had managed to cross Muller's three books off Simes's list of necessaries, probably added the authorized manuals of his profession: the King James Bible and the Book of Common Prayer of the Church of England. As an afterthought (because the fathers of teenage boys do tend to live in hope), the good parson might also have thrown in some weighty volume containing the collected, dry and dusty moral sermons of some long-dead churchman. And then, accompanied by a trusty man servant, it was into the waiting wagon and off to Ilchester to catch the mail coach for Chatham, the current station of the 23rd Foot.

As Thomas Pearson was to serve in this regiment for most of his career and remain ferociously loyal to it throughout his life, it is fitting that we take a brief look at its history. His Britannic Majesty's 23rd Regiment of Foot (Royal Welsh Fuzileers), to give the correct title, had been in existence for more than a century when grass-green Second Lieutenant Pearson joined it in early 1797. Raised by order of King William III in 1689 as Lord Herbert's Regiment of Foot, its first colonel had been Henry, 4th Baron Herbert of Chirbury, who had extensive holdings in Wales and thus the Welsh connection, although for the first century or so of its existence the regiment rarely recruited in that part of Britain. Herbert's Regiment fought under William III in Ireland against his Stuart counterpart, James, and was present at the Battle of the Aughrim in 1691 which left William master of that island.

In 1702 Lord Herbert's Regiment was renamed the Welch Regiment of Fuzileers, a title that requires some explanation. In the early 18th century, the spelling "Welch" was commonly used to distinguish people from Wales but it was later overtaken by the modern spelling, "Welsh." Given that one of the hallmarks of Thomas Pearson's new regiment is a certain obstinacy concerning matters of dress and tradition, when the title was officially changed to "Welsh" in 1751, they vigorously and, ultimately, successfully campaigned well into the 20th century to have the archaic spelling "Welch" restored. The word "fuzileer" or "fusilier" dates from the introduction of the flintlock musket (*fusil* in French) in the late 17th century. Most infantry at this time carried matchlock muskets, which were dangerous around the quantities of open powder in artillery positions, and so special units, raised to escort and protect the gunners, were issued with "fuzees" or flintlocks, which were safer weapons. They became known as "fusiliers" or, given the vagaries of period spelling, "fuzileers," "fusileers" or "fuziliers." Two other British regiments were converted to fusiliers at this time, the Royal Fusiliers and the Royal North British Fusiliers, and while the Welch Fusiliers generally looked down on every other unit in existence, if pressed they might grudgingly admit that these two regiments were a cut above the rest.

From 1701 to 1711 the Welch Fusiliers campaigned on the continent under the Duke of Marlborough and won the Battle Honours "BLENHEIM" (1704), "RAMILLIES" (1706), "OUDENARDE" (1708) and "MALPLAQUET" (1709). These were emblazoned on the Regimental Colour, which shortly thereafter changed to blue, the colour of the royal family, as the unit was re-titled the Prince of Wales's Own Royal Regiment of Welsh Fusileers in 1713. The regiment had lost "The Prince of Wales's Own" from its title when it participated in the War of the Austrian Succession in 1746 but the Battle Honour "DETTINGEN" (1743) marks its presence at the last battle fought by a British army commanded by its king, in this case George II. In recognition of this, the Welch Fusiliers, along with the other regiments present at that action were permitted to add the White Horse of Hanover, the emblem of the royal family, to their Regimental Colours. When British regiments were numbered in 1747, the Welch Fusiliers became the 23rd Regiment of Foot (Royal Welsh Fuzileers), a title they would retain until 1881.

In the Seven Years War of 1757-1763, the 23rd Foot fought in Europe, adding the rare Battle Honour "MINDEN" (1759) to its Colour but the next war brought no Battle Honours and precious little glory. The 23rd Foot was sent to America in 1773 to fight against the rebellious colonists, and though it performed well

Soldiers drilling
As a mounted officer looks on, two platoons of soldiers drill in this aquatint by J.A. Atkinson. In a well-commanded infantry regiment, drill was incessant and in the British army it was reckoned that nearly two years of such training was necessary before a soldier was ready for battle. (Author's collection)

at Lexington, Bunker Hill, Brandywine, Charleston and Guilford Court House, most of the regiment was forced to surrender at Yorktown in 1781. The return of peace brought a spell of garrison duty in Ireland in the 1780s and then came a new war and the horror of the West Indies. On 8 March 1794 the 23rd Foot, 665 officers and men, with 48 women and 48 children, embarked at Cork for St. Domingo, Just over two years later, on 27 April 1796, a captain and 45 enlisted men disembarked at Spithead. The remainder were dead, almost all killed by yellow fever, not the enemy.

When Thomas Pearson joined the 23rd at Chatham early in 1797 it was a skeleton military unit, 229 officers and men strong, trying to recruit back to health. This may actually have been a blessing for a new officer as there would have been few lieutenants senior to him and, as many new officers arrived at the same time, all had to start from the beginning. As was traditional, Pearson and the other newcomers first joined an awkward squad of recruits to learn the manual and platoon exercises under the guidance of an experienced sergeant or corporal, who would teach them how to stand and march, and the various facings, turnings, paces and wheelings. This process was not always

31

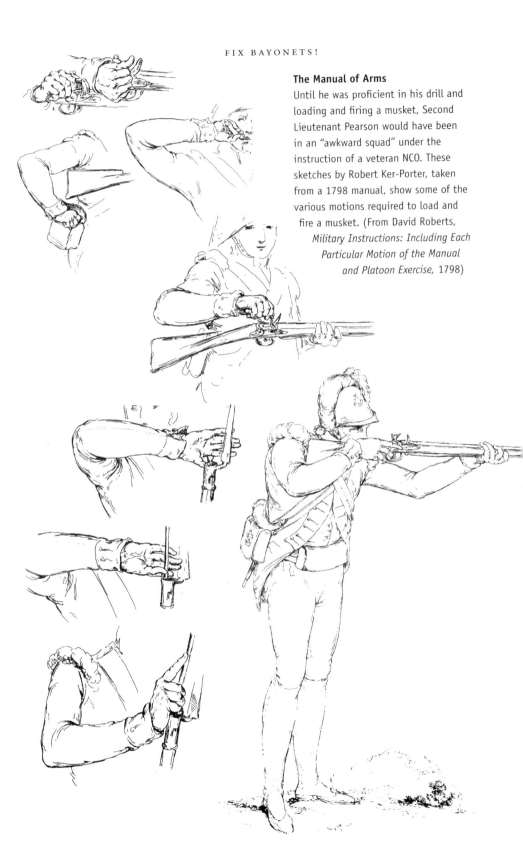

The Manual of Arms

Until he was proficient in his drill and loading and firing a musket, Second Lieutenant Pearson would have been in an "awkward squad" under the instruction of a veteran NCO. These sketches by Robert Ker-Porter, taken from a 1798 manual, show some of the various motions required to load and fire a musket. (From David Roberts, *Military Instructions: Including Each Particular Motion of the Manual and Platoon Exercise,* 1798) popular with new officers, who tended to agree with the witty author of that classic period piece, the tongue-in-cheek but still accurate *Advice to Officers of the British Army*, which suggested that, if told by their superiors that it might be a good idea to master "the manual, the salute, or other parts of the exercise," they should reply that they did "not want to be drill-serjeant or corporal" and that, having purchased their commissions, they "did not come into the army to be made a machine of."[30] Such a response would not have gone far in the 23rd Foot (although it might have in other regiments) and Pearson would have learned what he was required to learn. Much time would have been spent on the drill for loading and firing the musket, that often unreliable weapon which was the basis of the infantry tactics of the time. Recruits first learned the slow but complete drill: "Handle Cartridge! … Prime! … Load! … Draw Ramrods! … Ram Down Cartridge! … Return Ramrods! … Make Ready! … Present! … Fire!"[31] When they had mastered this so they could function like automatons, they would next be taught the "quick loading" drill which consisted of only four commands – "Prime and load!" … Make Ready! … Present! … Fire!" – all motions carried out "with as much dispatch as possible."

When he was proficient in the manual and platoon exercises, Second Lieutenant Pearson would next progress to company drill. When that was mastered, he might be judged fit to participate in battalion drill under the eagle eye of the adjutant, usually a veteran sergeant commissioned from the ranks, whose main duty was to drill the battalion for the lieutenant-colonel who commanded it. Pearson would now encounter the arcane mysteries of the *Rules and Regulations for the Formation, Field-Exercise, and Movements of His Majesty's Forces*, hundreds of pages of closely-printed and tightly-written script replete with such long and breathless sentences as:

> The deployment of the close column into a line OBLIQUE to the one on which its head then stands, may in some situations be required, where circumstances do not permit of the previous operation of placing the column perpendicular to such a line; as when a wing is to be lengthened out but refused, or an enemy's flank is to be gained by throwing forward one or more battalions which have advanced in close column behind the point a wing; or when the nature of the ground on which the column stands demands a deployment that will give a support to a flank, or preserve the advantage of position.[32]

Many were called to read Dundas but few chosen to fully understand him. Second Lieutenant Pearson would have spent many hours attempting to interpret the obfuscation of the text and staring in vain at the plates trying to comprehend how to transform a group of human beings into the precise geometric shapes illustrated in them. A lieutenant senior to Pearson would probably assure him that it was all so easy that only a simpleton would fail to grasp it.

As one of the most junior officers, Pearson and a fellow second lieutenant who enjoyed the same insignificant status would have carried the Colours on battalion parade. This was no easy task, particularly on windy days, as each of these heavily-embroidered articles was 6 feet, 6 inches on the hoist and 6 feet long on its shaft or pike, which measured 9 feet, 10 inches long. The most senior of the two second lieutenants carried the King's Colour, which was the Grand Union flag with the combined St. George and St. Andrew's cross, while the jun-

Maintaining discipline
Discipline in the British army was maintained by flogging, a punishment that had its opponents and proponents but was used throughout the war. For serious offences, such as desertion in the face of the enemy, a soldier might receive up to a thousand lashes. The amount of flogging varied from regiment to regiment and Lieutenant-Colonel Henry Ellis of the 23rd Foot, for example, was a humane commanding officer who remitted five of every six lashes he handed out, but he still flogged his men. (Drawing by Eugene Leliepvre, courtesy Parks Canada)

ior carried the blue Regimental Colour on which were emblazoned the Battle Honours of the 23rd as well as other heraldic devices, including the Prince of Wales's crest and the White Horse of Hanover.

When not spent drilling, the remainder of Pearson's day would have been devoted to the activities of garrison routine, such as mounting guards, barrack inspections and all the many and varied minor military tasks junior lieutenants receive to teach them flexibility and responsibility but which they are really given because no officer senior wants them. One event that would have become depressingly familiar would be a punishment parade, as the discipline in King George's army was ferocious and it was maintained by the lash.

To save money, Pearson would have joined the officers' mess of the 23rd Foot. Created as a temporary expedient to provide a more economical and enjoyable way for officers to dine, a mess was partly a private club in which all officers were equal regardless of rank (although this was not entirely true) and partly a dining establishment. As there were very few purpose-built military buildings at this time, messes were usually located in rented premises, often a hotel or tavern. The quality of the officers' mess, like much else, varied from regiment to regiment and many did not have them. The Welch Fusiliers did have a mess and it would have cost Pearson £3.10.0 to join, plus his share of the expenses – in 1787, an officer paid 10 shillings and sixpence each week to daily receive "a good dinner and small beer, one good fire in the Mess Room, and as many candles as may at times be thought necessary."[33] Wine was additional but as the mess bought in quantity, it was cheaper than elsewhere and a trustworthy soldier was usually appointed messman and allowed a small but controlled profit on sales of alcohol not provided for in the weekly fee. In any case, the purpose of a mess was not to make money, and any profits were usually drunk or eaten or ploughed back into improving conditions.

In a time when heavy drinking was normal, behaviour in messes could get out of hand. *Advice to Officers* suggests that officers belonging to a mess should

> eat with it as seldom as possible, to let folks see you want neither money nor credit. And when you do, in order to shew that you are used to good living, find fault with every dish, that is set on the table, damn the wine, and throw the plates at the mess-man's head.
>
> If the dinner is not served up immediately on your sitting down, draw circles with your fork on the table; cut the table-cloth; and, if you have

pewter plates, spin them on the point of your fork, or some other mischief, to punish the fellow for making you wait.[34]

In contrast, as its rules illustrate, the Welch Fusiliers officers' mess was well regulated:

The President and Vice-President shall be appointed daily in rotation: each of whom is to bring his [soldier] servant to assist in attending at dinner.

The President is to order dinner for the number the Mess consists of: each of whom is to pay 1 shilling, sixpence for dinner and beer, whether he comes or not. ......

The President is to order in a bottle of wine for every three persons present, and a bottle for any over. When that allowance is drank, the bill to be called and paid, charged as usual. ......

It is expected that no member of the Mess drinks more than one glass of wine during dinner. ......

No dogs to be admitted into the Mess room at any time.[35]

Shortly after his arrival, Second Lieutenant Pearson would have been inculcated into the regimental distinctions and traditions of the Royal Welch Fusiliers. Their bearskin headdress, unique to fusilier regiments among the infantry of the line, has been mentioned, but there was also the matter of his rank of second lieutenant, which was a fusilier oddity as the most junior officer's rank of the common herd – that is to say, all non-fusilier infantry regiments – was ensign.

Among regimental traditions, first and foremost was the Goat. By the 1790s, the Welch Fusiliers had forgotten just when and why they acquired the Goat – 20 years earlier they were already priding themselves "on the ancientness of the custom."[36] The Goat, which was not a mascot and never called such, accompanied the regiment wherever it went, and when the regiment passed in review, the Goat had the privilege, attended by his Goat Major, of leading them "with gilded horns, and adorned with ringlets of flowers."[37]

Another tradition was the celebration of St. David's Day, the first day of March, as St. David was the patron saint of Wales. An important part of the festivities was a curious ceremony known as "eating the leek" (a leek is a prominent

"Dreadful times are approaching."

Eating the leek in the Royal Welch Fusiliers' mess on Saint David's Day
The origin of the Welch Fusiliers' custom of eating a leek during the annual Saint David's Day celebration on the first day of March is lost in the mists of antiquity, which is to say that nobody knows when or why it started although the tradition is believed to be some three centuries old. In this fine painting by R. Caton-Woodville, two guests to the Fusiliers' mess eat a leek while standing on their chairs as the Goat, attended by two drummer boys and the Goat Major, circles the mess table. (Painting by R. Caton-Woodville, courtesy of The Royal Welch Fusiliers Museum)

member of the onion family) in the officers' mess after the celebratory dinner had concluded. This ceremony, which was believed to have originated when Lord Herbert's Regiment was raised in the late 17th century, is carried on to this day and has been well described by an officer who served with Pearson:

> The custom of the corps is, that on the day, immediately after dinner, when we are in barracks, one of the little drummer-boys, rides a large goat, with which the regiment is always provided, round the Mess-room, carrying in his hands a dish of Leeks. Each Officer is called upon to eat one, for which he pays the drummer a shilling. The older Officers of the regiment, and those who have service with it in the field, are favoured only with a small one, and salt. Those who have before celebrated at St. David's day with the regiment, but have only seen garrison duty with it, are required to eat a larger one

Learning how to smoke and drink grog
This drawing by Thomas Rowlandson for the marvellous little book *The Adventures of Johnny Newcome* illustrates the dangers inherent in young officers trying to keep up with their more experienced comrades at the mess table. The Georgian and Regency periods were hard-drinking times and men thought little of having a glass of whisky for breakfast – if it was available. (From *The Adventures of Johnny Newcome,* 1816)

without salt, and those unfortunates, who for the first time, have sat at the Mess, on this their Saint's day, have presented to them the largest Leek that can be procured, and unless sickness prevents it, no respite is given, until the last tip of its green leaf is enclosed in the unwilling mouth; and day after day passes by before the smell and taste is fairly got rid of.[38]

Goats being obstinate creatures, not unlike the Welch Fusiliers, they can sometimes get out of hand. At Boston in 1775 the Regimental Goat mutinied during the eating of the leek, giving "such a spring from the floor, that he dropped his rider upon the table, and then bouncing over the heads of some officers, he ran to the barracks with all his trappings, to the no small joy of the garrison and populace."[39]

Second Lieutenant Pearson would have learned, as did every young officer of that time, that the first day of the month was the most important as on that the day the British army was mustered and paid. In his case, he would receive £5.11.6 before various stoppages and deductions – including poundage or primitive income tax, a fixed donation toward the upkeep of the Chelsea Hospital for veterans and probably a fixed contribution to the maintenance of the regimental band – which would reduce his pay by about a fifth, and then there were his mess bills to be paid and probably other outstanding accounts. The result might just be a politely desperate letter to the rectory at Queen Camel.

Given his upbringing with its emphasis on an orderly life-style and service to the community, Second Lieutenant Thomas Pearson probably did not engage in the favourite pastimes of many young British officers, described by one author as "hard drinking, gambling and heiress-stalking, enlivened by duels and mad cap wagers."[40] He was probably one of the more temperate young gentlemen in the 23rd Foot, but that could also invite trouble for, as *Advice to Officers* notes,

> If there should be a soberly-disposed person, or, in other words, a fellow of no spirit, in the corps, you must not only *bore* him constantly at the mess, but should make use of a kind of practical wit to torment him. Thus you may force open his doors, break his windows, damage his furniture and put wh___s in his bed; or in camp throw squibs and [fire] crackers into his tent at night, or loosen his tent-cords in windy weather. Young gentlemen will never be at a loss for contrivances of this nature.[41]

Reading, even military manuals, was frowned on by the more lively officers. If they had "to kill in that manner the tedious hours in camp or garrison," they were advised only to read titles that "warm the imagination and inspire to military achievements," including "*The Woman of Pleasure, Crazy Tales*," or "if you aim at solid instruction and useful knowledge you must study *Lord Chesterfield's Letters*," while "*The Trials for Adultery* will afford you a fund of historical and legal information."[42]

Second Lieutenant Thomas Pearson's experiences in his first months in King George's army in 1796-1797 would not have differed much from those of any other new officer. While he was mastering the oblique step, learning how to stretch his pay from the first day of one month to the first of the next, eat a large, raw leek without salt and hold his liquor, the most popular subject of conversation among his fellow officers would have been the course of the war with France.

Unfortunately, it was not going well for Britain.

Loading troops for an expedition, c. 1800

This caricature by George Cruickshank exaggerates the organized chaos that took place when troops embarked for overseas service. Cavalry officers, for example, were not loaded while mounted on their horses – but the attitudes of the sailors toward the military passengers, the "shifting ballast," as they were known in the navy, is entirely accurate. Britain's incomparable fleet gave her a tremendous advantage as sea power enabled her to project military power at great distances, something that France could not counter.

(From William Robinson, *Jack Nastyface,* 1836)

CHAPTER TWO

"THE FRENCH HAVE READ A LESSON TODAY THEY WILL NOT SOON FORGET."

ENGLAND, HOLLAND AND EGYPT, 1798–1801

Hark! hark! the drums do beat, my love, and I must haste away;
The bugles sweetly sound and no longer can I stay.
We are called up to Portsmouth, it's many a long mile,
All for to be embarked for the Banks of the Nile.

"Oh, cursed, cursed be the day that e'er the wars began,
For they've taken out of England full many a pretty man;
They've taken from us our lifeguards, protectors of our isle,
And their bodies feed the worms on the Banks of the Nile."

Let a hundred days be darkened, let maidens give a sigh,
It would melt the very elements to hear the wounded cry;
Let a hundred days be brightened, let maidens give a smile,
But remember Abercromby on the Banks of the Nile.[1]

In the spring of 1796, at about the time 15-year-old Thomas Pearson applied for his commission, a French officer some 12 years his senior was making a name for himself. Napoleon Bonaparte, a Corsican by birth who had obtained a commission in the French artillery, first came to prominence during the siege of Toulon, occupied by Britain and Spain in 1793. *Capitaine* Bonaparte worked out the weak point in the allied defences and the French besiegers, directing their efforts against it, forced a hasty evacuation of the major French naval base in the Mediterranean. The times in France being uncertain, Bonaparte was jailed briefly when a *coup d'état* overthrew the Committee of Public Safety in July 1794 and replaced it with a five-man Directory, but he was eventually released, promoted *général de brigade*, and was holding a staff position in Paris when he helped to foil a counter-coup against the Directory. His reward was further promotion and an appointment to lead the Army of Italy.

Général de division Bonaparte was all of 27 years of age in March 1796 when he assumed command of this rather tattered force, short on arms, uniforms, equipment, money and food, but in the space of nine months he defeated several Austrian armies and forced that nation, which had also suffered serious reverses in Germany, to sue for peace, bringing the First Coalition to an end. Deserted by her allies, Britain was now left alone against France and her position was made worse when Spain, under pressure from the republic, declared war on her in the autumn of 1796.

There was, however, a more serious threat. On Easter Sunday, 16 April 1797, the sailors of the Channel Fleet at Spithead refused to put to sea when ordered. They had legitimate grievances, the main one being that their pay, which had not been increased in more than a century, was often in arrears and, in any case, inadequate to feed their families in the face of wartime inflation. It was cruelly ironic that, while these men were defending Britain at sea, their families were starving on shore. The sailors had respectfully submitted their grievances to the Admiralty, the headquarters of the Royal Navy in London, but through some bureaucratic oversight their petition had been put aside. Getting no response, the sailors naturally assumed that the Admiralty was not prepared to listen and refused to sail until there was a resolution of their problems. In the meantime, they maintained discipline on their ships and treated their officers well.

As the Channel Fleet was Britain's main defence, there was shock and dismay when news of this "mutiny" spread through the country. The Admiralty sent some of its senior members literally post-haste to Spithead, where they listened to the men's problems, adjusted their grievances as best they could, and obtained them a Royal Pardon for their actions. This, however, was only the beginning of a wave of naval troubles which culminated in a full-scale mutiny at the Nore in May 1797 during which the sailors put their officers ashore or imprisoned them and threatened to sail the fleet to France. This was going too far, and the government stood firm until the mutineers, themselves divided, finally submitted. Four hundred were court-martialled of which 300 were pardoned, 29 executed and the remainder punished by flogging or imprisonment.

During the time of the fleet troubles, the 23rd Foot was stationed at Chelmsford in Essex. In September 1797 it moved to Deal in Kent, where it remained until December before moving to Norwich in Norfolk, not far from Parson Woodforde at Weston Longville. In April 1798, just as the spring was in full bloom, the Welch Fusiliers marched south to Canterbury in preparation to counter an expected French invasion. If it came, it would be led by young *Général* Bonaparte as, early in that year, the Directory had turned its attention northward and dispatched the republic's most victorious commander to lead *l'armée d'angleterre* or "the army of England" on the Channel Coast. Bonaparte had orders to conquer the "giant corsair that infests the seas" and with his usual energy immediately commenced the construction of large numbers of landing craft.[2]

Prime Minister William Pitt's government prepared to meet him and Pitt's first step was to secure the financial means to increase the size of the armed forces. Over the winter of 1797-1798, he nearly trebled taxation, and though this led to much grumbling on the part of the propertied classes where the burden fell most heavily, the increase was generally accepted. The government also instituted a voluntary defence fund, which was wildly popular among all levels of society from King George III, who contributed a third of his disposable annual income, down to the seamen of HMS *Argonaut,* who contributed 10 shillings each "to drive into the sea all French scoundrels and other blackguards."[3] In Norfolk, as his diary entries for April 1798 testify, even Parson Woodforde, usually more interested in his stomach than the course of the war, sat up and took notice:

Dinner to day, Fillett of Veal rosted &c. ... By the publick Papers, every thing in them appears very distressing & alarming. French Invasion daily expected.[4] ......

A great Meeting at Reepham to day, respecting all People arming themselves &c. against an Invasion of this Country from the French &c. which is much talked of at present by all kinds of People especially the poor. Pray God preserve us from our private Enemies at home. Dinner today, a Fillett of Veal rosted &c.[5] ......

Nothing talked of at present but an Invasion of England by the French. Great Preparations making all over England &c. against the said intended Invasion, especially all along the Sea Coasts every where. ...... [6]

Dinner to day, hash Mutton and a Suet Pudding, I made a very great Dinner to day indeed, was rather afraid I had eat too much but I rec[eive]d. no Inconvenience from it. A Meeting of the Parish this Afternoon at the Heart, respecting a sudden Invasion from the French &c. what was necessary and proper to be done on a sudden attack.[7]

With money in hand, the government made new efforts to increase the size of the army and by the spring of 1798 there were 97,000 regular troops in the British Isles. Of these, however, 25,000 were fencibles, who were not required to serve outside the home islands, while 40,000 of the regulars were stationed to keep the peace in Ireland, where there were signs of serious unrest. Unfortunately, many of these troops were green recruits, hastily enlisted to replace the losses suffered in the West Indies. The strength of the militia was also increased to 100,000 and, following a wave of patriotism that swept over the nation, hundreds of volunteer units composed of great landowners, squires, farmers, clerks, labourers, shopkeepers, members of parliament, civil servants and just about any other male who could put one foot in front of another and shoulder a musket, sprang into being. They were gloriously uniformed, poorly armed and totally untrained but they represented a national spirit of defiance against republican France and "Boney," its scarecrow general, a spirit exemplified by the popular song, "Snug Little Island," first sung in the spring of 1797:

> Since Freedom and Neptune have hitherto kept tune,
> In each saying, "This shall be my land";
> Oh the army of England to all they could bring land,
> Would show 'em some play for our Island.
>
> We'd fight for our right to the Island,
> We'd give 'em enough of the Island,
> Invaders should just – bite at the dust,
> But not a bit more of the Island.[8]

The Royal Navy, the main defence of that island, quickly demonstrated that the recent mutinies of 1797 had not blunted its efficiency. Holland, in the form of the Batavian Republic, was now an ally of France, and in October that year a British fleet under Admiral Sir Adam Duncan with 16 ships of the line engaged a Dutch fleet of equal strength at Camperdown off the coast of Holland. The Dutch, no mean sailors themselves, fought stubbornly but after a bloody battle which lasted more than three hours, Duncan had taken seven enemy warships prize (although they were too badly battered to be of much service) and blunted the threat of Dutch naval power.

The government now began to contemplate other offensive moves and on the advice of an ambitious but rather impractical naval officer, Captain Home

"The French have read a lesson today they will not soon forget."

Popham, a raid was planned against the Dutch port of Ostend. A canal had recently been completed that connected Ostend with the inland waterways to facilitate the transport of men, stores and gunboats to the city for an eventual invasion of Britain. Popham proposed to land a raiding force to destroy a vulnerable lock on this canal to render it useless, and the government, anxious to strike back, agreed to his plan. An expedition was assembled with Popham commanding the naval component and Major-General Eyre Coote the army component. The landing force consisted of about 1,400 men assembled from detachments of the Guards and the 11th, 23rd and 49th Foot. The Welch Fusiliers were ordered to contribute their light and grenadier companies but not their battalion companies because, as a senior officer had commented, there were "a great many Dutchmen in the regiment which I do not think exactly calculated for the intended service."[9] Nonetheless, it appears that most of the 23rd Foot embarked with the expedition at Margate in May 1798.

Among them was Thomas Pearson, who had just been promoted to first lieutenant. A vacancy for that rank having occurred within the 23rd Foot and Pearson being the senior second lieutenant, the commanding officer accepted his application to purchase and Pearson made the arrangements. No money actually passed hands between officers, all the financial transactions being conducted by the regimental agents, who accepted Pearson's payment of £560 for the higher rank while at the same time selling his second lieutenant's commission to an approved purchaser for the established price of £460. This meant that Pearson's father (for it was almost certainly he who put up the money) had only to pay the difference of £100, although this was no insignificant amount, as well as the agent's fees. There may have been, although it was strictly forbidden by regulation, an arrangement under the table to sweeten the deal, which may have raised the price to more than £100.

At Margate, as he went on board the frigate HMS *Champion*, Captain Henry Raper, RN, commanding, Thomas Pearson witnessed for the first time the scenes of organized chaos that took place when an army embarked. As another soldier recalled about this process:

All bustles in the former course of my life were nothing comparable to this! What by embarking the troops and baggage, and the men of wars' officers running, cursing, swearing, and driving the sailors out of the publick houses, and from one boat to another, there was nothing but noise and confusion. And yet it is astonishing, in how short a time several regiments, with their baggage, were embarked. As our regiment was the last of the brigade which embarked that day, it was near dark before we were on board our transport, the Constant Jean, about three hundred tons burthen, in which was stowed four hundred soldiers, besides officers, sergeants, drums and women, with the sailors who belonged to the ship, there were full five hundred souls on board, and therefore were extremely thronged; to remedy which as much as possible, one half were ordered to remain on deck at one time, and the other half at another, so that we changed alternately.[10]

The expedition sailed on 15 May 1798 but Pearson did not see any action. The Admiralty had always been somewhat suspicious of this venture and had warned Popham about the dangerous and unreliable winds off the Dutch coast, and such was the state of the weather that he decided to lie offshore until a better opportunity presented itself. Coote, however, having information that the garrison of Ostend was weak, requested that his men be put ashore no matter what the risk. Popham complied and the troops, including the light and grenadier companies of the 23rd, were landed late in the morning of 19 May. Coote was able to successfully blow up the locks but the Dutch commandant of Ostend refused to surrender and the landing force, having accomplished its objective, returned to the beach only to discover that, due to a shift in the wind, they could not re-embark. Coote therefore dug in among the sand dunes and took the time to write a dispatch to inform his superiors of the "complete and brilliant success attending the expedition."[11]

The following day a large French force arrived, and although Coote resisted for several hours, he was finally forced to surrender. As he was wounded during the fighting, his second-in-command had to write another dispatch to report "the painful Task of detailing our unavoidable surrender." The casualties were 1,295 killed, wounded, missing and captured, of which the Welch Fusiliers lost 4 killed, 11 wounded and 184 officers and men taken prisoner, including Pearson's commanding officer and seven of his fellow lieutenants. The only bright spot in this misadventure was that most of the prisoners were exchanged by the French and returned to the regiment a year later.

Three days after the raid on Ostend, rebellion broke out in Ireland, whose affairs had been seriously mismanaged for more than a century. For the next six months, the government's main concern was the suppression of this insurrection, a suppression carried out with such cruelty and bloodshed that

"The French have read a lesson today they will not soon forget."

Général Napoleon Bonaparte (1769-1821)
A Corsican by birth, Bonaparte became an officer in the French artillery and first came to notice during the siege of Toulon in 1793. His rise through the ranks was meteoric and by 1796, at the age of 26, he was commanding the *Armée d'Italie,* which won a number of brilliant victories over an 18-month period that knocked Austria out of the First Coalition. In 1798 Bonaparte commanded the expeditionary force sent to Egypt which conquered that country. By this time he was a household name in Europe but even greater glory lay in store for him. (From *Portraits des généraux français faisant suite aux victoires et conquêtes des Français,* 1818)

it left indelible scars on the Irish consciousness. In the meantime, Bonaparte, having concluded that it was impossible for France "to gain naval supremacy for some years" and that to invade Britain "without such supremacy would be to embark on the most daring and difficult task ever undertaken," advised the Directory to undertake an "expedition to threaten England's trade with the Indies."[12] The Directory approved and in May 1798 Bonaparte assembled most of his veteran Army of Italy at Toulon for the purpose of invading Egypt in an attempt to close the Middle East to British commerce.

In late 1796 the Royal Navy, stretched thin to meet its many commitments, had been withdrawn from the Mediterranean, but when the Admiralty received intelligence of a French military and naval build-up at Toulon early in 1798, it ordered Rear-Admiral Horatio Nelson to that place with a squadron to block any French movements by sea. Nelson was delayed by weather and Bonaparte, with 31,000 troops carried on 300 transports escorted by 44 warships, slipped out of Toulon and set course for Egypt, where he landed in the first few days of July 1798. His veteran army made short work of the ragged troops of the Ottoman sultan and Bonaparte began to draw up plans for the invasion of Palestine.

Nelson, arriving at Toulon to find the fox gone, spent much of July 1798 hunting him around the Mediterranean but it was not until the afternoon of 1 August that he caught up with the French at Aboukir Bay near Alexandria. The enemy naval commander, *Vice-amiral* François Brueys, had anchored his force of 13 ships of the line and four frigates in line astern in the bay but far enough from the shore that they could be attacked on both sides by Nelson's

Nelson's victory at the Nile, 1 August 1798
In August 1798 Nelson destroyed the French fleet that had accompanied Bonaparte's ex-
pedition to Egypt at Aboukir Bay, cutting off his army from the European mainland. (From
Thomas Gaspey, *The History of England*, 1856)

fleet, which consisted of 14 ships of the line. As was his custom, the British
commander sailed straight into the attack and his confidence was matched
by that of his sailors, who had absolutely no doubt they would be victorious.
Even before the first shot was fired, they were counting their prize money, as
is clear from the conversation of one gun crew recorded by an officer as their
ship approached the French line:

> Jack: "There are thirteen sail of the line, and a whacking lot of frigates and
> small craft. I think we'll hammer the rust off ten of them, if not the whole
> boiling."
> Tom: ...... "Now, if we knock up a dozen of these fellows .... d[amn] my
> eyes, messmates, we will have a bread-bag full of money to receive."
> Jack: "Aye, I'm glad we have twigged 'em at last. I want some new rigging
> d[amna]bly for Sundays and mustering days."
> Tom: "So do I. I hope we'll touch enough for that, and a d[amned]d good
> cruise among the girls besides."[13]

Jack and Tom, if they survived the battle, were not to be disappointed. The battle of the Nile began in the evening and lasted through the night, and although the French fought with desperate courage – Brueys continued to command after losing both legs to a roundshot – by morning all but two of the enemy ships of the line and two frigates were taken or sunk. Bonaparte was now isolated in Egypt.

Fortunately for the Royal Welch Fusiliers, after their return from Ostend in May 1799, they were not sent to Ireland but instead stationed on Guernsey in the Channel Islands. At this time, the regiment was far below its establishment – in January 1799 it was reported as having only 410 officers and men but an inspecting officer praised the Welch Fusiliers for being "extremely steady, the whole seems to possess the proper esprit de corps which leaves no room for doubt, that, in a short time, the regiment will be as excellent as possible."[14] That same month they were transferred to Southampton and, in July, to Barham Down Camp near Canterbury, where they made ready to embark on an expedition to the continent.

Nelson's victory at Aboukir Bay had caused tremendous excitement in Europe and it was not long before a Second Coalition against France came into being, almost of its own accord. By the early spring of 1799, Austria, Britain, Russia and Turkey had declared war on the aggressive republic, with only Prussia holding back. Pitt's government had tried hard to forge a diplomatic alliance with Prussia and Russia with a view to invading Holland, but when Prussia proved reluctant, Britain and Russia agreed to undertake the operation with 18,000 Russian troops who would be paid by Britain, herself contributing 30,000 men to the expedition. The Dutch royal family, exiles on British soil, assured the government that the people of Holland would rise up in arms the moment a redcoat stepped on their soil and the Admiralty, although it disliked operating inshore along the treacherous Dutch coast, was keen to acquire the remaining ships of the Dutch battle fleet. Last but not least, public opinion, buoyed up by Austrian and Russian victories in Italy and Germany that had pushed the republican armies back to their own borders, demanded Britain take a more active role in the war. The government listened to this clamour and, for political reasons, the Duke of York was taken from the Horse Guards where he had been doing good work and appointed to command the expeditionary force with Lieutenant-General Sir Ralph Abercromby as his second-in-command and chief advisor. Abercromby would make the initial landing with the duke coming later to take command of the combined British and Russian armies and the Dutch insurgents.

Lieutenant-General Sir Ralph Abercromby, 65 years old in 1799, was an interesting man. Educated as a lawyer, he had switched careers during the Seven Years War and had seen considerable service during that conflict. A man of liberal leanings, Abercromby had refused to serve in North America during the War of Independence, but when war with France broke out, he had volunteered for active service and had fought in the Low Countries and West Indies in 1793-1797. His personal views, which usually clashed with those held by Pitt's cabinet, did not endear him to the government, but in 1797 he was appointed to command in Ireland, whence he was soon recalled because of his sympathies for the downtrodden Catholic Irish and his dislike of the rule of the Anglo-Irish elite. He was also angered by the quality and discipline of the regular troops of the Irish Establishment, whom he once castigated in a general order as being "formidable to every one but the enemy."[15] Despite his liberal views, it was widely accepted that Abercromby was one of the army's most intelligent senior officers. Captain Henry Bunbury, who served on his staff, admitted that the short-sighted general was perhaps a little too old for active service but remembered him as "a noble chieftain" who was

> Mild in manner, resolute in mind, frank, unassuming, just, inflexible in what he deemed to be right, valiant as the Cid, liberal and loyal as the prowest of black Edward's knights. An honest, fearless, straightforward man; and withal sagacious and well skilled in his business as a soldier. As he looked out from under his thick, shaggy eyebrows, he gave one the idea of a very good-natured lion, and he was respected and beloved by all who served under his command.[16]

Abercromby spent much of July and August 1799 puzzling over the government's plans for the Dutch operation and, with impeccable logic, rejecting most of the suggested objectives. It was finally decided, somewhat hazily by all concerned, that the army would land on the tip of the Marsdiep Peninsula, which separated the North Sea from the inland waters of the Zuyder Zee and was close to the major Dutch naval base on Texel Island to the north. Abercromby was unable to obtain any intelligence on the strength of the enemy and he discovered that transport, both sea and land, was in short supply. Just to add to the disagreeables, the government did not have the 30,000 men it had promised the

"The French have read a lesson today they will not soon forget."

Lieutenant-General Sir Ralph Abercromby (1734-1801)

A Scot with a somewhat mixed background, Abercromby served in the West Indies and Holland in 1793-1795. During the Helder campaign of 1799, he was second-in-command to the Duke of York and the following year commanded the British expeditionary force sent to Egypt. A good officer and respected leader, Abercromby was the first British general during the war to have the opportunity to properly train his troops before committing them to battle. The result was that he won three victories in quick succession in Egypt in 1801 but lost his life at the battle of Alexandria. Almost forgotten today, Abercromby was respon-

sible for placing the British army squarely on the road that led to victory at Waterloo. (From John Richards, *Naval and Military Heroes of Great Britain*, 1860)

Czar it would contribute to the expedition, but it did have a solution – it hastily passed an act paying large bounties to militiamen who enlisted in 14 selected regiments of the line (the 23rd Foot was not among them) that would not be required to serve outside continental Europe and thus would avoid the perilous West Indies. This measure brought a supply of trained men "drunk and rolling riotously into the ranks" of the regiments chosen, but Captain Henry Bunbury questioned whether this move was wise as the new recruits were no longer "well-drilled, orderly soldiers of our Militia regiments" and not yet men "on whom their new officers could rely for regular service."[17] In fact,

> these men were hardly sobered from the riotous jollity of their volunteering; their minds were unsettled; to them their new officers and sergeants were utter strangers; everything was new and bewildering. In this condition they were hurried down to seaside, packed in transports, and sent off in a tempestuous season to engage immediately with the French armies in one of the most difficult countries in which war can be waged. These raw soldiers did not even bear the uniforms of the regiments whose colours they were expected to defend and whose honour they were to uphold. There had not even been time to provide clothing for them. …. If only three months had been gained for them to know something of their officers and sergeants, and the ways of the regiment into which they had entered, these men would probably

have done their duty well; but such was not the case, and ...... and these suddenly created battalions proved unfit to meet a brave and skilful enemy.[18]

As if this was not bad enough, the expedition was the subject of conversation throughout Britain – a week before it sailed, Parson Woodforde recorded that there was "Great doing going forward respecting our intended Secret Expedition. Many think it is designed for Holland to reinstate the Statholder."[19]

The initial landing force, which included the Welch Fusiliers, sailed on 13 August 1799. The fleet encountered such rough seas that it was not until 27 August that Abercromby was able to attempt a landing at a point some four miles south of the village of Helder on the tip of the Marsdiep. The 23rd Foot was one of six battalions chosen for the assault and, on the morning of 27 August, under cover of a heavy bombardment from the fleet, they boarded their boats and, rowing through a heavy surf that swamped some of the crowded craft, landed on a narrow beach surrounded by sand dunes. Almost as soon as the troops had formed, they were attacked by French and Dutch troops and 12 hours of heavy fighting followed until the obstinacy of the British gradually wore down the defenders. As Lieutenant John Hill of the 23rd recorded, the Welch Fusiliers advanced "cheering" and the French, "who did not like this movement … began to get off in quick time."[20] The casualties in this, Thomas Pearson's baptism of fire, were heavy: the Dutch and French lost 1,400 killed and wounded while the British also lost 1,400 with the 23rd Foot suffering the highest unit losses in Abercromby's command, 95 killed, wounded and missing. But the army was ashore.

Three days later a squadron of British warships entered the treacherous waters of the Zuyder Zee and procured the surrender of seven Dutch ships of the line and 18 smaller warships. Two more were captured afterward and, as one of the main objectives of the expedition had now been accomplished, it perhaps would have been well if it had returned to Britain at this point. This was not to be, and over the next week, as more troops and supplies were landed, Abercromby gradually advanced until he reached the line of the Zuype Canal, which bisected the Helder Peninsula. This gave the French commander in Holland, *Général de division* Guillaume Brune, the opportunity to mass 21,000 troops, of which one third were French, to defend that line. On 10 September he attacked Abercromby's positions along the Zuype but was repulsed with heavy losses.

The Duke of York now arrived to assume command of an army which, including the Russian contingent, had grown to 40,000 men. With such a force,

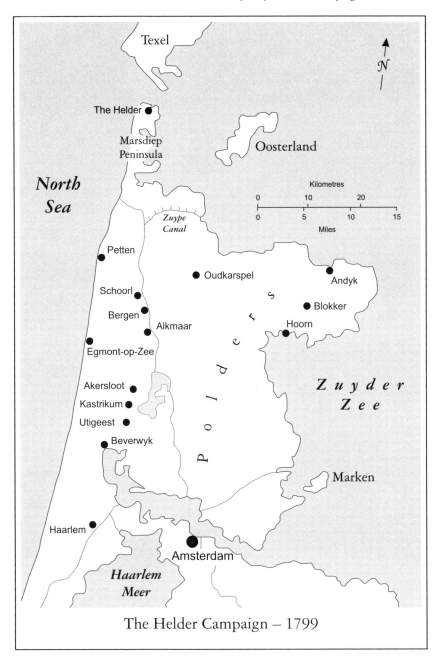

The Helder Campaign – 1799

York resolved to break out of the peninsula and take Amsterdam, about 25 miles to the south. He organized his army into four columns, the Russians to move along the sea coast, Abercromby along the shore of the Zuyder Zee, and two smaller columns to move in between to maintain contact. At 6 P.M. on 18 September, Abercromby set out to make a night march to Hoorn on the inland shore. At the head of his column of 10,000 men were the 18th Light Dragoons, an artillery detachment and the 23rd and 55th Foot – "hard biting soldiers" in Bunbury's opinion.[21] The march was a nightmare because, as Private William Surtees of the 56th Foot remembered,

> such was the state of the roads that it became the most trying and distressing march that I believe ever troops undertook; the roads were literally knee deep in mud in most places, while every now and then they were rendered nearly impassable, both by the enemy having broken down the bridges over the innumerable canals and dikes which intersect this country, and these canals in many places having overflowed their banks.[22]

By the time the advance guard approached Hoorn, it was four to five hours behind schedule and, when it did arrive, a comic opera scene took place. While the weary infantry of the 23rd and 55th Foot leaned on their muskets, staff officers pounded on the main gate of the town and shouted "Open your gates, or they shall be blown down by our cannons!"[23] To reinforce the effect, Bunbury remembered, the 18th Light Dragoons, who were at the head of the column, were ordered to open up their ranks and let two 6-pdr. guns come forward but,

> Instead of giving the word of command quietly, the leading officer shouted, "Back, back, make way for the guns!" – "Back, back," was loudly repeated by the dragoon officers. Our jaded infantry were roused from their unconscious slumbers by the sudden clatter of the horses on the pavement, the rattling of cannon wheels, and this unhappy cry of "Back, back." In an instant the 23rd and 55th broke like a flock of sheep, plunging into the deep mud at the sides of the causeway, and dreaming for some moments that they had been surprized and charged by a sortie of cavalry! The confusion was stopped in time; the Dutchmen opened their gates and the reserve recovered their senses and their ranks. Heartily ashamed of themselves they were, for there were no braver fellows in the army.[24]

The rest of the allied army fared as poorly. The Russians had started off two hours before the scheduled time and had pushed through the French, ignoring casualties that included their general, to enter the town of Bergen. Here they fell to looting and drinking, and when Brune counterattacked and drove them out of Bergen, the British infantry, which had moved at the correct time, were too far away to render support. The French hit the Russians hard and they broke and ran back through the British units behind, which, largely composed of militiamen, became infected by the panic and also made for the rear. The French kept advancing until they ran into four battalions of the Guards, which stopped them cold and restored the situation. For his part, Abercromby, who might have tipped the scales, remained at Hoorn waiting for information that never came and did not join the battle. The action ended with the loss of about 4,000 men per side but the overall result was that the British no longer trusted the Russians and York began to feel uneasy about many of his own units.

The Welch Fusiliers were engaged in this action and Lieutenant John Hill remembered it:

> they were engaged when we came up – we marched against a large body of the enemy posted along the top of the hills, with a gentle ascent without a hollow near them within musket shot; when I was ordered with the Col's company forward – to act as Light Infantry and give notice to the enemy yagers, to quite their lurking places, the first rifle shot fired from them hit the hairs of my bearskin … the third wounded one of the company, and we then began firing, when some more companies on the right coming up and, advancing on them, we soon turned them out of a wood, but before this their line moved off.
>
> We went on skirmishing a considerable way, till we came to a large hollow with a small wood between them on each side the hostile troops were, and the sharpshooters in the cover between. We were firing near two hours in this situation, when small parties of ours began to get into the wood against the enemy's rifle men. At this time our right was also gaining ground, and the enemy was passing off along the hills just before mentioned. Some troops on our left began to charge. We passed through the wood up the hills cheering as we passed through the copse. …… A spent ball afterwards hit the brass of my helmet [bearskin] as I was considerably in the rear of the Regt.[25]

York decided, however, to make another attempt to reach Amsterdam and again organized his army in four columns. Abercromby took command of a column of the best troops, including the 23rd and 55th Foot, which was to move along the shore of the North Sea, penetrate the French line and seize the town of Egmont-op-Zee. The other columns were to support him and the attack was set for 29 September, but a ferocious storm forced him to postpone it until 2 October. At 6 A.M. that day Abercromby's column moved off through a difficult terrain of sand hills and dunes, some as high as 150 feet, toward their objective.

Private William Surtees remembered that, as his company of the 56th Foot marched, they were passed by the 11th Light Dragoons, who shouted to their infantry comrades: "Go on, my lads, lather them up well, and we'll come up and shave them."[26] Surtees's company was in an *ad hoc* battalion commanded by Colonel George Macdonald, composed of light companies from various regiments which, with the 23rd and 55th Foot, moved on the left of Abercromby's main force as a flank guard. When Macdonald encountered a force of French *tirailleurs* or light infantry, he forgot his orders and ordered his troops to chase them, leaving Abercromby's flank wide open. Seeing this, Brune sent troops to threaten it and a confusing action took place in the sand dunes where units became dispersed and battalion commanders lost contact with some of their companies, which engaged in their own private war.

Meanwhile, the commander of Abercromby's advance guard, Major-General John Moore, despite being wounded, successfully fought off several French attacks but could advance no farther, and at nightfall Abercromby decided to hold his position. The other three columns fared no better, and although York was now in possession of Egmont-op-Zee, he was only a few miles closer to Amsterdam than he had been that morning.

Four days later York tried again. As the French were holding some villages north of their main line, he ordered the Russians to clear them. As Lieutenant Hill of the 23rd recalled:

> The Russian drove the enemy from all his entrenchments, 3 times he marched up at the beat of the Drum in ordinary time and turned the French out. The Russian afterwards advanced so far that ammunition could not be brought up to him, they were dispersed when the enemy came down on him with nearly all his Force.[27]

"The French have read a lesson today they will not soon forget."

French light infantry skirmishing, 1790s
The French army evolved a highly effective form of skirmish tactics using light infantry companies and regiments. In the Helder campaign of 1799 the superiority of French skirmishers over their British counterparts was marked, and the result was the creation of rifle and light infantry regiments in the British army and increased emphasis on this aspect of land warfare. (Drawing by Edouard Detaille from *L'Armée française,* 1888)

The Russians encountered so much resistance that the duke began to commit other units until, gradually, almost the entire army became drawn into a confused battle around the village of Kastrikum. York lost control of the battle and Bunbury, crippled with an attack of rheumatism, remembered,

> aide-de-camp after aide-de-camp was sent forth to make out what were the causes and objects of this off-hand engagement, and I was carried up and perched on the top of the tall steeple of Alkmaar, with a spying glass, to try to ascertain for the Duke what was the direction and where were the main points of the fight. But all was confusion, and in fact the troops were intermingled. ...... The country itself was extremely intricate, and the thick rain and the heavy smoke dwelling on the coppice-woods and enclosures of the villages made it impossible to distinguish anything.[28]

Private Surtees never forgot that day. His light infantry battalion had advanced along the shore of the ocean only to run into a French force, including

Général (later _Maréchal_) Guillaume-Marie-Anne Brune (1763-1815)
The French commander in the Helder campaign, Brune successfully defended Amsterdam against several attempts by the Duke of York to capture the city. Brune was in despair about the outcome of the campaign but York's decision to abandon the expedition left him justifiably claiming a victory. (From _Portraits des généraux français faisant suite aux victoires et conquêtes des Français_, 1818)

cavalry, four times their number. They were pushed back steadily until "our young [green] troops fell into considerable disorder and confusion" – in fact they took to their heels – and "what was at first a rather regular retreat, became at last a disorderly flight" which, in turn, "became more like a race than anything else."[29] As his comrades ran back, closely pursued by enemy cavalry and light infantry, Surtees saw some British infantry advancing. It was the 23rd Foot, which formed in line "and showed so good and steady a front as quite delighted us."[30] On the arrival of the Welch Fusiliers, the green militiamen

> which had been so woefully beaten, now united, and again advanced upon the enemy; and when the 23d had given them a volley or two, the French gave way and retreated with as great precipitation as they had advanced. In short the tables were turned upon them, and the pursuit of them now was equally rapid with our retreat before them a short while previously and before the action ceased, we had driven them considerably beyond where we had encountered them in the morning.[31]

The Welch Fusiliers had saved the day and Surtees, who would end his military career as a captain, had nothing but admiration for their "steadiness and fine appearance" but added that they "were all old soldiers, while our two battalions were composed altogether, I may say, of volunteers from the militia, who had as little idea of service in the field, as if newly taken from the plough."[32] The 23rd Foot's losses in this engagement were light, being only 6 dead and 34 wounded.

The battle of Kastrikum crushed the hopes of allied commanders, who believed no further offensive action was possible and advised York to retreat to the line of the Zuype Canal. This was duly done on 9 October, and when the Royal Navy informed the duke that it would be almost impossible to land supplies on the windswept beaches of the North Sea during the winter months, Pitt's government decided to withdraw his army to avoid a disaster. The duke contacted Brune to arrange an armistice and the French commander, himself in despair over the future, was only too happy to conclude an agreement that permitted the allied army to embark unhindered with the captured Dutch warships, after restoring 8,000 prisoners taken during the campaign. Yet another expedition had ended badly for the British army and yet another dispirited body of troops sullenly boarded their transports and sailed for home. Most disembarked at Yarmouth, including the Russians, who promptly drank the oil from the street lamps, a curious practice which caused much alarm among the good citizens of that port.

For the Welch Fusiliers, the end of the profitless Helder campaign was marked by a particular tragedy. On 29 October 1799 the regiment, 650 all ranks, boarded a number of captured Dutch ships, with 5 officers, 262 men, and 25 women and children going on board the former Dutch 24-gun frigate *Valk*. Delayed from sailing with the main convoy because of the tide, the *Valk* set off alone for Yarmouth next day and came within 30 miles of that place when the vessel was forced back by contrary winds which, over a period of days, drove her clear across the North Sea. The captain lost track of his position but estimated that he was off the coast of Norway when, on 10 November, the *Valk* ran aground on a sand bank some six miles from the Dutch coast. The crew, most of whom had never been to sea before, proved almost entirely useless and "gave themselves entirely up, and trusted more to their prayers than their exertions."[33] This being the case, the officers of the 23rd assumed command:

> Lieutenant Hoggard, who had some little knowledge of nautical affairs, took some of the soldiers down to the pumps, and Lieutenant Hill, having failed in an attempt to break open the powder-magazine, fired several rounds from a soldier's musket [to attract attention from the shore]; the ship's guns had all been drawn, and the gunner could not be found. The ship now beat over the bank and drifted among some breakers, the mainmast went overboard, severing the long-boat in two in its fall; the mizzen and foremasts soon followed, carrying with them numbers of people who had been crowding into the rigging. Lieutenant Hill now hearing the ship going to pieces, took his

station in the forecastle, where he lay down, and from whence he witnessed the unhappy fate of most of his companions, the afterpart of the ship having soon broken away. The forecastle seemed to be fast bedded in the sand, but it soon fell over, when Lieutenant Hill quitted it, and after many fruitless and fatiguing efforts, succeeded in fastening himself with his braces to a fragment of the wreck, on which he at length reached the shore, when he found that of the four hundred and forty-six souls which had sailed in the *Valk*, only twenty-five survived – himself, nineteen men of the Royal Welsh Fusiliers, and five Dutch sailors.[34]

Lieutenant Hill, the sole officer to survive, recorded a sad footnote to this tragic affair:

On the mast on which Lieut. Hoggard [who did not survive] floated to the beach, a dog also got on shore with the men on it; the dog formerly belonged to Major James Mackenzie, but latterly always lived with a private of the name of Wingfield; the animal would naver leave the beach up and down which it used to walk howling, but when disturbed, or attempted to be caught, used always to run in among the sandhills. Every exertion that was made by the survivors to make him follow them or to catch him were ineffectual and the dog remained there when we left the island [of Ameland].[35]

The Fusiliers' losses in the *Valk* disaster were heavy, being 247 officers and men or about 38% of the regiment's strength.

Lieutenant John Hill (commonly known in the Welch Fusiliers as "Jack" Hill) continued to serve with the regiment but, after the wreck of the *Valk*, he began to display some eccentricities such as never hanging up his uniforms or putting his possessions away but simply strewing both on the floor of his quarters, and keeping his personal financial accounts in chalk on the walls of his room. As these habits did not interfere with his military duties, however, and since he was a jovial fellow at the mess table, his brother officers overlooked them.

Although everyone mourned the comrades lost at Ostend and the Helder, the simple fact was that such casualties created opportunities for promotion; as the traditional mess toast "A bloody war and a sickly season" implied, promotion increased with casualty rates. Within 18 months, the Welch Fusiliers had lost 20 officers at Ostend and the Helder, nearly two-thirds of their commissioned complement, and this left vacancies that worked in the favour of Pearson and the other junior officers. In 1799 Pearson was 12th in seniority among the first lieutenants in the 23rd Foot. By the following year he had moved up several notches and, as there were now vacancies for captains, he began the paperwork to purchase his next step.

It would be more expensive than his last as the official price of a captain's commission in a fusilier regiment was £988, of which only £560 would be recouped from the sale of his first lieutenant's commission, leaving a difference of £428 plus fees for his father to pay. This was possibly as much as the good parson's annual income, which must have entailed some scratching around in Somerset – and that was only the official price as more money may have been paid under the table. The good news, although Reverend Pearson could not know it at the time, was that this was the last promotion his son would have to purchase. On 7 August 1800 Thomas Pearson was gazetted as a captain.

On their return from Holland, the 23rd was stationed over the winter of 1799-1800 at Battle Barracks near Hastings on the Sussex coast. Their losses from the *Valk* disaster and the Helder campaign were made up by a large draft of poorly disciplined volunteers from Irish militia regiments and the Duke of York judged it would be some time before the 23rd would be fit for service. Lieutenant Jack Hill noted that the regiment was weaker in strength than it had been in Chatham in 1797 and that its musketry was poor because so many of the new men "do not know how to load their piece" or muskets. It was Hill's wish that the Welch Fusiliers would go "abroad for some time" as he "would get high up among the Lieuts. [as] some are about to retire, some to purchase [additional rank], it will hasten them off, and make many steps for me."[36]

Training the new recruits and normal garrison duty occupied the regiment that winter. Hill recalled that they had "two or three times a week a field-day" and that two small artillery pieces were attached to the regiment and the men were taught "the great gun exercise."[37] Something out of the ordinary occurred in March 1800 when the 23rd received an order from the Horse Guards to send a subaltern, two sergeants, a drummer and 32 fusilier privates to Horsham to train with an experimental rifle corps being organized at that place. This specialized unit had resulted from proposals made by Colonel Coote Manningham of the 41st Foot and Lieutenant-Colonel William Stewart of the 67th Foot, who had seen at first hand how difficult it had been for the British infantry, even the light companies, to counter the French *tirailleurs* in the sand dunes of the Helder. They proposed that a rifle detachment be included in the establishment of each line regiment to improve its skirmishing abilities and the 23rd was one of the 14 regiments chosen to provide men for rifle training. Although this system was soon afterward abolished, a rifle company or detachment was to remain on the strength of the 23rd Foot for much of the next decade while the experimental unit created by Manningham and Stewart evolved into the 95th Foot (Rifles), which in a few years would win undying fame in Portugal and Spain.

While the Welch Fusiliers tried to recover their strength, major events took place in Europe. The Austrian and Russian armies had gained notable successes against the French in the previous summer but the pendulum began to swing back in October 1799 when Bonaparte, having deserted his army in Egypt, landed in France with a few selected officers. The hero of the republic had not bothered to inform his second-in-command, *Général de division* Jean-Baptiste Kléber, that he was leaving Egypt but had simply written him a letter that Kléber received only after Bonaparte had sailed. This cavalier abandonment infuriated Kléber, a blunt veteran, causing him to exclaim to his staff: "*Mes amis, ce baiseur-là a laissé ici ses culottes pleines de merde! Nous allons retourner en L'Europe et les lui foutre sur la gueule!*"[38]* For his part, with the assistance of some highly-placed conspirators, Bonaparte overthrew the Directory the following month and replaced it with a Consulate of three, of which he was First Consul and virtual dictator of France. He spent the winter impelling energy into the republic and its armies and preparing to take the offensive in the spring of 1800. Meanwhile, the unstable Czar Paul of Russia, wearying of the war, more or less withdrew from it, leaving Britain and Austria to continue the conflict. In May 1800 Napoleon launched an offensive against Austria in northern Italy which ultimately culminated in a near-run victory at Marengo in June and was followed by other French victories against the Austrian armies in Germany. In January 1801 Austria made peace, leaving Britain to again stand on its own, with a few weak allies, against France.

In the summer of 1800, while the French won victories on the mainland of Europe, Pearson and the Welch Fusiliers were touring in troop transports. Throughout the previous winter and spring Pitt's government had searched for ways to strike at France and most of the suggestions put forward were based on a need to assist Britain's weak allies: Portugal, Naples and Sicily. Objectives were selected and discarded as the government, in the words of a later critic, "instead of striking at the core of the evil" continued to merely nibble "at the

---

* Perhaps most delicately translated as "Comrades! That rascal has left his trousers here with an awful mess in them and we should return to Europe and shove it down his throat."

rind" of France.[39] Finally, it decided to try to carry out all of them, and when Lieutenant-General Sir Ralph Abercromby sailed from Britain with an expeditionary force in the spring of 1800 he was under orders to reinforce Malta, succour the garrison of Minorca, assist the Austrians in Italy, support a possible rising in France, defend Portugal, protect Naples and, if possible, attack Tenerife. As Spain was now a nominal ally of France, another force under the command of Lieutenant-General James Pulteney set sail from Plymouth in mid-July 1800 with orders either to support a rising in France or attack the Spanish naval base at Ferrol. Despite the Duke of York's misgivings about their strength and fitness, the 23rd Foot were chosen as part of this expedition, which arrived off Ferrol in late August 1800.

When Pulteney made a landing with 13,000 troops on 25 August, including the newly-promoted Captain Thomas Pearson, the operation was covered by three companies of the Experimental Rifle Corps under the command of Lieutenant-Colonel William Stewart, who was wounded in a day of skirmishing. When Pulteney and his staff made a close examination of the Spanish naval base they realized that it was too strong to be taken with the means at hand and the Ferrol force therefore joined Abercromby at Gibraltar in early September. Abercromby had just received new orders from London to attack the Spanish naval base at Cadiz and the combined force then sailed for that place but, on arriving, Abercromby wisely cancelled the operation after the navy refused to guarantee that they could supply his troops once ashore. Instead, he sailed back to Gibraltar, his arrival being delayed by a storm which drove the fleet out into the Atlantic for nearly two weeks. It was only on 24 October 1800 that Abercromby finally arrived at Gibraltar to find new orders waiting – he was to invade Egypt.

He dutifully sailed for Malta, which was selected as the rendezvous for the expedition. Fortunately for the troops on board the transports – some of whom had been at sea eating salt pork and ship's biscuit for nearly seven months – the need to overhaul many of the transports meant they spent most of November 1800 ashore. Abercromby took the opportunity to carry out a thorough inspection of all his units and "passed a very severe censure" on the 23rd Foot.[40] At this time, the regiment, which mustered 29 officers and 569 men, was under the command of Major Philip K. Skinner in the absence of Lieutenant-Colonel John Hall, who was on his way from Britain to the Mediterranean. After the reprimand, Skinner departed the scene and the 23rd Foot was temporarily placed under the control of their brigade commander until Hall arrived. As Lieutenant Hill recorded about this time: "Credit we [the 23rd] get nowhere, at least not from J.R. Abercrombie" who had "expressed his astonishment at the state of the Regt."[41]

In the middle of December, Abercromby sailed for Marmoris Bay on the southwest coast of Asia Minor near Rhodes, the jumping-off point for the attack on Egypt. There he expected to find supplies and horses that the Turks had promised to gather but was disappointed. As the attack on Egypt would have to be delayed until these requirements arrived, he put the time to good use by intensively training the 15,000 troops under his command and making preparations for an amphibious landing. Although the government's muddle had left his men at sea for many months, it had also resulted in Abercromby being the first British commander since the war with France had commenced nearly eight years before to have the opportunity to properly prepare his army for combat without interference by meddling politicians.

He put a great deal of effort into the amphibious aspect of the operation. Two officers from either service, Captain Alexander Cochrane, RN, and Colonel Robert Anstruther of Abercromby's staff, spent considerable time working out how to accomplish one of the most difficult of all military operations – an amphibious assault against a defended shore. After much discussion and experimentation, they compiled detailed and almost flawless instructions for the 200 landing craft with the fleet and conducted live rehearsals in Marmoris Bay to make sure every officer and soldier knew what to do, how to do it and when to do it. Lieutenant Thomas Evans of the 8th Foot recorded in his diary on 22 January 1801 that

This morning the Reserve of the Army under the Command of Major Gen'l Moore and the first brigade of the Line under Major Gen'l Coote, with a considerable proportion of Artillery from the different Men of War disembarked for practice; after going through the movements, it is intended they should execute, in presence of the Enemy they re-embarked. From the Great Endeavours making in all Departments to get our preparation in a state of forwardness, it is infer'd that our continuance here will be but short.[42]

The Royal Artillery and Royal Engineer officers, for their part, experimented with novel ways of landing supplies and lightening the artillery's field carriages and horsed transport. Effort was also put into drawing up loading tables for the cargo ships and, although the term would not come into vogue for nearly another century and a half, these vessels were "combat loaded" – what was needed first was loaded last and care was taken to spread important items such as artillery among a number of ships so that if one vessel was lost, the result would not be disastrous.

Marmoris proved to be a healthy place and the troops soon got their land legs. Abercromby held frequent unit inspections and came down hard on commanding officers he felt were not doing their jobs properly in looking after their men. He drilled his regiments rigorously in battalion and brigade-level exercises and he was assisted in this by 39-year-old Major-General John Moore, who had performed so well in the Helder campaign of 1799, and Lieutenant-Colonel Kenneth Mackenzie of the 90th Foot, widely regarded as one of the leading light infantry specialists in the army. Abercromby was not a proponent of either the "German" or the "American" schools of tactics. With the plain common sense that always marked his leadership, he realized that what was needed was a fusion of the two so that British infantry could either fight in close order or as detached skirmishers. Nonetheless, he used the authorized manual, Dundas's 1792 *Regulations*, as the tactical basis for the army's training at Marmoris, although he reduced its many complicated manoeuvres.[43] Moore was impressed by his superior's attention to detail:

> The Commander inspected the regiments and brigades separately. He gave praise where it was due, and was severe in his animadversions wherever he observed carelessness or inattention. He became thus acquainted with the state of every corps and the character of its commander. Discipline was improved and emulation excited. Corps were landed daily for exercise. The men were warned of the importance of preserving invariably their order in an open country exposed to the attack of the cavalry; and the attention of general officers was called to adopt the simplest and most speedy modes of forming from the column of march columns to resist the shocks of cavalry. The troops, particularly those intended for the disembarkation, were placed in the boats in which they were intended to disembark, and arranged with the guns in their proper order, and the landing practised several times in the order in which it was afterwards executed.[44]

When the troops at Marmoris sailed for Egypt on 22 February 1801, Abercromby was confident that he commanded the best army that Britain had assembled since 1793. But he and his soldiers also knew, as Evans of the 8th Foot recorded, that it was

no common Enemy we have to contend with, but an Army full of confidence from repeated victories gained in Italy &c. inured to a climate to be
the scene of action so fatal to the European constitution, and possessed
of all the strong-holds, so extensive a country must abound with, we shall
have to ... secure to ourselves all the advantages of courage, vigilance and
precaution, which both policy and wisdom point out as the only certain way
of obtaining (or at least) meriting Victory.[45]

Delayed by weather, it was not until 7 March 1801 that the warships and
transports were off the chosen landing site, Aboukir Bay near Alexandria,
where Nelson had destroyed the French fleet in 1798. At 2 A.M. on 8 March a
blue signal rocket was fired as the sign for the troops to embark in the landing
craft and, as Evans of the 8th recorded, "the brilliant career of the British army
in Egypt may be said to commence."[46] An hour or so later, a second rocket was

The Egyptian Campaign – 1801

let off as the signal for the boats to begin moving toward the shore and nothing, Evans remembered, "interrupted the solemn stillness that reigned throughout but the busy hum of preparation, and dipping of oars as the Troops were rowed to the last place of rendez-vous, about four miles distant from the shore."[47] The long pull had been forced on Abercromby because the shallow water near the landing site prevented the larger ships from approaching the shore. The 23rd Foot, 553 all ranks, under the command of Lieutenant-Colonel Hall, was in the "Reserve," commanded by Moore, this being something of a misnomer as this formation was actually part of the assault wave. Moore had the 23rd, 28th, 42nd and 58th Foot, the Corsican Rangers and the four flank companies of the two battalions of the 40th Foot. His task was to secure the right flank of the beach-head, a brigade of Guards would take the centre, and another brigade would land on the left. In all, the first assault numbered some 5,000 troops, who would be landing against 1,800 French troops well equipped with field artillery.

As the sailors commenced the long row, the soldiers in each craft, sitting with their muskets between their knees, were silent and, as one recalled, nothing was to be heard "but the hollow and dismal sound of the oars as they dipped into the water."[48] It was daylight by the time the boats were near the shore and they halted just outside enemy artillery range while Captain Cochrane made some final adjustments to their formation. Just before 9 A.M., all was ready. Cochrane gave the signal by firing a musket and the landing craft pulled hard for the beach. A soldier of the 28th Foot recalled that

> The boats were pulled off at the same moment presenting an awfully grand and impressive appearance; immediately the French began to fire shells and heavy shot; as we got nearer, they began to pour in grape, and General Moore and Captain Cochrane taking off their hats, were followed by all the army, rending the air with continuous cheering; as we approached, in addition to their grape-shot, the French began a sharp fire of musketry; the effect on the water was much like a hail storm.[49]

Moore, for his part, could see the French drawn up with field guns ready "to oppose us." As soon as Cochrane had ordered the advance, Moore recalled that,

> we were fired upon from fifteen pieces of artillery as soon as we were within reach, first with round shot, afterwards with grape, and at last by the infantry. The boats continued to row in steadily, and the sailors and soldiers

occasionally huzzaed. Numbers were killed and wounded and some boats were sunk. The fire of grape-shot and musketry was really most severe.[50]

As the boats grounded in the surf, Moore's men sprang out, splashed onto the beach and formed, all the while under a heavy fire. His major objective was a large sand hill, about 180 feet high, immediately in front of his landing place, and as soon as the 23rd, 28th and 40th were on land and ready, he placed the eight grenadier and light companies of the three battalions in line and led them straight up it. His men slipped and slid in the loose sand and came under fire from the French at the summit. It was at this point that Captain Thomas Pearson, commanding the light company of the 23rd, received a musket ball in the thigh, but kept going. The eight companies did not stop to return fire but went straight at the enemy with the bayonet and the French, seeing they meant business, decided it was time to go and ran down the reverse slope, leaving four field guns to be taken by the oncoming British, who cheered when they reached the summit. The right flank of the beachhead was secure.

Despite heavy casualties, the centre and left brigades also got ashore, although part of the left brigade was delayed when the merchant seamen rowing their boats proved to be somewhat gun shy. The French, taken aback by the speed of the landing and the loss of the sand hill, sent cavalry and infantry against these two brigades. French dragoons rode into the water to slash at the Guards of the centre brigade in their boats but the 58th Foot on their right, which had been able to form on the beach, poured several volleys into the enemy, causing them to retire and permitting the Guards to land. The fighting did not last long and, as the second wave came in, the 1,450 French survivors withdrew in the direction of Alexandria, 12 miles to the west.

A beachhead had been gained and the hero of the day was Major-General John Moore, whose "heroic conduct was highly conspicuous heading the Troops considerably in front up the sands, thereby setting the most encouraging example."[51] Abercromby had personally witnessed the Welch Fusiliers' assault on the sand hill and one of the first things he did after he landed was to seek out Lieutenant-Colonel Hall of the 23rd Foot. Referring to his severe criticism of the regiment at Malta, Abercromby shook Hall's hand and said, "My friend Hall, I am glad to see you; I shall never abuse you again," meaning that never again would he speak ill of Hall's fusiliers.[52]

When it was all over, the assault troops rested and consumed a breakfast of cold bacon, biscuits and water. Sergeant Benjamin Miller of the Royal Artillery

"The French have read a lesson today they will not soon forget."

Assault landing at Aboukir Bay, 8 March 1801

On 8 March 1801 the British army under Lieutenant-General Sir Ralph Abercromby carried out one of the most difficult of all military operations – an assault landing against a defended shore. The casualties were not light but when the fighting ended, Abercromby had a beach-head. During this action, Captain Thomas Pearson of the 23rd Foot received the first of five wounds in combat he was to suffer during his career. (Print after painting by Edward Dayes)

remembered that they amused themselves by piling "up no less than 200 human skulls in the space of a few hundred yards, supposed to be the bones of the men who fell" in Nelson's naval victory three years before.[53] The casualties had not been light. Abercromby had lost 748 soldiers and sailors getting ashore, with the 23rd Foot's share being 6 killed and 41 wounded. Among the latter was Pearson, whose wound seems not to have been serious enough to warrant hospitalization, and he therefore remained with his company. The landing had been a desperate venture but it had ended well and the naval commander, Admiral George Keith, was so impressed by the army's performance that he reported to the Admiralty: "The French have read a lesson today they will not soon forget."[54]

After taking four days to unload artillery and stores, on 12 March Abercromby advanced toward Alexandria along an isthmus, about a mile wide, between the sea and two salt lakes. As the British moved forward in two large columns with the 23rd leading the right column under Moore's command, the French withdrew to a strong position among some ruins which became known as the "Roman Camp." Abercromby came up on this position in late afternoon but, wishing to rest his troops, pulled back some distance for the night. Many in the army were impressed at how well it manoeuvred and how the light infantry which had preceded it had experienced little trouble with French skirmishers.

The light infantry were to prove themselves again the following day, 13 March 1801. Before the British could move the French attacked with cavalry and infantry. An enterprizing French cavalry officer, *Colonel* Marie-Victor-Nicolas de Fay, marquis de La Tour-Maubourg, seeing a skirmish line consisting of British troops wearing the Tarleton headgear, mistook them for dismounted dragoons and swept down on them at the head of the 22nd *Chasseurs à Cheval*. Unfortunately for La Tour, they were not dragoons but the 90th Foot, the only regular infantry regiment in the army to wear this headgear and a highly-specialized light infantry unit trained by Lieutenant-Colonel Kenneth Mackenzie himself. The 90th were not shaken and La Tour-Maubourg's *chasseurs*, beaten off by their musketry, then tried the 8th and 18th Foot only to be repulsed again by accurate fire which wounded La Tour-Maubourg himself. This, however, is not the last we shall hear of him.

Abercromby had no problem beating off a French infantry attack which followed, but when he advanced, his troops came under accurate artillery fire that inflicted heavy casualties. There was some confusion over how far the army should move, and while the generals sorted it out, the forward troops suffered from accurate bombardment. Finally it was decided to pull back to the original French position, the "Roman Camp." "Halting to deliberate," Moore later noted, "exposed us to the guns of the heights, and, when the attack was deemed imprudent, obliged us to a retrograde movement which was mortifying to troops who had displayed such spirit, and who had been successful."[55]

The battle of Mandara, as it came to be known, cost Abercromby 1,300 killed and wounded, mostly from artillery fire, as the French musketry had proved remarkably ineffective. Throughout the army, however, there was pride in the fact that the units had performed well under heavy fire with the possible exception of an *ad hoc* battalion of Royal Marines, which was clearly unused to land warfare. Lieutenant-Colonel Edward Paget of the 28th Foot thought "it was impossible for troops to have behaved better," as they had displayed a "cool intrepidity that never was exceeded."[56]

The next week was spent in the "Roman Camp" position while supplies were brought up in preparation for a further advance against Alexandria. In the meantime, the French commander in Egypt, *Général de division* Jacques Menou, assembled every man he could, about 11,000, and prepared to launch a major assault on Abercromby, whose army, reduced by casualties and sickness, was not much greater in strength. The British position was along a ridge with Moore's command, including the 23rd Foot, holding the right flank around the ruins while the 28th held a redoubt somewhat in advance. The remainder of the army was stationed along the ridge to Moore's left. The French plan was to make a diversionary attack against the British left, while the main assault went in against Moore. Menou launched his attack at about 3.30 A.M. on 21 March, but unfortunately for him, the British were standing to their arms and he did not achieve the surprise he was seeking. Furthermore, the diversionary attack, which took place at almost the same time as the main attack, failed to achieve the effect intended.

Moore's troops were therefore ready when French infantry advanced directly against their position and they repulsed them, inflicting heavy losses, including the divisional commander who led them. At this point, however, two *demi-brigades* or regiments from the French centre division, which had lost their way, managed in the darkness and the confusion to get between the British centre and right, and one battalion actually penetrated the ruins, surprising the 58th Foot defending them. Seeing the enemy's success, the Welch Fusiliers, formed in line behind the ruins, fired a volley at short range and then charged the intruders with the bayonet while, at the same time, the 42nd Foot cut off their escape. "Our men attacked them like wolves," Lieutenant Jack Hill of the 23rd recalled, "transfixing the Frenchmen with their bayonets against the walls of the building."[57] Moore agreed about the brutality of the fighting. "The contest was so severe," he remarked, "that little of the humanity which mitigates the usual horrors of war was shown."[58] The 42nd pursued the fleeing survivors back toward their own lines until they were charged in turn by French cavalry and forced to return to their position on the left of the ruins.

But the battle was not yet over. The French launched another infantry attack on Moore which was again beaten off with heavy enemy casualties. In frustration, Menou then ordered three regiments of dragoons to charge the redoubt and the ruins, and although the cavalry commander protested the order, he obeyed it. The dragoons came on hard, cutting through the 42nd and surrounding the 28th in the redoubt, which was open to the rear. As Paget had been wounded, the 28th was under the command of a Lieutenant-Colonel Chambers who, seeing he was being attacked from front and rear, issued a fa-

Général Jacques-François Menou (1750-1810).
The French commander in Egypt in 1801, Menou had married a Muslim and converted to that religion. He was not a particularly experienced nor a particularly good commander and his troops deserved better leadership. Nonetheless they fought hard at the battle of Alexandria on 21 March, inflicting heavy casualties on the British army before being beaten. On his return to France Menou was give a series of administrative and diplomatic posts but never held another important military command. (Courtesy, Tony Broughton)

mous order: "Rear Rank, 28th! Right About Face!"[59] While the front rank fired on the enemy infantry, the rear rank of the 28th fired into the oncoming horsemen and emptied so many saddles that the threat was ended. This deed created a regimental distinction which the 28th were proud to bear thereafter – permission to wear their badge on both the front and back of their headgear.

It was now dawn and although Menou had been rebuffed all along the British line and his infantry were in great disorder, he remained unwilling to give up. He sent out skirmishers to annoy the British while at the same time keeping them under a heavy artillery bombardment. By this time, most of the British units were either out of ammunition or running low, and some men were actually reduced to throwing stones at the French. As Moore remembered,

> Our artillery could not return a shot, and had their infantry again advanced we must have repelled them with the bayonet. Our fellows would have done it; I never saw men more determined to do their duty; but the French had suffered so severely that they could not get their men to make another attempt. They continued in our front until the ammunition for our guns was brought up. They then very soon retreated.[60]

It was about 9 A.M. when the battle of Alexandria ended in total defeat for the French, who, as one British officer remarked, had been given as "complete a dressing as they ever got."[61] Lieutenant Evans of the 8th Foot was perhaps more charitable toward his opponent:

"The French have read a lesson today they will not soon forget."

The Enemy after an unsuccessful contest of eight hours retired, and I must do those engaged the justice to say they fought well, not omitting their Artillery which was served to admiration, by it our Tents were pretty well riddled, I wish I could say as much for that part of our own force, or at least for the Commander of it, for such was his want of foresight, that our Guns were twice without ammunition during the action, and at those periods when it would have proved most destructive.[62]

There was particular pride among the British troops that the victory had been gained over the veterans of Bonaparte's famous Army of Italy.

Menou had lost about 2,500 men while Abercromby's casualties were 1,430 killed and wounded, with both the British commander and Moore being among the wounded. Moore recovered but Abercromby died seven days after the battle, universally mourned by his soldiers because, after years of humiliating defeats, he had given them three victories in quick succession.

Over the next few days, a truce was called so that the dead could be buried and the wounded collected. Sergeant Miller of the Royal Artillery took a walk

The 28th Foot at the battle of Alexandria, 21 March 1801
At the battle of Alexandria the 28th Foot gained immortal fame when, attacked in both front and rear, the rear rank calmly turned about and defeated the enemy while the front rank did the same. This bloody engagement, which ended in a British victory, doomed the French army in Egypt but it also cost the life of Lieutenant-General Sir Ralph Abercromby.

among the grave sites to think about "the implacable lot of men."⁶³ When he
came to the graves of his some his fellow gunners, he reflected that

> here lie the mangled remains of a comrade, who but the other day, he and
> I were very jovial, drinking wine together, and perhaps the next destructive
> day of carnage it may be my lot at no great distance from this awful spot
> to be laid where no relation or friend will ever have the melancholic satis-
> faction to drop the sympathetic tear. Then I would reflect how dreadful it
> was to be cut off so suddenly and so neglectful as soldiers are in regard of
> religion. But, a soldier's life of honour is subject to so many changes that he
> has not time to think of religion like another man, for no sooner, perhaps,
> does he think of prayer than the drum beats or the trumpet sounds to arms
> – and how can he talk of forgiving his enemy when it is his whole duty to
> destroy them.

The defeat on 21 March 1801 marked the beginning of the end for the French
in Egypt. Menou withdrew into Alexandria with part of his forces and the
remainder retreated to Cairo. Abercromby's successor, Lieutenant-General Sir
John Hely-Hutchinson, conducted operations at a slower pace because he was
aware, as Menou was not, that another British force was on its way from India
to advance on Cairo from the east, ultimately to crush the enemy between
two forces. In the meantime, bypassing Alexandria, Hely-Hutchinson moved
against Rahmanieh on the Nile, which he secured in early May with the help
of 4,000 wild and ragged Turkish troops. They provided much entertainment
for the British for, as one officer remarked,

> Such confusion as was exhibited that day never appeared at Drogheda Fair
> …… you see thousands of small white and coloured standards around
> which you observe multitudes of men, apparently possessed by the devil,
> screaming and running towards the enemy, until the whistle of a ball, like
> magic, brings them to their recollection; the next discharge is the certain
> order for retreat.⁶⁴

This preliminary accomplished, on 11 May Hely-Hutchinson commenced
a slow advance up the Nile. It took nearly a month for the army, marching in
the relative cool of the night and early morning, to reach Cairo, and the heavily laden infantry suffered from heat that at midday was rarely less than 100

degrees Fahrenheit, making the sand so hot that the drummer boys sometimes roasted eggs in it. Despite these conditions, the average infantryman had to carry about 60-65 pounds of weight and one veteran has left a description of his load during that march:

> The first thing after dressing he puts on his side belt, then his pouch, containing sixty rounds of ball cartridges, then his haversack with four days' provisions, then his canteen with water, if he chooses to fill it, but in a short time it gets too warm to drink with pleasure or to quench the thirst; then his knapsack, containing two shirts, two pairs of stockings, one pair of shoes, jacket and trowzers for fatigue dress, three brushes, black-ball, razors and shaving box, and a blanket or great coat buckled on the top; then his flintlock with bayonet, and marching among so many, you will judge of the difficulty under which he labours, compared with a person walking in a cool climate unencumbered.[65]

On 8 June 1801, the army was in sight of Cairo and in a few days the city was completely invested by British and Turkish troops. The French commandant, *Général de division* Augustin-Daniel Belliard, had no stomach for a fight and surrendered under very generous terms, stipulating that his army of 13,672 men would be transported to France at British expense. The occupation of Cairo was turned over to Lieutenant-General Sir David Baird's force from India and Hely-Hutchinson's army then escorted Belliard's troops, which retained their arms, down the Nile to Rosetta, where they embarked for France. Hely-Hutchinson next turned to Alexandria but, after some skirmishing outside the walls, Menou surrendered on 1 September under terms similar to those of Belliard. In a few weeks, 10,524 more French troops sailed for France and they were shortly followed out of Egypt by Hely-Hutchinson's army, which the government broke up and dispersed to Malta, Gibraltar and Britain. The 23rd Foot and its light company commander, Captain Thomas Pearson, who had participated in every action and movement of the campaign, were ordered to Gibraltar.

News of the victory in Egypt took nearly a month to reach Britain, which, reeling from high taxation, inflation and a succession of bad harvests, longed for peace. A new government was prepared to give it to them because, after 16 years as prime minister, William Pitt had resigned early in 1801 over a political crisis caused by the Catholic Emancipation Bill. He was replaced by

Henry Addington, a man who lacked his capacity as a leader. Acknowledging the general wish for an end to the war, Addington opened secret negotiations with Bonaparte, who was also seeking peace so that he could consolidate his internal position in France and create the large navy he knew was essential for the conquest of Britain. The French ruler prolonged the negotiations through most of the summer of 1801, extracting concession after concession from the British government including the return to France, Holland and Spain of most of their colonial possessions taken since 1793 and the British evacuation of Malta, the strategically-located naval base in the Mediterranean. On 17 September, however, the First Consul secretly learned of Menou's surrender at Alexandria and, realizing that this news would stiffen British resolve, informed Addington that unless a preliminary treaty was signed by 2 October, he would suspend all negotiations and continue the war. The bluff worked and the document was duly signed on 1 October 1801, one day before London learned of the victory in Egypt. Although negotiations over the form of the final treaty lasted until the following spring, the fighting between Britain and France now ceased.

The Peace of Amiens, however, did not overshadow the British army's triumph in Egypt, a success which did much to retrieve its battered reputation. As Captain Bunbury remarked, that campaign

revived confidence and an honourable pride in our military service. The British nation, exulting in the proved valour and the triumphs of their army, felt once more that they might rely upon their officers and soldiers as securely as they had relied upon their seamen. The high characters of the British army shone brightly forth after the clouds which had hung heavily over it. The miserable warfare in America, the capitulations of Saratoga and Yorktown, and the more recent disasters of our troops in Flanders and in Holland had fixed a deep distrust in the public mind of our military men. It was believed that our commanders, nay, even that our officers and soldiers, were degenerate, and unequal to cope in battle with the conquerors of Italy and Germany. The trial which had now been made under great disadvantages first dispelled this prejudice. Our service regained its ancient standing in the estimation of the British people.[66]

Britain's new-found pride in her army was reflected by the fact that the regiments which had fought in Egypt were granted the distinction of being able to place on their Colours a badge consisting of a sphinx with the word "Egypt" underneath "as a distinguished mark of His Royal Majesty's approbation, and as a lasting memorial of the glory acquired to his Majesty's arms by the zeal, discipline and intrepidity of His troops in that audacious and important campaign."[67] In addition, the ruler of the Ottoman Empire presented all British officers who had participated in the campaign with the Order of the Crescent, a gold medal that came in four different sizes according to rank, worn with an orange ribbon. As there were very few awards or distinctions available to the junior officers at this time, they were glad to receive this item, even though the orange ribbon contrasted vividly with the scarlet of their uniform coats. Being a captain, Thomas Pearson would have received the middle-sized variant.

More important, the Egyptian campaign provided excellent training for a generation of young officers, many of whom we will meet again as Thomas Pearson was to serve with veterans of Abercromby's army for the remainder of his career. Among those who would gain high rank were Lowry Cole, John Colborne, Gordon Drummond, Rowland Hill, James Kempt, John Moore and Edward Pakenham, while among those officers who were not so prominent but who will still play a part in our story, were Francis Battersby, Thomas Evans, John Harvey, George Macdonell and William Robinson. Although he soon faded from public memory, those officers who served in Egypt under his command never forgot Lieutenant-General Sir Ralph Abercromby, the elderly and shortsighted general who set them squarely on the road that would end, 14 years later, at Waterloo.

Captain Thomas Pearson, 23rd Foot, c. 1803
After his return to Britain following his service in the Mediterranean, Pearson had his miniature painted by Charles Buncombe of Newport on the Isle of Wight. This was probably done when the 23rd Foot was briefly stationed on the island between October 1803 and May 1804. Pearson wears his full dress uniform, including black cocked hat and scarlet coat with blue facings and gold lace. The epaulette on his right shoulder carries the Prince of Wales's three feathers insignia as does his belt plate. The Royal Welch Fusiliers were the senior Welsh regiment in the army. (Miniature by Charles Buncombe, courtesy of the Director of the National Army Museum, Negative 9730)

CHAPTER THREE

"GOD BLESS THE KING
AND DAMN THE FRENCH."

GIBRALTAR, BRITAIN AND DENMARK, 1801–1807

When I was young and in my prime
Twelve years I was recruiting
Through England, Ireland, and Scotland, too,
Whatever it was suiting.
I led a gay and splendid life,
In every town a different wife,
And seldom was there any strife
With the roving, rambling soldier.

With the blooming lasses in each town
No man was ever bolder;
I thought that I was doing right,
As the king did want young soldiers.
I told them tales of fond delight,
I kept recruiting day and night,
And when I had made all things right,
Off went the rambling soldier.[1]

I n the middle of December 1801 the 23rd Foot, 469 officers and men strong, landed at Gibraltar. The Welch Fusiliers had many sick and Lieutenant Jack Hill noted that there were only about 180 enlisted men fit for duty. But the Fusiliers at least got a good Christmas dinner – "boild beef, plum-pudding, potatoes, and a bottle of porter each."[2]

Four months later, Prince Edward, Duke of Kent and the fourth son of the King, assumed command of the garrison at that place. Kent was a rigid martinet whose father, angered by his profligate lifestyle, debts, public love affairs and political views, had more or less exiled abroad in 1789 to keep him out of

Edward, Duke of Kent (1767-1820)

The fourth son of George III, Kent was more or less exiled overseas in the 1790s by his father for his profligate life style, political views and massive debts. He was a martinet, obsessed with military minutiae and such a tyrant that he came close to inspiring a mutiny at Gibraltar when the 23rd Foot was serving at that station. Recalled by his father, Kent was never again given an active command and is best remembered today for being the father of the future Queen Victoria. (Print after painting by William Bate)

sight and out of trouble. Kent brought with him to Gibraltar his mistress of more than a decade, the charming Thérèse-Bernandine Mongenêt, known to everyone as "Madame St. Laurent," who, unlike her consort, possessed both common sense and a common touch that made her very popular.

Kent shortly began to display his obsession with military *minutiae*, as demonstrated by the following extracts from the garrison orders he promulgated at Gibraltar:

AS NOTHING tends more to the good appearance of Military Dress, than an exact uniformity in the mode of having the Hair cut & dressed, & as this is a point, to establish which much attention will be required, the Commg. Officer of each Corps is expected to be *most particular* in enforcing the following directions on the subject.

THE HAIR of the Officers to be at all times cut, in the *course of the first week of every Month, & no oftener, by one Established Regimental Hair Dresser,* who is to be responsible to do it according to this simple Rule, vis. The top to be cut as close as possible, being left no longer than is necessary to admit of its being turned with Curling Irons of the smallest size; the back line of the top is not to exceed a line formed by passing a packthread from the back of one Ear to that of the other vertically over the crown of the head; the hind hair to be parted from that of the top in the shape of a Horse shoe, which will occasion the sides to extend to half an inch behind the Ear ......[3]

Whenever the Troops are drawn up for the purpose of hearing Divine Service, & the Ranks are properly dressed, the Whole Parade, comprehending Officers, Non Comd. Officers, & Privates, is to remain correctly steady with their Bodies erect, their Heels square, & their Knees perfectly straight,

...... The Non. Comd. Officers & Privates are to have their hands behind their backs, passed under their Bayonet, the right wrist, firmly grasped in the left hand, the palm of the right being turned upwards, & the Fingers of that hand perfectly extended with the Knuckles toward the body. In this position the whole is to remain, from the moment the Ranks are dressed, during the time Divine Service lasts ......[4]

NO CORPORAL is at any time to Drink with a Drummer or Private man, nor is he to be allowed to hold conversation or be seen in Company with *them out of his Barracks except on Duty,* under pain of being punished for Disobedience of Garrison Orders should he deviate from this Rule. ......[5]

Kent seems to have thought well of the 23rd Foot, however, and when he carried out its half-yearly inspection, he had no complaints and – a rare thing for him – considerable praise:

Officers: acquitted themselves very respectably of every part of their field duty and were dressed in exact conformity to the King's regulations except having no gorgets and their not being completed with uniform swords which they had been unable to procure since leaving Egypt.

Non commissioned officers: of good appearance and thoroughly masters of their duty

Men: Very low [short], but stout, active and fit for army service ......

Arms: All bad, but clean and kept in the best order possible ......

Recruits: Low but perfectly suited to the rest of the Battn and well instructed both in the use of their arms and in their movements ......

Movement Evolutions: Well performed and strictly according to regs laid down

Manoeuvres: Highly creditable to the Corps

Remarks: The Adjutant of this Regiment and the Sergeant Major having both particularly distinguished themselves by their persevering attention to the instruction of their men at the different periods of drill, claim that I should name them to the Commander-in-Chief accordingly, and I feel I should be wanting in what is due to them were I not to state that they merit any mark of favour which he may choose to bestow upon them.[6]

Kent was harder on the other regiments and there was soon a great increase in the number of punishment parades for, as a sergeant in the 5th Foot remembered, the duke's "tyranny was exerted with all the power and force that he could suggest."[7] The result was that a riot, bordering on a mutiny, followed and several men were killed. Learning of this, King George immediately removed him from command and Kent returned to England, where he sought an interview with his brother, the Duke of York, at the Horse Guards at which he pleaded for a new appointment. It did not go well and ended in a shouting match. Kent was never again employed and if he is remembered at all today, it is for fathering the future Queen Victoria.

Captain Thomas Pearson luckily did not have to serve under the tyrannical Kent for long, since in September 1802 he received permission to take six months of home leave, the first leave he had been granted since joining the army in early 1797. Pearson would have spent much of it at Queen Camel with his family, and when it was over, he was sent on the recruiting service, as his regiment, depleted in Egypt, was trying hard to raise its strength to the new peacetime establishment of 750 enlisted men.

Few in the army or navy expected the peace to last and events proved them right. In August 1802 a plebiscite in France made Bonaparte First Consul for life – king in all but name – because, after 13 years of revolution, war and strife, France welcomed any form of government that promised stability and peace. Unlike Britain, which faithfully carried out the terms of the Treaty of Amiens, with the exception that it did not evacuate Malta, the aggressive Bonaparte violated it by annexing several small Italian principalities and re-occupying Switzerland. British protests were countered by French insistence that Malta be given up, but not trusting the First Consul's intentions, Britain refused. By early 1803, the British government concluded that a resumption of the war was inevitable and quietly began to prepare for it. Although he had never demobilized the French army but actually increased its strength, this caused complaints from Bonaparte, though he wanted to avoid outright war until he had finished building up his navy. The French leader had overestimated British patience, however, and when he made no reply to a final offer from London to evacuate Malta in return for French evacuation of Switzerland and Holland, Addington's government declared war on France on 17 May 1803.

Britain found it easier to commence hostilities in 1803 than it had in 1793, as its armed forces were in much better order. The Royal Navy re-instituted a blockade of French-controlled ports and, with the assistance of the army, occupied most of the French possessions in the West Indies. Bonaparte's response was to mass 150,000 men on the Channel coast and also to invade Hanover, linked to the British royal family by dynastic ties. This latter move brought most of the excellent Hanoverian army to Britain, where it was reorganized as the King's German Legion, a force that would prove a great asset in the future. Bonaparte again commenced constructing landing craft in great numbers and, under the terms of a previous treaty, called on Spain to provide warships to strengthen his fleet. The Spanish instead chose to give him a financial subsidy and Britain, angered by assistance being rendered to France by a supposedly neutral power, retaliated. Aware that Spain's wealth was based on a supply of precious metals from her American colonies, in October 1804 British warships attacked and captured the Spanish treasure fleet, which, two months later, brought Spain and her navy of 30 ships of the line into the war on the French side.

Bonaparte's actions prompted a second "invasion scare" in Britain, a mild panic with frequent rumours of French landings on the coasts and French spies moving about the towns and cities. "Boney" or "Nappy," as he was called, had by now acquired a considerable reputation among the British people, to the point where nursemaids frightened ill-behaved children with doggerel about the French ruler:

> Baby, baby, naughty baby,
> Hush, you squalling thing, I say;
> Hush your squalling, or it may be
> Bonaparte may pass this way.
>
> Baby, baby, he's a giant,
> Tall and black as Rouen steeple;
> And he dines and sups, rely on 't,
> Every day on naughty people.
>
> Baby, baby, he will hear you,
> As he passes by the house,
> And he limb from limb will tear you
> Just as pussy tears a mouse.[8]

Although Admiral Lord St. Vincent, First Sea Lord or commander-in-chief of the Royal Navy, stated bluntly that "I do not say that the French will not come, I only say that they will not come by sea," this did little to assuage the fears of the civilian population, who instead began to fear that the enemy might launch an aerial invasion by means of hot air balloons.[9]

As in 1797-1798, one positive result of this new invasion scare was a marked increase in patriotism which saw 300,000 men join the volunteer units that again sprang up across the nation, among them William Pitt and many members of the House of Commons. Although Bonaparte's veterans would have made short work of them, the volunteers proved useful in releasing the regular army and the militia from garrison duties. Enlistments in the militia, as opposed to the regular force, increased and some brave but deluded men actually went so far as to voluntarily join the Royal Navy. On his side of the Channel, the First Consul rigorously trained a large army camped around Boulogne to a state of near perfection and built landing craft at such a furious pace that they began to choke the coastal ports of France and the Low Countries. By August 1805, it was estimated that Bonaparte had assembled enough shipping to transport 167,590 soldiers and 9,149 horses in a single lift – but he still had to get past the Royal Navy. The Welch Fusiliers were not overawed by this; as Lieutenant Hill noted in September 1803, "Every week they are looking out for the French" but "everything is prepared to give them a warm reception."[10]

For the British army, a beneficial development during this anxious period was the establishment of camps of instruction to undertake training at the brigade level. Major-General John Moore was placed in command of Shorncliffe Camp near Hythe on the Kent coast, a crucial position if the French should land. Moore assembled a brigade comprising the 43rd and 52nd Foot and the new 95th Rifles, which Lieutenant-Colonel Kenneth Mackenzie instructed in light infantry tactics adapted from the various systems put forward since the beginning of the war, with the emphasis being on what was workable. Moore also

Lieutenant-General Sir John Moore (1761-1809)
One of the most professional officers in the army, Moore performed well in the Helder and Egyptian campaigns. In 1803 he was commanding an experimental brigade at Shorncliffe in Kent where he and his subordinates trained the 43rd and 52rd Light Infantry and 95th Rifles into an elite formation. Beloved by his troops Moore believe in treating the common soldier as an intelligent, rational human being and emphasized rewarding good behaviour rather than punishing bad. He was killed in battle at Corunna in 1809 and was universally mourned by the army. If he had lived, Moore might have continued to hold Wellington's command in the Peninsula. (From John Richards, *Military and Naval Heroes of Great Britain*, 1860)

British riflemen, c. 1811

In 1797, the 5th Battalion of the 60th Foot became the first permanent rifle unit in the British army and rifle companies were added to the other five battalions of that regiment. In 1800, as a result of the Helder campaign, an Experimental Rifle Corps was formed to train a rifle company to serve in selected regiments of the line, including the 23rd Foot. This innovation evolved into the elite 95th Foot (Rifles) of three battalions, which won undying fame in the Peninsula. The standing figure in this painting by Charles Hamilton Smith is from the 60th Foot, the kneeling figure from the 95th. (From C.H. Smith, *Costume of the Army of the British Empire,* 1814)

strove to inculcate in the minds of his officers the concept that the soldier was a thinking human being who would perform better if rewarded for good behaviour rather than punished for bad, a radical idea in the extremely conservative British army. When that army faced its major test a few years later in the Iberian Peninsula, the value of Moore's training became readily apparent, as not only did the three regiments he instructed at Shorncliffe become elite in every sense of the word; his ideas began to spread as their officers were promoted in rank.

During the "invasion" years of 1803-1805, when the defence of the home isles was the paramount concern, manpower became crucial. In contrast to the Royal Navy, the regular army was recruited by voluntary enlistment, and although past governments had imposed conscription for brief periods, it was highly unpopular. Britons would accept the press gang for the navy because it was the vital first line of defence, but they would not accept conscription for the army. Patriotic feeling was high but there was too much competition from the volunteers and militia, who, unlike the regulars, were not required to serve outside Britain in such dreaded places as the West Indies. The army's need for men was constant. Its average annual death rate from all causes between 1803 and 1807 was about 14,500 out of a total strength that rose from 100,000 to 200,000 and this did not include losses from desertion, which cost it nearly 10% of its strength every year. Recruiting was therefore unceasing and every regiment stationed in Britain was engaged in it, including the Welch Fusiliers, who, in 1803, never had less than two recruiting parties in England and Wales, with Captain Thomas Pearson leading one of them.

By this time in the war, recruiting was a highly developed business. When ordered on it, an officer would proceed with a small and specialized detachment usually consisting of a veteran sergeant experienced in fishing for men, a corporal and several soldiers who could be trusted not to desert, and a fifer and drummer. The men of the party would wear their best uniforms, which they would adorn with coloured rosettes and ribbons to increase their martial splendour. The officer would be given a substantial sum of money to pay bounties to new recruits, publish advertisements or print handbills, reward those who brought in men, pay the magistrate who attested recruits and the surgeon who examined them, and cover other necessary expenses. This included not only food and lodging for his party but also the purchase of copious amounts of liquor and beer, because alcohol played an important role in the matter of personnel acquisition.

When ready, the party would march to one of the recruiting districts in Britain for which a "beating order," or permission to recruit, had been granted. On his arrival, the officer would report to the inspecting field officer supervising that district, who would assign him a specific area within it, as having too many parties "beating" in the same area was not productive. Once in the assigned area, the officer's first task would be to rent premises for a rendezvous in a central town or village, usually near a prominent landmark such as a church, hospital or market. After contracting with a magistrate and doctor to carry out the formalities, he would then print handbills to be distributed, posters to be displayed and insert an advertisement in the local newspaper such as the following:

WANTED immediately Four Young MEN of good character, to complete Captain Smith's Company in that excellent Corps, the 10th of Foot. Now, my lads, lose not time, the Company are Light Infantry, which are always the most dashing brave young fellows in the service. The Bounty is SIXTEEN GUINEAS. No more can be given, that being the utmost. Those who offer a greater sum are impostors, and wish to impose on the public. The above bounty paid on the moment of approval. Apply without delay to Captain Smith at No. 44, Greenfield Street, near the Church. – – N.B. The above Four Men will complete Captain Smith's Company. – – Any brave fellow who will step forward *any day* this *week,* will be entertained comfortably till approved of, exclusive of his bounty. – – Bringers of good Recruits handsomely rewarded and immediately paid.[11]

Captain Smith almost certainly needed more than four men, but stating that vacancies were limited was always sound psychology, while rewarding and immediately paying those who brought in men was also a good tactic. Smith added the additional incentive that any possible recruit would be "entertained

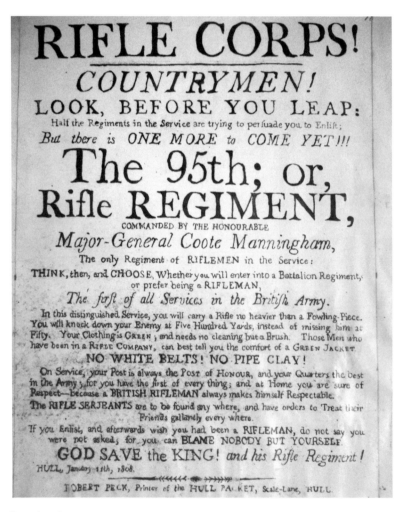

Easy cleaning
Any inducement was used to get men. The 95th emphasized the fact that because they wore black leather belts, their men did not have to resort to pipe clay. (Courtesy, Royal Greenjackets Museum, Winchester)

British army recruiting party, c. 1815
A recruiting party of the 33rd Foot, bedecked with rosettes and ribbons, fishes for men. The oatcake on the sergeant's sword was apparently unique to the 33rd Foot, a West Riding regiment, where oatcakes were regarded as a delicacy. Note the use of alcohol to entice the fish. (Print after George Walker, 1815)

comfortably," meaning free drinks, until he was attested, but the cost would not be taken out of his bounty.

Much attention was paid to the wording of recruiting posters and handbills. Their texts emphasized the drudgery of civilian life (boring, low wages, hard bosses), marriage (already contracted or legally impending), the inducements of the service including high bounties, good wages, smart uniforms, clean barracks and good eating (all lies) and the glory of the particular regiment (debatable). They were also unabashedly patriotic and nationalist in tone, and not a little racist. Consider the following examples:

A Year's Wages advanced or Twenty Guineas For a Day's Pay.
Lincolnshire Heroes having always been remarkable for zealously Supporting their KING & COUNTRY, they are now presented with a glorious and never-returning Opportunity of distinguishing themselves in the Loyal Lincolnshire REGIMENT OF FOOT ...

All those whose delight in their Honourable Profession of Arms and disdain the Drudgery of Servitude, repair without loss of Time, to Capt. Tho. Hornby Morland, Or Mr. Lloyd of the above Regiment, At their Rendezvous, the George Inn, Horncastle ... where they may exchange their Whips and Smocks for Laced Coats and Silver-Hilted Swords.

Spirited Lads of Size, Character & Qualifications, may acquit themselves of all women Labouring with Child and young Children, & enter into the direct road to Honour and Preferment. ......

GOD BLESS THE KING

And Damn the French ......[12]

[Our] Regiment has been one year and a half in Ireland, constantly employed in exterminating the Croppies, who are now, damn their bloods, about finished. So much so that these gallant light dragoons are at present eating their beef, bread and potatoes (which by the way are not got for nothing) in peace and comfort, in one of the most delightful, plentiful and cheapest Counties in Ireland...... [13]

A Horse! a Horse! my Kingdom for a Horse!

Now my lads for the 14th Light Dragoons or the Duchess of York's Own. All you who are kicking your heels behind a solitary desk with too little wages, and a pinch-gut Master, – all you with too much wife, or are perplexed with obstinate and unfeeling parents, may apply ...... [14]

GLENGARRY

LIGHT INFANTRY FENCIBLES

Every Young Man who aspires to serve His Majesty in this fine Regiment now raising, will ...... receive FIVE GUINEAS BOUNTY, and ... an allotment of the rich and fertile Lands of Upper Canada, or Lower Canada, if more convenient. This important Grant will make every Soldier of the Corps an Independent Man, at the expiration of his Service; enabled thereby to settle comfortably on his own Farm, in a short time he will have every Luxury of Life about him; he will be able to take his Wife and Family to Church or Market in is own Cariole, and if has not a Wife, it will be the sure means of getting him a good one, for Fortune always favors the Brave, and flinty must be the heart of that Damsel, and vain her pretensions to taste, who could resist a *Light Bob of the Glengary's*, when equipped in his new *Green Uniform*, which will unquestionably be the *neatest in Service.* ......[15]

The officer commanding the recruiting party supervised the process but it was the sergeant who did most of the work. This worthy would first survey the local taverns to find which publicans were friendly and which were not, a process that of necessity usually involved some coins passing hands. Hav-

Fresh fish – recruits for the army
Although this Henry Bunbury drawing is dated 1780, things had not changed more than two decades later when Pearson was on the recruiting service except that the demand for men was even more crucial. Outside the pub where he acquired them, a sergeant lines up his latest catch (who are not a very likely looking lot) for the inspection of the recruiting officer. Note the gleeful onlooker on the left – clearly he was not gulled by the sergeant's sales pitch. (Print after Henry Bunbury, 1780)

ing settled on the most likely spots for business, the sergeant would then seat himself in one of them, strike up a conversation with a likely prospect and buy him a few drinks. Recruiting sergeants were rough but ready psychologists and as one remembered:

> It was never much trouble enticing them to enlist. The best way was to make up to the man you had in your eye … and ask him what sort of a web he was in. You might be sure it was a bad one. …… Ask him how a clever, handsome-looking fellow like him could waste his time hanging seesaw between heaven and earth in a damp, unwholesome shop no better than one of the dripping vaults in St. Mungo's church …… weaving was going to ruin and he might soon be starving ……
>
> Ploughboys had to be hooked in a different way. Tell your man how many recruits had been made sergeants, how many were now officers. If you see an officer pass tell him that he was only a recruit a year ago, but now he's so proud he won't speak to you. …… Don't give up the chase: tell him that where your gallant, honourable regiment is lying everything may be had for almost nothing, that the pigs and the fowls are lying in the streets ready roasted, with knives and forks in them, for the soldiers to eat whenever they

pleased. ...... keep him drinking – don't let him go to the door without one of your party with him, until he is past the doctor and attested. ......

Your sentimental chaps are the easiest caught of all. You had only get into heroics, and spout a great deal about glory, honour, laurels, drums, trumpets, applauding world, deathless fame, immortality and all that, and you had him safe as a mouse in a trap.[16]

Once he hooked a fish, the sergeant wasted no time reeling him in. The potential recruit would be taken to the rendezvous to sign the enlistment papers and accept the "King's shilling." He would next be brought before a local doctor who would certify him fit for service, and the sergeant would know which doctors to use, men who would pass almost anyone who could walk and breathe. The next step was a visit to a magistrate or justice of the peace, but this was not supposed to take place until 24 hours after the man had signed his papers – a necessary precaution against drunkenness. Just as there were friendly doctors, however, there were also friendly magistrates and the sergeant would know them. The magistrate would read the Articles of War to the recruit and have him swear oaths testifying to his correct name and particulars, and that he was not already serving in another regiment. Finally, the recruit would swear the oath to serve the King and obey his officers.

After that the man was a soldier and, in 1803, a man enlisted for life or until he was killed, died, became unfit or was no longer needed. A few years later the Horse Guards reduced the term of service for infantrymen to seven years with an opportunity to re-enlist for two further periods of seven years. This was a wise move but it was not law in 1803. Having been sworn, the recruit now received his bounty, from which (and this was rarely explained to him) deductions were made for his "necessaries," small articles of kit and clothing. Intense pressure would be put on him to wine and dine various members of the recruiting party, and if he still had money when he arrived at his regiment's barracks, it would be quickly siphoned off by various private and illegal levies. It was the rare recruit who had retained any part of his bounty a few weeks after joining the army for, as the old soldier's song put it:

> Your sergeants and officers are very kind,
> If that you can flatter and speak to their mind,
> They will free you from duty and all other trouble,
> Your money being gone, your duty comes double.[17]

There were infinite variations on the process. Sometimes one or two of the soldiers from the recruiting party would don civilian garb and sit with the sergeant while he worked on a prospect, pretending to be interested in a glorious future in the army. Or they would go to another tavern, buy a few drinks for some likely looking lads and then tell them they were off to enlist and why not come along and join the adventure? The party would usually make a circuit of outlying villages, particularly on market or fair days, and here the drummer and fifer would come into their own as, splendidly dressed, they drew attention to arrival of the party. In Norfolk, Parson Woodforde was about to conduct a funeral one day and

> The Corpse was carried by my House, and what was remarkable a recruiting Party with a Drum and fife and Flag flying, passed just before all by chance – Drum beating and fife playing. They came from Lyng, Lyng fair being Yesterday in pursuit of a young Fellow who had listed Yesterday and had run away, and who sh[oul]d that young Fellow be but Barber, Mr. Hardy's the Mason's Lad, to whom I gave a Shilling to last Saturday, hearing he was a good sober Lad and particularly kind to his aged Mother.[18]

When the recruiting party reached a village or local fair, the officer might make a speech but more often it was the sergeant, and he knew just what to say. A young boy who heard one of these discourses remembered that it was all about "Gentlemen soldiers, merry life, muskets rattling, cannons roaring, drums beating, colours flying, regiments charging and shouts of victory! victory!"[19] Free drinks in a nearby tavern would follow and the fishing would then begin. Recruiting for the British army during the Napoleonic wars was a process that attracted the young, the gullible, the stupid and the desperate but it actually worked. Parson Woodforde was shocked to find that his servant lad, Tim Tooley,

> who was supposed to have been gone to bed was not to be found – All his Cloaths gone also. It is thought that he is gone to Norwich to enlist himself, as his Head has long run on a Soldier's Life. His being at Norwich last Saturday & then offered ten Guineas if he would go for a Soldier, determined him. ……[20]

> My late Servant Lad, Tim Tooley, called on us this Morning. He came from Norwich with a Cockade in his Hat, and says he has entered himself in the thirty third Regiment of Foot. Poor Fellow, he appeared happy & looked well.[21]

Woodforde should not have been too surprised because he was only paying young Tooley £2.2.0 per year while the 33rd Foot not only offered a bounty of 10 guineas (£10.10.0) but also an annual wage of £18.5.0. To an impressionable lad from rural Norfolk, whose "Head" had "long run on a Soldier's Life," it looked like a sure thing. Alas poor Tim, he would soon find his bounty drunk by the recruiting party or his comrades at the barracks and, from his £18.5.0 a year, £3.5.5. would be stopped from his pay for "necessaries" including certain items of clothing, a knapsack, pipe clay and whiting, a clothes brush, three shoe brushes, black ball (shoe blacking), worsted mitts, powdering bag and puff, two combs, grease and powder for hair and charges.[22] What with stoppages, charges for the replacement of lost or damaged items of kit provided by the Crown and various other charges, Norfolk Tim would be lucky to receive a few shillings on the first of every month. This is not to mention, of course, the other inconveniences of the service, including salt pork and beef, mouldy biscuit and bread, brutal discipline enforced by the lash, shipwreck, disease and, finally, the French. Six months after he enlisted, Private Timothy Tooley sailed for India with His Majesty's 33rd Regiment of Foot under the command of a Lieutenant-Colonel Arthur Wellesley who had recently changed his name from Wesley, and of whom we shall hear more. In the years that followed, if he survived, Tooley must have wistfully remembered his days in rural Norfolk working for a lenient employer in a house where the average weekday dinner not infrequently included a "very fine Sirloin of Beef rosted and plenty of plumb Puddings … & strong beer after."[23]

Captain Thomas Pearson spent most of 1803 on the recruiting service but his efforts and those of the other Welch Fusilier officers who joined him did not meet with much success. Shortly before it left Gibraltar in June 1803, the 23rd Foot had an enlisted strength of 469 men, with 346 needed to complete to establishment; seven months later it had an enlisted strength of only 389 although four parties were beating in Wales, Somerset and the Midlands. The fact that the 23rd was nominally a Welsh unit meant little when it came to recruiting as regiments took men where they found them and there was always a high proportion of Irishmen – the poverty of the Emerald Isle making it a particularly good source of soldiers – throughout the army. The Welch Fusiliers' difficulty in raising men was mirrored by other line infantry regiments, and in late 1803 the government decided to create a new force called the Army of Reserve, composed of men not required to serve outside Europe. The intention was that, after becoming used to military life, many of the new entrants would volunteer for universal or global service, and many regiments, including the

23rd Foot, raised 2nd Battalions in the Army of Reserve to function as depot or replacement units for their 1st Battalions.

Through 1804 and 1805 Pearson was employed in increasing the size of the 2nd Battalion. It was uphill work. A reviewing officer reported in October of 1804 that the 23rd Foot "has not been successful in recruiting for a second battalion" as all "their London recruits" had deserted.[24] The creation of a new battalion, however, resulted in vacancies for a lieutenant-colonel and two majors to be promoted from those serving in the 1st Battalion. Pearson was the senior captain of the 1/23rd and when a vacancy for a major occurred in the 2nd Battalion, he was promoted without purchase to fill it on 8 December 1804. He marked the occasion by having a new portrait painted in which he wore two epaulettes, the distinction for his new rank.

In February 1805, the 2nd Battalion of the 23rd was reported under Pearson's command at Wrexham in Wales with a strength of 4 officers, 2 sergeants, 28 rank and file, 3 sick and one on furlough – a total enlisted strength of 34. Things did not improve much during the spring of 1805 and, in June, the War Office lowered the establishment of the battalion to 400. Thereafter, progress was made and in November 1805 the 2nd Battalion reported an enlisted strength of 253. A year later it had 400 sergeants, corporals, drummers and privates, of whom 189 were English, 7 were Scots, 85 Irish and 56 Welsh.

While Pearson was fishing for men, the war continued in its course. In May 1804 the French senate declared Bonaparte emperor of France and he took the throne as Napoleon I. Despite his threats, there was still no sign of an invasion of England and many Britons became weary of the whole business of perpetual alarm that the French ogre would soon cross the Channel. The doggerel making the rounds now changed in tone:

> This little Boney says he'll come
> At merry Christmas time,
> But that I say is all a hum
> Or I no more will rhyme.
>
> Some way in wooden house he'll glide
> Some say in air balloon,
> E'en those who airy schemes deride
> Agree his coming soon.

Now honest people list to me
Though income is but small,
I'll bet my wig to one Pen-ney
He does not come at all.[25]

The efforts made to raise the strength of the army were starting to show results. By December 1804 there were 92,000 regulars, 80,000 militia and 343,000
volunteers – a total of 515,000 men ready to defend the home isles, while another 60,000 regulars garrisoned the empire. Nonetheless, this contrasted poorly
with the 450,000 men in the French army, not to mention the contingents
of the French-allied states. Prime Minister William Pitt, who resumed leading the government in May 1804, knew that the war would never be brought
to a successful conclusion unless Britain went on the offensive and began to
pursue diplomatic initiatives to put together a new alliance. Although he was
again rebuffed by Prussia, who had been promised Hanover by Napoleon, Pitt
managed to cobble together a Third Coalition of Austria, Britain and Russia to
defeat the new emperor.

For his part, Napoleon had his own plan to defeat his maritime enemy. It
involved having the French naval squadrons blockaded in various European
ports break out and rendezvous in the West Indies, forcing the Royal Navy to
disperse to hunt them. Once concentrated, the French navy would then join
with the Spanish navy and dominate the Channel long enough for Napoleon to
land an army in Britain. It was a sensible plan which, initially, seemed to work
well, as two squadrons were able to get out during the spring of 1805 and reach
the Caribbean while Vice-Admiral Horatio Nelson hunted for them vainly in
the Mediterranean before following his prey across the Atlantic. Other squadrons were unable to escape, however, and when the French commander, *Vice-
amiral* Pierre Villeneuve, returned to the eastern side of the Atlantic, he realized he was outnumbered and took shelter in the Spanish naval base at Cadiz.

In September 1805 Napoleon ordered Villeneuve to leave Cadiz with a Spanish squadron and enter the Mediterranean but he was not able to do so until 18
October. When he emerged with 33 French and Spanish ships of the line, Villeneuve found Nelson waiting for him with 27 ships of the line, superbly crewed,
trained and commanded. The two fleets made contact off Cape Trafalgar on 21
October 1805 and Nelson, as usual, sailed straight in to attack the enemy line,
hoisting a famous signal just before action commenced, which did not please
Vice-Admiral Lord Cuthbert Collingwood, his second-in-command. As the

Vice-Admiral Horatio, Lord Nelson (1758-1805)

The greatest naval commander of his time, Nelson's victory over a combined French-Spanish fleet at Trafalgar in October 1805 made Britain the undisputed ruler of the waves. Although Napoleon began a massive naval construction programme and tried to obtain the fleets of smaller nations, he was never able to achieve naval parity with Britain and was thus unable to defeat his most steadfast and dangerous enemy. Trafalgar also led Napoleon into an invasion of Portugal in an attempt to secure that nation's fleet, a step that ultimately brought on the Peninsular War of 1808-1814, which, with the failed invasion of Russia in 1812, ensured the collapse of his empire. (Print after painting by L.F. Abbot)

signal lieutenant on HMS *Royal Sovereign*, Collingwood's flagship, read the hoist on Nelson's *Victory* – "England … expects … that … every … man … will … do … his … duty" – the fretting Collingwood snapped: "What's Nelson signalling about? We all know what we have to do."[26]

The Royal Navy certainly did and by nightfall 18 French and Spanish ships were sunk or captured. The victory, however, was not bought cheaply – Nelson was dead and 1,700 British sailors were killed or wounded, and among the severely wounded was Pearson's younger brother, Lieutenant George Pearson of HMS *Bellerophon*. Trafalgar, nevertheless, spelled the end of Napoleon's invasion plans and left Britain quite literally ruling the waves.

But the armies of France remained superior on land, a fact that Napoleon quickly demonstrated to his enemies. Learning of the formation of the Third Coalition, he sent an ultimatum to Austria in August 1805, and when the reply was unsatisfactory, began to move his newly-titled *Grande Armée* east from the Channel coast in late August. The new emperor destroyed one Austrian army at Ulm and occupied Vienna before winning one of his greatest victories at Austerlitz on 2 December 1805, where he defeated a combined Austrian and Russian army. Although Russia continued in the war, this defeat forced Austria to seek peace, and the Third Coalition began to unravel. When William Pitt died from exhaustion in January 1806, Britain was safe from invasion but no closer to defeating her opponent.

Napoleon tried to conclude peace with Russia but Czar Alexander I would not agree to his terms, preferring instead to make a secret treaty with Prussia that would see each nation render the other mutual aid. Pitt's successor, Lord

Grenville, who headed a coalition government somewhat derisively known as the "Ministry of all the Talents," had recently opened secret negotiations with France. When the Prussian government learned that Napoleon had offered to restore Hanover, currently occupied by Prussia, to Britain, it became incensed. The timid King Frederick William III agonized for months before finally sending an ultimatum to Napoleon in October 1806 ordering him to remove all French troops from the German-speaking states, on threat of war. Napoleon's response was to invade and crush Prussia in a matter of weeks, bringing to an abrupt end a myth of military superiority founded by Frederick the Great. Russia, however, remained truculent and the French emperor became involved in a costly winter campaign in Poland that lasted from December to February 1807 and, after heavy casualties on both sides, ended in a stalemate.

The "Ministry of All Talents" quickly demonstrated that it was no such thing. Britain's major contribution to the campaigns in Europe was to send 26,000 troops, including the 1/23rd Foot, to Cuxhaven in December 1805, where they more or less sat for two months before being withdrawn, having accomplished absolutely nothing. For the rest of its short term, which ended in March 1807, the talentless government planned various expeditions, including an invasion of Egypt and an attack on Buenos Aires. Both of these operations ended in ignominious defeats, caused more by the incompetence of the British commanders than by the prowess of their enemies, but an invasion of the Italian mainland from Sicily, under the command of Lieutenant-General Sir John Stuart, had a more positive result. At the battle of Maida on 4 July 1806, Stuart defeated a superior French force, although the victory owed more to the professionalism of his brigade and regimental commanders than to his own generalship. Many of these officers, such as Brigadier-General Lowry Cole, Colonel James Kempt and Captain John Colborne, were veterans of Egypt, and Maida demonstrated that the British army had not lost the tactical skills it had acquired under Abercromby. Unfortunately, having won this signal triumph, Stuart then withdrew his army to Sicily.

In May 1807 Napoleon resumed his campaign against Russia and in the following month gained a major success at the battle of Friedland, which brought Czar Alexander to the negotiating table. In July the two emperors met at Tilsit in eastern Prussia to end the war of the Third Coalition and in doing so redraw much of the map of Europe, creating a new Polish nation, the Grand Duchy of Warsaw, and a new entity termed the Confederation of the Rhine, which incorporated many of the independent small German states and principalities. Napoleon and Alexander also agreed on a number of secret clauses in the resulting Treaty of Tilsit, signed on 7 July 1807, in which Russia promised to support Napoleon's plan to acquire the Portuguese, Danish and Swedish fleets, which, combined with the rump of the French and Spanish fleets remaining after Trafalgar, would not only give him naval parity with Britain but also deny the Royal Navy the supplies of Scandinavian timber necessary to maintain its fleet.

Napoleon also decided that the most effective way to bring intransigent Britain to its knees was to destroy, by any means possible, that nation's maritime commerce. Toward this end he issued the Berlin Decrees in November 1806 which declared that any British goods found in France or French-occupied nations on any vessel, British or otherwise, would be subject to seizure. Since France controlled nearly the entire coastline of Europe and one-third of British exports went to the continent, this move was aimed squarely at British trade. Britain responded in January 1807 with the Orders-in-Council which proclaimed that any vessel carrying cargoes to or from a French-held port would be subject to seizure. Napoleon fired back with the Milan Decrees, which declared that any vessel obeying the Orders-in-Council or allowing itself to be boarded by the Royal Navy would be subject to French seizure. Napoleon knew that Britain could only be defeated by a superior naval force but, until it was available to him – and he again accelerated his naval construction programme – his intention was to bring such economic pressure to bear on his mortal enemy that she would be forced to seek peace.

Unfortunately for his plans, the British government, now headed by the Duke of Portland, learned of the secret clauses of the Treaty of Tilsit and was quick to react. Exactly three weeks to the day after the treaty was signed, a British expeditionary force with 18,000 troops was ordered to sail for the Baltic with the purpose of convincing Denmark to turn over its fleet to Britain for safekeeping. Among the regiments on board the transports was the 1/23rd Foot, and among that battalion's officers was Major Thomas Pearson, who was about to see his first action in more than six years.

Major Thomas Pearson had rejoined the 1st Battalion of the 23rd Foot at its station at Colchester in February 1807 when it received a large draft of officers and men from the 2nd Battalion. By now the senior battalion was up to strength and in fine fettle as it had had nearly four successive years of training. The newly-promoted Captain Jack Hill recalled that the 1/23rd had a reputation as an elite unit, as he boasted to his parents: "We are indeed a very favourite Regt" and "H.R.H. the Prince of Wales paid the Regt. and Bury the most marked compliments, the Duke of Kent pleas'd as Punch at the Regt. coming off with so much credit."[27] Of course the royal personage who really counted was the Duke of York but even that not-easily-fooled officer thought the 1/23rd "was in the highest order possible."[28]

Among the new arrivals who came from the 2nd Battalion with Pearson was 19-year-old Second Lieutenant Thomas Henry Browne from Denbighshire in Wales, who had been commissioned without purchase in September 1805. A literary-minded man, Browne kept a diary which, in later life, he expanded into a memoir, and this is fortunate as he was to serve with Pearson for several years. Although he provides only a few glimpses of the subject of our story, he does provide much interesting and colourful detail about the daily life of the officers of the Welch Fusiliers, in garrison and field.

The naval component of the Copenhagen expedition was under the command of Admiral James Gambier, nicknamed "Dismal Jimmy" in the navy because he was "a man of extreme Evangelical opinions in the matter of religion, who would heave to his fleet for prayers and distribute tracts about the lower deck."[29] His army counterpart was Lieutenant-General Lord Cathcart, described as being "dejected and downcast, full of apprehensions and ominous forebodings, which did not promise well for the speedy accomplishment of his task."[30] Fortunately, Cathcart had some very good subordinate officers, including 38-year-old Major-General Sir Arthur Wellesley, last met as Private Timothy Tooley's commanding officer when the 33rd Foot sailed for India in 1796, who had acquired an excellent reputation during several successful campaigns in the subcontinent. Since Portland's government did not expect that the Danes would resist the British demands, Cathcart hoped to be able to accomplish his task without loss of life. Unfortunately, this was not to be so but this should have come as no surprise to London, as a previous attempt to acquire the Danish fleet in 1801 had been rejected, forcing the Royal Navy to destroy much of it by bombarding its base at Copenhagen.

After remaining six days on their transports at Harwich, the 1/23rd Foot sailed on the 30 of July 1807. As 19-year-old Lieutenant John Harrison of the Welch Fusiliers recalled, their destination "was kept very secret, but it is supposed that we are going to make a great dash somewhere."[31] It was not an unpleasant voyage and young Harrison, who was on board the transport *Louisa* with the commanding officer, recalled a typical day:

At 6 a.m. rose, walked the deck while the cabin was cleared for Breakfast, which consisted of Tea, Coffee and Hot Rolls, the latter luxury we were indulged with by lucky circumstance of our having the mess cook on board the Louisa. If the weather was tolerably calm we fished and one day we caught five dozen mackerel. Amused myself on my violin and sometimes read. Making our observations of the Fleet and frequently coming alongside a Transport with some of our Regt on board afforded us great pleasure. At 4 pm were summoned to dinner. We limited ourselves to a pint of good port and rational conversation and when candles were lighted, passed the evening with a social game of Whist. At half-past nine for those who wished a little cold meat introduced for supper, which meal being concluded with a glass of grop, we retired to rest.[32]

The fleet made good time and by 9 August rendezvoused off Elsinore, where they waited a week while the British ambassador to Denmark tried to convince the Danes to agree to London's demands. By now, the Welch Fusilier officers on board the Louisa were running low on their "sea stock," the food that they had to purchase themselves while travelling by sea. It was one of the curiosities of the service that, while on a sea voyage, army enlisted personnel received their rations cooked by the navy while army officers received only the raw, uncooked ration and were not even provided utensils with which to eat it. Naval officers, of course, had their own messes on board and sailors assigned to do their cooking. As one officer complained:

> The intention of government was no doubt to consult as much as possible the convenience of the Officers; but, the arrangement *was*, and *is*, shameful, respecting their treatment when embarked and on board Transports. In the first instance, hurried to get on Board, they immediately find they have nothing to expect but a hard berth, the use of a Cabin, and Rations; not utensils to cook with, or to use; no person to cook for them; in short, all must depend on their individual exertion. Conceive a young Lad, without a servant, and with a scanty purse, thus situated, expecting a voyage of a month or six weeks' continuance![33]

The Welch Fusilier officers, being an adaptable lot, took advantage of the delay at Elsinore to re-provision and Lieutenant Harrison recorded that they were allowed

to send an officer with a boat on shore to purchase and bring off what necessaries were wanting, but not to allow the soldiers or sailors to land on any
account. In consequence of this order we sent our boat and procured one
Dozen of Port and do. [ditto] of Claret, the latter at the easy rate of 29/ [29
shillings] a dozen, a couple of poor duck and a few eggs, also some brandy
tolerably cheap.[34]

On 16 August 1807, having had no success with his negotiations, Cathcart
began to disembark his army at Vedboek, about four miles from Copenhagen.
The landing was made "without any noise or confusion" and Lieutenant Harrison remembered that

We had just furnished each man with eighty rounds of Ball cartridge, and two
days provisions ready cooked with their usual allowance of grog. When the
Boats came alongside to receive us I instantly buckled on my Knapsack and
slung my Haversack and Canteen across my shoulder, well stored with Ham,
Biscuit and Grog, and took my leave of the Louisa. We reached the shore in
very good style. The Landing was flanked by our Bomb and Fire ships.[35]

When the 23rd Foot landed, unopposed, Second Lieutenants H. Stanyford
Blanckley and Thomas Browne were carrying the Colours. As Browne fondly
recalled, "when we planted them on the Danish shore, we had by no means
an indifferent opinion of ourselves."[36] Over the next few days Cathcart moved
toward the Danish capital, and during this movement Pearson commanded the
light companies of the 4th and 23rd Foot, the two regiments being brigaded
together under the command of Major-General Thomas Grosvenor.

Copenhagen, a city of some 100,000 souls, possessed formidable defences
on both its landward and seaward sides but the Danish commandant had neglected to assemble large forces of regular troops to increase its garrison. This
is not surprising as, from Browne's account of the army's first days ashore, it
seems that the Danes were completely bewildered by the sudden appearance
of armed and redcoated visitors in their midst. The garrison only attempted
one serious sortie against the batteries that the British gunners and engineers
began to construct around the landward extent of Copenhagen and it was easily beaten off while other half-hearted attempts to attack the besiegers from the
north were brushed aside by Wellesley. There was constant skirmishing on the
outskirts of the city, however, and, as a light infantry commander, Pearson was
frequently involved in it.

Despite the fact that he had considerable artillery, Cathcart did not feel that he had the means to mount a regular siege of Copenhagen, but when he expressed his concerns to Gambier, that God-fearing officer replied that, "in this case the Navy would be happy to take the matter in hand" as indeed, they had six years earlier.[37] In fact Cathcart knew that, if the Danes did not accede to the British demands, he would have no choice but to destroy their capital.

By 1 September 1807 the gunners were ready to fire. Cathcart sent a final demand to the governor warning him that he would bombard the city unless he delivered up the Danish fleet, which would be taken to Britain, where it would be held until the war with France had ended and then returned in a good state of order. Not unreasonably, the governor replied that the Danish fleet was safer in the hands of the Danish king than in those of George III and refused the ultimatum. Hoping the man would change his mind, Cathcart refrained from firing until the evening of 2 September and then reluctantly, at about 7.30 P.M., gave the order. Eighty guns, mortars and howitzers, and a Congreve rocket detachment under the command of the weapon's inventor, opened up and within an hour or two Copenhagen was a mass of flames. The Congreve rockets, which, despite being very erratic, could hardly miss such a target, proved effective and terrifying. A Dane who was bombarded that night later complained that "when I saw the air gingling [sic] with the never to be heard of inventions, carrying fire thro' the air, not to be extinguished, down upon our dwellings, oh Britain, Queen of Nations, Mother of such noble and manly sons, said I to myself, is this thy work."[38]

After 12 hours, the British batteries fell silent but resumed firing on the evening of 3 September. Gambier's fleet, which included several bomb vessels, joined in by attacking the Danish batteries along the waterside. The Danes sent gunboats against this inshore squadron and Gambier countered this with ships' boats armed with light ordnance, which were no match for the Danish vessels armed with two 24-pdr. guns. It was during this unequal contest that Lieutenant Charles Pearson of HMS *Spenser*, Tom Pearson's brother, who had joined the Royal Navy in 1801, was forced to swim after the launch he was commanding was sunk by a direct hit.

On land, as the bombardment continued, Lieutenant Browne and the officers of the 23rd watched spellbound as

The fire from our batteries, and from the Danish ramparts, resembled a constant succession of flashes of lightning, and the very firmament shook

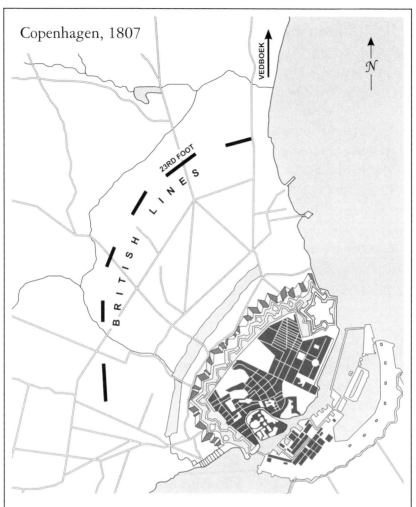

Copenhagen, 1807

After landing in Denmark, Cathcart's army, including the 23rd Foot, set up a siege line around Copenhagen which included numerous artillery positions. When the Danes refused to surrender their fleet, the British gunners opened fire and destroyed much of the city.

with unceasing explosions. A Church steeple was set on fire by a shell lodging in the Belfry, and it fell, a mass of flame, with a tremendous crash, on the houses near it, and communicated flames to a whole street. The number of houses on fire, before day break exceeded four hundred. ...... The blaze of Copenhagen thus on fire, and the incessant roaring of guns, pouring destruction on other parts of the City which did not give evidence, in flames, of the effect produced by them, continued thro' the night. Day-break showed a white flag on one of the ramparts, and our firing ceased.[39]

To Cathcart's relief, the Danish commandant capitulated and terms were quickly agreed – the Danish fleet and naval stores would be rendered up and the British would evacuate Denmark within six weeks. Over the next few days the soldiers occupied the outlying defences of the city while naval shore parties landed to make the Danish fleet – 18 ships of the line, 15 frigates, 6 brigs and 25 smaller vessels – ready to sail to Britain with prize crews. Officers were permitted into Copenhagen, so Browne toured the ruined city and, with all the self-proclaimed knowledge of any 19-year-old male, decided that he "did not observe much beauty in the women, but much taste and elegance in dress, and good figures."[40] Considering what these women had just gone through, this can hardly come as a surprise. For his part, Pearson almost certainly had a reunion with his brother Charles.

By 18 October 1807 all was ready, and the combined fleets sailed for home. It being a Sunday, Gambier, true to his reputation, signalled for the fleet to "to lay to, for prayers" near Elsinore. This order was not popular because, given the season and state of the sea, "the safe return to England of so valuable a fleet, having on board more than 40,000 souls, should not have been delayed an instant."[41] It also led the "irreligious and profligate" part of the soldiery "to blaspheme and storm at a terrific rate, for being so long detained when the wind was so fair."[42] As it was, the passage home was rough and some of the captured vessels were lost during a storm in the North Sea. Browne's transport accidentally rammed one small craft, sinking it, before running afoul of a frigate, and it was not until 6 November that the 23rd Foot landed at Deal.

The British army was not particularly proud of its participation in the Copenhagen expedition – one soldier wrote that he pitied the Danes "from the bottom of my heart" – but for some reason Portland's government was surprised when Denmark immediately declared war on Britain.[43]

Napoleon was furious. The Danish fleet had been snatched from under his nose and as the Swedes resolutely refused to give up their vessels, he now began to put pressure on Portugal, demanding that that small nation close its ports to British trade – its economic lifeline – and declare war on Britain. In response, Britain threatened Portugal, a country dependent on imported food, with blockade, and thus unoffending Portugal and its ruler, Prince John, were roasted between two fires. Not satisfied with the Portuguese response to his demands, Napoleon declared war in the autumn of 1807 and, with the cooperation of Spain, a French army marched across that nation and entered Lisbon in late November, just in time to see the Portuguese fleet disappear

The bombardment of Copenhagen, 2-6 September 1807
A secret clause in the Treaty of Tilsit between France and Russia in July 1807 agreed that
Napoleon would take possession of the Danish fleet. Learning of this, the British government sent an expeditionary force to Copenhagen to demand that the Danes turn their fleet
over to Britain for safekeeping until the war ended. Not unnaturally, they refused and much
of Copenhagen was destroyed by a five-day bombardment until they capitulated. Both Pearson and his brother Charles, a naval officer, participated in this operation, which was not
exactly Britain's proudest moment. (From James Grant, *British Battles on Land and Sea*)

over the horizon with the Portuguese royal family, who had decided to escape
to Brazil.

Napoleon also began to take a closer look at Spain, a nation racked by internal dissension, and started to contemplate placing one of his brothers on the
Spanish throne. Although the French ruler was at the height of his power, with
every nation in mainland Europe either part of his empire, nominally allied
with it, or occupied by his troops, Napoleon was still not satisfied for, as he remarked: "Conquest has made me what I am and only conquest can enable me
to hold my position."[44] The war would continue until either Britain or France
was completely victorious.

On their return from Copenhagen in late October 1807, the 1/23rd Foot went back to Colchester. For a while the Fusiliers had an easy time as winter set in and the weather was too cold and wet for drill, while the garrison, which included three other regiments, was so large that guard and post duties were light. The regiment therefore sent a proportion of its officers, and ten men from every company, on leave and settled down to a quiet life. The officers busied themselves having their mess room repainted, laying in a winter stock of wine, improving the mess's supply of newspapers and periodicals, organizing a "glee club" or choir from the enlisted men and subscribing for new instruments for the band. Furthermore, in anticipation of the prize money they would be receiving after the ships and naval stores captured at Copenhagen were purchased by the Crown, which active imaginations nearly trebled in size, the Fusilier officers invited guests to their mess "much more frequently than was usual."[45] Still being at a loss "to dispose of money which we had not received," they decided, along with the officers of the 4th and 28th Foot, to give a ball at the Three Cups Inn in Colchester.

A major from each regiment was appointed to a management committee, which began to hold meetings at the Three Cups. Either Pearson or Major

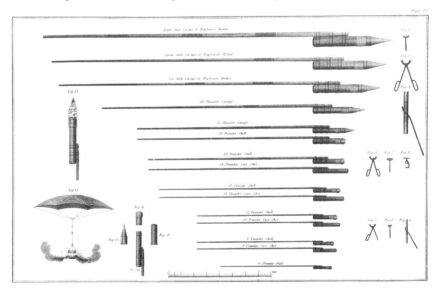

Britain's secret weapon – the Congreve rocket
Invented by William Congreve, these weapons were used extensively during the bombardment of Copenhagen in September 1807. They were highly inaccurate but a city was a hard target to miss and they did much damage to the Danish capital. (From William Congreve, *Details of the Rocket System*, 1814)

Richard Offley would have represented the 23rd on this hardworking group but disquiet shortly spread among the junior officers when, after several meetings, the committee had nothing to report and discreet inquiries revealed that the three majors had been enjoying capital dinners at the Three Cups "with the very best wines, to be paid for, from the funds destined for the ball."[46] The junior officers tactfully steered the erring committee back on course and the event was a great success. As its costs did not consume all the expected prize money, however, the officers of the 23rd followed it with a "masquerade" in their own mess room which proved so expensive that, when the anticipated prize money did come, "it would not prove particularly burdensome." Having spent much of their bonanza on these two social events, the Fusilier officers squandered the rest on less elaborate activities.

It was all great fun and the officers of the 23rd were eagerly anticipating at least another six months of such fine life but the war caught up with them on 16 January 1808. That day, Pearson was commanding the regiment in place of Lieutenant Colonel Henry W. Ellis, who was on leave, and Lieutenant Browne never forgot the fateful evening when the idyll came to a crashing end:

> Winter was in its glory ... the mess room fire was burning unusually bright – the wine was voted unusually good, and an officer had just remarked, "this is really too comfortable to last long" – for which we thought him a real croaker, when the Drum-Major came in, and delivered to the Commanding Officer a letter of Official form. A sort of chill passed thro's us all, and the blue-devils had evidently entered the mess-room, with the Drum-Major.[47]

Pearson broke the seal on the letter and read it. He then looked up and, seeing the curious faces of the assembled officers, read its contents aloud:

> The 23rd regiment will march in three divisions, to Portsmouth for embarkation for foreign service. The 1st division will move by the enclosed route, on the 17th [the following morning] and the remaining divisions on the 18th and 19th. All officers and men on leave of absence, to join the regiment at Portsmouth.[48]

Within minutes, the Welch Fusiliers' barracks at Colchester were a scene of frantic activity. Personal belongings had to be packed, a task made the more difficult by the fact that no one had the slightest idea of their eventual destination. There was the mess wine, silver and other furnishings belonging to the regiment to be properly crated, as well as the government property that would be taken along. Arrangements had to be made to pay outstanding bills to local merchants and return furniture hired for the mess room and officers' quarters. Letters had to be written to those on leave, including Lieutenant-Colonel Ellis, directing them to proceed immediately to Portsmouth to meet the regiment there. The quartermaster was probably driven half crazy with worry, the pay-master bewailed the state of his records, the adjutant harassed everyone and it is likely that the sergeant-major lost his voice from shouting. The entire bat-talion, officers and men, worked through the night to have the first division ready to march by morning.

There was also a sad task to be performed: choosing which of the soldiers' wives would be permitted to accompany their husbands. As the regulations al-lowed only 12 wives and their children per company at best on foreign stations, the remainder would be sent to their home parishes, where many would inevi-tably end up in the local workhouse. Knowing this, there was keen, even vicious, competition among the wives to be chosen to accompany the regiment, and the 23rd Foot, through long experience, probably resorted to the time-honoured method of drawing lots. Pieces of paper with "To Go" or "Not to Go" written on them were placed in a hat and each wife in turn drew her fate. A soldier who wit-nessed this heartrending process has left a moving account of what took place:

The first woman, the senior sergeant's wife, drew "Not to go." Nobody cared, for she was no favourite, neither was her husband. A corporal's wife came next – again, "Not to go." Not a sound of regret, for she was no more popu-lar than her man. The third put in her hand – an outrageous virago, who thought nothing of knocking down her husband, and was hated about the barrack-room fire at cooking times. The wishes of the assembly that she be left were almost audible. Boldly she plunged her hand into the hat; trium-phantly she waved the scrap inscribed "To go." "Hurrah," she shouted, "Old Meg will go yet and live to scold more of you round the fireside." "Hang the old wretch!" came from behind, "she has the devil's luck and her own."

Then came a modest young woman, wife of the model of the company, beloved of her husband, and esteemed by the roughest of his barrack-mates. Trembling she drew out her ticket. "Not to go," it read, but she could not see for her emotion. "Tell me, for God's sake, what is it! Oh, God help me! Oh Sandy," came her cry as she sank fainting on her husband. "Oh, Sandy, you'll no leave me and your poor baby." Her agony touched deeply the hardest of them all, but Old Meg burst out: "What are ye making sic a wark about? Let the babie get her greet out. I suppose she thinks there's naebody ever parted with their men but her, wi' her faintin' and her airs, and her wark."[49]

According to Lieutenant Browne, the "wailings" of the abandoned Fusilier wives "resounded in the barrack yard."[50]

When morning came, the first division marched off on time and it was followed in due course by the second and third. As they arrived in Portsmouth after a journey of a hundred miles, each division embarked on a waiting transport. The Fusilier officers formed partnerships to acquire sea stock for the voyage and Browne recorded that his group purchased port, sherry, tea, sugar, coffee, biscuits, plenty of potatoes, some oranges and lemons in case of sickness, as well as live sheep, pigs, fowls and ducks and, to pass the time, a chess board and some decks of cards.

The Welch Fusiliers were not the only regiment embarking as the 1/7th, 1/8th and 13th Foot were also under orders for foreign service but, although the rumour mills ground furiously, their destination remained a mystery. Lieutenant-Colonel Edward Pakenham, commanding the 1st Battalion of the 7th Foot or Royal Fusiliers, was certain that it was British North America, but since the Atlantic shipping season normally began only in late March, he shrewdly calculated that "some time must be passed else where for we set out at least two months earlier than we ought to do for the Quarter supposed."[51]

Pakenham was right. The 13th Foot was bound for Bermuda while the other three regiments, under the command of Major-General Daniel Hoghton, were heading for Halifax, Nova Scotia. The transfer of this number of troops, about 4,000 in all, across the Atlantic resulted from growing tension between Britain and the United States, tension caused by the war in Europe. The tit-for-tat conflict of economic sanctions on each other's maritime trade played by Britain and France – Napoleon's Berlin and Milan decrees and Britain's Orders-in-Council, not to mention the Royal Navy's active blockade of European ports – had adversely affected the young republic. Its merchant marine, the second largest in the world after the Royal Navy had swept French and European competition from the seas, was caught in this economic crossfire. Even more galling to the United States was the custom of Royal Navy captains, desperate for manpower, of stopping American merchant vessels and impressing or conscripting members of their crews on the dubious grounds that they were British citizens.

In June 1807 Britain and the United States came to the brink of war after a British 50-gun ship, HMS *Leopard,* fired into the unprepared American frigate, USS *Chesapeake,* when the latter refused to be boarded for an inspection, killing or wounding 21 persons. Although Britain apologized for this incident, Americans were understandably outraged and demanded armed retaliation, but President Thomas Jefferson decided to use economic measures of his own and in December 1807 proclaimed an embargo against the European belligerents, which forbade American ships to sail to their ports. This measure actually had a more harmful effect on the American economy than on that of the belligerents, but the rising tension was such that the British government felt compelled to reinforce its North American garrisons.

At the same time it also decided to send a soldier, Major-General Sir George Prevost, to assume the appointment of lieutenant-governor of Nova Scotia. The 41-year-old Prevost, with whom Pearson was to become closely associated, was the son of a Swiss Protestant officer who had helped to raise the 60th Regiment of Foot (Royal Americans) in the Seven Years War. Commissioned at the end of the American Revolutionary War, Prevost had seen considerable service in the West Indies and being fluent in French, had been a popular and effective governor of St. Lucia, a former French colony. Although he possessed diplomatic skills, Prevost was also a capable commander and had successfully defended Dominica in 1805 against a determined French assault. He thus appeared to be an ideal choice for the position of lieutenant-governor of Nova Scotia, which brought with it responsibility for defending Halifax, the Royal Navy's major base in North America.

The result was that the 1/23rd Foot had their pleasant sojourn at Colchester rudely interrupted one winter evening. Although the regiment boarded the transports on schedule, they had to wait nearly a month in Portsmouth before their convoy weighed anchor on 13 February 1808. It took the ships 12 days to make the Azores and by St. David's Day, 1 March, the convoy was far out in the Atlantic. Due to the circumstances, the Welch Fusiliers had to forgo their traditional festivities but the officers at least had their cabins "dressed in Onions, and drank an extra glass of grog on the occasion."[52] If the officers had laid in enough sea stock, these trans-Atlantic troop movements could sometimes be uproarious, as was the case with the infamous passage of the 10th Foot from Ireland to Quebec in 1767, immortalized in a song sung for years around the mess tables of many regiments:

On the third day of June of the year '67
The Tenth in three transports sailed out of Cork Haven.
All jovial and hearty like sailors so valiant,
And Commodore Holmes was top and top-gallant.

But of all jolly fellows, the first to be reckoned
Was Marmaduke Savage of the Fifty-Second;
For he of the bottle was such a brisk shover,
That before they left land, they were near half seas over.

Fitzgerald was hearty, and Kelly was rosy,
And Thompson was rocky, and Vertis was boozy;
And all were as merry as ducks in a shower,
And thus they sailed on, at nine knots by the hour.

But such was their loyalty, such was their boozing,
That in nine weeks, of wine they drank eighty-one dozen
Of rum, shrub and brandy, just fifty-six gallons,
And ninety-eight dozen of porter, to balance![53]

As befitting an elite fusilier regiment, the officers of the 23rd were possibly more temperate.

On 12 March, the convoy was becalmed in mid-ocean so Lieutenant Browne and his comrades took a boat over to the *Lord Collingwood*, the regimental headquarters ship. As the other ships came as close as they dared, the band of the 23rd played "country dances, and the soldiers with such women as were embarked, danced till past midnight," a scene that "was repeated whenever the fineness of the weather permitted."[54] The convoy raised Bermuda, the summer station of the Royal Navy's North America squadron, on 24 March, where it disembarked the 13th Foot before turning north for Nova Scotia, which was sighted on 7 April. A pilot came on board to guide the lead vessel along the 15 miles of the Eastern Passage, fringed with rocky hills and redolent with the scent of pine, into the harbour proper, and thus the Royal Welch Fusiliers, along with 12 dogs belonging to the officers of the regiment, arrived in North America.

The "Flash," 1814

The Welch Fusiliers' mark of distinction, the "Flash," originated in an incident that took place in Halifax in the late spring of 1809. When the regiment received an order to cut its queues, it grudgingly obeyed but, as a sign of protest, began to wear the ribbons that had formerly been used to tie the queue as a decoration on the backs of their coats. The picture of this Welch Fusilier sergeant, painted in 1814, illustrates this unique distinction which is worn by the regiment to this day. (Courtesy of The Royal Welch Fusiliers Museum)

CHAPTER FOUR

"FAIR COMPLEXIONS LIT UP BY SOFT BLUE EYES."

NOVA SCOTIA, MARTINIQUE AND NEW BRUNSWICK, 1808–1810

I'm lonesome since I crossed the hill,
And o'er the moor and valley,
Such grievous thoughts my heart do fill,
Since parting with my Sally.
I seek no more the fine or gay,
For each does but remind me,
How swift the hours did pass away,
With the girl I've left behind me.

Oh, ne'er shall I forget the night
The stars were bright above me,
And gently lent their silvery light,
When first she vowed to love me.
But now I'm bound to Brighton Camp
Kind heaven, then, pray guide me,
And send me safely back again
To the girl I've left behind me.[1]

There was great excitement in Halifax as, one by one, the ships of the Welch Fusiliers' convoy dropped anchor. The *Nova Scotia Gazette* confessed itself "happy to report that of the transports, which left Portsmouth, … not one is missing, and that considering the early season of the year, they have arrived in the best order imaginable."[2] The *Gazette* was also impressed by the regiments that landed for they appeared to be "in the highest state of military order." Nova Scotians were particularly pleased that the convoy had brought a new lieutenant-governor as the incumbent, the corrupt Sir John

Wentworth, was universally despised – his greatest accomplishments had been to enrich himself at the expense of the people of the province and to erect a fine official residence, Government House, on Barrington Street, the main thoroughfare of the town. Sir George Prevost and Wentworth never officially met; the general stayed at Government House, which he found "an edifice out of all proportion to the situation," while the latter remained at his country residence before boarding a ship for the return voyage to Britain.[3]

Having only been founded in 1749, Halifax was a relatively recent phenomenon. It existed because of its long, wide, deep and well-sheltered harbour, 13 square miles in extent and one of the largest in the world. It was a busy port and its economic livelihood depended on the sea, in the form of fishing, maritime commerce, privateering, the naval base and the large garrison which defended it. The military and naval presence in the town was overpowering – there were approximately 9,000 civilians in Halifax in 1809 while, depending on the season, there could be as many as 6,000 service personnel. Compared to Britain, the cost of living was low, alcohol was cheap – a gallon of West Indies rum could be had for 50 cents and some storekeepers gave it away free to their customers – and it was estimated that there was one drinking establishment

Halifax, c. 1817
Possessing one of the best natural harbours in the world, Halifax was the Royal Navy's major base in North America. When Pearson and the Welch Fusiliers arrived in the spring of 1808, the town was just over a half century old but was a booming sea port with a reputation as a good station in both the navy and the army. (Aquatint by George Parkyns, National Library and Archives of Canada, C-000981)

Lieutenant-General Sir George Prevost (1767-1816)
Seen here as a major-general in a portrait done by Robert Field of Halifax, Prevost was sent to Nova Scotia in 1808 as lieutenant-governor. In late 1811 he was promoted lieutenant-general and appointed Governor-General and Captain-General of the Forces in British North America. He successfully defended Britain's North American possessions during the War of 1812. Nearly forgotten today, at one point Prevost had more British regular troops under his command than the Duke of Wellington. (National Library and Archives of Canada, C-6512)

for every hundred civilians but only one school for every thousand. It is small wonder that Halifax had the reputation in the Royal Navy for being the liveliest, cheapest and most friendly port for a run ashore after Portsmouth. The army liked the place not only for the liquor and the prices, but also the fact that it was a healthy station with little disease. Halifax thrived in wartime and suffered in peacetime but in 1808, although the American embargo had put dents in its economy, thanks to the lengthy conflict in Europe it was bustling.

The town was no stranger to the famous and infamous. General James Wolfe had used the marvellous harbour to train his troops in amphibious landing exercises before undertaking successful attacks on Louisbourg in 1758 and Quebec in 1759. Horatio Nelson had walked its muddy streets as a young frigate captain, and Sir John Moore had briefly served in the garrison. In the late 1780s and early 1790s, His Royal Highness Prince William Henry, another of the many sons of George III, had been a frequent visitor in his frigate, HMS *Pegasus*. When "Coconut Head" (as William was universally known in the Royal Navy) made a run ashore, it was almost always a riotous occasion marked by heavy drinking and serious wenching on the part of the prince. Not infrequently he ended up in the arms of Lady Frances Wentworth, whose services to the fleet were such that they ultimately gained her husband, Sir John Wentworth, the appointment of lieutenant-governor and kept him there for 16 years despite his flagrant corruption. On one visit, William hosted a dinner for 20 guests including the lieutenant-governor, the naval commodore on station and the commanding general, which ended in 23 bumper toasts that the duke insisted his guests drink while standing on their chairs. "I think it was the most laughable sight I ever beheld," remarked one of the prince's friends, "to see our Governor, our General and the Commodore all so drunk that they could scarcely stand on the floor, hoisted up on their chairs each with a bumper in his hand; three times three cheers was what they were afraid to attempt for fear of falling."[4] Sixty-three bottles of wine were consumed that night.

A few years later Prince William was followed by his younger brother, Prince Edward, Duke of Kent, exiled from Britain by his father for his many transgressions. Edward was more sober than William and oblivious to the attractions of *la Wentworth* as he had brought his own mistress with him, the charming Madame St. Laurent, 20 years her junior. Wishing perhaps to emulate the ancient pharoahs, Kent embarked on a military construction programme that lasted the six years of his command and distributed forts, batteries, barracks, storehouses and a semaphore telegraph system in and around the town – and also a fine Georgian clock tower on Citadel Hill that remains to this day. But Kent was also a cold-blooded and brutal martinet who flogged hundreds of men for the most trivial offences and was unpopular with soldiers and civilians alike. When he was transferred to Gibraltar in 1802, his father, that most unfortunate of parents, warned him "not to make such a trade of it as when you went to Halifax!"[5] As we have seen, Kent disregarded this paternal advice.

Unfortunately for the Welch Fusiliers, who were fully aware of the town's reputation for fun, they did not long linger at Halifax. Immediately on its arrival, the 23rd Foot was ordered to Annapolis Royal, on the far side of the province, to garrison the outpost defences of the port. The young officers had time only to hold a single ball in Halifax to which they invited all the local belles, but were forced to cut short their dancing and go aboard the transports in silk stockings and shoes when a favourable wind suddenly came up. For the next five months the Fusiliers were stationed at Annapolis Royal, the village of Digby on the Fundy shore and on the western side of Halifax harbour, where the officers spent their time reading, fishing, hunting (shooting) and acquiring pets – Captain Jack Hill proudly informed his parents that the regiment had a fox but their bear ran away while he was the master of "a pony, 4 cats, 2 ducks but not yet a dog."[6] Life was actually rather boring, Hill recorded, with only "an hour and a half of drill before 8 every morning." Fortunately, the custom was to regularly rotate units between the port and the outposts, and the 23rd was back in the town by October 1808, well before the onset of winter, which in the country meant temperatures in January averaging -15 degrees Fahrenheit and snow four to six feet deep.

The official record is silent as to Thomas Pearson's whereabouts during his first six months in Nova Scotia, but for a time it would seem that he was at Sackville, west of Halifax, because the following notice appeared in the 23 August 1808 edition of the *Nova Scotia Gazette*:

Deserted

From a detachment of the 1st battalion 23rd regiment of foot, or Royal Welsh Fusiliers, at Sackville on the 15th August, 1808.

John Griffin, aged 27 years; 5 feet 6 inches high; swarthy complexion; brown hair; round visage; hazel eyes; stout made.

Richard Walsh, aged 24 years; 5 feet 8 inches high; fresh complexion; brown hair; round visage; grey eyes; slender made; both natives of Ireland.

For the apprehension of the above Deserters, so that they may be lodged in any place of safe confinement, or any party bringing the above men to Halifax, shall receive the following reward; three guineas, by regulation; three pounds, ten shillings, currency, from the Treasury of the Province; and two guineas and a half for each man, to be given by the regiment on their arrival in Halifax.

T. Pearson, Major

The substantial reward offered for the return of these two men is an indication of how serious a problem desertion was for the British army and navy in North America. The continent was an attractive place for men recruited from the lower strata of society and often forced into the service by economic hardship because it offered employment, a low cost of living and plenty of good and cheap land, while the nearby United States offered both a refuge and a brighter future. The punishments for desertion were extreme, however, and, if they were apprehended, matters would not bode well for Griffin and Walsh because Pearson would do his duty as he saw it and the best they could hope for was the remission of a few hundred lashes.

Having had enough of the rustic charms of rural Nova Scotia, the 23rd Foot was glad to be back in Halifax. It was a good station, everyone was agreed on that, but since the tension with the United States had subsided, the regiment was getting restless, particularly as it followed the news from Europe, where in early 1808 Napoleon had deposed the king of Spain and replaced him with his

brother Joseph, which led to a massive uprising of the Spanish people. The following summer, Lieutenant-General Sir Arthur Wellesley was sent to Portugal
to assist both that nation and Spain. Wellesley had won two notable victories
at Rolica and Vimiero and cleared Portugal of the French. For professional
soldiers, it looked like the place to be was the Iberian Peninsula and the Fusiliers fretted as they knew it was usual to keep regiments in North America for
a considerable length of time and there was great concern that the 23rd Foot
would be forgotten in a colonial backwater.

In the autumn of 1808, however, rumours began to go around about an expedition to the West Indies, but, as Lieutenant Thomas Browne recalled, they
were "repeated and contradicted so often, that we began to pay little attention
to them, and perhaps the less, as there was no particular disposition in the
Regiment for West-Indian service," which was not surprising considering the
Welch Fusiliers' experience there in the 1790s.[7]

On 27 November 1808, eight months after it had arrived in Halifax, the 23rd
Foot mustered on the grand parade in the town, 884 rank and file strong, and
marched down to the harbour to embark, along with the 7th and 8th Foot, on
waiting transports. There being no definite information as to their destination, the rumour mill was active, with the favourite bets being the West Indies
or Portugal. The shrewd Pakenham of the 7th Foot, noting that each regiment
was ordered to leave a company behind in Halifax, thought that this indicated
that the three battalions would eventually return to that place. He favoured a
North American destination and, in fact, the troops were bound for the West
Indies.

B y this time Britain had conquered most of the major French possessions in
the West Indies with the exception of Guadaloupe and Martinique, which
they kept under blockade. In 1808 a dispatch from the governor of Martinique
describing the weak state of the island's defences was intercepted and Rear-Admiral Alexander Cochrane, the senior naval officer on station, suggested to his
army counterpart, Lieutenant-General Sir George Beckwith, that an amphibious expedition be launched against that island. Beckwith was less keen to undertake this operation because his limited forces were stretched thin to garrison
various British possessions in an area that covered a thousand miles from the
Leeward Islands to Surinam on the northeast coast of South America. He was
somewhat mollified when he learned that he was going to get reinforcements
from Nova Scotia and therefore agreed to plan an assault on Martinique.

"Fair complexions lit up by soft blue eyes."

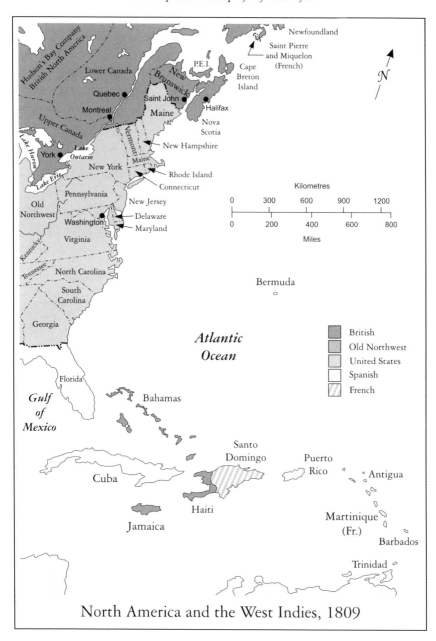

North America and the West Indies, 1809

It was not until 6 December that the Welch Fusiliers' convoy weighed anchor and sailed for the south under naval escort. It took just over three weeks to reach Barbados, the assembly point for the expedition, and it was not an unpleasant voyage, despite some winter gales that briefly scattered the ships and a lightning strike on one transport that killed one man and injured several others.

Lieutenant-General Sir Edward Pakenham (1778-1815)
The brother-in-law of the Duke of Wellington, Pakenham commanded the 1/7th Foot or Royal Fusiliers in Halifax and fought alongside Pearson and the Welch Fusiliers in Martinique in 1809. Promoted colonel in 1810 he joined Wellington's staff and was instrumental in getting the 1/7th and 1/23rd Foot transferred to the Peninsula. He commanded the Fusilier Brigade in 1811 and ended up as a divisional commander. Reluctantly, he took over command of the army besieging New Orleans in 1814 and was killed during the ill-fated attack on that city in January 1815. (Author's collection)

By Christmas Day, the convoy was near Bermuda and the temperature became so warm that everyone slept without blankets. On Lieutenant Browne's ship, the officers celebrated the day by playing their flutes for the married soldiers "and such few of their wives as were on board" who "danced and sang songs until late at night."[8] A few days later, one of the accompanying warships hailed two merchantmen, which passed over recent newspapers containing the interesting information that a second British army had landed in Spain under the command of Lieutenant-General Sir John Moore, the Welch Fusiliers' brigade commander in Egypt. Late in the evening of 29 December 1808, the fleet anchored in Carlisle Bay off Bridgetown, the capital of Barbados, and the ships were immediately surrounded by bum boats selling fruit, spruce beer and milk.

The 23rd Foot remained at Bridgetown for a month while the final preparations were completed for the attack on Martinique. The great fear among senior officers and medical staff was that the troops would be decimated by disease, as memories of the disastrous campaigns of the 1790s were fresh in memory. The surgeons put into effect regulations requiring the enlisted men to bathe daily and to avoid any exertion during the hottest part of the day and in the damp of the evenings. These precautions were ignored, however, by most of the young officers of the 23rd, who went ashore to explore the fleshpots of Bridgetown. Lieutenant Browne was somewhat taken aback when a native woman, seeing his pale visage in the marketplace, gave him some sobering advice: "Ah Massa Johnny Newcome go back to Shippy, too hot for him here, kill him."[9]

Nor was Browne consoled the first time he and his comrades entered Nancy Clarke's notorious hotel-tavern in Bridgetown when the proprietress, identify-ing his unit from his buttons, exclaimed, "Twenty-third twenty third! Ah me shew you plenty of twenty-third in Church-yard dere."[10] The young gentlemen gamely shrugged off such grim portents and enjoyed life ashore to its fullest at the establishments of Nancy and her competitor, Susan Austin, who offered such good food, fine drink (and certain other attractions) that they were the subject of song:

> If you go to Nancy Clark,
> She will take you in the dark;
> When she get you in the dark,
> She will give you aquafortis.
>
> If you go to Susy Austin
> She will take you in the parlour;
> When she take you in the parlour,
> She will give you wine and water.[11]

All good things must end, however, and a week later a lieutenant in the light company of the 23rd, taken ill with yellow fever in the morning, was dead by nightfall. He was followed by others and thereafter, as Browne commented, the subalterns "behaved remarkably well during the remainder of our stay in Bridgetown."[12]

In the first weeks of 1809 there was considerable discussion and argument by the senior commanders, and for a time it looked as though the operation against Martinique might be cancelled. Browne and his comrades, unable to bear the thought of returning to the admiring belles of Halifax after such an embarrassment, promptly went out and drowned their sorrows in a splendid dinner at Nancy Clarke's place. On 28 January 1809, however, the expedition sailed for Martinique under Beckwith's command. He had 12,400 troops and 36 pieces of artillery organized in two divisions, the larger being commanded by Prevost, and the smaller by Major-General Thomas Maitland. The 7th and 23rd Foot were in Prevost's division, being brigaded with the 1st West India Regiment, all under the command of Major-General Daniel Hoghton. At this time, the French garrison of Martinique consisted of 6,250 regular troops, sailors and *Garde Nationale* or militia. The island was well fortified, including the very strong Fort Desaix, mounting more than a hundred artillery pieces, which was sited in rugged hills that overlooked Fort Royal, Martinique's capital.

The fleet arrived off the island on 30 January 1809. Beckwith's plan of attack was simple. Maitland's division would seize the outlying forts that protected Fort Royal to permit Cochrane's transports to enter Fort Royal Bay and unload the thousands of tons of stores necessary to undertake a siege of Fort Desaix. Prevost, in the meantime, would come ashore on the opposite coast and make for the French stronghold. Prevost's troops began landing at Bay Robert on the northeast side of the island late in the afternoon of 30 January and his first task was to capture Morne Bruneau, a pass through the mountainous country that formed the spine of Martinique. He wasted no time. Under a downpour of rain, his advance guard, consisting of Pakenham's 7th Foot, the grenadier company of the 23rd and a light infantry battalion formed from the light companies of all the units in Prevost's division, pushed forward through massive sugar cane plantations. It was found that the horses for the divisional artillery were not fit after being cooped up on the transports for so long, and teams of soldiers dragged two 6-pdr. field guns the five miles to Morne Bruneau.

By dawn on 1 February 1809 Hoghton's entire brigade was up to support Pakenham. As expected, Morne Bruneau was defended and, on Prevost's orders, Hoghton immediately sent Pakenham to take this position with the 7th Foot, supported by the grenadier company of the 23rd Foot. The enemy, who turned out to be *Garde Nationale*, were pushed aside, and Pakenham's troops advanced but were counterattacked by a strong force of French regulars, who were repulsed, but returned to the attack, "with drums beating" before finally being rebuffed.[13] The grenadier company of the 23rd Foot lost 26 killed and wounded in this seven-hour action, which terminated when the remainder of the regiment came up to assist the 7th Foot and the light infantry battalion drive the enemy back toward Fort Desaix. During the latter part of the action, Pearson commanded the left wing of the 23rd. When the fighting had ended, Prevost held Morne Bruneau and the high ground overlooking his objective. In his report on this engagement, Prevost wrote that he had

innumerable proofs of the valour and judgement of the Honourable Lieu-tenant-Colonel Pakenham, of the excellence of the Fusilier Brigade, and of the spirited and judicious exertions of Lieutenant-Colonel Ellis and Majors Pearson and Offley of the 23rd Foot … also of the bravery of Major Camp-bell and the light infantry battalion all of which have enabled me to retain this valuable position without artillery, within three hundred yards of the enemy's entrenched camp covered with guns.[14]

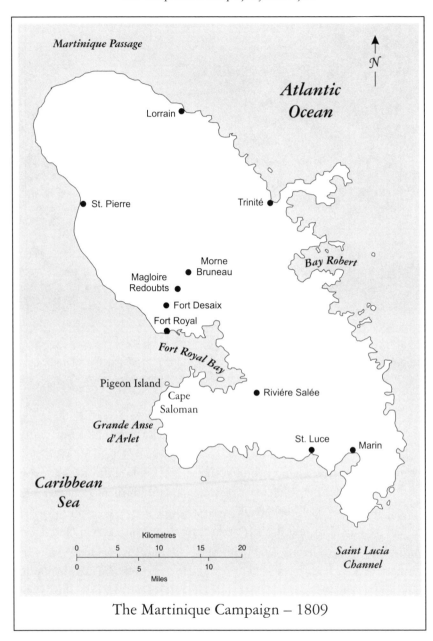

The Martinique Campaign – 1809

The next morning Prevost consolidated his position and began to plan an attack on two outlying redoubts of Fort Desaix at Magloire, north of the fort. Each of these positions was defended by 150 regular French troops and three 12-pdr. guns, and protected by an abattis of fallen trees. Strong detachments from the two Fusilier regiments attacked each of the redoubts but were repulsed after

Martinique, 1809
Troops from Prevost's division attack and capture a bridge on the approaches to Fort Desaix.
Prevost's division, which landed on the opposite side of the island from the main force,
undertook the heaviest fighting in this campaign and suffered the worst casualties. Both
Pakenham and Pearson were wounded. (Author's collection)

heavy fighting and heavy losses, including Pakenham who took a musket ball
in the neck. As the Royal Fusiliers and Welch Fusiliers reformed for another assault, Beckwith arrived and, encountering the 23rd Foot waiting to go forward,
asked Lieutenant-Colonel Henry Ellis if he thought his men could take such
difficult objectives. "Sir," replied Ellis, who was mildly insulted by the question,
"I shall take the flints out of their firelocks and they shall take them," meaning that he was prepared to send in his men with only the bayonet.[15] Beckwith,
however, decided not to renew the attack and that night the French abandoned
the redoubts and drew back into Fort Desaix proper. Prevost published a general order praising the two Fusilier regiments and promising that he would
"not fail to lay their meritorious exertions before the King," but cautioning that
"their spirit and determination," if "tempered by less impetuosity, will lead to
the happiest results."[16]

There was now a lull of more than two weeks while the artillery and engineers constructed siege batteries around Fort Desaix. Sailors dragged the
heavy guns, their ammunition and equipment, along wretched and muddy

tracks over steep and rugged hills to the fort under a steady downpour of rain. There was much squabbling between British and French patrols who tried to surprise their opponents' outposts. Pearson was prominently involved in this skirmishing as he had assumed command of the Light Battalion, which consisted of between seven and nine companies with a total strength of 550 all ranks, after its former commander had been wounded. This was Pearson's first real independent command and he seems to have performed well – a report he submitted to Prevost after one of the outpost actions gives some idea of the fighting involved:

> In obedience to your orders of yesterday, I proceeded with the two flank companies of the 25th Regiment, in order, if possible, to surprize the advanced picquet of the enemy, which, I am happy to say, was effected after a very intricate and difficult march of two hours. The enemy left 5 or 6 killed on the ground, and the rest made a most precipitate retreat to their fort.[17]

Attacking a redoubt, Martinique, 1809
The mountainous approaches to Fort Desaix were defended by outlying redoubts such as those shown here, surrounded by abbatis. They were difficult objectives to take and casualties were heavy. (Author's collection)

For his efforts in this action, Pearson was officially thanked by Prevost in the orders of the day but unfortunately, during one of these encounters, on 21 February 1809, he came too close to Fort Desaix and received his second wound in combat, a canister bullet in the leg. It was not serious but it placed him *hors de combat* for the remainder of the campaign.

On the morning of 19 February 1809 the Royal Artillery opened fire on Fort Desaix with 46 pieces of ordnance ranging from 24-pdr. guns down to 5.5-inch howitzers and, once started, the bombardment continued day and night. At noon on 23 February, a flag of truce came out of the fort with an offer to capitulate, but the terms suggested by the French were not acceptable to Beckwith and the bombardment resumed. On the morning of 24 February, after 4,000 round-shot and 10,000 shells had been fired, two field magazines in the fort exploded and the French commandant capitulated on British terms. The defenders, some 2,200 officers and men, had fought bravely and were accorded the full honours of war, Lieutenant Browne of the 23rd recorded, and marched out of the fort "with drums beating, colours flying and matches lighted, having at their front four field pieces with their artillerymen."[18] The 7th and 23rd Foot replaced them in Fort Desaix, which was "a shocking spectacle of ruins, and blood, and half buried bodies," and the King's Colour of the Welch Fusiliers was soon flying over one of its bastions in place of the tricolour of imperial France.

The capitulation stated that the senior French officers would be sent directly to France, while the remainder of the regular troops would be exchanged, rank for rank, for British prisoners in French hands. Naturally, the French were extremely happy about this arrangement and Browne of the 23rd Foot, who saw them on board British ships at Fort Royal, remembered that the prisoners were

> laughing and singing & dancing on the decks, just as they would have done in any little Cabaret near Paris, and in observing this, we could hardly refrain from envying their happy frivolity. ...... The chattering of the fellows is really quite impossible to describe, and the whole scene presented much more the spectacle of elated & victorious Troops, than of men going to England as prisoners of war. They sailed next morning, making all sorts of grimaces and bows to us. I never saw so merry a set of fellows.[19]

The smiles left the faces of this "merry set of fellows" when their emperor refused to honour the agreement to exchange them, and they were thus condemned to five years on the prisoner of war hulks in Britain.

Lieutenant-General Sir George Beckwith was proud of the efforts of his men and stated in his official dispatch that the "honour of commanding such an army will constitute the pride of my future life."[20] His total losses were 550 killed, wounded and missing, of which no fewer than 529 were suffered by the 1/7th Foot, 1/23rd Foot and the Light Infantry Battalion of Prevost's division, an indication of how heavily these units had been engaged. The regular units who served in the third British attack on Martinique in half a century were granted a Battle Honour, "MARTINIQUE 1809," and the Patriotic Fund of Lloyds of London voted £850 for the benefit of the wounded, of which £250 came to the grenadier company of the 23rd Foot, who used part of the proceeds to erect a plaque in a church in Halifax to honour their fallen comrades. There was excitement over the fact that the regular units in the French garrison, the 28th and 82nd *Régiments de Ligne*, surrendered their Eagles, the first such trophies to be taken by the British army during the war. There was great interest in these objects which Browne described as being "about the size of a Pigeon with its wings displayed" and "screwed upon the pole which bore them, so that in case of reverse, nothing was easier than to unscrew the Bird, pocket it and save the disgrace which its capture might bring it."[21] The Eagles were eventually sent to Britain with Beckwith's dispatch about his victory and when they arrived, the King "was pleased to command that they should be escorted in state by the regiments of the Household Brigade to St. Paul's Cathedral where they were received with due solemnity."[22]*

Prevost's force remained in Martinique until 15 March 1809 when it sailed for Halifax. The convoy made good time but the Welch Fusiliers were sad to learn from a passing ship that Sir John Moore, a man many in the regiment still fondly remembered, had been forced out of Spain by superior numbers and killed while fighting a successful battle at Corunna to permit the embarkation of his troops. As the convoy moved north, the weather grew colder and

---

* The Eagles ultimately ended up in the Royal Hospital at Chelsea where they remained until 1947 when one Eagle of the 82e *Ligne* was presented to the Royal Fusiliers (late the 7th Foot). Although it was intended that a second Eagle from this same French unit be given to the Royal Welch Fusiliers, the exigencies of service prevented the regiment from receiving it until 17 December 1957, when the governor of Chelsea Hospital presented it to a party from the unit to "serve as a memorial to the gallantry of the past members of the Regiment, and as an incentive and inspiration to their successors, the young soldiers of the future." This proud memorial of the Martinique campaign is currently on display in the regimental museum at Caernarvon Castle in Wales. See *Y Ddraig Goch* (Winter 1957), 38-39.

many of the sick and wounded, unable to stand the abrupt change in temperature, began to die. By 12 April it was off Halifax but was then becalmed for three
days in a cold, thick fog and not until Saturday, 16 April 1809, did it enter the
harbour to an enthusiastic reception:

> Early on Saturday morning the [semaphore] Telegraphs announced the ap-
> proach of a Frigate and a fleet of transports; it was soon ascertained that the
> Frigate was the Penelope, and that his Excellency [Prevost] was on board
> – at nine she passed the wharves, and was successively cheered by crowds of
> Inhabitants – at ten Sir George Prevost quitted the Penelope, when a salute
> of seventeen guns was fired from her … he landed at the King's wharf …
> the Soldiers, on board the Transports, as his Excellency passed in the barge,
> most heartily cheered him.[23]

The weather was cold – in fact the three regiments which had fought in
Martinique had just missed the worst winter in Nova Scotia in living memory
– and Lieutenant Thomas Browne could not get used to seeing comrades who,
a few weeks before, had been sporting straw hats, vests, and shirtsleeves, now
bundled up in fur-lined greatcoats and fox-skin caps. Captain Hill recorded
that there was much illness in the 23rd, with 320 men on the sick list in April
and in his opinion,

> The principal part which have fallen ill … in my opinion have caught it
> by infection, not, as some of the wiseacres say, owning to new rum bought
> in Halifax. My company never were so sober, I do not think, and the Ser-
> geants tell me the same, that not five have been drunk since we landed, and
> that, under the temptation of having it for nothing, as every one tried who
> should give them drink, the people being so glad to see us back again.[24]

Hill was not exaggerating about the Welch Fusiliers' warm reception from
the citizens of Halifax. Sir George and his troops were heroes to the Haligoni-
ans, who had taken them very much to heart, and on 28 April the townsfolk
honoured the victors of Martinique with a ball at the Masonic Hall. It was
opened at 9 P.M. by Sir George and Lady Prevost and the guests found the ball
room "decorated with laurel, and filled with transparencies of Battles fought,
and breaches mounted, and every other description of military honour."[25] The
bands of the 7th and 23rd Foot provided music for the dancing, which con-

Sleighing, Halifax

Winter was the social season in Halifax and sleighing was a popular activity that often led to romances. Contemporaries noted the beauty of Canadian women and many British officers wed local belles, among them Thomas Pearson, who married Ann Coffin from New Brunswick. (Painting by William Eagar, National Library and Archives of Canada, C-013362)

tinued past midnight, and which was followed by toasts that did not end until about 4 A.M. Everyone then sat down to a splendid supper that included "every dainty the season offered also various fruits, wines, etc." with the centre piece on the table being "a correct pastry figure of Ft. Bourbon [Desaix]."[26] As the guests dined, the musicians of the two Fusilier regiments played popular songs. We can gain some idea of the musical repertoire that evening from the programme of a similar function held a few weeks earlier which featured "The Duke of York's March," "Rule Britannia," "Paddy O'Rafferty," "O Lady Fair," "Britons Strike Home," "The British Grenadiers," "The Heaving of the Lead," "Yankee Doodle," "Hearts of Oak," "The Rakes of Mallow," "The Wounded Hussar," "Roast Beef of Old England," "See the Conquering Hero Come" and "Garry Owen."[27] In the opinion of Lieutenant Browne, the victory ball "went off capitally."[28]

Five days later, a wealthy Halifax merchant gave a supper to the NCOs of the units that had fought in Martinique. Sir George's daughter Anne Elinor, who was 14 at the time, remembered that my Father accompanied by his suite and my Mother and myself, went in for a few minutes to look at them [the NCOs]. It was one of the most gratifying sights I ever saw. My Father's entrance was hailed with tumults of applause; he gave [toasted] the King's health, and afterwards "The Soldiers who did their duty." It was echoed round and round the room, every individual repeating the sentence, and many a hearty cheer followed the libation. I remember clinging to [Captain] J[ames]. P.[Prevost]'s arm and scarcely knowing whether to laugh or cry with delight.[29]

On their return from the West Indies, the Welch Fusiliers received the welcome news that they were to be stationed in Halifax, as duty in a town so dependent on the two services, and rather fascinated by them, was certainly better than being in the countryside. To a great extent, one townsperson recalled, Halifax tolerated the excesses of soldiers and sailors because

The army and navy on station were very important. They were the patrons of the place. Great deference was paid to them. Shopkeepers found them their best customers, but the manners and usages of men who had been long in active service were not such as would improve those who companioned with them. Young officers were abroad at night, tearing down and misplacing sign boards, breaking windows and engaging in mischievous pranks. Large gangs of men were on shore on liberty on Sunday from the war vessels, sometimes 200 from one ship, whose crew was 600, who made the town lively with their drunkenness and noise; for man-o'-war's men were not then such as we know to-day, and drunkenness did not offend our citizens as it does now. Jack's frolics and drollery were amusing, though sometimes indelicately exhibited.[30]

There was, however, a darker side to life in wartime Halifax. From time to time, if circumstances demanded it and the town magistrates agreed, a warrant was issued for the press and naval shore parties combed the streets looking for manpower to fill the lower decks of the Royal Navy. There were so many exemptions from the press, including most middle and upper class males, tradesmen, farmers, watermen (ferry boatmen), members of the merchant marine engaged in a voyage, fishermen, naval and military civilian staff, persons engaged in government work and so on, that its weight fell most heavily on the unemployed or underemployed. Mistakes in identification, however, were common and the occasional exempt male was caught up in the net – not that the townspeople cared unless they themselves were ensnared for, as one remarked, the positive result of the press was that "many of the idle and worthless vagabonds of the town were happily secured for His Majesty's service, where they would be brought under wholesome restraint."[31]

The army, recruited from volunteers, had a marginally better reputation but still respectable women did "not venture homeward alone after dark, until after gun-fire [tattoo], when soldiers were not abroad."[32] Nighttime could be dangerous and both life and property "were considered insecure after nightfall, and townsmen were summoned for patrol duty by the magistrates, and went about their rounds with a cudgel, to check rioting, violence and robbery."[33]

There was also the matter of military and naval punishments, which were common and public occurrences. One Haligonian recalled that,

In the army and navy men were sentenced to receive hundreds of lashes for misconduct, and on some occasions I have stood with the boys outside the Barrack Gates while the poor fellows were being flogged within and a wife and children were crying on the street, knowing what was being done. I remember a poor fellow being flogged through the fleet in the harbour. There were seven ships, and he received a portion of his punishment in each ship. I stood on a wharf and saw the hammock in which he lay hoisted and lowered at each ship, and my heart sickened at the thought of his sufferings. Three days after he died in the hospital, but whether from the flogging or other cause I did not learn.[34]

Officers, however, were very welcome in polite society. In fact, so much so that one recalled that the average young gentleman posted to Halifax "finds himself at once raised to a level above that accorded to the scarlet cloth at home [in Britain]" with "his society generally sought, frequently courted, and himself esteemed as a personage whose opinions are regarded with no little degree of attention."[35] Army and navy officers were regarded as prize catches by Canadian mothers with marriageable daughters, and the custom was for young ladies from remote areas to spend a winter or two with friends or relatives in Halifax to see if they could get their hooks into suitable prey. Apparently it wasn't difficult because, as one officer wistfully recalled, young Canadian ladies possessed "fair complexions lit up by soft blue eyes" and were "endowed with great natural abilities and lively dispositions."[36] Winter was the prime social and matchmaking season and there was just something about those two-person sleighs "filled with *élégantes* and driven by monstrous-looking exquisites, muffled up to the eyes," which dashed over the snow "at a wonderful pace," bells tinkling to warn pedestrians.[37] Of this pastime, the same officer bemused by "soft blue eyes" commented that "though a nose may be frost-bitten – there are no cold hearts" on such winter rides and the result was that it was not uncommon for sleigh bells to be replaced by wedding bells.[38]

One of the young ladies at Halifax during the winter season of 1808-1809 was 20-year-old Ann Eliza Coffin, the second daughter of General John Coffin. A native Bostonian, John Coffin had served in a Loyalist regiment during the American Revolution and reached the rank of brevet lieutenant-colonel by 1783 when his active military career ended. This rank, however, enabled Coffin to obtain steady promotion by seniority and when he died in 1838, he was one of the most senior generals in the British army – although he had not heard a shot fired in anger for more than five decades. For his services to the Crown, Coffin received a large grant of land near Fredericton, the capital of New Brunswick, and, by hard work, had turned it into a respectable estate which he named Alwington Manor. A longtime member of the Legislative Assembly of the province, by 1809 Coffin had become one of the wealthiest and most powerful men in New Brunswick. Eight of his children survived to adulthood: his three sons entered the Royal Artillery, with one dying as a general, while the five daughters married either British or Canadian army officers. Two of the husbands reached the rank of general; the other three sisters had to be content with mere colonels.

Ann, commonly called "Anna," was Coffin's second daughter and, by all accounts a raving beauty who was one of the belles of the Halifax season of 1808-1809. As the brother of some of her lady friends in New Brunswick informed his sisters:

> You all conclude your letters with a quiz about Anna Coffin. That good girl seems to have had a multiplicity of admirers. I am told Wallop renewed his attack after I came away, and a friend of mine wrote me that two more red coats (a Capt. and a Sub.) had put in their claims and laid a regular siege. However it appears these sons of Mars were all retired in their turn and I understand that the Forum has produced a champion who will probably bear off the Prize.[39]

That champion was Thomas Pearson.

Government House, Halifax
The residence of Major-General Sir George and Lady Prevost at Halifax. Both Major Thomas Pearson and Ann Coffin would have been frequent visitors here and perhaps this is where they met. (Painting by John Woolford, National Library and Archives of Canada, C-003558)

Pearson may have met Ann Coffin at a function at Government House as both would have been on the Prevosts' invitation list, or they may have met at the Martinique victory ball as Ann Coffin would certainly have been at such a prominent event. Perhaps the two danced together in a room decorated with laurel and transparencies of "Battles fought, and breaches mounted" or their eyes met across the "correct pastry figure" of Fort Desaix while the band played "O Lady Fair" or "See the Conquering Hero Come." Whatever the circumstances or wherever the place, Ann Coffin and Thomas Pearson fell in love.

Unfortunately, little is known about Ann.[40] Apart from her beauty, she was doubtless intelligent and strong-willed, necessary qualities to attract and hold a man like Thomas Pearson. The Coffin girls seem to have been a determined lot and Ann may well have resembled her younger sister Sophia, or Sophy, admired for her courage by one officer who thought her "a splendid girl."[41] This quality was certainly evident the day Sophy and her father were crossing the St. John River near their home in a boat

when a great Bear attacked them, and would have swamped the boat if Sophy had not stood by the General with discretion and courage. For while the General was battering Bruin with the Butt end of an oar, Sophy pushed the point of the boat hook into his Eye which made Bruin scratch it and retreat. If I had been a rich Captain I should certainly have tried to captivate, if not capture, such a brave girl.[42]

On the other hand, as the officer so bemused with soft blue eyes had noted, these Canadian girls did tend to possess lively dispositions.

Although the winter season was over when Tom and Ann got together, society was still active in the spring and summer; in fact society in Halifax during the war with France was fairly active year round. There were picnics in the countryside at Myrtle's Farmhouse and delightful dinners at the Rockingham Club, on the waterfront some miles south of the town. There were assemblies – or dinner, dance and card evenings – supervised by Mr. Charles Powell, who, along with his wife and daughters, also taught dancing to the children of the upper strata of Haligonian society. Mr. Powell, it seems, was an eminently useful man as he also managed the Theatre Royal, where plays were often performed by the officers of the garrison or the fleet. This was an activity that Sir George Prevost encouraged as he believed that "Theatrical amusements … broke up long sittings in the Mess Rooms, and gave the young officers an employment for their leisure hours far better than many others to which they might have recourse."[43] In May 1809, the Theatre Royal presented the officers of the garrison performing in "John Bull, or, An Englishman's Fire-Side" and "Love Laughs at Locksmiths," the proceeds of which went "for the relief of the Widows and Children of the Soldiers who fell at Martinique."[44] Later in the year came "Barbarossa, Emperor of the Turks … performed by Gentlemen belonging to HM Ship Pompee [*Pompée*]."[45] When he ran out of unpaid actors, Mr. Powell sometimes took the stage himself to give "readings and recitations." On 5 September 1809 for example, he presented Gray's "Elegy" and Shakespeare's "Hamlet" followed by the not-to-be-missed "Darby Logan's Passage from Ireland to England."[46]

Besides the theatre, Halifax had other attractions. There was the Museum of Wax Works featuring figures "as large as life, among which is 'Lord Nelson in the last moments of his life attended by his officers.'"[47] Also popular was a visit to the naval prison on Melville Island, south of the town, which housed hundreds of French sailors taken on enemy warships and merchantmen. A stroll or carriage ride out to Melville Island was interesting because the prison was basically a craft bazaar that sold the work of the industrious prisoners, who, as one inmate recalled, were always busy:

Some were knitting stockings, mitts, gloves or purses, and some were spinning. Some were making model battleships rigged with silk and armed with cannons made with pennies. It took almost six months to make some of these models, and they sold for as much as twenty dollars.

Other Frenchmen made hats from birchbark, all kinds of crafts from bones, such as snuff boxes, knives, forks, dice, dominoes, and even ships. ......[48]

If the articles on display did not take one's fancy, you could always commission special items such as handmade gloves, shoes, boots, umbrellas, fans or a model of a certain ship.

For Ann and Thomas most of their social activities would have revolved around the life of the garrison. Every afternoon at 3 P.M., one of the regiments in the town would be under arms for review on the grand parade and this was a popular event usually attended by officers and their ladies as well as officers with not-quite-ladies, as the gaily-attired women of the "demi-monde" were often there "and could be seen abroad on other days, shopping and accompanied by gentlemen."[49] There were special occasions like the celebration of the King's Birthday on 6 June 1809, which featured all the regular, militia and volunteer units in the town, who fired a "royal salute and a *feu de joie*" on the Grand Parade, followed by a levée at Government House a few short blocks away.[50]

Sir George and Lady Prevost liked to entertain and regularly had the officers of the garrison at their table, and it is clear that Pearson enjoyed good relations with the vice-regal family. Sir George's daughter, Anne Elinor, noted in her diary that he "found a steed for me," meaning that he chose the pony she desired.[51] Four of Prevost's American-born nephews were serving in the British army and two of them, 25-year-old Captain James Prevost of the 60th Foot and 21-year-old Lieutenant Henry Prevost of the 7th Foot, were in Halifax in 1809. It appears that James came perilously close to being bewitched by the owner of a pair of those soft blue eyes. As his cousin Anne Elinor remembered, "he was giving symptoms of being seriously in love with a Halifax Belle, and as he was young and extravagant, and had nothing in the world but his pay, my Father thought the kindest thing he could do for him would be to send him to his Regiment" in Spain.[52] With Prevost's permission, Pearson went on leave in June 1809 and it is possible that he paid his first visit to New Brunswick as Ann Coffin returned to her parents' home at about this time.

Major Thomas Pearson would never have let the fact that he was in love interfere with his duties – although his new and blissful state might have led to the self-satisfied expression visible in a portrait painted during his service in Halifax – and there were always duties to be performed. On their return from Martinique in April, the 23rd was retained at Halifax with about one half the regiment stationed in the town while the remainder were scattered about the nearby fortifications and defence works: Fort Clarence, at Melville Island to guard the prisoners, York Redoubt, Sackville Fort, and George's Island, with a regular rotation between posts. Garrison routine prevailed and life was actually quite enjoyable, if rather quiet. On 14 June 1809 Sir George Prevost carried out the half-yearly inspection of the regiment and found everything satisfactory – in fact he was full of praise:

> This battalion was commanded by Lt Colonel Ellis, an intelligent, active and zealous officer. ......
>
> The subordinate officers whom I called upon to take charge of the Battalion in the field executed and combined such movement as were required of them, in conformity with the Rules and Regulations, established for His Majesty's Forces and evinced an acquaintance of the principles which constitute them.
>
> I find the Commissioned Officers intelligent and carefully instructed. On the following day I inspected the clothing for the present year which, in consequence of the Battalion having been upon service [in Martinique], was not completely fitted to the Men. I found it to confirm with the sealed patterns produced. The Arms with the exception of those specified in the enclosed Return, are serviceable and those lost upon service, as well as the number requisite to complete the Battalion to its establishment, can be supplied from the Ordnance stores of this place.
>
> The accoutrements are in good condition.
>
> The Officers, Non-commissioned Officers and private soldiers are orderly and regular in quarters.[53]

Prevost found 17 muskets, 16 bayonets, 8 rifles and 5 swords unfit for service, the presence of the rifles being an indication that the 1st Battalion still possessed its rifle detachment. Unfortunately, the methods of punishment in the British army at this time are sadly evident from Prevost's statement that, between 26 October 1808 and 31 May 1809, there had been 32 courts martial in

"Fair complexions lit up by soft blue eyes."

Lieutenant-Colonel Henry Walton Ellis (1783-1815)
The son of the commanding officer of the 23rd Foot, Henry Ellis, through the vagaries of the purchase system, was a captain at the age of 11 although he did not serve. In 1795 he joined the 23rd Foot at the age of 14 and stayed with them for 20 years, assuming command of the 1st Battalion in 1807. Henry Ellis saw action in the Netherlands, Egypt, Denmark, the West Indies and the Peninsula, being wounded no less than eight times. Tragically, he was mortally wounded at Waterloo, the last major battle of the war with France and died two days later. (Courtesy, Royal Welch Fusiliers Museum)

the 1/23rd Foot "by which 101 men have been tried, 5 Sergeants and 3 Corporals reduced, 36,550 lashes sentenced and 5,950 inflicted."[54] The best thing that can be said about this is that Lieutenant-Colonel Ellis was remitting five of every six lashes he handed out, an indication of his humanity – other battalion commanders were far worse.

It was around this time, while the regiment was at Halifax in the spring or summer of 1809, that an incident occurred that created one of the Welch Fusiliers's most famous distinctions – indeed, their badge of honour. On 20 July 1808 the Horse Guards had issued an order abolishing the wearing of queues in the army. A queue was a pigtail which, by regulation, could be no longer than seven inches, and it had been worn by officers and soldiers alike for more than a century. The practice of powdering the hair and queue had ceased in the 1790s but the queue was still pulled out and combed daily before being set with candle tallow or pig's grease, depending on availability. The wives of married soldiers dressed their husband's hair each morning and there was keen competition among the women to turn out the best queue in their husband's company. Bachelors, poor fellows, had to do each other's hair and no one questioned the fact that the use of candle or pig's grease was hardly sanitary; it was matter of ingrained daily routine. Although the order abolishing queues was issued in July 1808, the 23rd Foot had been on outpost duty for much of the remainder of that year and had then gone to Martinique, and it seems not to have caught up with them until the spring of 1809. Perhaps Lieutenant-Colonel Henry Ellis, who himself favoured the queue, tried to stave it off as long as he possibly could but was finally forced to bow to higher authority.

According to Lieutenant Thomas Browne, Ellis broke the sad news to the officers in the mess one evening after dinner. As the assembled company had "perhaps taken an extra glass by way of softening our vexation, one of the officers proposed that we should, then and there, cut off each other's plaits with a carving knife and should make a grand friz of them in the fire."[55] It was immediately done. The problem came the next morning when the order was read out to the enlisted men as "the row which this order produced in the barrack yard amounted to very little short of mutiny" because their wives "swore by every oath that a soldier's wife has no difficulty in uttering that the order should not be carried into execution, and that they would murder the first operator who should dare touch a hair of their husband's head."[56] When the adjutant communicated this to Ellis, he immediately assembled one company, commanded them to sit down on benches that were brought from the barracks, and had their queues cut *en masse* by the company barbers. The wives "cursed and muttered" but were silenced by a single stony stare from Ellis, who had the power to expel them from the regiment. The process was repeated on each company in turn until the enlisted men of the 23rd Foot were as shorn as their officers.

However, this did not end the matter. As a mark of protest, perhaps, the officers took the ribbons with which they had tied their queues and fashioned them into a "flash" or badge which they wore on the backs of their uniforms in the same place where a small patch had formerly been worn to protect the cloth from the grease and oil of the queue. This quickly became an established Welch Fusilier tradition and we shall hear more of it.

The 23rd Foot continued to serve at Halifax until mid-October 1809 when their turn again came for outpost duty. Pearson, however, was sent even farther abroad – he was ordered to take three companies to Saint John, New Brunswick, to provide a garrison at that place. Since Ann was with her family at Alwington Manor just under a hundred miles away, it might be thought that Pearson managed to persuade Lieutenant-Colonel Ellis to give him the duty at New Brunswick because of her, but more likely it came his way since he was the senior major in the battalion and therefore the first to be considered for an independent command. His detachment, consisting of 8 officers and 227 enlisted men, boarded the military schooner *Lady De Laval* on 13 October and made a rather rough passage around the southern tip of Nova Scotia and across the Bay of Fundy to Saint John, where they arrived ten days later almost out of food. Lieutenant Thomas Browne, who sailed with Pearson, was not impressed with the first view of his new station and thought the town "rather a miserable looking place" with only three or four streets lined with wooden houses.[57]

It quickly became clear that Saint John offered few off-duty attractions. For one thing, the theatre closed down on almost the same day that Pearson's command arrived and, for another, the monthly assembly evenings were cancelled for a lack of subscribers. Not only that, but winter was coming on and although winters there were moderately better than in Nova Scotia, they were still very cold. Fortunately, the British army in North America provided its officers with a generous allowance of wood and if they chose not to use all of it, the Commissary would pay for any left in his store as it saved him having to procure more. Pearson adopted this system for his enlisted men and used the money received to buy each soldier a new flannel shirt or a new pair of shoes, a wise measure that "did not in the least diminish the abundant warmth" in the barrack rooms.[58]

After a few weeks, Pearson's eight officers began to think

Saint John, New Brunswick

In 1809-1810 Pearson commanded the garrison in New Brunswick from headquarters in this town. It was not as large as shown in this view done in the 1830s and one his officers recorded that it was rather a dreary place, but that would not have bothered Pearson as his fiancée, Ann Coffin, was only a hundred miles up the St. John River at her father's manor near Fredericton. The couple were married in June 1810, less than four months before Pearson sailed for the Peninsula. (Painting by Mary G. Hall, courtesy National Library and Archives of Canada, C-030959) our residence at St. John's rather dull, and therefore determined to give the natives a dance, & with our usual activity, decorated our Messroom with spruce fir, almost the only evergreen of the country. It was a cold snowy night & we almost began to fear that our Company could not reach us, but about eight o'clock, the gingling [sic] of the bells of their sledges [sleighs], put an end to our apprehensions, & we had a right merry dance, which did not finish before early the next morning. This set the society of the place in motion, & dinners & parties were given by the respectable families, to those Officers who had danced with their daughters or kins-folk, and it ended by the inhabitants clubbing together to give us a handsome ball & supper, which they did & a whole round of gaieties & amusements succeeded.[59]

As Saint John was a Loyalist settlement, the experience of Pearson's officers during the winter of 1809-1810 would have been akin to that of another British officer who wintered in a similar community in Canada. He and his comrades

found ourselves in very agreeable society, composed principally of old officers of the revolutionary war, who had obtained grants of land in this neighbourhood, and had settled down, as we say in this part of the country and its neighbourhood, with their families. An affectation of style, and set entertainments that follow so rapidly the footsteps of wealth, were then and there unknown, and we immediately become on the best possible terms with the highest circles (for these exist in all societies, and the smaller the society, the more distinctly is the circle defined). ...... The old gentlemen when in town came to Our Mess, and when they had imbibed a sufficient quantity of port, they regaled us with toughish yarns of their military doings during the revolutionary war. And when a tea-drinking party called a sufficient number of the aristocracy together, an extemporaneous dance was got up, a muffled form of drum and fife furnishing the orchestra.[60]

As they always did when a new regiment arrived in the province, the local belles had great hopes because, as one remarked, the coming of the 23rd meant "a great supply of hearts" to be broken.[61] It appears, however, that the most afflicted military heart in the Saint John garrison was that of its commanding officer. Browne, acting both as Pearson's adjutant and the town major, was puzzled one day that winter when an invitation came from Major-General Sir

Martin Hunter, the lieutenant-governor of New Brunswick, to a ball he was holding at Fredericton, the provincial capital. "None of the Officers," Browne recalled, thought "it worthwhile to go a hundred miles to a ball except the commanding officer who thought he could not well decline the governor's invitation."⁶² The fact that Alwington Manor was close to Fredericton and that the most interesting member of the Coffin family would surely be at the ball did not enter into consideration or, if it did, Pearson certainly didn't tell the mystified Browne, who loyally volunteered to accompany him on the journey. As the St. John River

was completely frozen over, & the only conveyance we could use was a sledge [sleigh]. It was lined with bear skin, and fastened on all sides so closely, that the snow could not get in. There was no head to it, but we were muffled up almost to the eyes in fur cloaks, on the collars of which, during the journey, our very breath shewed itself in Icicles. The Sledge was drawn by a pair of horses, yoked abreast, which trotted at the rate of ten miles an hour. There were post houses, or stations, as they were called, every fourteen or fifteen miles, close at the edge of the river. At these places, we changed our horses. We had left St. Johns' at about nine oclock in the morning & arrived at Frederic Town at seven in the evening.⁶³

Lieutenant-Governor Hunter was exceedingly pleased that Pearson and Browne had come "so far to his entertainment" and, of course, there was another guest who was even more happy. Everyone asked the two officers to stay on for a few days but, as Browne recalled, "some pressing Regimental duty, made it impossible for Major Pearson to remain, and we retraced our steps on the ice immediately after breakfast."⁶⁴ This should come as no surprise as Thomas Pearson tended to view the world through the prism of his military responsibilities and they had precedence above all else – even the lovely Ann.

That winter Pearson took the opportunity to reply to a circular sent out by the Horse Guards asking field grade officers to compile a summary statement of their services. Stressing that, in his 13 years and 3 months in the army, he had taken only six months leave during the Peace of Amiens in 1802, Pearson itemized his four campaigns in Holland, Egypt, Denmark and Martinique and noted that he had commanded a "Light Brigade" in the latter operation, which was not quite accurate but, on the other hand, he had commanded a rather large battalion. Pearson only listed one of his wounds, that suffered in Egypt,

but not that received in Martinique, an indication that either it was not serious or that he did not want to detract from the importance of his "brigade"
command. One should not be too critical of Pearson because padding one's
résumé is common practice both in the military and civilian worlds and, in this
respect, probably few of the readers of these words will be without sin – the
author of them certainly is not. Having summed up a professional career with
commendable economy (because lengthy résumés were no more popular in
1809 than they are today), Pearson submitted it with the humble hope that "the
Commander-in-Chief will vouchsafe to take to his gracious consideration my
claims for promotion."[65] As we shall see below, promotion was in the offing for
Pearson but he would earn it the hardest way.

In late March 1810, when the days were getting marginally longer and the
temperature marginally warmer, the intrepid Mr. Powell arrived in Saint John
from Halifax with his wife and daughters to give dancing classes to the young
people of the town. At the end of their instruction in early April he held a
"Dancing School Ball," attended by all proud parents and interested visitors, to
show off the results. He also took the opportunity to present the culturally-de-
prived people of the town with "The Evening Brush for Rubbing off the Rust of
Care" at the Drury Theatre, re-opened for the occasion, which featured "several
appropriate Comic songs" as well as the immortal "Darby Logan's Passage from
Dublin to London," "The Coach Box" and "The Golden Days of good Queen
Bess" to which he added a "Critical Dissertation on Noses … the whole to be
concluded with a SONG giving a whimsical description of the Battle of the
Nile to be Sung in the Character of a French Officer."[66]

Darby Logan and Mr. Powell aside, by the spring of 1810 the 1st Battalion of
the 23rd Foot was getting very restless. The tension between the United States
and Britain which had brought the regiment to North America had lessened,
and they wanted to get back to Europe, where the war had heated up in 1809
after Britain and Austria had formed a Fourth Coalition against France. When
Napoleon invaded Austrian territory, he suffered his first major defeat at the
battle of Aspern-Essling in May but managed to win a very hard-fought and
bloody battle at Wagram in July, forcing Austria again to sue for peace. Britain
tried to assist her ally by launching an invasion of the Scheldt Estuary to take
Antwerp and destroy or capture the warships being built in that great port.
Nearly 40,000 troops, including the 2nd Battalion of the 23rd Foot, landed
in August 1809, but although progress was initially good, the operation was
doomed by the dilatory attitude of its commander, sickness and the strong

fortifications in the area. The army was evacuated a few months later and of the 40,000 men who participated, 106 died from enemy action and 4,066 from sickness, and there were still 11,000 men on the sick list a half year later.

Things went better in the Peninsula, where Wellesley, having expelled the French from Portugal, invaded Spain in the summer of 1809 and won a very close victory at Talavera, which gained him the title of Viscount Wellington, before being forced back to Portugal by superior numbers. In the spring of 1810, however, it looked like the campaigning in the Peninsula during the coming summer would be very active, and what was particularly galling to the officers of the 1st Battalion of the 23rd was that the 2nd Battalion had made a name for itself under Sir John Moore's command. The 2/23rd had been the last unit to embark when the Royal Navy rescued the remnants of Moore's army at Corunna and Captain Thomas Fletcher of the battalion, the last British soldier to leave that city, had brought home the keys to one of its gates to prove it. The reasoning in the 1st Battalion was that, if the junior battalion had done so well, they would almost certainly do better – if given the opportunity. Their restlessness increased after the recently-promoted Colonel Edward Pakenham was appointed to a position on Wellington's staff and left the 1/7th, turning over command to Lieutenant-Colonel Edward Blakeney. Pakenham's sister just happened to be Wellington's wife and, before leaving, he promised the officers of both the 7th and 23rd Foot to "spare no exertion" to induce his brother-in-law "to ask for the two Fusileer Regiments & thus to have them emancipated from the inactive scenes of a garrison life … and permitted to share in the interesting warfare of the Peninsula."[67]

There was great excitement, therefore, in the second week of June when Pearson's detachment in New Brunswick was ordered to rejoin the regiment in Halifax. With regard to this movement, Pearson had many tasks to complete but one was considerably more pleasant than the others and, as the *New Brunswick Gazette* reported on 2 July 1810, it was successfully accomplished: "Married on Thurs. last by the Rev. Mr. Vilts, at Alwington Manor, Thomas Pearson, Major of the Royal Welch Fusiliers, to Ann Eliza, second daughter of Lieut. Gen. Coffin."[68]

When the three New Brunswick companies disembarked in Halifax in mid-July 1810 they found that the 7th Foot had already sailed for Lisbon but that there were no orders concerning the transfer of the 23rd Foot. It was assumed that these orders would come on the next mail packet from Britain, but in the meantime there was nothing to do but wait. As the regiment had been much dispersed for the last year, Prevost took the opportunity of its concentration at Halifax to carry out his half-yearly inspection:

The 23d has been commanded by Lt Colonel Ellis since the beginning of 1808 [sic]. He is an officer of promising talents, uniformly zealous in the discharge of his duty and judicious in the enforcement of military discipline and well versed in manoeuvres which have been prescribed for the use of the Army by His Majesty's command, and in consequence the Battalion has made due progress in its field exercises.

The first [Pearson] and second major having been entrusted with separate commands as well as several of the Captains has afforded me an opportunity of appreciating their merit. Without exception they are active and intelligent. The captains present with the Battalion attend to the interior economy of their companies and appear competent to the command of them in the various situations of service. The subalterns appear to have acquired that degree of information which His Majesty's regulations declare to be indispensably necessary. Unanimity and good understanding [among the officers] prevails in this Corps. ......

The Non-Commissioned Officers are properly instructed and active. They are obedient to their superiors and are instructed to support their authority in a becoming manner. They promote to the very best of their abilities the discipline of the Regiment and perform their duty in the field and quarters with energy and promptitude. ......

The 23rd Regiment is a good serviceable body of men, with a general appearance of health – though many are under the fixed standard [of height]. The numbers in the field correspond with returns. They are well drilled and attentive. Their conduct in quarters is orderly and soldier like and there is no man kept on the strength of the Battalion who is not clothed. ......

The field exercises and movements were performed with precision. The formations were correct although some of them were executed with increased celerity.[69]

A commanding officer could not have asked for a better report.

During his last few months in Nova Scotia, Pearson sat for a second miniature. In a time before photography, this was a quite common measure for military officers about to go on active service, as their loved ones would have a memento in case they did not return. The artist was Robert Field, the leading society painter in Halifax, who also painted a portrait of Sir George Prevost. Pearson's picture shows a slim young man with a prominent nose and a receding hairline wearing a slightly self-satisfied expression – possibly a result of his recent nuptials or, knowing Pearson, possibly the result of Prevost's recent glowing inspection report of the 23rd Foot.

It was early September 1810 before the semaphore telegraph on Citadel Hill announced that the British mail packet was making its way up the Eastern Passage, causing great excitement. An hour after it had anchored, Sir George Prevost sent for Lieutenant-Colonel Ellis and informed him that the 23rd Foot was under orders for Portugal, and that night there was a great celebration in the officers' messroom and "many bottles were drunk," recorded Browne, "to assist getting off a stock which we did not choose to leave behind us."[70]

The happy news was announced to the enlisted men on parade the following morning and they greeted it with three cheers. The Fusiliers still had to wait, however, for the necessary transports to arrive from Britain, and during this time, which lasted more than a month, Pearson made arrangements for Ann to take passage to England, where she would live with either her relations or his parents while he served abroad. There was reason for him to take particular care with these arrangements because by the autumn of 1810 Ann was carrying a child. As the days, and then the weeks, passed with no sign of the transports, some in the regiment were close to despondency but, on 6 October 1810, the disarmed warships, HMS *Regulus* and HMS *Diadem*, arrived at Halifax with orders to transport the 23rd Foot to Lisbon.

There was the usual last-minute activity. Sir George Prevost reviewed the Welch Fusiliers one final time, wished all ranks the best of luck and praised them in a flattering garrison order. Not to be outdone, the merchants and magistrates of Halifax published a "tribute of respect" for a regiment "whose orderly and exemplary conduct and social manners, have endeared them to all ranks of people in this Province, and excited an earnest solicitude for their future welfare and glory."[71] Bills were paid, goodbyes said and then, on 11 October 1810, the 1st Battalion of the Royal Welch Fusiliers "embarked for the Peninsula, nearly a thousand Bayonets, and in the best possible service order."[72]

PRACTISING
THE TRADE,
1810–1811

The destruction of Colborne's brigade at Albuera, 16 May 1811
At Albuera, French cavalry, including Polish lancers, mounted a devastating attack against
a British infantry brigade that was not formed properly to receive cavalry. The result was
the destruction of three battalions and the loss of the Colours and an artillery piece.
(Contemporary lithograph by J. Atkinson)

The 23rd and 6th Regiments of Foot, 1812

This Hamilton Smith plate depicts the Welch Fusiliers as they would have appeared in full dress in 1812. The fur cap was unique to fusilier units among the infantry of the line; the common herd wore the shako. In the field in the Peninsula in 1810-1814 the 23rd Foot, however, wore a stovepipe-style black felt shako that was replaced the following year by the "Belgic" shako seen here worn by a private of the 6th Foot. (From Charles H. Smith, *Costume of the Army of the British Empire,* 1814)

CHAPTER FIVE

"JOHNNY NEWCOMES"

PORTUGAL AND SPAIN,
OCTOBER 1810 – MAY 1811

Come all you valiant soldiers and listen unto me,
Who has an inclination to face your enemy.
Never be faint-hearted but boldly cross the main,
Come and join Lord Wellington who drubbed the French in Spain.

> *With Wellington we'll go, we'll go, with Wellington we'll go*
> *Across the main o'er to Spain and fight our daring foe.*

All you that wish to have a peace, from heavy taxes free,
Pray for success to Wellington and all his grand army.
May he always gain the victory so that the war might cease,
Then trade again in England would flourish and increase.

> *With Wellington we'll go ...*[1]

The Welch Fusiliers' passage to Portugal on HMS *Diadem* was not as pleasant as some of their other sea voyages. *Diadem* was a warship, not a transport, naval discipline prevailed and her captain was extremely strict about the behaviour of the "shifting ballast," as the navy termed troops on passage. The result, as Lieutenant Thomas Browne remembered, was that he and his fellow officers were "perpetually transgressing some little point or other of etiquette, and incurring the Captain's displeasure."[2] Browne elaborated on the finer points of this naval "etiquette":

> Whenever an Officer came on deck from below, it was requisite for him to take off his hat, as a salute to the Pennant flying on the Main-top gallant mast head. It was also enjoined us that we should not on any account lean against the Capstan, or sit on any of the Gun-carriages. Then we were on no account to walk on the wind-ward side of the quarter deck, nor we were we to assemble into groups of more than two on the deck, with various little particularities of the same nature.[3]

Going to lay in stock for the field
One of the essential activities undertaken by officers who had just landed in Lisbon was to prepare for field service by acquiring horses, baggage mules, utensils, food and potables. In this Rowlandson cartoon, a newly arrived officer visits Senhor Cavigole's store in Lisbon, which sold everything needed for the comfort of the inner officer. (From *The Adventures of Johnny Newcome*, 1816)

The Fusilier officers tried hard to follow directions but the capstan, "being a most tempting thing to lean upon, in blowing weather," they often broke this particular rule – until the day they found it covered with thick, soft tar and "sure enough the flies were caught."

Thankfully, the 1/23rd Foot had only to endure about a month of such hospitality. On 11 November 1810, the *Diadem* and *Regulus* raised the mouth of the Tagus and the next day anchored in Lisbon harbour, which was crowded with warships and merchantmen, including many American vessels as the army in Portugal largely depended on American grain for its bread. Captain permitting, the Fusiliers crowded the deck to look at the pilot and fishing boats on the river with their painted awnings. There was also Lisbon with its dazzling white cathedrals, palaces, churches and convents and its suburbs adorned by orange groves. As the *Diadem* dropped anchor, it was surrounded by boats manned by swarthy watermen who offered fruit or other delicacies, or money-changing services at a high rate.

Next day the battalion landed and marched to a camp in the Prince's Park, in the Lisbon suburb of Belem. The Welch Fusiliers' first impressions of Portugal and the Portuguese likely echoed those of other newly-arrived British soldiers who, with their innate sense of Anglo-Saxon superiority (true or not) over all Latin races, were not impressed with the city and its inhabitants. Lisbon was still being rebuilt after a disastrous earthquake in the mid-18th century and magnificent buildings existed side by side with hovels while sanitation, both public and personal, was primitive. The city streets smelt vile because every evening after 9 P.M. chamber pots were emptied into them (and passers-by beware), where the ordure remained until washed away by rain. Lisbon seemed full of beggars, packs of mongrel dogs and members of the many religious orders resident in the city. Particularly offensive to British eyes was the sight of the locals, from all stations in life, picking fleas off each other in public, and there is only slight exaggeration in the doggerel composed by an officer of the 51st Foot:

> It is a fact well known, the Portuguese
> Cherish voluptuously both Lice and Fleas;
> Some Bramin-like, are influenced by Piety,
> But mostly for Amusement and Society;
> For Females oft in parties will arouse
> Scratching each other's Heads, t'entrap a Louse,
> Whilst on their skins, the Fleas will skip, & Scramble,
> And wanton Lice through all their ringlets ramble.[4]

One British officer thought Lisbon the "Sink of Sinks" while a veteran sergeant recommended that its dogs "all be destroyed, the able bodied Priests draughted into the Army, half the remainder should be made to keep the city clean, and the remainder if they did not inculcate the necessity of personal cleanliness should be hanged."[5] A more discerning and charitable witness felt it impossible to draw comparisons between Lisbon and London and stressed that the Portuguese, despite their different social customs and widespread poverty, were unfailingly polite and hospitable to the soldiers of *"O-grande-Lorde"* or Lieutenant-General Viscount Wellington, who had come from far away to "fight for us."[6]

Once ashore, the enlisted men of the 23rd Foot were issued with camp kettles, wooden canteens, well soaked to keep them watertight, blankets and bill hooks and a clasp knife that was both fork and spoon for active service in the field. Officers were left to their own efforts to equip themselves for campaigning, using either their *bât* and forage money (financial compensation for the feeding of their personal animals), or the contents of too-often-slender purses.

Lieutenant-General Arthur, Lord Wellington (1769-1852)
Wellington had learned his soldiering the hard way in the inglorious campaigns in the Low Countries of 1794-1795 before enjoying success as a general in India. In 1808 he was sent with an army to Portugal and quickly proved himself the superior of his French counterpart, winning a string of victories that culminated in his triumph at Waterloo when he defeated the first soldier of the age, Napoleon Bonaparte. Wellington's men respected rather than loved him but they wanted him around in a fight because they knew he would not sacrifice them needlessly. (Engraving by F.C. Lewis after an 1814 painting by Thomas Lawrence, from G.R. Gleig, *The Life of Arthur Duke of Wellington,* 1864)

It being the third year of war in Lisbon, the business of getting outfitted was well advanced and the first step was to repair to the weekly Rocio horse market in the northern part of the city to purchase riding horses and baggage mules or donkeys "as cheap as the Portuguese sharpers would sell, who next to Yorkshiremen are the greatest rogues known in regard to horses."[7] Because of the scarcity of forage, the number of animals permitted to accompany the army was strictly limited and regulated by rank. Being a major, Thomas Pearson would have been allowed five animals and five rations of forage to feed them. Junior officers, ensigns and lieutenants, were permitted only one baggage mule between two officers, and since a strong mule could only carry about 150 pounds, this severely limited the extent of their possessions.

The bargain struck and money paid, the officers turned their animals over to their "bâtmen," the soldiers who tended them, and then repaired to Smith's Repository or the many other shops that catered to a military clientele to purchase their field kit. What was purchased and what was taken varied according to personal taste, but one infantry officer listed the contents of what was probably a typical campaign kit:

Our little stock of tea, sugar and brandy was carefully hoarded in a small canteen, wherein dwelt a little tin kettle, which also acted the part of teapot; *two* cups and saucers (in case of company), two spoons, two forks, two plates of the same metal, a small soup-tureen, which on fortunate occasions acted as punch-bowl but never for soup. This was termed a rough-and-ready canteen for officers of the line only. Hussars, lancers and other cavalry captains would doubtless sooner starve than contaminate their aristocratic stomachs with viands, however exquisite, served on such plebeian utensils; however a frying-pan was common to all ranks.[8]

The final stop would be the store of the famous Senhor Cavigole or one of his competitors who sold potables, consumables and delicacies and where, in the words of the author of that witty little book *Johnny Newcome*, food for the inner officer was procured:

> "Pray, Sir," says John, "do you sell Hams, and Cheese?"
> "Si Senhor, I do sell all vat you please;
> Biscuits, & Porter, Tongues, Hollands, & Brandy."
> John crack'd his Whip, and swore 'twas all the dandy.
> "Tea, Sugar, Salt, and vat of all most nice is,
> Pickles and Soda, good Segars and Spices."
> "Well said, my Hearty! now I'll tell you what,
> "Pack some of all, but in a separate lot."[9]

Preparations for the field completed or not, on 16 November 1810 the Welch Fusiliers marched out of Lisbon and took the road north to join Wellington's army camped near Sobral. Unfortunately, Lieutenant Browne, our faithful witness to the activities of both the 1st Battalion of the 23rd Foot and Thomas Pearson for nearly three and a half years, did not go with them; taken ill with jaundice, he remained behind in Lisbon.[10]

The Welch Fusiliers' march up-country was pleasant and on the way they passed through Villa Franca with its 27 white convents and churches, their steeples and towers "full of hawks, storks and pigeons all living in splendour."[11] As they neared the positions of the two opposing armies, however, Captain Jack Hill recorded that

> The country is dreadfully ravag'd, I saw nothing except a few pidgeons left about the villages; the floors and rafters taken out either to burn or make huts. All the inhabitants had retire'd before our army, so that what a few months before had been a fine country is literally now a desert, with the exception of the roofs of the houses.[12]

The battalion finally arrived at the camps of the 4th Division of the Peninsular army, commanded by Major-General Lowry Cole, in and around the village of Azambuja, about 15 miles south of Santarem. Here they joined the Fusilier Brigade under Colonel Edward Pakenham, which included the 1/7th Foot or Royal Fusiliers, their former partners in the Halifax garrison, and the 2nd Battalion of the same regiment. The 2/7th had been in the Peninsula since the spring of 1809 and had distinguished itself at the battle of Talavera that year and at the battle of Bussaco in 1810, while the 1/7th, in country since the previous July, had also fought at Bussaco. The Welch Fusiliers were, therefore, very much "Johnny Newcomes" and as they marched into the brigade lines at Azambuja, the veterans greeted them with the usual derisory insults and unprintable witticisms.

In any case, the difference between the newcomers and the Royal Fusiliers would have been immediately discernable. The pale-faced Welch Fusiliers, only five weeks out of a long period of garrison service, were properly turned out according to regulation. The 7th Foot, lean and tanned, would have been wearing faded red coatees, patched with grey, white and brown cloth, with their officers, following current fashion in the Peninsular army, sporting thick mustachios and side whiskers, "waistcoats of all sorts, and colours, with filagree gold, or silver buttons, and what were called Forage Caps, of all fancies and shapes."[13] Wellington was not a stickler for uniform regulations and, as long as his officers brought their men into the field "well appointed, with sixty rounds of good ammunition each, he never looked to see whether their trousers were blue, black or grey."[14] This being the case, British officers in the Peninsula "might be rigged out in all the colours of the rainbow if we fancied" and "scarcely any two officers were dressed alike."

When the 23rd Foot arrived in Portugal in late 1810, the war was at a stalemate. Earlier that year Napoleon had become concerned about the size of French forces committed to operations in the Iberian Peninsula, a theatre of war he regarded as secondary, and their lack of success. Although his generals had beaten one Spanish army after another, that nation still refused to come to terms and accept the puppet kingdom of his brother Joseph. Convinced that this continued resistance was due to the presence of Wellington's army in Portugal, Napoleon decided to end the conflict by mounting a major offensive that would drive it into the sea. The task went to *Maréchal* Andre Masséna, who was given 70,000 men and ordered to conquer Portugal. During the summer of 1810, Masséna had been able to take Ciudad Rodrigo and Almeida, the two

The 23rd Foot in the Peninsula, 1810 – 1811

Marshal of Portugal Sir William Carr Beresford (1768-1854)
The illegitimate son of an Irish peer, Beresford had a solid record of achievement and had done very good work in reorganizing the Portuguese Army, which he commanded from early 1809. In the spring of 1811, Beresford was given his first important independent appointment when Wellington placed him in command of the Allied army in the Estremadura. A strong and personally brave officer, Beresford was an anxious commander who proved rather cautious in the field. He was also rather sensitive and was horrified by the price that had to be paid to win battles. (Print after painting by Thomas Lawrence)

key fortresses along the northern route into Portugal, but the resistance put up by their garrisons delayed him and it was September before he began his final advance on Lisbon.

Unfortunately for Masséna, for more than a year Wellington had been preparing to counter just such an invasion. The key to his strategy was the secret construction of a series of fortifications, the virtually impregnable lines of Torres Vedras, three of them in all, with 152 mutually-supporting strongpoints, stretching across the mountainous southern part of the Lisbon peninsula. North of these lines, Wellington was prepared to carry out a policy of "scorched earth," evacuating the civilian population and destroying all food stuffs, while organizing 45,000 Portuguese militia into guerilla bands to harass French communications and restrict their ability to forage for what limited food might be available. Wellington also had another asset. After hard work on the part of Marshal William Carr Beresford, the British officer assigned to command it, the Portuguese army had been revitalized and the British commander now had the services of 45,000 Portuguese soldiers, which effectively doubled the number of troops at his disposal.

The British commander was aided by the fact that when Masséna began his forward movement in mid-September 1810, he unwisely chose one of the worst routes possible which led over bad roads and through barren country. His army made slow progress and on 27 September they came upon Wellington deployed along a nine-mile ridge running through the village of Bussaco. Although his subordinates urged caution, Masséna persisted in launching a series of un-coordinated attacks, which were beaten off by Wellington, who inflicted 4,500 French casualties for 1,500 of his own. More importantly, Wellington "blooded" his Portuguese regulars, who performed so well in their first major engagement that "a French Officer who came with a flag of truce, asked if they were not British Troops in Portuguese Uniform."[15]

Having administered this rebuff, Wellington withdrew behind the lines of Torres Vedras and on 14 October a dumfounded Masséna gazed for the first time on these impressive defence works. As he reported to Napoleon, an attack on such positions would be certain to "compromise the army of His Imperial Majesty" and he therefore asked for instructions.[16] In the meantime, both armies sat down to wait, but in early November shortage of supplies compelled Masséna to pull back to a position around Santarem. Wellington promptly advanced but the deteriorating weather brought an end to major operations and the opposing armies went into winter quarters.

The 23rd Foot spent the winter of 1810-1811 trying to keep warm although, like the remainder of the allied army, they were better fed than their French counterparts. In the officers' mess of the 23rd that winter, the somewhat eccentric Captain Jack Hill of *Valk* fame was always sure to be a source of entertainment. As an officer who served with him in the Peninsula, remembered, Hill

> was accustomed to take wine very freely after dinner, and would then amuse us with the never-failing theme of the comparative merits, as leaders of armies, of Moses, Alexander, Bonaparte, and Wellington but he always gave the palm to Jewish leader, with whose camp regulations, he seemed greatly enamoured. Hill was wont to attribute a great deal of the sickness in modern armies to epidemics, occasioned by the effluvia arising from reservoirs for filth [latrines], ordered to be constructed in our camps, and cited the 23rd chapter of Deuteronomy, 13th verse, as a far preferable sanitary regulation. Thinking he was not serious, but only trying to pass of a joke on a

***Maréchal* André Masséna (1758-1817)**
An enlisted soldier in the pre-Revolutionary French Royal Army, Masséna had enjoyed a meteoric rise in rank – he was a lieutenant in 1792 and a *général de division* by the end of 1793. Possessing a brilliant combat record against the Austrians, Prussians and Russians, he did considerably less well when he came up against the Anglo-Portuguese army under Wellington. His invasion of Portugal in 1810 was thwarted by the Lines of Torres Vedras, and the British commander beat him at the battle of Fuentes de Oñoro in 1811. (From *Portraits des généraux français faisant suite aux victoires et conquêtes des Français*, 1818)

newcomer, I told him that I did not conceive Moses deserved the credit of the discovery [of frequently covering the contents of the latrines with dirt], since it had been the practice of the whole family of cats from the creation. "Ah," he replied, "Puss does it from instinct, but our leaders ought to be governed by more rational motives."[17]

The units of the Fusilier Brigade were in fine fettle although they were sad when Colonel Edward Pakenham left them in January 1811 for a staff appointment, to be replaced by Major-General William Houston, whom one 23rd officer thought "a pleasant old boy."[18] Houston did not remain long and was, in turn, replaced by Lieutenant-Colonel William Myers of the 1/7th Foot. Lieutenant Henry Prevost of the same regiment recorded that the officers and men of the formation were

all in villages and stay under canvas – in fact we are in the highest health and spirits. We have a fine British Army and in the Portuguese we put the highest confidence. Should Massena attack us, it would be a glorious day for Old England.[19]

But Masséna did not attack although, to everyone's amazement, he did not withdraw – as Wellington put it, it was "certainly astonishing that the enemy have been able to remain in this country so long; and it is an extraordinary instance of what a French army can do."[20] One reason Masséna held on was the hope that the political situation in Britain would bring a change in his favour. In October 1810, King George III had suffered a third and final relapse into madness and the government of Prime Minister Spencer Perceval was forced to bring in a bill to permit his son, George the Prince Regent, to rule in his stead. As the Prince Regent was known to favour the Whig opposition, which did not approve of British commitment in the Peninsula, it was expected that, if the Whigs came to power, they would abandon operations in Portugal. Many in the army were concerned that

If something is not done soon, it is probable the New Ministers will put a stop to all ulterior intentions by withdrawing the Army from the Peninsula. Their Organ, the *Morning Chronicle,* appears to be feeling the public Pulse on the subject. Such a proceeding would blot the Page of History, and should only be recorded as a memento of the infamy of those who could recommend and adopt such a measure.[21]

It was ironic that, when the regency bill was passed in February 1811, the Prince Regent abandoned his Whig friends and retained Perceval's government. But that government was itself concerned about the cost and value of a campaign which had dragged on for nearly three years without any decisive result, and had recently cautioned Wellington that it could not continue "exertion upon the present scale in the Peninsula for any considerable length of time."[22]

In late January 1811 the Fusilier Brigade changed quarters from Azambuja to Averias de Cima two miles to the north. The rigours of active service were already starting to affect the Welch Fusiliers – on 25 January, the battalion reported 653 officers and soldiers fit for duty at Averias but listed 218 officers and men sick, either at that place, in Lisbon or on their way back to Britain. By this time Thomas Pearson was the only major with the 1/23rd as Francis Offley had accepted a position in the Portuguese army, where, as a local lieutenant-colonel, he would eventually take command of a *batalhão de caçadores* or light infantry battalion.[23] It is notable that Pearson did not join Offley and so many other British officers in the Portuguese service, which offered swifter promotion, if only local. Certainly, his prospects would have been brighter because, in the 23rd Foot, he was two years older than his commanding officer, Lieutenant-Colonel Henry Ellis, who would probably have a long tenure of command – and the lieutenant-colonel of the 2nd Battalion was younger still. If there is one thing, however, that his record makes clear, it is that Pearson preferred service with the Welch Fusiliers over any other duty.

As winter turned to spring, the Fusilier Brigade and the rest of Wellington's army were "in high health, spirits and courage ... full of confidence in its Leader" and anxious for the war to come alive.[24] The Fusiliers did not have long to wait. In late February 1811, realizing that it was hopeless, Masséna prepared to retreat and in the first week of March withdrew from his position around Santarem. Wellington learned of this movement on 4 March and, the next day, the brigade left its lines at Averias de Cima and marched as part of Cole's 4th Division toward Cartaxo and on 6 March, to the cheers and *"vivas"* of the surviving inhabitants of that ruined city, they entered Santarem on its height overlooking the Tagus. Two days later the brigade passed through Thomar and moved on Pombal.

During the advance, Wellington's army saw terrible scenes of death and devastation and it became clear that Masséna's occupation policy in Portugal was nothing less than genocidal. The regiment picked up a French order book that contained directions "to burn every town through which the [French] rear guard passed."[25] Brigadier-General Robert Long recorded that, not only were such orders carried out, but the French did worse as

> men, women and little children were equally the objects of their insatiable cruelty. Their orgies in this particular out-rivalled those of the most savage Indian tribes, and will reflect eternal disgrace on the Troops and the officers who connived at such a[n] iniquitous proceedings [sic]. Mothers were hung up with their children by their sides, and fires lighted below them. Men and children, half-murdered, thrown upon the burning embers of the houses they had set on fire.[26]

There seemed no limit to the enemy's depravity. At Porto de Mas, Masséna's soldiers herded most of the two hundred inhabitants into the village church and burned them alive. They opened graves, overturned roadside shrines and, something the more sentimental British found particularly distressing, hamstrung but left alive transport animals too weak to carry their burdens.

But the French suffered in their turn. Such was Portuguese hatred for the invaders that stragglers who fell out from sickness, fatigue or hunger, or small detachments that got separated from their main body, could expect no mercy from the guerillas and peasants, who killed them without a qualm, often torturing them first. A private of the 71st Foot remembered that, in the spring of 1811, his company could not march a hundred yards "without seeing dead soldiers of the enemy, stretched upon the road or at a little distance from it, who had laid down to die, unable to proceed through hunger and fatigue."[27] He and the rest of the British army had no pity for the French because murder and devastation "marked their way, every house was a sepulchre, a cabin of horrors!" that contained "traces of their wanton barbarity."[28] Along the path of Masséna's fugitive army, it "was shocking to behold the number of dead bodies (chiefly of the French Army) with which the Highway was crowded," these being "in a horribly disgusting state of Nudity, and half devoured by Wolves, and Birds."[29] The best estimates are that the French invasion of Portugal in 1810-1811 resulted in the deaths of 80,000 Portuguese civilians from murder or starvation and 25,000 French soldiers, the greater part of whom succumbed to starvation and sickness.[30]

The Fusilier Brigade saw more of the enemy's handiwork than they did the enemy as the French rearguards generally kept ahead of the British. During the forward movement, Pearson commanded the advance guard of the 4th Division, which consisted of the light companies of all its regiments. In one village, his lead elements came up so quickly that the French were forced to leave their dinner and hastily exit out the opposite side. The enemy seemed to have kept their sense of humour, as the British found their dinner – a mule's head – had been left behind on a platter to which was attached a neatly-written note that read *"pour Monsieur Jean Bull."*[31]

On the whole, the French made good their retreat without serious molestation, although there were a few rearguard actions. At Redinha north of Pombal on 12 March, *Maréchal* Michel Ney, feeling himself pressed too closely, fought an action that held Wellington up for nearly half a day. Cole's 4th Division was the third British division to arrive on the scene and was formed in two lines with the Fusilier Brigade in the second, and the brigade's three light companies were sent out under Pearson's command as skirmishers. Redinha was the 1/23rd Foot's first action in the Peninsula, and although the regiment was not heavily engaged, it had a grandstand seat for the battle. As one Welch Fusilier officer remembered:

> The enemy's artillery played on us in high style, and many shot passed close to me. Our first line lost about 20 men killed and wounded. To have seen us deploy and march in line, as we did, you would have been highly pleased. I never saw better. The troops in the highest spirits, and to do justice to the Portuguese, they equalled us. When our first line had approached within about 400 yards, without firing but marching steady as a rock, in ordinary time, the enemy's infantry began to retire in double quick time, and the artillery and cavalry followed their example.[32]

When the Fusilier Brigade deployed, Corporal John Cooper of the 1/7th Foot remembered the sequence of orders issued:

> "Form close column;" "prime and load;" "fix bayonets;" "shoulder;" "slope;" "silence;" "steady;" "deploy into line;" "forward." We moved across the plain in three or four parallel lines towards the French batteries, which now opened on us briskly. This was immediately followed by as heavy a fire of musketry as I ever heard in the Peninsula. The balls flew from the combatants like hail. But this did not last long; the enemy gave way, and carried off their artillery at a rattling pace, followed by loud English hurrahs, and our skirmishers. We hurried through the burning village to overtake them; but they waded the river, and made good use of their legs.[33]

After Ney withdrew, the Fusilier Brigade was dispatched on a flanking movement through the mountains to the village of Epinhel. "We had to climb the most difficult places," an officer recalled, "and what with the heat of the weather, and being without provisions, I was nearly exhausted."[34] Fortunately, when it reached their destination, the brigade found that the French had left many ovens in Epinhel "full of Indian corn bread, which was very acceptable" and also the wood they had cut to build huts, "which fell to our lot."[35] On the afternoon of 15 March 1810, the Fusiliers were enjoying this bounty when orders arrived detaching the 4th Division and sending it on a forced march to the south.

These orders had resulted from a changing situation. In the spring of 1811 Wellington's objectives were to drive Masséna out of Portugal and recover the frontier fortresses of Almeida and Ciudad Rodrigo. At the outset of the campaign, these objectives seemed attainable but events elsewhere shifted matters against the British leader. In February *Maréchal* Soult, the commander of the French Army of the South, with headquarters at Seville, mounted an operation against Badajoz and Olivenza, the frontier fortresses that guarded the southern route into Spain as Almeida and Ciudad Rodrigo guarded the northern. Wellington did not think Olivenza worth defending but, as Badajoz had a strong garrison, he was confident it could hold out until he was able to relieve it.

When Soult approached Olivenza in late January, the Spanish commandant surrendered after token resistance and Soult then moved on Badajoz to commence a formal siege. He was forced to raise it after a stronger Spanish army under *Teniente-General* Gabriel Mendizabál advanced to the relief of the garrison. Instead of retreating, however, Soult remained in the vicinity and on 19 February attacked Mendizabál's army outside the city near the Gebora River. Although outnumbered, the French inflicted a crushing defeat on the Spanish commander, killing or capturing over 40% of his army and scattering the remainder. Soult then resumed the siege, and as soon as his gunners had blown a practicable breach through the walls, the commandant capitulated, despite being in receipt of a secret message from Wellington that help was on the way. Word that another Spanish army was threatening Seville and that an allied force had made an amphibious landing near Cádiz, however, caused Soult to turn over command to a subordinate and hurry back south.

Wellington had already issued orders for Marshal William Beresford, to whom he had given an independent command in the south, to move with the 2nd Division and relieve Badajoz when, on 14 March 1811, he received word of

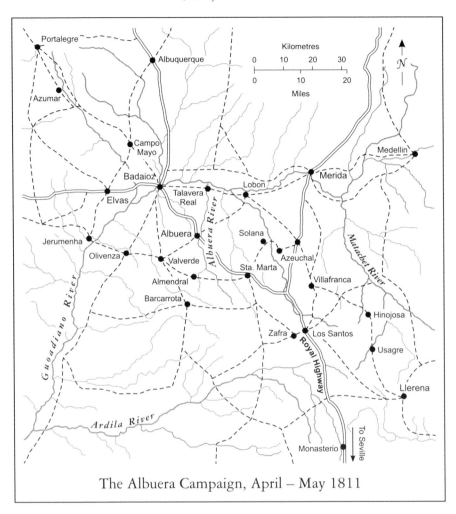

The Albuera Campaign, April – May 1811

the surrender of that place. The following day, he directed Cole's 4th Division and other elements of his army to join Beresford, who had orders to retake Badajoz and Olivenza. As soon as it received its marching orders, at about 3 P.M. on 15 March, the 4th Division set out and marched that day until dark. It went through Thomar, crossed the Tagus River at Tancos on a bridge of boats and then moved by way of Gavao and Garfete toward Portalegre.

As the Fusilier Brigade progressed south, the weather became warmer but food became scarcer as it began to outstrip its supply lines. Not that the rations were anything to boast about at the best of times – even when cattle were present with the army they were usually muscular, tough and stringy North African beasts. Bread was good if there were bakers and ovens available, but all too often recourse had to be made to biscuit or hardtack. The brigade carried its immediate reserve of food and ammunition on mules and had about 3-4 days of rations with it from which, by regulation, each soldier was to daily receive 1 lb. (including bone) of beef and 1 lb. of biscuit and a ration of rum, or wine or brandy if rum was not available. After rations were issued, each mess of three or four soldiers prepared their meal by cooking (actually boiling) their beef and then eating it with their hardtack. On the march south there were many days when beef and biscuit were not available – Corporal Cooper remembered one terrible night when there was nothing to eat but boiled bean tops. Like his comrades, however, Cooper "hobbled on" but "suffered dreadfully from hunger, thirst, little shoes, and blistered feet."[36] Lieutenant John Harrison of the 23rd Foot never forgot the day the regiment marched 30 miles although they "had no meat for two days before or spirits, only a small portion of biscuit and water to support us" and the soldiers "were in a poor way, as most of them were barefoot."[37]

On 22 March 1811, having covered 110 miles in six and a half days, the 4th Division arrived at the walled town of Portalegre with its fine cathedral. Here the soldiers received new shoes of local manufacture made of a dirty buff leather with the seams on the interior and, as by this time most men had no stockings, these items caused injuries until the skin of their feet toughened. Beresford granted the division two days rest at Portalegre and it then resumed its march to join his main force, which was moving on Campo Mayor. The rigours of the move south are demonstrated by the fact that the Welch Fusiliers had no fewer than 135 soldiers drop out, too tired or too ill to continue. Shortly after reaching Portalegre, however, the unit received a draft of 9 officers and 233 men from the 2nd Battalion, bringing its strength up to 787 all ranks.

As Beresford's army approached Campo Mayor, the French abandoned it and withdrew toward Badajoz. On 25 March, the 13th Light Dragoons caught up with the retreating enemy, scattering a French cavalry rearguard and chasing its remnants to the walls of Badajoz but ignoring the French infantry and artillery, which made an orderly withdrawal and largely escaped capture. This earned the 13th Light Dragoons a blistering rebuke from Wellington, who accused them of behaving like "a rabble, galloping as fast as their horses could carry them over a plain … and sacrificing substantial advantages, and all the objects of their operation, by their want of discipline."[38] For his part, Beresford blamed his cavalry commander, Brigadier-General Robert Long, for the fiasco and relations between the two soured.

Having secured Campo Mayor, Beresford was ready to move against Olivenza and Badajoz. First, however, he had to construct a bridge across the Guadiana River at Jurumenha as both places were on the south side of that waterway and the nearest bridge was at Badajoz itself. Because equipment was in short supply this took some time, and the first bridge, completed on 3 April, was washed away the following night by storm water. It was not until five days later, after the hardworking engineers had completed a second bridge, that the army was over the Guadiana and marching toward Olivenza. Leaving Cole's 4th Division to invest that place, Beresford then pushed east to cut communications between Badajoz and Seville. As Cole had no siege train, it took several days for his artillery commander, Major Alexander Dickson, to procure four heavy guns from the Portuguese fortress of Elvas, which finally arrived on 13 April.

Cole and Dickson planned to place these weapon in an abandoned earthwork about 300 yards from the main wall of Olivenza and this was duly done during the night of 14 April. Pearson commanded a force, consisting of the light companies of the Fusilier Brigade, that formation's attached company of

Spanish infantry
From 1809 onward, Britain began to supply the Spanish army with blue and grey uniforms which, as shown here, were simplified versions of the standard British uniform. Such were the vagaries of the Spanish supply system, however, that Spanish soldiers often wore an incredible variety of clothing and in 1811 would not have appeared so uniformly dressed as the subjects of this painting. Poorly supplied and armed, and often miserably commanded, the Spanish army nonetheless refused to give up the struggle against Napoleon and kept fighting. (From William Bradford, *Sketches of Military Costumes in Spain and Portugal,* 1814)

Teniente-General Joaquin Blake (1759-1827)
Of Irish descent, Blake was a professional soldier who had seen service during the American Revolutionary War and the campaigns of the 1790s. His strengths lay in training and staff work and, by 1808, he had achieved the rank of _teniente-general_. His record against the French was mixed; he achieved some successes but they were offset by more numerous defeats and it was said that he had won one battle and lost 15, finishing with the surrender of his army at Valencia in early 1812. Although personally brave, at Albuera Blake proved to be slow thinking and slow moving. (Print from portrait)

Brunswick riflemen, and elements of the 11th and 23rd Portuguese Regiments, which took position in woods nearer to the wall of Olivenza to cover the artillery. Just after daybreak on 15 April Cole sent a flag of truce to the defenders demanding a surrender. When this was refused, Dickson's gunners opened fire, and after a few hours the French commandant surrendered unconditionally. In his report to Beresford on this action, Cole credited the few casualties he suffered to "the fire kept up" by Pearson's men on the defenders.[39]

In this part of the Iberian Peninsula, the Guadiana formed the border between Portugal and Spain and Beresford's army was now operating in Spanish Estremadura. His soldiers noticed that the towns and villages in Spain appeared more prosperous than those in Portugal and they were also impressed with the agricultural bounty of the Estremadura plain which, stretching in all directions to the brown mountains in the distance, was covered with a healthy crop of wheat, barley and beans. Others were intrigued by the local costume as the Extremeños wore brown jackets and pantaloons ornamented with lace, red sashes, and cloaks while perpetually-hopeful junior officers made careful note of the young women in their black, tight-fitting dresses. As one recalled, these "dark-eyed and fine-formed damsels" made even the "unwilling Englishman confess the majesty of Spanish beauty."[40]

Not quite as appealing to the eye but still interesting was the Spanish army under the command of _Capitán-General_ Javier Castaños, which now joined Beresford. The first thing that struck British observers was the sheer diversity of dress worn by the Spanish, which was "of every variety of colour," and officers of the same unit often wore different coloured uniforms.[41] Although British officers were hardly better in this respect, the more discerning did note that, despite their rather fantastical and ragged appearance, the basic human materiel was good. One British officer thought the Spanish soldiers were "remarkably fine, possessing all the essential qualities to make good soldiers – courage, patience, and soberness."[42] Another concluded that "all in all, it would not have been easy to find a stouter or more hardy looking body of soldiers in any European service."[43] The Spanish soldier needed these qualities because, in three years of war, his army had suffered a dozen major defeats at the hands of the French but retained an uncanny ability to take a beating and come back for more, which was frustrating to the French. "In any other country of Europe," complained *Maréchal* Jean-Baptiste Jourdan, the defeats he had inflicted on his enemy "would have reduced the country-side to submission, and have enabled the victorious armies to press forward to new conquests," but not in Spain, where the reverse seemed to be true, as "the greater the disaster suffered by the national troops, the more willing were the population to rise and take arms."[44] Even though Spain was economically devastated and partly occupied, with much of her population either suffering from French repression or on the verge of starvation, the people of that nation refused to relinquish a struggle that by 1811 was costing Napoleon the lives of a hundred soldiers each day.

When he arrived from the north on 22 April 1811, the Spanish were much on the mind of Wellington. Masséna had been driven back to the area of Ciudad Rodrigo and the British commander found time to make a short five-day visit to Beresford. Badajoz was his major preoccupation and, after completing a personal reconnaissance of the fortress, Wellington wrote three memoranda to guide Beresford's actions. The first contained detailed instructions for the siege of Badajoz which directed Beresford to build a bridge over the Guadiana closer to the city and take the outerworks before trying to breach the main city wall.

Capitán-General of Andalusia Francisco Javier Castaños (1756-1852)
In 1808 Castãnos had won a great victory over the French at Bailen, forcing 18,000 of Napoleon's troops to surrender, one of the first serious reverses suffered by the French empire. After that, however, his record was dismal and he lost several major engagements but such was his reputation that he was retained in high command. Castãnos, unlike other senior Spanish officers, was ready and willing to work with the British army and his decision to place himself and his troops under Beresford's command eased a somewhat complicated command situation. (Print after portrait)

The second memorandum was addressed to the three Spanish commanders, *Generales* Ballesteros, Blake and Castaños, whose forces in Estremadura were under orders from the Cádiz *Junta*, the central government of Spain, to assist Beresford. Wellington asked them whether they would co-operate in the siege and requested information on the size of their forces. The final memorandum outlined the options available to Beresford should Soult advance from Seville to relieve Badajoz. Depending on how strong his forces were and whether or not he would have Spanish support, Wellington gave Beresford full authority to fight a battle, provided that he preserved all the vital siege material. If a battle was to be fought, Wellington expressed his belief that "the most central and advantageous place" for Beresford to position the allied army would be at Albuera, a village and road junction southeast of Badajoz. This done, the British commander returned to the north and Beresford gave orders for his somewhat scattered army to concentrate before Badajoz.[45]

By the end of the first week of May 1811, that fortress was invested on both sides of the Guadiana and a bridge had been built over that river. Unfortunately, Beresford did not possess a proper siege train and Major Alexander Dickson was again forced to use antique Portuguese brass 24-pdr guns, some nearly two centuries old, brought up from Elvas. By great exertions, he got 20 of these museum pieces and four mortars into position, but siege warfare was never popular in the British army. As Surgeon Charles Boutflower of the 40th Foot noted: "there is so much fatigue and so little glory attending a besieging Army, that it is rarely one meets a Military Man anxious to be engaged in such a service."[46] To add to the discomfort, the weather turned hot and the men sweating in the trenches under heavy and accurate bombardment from the defenders became even more discontented when news came of Wellington's victory over Masséna at the battle of Fuentes de Oñoro on 5 May. Lieutenant Moyle Sherer of the 34th Foot reflected their beliefs when he commented: "I know not how it is, death in the trenches never carries with it that stamp of glory, which seals the memory of those, who perish in a well-fought field."[47]

Although the greater part of Beresford's army was deployed on the south side of the Guadiana, his main effort was made on the north side against the outlying Fort San Cristóbal. This was the highest point of the defences and it was reasoned that, if it fell, the city would be dominated and would have to surrender. Unfortunately, San Cristóbal was also the strongest part of the defences and the ground around it so rocky that trenches could not be dug and the siege batteries had to be constructed out of gabions, or earth-filled wicker contain-

Badajoz from the north side of the Guadiana
The fortified city of Badajoz was the key to the southern invasion route from Portugal into
Spain and its retention was a cornerstone of French strategy. It was besieged three times by
British armies in 1811 and 1812 and was finally taken with very heavy casualties. The city's
commanding position and its fortifications are obvious from this view from the north of the
Guadiana River. (From James Grant, *British Battles on Land and Sea*)

ers, dragged into position. This work, carried out under constant fire, was so
dangerous that Beresford lost three of his nine engineer officers in a single
day. On 10 May, just after daybreak, the defenders mounted a sortie against
these batteries. Captain James Prevost, nephew of the general, was commanding the company of the 5/60th on picket duty but, "wisely foreseeing with his
great inferiority of force, that not suffering his flanks to be turned was of more
importance than a temporary loss of the Battery, fell back some paces."[48] Reinforcements were brought up and the French, "tho greatly superior in number
were driven down the slope with the rapidity of a torrent." The British then
pushed the enemy back into San Cristóbal but, unfortunately, as one witness
remembered, "our Troops pursued them with their wonted ardour to the very
Walls, where they were exposed to a most destructive Fire of Shell Shot and
Musquetry" and suffered heavy casualties.[49]

By 11 May the battery on the north side of the Guadiana was ready and it
opened up at dawn but was almost immediately overwhelmed by the defend-

ers' fire, which dismounted four of its five guns. At the battery, Captain George Ross of the Royal Engineers remembered, "everyone on duty lived (or died) in an atmosphere of shot, shell splinters and musket balls."[50] Morale began to droop – the men in Colonel James Kemmis's brigade were "in a complete state of despondency at having witnessed so much Blood shed in vain" and became convinced that their brigade were "the victims of some shameful mismanagement."[51] To make matters worse, the weather now perversely turned cold and wet, while rumours began to circulate that a strong French army was advancing to relieve Badajoz.

These rumours were true. By paring his garrisons to the bone, *Maréchal* Soult had managed to assemble a force of about 24,000 men and by 8 May he was ready to march. He gathered his officers together in a public place in Seville and told them that "they were destined to save Badajoz and drive the British from Estremadura, and that the force would march at midnight on the 10th."[52] This information, so obligingly provided by the French commander, was passed on by the Spanish to Beresford, who waited until 12 May to make sure that the French were actually on the move before he ordered the siege of Badajoz to be lifted. That day, Beresford moved his headquarters to Valverde, eight miles west of Albuera, to confer with his Spanish counterparts, *Capitán-General* Javier Castaños and *Teniente-General* Joaquin Blake.

Although he was senior to Beresford, Castaños had agreed to act in a subordinate capacity as the British general commanded more troops. The main topic of discussion between the three leaders was whether the allied army should fight or retire behind the Guadiana. Wellington had granted Beresford complete freedom of action, authorizing "him to fight the action if he should think proper, or to retire if he should not."[53] It would seem that on 12 May Beresford had not made a decision but was tending toward a withdrawal. *Teniente-General* Blake was firmly against a retreat because he believed that his army would "desert and disperse" if it crossed the border into Portugal.[54] Pointing out that, "whether the situation was good or bad," Wellington had indicated Albuera as the place where a battle should be fought, Blake threatened to fight alone at that place if Beresford retreated. Since such a move would end in disaster, the Spanish general was clearly bluffing, but his obstinacy forced Beresford's hand and it was agreed by all three commanders that the allied army would assemble at Albuera. The troops of Castaños, who were at Badajoz, would march with the British and Portuguese forces to that place while Blake promised to be there by noon on 15 May.

Maréchal Nicolas Jean-de-Dieu Soult, "Main de Fer," (1769-1851)

A private soldier in the French Royal Army, Soult experienced swift promotion after 1792 and by 1799 was a *général de division*. He was named a *maréchal* in 1804 and played a major role in the victory at Austerlitz in 1805. A good soldier but a somewhat cold and austere man, Soult was nicknamed *"Main de Fer"* or "Hand of Iron" by his troops. He was a dangerous opponent and had fought successfully in Spain for nearly three years against Spanish and Portuguese armies but had never fought a pitched battle against British infantry on ground of their own choosing. (From *Portraits des généraux français faisant suite aux victoires et conquêtes des Français,* 1818)

It was well these decisions were made because Soult was definitely on the move. On 12 May 1811, the same day that Beresford met with Blake and Castaños, the advance elements of "an army formed of the finest *matériel,* complete in every arm, and under the orders of the best officers of France," led by one of Napoleon's most able generals was just three days march east of Albuera.[55] *Maréchal* Jean de Dieu Soult, 42 years old, had joined the French royal army as a volunteer in 1785 and by 1792 had risen to *sous-lieutenant.* Thereafter promotion came swiftly as Soult fought on the Rhine and in Italy in the 1790s, reaching the rank of *général de division* by 1799. Promoted *maréchal* in 1804, he had played a prominent role in the Austerlitz campaign of 1805 and in Prussia and Poland in 1806 and 1807. Soult had accompanied Napoleon to Spain in 1808 and it was he who pursued Moore to the gates of Corunna in 1809 before leading an invasion of Portugal. Shoved out of that country by Wellington, he had rebounded to win a notable victory against the Spanish at Ocaña in November 1809 before assuming command of the Army of the South. As we have seen, he had mounted a successful campaign in Estremadura in early 1811 that left Badajoz in French hands. Soult, known as *"main de fer"* or "Hand of Iron" to his troops, was described by an officer who knew him well as being imperturbable "in good or evil fortune, … observing, seeing all, comprehending all" and "silent, but hard."[56] Soult was a very dangerous enemy.

His army, marching hard toward Albuera, was the best in quality that could be assembled from the French forces serving in Spain in 1811.* Most of the 19,000

---

* A detailed order of battle for the French army under the command of *Maréchal* Soult in May 1811 will be found in Appendix C below.

infantry were comprised of two divisions from the 5th Corps but Soult had also stripped 15 infantry battalions from the 1st and 4th Corps and formed them into two very strong brigades and a reserve of two battalions of grenadiers. His cavalry component was particularly strong – 12 regiments, all but two being French, with about 4,000 sabres. Finally, he had at least eight artillery batteries, equipped with about 30 pieces of artillery being a mix of heavy 12-pdr., medium 8-pdr. and light 4-pdr. guns, and howitzers. Almost all these troops were veterans and, what was unusual by this late period in the history of Napoleon's short-lived empire, with the exception of three small units, they were all French.

Preparing to meet them was an allied army under a commander who lacked Soult's experience. Not that Marshal William Beresford, aged 42, looked weak – he was a tall man with a powerful frame who had lost an eye in a youthful shooting accident and the "glare of this injured optic is said to have been discomposing to culprits whom he had to upbraid and admonish," a task Beresford "always executed with thoroughness."[57] The illegitimate son of an Irish aristocrat, Beresford had been commissioned an ensign in the 6th Foot in 1785 and had served in the occupation of Toulon in 1793 and in India, Egypt and South Africa, rising to brigade command as a colonel. He had fought in the Buenos Aires expedition of 1807 but his career was not blighted by that fiasco and in 1808 he joined Wellington as a major-general before fighting under Moore's command the following year. Rare among British officers because he spoke Portuguese, in 1809 Beresford was placed in command of the Portuguese army with the local rank of marshal and given the task of turning it into a force that could meet the French in battle – a task he had successfully accomplished. When Lieutenant-General Rowland Hill, Wellington's favourite subordinate, was forced to return to England because of illness, the British commander chose Beresford to replace him in independent command in the south. Competent but somewhat plodding, William Beresford was neither much liked nor disliked by his men but he had never fought a major battle as an independent commander and there was already some concern over his generalship at Campo Mayor and Badajoz. In the opinion of Colonel Edward Pakenham, Beresford was "a clever fellow but no general; as his anxiety is too great."[58]

Beresford's army, about 35,000 troops, was larger than that of Soult but it was not nearly as experienced nor as unified.* The single largest component was the 14,634 Spanish troops of *Generales* Blake and Castaños but such was

---

* A detailed order of battle for the allied army at Albuera will be found in Appendix B below.

the reputation of the Spanish army in British eyes that neither Beresford or his senior staff had much confidence in their ability to fight and certainly the record of these two generals did not inspire confidence. *Capitán-General* Javier Castaños, aged 54, had forced a French army to surrender at Bailén in 1808 but had been defeated more times than any other Spanish general, although he was always ready to return to the fight, while *Teniente-General* Joaquin Blake, age 51, had an even more dubious record. The greater part of the Spanish contingent consisted of infantry, five divisions in all, and there were some good troops among them, including a brigade of Spanish guards. The cavalry, however, was weak – just 1,886 sabres in two badly-mounted brigades – and the artillery consisted of only two batteries with a total of eight 4-pdr. guns.

If it came to a fight, Beresford placed his confidence in his 10,449 British and German troops and his 10,201 Portuguese soldiers. Here, the situation was much happier. He had 17 British and German infantry battalions in six brigades, three being in Major-General William Stewart's 2nd Division, two in Cole's 4th Division and two excellent King's German Legion light battalions in an independent brigade. All these were veteran units, with the exception of the 1/23rd Foot, which had not yet seen hard fighting in the Peninsula. Beresford had four Portuguese infantry brigades with 16 battalions, two comprising a division commanded by Major-General John Hamilton while a third brigade was part of Cole's 4th Division, and a fourth independent brigade usually marched with Hamilton's division. Beresford's British and Portuguese mounted troops consisted of about 2,000 sabres, formed in two British and one Portuguese brigades. Finally, he had six British, Portuguese and German artillery batteries with 32 pieces of artillery.

It was raining on the morning of 13 May 1811 when Soult's mounted advance guard encountered the Spanish cavalry of *Mayor-General* Conde Penne-Villemur at Llerena, about 55 miles southeast of Albuera. Outnumbered, the Spanish commander pulled back to Los Santos, where he met Brigadier-General Robert Long, the allied cavalry commander, who had with him his own brigade of British cavalry and Brigadier-General Loftus Otway's brigade of Portuguese cavalry. Long and Penne-Villemur ordered their men to withdraw to Santa Marta, 20 miles to the west but, standing with their staffs on high ground near the church in Los Santos, they watched the enemy approach and it was only when the French were about to enter the village that they mounted and rode away. On the following day, the enemy did not advance as quickly and Long's allied cavalry remained unmolested at Santa Marta. Long was concerned, however, about the safety of his third brigade under Brigadier-General George Madden, which was stationed in and around the village of Solana, about eight miles northeast of Santa Marta, particularly after a messenger sent to that officer was blocked by French patrols.

The dawn of 15 May brought no word from Madden but it did bring mounted French skirmishers, who began to trade shots with Long's vedettes. Long held steady at Santa Marta, but at about noon a strong column of French cavalry, which he estimated to be 3,000 sabres, followed by infantry and artillery, began advancing on his position. As it was clearly time to go, Long pulled in his vedettes and fell back at a walk toward Albuera, his rearguard skirmishing with the French who snapped at their heels. While on the road, Long received an order from Beresford directing him to "march immediately" to Albuera to await further orders, and as this movement was already being carried out, he continued his march west to that place.[59]

The village of Albuera lay at the junction of several roads that ran weblike from its centre toward Almendral, Badajoz, Santa Marta, Talavera la Real and Valverde des Leganés. Its most notable structure was the high-towered church of Nuestra Señora del Camino (Our Lady of the Road), an apt name as Albuera lay on the Spanish Royal Highway between Seville and Badajoz. Albuera had been occupied and looted so many times that most of its buildings were ruined and roofless, and one witness remembered that the only life to be seen on its streets was "an old man and a cat."[60]

The village stood on a low knoll about 150-200 yards west of the river of the same name (actually more a stream, although swollen by recent rain) which was formed by the junction of two brooks, the Nogales and the Chicapierna, south of the village. Two bridges crossed this river, an old and narrow 16th-century structure near the village and, farther to the south, a larger 18th-century bridge which carried the Royal Highway between Seville and Badajoz. All these waterways were fordable along most of their length by infantry but high banks in places limited the choice of crossings for artillery and cavalry.

Immediately behind, and to the west of Albuera lay a long, softly rolling series of low hills running north and south, with the highest point being directly behind the village. These hills were nearly bare of vegetation and their slopes so gentle that any one spot on their length could be seen from another – and also from the east side of the waterways. This chain of hills has been described as "simply an undulation above the general surface of the plateau which forms the north-west bank of the Albuera river" that extended "as far as the eye can

The 16th-century bridge at Albuera and the village
This view looks directly west and shows the narrow 16th-century bridge and the village on the heights behind. There was much fighting around this bridge during the battle.

The church of Nuestra Señora del Camino in Albuera
In the early morning of 16 May 1811, the brother of *Schütze* Friedrich Lindau of the 2nd King's German Legion Light Battalion was on look-out in the bell tower of this church. Seeing Lindau foraging in the village he shouted down to him to get back to his unit as the the French were on the move. (Photographs by Robert Malcomson)

The 18th-century bridge at Albuera
The more modern 18th-century bridge carried the Royal Highway across the river and into the village. It was wider than the 16th-century bridge, as can be seen in this view which looks directly east from the village.

The 16th-century bridge at Albuera and the high ground on the west bank of the river
This view, taken on the east bank of the river, looks southwest and shows the high ground on the west bank of the river and the village.

The Albuera River
This view, taken from the west bank, looks south up the river. Although it may have been somewhat higher in May 1811, the Albuera was not an obstacle to infantry, although cavalry and artillery were more restricted in their crossing points because of the high banks. (Photographs by Robert Malcomson)

reach, with varying altitude," its highest points being about 150 feet above the water's edge.⁶¹ On the eastern side of the river, the ground was much the same but a narrow tongue of land formed by the two brooks was covered in olive and cork woods that screened observation from the west side of the Albuera.

During the afternoon of 15 May, Long withdrew across the river and took post near the village. In retrospect, it might have been better if he had not given up the wooded tongue of land so easily – indeed, his doing so was to become a major topic of controversy in the pamphlet war waged among some of the British officers who would take a prominent part in the forthcoming battle. On the afternoon of 15 May 1811, however, nothing was said to Long about the withdrawal and, in fact, Colonel Benjamin D'Urban, Beresford's quartermaster general or chief of staff, had informed the allied cavalry commander shortly after he arrived at Albuera that, "if pressed," he might retire across the river but he was "to maintain his ground on the left [or west] bank to the extremity, as he would soon be relieved."⁶² With this order in hand, Long felt he had permission to abandon the east bank and did so.

For their part, Beresford and D'Urban were familiar with the ground around Albuera. Earlier that day the two had ridden along the line of hills on the west side of the river and marked the locations where the various allied formations, which began to arrive about noon, were to take position. The first troops to come up were Stewart's 2nd Division, which was shortly followed by Hamilton's Portuguese division, Brigadier-General Charles von Alten's King's German Legion brigade and Lieutenant-Colonel Richard Collins's independent Portuguese brigade. When they arrived, they were met by staff officers who guided them to their proper places under a steady downfall of rain.

It was Beresford's conviction that the French would try to seize what he believed to be the key parts of the allied position – the bridges, Albuera and the higher ground behind the village – and, accordingly, he deployed to defend them. Otway's cavalry brigade was posted on the extreme left and was eventually joined by two orphan squadrons from Madden's brigade which wandered in, although the rest of that formation had seemingly disappeared. Hamilton's division was placed to the left of Albuera with Collins's brigade behind it. Von Alten's German light battalions occupied the village itself, while Stewart's division was deployed on the high ground behind it, between the Badajoz and Valverde roads. When darkness fell about 7 P.M. on 15 May, there was still no sign of Blake's Spanish troops, now seven hours behind schedule, so Beresford directed the cavalry of Long and Penne-Villemur to occupy the position he had intended for Blake along the high ground bordering the Chicapierna, south of the Valverde road. When the artillery batteries arrived, they were placed in good firing positions along the length of the allied line.

While this was going on, French cavalry vedettes maintained a watchful eye from the east side of the river, just out of range of von Alten's Germans. More French troops appeared and, in the words of Lieutenant Charles Madden of the 4th Dragoons, during the course of the day the enemy began "to multiply in every part of the wood near our lines."[63]

The main body of Soult's army had halted at Santa Marta but the marshal and his staff rode on to Albuera, arriving in the early evening when there was still daylight enough for Soult to make a reconnaissance. Since he could see Alten's infantry in the village and Otway's cavalry to the north, the French marshal would have logically assumed that there were troops hidden behind the gentle hills in the centre. Looking to the allied right, he would be able to see cavalry guarding the southern flank of his enemy's position. Soult would have noted that there were hills south of the allied right flank that overlooked it and that the woods on his bank of the river would screen any movement he might wish to make in that direction. Taking all this into consideration, Soult

realised the impossibility of reaching all the points with an army that was also inferior in number, he had to concentrate on getting his forces on just one point to overcome it, and he chose the extreme right of the enemy line. ...... The motives that led him to make this choice were that, if he succeeded in overwhelming the right wing of the allies, they would fall back towards their left, leaving open the road to Olivenca [west of Valverde], the only one they could use for their retreat; and once that road was under French control, the enemy army risked being cut up or thrown back on Badajoz, whose brave [French] garrison could not remain motionless at such a decisive time.[64]

Utilizing a feint to distract an enemy from his main attack was a tactic Soult had used before in his career, particularly against the Spanish at the battle of Gamonal in November 1808, where it had worked to perfection. If his attack was successful, he would roll up Beresford's army and place himself between it and Blake, whom Soult believed was some distance away, giving him a chance to defeat both his enemies in detail. His decision made, the orders were issued and dispatch riders set out for the French camps in and around Santa Marta, which they reached about midnight. Cursing NCOs woke their grumbling men

French light cavalry skirmishing
One of the traditional roles of light cavalry was to form advance and rear guards for the main body of an army. This required a skirmishing capability and light cavalry regiments were trained to carry out such tactics. One of the *hussards* shown here is wearing a bearskin busby, indicating that he is from the elite company of his regiment. (Drawing by Edouard Detaille from *L'Armée française,* 1888)

and the companies, battalions, brigades and divisions formed in the dark under a steady downpour of rain and then marched for Albuera.

Allied troops were also on the move that wet and miserable night. Although his chief of staff later claimed that Blake's army moved "with speed and all imaginable order," that general was slow to arrive.[65] It was not until 11 P.M. that the first of his troops came up and it was 3 A.M. before his last units appeared. *Mayor* Andreas von Schepeler, a Westphalian serving as a staff officer in the infantry division commanded by *Mariscal de Campo* José Pascual de Zayas, remembered that his division actually marched through the bivouacs of Long's cavalry without being challenged before stopping to camp close to the Chicapierna. At Badajoz, meanwhile, Cole's 4th Division and Castaños' Spanish troops remained in their positions until all the siege equipment had been put safely on the road to Elvas and, as they had to call in their guards and pickets, it was 2 A.M. on 16 May before they were on their way to Albuera. The brigade of Colonel James Kemmis, stationed on the north side of the Guadiana, carried out similar tasks and then marched for a ford below the city. Unfortunately, the heavy rain of the past few days had rendered it impassable and Kemmis was forced to head for the bridge at Jerumenha, requiring a 30-mile circuit to get to Albuera. The light companies of his three battalions, which were on the south side of the river, however, marched with the Fusilier Brigade.

Corporal Cooper of the 2/7th Foot remembered that night march as a wretched business with a lot of grumbling in the ranks as everyone was "complaining of want of rest and sleep."[66] At daybreak, the Fusiliers halted briefly for a break to remove and roll their greatcoats and cook some breakfast.

When dawn came on Thursday, 16 May 1811, it brought a cold, misty, wet morning that, to *Teniente-Coronel* Antonio Burriel, Blake's chief of staff, "felt like November instead of May."[67] Beresford's first task of the day was to get the Spanish into proper position as they were too far forward, nearly at the Chicapierna. Under D'Urban's direction, the repositioning began about 6 A.M. and Major Charles Leslie of the 29th Foot, watching the slow movements of his allies, noted that they were "drawn up as for a grand parade, in full view of the enemy, so that Soult could see almost every man."[68] It took nearly two hours to complete this business and when it was over, the divisions of *Teniente-General* Francisco Ballesteros and *Mariscal de Campo* José Lardizábal formed an extension of the line of Stewart's division with their left flank resting on the Valverde road. About 500 feet behind, *Mariscal de Campo* José Zayas' division formed a second line while the cavalry brigades of *Teniente-General* Alfredo Loy and *Mayor-General* Penne-Villemur took post on the right flank. When the troops of Castaños arrived with Cole's division just before 8 A.M., his infantry were placed in the second line with Zayas while the Spanish artillery, eight 4-pdr guns, was positioned to support the infantry. For the time being, Beresford left Cole's 4th Division in column on the Badajoz road to act as a reserve.

As the morning wore on, the rain gradually tapered off and the sun made a brief appearance. From their positions, many in the allied army could see French troops marching in the distance – Lieutenant Moyle Sherer of the 34th Foot recalled watching "the whole of the French cavalry moving on the plain; but in a short time they retired into the wood" leaving only their vedettes visible.[69] *Teniente-Coronel* Burriel remembered that enemy cavalry were "discovered to be in the wood near the royal road" on the far side of the Albuera but, "for a long time nothing happened, so that a doubt was left as to whether the enemy army would approach."[70] This being the case, the troops were dismissed to get their breakfast, which Beresford, Blake, Castaños and their staffs ate on the high ground behind the village of Albuera. Long was ordered to send his

Colonel Benjamin D'Urban (1777-1849)

In 1811, D'Urban was functioning as Beresford's chief of staff. A competent soldier, his loyalty to Beresford may have blinded him to that officer's weaknesses. He enjoyed a later career as a colonial administrator and died in Canada in 1849. (Courtesy Mark Young)

British cavalry regiments to the rear to forage, an order he thought rash and delayed carrying out as long as he could.

Food was also on the mind of *Schütze* Friedrich Lindau of the 2nd King's German Legion Light Battalion, who entered Albuera to forage. He had not gone far when his brother, who was on look-out duty in the bell-tower of the church, spotted Lindau and called out for him to find some wine. The village appeared to be deserted but in one house Lindau came across an old man who had remained although he complained that "his wife had taken all the food with her."[71] The rifleman found no wine but did come across a sheep in a stable which he led back to the church tower. Lindau's brother was not impressed and shouted to

> kill the sheep quickly, hurry back to my company and tell them that the enemy was approaching. I thereupon slit the throat of the sheep and left it lying by the tower so that my brother could take it away. I informed our commander that the enemy was approaching and moved quickly back to the tower with the adjutant, from where he could observe the enemy on high. He soon came down quickly with my brother, and ordered us to hurry back to our company, taking none of the sheep with us, as the enemy was already in the vicinity. Nevertheless, I cut myself a leg of meat, and dashed back but hardly had I tied it inside of my knapsack, than our company advanced to skirmish.[72]

Sherer of the 34th had a similar experience. It looked as if it was going to be a quiet day so, after getting a bite to eat, he set out to take a closer look at his Spanish allies, but the sound of musketry brought him immediately back to his battalion, which he found "getting hastily under arms."[73] For his part, Leslie of the 29th remembered that he and his comrades scarcely had time to "get a little tea and a morsel of biscuit" when they heard shouts: "Stand to your arms! The French are advancing!"[74]

Polish lancer at work

The use of lancers at the 1811 battle of Albuera came as a nasty shock to the British army, which lost heavily as a result. Many eyewitnesses commented on the viciousness of the men of the Polish lancer regiment, who many claimed were drunk when they charged at Albuera. There were also many claims that they maltreated prisoners after they had surrendered. True or not, some British regiments vowed never to take prisoners from the Polish *Lanciers de la Vistule* should they encounter them. (Lithograph, courtesy of John Grodzinski)

CHAPTER SIX

"OH, WHAT A DAY WAS THAT."

ALBUERA, 16 MAY 1811 (1)

On va leur percer le flanc,
Ran-tan-plan, tire-lire lan.
Ah! ce qu'on va rire!
Ran-tan-plan, tire-lire lan.
On va leur percer le flanc,
Ran-tan-plan, tire-lire lan.

Le petit tondu sera content,
Ran-tan-plan, tire-lire lan.
Ca lui f'ra bien plaisir!
Ran-tan-plan, tire-lire lan.
On va leur percer le flanc,
Ran-tan-plan, tire-lire lan.

Car c'est de là que dépend,
Ran-tan-plan, tire-lire lan.
Le salut de l'Empire!
Ran-tan-plan, tire-lire lan.
On va leur percer le flanc,
Ran-tan-plan, tire-lire lan.[1]

The alarm had been raised by a vedette from the 13th Light Dragoons who sighted French infantry and cavalry advancing up the Royal Highway toward the bridges. This was Soult's feint and to carry it out, he had chosen *Général de brigade* Nicolas Godinot with the 16th *Léger* and 51st *Ligne* Regiments supported by *Général* André Briche with five squadrons of the 21st and 27th *Chasseurs à Cheval*, the 2nd and 10th *Hussards* and a battery of horse artillery. Following at some distance and just visible from the high ground behind the village were the infantry brigade of *Général* François Werlé and the cavalry brigades of *Généraux* André Bron and Joseph Bouvier

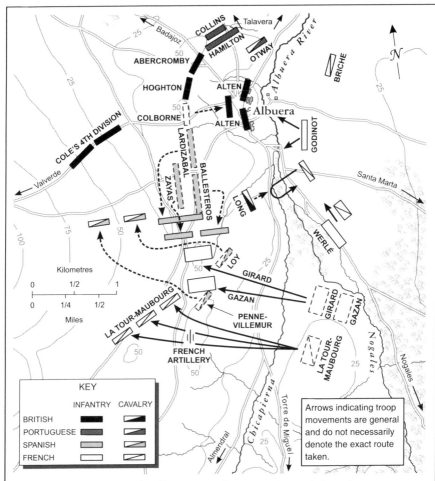

Battle of Albuera, 16 May 1811, Map 1

Due to the limited space, some units in both armies have not been shown and the size of those that do appear has been exaggerated to make them more legible.

Godinot opens the battle by making a feint attack on Albuera and in response Beresford orders Colborne's brigade to support Alten, who is holding the village. Meanwhile, an attempt by French cavalry to cross a ford above Albuera is thwarted by Long.

Seeing that Beresford has taken the bait, Soult then sends Girard with two divisions and most of his artillery and cavalry across the Chicapierna to attack Beresford's right flank. They push the Spanish cavalry back and move directly north.

As Beresford re-forms the allied army to meet this attack, Zayas and Ballesteros form a new front to face the oncoming French but come under heavy fire from well-positioned French artillery.

"Oh, what a day was that."

Portuguese cavalry

The mounted arm of the revitalized Portuguese army never matched the standards of the infantry and artillery. Part of the problem was a dire shortage of horses and forage in the Iberian Peninsula, and what was available often went to British mounted units. Another problem was lack of training. Although the Portuguese mounted troops behaved well on occasion, they were never completely reliable. (From William Bradford, *Sketches of Military Costume in Spain and Portugal,* 1814)

des Eclaz. The 46-year-old Godinot, a veteran light infantryman with more than 15 years experience in that branch, was a good choice, in Soult's words, "to fake an attack" on Albuera.[2] While Briche deployed some of his squadrons to cover the French right flank, Godinot advanced in open order to within 600-700 yards of the new bridge, sent out a strong skirmisher screen (probably a battalion or more of the 16th *Léger*) toward it and drove in the pickets of Alten's Germans posted on the east side of the river. This movement was supported by the horse artillery battery, which opened fire on the defenders of the village. Lieutenant John Clarke of the 66th Foot, who was on picket by the old bridge, remembered that "the enemy sent a brigade [battery] of guns and a force of cavalry towards" that bridge" and while the guns "commenced a smart fire," the French cavalry dashed forward, "as if they were going to charge the bridge."[3]

Just as Godinot's skirmishers moved forward, a column of French cavalry emerged from the woods near a ford over the river south of the new bridge and nearly facing the centre of the allied position. This threat was immediately countered by the 3rd Dragoon Guards deployed on the west side of this ford. They had only been in that position for a few minutes, having been placed there by Long, who, immediately after the French advance had been reported, countermanded the order for his cavalry to forage and sent them back to their original positions. The ford was narrow and the head of the French column, which consisted of squadrons from the 4th *Dragons* and the Polish 1st *Régiment*

Général de brigade Deo-Gratias Nicolas Godinot (1765-1811)
A veteran light infantry commander, Godinot was put in command of the feint attack against the allied left at Albuera. He managed to fool Beresford into believing that this was the main attack but he did not have enough troops to make much effect on his front nor could he prevent Beresford from switching troops from that flank to the more threatened allied right flank. Godinot was a sensitive man and criticisms by Soult and other senior French officers caused him to commit suicide in October 1811. He was depressed not only by the criticisms of his actions at Albuera but because he was charged with looting by Soult – a case of the pot calling the kettle black. (Author's collection)

de la Vistule Lanciers (Regiment of the Lancers of the Vistula), was forced to remain in column as they crossed the river. As the head of that column arrived at the west bank, it was charged by the Dragoon Guards and driven back to the eastern side. The French re-formed, tried again and although *Général de division* Marie-Victor-Nicolas de La Tour-Maubourg, the French cavalry commander, whom we met in Egypt in 1801, claimed they "did much execution and made several prisoners," they were again forced back.[4] At one point, *Lieutenant* Kajetan Wojciechowski of the *Lanciers* found himself, horseless, with a few of his lancers on the wrong side of the river. As the British closed in on him, Wojciechowski led his men back across the river, sabre in hand, "but the swampy ground delayed our retreat" so, throwing his sabre away, the 25-year-old Pole swam "happily to the other side."[5]

In the meantime, Godinot's troops were engaged in a "lively advance against the bridge."[6] His skirmishers tangled with Alten's in a cork wood on the east side of the river, while his supporting artillery bombarded the King's German Legion infantry in the village. *Schütze* Lindau of the 2nd Light Battalion remembered that his company

advanced through the village and occupied positions on the far side of it, one being a field of thistles eight or nine feet high, in which, virtually unobserved, we advanced to a small river [the Albuera]. On the other side were enemy skirmishers who fired on us continuously, and behind them stood troops of the line and cavalry. We also fired incessantly, but nevertheless, the enemy penetrated across the river several times and we drove them back at the charge.[7]

The French gunners supporting Godinot, however, did good work. Lieutenant-Colonel John Colborne's brigade of the 2nd Division, stationed on the heights behind Albuera, "suffered very considerably" from "random cannon shot that came over the hill in our front."[8] The French 4-pdr. guns were easily countered, however, by Major Alexander Dickson's two Portuguese batteries – a 6-pdr. battery commanded by *Capitão* Sebastião José de Arriaga and a 9-pdr. battery commanded by Captain Wilhelm Braun – positioned with good fields of fire near the church of Nostra Señora del Camino, and French witnesses recalled that their "murderous fire" caused heavy losses.[9]

This first demonstration did not seem to accomplish its purpose so Godinot next sent forward the remaining battalions of the 16th *Léger* in column and, to Lieutenant William Unger of the Legion artillery, stationed near Albuera, it appeared as if the French were launching "a grand attack."[10] Although the river was fordable for infantry along almost its entire length, Godinot directed this attack squarely at the two bridges, which permitted Alten to concentrate on their defence. As the French movement was aimed at precisely that part of his position Beresford considered most vital, he responded by ordering Colborne's brigade and Captain Andrew Cleeves's battery of the King's German Legion artillery forward to reinforce Alten. Colborne's lead battalion had just reached the village when the order was suddenly countermanded because there had been an ominous new development – the enemy was reporting advancing in strength against the allied right flank.

Watching from his side of the river, Soult had noted with satisfaction the British commander's reaction to Godinot's feint. It appeared to him that Beresford had taken the bait and the sight of Colborne's brigade moving down into the village would have confirmed the French commander's suspicion that there were British infantry in the centre of the allied line. He might also have presumed that some of Beresford's British and Portuguese troops were still occupied at Badajoz. That left the Spanish, and though Soult was later to claim he was not aware of Blake's presence at Albuera until so informed by a prisoner, he was too experienced a soldier not to have seen the large-scale movement of troops that had taken place just after dawn when Beresford and D'Urban re-positioned the Spanish and he would have made a fairly good estimate of their strength. Soult probably came to the decision he was facing more Spanish troops than expected but possibly fewer British troops and, in any case, the main consideration was that the Spanish were on the allied right

Général de division Marie-Victor-Nicolas La Tour-Maubourg (1768-1850)
An aristocrat, La Tour-Maubourg had reached the rank of lieutenant-colonel in the Royal Army when revolutionary turmoil forced him to emigrate in 1792. He returned to French service in 1799 and gained rapid promotion after fighting in the Egyptian campaign of 1801, the Austrian campaign of 1805, the Prussian campaign of 1806 and the Polish campaign of 1807. He had been wounded three times when he was promoted *général de division* and sent to Spain in 1808, where he enjoyed some success in independent command. In 1812 La Tour participated in the Russian campaign, which he survived only to lose a leg in 1813. (Courtesy, Tony Broughton)

flank – exactly where he intended to launch his main attack.

The French commander was confident that this attack would meet with success. Having won a number of victories against the Spanish and drubbed a rag-tag Portuguese army at Braga in the spring of 1809, Soult had no great respect for the armies of the Iberian nations. As for the British, Soult had chased Moore back to Corunna in late 1808, and while Wellington had manoeuvred him out of Portugal in the spring of 1809, Soult had not been present at Talavera in 1809 and Bussaco in 1810, where Wellington had beaten Victor and Masséna. On the other hand, given *Maréchal* Nicolas Soult's high opinion of his own talents, he would probably have attributed the French defeat in those engagements to the fact that he was not present. Today, however, Soult was not facing Wellington, only a subordinate commanding British and German troops, respected opponents, but also the despised Portuguese and Spanish.

To carry out the main attack, Soult had selected *Général de division* Jean-Baptiste Girard, temporarily commanding the 5th Corps in the absence of *Maréchal* Edouard Mortier. The 36-year-old Girard had been in the army since 1793, though much of his service had been spent on the staff, and was a fa-

Général de division Jean-Baptiste Girard (1775-1815)
A young officer whose background was in staff work, Girard had performed well against the Spanish but proved unsuccessful against British troops. At Girard's request, Soult gave him the major task at the battle of Albuera, which was to crush the allied right flank. He received two divisions of infantry to do so but handled them so clumsily that they were beaten by inferior numbers of troops. Personally very brave, the aggressive Girard was mortally wounded at Ligny in 1815. (Courtesy, Tony Broughton)

Waiting to advance: French infantry
The *infanterie de ligne,* the backbone of Napoleon's army, had won impressive victories against the armies of all the major European powers. Formidable in the attack, particularly if supported by their excellent artillery arm, the French *fantassins* were feared opponents. In the Iberian Peninsula, however, their offensive capabilities were matched by Wellington's sound defensive tactics and the disciplined obstinacy of his British infantry. Most of the infantry under Soult's command at Albuera had never before encountered their British counterparts and the battle was to prove a rude and bloody awakening for them. (Drawing by Edouard Detaille from *L'Armée française,* 1888)

vourite of Napoleon, who had been one of his early commanding officers.[11] An officer always "anxious for glory," in the words of a man who knew him, the previous day Girard had demanded for his corps "the honour of marching first to the attack" and Soult had granted this request.[12] To mount this attack Girard was given his own division and that of *Général* Honoré Gazan, who, although senior to Girard, was acting as Soult's chief of staff as *Général de division* La Tour-Maubourg, the officer who normally held that appointment, was commanding the army's cavalry. Girard's two divisions comprised four brigades with 19 battalions and just over 8,000 officers and men – nearly half Soult's infantry. As both Girard and Gazan were filling other appointments, the divisions were commanded by their senior brigadiers, *Général de brigade* Michel-Sylvestre Brayer for the 1st Division and *Général de brigade* Joseph Pepin for the 2nd Division. Support for the infantry *fantassins* of the two divisions would be provided by batteries of foot and horse artillery, comprising about 20 8-pdr. guns and howitzers, under the overall command of *Général de brigade* Charles Ruty, one of the most professional and accomplished gunners in the imperial service. All these generals were veterans of Peninsular campaigning and, like Soult, did not have a high opinion of the fighting ability of their enemies.

The men who would have to do the actual fighting were not quite so confident. Captain Edouard Lapène, serving in 5th Corps artillery, remembered that

Scarcely had the army and the preparations of its commanders caught our eye, than a muted unrest spread through our ranks: an indication of the sudden effect that this long expected encounter [with the British] produced. A few people, guided by old prejudices, considered with some disdain this [British] army that for two years has been bent on avoiding battle, and always swift to withdraw into the interior of Portugal. But most of us, preoccupied with the most recent details of the affair of 5 March [the battle of Fuentes de Onoro], and the memory of the murderous action at Talavera, felt no disgust in confessing that finally, the French were going to fight two rivals worthy of being opponents; and in fact, the impressive sight of the double English line, and the sudden comparison with our small number, was a measure of the complete inequality of the fight that we were going to sustain. Carried along, nevertheless, by the memory of past victories, and the latest brilliant successes in Estramadura and Andalousia, the soldiers were full of confidence, and prepared to tackle the troops of the coalition with their customary vigour.[13]

There was no subtlety about Soult's plan. La Tour-Maubourg, with Bron and Bouvier's brigades, the unbrigaded cavalry regiments and two batteries of artillery totalling 10 guns, would first cross the Chicapierna and clear the high ground on the west bank of allied cavalry before taking up a covering position for Girard's infantry, which would cross next and move directly west to the high ground before turning north against the allied right flank. Three batteries of foot artillery would then cross to support the infantry. Finally, Werlé's strong brigade, really a division with nine battalions, currently positioned near the right flank to support Godinot, would make use of the excellent lateral communications provided by the Royal Highway (which one British officer thought "equal to any turnpike in England") to move behind the woods and join Girard.[14] Girard and La Tour-Maubourg were able to assemble their units unobserved by the allies as they were screened by the woods and high ground on the east side of the Chicapierna.

It was about 9.30 A.M. when all was ready and the cautionary, *"en avant,"* was issued, followed by the executive order, *"marche!"*

At this time Beresford and Blake and their staffs were on a promontory just south of Albuera.[15] *Mayor* Andreas von Schepeler of the Spanish army recalled that most of the staff were watching Godinot's posturing against the bridges but Schepeler, "knowing Soult's reputation for bold maneouvre," was convinced the French marshal would try to turn the allied right and kept turning his telescope to the wooded tongue of land across the Chicapierana.[16] The German's scrutiny was rewarded when he "detected the gleam of bayonets" moving among the trees and his shout of *"There* they are, on the move, and *there* they will deliver their attack!" caused heads and telescopes to swivel. Almost at the same time reports began to come in from the centre and right that the French were in motion on the far side of the waterway. While the staff could make out movement in the trees, they were not sure of its direction so Blake ordered Schepeler to ride hard to the right, observe and report. As the German neared the end of the allied line, he saw massive infantry columns "descending from the opposite slopes" toward the Chicapierna and galloped back to Blake and Beresford, "making signs that the enemy was closing in."[17]

La Tour-Maubourg's cavalry advance guard, using a ford about three-quarters of a mile south of that defended by the 3rd Dragoon Guards, were soon over the stream. It had no problem driving away the small Spanish cavalry division of *Teniente-General* Casamiero Loy, only 1,000 sabres strong, and the two French horse batteries moved up and unlimbered in a position where they could fire at the allied cavalry on the plain to the west of the ridge and support Girard's infantry, which were now splashing across the stream. Once the leading infantry division was over and had climbed the higher ground at a point about three-quarters of a mile south of the allied right flank, it wheeled and moved directly north. Girard had chosen to form this division in a massive and clumsy variation of *l'ordre mixte* (see Diagram A). Its centre portion consisted of four battalions in column of double companies, while on each side of the front rank of this central column was a battalion deployed in line, and at both outer ends of their lines was a battalion in column of companies, ready to form square if the allied cavalry should threaten. This unwieldy mass, comprising more than 4,000 infantry, could move fairly quickly over broken ground but only the 1,200 men in its first three ranks would be able to bring their muskets to bear. The French marched at the *pas de charge* of 120 paces per minute beat by their drummers in a quick and persistent rhythm – "*one*, two-three, *one*, two-three, *one* two-three" – which had caused the British to call it, rather disrespectfully, "*Old* trow-zers, *Old* trow-zers."[18]

Realizing his right was in danger, Beresford rode in that direction. When he saw French cavalry on the west side of the Chicapierna with infantry behind them, he no longer had any doubts as to where the main enemy blow was going to fall and made preparations to meet it. He directed *Teniente-General* Blake to place his second line, formed by the divisions of *Mariscal de Campo* Zayas and *Teniente-General* Ballesteros, in line at right angles to the Spanish front, in a position that would occupy two knolls, about a half mile apart, which rose some 20-25 feet above the remainder of the ridge and formed a small summit south of the allied flank. Beresford did not wait to see this order carried out but next rode to Major-General William Stewart and ordered him to bring up the three brigades of his 2nd Division and their attached battery of King's German Legion artillery to support Blake. He then moved to Major-General John Hamilton and requested Hamilton to move his Portuguese division and Colonel Richard Collins's independent Portuguese brigade into the position vacated by Stewart, but to leave his troops in column so that they could quickly move to any threatened point. To Hamilton, Beresford emphasized that he was "to take care" that the village of Albuera "was maintained."[19]

Turning next to the cavalry, Beresford ordered Brigadier-General Robert Long to leave a small covering force near the fords and shift the remainder of his British mounted troops to the allied right flank. Long accordingly left two squadrons of the 4th Dragoons and a squadron and a half of the 13th Light Dragoons in place and moved with the rest of his command, an attached two-gun battery of Spanish horse artillery, and Captain George Lefebvre's troop of Royal Horse Artillery, to the right where he formed with Loy and Penne-Villemur's cavalry. Long had just completed this movement when Major-General William Lumley rode up to inform him that, on Beresford's orders, he was assuming command of all allied mounted troops. This change was supposedly made because Penne-Villemur was senior in grade to Long, which made the issue of cavalry command somewhat tricky, but more likely it was ordered because Beresford had been dissatisfied with Long for some time and had taken advantage of the presence of Lumley, a former cavalry officer currently commanding an infantry brigade in the 2nd Division, to supersede him. The change had been delayed because Lumley had only caught up the army that morning and it pleased neither officer, particularly Long, because as he complained, it took place "after the action had commenced, and whilst I was manoeuvering the Troops."[20] Nonetheless, he explained his dispositions to Lumley and faithfully assisted him throughout the day.

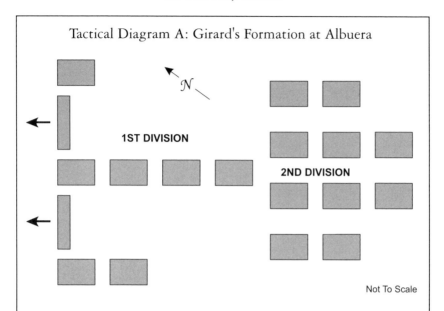

Tactical Diagram A: Girard's Formation at Albuera

1ST DIVISION

2ND DIVISION

Not To Scale

To carry out his attack on the allied right flank, *Général de division* Jean-Baptiste Girard used a massive but clumsy formation. His first division was deployed with a front of five battalions (three in columns of double companies, connected by two battalions in line) with two battalions in column on the left flank, one on the right flank and the remainder in the centre. The 2nd Division was deployed in four massive columns. While this deployment permitted his 19 battalions with more than 8,000 men to move quickly, it put them at a disadvantage if they encountered troops formed in line who could bring more muskets to bear. In fact, that is exactly what took place.

This left only Major-General Lowry Cole's 4th Division, which had arrived from Badajoz shortly before Godinot had started his attack. Having been on the move through most of a rainy night, Cole's men were not in a happy mood but, as they neared Albuera, Corporal Cooper of the 1/7th Foot remembered that his comrades

heard distant sounds, and though they grew more frequent, yet we did not think that they were the noises of a battlefield, as we were quite ignorant of any enemy being nearby. But so they proved, for in a few minutes the words, "Light infantry to front," "trail arms," "double quick," were given. We then knew what was astir. Being tired, we made a poor run up a steep hill in front; but on reaching its summit we saw the two armies engaged below, on a plain about three quarters of a mile distant. ...... We were now quite awake and roused in earnest.[21]

Beresford had earlier directed Cole to take up a position behind the 2nd Division. He now ordered him to form the 4th Division "at right angles to its original front," with its left flank resting on the foot of the hills and its right in the plain, and told him not to move from that position without orders from Beresford himself.[22] Cole deployed his two brigades* in line facing south and then permitted his men to sit or lie down in rank and they did so "in a storm of hail and rain waiting for orders."[23]

As a result of Beresford's orders almost the entire allied army was shortly in motion. He had just finished issuing them when one of Blake's aides-de-camp arrived with the disturbing information that the Spanish commander had halted his redeployment because he suspected that the main French attack would actually come against the centre. Why Blake came to this conclusion is unknown but the Spanish general may have been led astray by glimpses through the woods of Werlé's infantry and Bron and Bouvier's cavalry moving south on the Royal Highway, and assumed that the French were about to assail his front as well as his right. When a horrified Beresford arrived to remonstrate with him, Blake "positively refused" to carry out a major redeployment and the two men argued about the matter for some time. Blake finally agreed to shift his troops but, as Lieutenant-Colonel Henry Hardinge recalled, the Spanish commander "gave such tedious pedantic orders of counter march that Beresford was obliged to interfere and direct the movement himself."[24]

Fortunately for the allied cause, one Spanish general had grasped the seriousness of the situation and moved more swiftly. *Mariscal de Campo* José Pascual de Zayas, 39 years old, was one of the more competent and aggressive senior officers in the Spanish army. A native of Cuba, Zayas had been commissioned in the late 1780s and had fought against the French in 1793-1795, and had been a member of the garrison of Ferrol when the British landed near that place in August 1800 at which time he fought against Pearson. He had later served as a major with the Marquess La Romana's army in Germany under French command in 1807-1808. Promoted to battalion command in the latter year, Zayas had seen much fighting during the current conflict and had been prominent in almost every major battle, nine in all, gaining steady promotion.[25] It was Zayas whose performance as a divisional commander in

---

* Kemmis's brigade, it will be recalled, had been caught on the wrong side of the Guadiana and was in the process of making a roundabout march to Albuera. Kemmis's three light infantry companies, however, were present with the Fusilier Brigade.

French artillery in action
Throughout the Revolutionary and Imperial periods, the artillery was the most professional and effective arm of the French army as it had suffered less than the infantry and cavalry from political turmoil. In the Peninsula, although the British, King's German Legion and Portuguese artillery had superior weapons, the French artillery had superior tactics, honed in nearly two decades of continuous warfare, and possessed an ability to move and mass firepower that could not be matched by Wellington's gunners. At Albuera, the French gunners ended up covering the retreat of Soult's army and did so most effectively. (Drawing by Edouard Detaille from *L'Armée française,* 1888)

Général de brigade Charles-Etienne-François Ruty (1774-1828)
One of the most experienced senior artillery officers in the French army, Ruty had fought continuously since 1793 when he graduated as a lieutenant from the Artillery School at Chalons. In 1808 he was sent to Spain, where he played a prominent role in a number of sieges and had also enjoyed independent command of troops of all three arms before becoming Soult's artillery commander in late 1810. Ruty and his gunners were primarily responsible for the heavy allied casualties at Albuera. (Courtesy, Tony Broughton)

the Talavera campaign in the summer of 1809 provided one of the few bright spots in an otherwise dismal episode for the Spanish army. It was Zayas who commanded the hard-fighting rearguard which saved the remnants of the Spanish army after the disaster at Ocaña in November 1809, and it was Zayas who unsuccessfully pleaded with his superior at Barosa in March 1811 for permission to help Lieutenant-General Thomas Graham's hard-pressed British troops. Despite his impressive combat record, Zayas had not neglected

Teniente-General José de Zayas (1772-1827)
A North American, Zayas was born in Havana,
Cuba. He joined the Spanish army at a young
age and saw considerable action in the 1790s
fighting both France and Britain. At the outbreak of the Spanish war of liberation against
the French in 1808 he served as chief of staff
to Castaños and over the next three years
fought ten major engagements. It was Zayas'
decision to move quickly and without orders to
counter the massive French attack on the allied
right that saved the battle for Beresford. His
division fought well and suffered heavy casualties. (Print after portrait)

the theoretical aspects of his profession and had found time to write a useful
military manual.*

Seeing the French bearing down from the south, in "massy columns" as
one eyewitness put it, Zayas moved quickly to form a new allied right flank.[26]
He used the closest units in the Spanish second line and the 2nd and 4th Battalions of the *Reales Guardias Españolas*, the Spanish household troops, and
the *Regimiento Irlanda* from his division and the *Voluntarios de Navarra* from
Brigadier-General Carlos de España's division. Zayas placed the two battalions
of guards in line just north of the two knolls he had been ordered to occupy,
with the 2nd Battalion on the right, and formed the other units in column
behind them, with the *Voluntarios* on the right. He then ordered *Teniente-
Coronel* José Miranda to place two of his 4-pdr. guns on the left flank of this
line and four on the right. A few minutes later, *Teniente-General* Ballesteros
brought up three units from his division, – the 1st Battalion of the *Regimiento
de Cataluña*, the *Regimiento Barbastro* and the *Regimiento Pravia* – and placed
them in line on Zayas' left flank. As they came into position, the Spanish could
see the French marching steadily toward them and, from their standpoint, it
appeared as though the French cavalry were moving forward on the right, the
artillery in the centre, and the infantry on the left.

While carrying out these movements, the Spanish were hit by French artillery fire. It came first from La Tour's two horse batteries, which were deployed
on rising ground about 800 yards to the south, fairly long range for that cali-

---

* *Instrucciones Sobre el Buen Orden Militar* (Instructions on Good Military Order), published
at Cadiz in 1811.

bre. Nonetheless La Tour-Maubourg reported that their fire "must have done considerable mischief."[27] In a few minutes, *Général de brigade* Ruty arrived with ten more pieces and assumed command of all the guns on the west side of the Chicapierna, a total of about 20 weapons. This veteran gunner recognized at a glance that his position was a good one, being on slightly elevated ground which sloped toward an enemy line that was well within range. On ground like this, one French artillery authority believed, it did not matter whether the gunners used "raking shot or direct fire;" the effect would "be powerful, if kept up with cool and steady regularity, and careful pointing [aiming]."[28]

Ruty gave the order and his batteries went into position, their four-horse teams drawing the green-painted carriages of the brass 8-pdr. guns and 6-inch howitzers into positions selected by the battery commanders. Once in place, the gunners unhooked the *avant-trains*, or limbers, which were driven off to a safe distance and then man-handled the guns to the correct position which was no easy job, as an 8-pdr. gun complete with carriage weighed 1,200 pounds. Ruty had at least eight of these weapons and their detachments had the additional task of pulling the tube forward on its carriage from the travelling trunnion holes to the firing holes. Next, the ready-use ammunition chest stowed between the brackets of the trail of each piece was unshipped and, everything being ready and the gun implements to hand, the order *"Chargez!"* was issued, causing the weapons to be loaded, probably with roundshot, given the range. The gun was then "laid" or aimed by the gun commander, who when all was ready would step back and give the order, *"Feu!"* at which point the gunner on the left of the breech ignited the weapon with his portfire, causing a short, sharp bark that pressed on the eardrums, and a prodigious amount of dirty white smoke. While the weapon recoiled about six to eight feet, the iron roundshot, weighing 8.8 pounds in the case of the larger calibre and 6.6 pounds in the case of the smaller, was propelled toward the target at a velocity of between 1,600 and 1,700 feet per second and, given the range, the Spanish targets would see the puff of smoke from each gun about a second before they heard the noise of its firing. Although some of the first few shots may have been short or over, Ruty's gunners soon had the correct range. Their task was to lighten the work of their infantry comrades by weakening Zayas' line before Girard's column closed within musket range and they set about the job methodically, trying to conserve ammunition as they had just under a hundred roundshot and canister rounds in their immediate supply.

Being on the receiving end of such fire was a terrible experience. Under optimum conditions an 8-pdr. roundshot fired at the range of Ruty's guns could penetrate 28 human beings and it went through men and animals with a sound not unlike that of a large, rotten grapefruit thrown hard against a brick wall. Not only was a victim's fate immediately known to his comrades on either side of him, they were often splattered with the results – in some cases with such velocity that they were wounded by the residue. Roundshot was the subject of many soldiers' myths, including one that a man hit by it did not feel much pain – at least immediately. This was denied by a recipient who lost a great part of the flesh of one thigh to a shot and who recalled his sensations at the time the wound occurred as "being a confused sense of severe injury, followed immediately by great pain in the part affected."[29] Surgeon George Guthrie, who treated the wounded at Albuera and almost every other major battle fought by the British army in the Peninsula, concluded that when wounds were inflicted by roundshot, the pain was immediate but that, mercifully, there was less chance of major bleeding:

> When a limb is carried away by a cannon shot, any destructive bleeding usually ceases with the faintness and failure of strength subsequent on the shock, and a haemorrhage thus spontaneously suppressed does not generally return; it is the effort of nature to save life. The application of a tourniquet is rarely necessary, unless as a precautionary measure, when it should be applied loosely, and the patient, or someone else, shown how to tighten it if necessary.[30]

This knowledge, of course, was cold comfort to the Spanish infantry who were suffering from Ruty's gunners and Schepeler remembered watching the enemy artillery fire "tearing gaps in the right of Zayas' line."[31] *Teniente-Coronel* Miranda tried to reply with his 4-pdrs. but they were no match for the heavier French weapons. His two guns on the left of Zayas' line were soon put out of action and the detachments manning the four pieces on the right took heavy casualties. The weight of the enemy artillery fire was too much for the *Voluntarios de Navarra*, whom Zayas was trying to form in line on the right of the two guards battalions, and they gave way. Zayas was eventually able to rally them but he replaced them in his front line with the *Regimiento Irlanda*.

By this time it was after 10.00 A.M. and now came the floodtide of Girard's infantry. Since it had been overcast or raining since dawn, the French were probably wearing their dun or beige woollen overcoats, the bulky sleeves slashed off at the elbow so that they could load and fire their muskets. Marching

Teniente-General Francisco Ballesteros (1770-1832)
A professional soldier from Asturias, Ballesteros commanded a division which had harassed the French in Andalusia and saw heavy fighting at Albuera but did not suffer as many casualties as Zayas' division. Unlike Zayas, Ballesteros was a skilled politician and ended his military career as a very senior commander. (Print after portrait)

steadily in their crowded columns to the beat, "*Old* trow-zers, *Old* trow-zers," and preceded by a battalion or more of skirmishers drawn from the light infantry companies of the four regiments in the division, the French "began to pour down on us," an eyewitness remembered, "like an immense torrent."[32] *Capitaine* Lapène of the 5th Corps artillery remembered proudly that his infantry brothers "marched steadily with their muskets on their shoulders, crossed the stream [the Chicapierna] and mounted the escarpment on which the enemy was positioned and, with great vigour, closed with him."[33]

If *Général de division* Jean-Baptiste Girard intended to deploy his clumsy formation into line before he closed on his enemy, now was the time to do it. Girard, however, appears to have abandoned any such intention as both he and Soult, who was with him, were convinced that the withdrawal of the allied cavalry from the far right and the re-alignment of the Spanish troops were signs of an allied retreat. In addition, since Girard quickly identified the troops facing him as Spanish, he was confident that the day would be his as he had seen the Spanish run away from too many battlefields to have any fear of them. He therefore did not make a serious attempt to deploy, probably thinking his men would march straight through the enemy, as indeed they had on previous occasions.

This was a fatal miscalculation. Girard was attacking not only one of the best generals in the Spanish army; he was also attacking some of the best troops in that army. The *Reales Guardias Espagñolas* were the elite soldiers of Spain, and although they had shared in many bitter defeats at the hands of the French, they had always performed well in battle. The *Regimiento Irlanda* or Regiment of Ireland was a holdover from the 18th century when young Irishmen fled abroad to serve in the armies of European states, hoping to get a chance to fight the detested redcoats. There were few real Irishmen in the *Irlanda* now (there was, however, a *Sargento* Carlos Nolan with the regiment at the battle) but the *Irlanda*, along with its sister units, *Hibernia* and *Ultonia* (Ulster), was a cut above the average Spanish line infantry unit and considerably better than many of the recently raised units of *voluntarios*. Formed in a line of three ranks, the men of the *Guardias Españolas* in their dark blue uniforms and those of the *Irlanda* in their light blue waited impassively as the rain dripped off their bicornes and the French bore down on them.

As the enemy column moved closer, Zayas sent out the *cazadores* or light infantry companies of the three units to counter Girard's skirmishers. So eager were they to get to grips with the enemy, Schepeler remembered, the *cazadores* actually drove the French back with the bayonet, "forcing them to retreat to the main body of their army."[34] The enemy hesitated for a moment while Girard's skirmishers filed off to either flank, and then came on again, forcing the Spanish skirmishers to shelter within the lines of their units. When the French approached maximum musket range, about 60 yards, Zayas gave the orders and the battalion and company commanders repeated them: *"Prepárence para hacer fuego! ... Apunten! ... Fuego!"** and the three regiments were shrouded in white smoke as, individually, they delivered the first and crucial volley – because it had been calmly loaded out of the heat of action – into the oncoming French.[35] As Zayas remembered it,

> the fourth battalion of our Royal Spanish Guards opened fire under their officers' commands, displaying an incomparable courage and perseverance in this battle; the second battalion lost no time carrying out the same action [musketry]; as did the Irish regiment ...... The crash was so terrible and tenacious that only men very determined to gain had been able to resist it; but at last the French, fierce soldiers but instruments of the tyranny, could not resist the Spanish courage.[36]

On Zayas' left, Ballesteros' units joined in the musketry, which, after the first few disciplined volleys, deteriorated into "running fire," basically every man doing his best. Zayas thought the French recoiled from these opening rounds but what probably happened was that the front ranks of Girard's column shuddered from the shock of the Spanish fire and came to a halt while the rearward ranks continued onward, colliding with those in front and causing confusion. After they got themselves sorted out, the French began to open a ragged return fire and a musketry duel began. More men in the Spanish

* "Prepare to fire ... present ... fire!"

line, which numbered between 2,800 and 3,000, could use their muskets but this advantage was partially offset by the fact that the French being lower on the ridge, the centre ranks in their "dense column could direct their musquets against it [the Spanish line] with effect; as they levelled far above the heads of those in their front."[37]

This exchange at close range continued for perhaps 30 to 45 minutes. Despite the best efforts of their officers, the French were reluctant either to move forward or deploy into line. On the Spanish left flank, *Teniente-General* Ballesteros noted that the enemy units opposite did make unsuccessful attempts to deploy, but on Zayas' front the French preferred to remain in the comforting shelter of their column and to keep up individual fire. Although the Spanish were taking heavy casualties, they did not flinch but stolidly returned fire and *Teniente-Coronel* Antonio Burriel, Blake's adjutant-general or chief of staff felt that their behaviour created "large hopes of success on this day."[38] But the Spanish suffered cruelly from the French artillery as, by now, Ruty had about 20 guns in position to support Girard. The enemy's artillery fire, Burriel recorded, was "continuous" and the range so close that the second Spanish line was being affected by it. Miranda's *artilleros* were hopelessly outgunned and he lost an ammunition wagon exploded by a French howitzer shell, which "caused disorder" among the mule teams pulling his guns and vehicles.[39] His remaining four guns were hit by roundshot, one shot cutting down *Teniente* Joaquin Moscoso and wounding *Teniente* Antonio Arderius, another wounding three gunners manning a 4-pdr. piece. The Spanish gunners gamely tried to do their best but one by one Miranda's guns fell silent.

Zayas' infantry kept up their fire, however, and one can hear the pride in their commander's voice when he later reported that, although,

> the enemy repeated their attacks … many times and always with bayonets; … the fourth battalion of Guards, similar to the three hundred Spartans, was immutable at its post: the second battalion forced by the enemy's superiority and the disadvantage of the land had to concede some steps but without turning their heads, in order to emphasize their discipline and courage, only a brief moment was enough to recover and attack the enemy again. The Irish [*Regimiento Irlanda*] were also in good spirits and the last charge that they carried out against the enemy with bayonets having lost fifteen officers was very well considered in our opinion.[40]

It is a tribute to the quality of *Mariscal de Campo* José de Zayas, both as a soldier and as a man, that in his official report on the battle of Albuera he listed by name no fewer than 17 enlisted men from the two guards battalions and the *Irlanda* who he felt deserved either promotion or some other distinction. The Spanish were clearly living up to the motto *"Vencer o Morir"* ("Victory or Death") embroidered in large red letters on the white Colour of the 4th Battalion of the *Guardias* which could sometimes be seen through the smoke of the firing.

As men fell, cut down by French musketry or artillery, the units of Zayas and Ballesteros closed in to their centre and the gaps between them began to widen. Their ammunition also began to run low as Spanish unit supply was always somewhat shaky and the men in the ranks were forced to root around among the dead and wounded for cartridges. Despite their courage, the situation was beginning to deteriorate and, after suffering considerable loss, some of Zayas' men ceased firing and his units became crowded together "in two irregular masses."[41] Seeing this, a clear indication that his allies were nearing the end of their tether, Beresford began anxiously to look for the arrival of Stewart's 2nd Division.

A t that moment, the lead brigade of that formation, commanded by Lieutenant-Colonel John Colborne, was approaching. Earlier, Colborne had been ordered to take his brigade down into Albuera and it had required some time for him to extricate it and move to the right flank, but he finally got his men marching south in column of half companies in what Colborne, a veteran of the Egyptian campaign and Maida, thought were "very disadvantageous circumstances."[42] Moving beside the head of the brigade column were three 6-pdr. guns and a 5.5-inch howitzer of Captain Andrew Cleeves's battery of King's German Legion artillery, his remaining two 6-pdr. guns marching at the rear of the formation.

When Colborne had moved down into the village, the other two brigades in Stewart's division, commanded by Major-General Daniel Hoghton and Lieutenant-Colonel Alexander Abercromby, a son of the victor of Egypt, had remained in their original positions, standing at ease while "exposed to a heavy, chilling, and comfortless rain" and, occasionally, taking casualties from roundshot fired by the French battery supporting Godinot which bounced over the hill in front of them.[43] Lieutenant Moyle Sherer of the 34th Foot remembered that, after about 90 minutes of this, sounds "which breathed all the fierceness of battle, soon reached us from the right" and artillery and musket fire indicated that "the real attack was in that quarter."[44]

After Colborne had pulled out of Albuera and moved south, Hoghton formed his brigade in column and followed him, he being followed in turn by Abercromby. Lieutenant John Clarke of the 66th Foot remembered that Colborne moved his brigade "in open columns of companies at the double" and that the rain "was falling fast and the ground was very heavy" or muddy.[45] It is an indication of how unexpected was the order to move that Hoghton was still wearing a green frock coat when his brigade moved off as he had thought there would be little fighting that day. His servant had to fetch his red uniform coat and catch up with him on the run so that his brigade commander was properly dressed to kill.

Just as Stewart's three brigades neared the scene of the Spanish struggle with Girard's column, they came under artillery fire. Ensign Benjamin Hobhouse of the 57th Foot in Hoghton's brigade recalled that the "incessant and well-directed fire" of the French artillery "mowed down many of our poor fellows" as the 2nd Division marched up.[46] A roundshot carried away the hip of Captain John Humphrey of the 29th Foot and killed two men behind him. Humphrey had suffered a dreadful and mortal wound but neither his comrades nor those coming behind could stop to assist him – Lieutenant Sherer never forgot the sight of Humphrey and "the heart rendering tone in which he called out to us for water, or to kill him."[47] But, as Sherer noted, "on this trying day, such of the wounded as could not walk lay unattended" because "all was hurry and struggle" and "every arm was wanted in the field."

Stewart had ridden with his staff ahead of his troops to assess the situation. In an army that had more than its share of such men, William Stewart, aged 37, was a notorious "character." A passionate hater of Napoleon's France, which he believed desired "nothing less than the subjugation of the whole civilized world," Stewart had been one of the creators of the experimental rifle corps which later evolved into the 95th Foot and had written that unit's first manual.[48] Stewart believed that "duty should be done with cheerfulness and inclination, and not from mere command and the necessity of obeying" and his practice of authorizing frequent double rations of rum for his men (for which he was later forced by Wellington to reimburse the commissary out his own pocket) earned him the fine soldiers' nickname of "Auld Grog Willie."[49]

In battle William Stewart was absolutely fearless. A favourite anecdote about "Auld Grog" came from an officer who was tasked to give him a message dur-

Lieutenant-Colonel John Colborne (1778-1863)
John Colborne was a protégé of Sir John Moore and fought with distinction in Egypt, at Maida, and throughout the Peninsular War, gaining steady promotion. The battle of Albuera was not a happy affair for him as his brigade was broken, through no fault of his own, by French cavalry. By 1815 Colborne was a colonel and his 52nd Foot played a memorable role in the battle of Waterloo. Colborne also enjoyed a notable career as a colonial administrator and served as governor-general of Canada in the 1830s. (Toronto Reference Library)

ing the middle of an intense artillery bombardment. The two were conversing when a French shell landed at Stewart's feet and exploded, fortunately not wounding either man. "A shell, sir, very animating," remarked "Auld Grog," who then continued with the conversation as if nothing had happened.[50] But Stewart's courage was sometimes greater than his judgement, and although he was possibly one of the best battalion commanders in the British army, he may have been one of the worst division commanders. Certainly, he was a continual trial to Wellington, who complained of Stewart that, even though he possessed the "utmost zeal and good intentions," the man simply "cannot obey an order" and needed to be under "the particular charge" of a superior lest he get carried away.[51]

Unfortunately, at about 11 A.M. on 16 May 1811, there was no one to check Stewart and he did get carried away. A glance was enough to tell him that Zayas' battalions could not take much more but also that the long left flank of Girard's column was vulnerable. Although his orders were only to support the Spanish, Stewart decided to attack the enemy flank with Colborne's brigade, which was just coming up. He rode to that officer and ordered him to move his four battalions (the 1/3rd, 2/31st, 2/48th and 2/66th Foot), just under 2,000 bayonets, to the right of Zayas' line, wheel them to the left, form line and attack. Hoghton and Abercromby's brigades, meanwhile, would deploy into line behind the Spanish so as to eventually replace them in position (see Diagram B).

Lieutenant-Colonel John Colborne, aged 35, was a gifted soldier and a protégé of Sir John Moore. After hearing Stewart's orders, Colborne pointed out that the right flank of his brigade, if deployed in line, would be vulnerable to the masses of French cavalry both officers could see out on the plain to the south and west. He therefore requested permission to leave the right wing (or half battalion) of his lead unit, the 3rd Foot, in column so that it would be in better formation to repel a possible cavalry charge. Stewart, excited and anxious to get stuck into the French, refused to hear of it and as Colborne later noted, he had "nothing to do with the arrangement" of his brigade but "merely obeyed the orders of General Stewart."[52] Colborne therefore moved in column to the right of Zayas' line and deployed into line while Captain Andrew Cleeves positioned his three 6-pdr. guns and 5.5-inch howitzer on the right flank of the Spanish, about 90 yards from the French infantry, which to the British appeared to be in three "immense columns."[53] Other witnesses claimed there were more but Major Georg Julius Hartmann, commanding the British and German artillery, noting that observers often "see what they want to see," only remembered there being three columns and a reserve.[54] As soon as his artillery brigade appeared on the crest of the higher ground, Cleeves came under heavy fire from Ruty's batteries.

Stewart attacked immediately. Major William Brooke of the 2/48th Foot remembered that the first three battalions in the brigade deployed into line and moved to within musket range of the French where they "halted, and fired two rounds," their fire being returned by the front and flank of the French columns, which fired "three deep, the front rank kneeling."[55] It was during this exchange of fire that 23-year-old Lieutenant-Colonel John Duckworth, commanding the 66th Foot, who had somewhat rashly remained mounted while leading his regiment forward, was hit in the chest by a musket ball. The son of a distinguished admiral in the Royal Navy, young Duckworth "could not be induced

Major-General William ("Auld Grog Willie") Stewart (1774-1827)
A somewhat eccentric but very aggressive officer, Stewart was first commissioned in 1786 and saw much active service in the 1790s. In 1800 he and Colonel Coote Manningham raised the Experimental Rifle Corps, which evolved into the 95th Rifles. Stewart was an excellent regimental officer but he proved less successful as a brigade and division commander because he tended to be somewhat rash in action. Stewart commanded a division in the Peninsula under Wellington for three years, and although the Duke did not like him, he could not get rid of him. Stewart retired in 1818 but died young, worn out by having fought 17 campaigns during which he suffered nine wounds or contusions. (From *The Cumloden Papers,* 1871)

to leave the field" and continued in command until shortly afterward, a second musket ball hit him in the throat, severing his carotid artery and causing him to bleed to death within minutes.[56]

Finding that the French columns "were not to be shaken by fire," Brooke of the 48th remembered,

the three leading battalions of the brigade prepared to charge with the bayonet, by order of Major-General the Hon. William Stewart, who led them on in person to the attack in the most gallant manner. The charge being delivered, the French 28th *Léger* gave way, as did also the front ranks of their Grenadiers. In the latter we could see the officers trying to beat back the men with the flats of their swords.[57]

Mayor Schepeler, who watched this charge with Zayas' staff, noted that Colborne's front rank never truly crossed bayonets with the enemy, but when they "they brought their bayonets down the French gave way, and began to fall back along the slope."[58] Stewart's charge removed the pressure on Zayas, and Hoghton and Abercromby prepared to take over the Spanish battle against the front of Girard's column.

It was at this moment that the drizzle, which had been continuous for much of the morning, turned into a downpour that, "combining with the smoke of the firing, caused such a darkness, that it was impossible to distinguish any object, even at a few paces' distance."[59] So heavy and high were the clouds of smoke being produced by the battle that, despite the rain, it could clearly be seen in Badajoz 14 miles away, where fascinated Spanish observers estimated that the battle line "occupied there [at Albuera] seemed to be more than two leagues in length" or about six miles, a fairly accurate estimate.[60]

With their vision thus obscured and their attention focused on the enemy infantry columns, which appeared to be faltering, many in Colborne's line did not notice a body of French cavalry moving toward the rear of their right flank.

After crossing the Chicapierna, *Général de division* La Tour-Maubourg had deployed most of the French cavalry on the French left flank. As he later reported:

After having assembled the 2nd and 10th Regts of *Hussards*, the 4th, 20th, 26th, 14th, 17th and 27th *Dragons*, and the 4th Regt of [Spanish] *Chasseurs à Cheval* in the service of His Christian Majesty, I placed the cavalry in columns by regiments being in echelon and well spread out from each other. …… This position gave our cavalry the opportunity to focus [concentrate] on the enemy's right, their cavalry stretched fairly far to the right, to the rear of their infantry.[61]

La Tour had watched with growing concern the battle on the ridge where the Spanish had first stopped Girard's column cold and it now appeared to be giving way before Colborne's brigade. An aristocrat who had reached the rank of lieutenant-colonel in the royal army prior to 1789, the 52-year-old La Tour had left France for seven years during the time of worst revolutionary excesses but had rejoined the army in 1799. As we have seen, he had campaigned in Egypt before serving in the light cavalry division of the famous *Général* Antoine Lasalle and had fought at Austerlitz in 1805, Jena in 1806 and Friedland in 1807, suffering three wounds but gaining steady promotion. An experienced cavalry commander, La Tour saw the golden opportunity presented by Colborne's open flank and ordered *Colonels* Jan Konopka and Gilbert-Julian Vinot, commanding the *Lanciers de la Vistule* and the 2nd *Hussards* respectively, to attack it with *Colonel* François de Laval's 10th *Hussards* acting in support.

The two leading units were probably in a position about three-quarters of a mile south of Colborne's right flank. Because of intervening high ground and the poor visibility, neither Colborne nor Stewart would have seen them begin to move. As one squadron of the lancers was serving with Briche on the French right flank, Konopka had only three squadrons under command, about 450 men, while Vinot had four squadrons, 22 officers and 282 men, and de Laval 262 all ranks, according to one strength return, making a total of 1,000 sabres. At the last minute, *Lieutenant* Guadelet of the 2nd *Dragons*, who commanded La Tour's escort troop, which consisted of men from different regiments, asked and received permission to join the charge and formed with Konopka's lancers.

As the three regiments, with the *Lanciers* leading, rode north on the convenient road from Almendral, the horse soldiers made last-minute adjustments, checking pistol flints, loosening swords in scabbards, and the lancers tightening the sling, or tethering strap, of their 9-foot-long weapon with its 8-inch blade, above their right elbow. Despite the rainy weather, the men would have rolled their overcoats and tied them banderole fashion over their right shoulders as protection against sword cuts. In any case, on a miserable day like this, the hussars of the 2nd and 10th would have donned their pelisses or outer jackets, brown and light-blue respectively, while the lancers, as was their custom before going into action, would have buttoned across the yellow plastrons of their blue *kurtkas* or coats to render the garment not only less conspicuous, but also double-breasted for warmth. The final adjustment would have been to tighten the cords that held the shakos of the hussars and the *rogatywki* of the lancers, their distinctive four-cornered headgear.

Just before his regiment emerged onto the open "plain," Konopka halted and formed it for the charge, while behind him Vinot and de Laval did the same for their regiments. Given the narrow aspect of his objective, the end of a two-rank line of infantry, Konopka probably opted to attack with the three squadrons of lancers in line so they would hit and wrap around the flank, and then cut down the companies of the right-hand British battalion (the 3rd Foot) in sequence. Only the first rank (or half) of each of his three squadrons was armed with lance and sword, the second had only the *arme blanche*, but swords were not normally drawn in a charge until the last few hundred feet lest their sudden flashing appearance in a moving cavalry unit give away its intentions to the enemy. Vinot and de Laval would have used a similar deployment or more likely echelon of squadrons behind each other, so that the target infantry would be hit in "waves" – in fact they would be overwhelmed.

When Konopka was satisfied, he took position in front of the centre of his regiment's first rank and issued the cautionary, *"En avant!"*, which was sounded by the trumpeter riding beside him, and then *"promenez!"* or "walk!" These orders were repeated by the three squadron commanders and the regiment moved forward, taking its direction from Konopka, who moved straight at the redcoated infantry some 900 yards away. After the regiment had advanced about 50 yards

Beau sabreur: Colonel Pierre-Joseph Farine (b. 1770)
Farine joined the army in the early 1790s as a cavalry-man and was a colonel and commanding officer of the 4th *Régiment de Dragons* when he was sent to Spain in 1808. He charged with his regiment at Albuera and survived the battle only to be captured a few weeks afterward. He was sent to Millprison in England but escaped in December 1811 and returned to France, where he was created a baron of the empire by Napo-leon as a reward. Farine was promoted *général de bri-gade* in 1814 but again taken prisoner. Farine rallied to the emperor in 1815 but was wounded by a sabre cut at the battle of Ligny and shot in the head at the battle of Waterloo. He continued in the army until his retirement in 1832. (From *Portraits des généraux français faisant suite aux victoires et conquêtes des Français,* 1818)

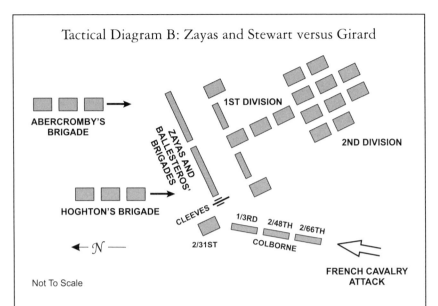

Tactical Diagram B: Zayas and Stewart versus Girard

When Girard's leading division encountered the troops of Zayas and Ballesteros formed in line, they were stopped by the Spanish. A musketry duel ensued and, seeing that the Spanish were taking heavy casualties, Beresford ordered Stewart to support them with his division. When he arrived with his leading brigade under Colborne, Stewart exceeded his orders by attacking the left flank of Girard's leading divsion in line. Although this attack was successful, it resulted in the right flank of Colborne's brigade being vulnerable to a French cavalry attack which destroyed three of his four battalions.

or so, Konopka ordered his trumpeter to sound the call and the squadron commanders ordered *"au trot, Marche!"* and the moving mass of men and horses accelerated to about 200 yards per minute, the horses' hooves throwing up clods of earth as the rank of *serre-files* or file closers riding behind each squadron discouraged any reluctant rider who slowed down by pushing him forward. After another 150 yards, or when he was most comfortable, Konopka had his trumpeter sound the correct call and the squadron commanders repeated, *"au galop, Marche!"* as the speed increased to about 300 yards a minute. It was now too late for any reluctant heroes as they were simply caught up in the moving mass.

This pace, however, could not be sustained for long and when Konopka could make out the buff facings on the coatees of the last righthand file in the grenadier company of the 3rd Foot (the company holding the threatened flank) – probably at a distance of 75-100 yards – he had his trumpeter sound the final order: *"Chargez!"* At this, the lances with their fluttering pennants of greyish-yellow chamois came down from the vertical to the horizontal and those horsemen armed only with swords drew them from their scabbards and held them straight out at eye level with "the sharp edge of the blade to the right, the point a little lower than the wrist."[62] The carefully maintained formation now began to come apart at its edges as the lancers changed from controlled movement to the "*charge à la sauvage*" and rode hard at the redcoated soldiers in their front.[63]

They were seen at the last minute and Colborne made an attempt to form for a proper defence. Clarke of the 66th Foot recalled that the 3rd Foot was "ordered to reform column, their right wing to cover the rear of the brigade" and, "to effect this they faced about, a very dangerous manoeuvre when near an enemy."[64] Unfortunately, confusion over the identification of the oncoming horsemen – some believed them to be Spanish as the Spanish army had lancers – delayed things until it was too late.

Neither the lancers nor the hussars were on particularly big horses, as the French remount situation in Spain was difficult, and the light cavalry had to take what they could get, usually rather stringy beasts of about 14 (or less) hands weighing 850 to 900 pounds. Still, with the weight of the rider, saddlery, weapons and equipment, the combination of man and beast totalled about 1050 to 1100 pounds and that combination with "*élan admirable*" slammed into the British line at a speed of about 10 miles per hour.[65] In effect, Konopka's lancers, and the hussars coming behind, hit the right flank of the 3rd Foot like a blue and brown wave and simply rolled over the Buffs, who were immediately "broken, and suffered immensely."[66] Behind the two leading units came de Laval's 10th *Hussards* in their light blue to mop up. The lancers were particularly effective; Captain Arthur Gordon of the 3rd Foot remembered that "the enemy's cavalry (Polanders) armed with long spikes, charged over our dead and wounded men, it was this circumstance that ensured the destruction of so many of the Buffs."[67] Gordon was stabbed "in the breast, in the back, and elsewhere" as "the enemy's cavalry galloped over me."

In a matter of a few minutes the 3rd Regiment of Foot dissolved into a mass of fleeing fugitives. Even where an officer or NCO was able to cobble a few men together to make a fight, the heavy rain affected the priming of their muskets, causing misfires, and in any case the longer weapons of the lancers gave them a tremendous advantage in reach against men armed with a musket and bayonet. If the lancers saw a small knot attempting a stand, they would pick out a human target, point their lanceheads at his body mass and "attack at full speed" to "obtain full advantage of the terror which the lance inspires."[68] "When delivering the charge," a lancer manual of a later period advised, "the body should be inclined forward, the weight being taken off the seat bones; the grip of the thighs and knees should be as strong as possible, the right shoulder well forward, the head inclined forward, and the eyes directed at the target."[69] The lancer did not thrust his weapon at his target but simply let his impetus drive the point home and then relaxed his grip, letting the lance, which he retained by means of the tethering strap above his right elbow, be pulled behind him by his victim's weight and then out of the victim by his forward motion. Weapon recovered, the lancer then circled, looking for more opportunities. Once a defensive knot was broken, the hussars of Vinot and de Laval and the sword-armed lancers swept in to cut down the survivors. A private of the Buffs remembered being

> knocked down by a horseman with his lance, which luckily did me no serious injury. In getting up I received a lance in my hip, and shortly after another in my knee, which slightly grazed me. I then rose, when a soldier hurried me to the rear a few yards, striking me on the side of the head with his lance. He left me and soon another came up, who would have killed me had not a French officer came up, and giving the fellow a blow told the fellow to spare the English, and to go on and do his duty with those of my unfortunate comrades. The officer conducted me to the rear of the French lines and here, the sight that met the eye was dreadful! Many dead, where the column [of Girard's infantry] had stood, heaped on each other; the wounded crying for assistance and human blood flowing down the hill![70]

Desperate fighting took place around the Buffs' colours. That day the Regimental Colour was being carried by 16-year-old Ensign Edward Thomas, who was immediately surrounded by enemy horsemen and summoned to deliver over his charge. "Only with my life," young Thomas replied, and was cut down.[71] Ensign Charles Walsh, carrying the King's Colour, was about to be taken prisoner when his precious burden was seized by Lieutenant Mathew Latham, who bravely defended it against a knot of enemy horsemen, receiving a disfiguring sword cut across his face and a sabre blow that nearly severed his left arm. Latham continue to fight until he was ridden down, trampled and stabbed by lancers, who triumphantly bore off the shaft of the Colour but not the cloth itself, which shortly before he fell Latham had managed to tear from its fastenings and conceal in his coatee.

Lieutenant Latham defends his regiment's Colour. Lieutenant Mathew Latham bravely defended the King's Colour of the 3rd Foot against French horsemen, who were determined to take it. He suffered a sword cut across his face, his arm was nearly severed by another cut, and he was stabbed by lance blade before being trampled after he fell to the ground. The French triumphantly bore off its staff but not the Colour itself, which Latham managed to conceal beneath his coat. Amazingly, he survived the battle and the Colour was restored to his regiment. (Detail, contemporary lithograph by J. Atkinson)

After the Buffs disintegrated, the French and Poles continued forward into the next unit, the 2/48th Foot, and the scene was repeated. The lancers were particularly vicious, leading Major Brooke of the 48th to conclude that "from the conduct of this regiment on the field of action I believe many of them to have been intoxicated, as they rode over the wounded, barbarously darting their lances into them."[72] There may be some truth to this statement as the ratio of killed to wounded in Colborne's brigade was unduly high, being about one dead to two wounded in the three battalions that were most afflicted by the French attack – an indication that the French and Poles gave the wounded special attention. Stewart and his staff were near the position of the 48th, and as the enemy bore down on them, "Auld Grog" quietly remarked to the officers around him that it was "no use, gentlemen, we must make the best of our way" and the group split and galloped off in all directions.[73]

The third regiment to be hit was the 66th Foot. When the enemy cavalry swept over his company, Lieutenant John Clarke of the 66th recalled that

Our men ran into groups of six or eight, to do the best they could. The officers snatched up muskets and joined them, determined to sell their lives dearly. Quarter was not given. Poor Colonel Waller, of the Quartermaster-

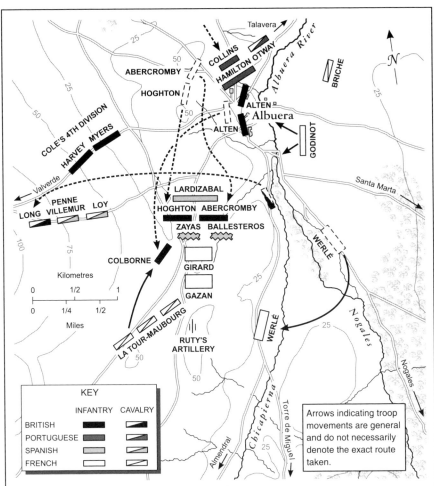

Battle of Albuera, 16 May 1811, Map 2

Due to the limited space, some units in both armies have not been shown and the size of those that do appear has been exaggerated to make them more legible.

As the allied army takes up new positions to meet the French attack, the brigades of Ballesteros and Zayas engage Girard's massive column, bringing it to a halt. In the meantime, Werlé's strong brigade, which had been in a position to support Godinot, moves to the French left, to support Girard.

As the Spanish take heavy casualties, Stewart's division arrives, on Beresford's orders, to support them. Seeing an opportunity, Stewart orders Colborne's brigade to attack the French left flank while Hoghton and Abercromby prepare to move up and take over the battle from the Spanish. Colborne's attack is successful but his brigade is all but destroyed when La Tour-Maubourg, seeing a marvellous opportunity, sends the Polish lancers and two mounted French regiments against his open flank.

General's Staff, was cut down close to me. He held up his hands asking for mercy, but the ruffian cut his fingers off. My Ensign, Hay, was run through the lungs by a lance which came out at his back. He fell, but got up again. The lancer delivered another thrust, the lance striking Hay's breastbone. Down he went, and the Pole rolled over in the mud beside him. In the mélée, when mixed up with lancers, *chasseurs à cheval* [sic] and French infantry, I came into collision with a lancer, and, being knocked over, was taken prisoner.[74]

For his part, Lieutenant George Crompton of the 66th never forgot that terrible day:

It was then that our men began to waver, and for the first time (and God knows I hope the last) I saw the backs of English soldiers turned upon [the] French. Our Regiment once rallied, but to what avail! we were independent of Infantry: out-numbered with Cavalry. ......

Oh, what a day was that. The worst of the story I have not related. Our Colours were taken. I told you before the 2 Ensigns were shot under them; 2 Sergeants shared the same fate. A Lieutenant seized a Musket to defend them, and he was shot to the heart; what could be done against Cavalry?[75]

Colborne's fourth battalion, the 2/31st Foot, was more fortunate. The brigade had gone into action before it had cleared the right flank of the Spanish line and it was still in column behind that line when the cavalry destroyed its sister units. Its commanding officer, Major Guy L'Estrange, "quick as thought, formed square by an original manoeuvre of his own devising" and the sight of the unbroken ranks of the 31st Foot bristling with bayonets caused the lancers and hussars to veer off in search of easier prey.[76] Stewart later praised the 31st for retaining

by its steadiness and spirit, the summit of the hill which had been gained by the rest of the brigade. The conduct of this small corps (it had only 320 firelocks in action), under the command of Major L'Estrange, was so particularly remarked by me during the whole of the action that I feel it to be my duty to state the same in the warmest terms.[77]

The last element to be overrun was Captain Andrew Cleeves's battery on the right of Zayas' line. Seeing trouble coming, Cleeves tried to limber up and move out of harm's way but his position was overrun with fugitives from the infantry regiments, which made escape difficult if not impossible:

I had then no other chance left to cover our soldiers and save the guns (the men ran through our intervals [between the guns], which prevented our limbering up) but to stand firm, and to fight our ground. We prevented the cavalry from breaking our centre; but finding no opposition on our right, they turned us, and cut and piked the gunners of the right detachment down.[78]

Owing to "the bravery and presence of mind" of Sergeants Hebecker and Bussmann of the battery's left division, its two guns were limbered up. According to Cleeves, both pieces would have escaped

but the shaft horses of the right gun were wounded, and came down, and the leading driver on the left gun got shot from his horse. Corporal Henry Fincke had presence of mind enough to quit his horse, to replace the driver, and then galloped boldly through the enemy's cavalry; his own horse, which ran alongside of him, secured him from the enemy's cuts and saved the gun,

French cavalry and lancers destroy Colborne's brigade.
Covered by mist and rain, three regiments of French cavalry, including a regiment of Polish lancers, destroyed three battalions of Colborne's brigade, which were badly positioned on the orders of their divisional commander. As shown here, the lancers were particularly effective and this event so impressed the British army that lancer regiments were eventually introduced into that service. (From James Grant, *British Battles on Land and Sea*)

which I immediately made join the fight again. At this moment I was then made prisoner, but had the luck to escape unhurt.[79]

The two 6-pdr. guns and the howitzer lost by Cleeves were dragged away by the triumphant French.

A small group of lancers continued on past the ruins of Cleeves's battery, riding between Zayas' battalions and Hoghton's brigade, which had just deployed into line behind the Spanish. This was where most of the senior commanders and their staffs were located and their arrival caused tremendous excitement. Schepeler remembered that there was little warning:

> I was in the rear of the 4th battalion of the Spanish Guards, intent on the frontal fighting, when I received a thrust in my back from a lance – which fortunately did me no harm – and discovered that two French horsemen were galloping past me. Colonel von Oppen (who had come along with me to Spain) cut one lancer off his horse: the brigadier, Carlos de España, wanted to shoot the disabled man – so plucky of him! but my gallant German friend prevented him from doing so.[80]

Blake and Zayas and their staffs had to scramble to avoid the lancers as on they swept toward Beresford's position. Grenadier Juan Pastor of the 2nd Battalion of the *Guardias* was attacked by a lancer who fouled his blade in Pastor's greatcoat, giving Pastor a chance to pull the Pole from his horse. One Pole went straight at Beresford with his lance but the marshal "grappled his adversary by the throat and threw him from the saddle."[81] Another lancer charged the staff officers around the marshal and "knocked down one with the butt of his pike [lance], overset another man and horse, and gave ample employment to the entire head-quarters before he was finally dispatched."[82] Eyewitnesses remarked that the Pole "seemed possessed of an evil spirit; and that when he fell at last, he literally bit the ground."

When the intruders galloped by the 29th Foot, it opened fire on them, unfortunately also hitting the rear rank of the Spanish unit in front of them. This caused some confusion and Major Charles Leslie of the 29th remembered that troops from the *Regimiento Irlanda* came pouring back

> mixed pell-mell with a body of the enemy's lancers, who were thrusting and cutting without mercy. Many of the Spaniards threw themselves on the ground, others attempted to get through our line, but this could not be per-

mitted, because we being in line on the slope of a bare, green hill, and such a rush of friends and foes coming down upon us, any opening made to let the former pass would have admitted the enemy also. We had no alternative left but to stand, firing in self-defence on both.[83]

This fire was taken up by the right-hand companies of the 57th Foot, the next unit in line, before Lieutenant-Colonel William Inglis, their commanding officer, could prevent it. He was able to stop it, however, before much damage was done and, as he remarked, the Spanish "had happily not suffered much" as they were higher on the hill than the firing units.[84] Not to be outdone, some of Zayas' rear ranks faced about and also opened fire at the lancers, fortunately inflicting few casualties, either on the enemy or the British troops behind them. The enemy cavalry were unrelenting. Lieutenant John W. Dixon, adjutant of the 48th Foot, who was with Stewart's staff when the attack began, was pursued by two horsemen as far as the lines of the 7th Foot, nearly three-quarters of a mile. Just as the Royal Fusiliers brought their muskets up to fire a volley that cut down the enemy riders, Dixon threw himself off his horse and took shelter on the ground at their feet.[85]

The Polish lancers, remembered many British witnesses, were extremely vicious, rarely giving quarter. Nonetheless, several hundred men of Colborne's brigade, including the brigade commander, were taken prisoner and led to the rear. The Poles treated them particularly badly, Brooke of the 48th claiming that they murdered some of the prisoners in cold blood after they had surrendered and he himself had a close call:

I was being led as a prisoner between two French infantry soldiers, when one of these Lancers rode up, and deliberately cut me down. Then, taking the skirts of my regimental coat, he endeavoured to pull it over my head. Not satisfied with this brutality, the wretch tried by every means in his power to make his horse trample on me, by dragging me along the ground and wheeling his horse over my body. But the beast, more merciful than the rider, absolutely refused to comply with his master's wishes, and carefully avoided putting his feet on me![86]

Brooke was rescued by French soldiers and escorted safely away but his was not the only case of poor treatment. Among the stories that made their way through the ranks of Beresford's British troops was that of an officer who had fallen into their hands, was, as usual, stripped of his watch and money, of which I suppose he had rather a small stock, as there had been no pay issued for some time, on being asked if that was all, and replying in the affirmative, they deliberate cut off one or both of his ears. ......

Another who had singly brought one of the artillery drivers who had been taken, into the wood, after praising his jacket, desired him to take it off, and exultingly went on with every article, individually, in the same way, except the boots, the feet of which being too small, he said were of no use, he might therefore cut them off, give him the legs, and keep the feet as slippers, and when reduced to this state, without the smallest addition of dress, he told him he should take some *mark* to his comrades that he had been in their power, and giving him a stab in the back with his lance, bid him go.[87]

True or not, tales like these led the British to believe that the Poles were "guilty of such atrocities" that several regiments in Beresford's army resolved that, "if they ever meet with them again they will give no quarter."[88]

The destruction of Colborne's brigade had taken place so quickly that there was almost no time for the allied cavalry to react. When the French fell back with their prisoners to regroup, however, Major-General William Lumley and *Mayor-General* Penne-Villemur mounted a counterattack. The visibility being so bad, it had taken some time before the Spanish cavalry commander realized that there was "some kind of disorder" among the British troops on the high ground.[89] Seeing the lancers and hussars retiring from their highly successful attack, he sent *Teniente-Coronel* Antolin Riguilon with half his brigade to attack them, an attack that Riguilon "carried out with so much precision, that the lancers became disordered and were forced to withdraw hurriedly, suffering many losses." At least that is how Penne-Villemur reported it. Captain William Light of the 4th Dragoons, who participated in that charge, had a somewhat different recollection – as he remembered: "we all started, as I thought, to do the thing well; but within a few paces of the enemy the whole [of the Spanish] pulled up, and there was no getting them farther; and in a few moments after I was left alone to run the gauntlet as well as I could."[90]

Lumley then ordered two squadrons of the 4th Dragoons to attack and it seems they did better work. Although the lancers formed to face them, the dragoons were not fazed by the Poles, whose front rank was armed "with long spears, with flags on them, which they flourish about, so as to frighten our horses, and thence either pulled our men off their horses or ran them through."[91] The dragoons discovered that if they could get behind the lance head, their sabres made short work of the man wielding it. The dragoons' attack also took the attention of the French and Poles away from their prisoners, many of whom, including Colborne, took the opportunity to escape. La Tour-Maubourg, however, had been anticipating just such a move by the allied cavalry and was ready to meet it; as the two squadrons of the 4th Dragoons got to grips with the lancers and hussars, he ordered the 20th *Dragons* to attack them in turn. The result was a swirling mélée but the outnumbered British had the worst of it, suffering heavy casualties that included both squadron commanders and "a great proportion of men and horses killed and wounded."[92]

La Tour-Maubourg was proud of his men, who had "charged the English infantry with complete success and in a way that reflects the greatest honour upon those regiments."[93] In his report on the battle, Soult exalted that "three English infantry brigades were entirely destroyed" and "six cannon, 1,000 prisoners and 6 colours (those of the 3rd, 48th and 66th English regiments) were ours for the taking."[94]

It was now about noon and the battle appeared to be going well for *Maréchal* Soult and his army. As *Capitaine* Lapène put it:

This early success predicted the most brilliant outcome, and the day had begun under the most favourable auspices. The right of the enemy, in the second position, could be seen hurriedly forming a square in front of General Latour-Maubourg's cavalry, which, having received its order, was going to outflank this right position, a part of which had already been overwhelmed in the first charge. Hope of a quick victory sparkled in our ranks.[95]

Lieutenant Charles Madden of the 4th Dragoons naturally had a somewhat different view – it was his feeling that the day was starting to take on "an awful unfavourable appearance."[96]

A souvenir of Albuera

A shako plate from the French 55th *Régiment de Ligne* of Werlé's brigade, a
veteran unit with Battle Honours going back to Ulm in 1805, which was picked
up on the battlefield and passed down through the Prevost family. (Courtesy of
Sir Christopher Prevost and the Royal Greenjackets Museum, Winchester)

CHAPTER SEVEN

"FALL IN FUSILEERS!"

ALBUERA, 16 MAY 1811 (2)

Our regiment has conquered but never in vain,
Bear witness those hills and the mountains through Spain,
Bear witness the shades of those hundreds who fell
At red Albuera, and our victory can tell
How Soult and his Frenchmen were beaten and sank,
As we fell on them fiercely, rank after rank,
Invincible seemed those brave children of Mars,
When Lord Beresford styled us the "Gallant Die-Hards."

For Highlanders, Riflemen, Lancers or Guards,
Are not like the boys called the jolly Die-Hards.[1]

fter the destruction of Colborne's brigade, a brief lull descended on the battle. Despite the disaster, Stewart's earlier attack on Girard's left flank had let the steam out of the French column, and although it continued to exchange musketry with the Spanish, the *fantassins* did not advance. In the meantime Major-General Daniel Hoghton and Lieutenant-Colonel Alexander Abercromby, who had deployed their brigades in line behind their allies, prepared to move up and take over the battle. Ensign Hobhouse of the 57th recalled that his regiment was about 20 yards "in the rear of the right of a small body of Spaniards, who were supporting and returning the enemy's fire with the greatest bravery."[2] This "small body" was probably the surviving remnant of Zayas' four battalions as by now their casualties were so heavy that the troops of Zayas and Ballesteros had "clubbed together" into two small bodies.[3] Stewart's two remaining brigades would have to replace the Spanish but it would not be an easy change to carry out as it would involve a "passage of the lines," the movement of different military formations through each other, while under fire.

For his part, *Général de division* Jean-Baptiste Girard was certain he had forced the allies back from their first position and that they would shortly give way in confusion. For this reason apparently, he did not attempt to deploy his massive column into line but, as *Capitaine* Lapène noted, decided

> to continue his advance in the same order, firmly convinced again that the movements of the enemy, on the right and centre of his line, were preparations for retreat. *Général* Girard believed that there was no time to be lost to extend disorder and confusion throughout all the [allied] right. This belief and the fact that the general-in-chief [Soult] and all the army had a perfidious confidence in him, led Girard to the conclusion that there was no point in stopping his attack to deploy his columns …… and, as a result, committed with fatal imprudence, to send the 5th Corps forward again in massed columns and to attack the enemy using the same formation.[4]

The French column, some men in the front ranks shouting "now there are only *Gavachos*," derogatory French slang for Spaniards,* began again to move forward.[5] Unfortunately for the French, instead of *gavachos*, they ran into a two-rank line of His Britannic Majesty's infantry as Hoghton and Abercromby had, with some difficulty, successfully accomplished a "passage of the lines."

Hoghton's brigade (1/29th, 1/48th and 1/57th Foot) was the first to undertake the manoeuvre and Hoghton ordered Lieutenant-Colonel William Inglis of the 57th not to advance until the brigade commander took off his hat "as a signal to him when he wished him to commence."[6] When Inglis saw the signal, he returned it by waving his own hat and then ordered his regiment forward with shouldered arms. Stewart was with the 29th Foot and shouted: "Now is the time – let us give three cheers!" and the 29th then went forward.[7] As the British infantry moved through the Spanish, Schepeler observed that some of the latter were so reluctant "to give back, that I saw the British obliged to elbow them away almost with actual violence."[8] The result was that the manoeuvre was not accomplished smoothly and Hoghton's three battalions became "separated, and fought alone during the remainder of the action."[9] To Hoghton's left, Abercromby's brigade (2/28th, 2/34th and 2/39th Foot) carried out the move-

---

* Curiously enough, *gabachos* (with a "b") was the Spanish derogatory term for the French during the Peninsular war and this is obviously a case of a taunt being thrown back at its originators. A *gabacho* was an uncouth person who spoke badly and the word originated in the Pyrenees region of Spain, where it was often used by the Spanish to describe the French.

ment somewhat more smoothly, although the proud Spanish were no happier about being replaced. Just before his regiment advanced, "a very noble-looking young Spanish officer rode up" to Lieutenant Sherer of the 34th and begged him, "with a sort of proud and brave anxiety, to explain to the English, that his countrymen were ordered to retire, but were not flying."[10]

When the two brigades came into their new position, for the first time they got a clear view of the enemy. Sherer recalled that the "smoky shroud of battle" was "blown aside, and gave to our view the French grenadier caps, their arms, and the whole aspect of their frowning masses."[11] Abercromby formed his three battalions somewhat down the eastern slope of the hill while Hoghton formed where Zayas' troops had made their stand, with the 31st Foot, the sole surviving battalion from Colborne's brigade, on his right. Both brigades immediately came under heavy fire – the 57th Foot received "a most raking and continued cross-fire of musketry from a large body of the Enemy's infantry whose heads were scarcely exposed above the brow of a hill" and Ensign Hobhouse watched as "poor fellows dropped around us in every direction."[12] For its part, the 29th Foot

> advanced up the hill, under a sharp fire from the enemy's light troops, which we did not condescend to return, and they retreated as we moved on. On arriving at the crest of the height, we discovered the enemy a little in rear of it, apparently formed in masses or columns of grand divisions, with light troops and artillery in the intervals between them: from the waving and rising of the ground on which some of these stood, the three or four front-ranks, in some cases, could fire over the heads of one another, and some guns posted on a bank fired over one of the columns.[13]

Hoghton and Abercromby gave orders to return fire and now commenced "a murderous and desperate battle."[14]

After the first few volleys it deteriorated into individual fire as men on both sides loaded, presented and discharged their muskets, almost in a trance. The slaughter was "dreadful," thought Sherer, as "every shot told."[15] As a French commentator noted,

> the English battalions, having completed their movement, began a continuous and well directed firing of two ranks: not one blow [ball] was lost on the tightly massed French column, whose only return fire, which came from its front, was light and insufficient; the soldiers in the rear ranks, seeing their comrades fall without being able to avenge them, became discouraged.[16]

FIX BAYONETS!

Despite the close range, however, the musketry of both sides may not have been that destructive. For one thing it was raining "most violently" and, according to Hobhouse, "the wind blew in our teeth, which prevented us from seeing the enemy during the thickest part of the fire."[17] The rain soaked the vulnerable priming of the muskets, causing a great number of misfires, which the soldiers, functioning like automatons, may not even have noticed. The crowding, the jostling, the tension and the smoke, combined with the attendant inefficiencies of the musket – loose or blunt flints, plugged touch holes and bores, ramrods dropped or fired away – resulted in many rounds being wasted. This was not surprising for, as one British officer put it,

What precision of aim can be expected from soldiers when firing in line? One man is priming; another coming to the present; a third taking, what is called aim; a fourth ramming down his cartridge. After a few shots, the whole body are closely enveloped in smoke, and the enemy is totally invisible; some of the soldiers step out a pace or two, in order to get a better shot; others kneel down; and some have no objection to retire a step or two. The doomed begin to fall, dreadfully mutilated perhaps, and even bold men shrink from the sight; others are wounded, and assisted to the rear by their comrades; so that the whole becomes a line of utter confusion, in which the mass only think of getting their shot fired, they hardly care how in what direction.[18]

Given these problems, it was probably the artillery on both sides who were inflicting a great if not the greater part of the casualties. Major Alexander Dickson of the Royal Artillery, a very professional and experienced gunner, later stated that "on few such occasions had there been more casualties from artillery fire" than at Albuera.[19]

Whatever the cause, the losses were heavy. Hoghton, bravely but perhaps not wisely, remained mounted and "was in the act of cheering on his men" when he was hit several times and fell dead from his horse.[20] "Auld Grog Willie" Stewart, absolutely fearless in action, was also mounted and, although lightly wounded, continued with his men as they fought, loading and firing, closing in as casualties were taken, occasionally advancing a few feet to clear the ever-present smoke, but never taking a backward step. The officers steadied them, closed them in to the centre and attempted to supply them with ammunition from the casualties, which were so numerous that Hobhouse recalled that "you could scarcely avoid treading on the dying and the dead."[21]

224

Artillery in action
A Royal Artillery detachment mans a field piece in action in this sketch by George Jones. The artillery of both sides played a major role in the battle of Albuera, inflicting massive casualties on their opponents. (From George Jones, *The Battle of Waterloo,* 1852)

It was in the middle of this hellish battle that a King's German Legion artillery officer arrived in the lines of the 29th Foot to say "he had brought two or three guns, but that he could find no one to give him orders (our superior officers being all wounded or killed)."[22] "It was suggested" in no uncertain terms by the officers of the 29th "that he could not do wrong in opening directly on the enemy, which was accordingly done." Unfortunately this officer and his gunners did not last long – as Schepeler watched, two field pieces "were run up to replace the English pieces lost in Colborne's rout: they put several telling discharges into the flank of the French column, but ere long their officer and very nearly every one of his gunners were shot down."[23]

Stewart's remaining two brigades fought with steady courage and in his report to Beresford, written two days after the battle, Stewart wrote that,

On none of the many occasions on which British armies have been accustomed to evince high conduct in battle has there been more high or, I believe, more general good conduct than was shown on the 16th instant. The contest was arduous, and our situation was critical. The enemy was more obstinate than usual; and your own expression of determination to myself on the field called forth a more than ordinary degree of exertion and of self-devotion from all. It is my hope that the 2d Division did its duty on that day.[24]

The behaviour of Stewart's men excited the admiration of *Mariscal de Campo* Zayas, who praised the "intrepidity and courage" of his British allies as they loaded and fired, loaded and fired.[25] Inglis of the 57th, who had taken over Hoghton's brigade after that officer was killed, was struck in the chest by a canister bullet but, refusing to be carried to the rear, remained on the ground close to his men, exhorting them to "Die hard, 57th! Die hard!" – thus giving birth to a splendid regimental nickname.[26] By this point, about half an hour after the duel had commenced, the 57th was down to about a third of its strength while the 29th was "so reduced that it resembled a chain of skirmishers in extended order."[27] Major Gregory Way, who succeeded to command of the 29th after White was mortally wounded, was knocked off his horse, "Black Jack," by a musket or canister ball and the senior captain, Captain Thomas Fell, took over that regiment. In a similar fashion, command of the 1/48th devolved on Captain Gilbert Cemetière, a native-born Frenchman who had taken more than 15 years to work his way up from the enlisted ranks. Ensign Richard Vance, carrying the Regimental Colour of the 29th, becoming fearful that it might be taken by the French, tore the cloth from its shaft and concealed it in his coatee, where it was found after his death. His comrade, Ensign Edward Furnace, all of 17 years, "received a severe wound, but declined to leave the field, soon after received another, which proving fatal, terminated his short but honourable career."[28] In the lines of the 57th Foot, musket fire broke the shaft of the King's Colour while the Regimental Colour was pierced by no fewer than 21 balls. As men fell and the battalions closed in toward their centre, the intervals between them grew wider – "there we unflinchingly stood," recorded Leslie of the 29th, and "there we fell, our ranks were at some places swept away by section."[29]

The French, however, had problems of their own. As a French commentator described it:

No blow was lost on our column which, in closed ranks en masse, could only put forward the insufficient and poorly fed fire of its first two ranks. Beyond these positions, our soldiers fell to the right and left, defenceless, and those who survived gave themselves over to the most grievous despondency. The commanders tried in vain to restore confidence to the troops and revive them by their example.[30]

Too late, Girard decided to deploy into line. All his efforts and those of his brigade and regimental commanders to do so, however, were ineffectual. Too many officers had become casualties, the four regiments of the 1st Division had become mixed together and control of the formation was beginning to erode. Girard had violated an important tactical precept of the French army, which was that, if "your men stop in spite of your energetic exhortations and efforts … do not endeavor to keep them near the enemy when their courage fails."[31] Giving up trying to deploy the 1st Division as hopeless, Girard then attempted to have the ten battalions of the 2nd Division execute a "passage of the lines" through that formation but this manoeuvre, "difficult enough when it was calm and there was space available," was impossible under heavy fire and the two formations became inextricably jumbled together.[32] Attempts by the officers to separate them proved costly as three of the four brigade commanders in the two formations were killed or wounded and *Général de division* Honoré Gazan, who appears to have come forward to assist Girard, was wounded.

Major Robert Saint-Chamans, an officer who served on Soult's personal staff for many years, was critical of the clumsy formations used by Girard and his conduct of the battle. As he noted, if the 5th Corps had advanced immediately after the destruction of Colborne's brigade, "we would have achieved a most complete victory, but it had barely arrived at the line of battle, its columns were poorly formed and it did not attack quickly enough to take advantage of the fine cavalry movement."[33] It is curious that Soult, although he was up with the forward troops, did not take a greater hand in the battle. But Soult, too, had his weaknessess. As an officer who had served with the *maréchal* remarked:

This proud man of borrowed reputation was full of confidence the day before a battle; he recovered this confidence the day after a defeat; but on the day of combat, he couldn't give an order, take a position, or have a movement of troops carried out. It seemed that a plan devised and organized at his desk was a decree from above, no part of which could be changed.[34]

Saint-Chamans, echoing this assessment, noted that Soult loved "vigorous enterprises and when once committed to a scheme stuck to it with obstinacy.[35]"
In his report on the battle, Soult rather weakly explained away his failure to

push home his attack by stating that, since the allies had "left us the position we had taken from him," they did not dare "to attack again."[36] The result was that, crowded into dense ranks, barely able to move and nearly unable, except in the front or side ranks, to fire, the *fantassins* of the 5th Corps began to shift from side to side as the casualties mounted and unease spread through their ranks because, not unnaturally, many regarded themselves as "victims to be sacrificed."[37] They did not break, however, but stood their ground, partly because they were so tightly massed together but "chiefly because they were soldiers of the Emperor and brave children of France."[38]

It was now about a half hour after midday and it was very clear to both Beresford and Soult that the deadlock on the hill could only be broken by fresh troops. On his side, Soult ordered *Général de brigade* François Werlé to bring forward his nine battalions to support Girard, while Beresford tried unsuccessfully to get Spanish troops from España's division to advance. They proved so reluctant, however, that the allied commander actually "laid hold of a colonel commanding one corps, and taking him somewhat forcibly to the front, desired him to order his men to follow … declaring that he would lead them on. All was in vain."[39] The closest British or Portuguese troops were Cole's 4th Division on the Valverde road about a mile and a half back, but Beresford did not want to move Cole as he was propping up the outnumbered allied cavalry and also protecting his line of retreat – and Beresford was by this time beginning to seriously think of withdrawing. He therefore sent Major Robert Arbuthnot of his staff to Major-General John Hamilton to order him to bring his Portuguese division forward to support Stewart. Arbuthnot had some difficulty in finding Hamilton as that officer had taken advantage of the discretionary orders given him earlier by Beresford and had become involved in the fighting around the village of Albuera. When the staff officer finally caught up with him, it took Hamilton some time to get his brigades out of Albuera and on the move to the south. Growing impatient at the delay, Beresford himself went to find Hamilton and urge him to hurry.

At this point, one of Beresford's staff officers decided to take matters into his own hands before Stewart's dwindling line on the hill simply melted away. In the opinion of Lieutenant-Colonel Henry Hardinge, Beresford's deputy quartermaster-general, the "desperate state of things" required "an instant remedy."[40] As Beresford was absent, the Spanish apparently could not or would not move and there was no sign of Hamilton's Portuguese division, Hardinge rode to the 4th Division to get help.

He found Major-General Galbraith Lowry Cole, commanding that formation, in rather a bad mood. Cole was under orders from Beresford not to move his division, positioned along the Valverde road, without orders from the marshal himself. In obedience Cole and his regiments had remained as distant spectators of the ferocious battle being waged east of their position. Given rain, smoke and the contours of the ground, they could not see much of the fighting on the hill but were able to gauge, from the noise and the human wreckage limping or crawling back, that it was severe. When no orders came, Cole sent one of his aides, Captain Alexandre de Roverea, to wait on Beresford but Roverea had not returned and, as one of Cole's staff later remarked, the commander of the 4th Divison "continued anxiously to watch the progress of the contest" because without orders he could do nothing.[41]

When a somewhat excited Hardinge rode up and proposed that the 4th Division should attack the French flank, Cole was not at all amused. A competent and professional but somewhat conservative soldier, the 39-year-old Cole had fought in the West Indies, Egypt and at Maida and for two years had commanded a division under Wellington, with whom he had unsuccessfully vied for the hand of Kitty Pakenham. He could sense that the battle was at a crucial point and did not need to be told so by some jumped-up puppy on the Portuguese staff, nor did he need to have a course of action proposed to him by that same puppy because Cole knew, better than Hardinge, what had to be done. Decades later, he would somewhat primly remark that "the advice of Colonel Hardinge, at [age] twenty-three or twenty-four ... without much professional experience," did not carry "the authority which in later years it might have been entitled to."[42] Cole therefore told Hardinge plain that he was under "positive orders" from Beresford "*not* to leave the position" in which he was placed without the marshal's "special instructions."[43] Things were thus at an impasse that was only broken when Lieutenant-Colonel John Rooke, Beresford's deputy adjutant-general, arrived and Cole asked his opinion. Rooke replied that if Stewart's troops were not soon reinforced, the battle would be lost. This seems to have tipped the balance and Cole decided to advance to support the 2nd Division, thus disobeying a direct order but acting, in the words of one of his staff officers, "with a moral courage of which few English generals have given an example."[44]

Cole was fully aware that this advance would be both "hazardous and difficult."[45] His two brigades would have to cross nearly a mile and more of open ground swept by French artillery fire and then move up a slope with their right flank vulnerable to the masses of enemy cavalry. Although he intended to at-

Lieutenant-Colonel Henry Hardinge (1785-1856)
Just 26 years old in 1811, Hardinge served as a senior staff officer to Beresford during the battle of Albuera. Realizing that Stewart's division on the hill would have to be reinforced or the battle was lost, he rode to Major-General Lowry Cole, the commander of the 4th Division and proposed that he move forward and support Stewart. Cole, who was under orders from Beresford only to move on the marshal's personal word, was not amused by this proposal but finally came to the conclusion that he would have to disobey orders and attack. (From W.H. Maxwell, *Life of His Grace, the Duke of Wellington,* 1839)

tack in line, Cole had no intention of marching in that formation because his division would have to move slowly so its units could maintain their alignment. There was also the consideration that, although Lieutenant-Colonel William Myers's Fusilier Brigade was composed of first-class troops, Brigadier-General William Harvey's Portuguese brigade (*Regimentos de Infantaria* nos 11 and 23) was about to fight its first major action. Taking all these factors into consideration, Cole decided to advance in battalion columns in echelon from the left – that is, staggered back from the left to the right – as this would not only allow the two brigades to move faster but would also permit them to deploy into line or square more quickly to counter any threat from the French cavalry. But it was not going to be an easy manoeuvre to execute. As Cole explained it, the 4th Division would have to carry out an evolution "difficult to perform correctly even in a common field-day" and Harvey's brigade would have the worst of it as it would have "to show front to the enemy's cavalry" while at the same time, preserving "its distance from, and cover the right flank of, the Fusilier Brigade."[46]

To provide flank guards for the division, Cole placed the Loyal Lusitanian Legion of battalion strength in column on his left while Major Thomas Pear-

Major-General Lowry Cole (1772-1842)
A professional but somewhat conservative soldier, Cole had once vied unsuccessfully with Wellington for the hand of Kitty Pakenham. A veteran of the Egyptian campaigns and Maida, Cole had the moral courage to disobey a direct order and move his division forward into the battle on the hill. The result was a British victory and one of the most famous prose passages in the English language. (Print after painting by Thomas Lawrence)

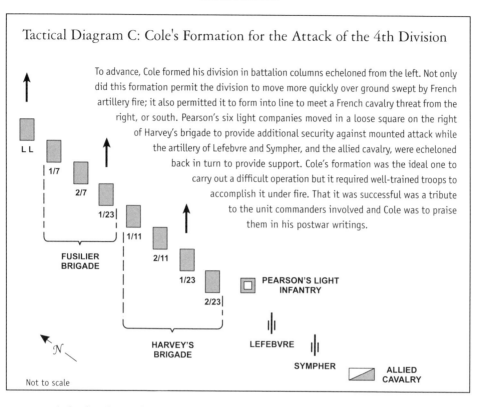

Tactical Diagram C: Cole's Formation for the Attack of the 4th Division

To advance, Cole formed his division in battalion columns echeloned from the left. Not only did this formation permit the division to move more quickly over ground swept by French artillery fire; it also permitted it to form into line to meet a French cavalry threat from the right, or south. Pearson's six light companies moved in a loose square on the right of Harvey's brigade to provide additional security against mounted attack while the artillery of Lefebvre and Sympher, and the allied cavalry, were echeloned back in turn to provide support. Cole's formation was the ideal one to carry out a difficult operation but it required well-trained troops to accomplish it under fire. That it was successful was a tribute to the unit commanders involved and Cole was to praise them in his postwar writings.

L L
1/7
2/7
1/23
1/11
FUSILIER BRIGADE
2/11
1/23
2/23
PEARSON'S LIGHT INFANTRY
HARVEY'S BRIGADE
LEFEBVRE
SYMPHER
ALLIED CAVALRY
𝒩
Not to scale

son (who has been absent from our story for quite some time), was stationed on the right of Harvey's brigade with the three light companies of the Fusilier Brigade and the three "orphan" light companies from Kemmis's brigade. Artillery support would be provided by Captain George Lefebvre's troop of Royal Horse Artillery with four 6-pdr. guns, and Captain Frederick Sympher's No. 2 Company of King's German Legion artillery with five 6-pdr. guns and one 5.5-inch howitzer, which would take position to the right rear of Harvey's brigade and move in tandem with it. Finally, Major-General William Lumley's allied cavalry would move on the far right.

Once made, these decisions were quickly put into effect. Corporal Cooper of the 7th Foot remembered that the shout of "Fall in Fusileers!" brought him and his comrades, who had been sitting or lying under a downpour of rain for the last few hours, to their feet.[47] Obeying the orders of officers and sergeants, the men of the three Fusilier battalions formed close columns of companies, each column consisting of a single company breadth and a nine-company depth (the tenth or light company having been detached under Pearson) with only a few paces between companies. The two regiments of Harvey's brigade, each with two battalions, adopted a similar formation and, finally, the Lusitanian Legion took post on the left of the division while Pearson did the same on the right with his six light companies.

We will never know, of course, what was going through Thomas Pearson's mind at this moment. Perhaps he thought of Ann and the son which she had recently brought into the world, but more likely, having just been given an important independent command, he was too busy to think about anything other than his duties. Although Pearson was not a man given to introspection (which, under the circumstances, was just as well) it must have crossed his mind that he was about to enter the toughest action of his career. As a veteran who had seen combat on three continents and was now at the height of his abilities after 14 years of professional preparation that had begun at Chatham in 1797, Pearson likely did not spare a thought about anything other than getting his six companies, with a total strength of about 300 all ranks, into proper position on the right of Harvey's Portuguese.

As the two brigades were forming, Lieutenant John Harrison of the 23rd Foot arrived, looking for his commanding officer. Harrison had been a mile or so in the rear as part of the brigade baggage guard of about 50 men drawn from all three Fusilier battalions. Just 23 years old and anxious to see action, Harrison was desperate to get rid of this "troublesome office" and join his unit and was, it appears, an enterprising young officer because, ignoring the protests of both the commander of the baggage guard and Major-General Lowry Cole himself, he managed to ride forward to his regiment.[48] When Harrison found it, Lieutenant-Colonel Henry Ellis of the 23rd told him to go "and bring the drums [drummers] up and all the spare hands I could collect from the baggage." Harrison departed on this mission and returned to the unit just in time to take over a company whose captain was absent.

All being ready, Cole and his staff took their proper place in the front of the division, which was now in a line of close columns, nine blocks of red or blue uniforms with about 5,000 men in their ranks. While the battalion commanders at the front of each unit waited for orders to advance, Lieutenant-Colonel Edward Blakeney, commanding the 2/7th Foot, remembered that the fog and heavy rain, which had obscured his vision of the battle on the hill, cleared for a few minutes and suddenly Blakeney could see "the French columns placed in echellon on our side of the hill, with the artillery – twenty-three pieces – above, and an echellon of cavalry on their left flank, covering the whole plain with their swords."[49]

It was about 1 P.M. when Cole issued the cautionary order "The division will advance!" It was repeated by the commanding officer of each unit with the words "The battalion will advance!" and each officer no doubt took care, as the manual of the army advised, to issue these orders "short, quick and loud … to the full extent of his voice, and in a sharp tone" so as to be heard clearly by all those "dependent on his motions."[50] The cautionary was then repeated by the company commanders in each battalion column. Not long afterward came the executive order, "March!" and since the order of march was left in front, the units on the left flank, the Lusitanian Legion and the 1/7th Foot, moved off at the quick step of 108 paces per minute, so as to cross the required distance in the shortest possible time. They were followed, as soon as their predecessors had reached the correct interval, by the 2/7th Foot, the 23rd Foot, the two battalions of 11th Portuguese Line, then of the two of the 23rd Portuguese Line and, finally, Pearson's light infantry companies (see Diagram C).

As the division moved toward that fatal line of hills where the smoke of battle was clearly visible, Private Horsefall of the 7th Foot marching beside Corporal Cooper suddenly asked, "Whor's ar *Arthur?*" meaning Wellington. Cooper replied that he didn't know and hadn't seen him, to which Horsefall responded, "Aw wish he wor here." As Cooper later remarked, "So did I."[51]

As the 4th Division advanced, the Fusilier Brigade almost immediately began to pull ahead of Harvey's brigade. "The remainder of the division followed the movement of the Fusiliers," Major Charles Broke Vere of Cole's staff recorded, "but could not make the same forward progress, and also to keep its order, so as to preserve its echellon to the Fusiliers" but "every effort was made, and effectually," to have the Portuguese brigade cover the right flank of the Fusilier Brigade which "at every step became more exposed."[52] After the 11th and 23rd Portuguese Regiments had gone forward, Pearson's six light companies moved in a hollow square on their right and rear. Then, while Sympher covered his movement with his battery, Lefebvre moved his troop of RHA to a new position to support the advance of all the infantry.

Cole's advance was a complicated business that required technical skill, a high level of training and correct timing lest the disparate parts of the division stray too far apart and be unable to support each other. Cole later generously remarked that, in "the very high state of discipline of the Fusilier Brigade, commanded by officers of acknowledged professional merits and talents … I can claim little merit for the execution of this movement."[53]

The area of the Fusilier Brigade advance
This photograph, looking southeast from the approximate area where the Fusilier Brigade began its advance, shows the open ground over which the formation had to move to reach its objective, which was in the far distance behind the three trees in the right middle-ground. (Photograph by Robert Malcomson)

This statement is perhaps unfortunate for the honest Lowry Cole's military reputation as the attack of the Fusilier Brigade at Albuera was to become a celebrated event in the long and illustrious history of the British army. This was partly because it was a superb feat of arms and partly because it was immortalized in magnificent and sonorous prose written by an author who was both a gifted writer and a contemporary of the men who carried it out. The reality was, however, not quite as dramatic as William Napier would have us believe and the following description, in contrast to Napier's marvellous skill with the language, is a rather plodding but possibly somewhat more accurate account of what really took place in the early afternoon of 16 May 1811.*

The two brigades had not moved a quarter of a mile when they came under artillery fire from the French guns on the ridge. The distance was about 900 yards, extreme range for canister, but the sight of about 5,000 infantry advancing steadily toward the flank of Girard's confused mass on the low hill attracted Ruty's attention. He brought his guns to bear on the new target and it was not long before Myers and Harvey's brigades began to take casualties. Harrison of the 23rd had a close shave when a canister bullet "passed through the centre of my cap, taking the point of my hair and went through several folds of my pocket handkerchief which was in my cap."[54] The battalion columns presented good targets and the fire increased as they began to near the slope. Lapène, who was possibly with Ruty's batteries on the hill, thought that

---

* See Appendix D below for William Napier's famous text describing the attack of the Fusilier Brigade at the battle of Albuera.

Our guns, served thoroughly as opposed to quickly, produced the most terrible effects. Despite his obstinacy in continuing his march onto the ground he had lost, the enemy was stopped by the roundshot and the discharges of canister which rained down on his ranks and ravaged them. The field of battle was furrowed in all directions by our projectiles and their ricochets scoured elongated gaps through their lines.[55]

The Fusiliers may have halted for a moment to re-align their ranks as casualties were taken, but they soon went forward again. Although Cooper saw men "knocked about like skittles" by roundshot, it was clear in his memory that "not a backward step" was taken.[56] The two brigades continued to advance, behaving "most gloriously, never losing their ranks, and closing to their centre as casualties occurred."[57] In the opinion of one historian of the battle, the reason for their cohesion was that

the individual bravery of the soldiers and platoon officers so strongly manifested itself by continuing to advance with unabated ardour and steadiness, after their commanding officers had been mowed down, and while the line was raked so terribly by the destructive fire of the enemy's grape and musketry, which appeared only to increase if possible, their enthusiasm, steadiness, and perseverance.[58]

Smoke and rain limited visibility and Blakeney of the 2/7th Foot "could perceive very little but what was immediately in my front" – but perhaps that also was just as well.[59]

It took the 4th Division about half an hour to cross that fire-swept piece of ground and it would have seemed like an eternity to the men in the ranks. When the Fusilier Brigade was nearly within musket shot, about 100 yards from Werlé's brigade, which had just come over the brow of the ridge, Myers gave the order and it deployed from column into line. At almost the same time, Myers took a canister bullet through his thigh which would ultimately prove mortal, and command devolved on Lieutenant-Colonel Ellis of the 23rd Foot, the next senior officer. Seeing the Fusiliers deploy, Harvey followed suit with his brigade but kept somewhat to the rear, with Pearson keeping his six companies in square on the Portuguese right flank. Lefebvre and Sympher now brought their guns up, probably in echelon to Harvey, and, finally, on the far right, Lumley advanced the allied cavalry. All three arms of the allied army were participating in the counterattack.

Général de brigade François-Jean Werlé (1763-1811)
A veteran soldier who began his military career as an
enlisted man in the French Royal Army in 1781, Werlé was
commissioned in 1792 and had reached the rank *général
de brigade* by 1803. At Albuera he commanded a strong
brigade of nine infantry battalions which fought a desperate
battle with the three battalions the Fusilier Brigade. Werlé
was killed during the battle and his brigade put to rout.
(Courtesy, Tony Broughton)

Werlé had been ordered forward by Soult some time before but his lead units,
the 12th *Léger* and 58th *Ligne,* had become tangled up with the seething mass of
Girard's two divisions and had to be extricated, which took time and hindered
their progress. For this reason Werlé did not come over the ridge in line as he
had apparently planned, but with his nine battalions in three regimental columns, each with a front of two companies (see Diagram D). Soult, who was with
Girard's infantry and fully aware that they were becoming shaky, "hoped, with
the aid of this reinforcement to reassure the morale of the troops engaged and
to re-establish the attack."[60] Werlé halted at the top of the ridge and, to Captain
Jack Hill, commanding the light company of the 23rd Foot under Pearson, it
appeared that the three Fusilier battalions had taken a position "commanded by
another still higher which the enemy occupied, distant about 60 yards."[61]

The Fusilier Brigade faced off almost squarely against the French (see Diagram E). To Blakeney, commanding the 2/7th, the centre battalion of the brigade,
it appeared that the 1/7th on his left was about to engage the left-hand enemy
column, while he faced the centre column and the 23rd the right-hand column.
Harrison, commanding No. 7 Company of the Welch Fusiliers, noted that, because the French "were formed on an eminence," the brigade "had every disadvantage of the ground."[62] He remembered that the enemy opened fire first but the
Fusiliers "returned it handsomely, came down to the charge, and cheered" before
advancing with the bayonet. The French line recoiled, with "others coming to
their assistance" – probably the regiments behind – and the exchange of fire "became general" being "kept up on both sides, so near almost *muzzle to muzzle.*"[63]

Watching from his position on the French left, La Tour-Maubourg sensed
opportunity. After the destruction of Colborne's brigade he had fully "expected
there would be an engagement of cavalry, but that of the enemy, placed in the
rear of a considerable line of infantry, in front of which was a ravine, remained
in its position and offered me no opportunity of attacking it, but at a positive

disadvantage owing to the nature of the ground."[64] Now that "considerable line of infantry" had advanced and the right flank of the Fusilier Brigade, somewhat in advance of Harvey's brigade, offered a tempting target. La Tour therefore decided to send in the veterans of the successful attack against Colborne: Konopka's *Lanciers*, Vinot's 2nd *Hussards* and de Laval's 10th *Hussards*, who swept down on the Fusilier Brigade (see Diagram D).

Captain Jack Hill, stationed with Pearson on the right, watched as the enemy horsemen galloped across his front. Pearson gave them a volley from those of his companies that could bring their muskets to bear, and this may have emptied some saddles. But it did not stop the French who, in Hill's words, "put themselves in order and prepared to charge" the right flank of the 23rd Foot, thinking "the whole unloaded."[65] That flank was held by the Royal Welch Fusilier grenadier company and, as Hill remembered it, the spurs of the enemy cavalry "were in the horses' sides" and "they were coming on," when the grenadiers "fired on them at about 15 paces distant and the file fire recommenced from those who had first fired." It was too much for the horsemen and "they went to the right about and galloped off." Harrison, watching from the centre of the 23rd Foot, thought it happened somewhat differently – he later recorded that the enemy cavalry "advanced *au pas de charge* on our line, but observing us so unshaken and so little

French infantry advancing
At almost the same time Cole moved forward, Soult ordered Werlé to bring up the nine infantry battalions of his strong brigade and the result was a vicious and bloody battle between the Fusilier Brigade and Werlé's infantry. In this drawing, French infantry advance in column wearing the buff or grey wool overcoats that were their common campaign uniform. French soldiers often chopped the sleeves off at the elbows so that they could load and fire their weapons more easily. (Drawing by Edouard Detaille from *L'Armée française*, 1888)

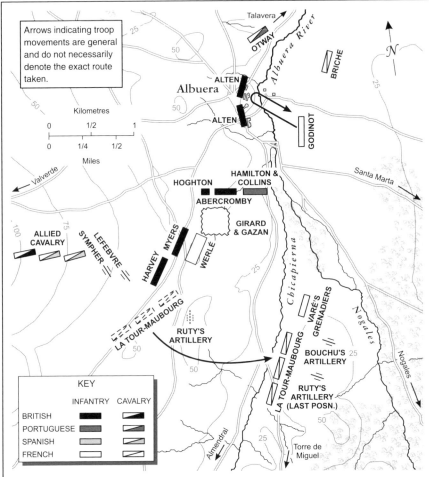

Battle of Albuera, 16 May 1811, Map 3

Due to the limited space, some units in both armies have not been shown and the size of those that do appear has been exaggerated to make them more legible.

Hoghton and Abercromby's brigades take over the battle against Girard. Girard first attempts to deploy into line and then to replace his division with that of Gazan but the two formations become jumbled and confused. Seeing that the two outnumbered British brigades are taking heavy casualties, Beresford orders Hamilton's division to support them but, before this takes place, Cole, sensing the urgency, moves against the French left flank. The Fusilier Brigade meets Werlé's brigade, which Soult has ordered up to support Girard, and a vicious musketry duel ensues.

Beresford, somewhat shaken by his losses, orders Alten to withdraw from the village, which is occupied by Godinot's troops, in preparation for a retreat but soon countermands this order and Alten retakes Albuera. On the hill, the French break and retreat, covered by La Tour-Maubourg's cavalry, Ruty and Bouchu's artillery and two battalions of grenadiers under Varé. The victorious allied army pursues them to the Chicapierna but halts on Beresford's orders.

dismayed at their forceful appearance, when within about one hundred yards, they wheeled about and we saluted their *derrières* with a smart fire."[66]

Notwithstanding the rebuff, La Tour decided to try again. This time the objective was Harvey's brigade and the French cavalry commander may well have thought that the Portuguese would be an easier target than the rock-steady Welch Fusiliers. In any case, he ordered *Colonel* Jean-Baptiste Bouquerot des Essarts' 4th *Dragons* and *Colonel* François Chabert's 20th *Dragons* to charge. As the French horsemen swept down on Harvey's blue line, he saw them coming, and there being no opportunity or time to form square, relied on Pearson's light infantry to preserve his vulnerable flank as Lieutenant-Colonel Donald MacDonald, commanding *Regimento de Infantaria* no. 23 on the right, and Lieutenant-Colonel William Stubbs, commanding the *Regimento de Infantaria* no. 11 on the left, held their men steady. As the dragoons moved toward the waiting Portuguese, they were hit by canister from Lefebvre's RHA troop, which had brought its four 6-pdr. guns into action on Pearson's right rear. Brigadier General Robert Long, who was watching, thought Lefebvre's gunners did "considerable havoc" among the French squadrons.[67] Madden of the 4th Dragoons was more descriptive – he remembered that the horse gunners "mowed them down in six and ten at a time."[68]

The green-uniformed dragoons ignored their losses and came on. At the right moment, and the right range, Harvey gave the order and his two regiments fired a single devastating volley into the horsemen, inflicting heavy casualties. The charge

Portuguese infantry, 1811
Thanks to hard work by Beresford and a select group of British officers, the Portuguese army had been reorganized, re-equipped and properly trained in 1809-1810. At Albuera, Harvey's Portuguese brigade performed very well and by the later years of the Peninsular War the "Johnnies," as the British called their Portuguese comrades, had become excellent soldiers. (From William Bradford, *Sketches of Military Costume in Spain and Portugal,* 1814)

fell apart as the survivors wheeled about and rode away, with Lefebvre getting a second chance to put some canister into them. The two Portuguese regiments displayed such steadiness, Beresford later reported, that their behaviour "would have done honour to the best and most experienced troops."[69] La Tour, for his part, claimed his dragoons had "penetrated the enemy's ranks, sabred some and made some prisoners, though at a considerable sacrifice of men," but the charge failed "because of the nature of the ground."[70] This was the last French cavalry attack of the battle, however, and Harvey gradually brought his brigade forward into line on the right flank of the three Fusilier battalions, which had all the while continued to exchange musketry with Werlé's brigade.

On the hill, meanwhile, Blakeney thought the "firing was most incessant" as the two opposing formations exchanged fire at very close range.[71] Cole recorded that men who had fought at Talavera and in Egypt thought the musketry at Albuera "was more tremendous than at either" and for his part, the commander of the 4th Division "certainly never saw anything like it and I hope I never shall."[72] A few minutes later, Cole was knocked off his horse by canister. Cooper remembered that the 1/7th was taking so many casualties that the orders to "close up" and "close in" were almost continuous and then it was "fire away" and "forward" as the Fusiliers opened up and then moved forward a few paces to clear the smoke of their volley.[73] On the far right of the division, Hill of the 23rd thought this forward movement caused the French to fall back but noted the Fusiliers were suffering heavy casualties not only from musketry but also from the enemy artillery, "which kept up a heavy fire with grape shot and round shot on our line at a very short distance."[74] Harrison, also of the 23rd, recalled that the enemy "again drew us on by showing us their backs, and we twice repeated our former treatment."[75] "This work," he added, "lasted some time, they continuing to bring up fresh regiments, our brigade being much broken by its loss, *not above one third of our men were standing.*" Unfortunately, at this point Harrison received his "reward for the day," a musket ball through the thigh, and had to leave the field.

In the ranks of Werlé's columns things became confused as the officers tried to get their men to cease firing and deploy into line. Blakeney watched

the French officers endeavouring to deploy their columns, but all to no purpose; for, as soon, as the third of a company got out they immediately ran back, to be covered by the front of the column. Our loss was, of course, most severe; but the [three Fusilier] battalions never for an instant ceased advancing, although under artillery firing grape the whole time.[76]

Tactical Diagram D: The 4th Division versus the French

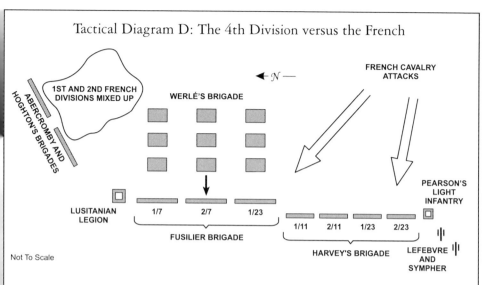

While Hoghton and Abercromby's brigades held off Girard's two divisions, which by this time had become jumbled in confusion, the Fusilier Brigade formed in line and engaged the nine battalions of Werle's brigade in column. The left flank of the Fusilier Brigade was protected by the Lusitanian Legion formed in square and they were supported by the four battalions of Harvey's Portuguese brigade stationed slightly to their rear. Harvey's flank was in turn protected by Pearson's light infantry formed in square and the whole was supported by allied artillery. La Tour-Maubourg's cavalry made two attacks against the 4th Division, one on the right flank of the 23rd Foot and another straight against Harvey's brigade. Both were beaten off.

In such a situation the experience of Werlé's men may have mirrored that of a another French column in the 1809 battle of Talavera:

> The officers and NCOs shouted at the soldiers, "Forward, March; don't fire". Some even cried, "They're surrendering". The forward movement was therefore resumed; but it was not until extremely close range of the English line that the latter stopped its movement, and produced some disorder. While the officers shouted to the soldiers "Forward: Don't open fire" (although firing set in nevertheless), the English suddenly stopped their own fire, and charged with the bayonet. Everything was favourable to them; orderliness, impetus, and the resolution to fight with the bayonet.[77]

While trying to encourage and deploy his men, *Général de brigade* François Werlé, 48 years old and a veteran of three decades of service who had been with Soult since the 1790s, was mortally wounded.

The opposing lines shifted back and forth but the general trend was that the Royal and Welch Fusiliers slowly but surely pushed the French back. At the same time, the enemy centre also came under heavy pressure from the 2nd Division. Captain Alexandre de Roverea, who was with Beresford, recalled that the marshal "gave me the first and only order I received from him, which was to go to the rear and find a Spanish regiment which hadn't suffered much and take it to support the 4th Division."[78] Roverea executed this order by bringing up the *Guardias Walonas* (Walloon Guards) and then rode to the Fusilier Brigade to join the fight.

At this point, however, Beresford took counsel of his fears and prepared for a retreat. The unauthorized attack of Cole's 4th Division, which he had been holding in reserve, seems to have momentarily unnerved the allied commander, and his probable state of mind at the moment has been aptly summed up by one historian of Albuera:

Since his whole strategy was based on keeping the lines of retreat secure using the 4th Division, whilst fighting with the remainder of his troops he must have immediately become concerned to see the last of his British troops [Cole's division] moving forward without orders into the maelstrom on the right. Although hotly contested by Beresford [in later years], his subsequent actions suggest that he had retreat in mind.[79]

Lieutenant-Colonel Sir William Myers (1783-1811)
The commanding officer of the 1/7th Foot, Myers led the Fusilier Brigade throughout the campaign in Estremadura in the spring of 1811. He was killed at Albuera and his two successors as brigade commander, Lieutenant-Colonel Henry Ellis of the 1/23rd Foot and Lieutenant-Colonel Edward Blakeney of the 2/7th Foot, were wounded, at which point Pearson assumed command of the brigade. The commanding officer of the 1/7th Foot during the battle, Major John Nooth, was also wounded. (The Royal Regiment of Fusiliers (City of London) Museum, Tower of London. Photo by John R. Grodzinski)

Beresford's decision, remarked Roverea, happened because the marshal was "frightened by his losses" and had "no further hope of victory." In Roverea's understated but acid opinion, such a retreat "with an enemy fortress (Badajoz) and a river (Guadiana) without a bridge in our rear, and considering the superiority of their Cavalry" would have been difficult, if not disastrous, to carry out.[80]

But Beresford had decided on a retreat and issued the relevant orders. He directed Alten to withdraw his brigade from Albuera to a position on the high hill behind it while Dickson's two Portuguese batteries, which had been supporting it, were ordered to pull back to the Valverde road. The Germans and the units in support had been scrapping with Godinot's infantry and Briche's cavalry around the village and its bridges since 8.30 A.M. that morning but had not had a particularly hard time of it. Lieutenant Madden was sure that the battle on the left flank meant that the allied army was forced "to keep a large portion of our cavalry to keep in check a column which menaced that part, and seem determined to force the bridge."[81] Madden summed up the fighting near the bridges:

> I was stationed near the bridge with the left wing of my regiment, and a squadron and half of the 13th, to cover some guns and defend the ford against a column of cavalry in our front. We had a brigade of Portuguese cavalry in our rear as our support. The enemy moved forward with the intention of attacking us, on which we advanced near the ford, when an immense fire of artillery was opened on us, every shot told; however, our advance had the effect of checking their cavalry. We remained for five hours exposed to a heavy fire of artillery and musketry. We had nine guns playing on them from the church over the bridge, which did great execution. We had also near us a brigade of German rifle men. The uproar and confusion was dreadful, each party cheered when they came to the charge, and every inch that was gained could easily be discovered on which side it went by the immense shout of the parties engaged. They were like an immense body of water ebbing and flowing. Had a man time to reflect, one's situation must have been dreadful, but each man had his point to watch, which took up his whole operation. Wretched objects in all shapes and descriptions were to be seen in every direction, some creeping on their hands and knees, with both their legs shot off, and others in equally a distressing situation.[82]

Despite the colourful language, the casualties on the Allied left were not nearly as heavy as those on the right nor was the fighting as severe. An officer of Alten's 2nd Light Battalion recalled that the French "brought two field-pieces and cavalry three different times to the attack, and got upon the bridge, but were in every instance driven back, and in one they left fifteen behind them."[83] As a German enlisted man expressed it in heavily accented English: "Three times the French was take the bridge; three times they must leave it."[84] It was Lapène's opinion that, if Godinot had pushed his attacks more vigorously, he would have relieved the pressure on Girard and Werlé and prevented Beresford from sending reinforcements against them. This is somewhat unfair because Godinot only had two regiments of infantry with six battalions, supported by Briche's five squadrons of cavalry and a battery of horse artillery. This was not enough to pry Alten's Germans out of their good defensive position, particularly as they were supported by Braun's 9-pdr. battery and Arriaga's 6-pdr. battery positioned near the church of Nostra Señora del Camino. As Lapène noted, the Portuguese gunners had done good work that day, more or less neutralizing Briche's mounted troops:

> Our columns, in their turn, could not fend off the murderous volleys of the cannon placed beside the church, while we were trying to hold on in the village. This cannon wrought no less havoc on General Briche's chasseurs, who were forced, during the greater part of the action, to remain motionless to the right of Godinot's brigade.[85]

It appears that Albuera was never seriously threatened during the battle but, nonetheless, Alten obeyed orders and began to pull his brigade by detachments out of the village. Godinot's troops, seeing their backward movement, "immediately pursued closely and most vehemently, passed the river and bridge on the run and pressed into the village, even before the brigade had completely evacuated it."[86] The withdrawal did not last long. Alten recalled that "just about the time the last detachments were in the act of quitting the village, the battle had been decided in favour of the Allies; and the Marshal's countermand arrived."[87] He "instantly faced about and retook the village, cheering and advancing in double quick time, without meeting with any serious opposition" as the enemy "was found to have thrown only a very few straggling Tirailleurs into the place: and even these were not met with, till the church yard, situated in the centre of the

Général de brigade Jean-Pierre Maransin (1770-1814)
A veteran soldier commanding a brigade under Gazan,
Maransin was grievously wounded at Albuera. He returned
to active service before he was completely recovered, was
wounded twice more and died unseasonably young just
before Napoleon's empire collapsed in the spring of 1814.
(Courtesy, Tony Broughton)

village, had been passed."[88] Although somewhat confused over the reasons for
the withdrawal, *Schütze* Friedrich Lindau of the 2nd Light Battalion remembered retaking the village:

> We had fought for about 1½ hours and lost a lot of people and the enemy
> even more, and then we had to withdraw because the Portuguese positioned
> behind us were to take our place. At this point we were under fire from two
> sides, since the Portuguese, who took us for French, also shot at us until our
> *Oberst* [Colonel] Halkett rushed off to the Portuguese and threatened their
> commander with his sabre; at that moment a ball tore from me my piece
> of mutton that I had put in my knapsack several hours earlier, and another
> went through my canteen.
>   We pulled back through the Portuguese lines and positioned ourselves
> behind the village, where we at once received orders to resume our earlier
> position, since the Portuguese had given way before the French. We fixed
> our sword bayonets on our rifles and with a "Hurrah", went into the village,
> which was already occupied by the French. In the beginning they shot at us,
> but they yielded and retreated, indeed in such a hurry that I alone chased
> ten Frenchmen out of the ruins of a house and only managed to get my
> sword-bayonet into the last of them, running him through as he jumped
> over the wall.[89]

Colonel Annet Morio de l'Isle, commanding the 16th *Léger*, whose unit had
done the greater part of the fighting on the French right flank, obstinately defended the village but was finally forced out of it.[90] Albuera was secure and any
danger to the allied left had dissipated.

B y this time, about 2 P.M., *Mayor* Andreas Schepeler recorded, there was
"fighting going on upon a very long front" with the "allies all in line, according to old custom, the French in column."[91] On the left flank of the allied
line, somewhat down the slope to the Chicapierna stream, was Abercromby's
British brigade with Ballesteros' Spanish units immediately behind. Between
Abercromby and Hoghton's brigades (the latter now commanded by Lieutenant-Colonel Duncan MacDonald of the 57th), both considerably reduced but
still gamely fighting, was Captain James Hawker's battery of four 9-pdr. guns,
which were firing at close range into Girard's wavering columns. On the right
of Hoghton's former brigade was Cleeves of the King's German Legion artillery, who was trying to keep his remaining two 6-pdrs. in action. Major Georg
Julius Hartmann, the British artillery commander, attempted to co-ordinate
the fire of both batteries on the hill with Lefebvre and Sympher's batteries out
in the plain. Coming up behind the two reduced British brigades were Hamilton's Portuguese division and Collins's independent Portuguese brigade. Some
distance to their right was the Fusilier Brigade, now under the command of
Blakeney as Ellis had been wounded, and on the Fusiliers' right was Harvey's
Portuguese brigade. Lumley's cavalry maintained the far right flank on the
plain but La Tour's two recent failed charges seemed to have dampened the
spirit of the French horsemen, although Hill of the 23rd Foot remembered
"some small parties" of enemy cavalry occasionally getting "in our rear" to take
prisoner "the wounded who were getting away from the fire."[92]

The British and Portuguese troops blazed steadily away at the French infantry columns which had become so "closely crowded" that their fire had slack-
ened.[93] Girard's infantry now reached the breaking point:

Colonel [Jean-André] Praefke, of the 28th Léger, forming the head of the
column, was mortally wounded as were almost all his battalion commanders; the despondency could not have been greater: the chasseurs of the 28th,
who were receiving death blows without being able to give any back, felt like
victims of sacrifice; and soon this regiment, already having lost six hundred
men, and in the midst of the most hopeless situation they had ever found
themselves in, without their commanders, whirled in upon itself and disbanded; … finally, the Fifth Corps looked no better than a confused mass
of runaways, the greater part of which threw down their arms and hurried
to rejoin one another far from the battlefield, sheltered from danger on the
other side of [the] Albuhera [River]. The bed of the stream, turned into a

quagmire by the crossing of troops and artillery, posed more obstacles and left the battalions exposed to enemy fire during their hurried escape.[94]

Schepeler, moving forward with Zayas, who had reformed his division behind the right flank of Hoghton's brigade (actually now MacDonald's brigade), was an observant witness of this final stage of the battle:

the foes were blazing into each other at fifteen yards distance only! Zayas brought up his division for the final push: though there were few cartridges left they [the Spanish] came on shoulder to shoulder, the muskets at the slope. When we were hardly ten yards from the French, they suddenly turned and fled – a Portuguese *Cazador* battalion [the Lusitanian Legion] suddenly ran across our flank from the right, and smashed in upon the left of the enemy's mass. The French in the rear, unable to fire from the dense ranks before them, yet suffering many casualties, gave way under the pressure of the recoiling crowd in front. Then the battalions next them on their left, already much thinned and disordered, gave way and followed the first mass of fugitives. We witnessed a rout with complete dispersion! It was like a sudden change of action on the stage of a theatre – from the river bank to the right slope of the hill we could see nothing but the backs of flying Frenchmen.[95]

Captain Alexandre de Roverea saw it much the same: "The French officers made every effort to keep their men, but the first ranks of their column threw themselves on those behind," crying out that "it was butchery and were soon in full flight."[96] Lieutenant Moyle Sherer with the 34th thought that the enemy, "alarmed by our preparatory cheers, which always indicate the charge, broke

Général de brigade Michel-Sylvestre Brayer (1769-1840)
One of Girard's brigade commanders at Albuera, Brayer began his career in a Swiss regiment of the French royal army at age 13. He was commissioned as an officer in the revolutionary army in the early 1790s and fought in the campaigns of 1800 and 1805-1807. Sent to Spain in 1808 as an infantry *colonel*, he was promoted *général de brigade* in 1810. Badly wounded in the leg at Albuera, he did not return to active service until 1813. He rallied to Napoleon during the "One Hundred Days" and for his efforts on the emperor's behalf was arrested and condemned to death by the Bourbons. He escaped to America and later fought in Chile and Argentina as a mercenary. Returning to France in the 1820s, he was reinstated in the army and ended his career as a *général de division*. (From *Portraits des généraux français faisant suite aux victoires et conquêtes des Français*, 1818)

and fled, abandoning some guns and howitzers about sixty yards from us."[97] In the remnants of Hoghton's brigade, Ensign Hobhouse of the 57th recalled that a "general shout" passed down the allied lines, and immediately afterward, came a loud cry of "they run, they run!"[98]

Just as Hamilton, Collins and the Spanish were approaching the front line, a general allied advance began. By this time Pearson was commanding the Fusilier Brigade. He had woken up that morning as one of a number of majors in the brigade but such were its officer casualties – including Myers, Ellis of the 1/23rd and Blakeney of the 2/7th, who had successively taken over command of the formation – that he ended the day as the brigade commander. As the enemy columns begin to dissolve and the allied line moved forward, Pearson, realizing it was no longer necessary, would have commanded the Fusiliers to cease firing before giving the order "Fix Bayonets!" This command was repeated by the battalion and company commanders down the line, and as soon as each soldier in the two ranks heard it he drew his bayonet out of his scabbard with his left hand and fixed it on the muzzle of his musket "with the utmost celerity."[99] The resulting metallic clatter was audible over the noise of battle. Next came the command "Charge Bayonets!" and the two ranks of Fusiliers transformed into a steel-tipped line as the men brought their weapons up, ready for the order to advance against the French. It would have shortly followed and the brigade then moved slowly but steadily forward against the men in Werlé's columns who, not having need of any more encouragement, gave way before them and headed at best possible speed for the eastern bank of the Chicapierna.

The 57th Foot, which had taken such tremendous casualties that it was reduced to the strength of a large company, was about to join in this general advance when Beresford, who had returned to the battle, brought it to a halt with the shout: "Stop! stop the 57th; it would be a sin to let them go on!"[100] At almost the same moment a French artillery shell wounded the unit's last surviving major. A soldier from *Teniente-General* Ballesteros' division found a bloody uniform coat belonging to one of the five French general officers killed or wounded on the hill, and Ensign Hobhouse recalled that Ballesteros promptly

seized it and cried out, though I believe he knew to the contrary, "Soult is dead, my lads, look at this coat," as he rode in front of the lines, and he held up the embroidered coat. He said this in my hearing, and it produced an admirable effect; for both Spaniards and British advanced to the attack with redoubled vigour.[101]

248

A general's coat was not all that was found. Cleeves recovered the three 6-pdr. guns he had lost during the French cavalry charge although the French managed to drag his light 5.5-inch howitzer away. According to *Capitaine* Lapène of Soult's artillery, a determined effort was made to get the 6-pdrs. off the battlefield, but the weak horses and poor drivers assigned to this task, became caught up with the confused mass of Girard and Gazan's infantry and finally cut the traces to the guns and made their escape. The advancing troops also recovered the King's and Regimental Colours of the 3rd Foot, the King's Colour being found on Lieutenant Mathew Latham, who miraculously was still alive, and the Regimental Colour being found on the field. There has been some controversy over the recovery of these trophies as the French insisted that they captured six Colours from the three battalions of Colborne's brigade.[102]

The French retreat, however, did not become a rout and on the enemy left flank it was Ruty's gunners who formed the rearguard for the fleeing infantry – a highly unusual event as *Capitaine* Lapène emphasized:

> There were no columns of French infantry left intact to the left of our line and the skirmishers, just a few of whom remained between the batteries, were only able to offer weak protection to our cannon. The officers and gunners therefore find themselves exposed to a horde of enemy skirmishers; and the number of our artillerymen disabled in battle is considerable; even the ammunition began to run out; a decision had to be made finally, therefore, to end this extraordinary cannon battle against the infantry, and to withdraw conclusively from the battlefield.[103]

To prevent a disaster, Soult now threw in his last reserves, two battalions of grenadiers under *Colonel* Pierre-Louis Varé of the 45th *Ligne*, which formed in line on the east side of the Chicapierna to screen the retreating army. La Tour-Maubourg formed his cavalry on Varé's flanks and the grenadiers were also supported by a reserve battery of two 12-pdr. guns commanded by *Colonel* François-Louis Bouchu. When Ruty got all his guns safely across the Chicapierna, they began to fire at the advancing allied troops to keep them back and the French bombardment, which one officer felt "annoyed us most dreadfully," cost Colonel Richard Collins, commanding the independent Portuguese brigade, a leg.[104] Hartmann moved his batteries forward to return this fire and Sergeant Thomas Bennett of the 13th Light Dragoons, watching the result, thought "the carnage caused by our musketry and shrapnell-shells was immense" with "whole ranks of the enemy mowed down like hay."[105]

The first allied troops to arrive at the Chicapierna were Pearson's six light companies. The other allied infantry came up in turn and Sherer of the 34th noted that, as the French cavalry did not permit "us to pursue, we halted and recommenced firing" at the enemy infantry.[106] "The slaughter," he thought was "for a few minutes, dreadful; every shot told; their officers in vain attempted to rally them; they would make no effort." As the last of Girard and Werlé's *fantassins* splashed across the stream, the Portuguese and Spanish took over the skirmishing but Beresford, mentally overwhelmed by a battle he had never wanted to fight and at one point thought was lost, gave the order not to cross the Chicapierna. It was between 2.30 AND 3.00 P.M. and, although there was scattered firing until nightfall, for all intents and purposes the battle of Albuera, which had lasted about six hours, ended.

Beresford was later criticized for his decision not to keep attacking Soult. For his part, Roverea thought that the French superiority in cavalry, "our immense loss, the irresolution of the Marshal, who should have advanced the Portuguese, were the reasons we were unable to pursue them."[107] *Mayor* Andreas Schepeler, a veteran of the Prussian army, also thought the victory incomplete and explained why:

I have no doubt that if the allied centre had pushed on without hesitation, the whole French army would have been cut in two and dispersed. But we had not a single squadron on this part of the field, and the victorious infantry, to the right of the hill, surprised by the suddenness of the rout, came on slowly and with pauses. I rode up twice to the Portuguese brigades in the centre, and begged their brigadiers to charge on without hesitation – once when the French infantry were streaming down back of the heights, and on the second occasion when the French cavalry were recrossing the Albuera bottom. On each occasion I was told that no orders had come from the Marshal. I got together some Spaniards who had still cartridges left, and sent them firing into the flank of the disordered cavalry who were fording the river. From the effect of this trifling diversion one saw what tremendous results would have been produced by the attack of a few battalions accompanied by any sort of a cavalry charge.

The Mass of Latour Maubourg's horsemen, passing the Albuera at two fords in demoralized groups, might thank the kind General Lumley for their escape from complete destruction. He cautiously drew up his squadrons in line above the river, and set his battery to shell the crowd. But not one battalion was sent forward to blaze into the jammed masses of horsemen. And when the infantry had won the victory the cavalry ought to have completed it! Lumley might have dared anything, considering the marked disorder of the close-pressed throng. ......

But Beresford also was letting the enemy off too easily! It took the French some time before they could get a few battalions reformed on the further bank of the Albuera, under cover of their artillery. We were in those days too little acquainted with the Goddess of Victory – we stood astounded at Fortune's smile, and were contented with having inflicted a complete repulse on the enemy![108]

The British and Spanish units which had born the brunt of the fighting were replaced by the fresher Portuguese troops and withdrawn to the rear. After the French had been pushed out of the village and over the river, Lindau remembered that scattered shooting continued around Albuera until almost evening when "the enemy called over to us – they were Alsatians and spoke German – saying that they had had more than enough for today" and "wanted to cease firing, and we wanted to do the same" so "peace and quiet descended on our flank, but the rain, which had not stopped the entire day, poured down in torrents."[109]

The shooting eventually tailed off and the soldiers of both armies, most of whom were soaking wet, were not cheered by the fact that, as night came on, the rain became quite heavy. In the area of the greatest fighting on the ridge, one witness later wrote that the blood "was so profuse, that in several places, mingling with the rain, it ran in torrents like blood itself; but recollect, at this moment, it had, *within* the space of three-quarters of a mile, flowed from the veins of upwards of 8000 men ... the scene may be imagined, but I will not attempt to describe it."[110] The exhausted survivors of the battle, staring at sights like this, wondered why they were still alive.

But the human spirit is an amazing thing and they soon recovered. Ensign Benjamin Hobhouse, probably all of 17 years old, had just fought his first major battle, and he and one other officer of the 57th Foot "were the only ones who had not some scratch or shot through their cloathes."[111] Determined to prove that they had tried just as hard as their comrades, the two officers searched diligently "for some hole" in their uniforms to prove their determination and their "anxiety to find one, and our want of success, created a great laugh against us."

The paths of glory lead but to the grave.
As darkness fell and the shooting died away, the fields and hills around
the ruined village of Albuera were littered with the bodies of about
14,000 dead and wounded soldiers. Albuera was the bloodiest battle
of the Peninsular War fought by British troops and its very name has
become a watchword for the steadiness and courage of the British
infantry. (Drawing by George Balbar, reproduced with permission from
Robert Foley, *The War of 1812*)

"THE ROYAL WELCH FUSILIERS ... THE VERY THING"

SPAIN AND PORTUGAL, MAY – NOVEMBER 1811

Frae a' lang marches on rainy days,
And frae a' stappages out o' our pays,
And frae the washerwoman's bills, on the damned claise,
Gude Lord deliver us.

Frae a' bridewell cages and blackholes,
And officers' canes, wi' their halbert poles,
And frae the nine-tailed cat that opposes our souls,
Gude Lord deliver us.

May a' officers who make poor men stand,
Tied up to the halberts, foot, thigh and hand,
Die rotten in the pox, and afterwards be damn'd,
Gude Lord deliver us.[1]

Whinen the fighting ended, the area around the little village of Albuera was a vista of unrelenting horror. Nearly 14,000 men lay dead and wounded in the fields about the place, with about 6,500 sprawled in the location of the heaviest fighting, an area no greater than a half mile square. Never, wrote Brigadier-General Robert Long, had he witnessed such "carnage in the same space of ground," it was "a human slaughter house."[2] Corporal Cooper of the 7th Foot remembered that "the dead were in heaps" with one pile being nearly three feet high.[3] Another observer noted that the bodies "were seldom scattered about, as witnessed after former battles, but lying in rows or heaps; in several places whole subdivisions or sections appear to have been prostrated by one tremendous charge or volley."[4] *Mayor* Andreas von Schepeler recalled that the worst slaughter was to be found where Zayas and Stewart's men had fought Girard's columns:

For a depth of about 100 yards the ground was absolutely covered with dead, on the part where the two parties had stood opposite each other for so long. I noted a complete line of blue corpses where the Spanish Guard battalions had stood, and a corresponding line of red-coated corpses where Hoghton's British brigade had fought, the two ranks were in each case clearly visible.[5]

The casualty figures were frightful. Beresford had lost 5,916 men from a total strength of 35,284, or 17% of the allied army. The heaviest toll, however, fell on his British infantry, the troops he could least spare, who had suffered 4,159 killed and wounded, or 40% of their numbers. The Spanish and Portuguese loss was less, being 1,368 and 359, or 9% and 4% respectively of their totals present, the greater part in Zayas' Spanish division and the Portuguese units of the 4th Division – the Lusitanian Legion suffering nearly half of all the Portuguese casualties. Stewart's 2nd Division had been dreadfully cut up. Colborne had 1,413 men killed, wounded or missing in his brigade, 69% of his strength, with the 3rd Foot reporting the loss of 85% of its numbers,[6] while Hoghton's brigade lost 62% casualties. Abercromby's brigade suffered less but still lost 24% of its number. Officer casualties were also very high in the 2nd Division and at the end of the battle the remnants of Hoghton's brigade were commanded by a captain from the 48th Foot with the appropriate name of Cemetière.

The losses of the Fusilier Brigade were as grim: 1,045 of its strength of 2,015 officers and men had fallen, or a 52% casualty rate. The 1/7th Foot suffered 50% losses, the 2/7th lost 62% and the Welch Fusiliers 46% of their numbers. Again, officer casualties were heavy: 43 of the 96 officers present with the brigade that morning were casualties, with Myers, the brigade commander, being killed, while the commanders of the 1/7th, 2/7th and 1/23rd, Nooth, Blakeney and Ellis, were wounded. Cole, the divisional commander, was wounded, as were five of his six staff. In the Welch Fusiliers, two officers and 74 enlisted men were killed and 12 officers and 341 enlisted men wounded or missing. The losses of the three Fusilier light companies under Pearson's command were not separated from the totals for their battalions, but as the three orphan light companies from Kemmis's brigade reported 20 killed and wounded, the total for Pearson's command would probably have been 40 to 50 men. So heavy was the officer loss in the Fusilier Brigade that Major Thomas Pearson was the only field officer in that formation still standing when the battle ended.

Soult's losses were as high, if not worse. Although the French commander at first claimed that he only suffered 2,800 killed and wounded, this figure has

On the march in the Peninsula
In this 1811 cartoon by Thomas Rowlandson, soldiers' wives accompany a regiment on the march. Note the young officer being carried by one wife and the children clinging to their mothers as they cross a stream. Although they were difficult to discipline and often the cause of trouble, women and their children accompanied the British army throughout its campaigns in the Peninsula. (Author's collection)

been steadily revised upward by historians, and possibly the most accurate estimate is that of nearly 8,000 French casualties made by Charles Oman. The *Lanciers de la Vistule*, who had played such a significant part in the battle, lost 130 of 591 men, or 22% of their strength, but the heaviest French losses were in the infantry divisions of Gazan and Girard, 3,128 from a total strength of 8,437, or a 37% casualty rate.

The arithmetic, however, does not convey the true horror of the bloodiest action to be fought by British troops during five years of campaigning in the Peninsula. Medical personnel were few in numbers – at best each infantry battalion had a surgeon and two assistant surgeons – and the medical services were neither organized nor equipped to cope with the numbers of wounded. Even finding, collecting and transporting them to the surgeons was difficult. The Welch Fusiliers, for example, had 404 very tired officers and men on their feet at the end of the day to assist the 257 casualties of their regiment. Beresford requested help from Blake to transport the British wounded and bury the dead, only to receive the reply that each nation should be responsible for its own casualties. "To be short," Cooper of the 7th Foot noted, "the wounded that could not walk were carried in blankets to the bottom of the bloody hill, and laid among the wet grass. Whether they had orderlies to wait on them, or how many lived or died, I can't tell."[7]

Lieutenant John Harrison of the 23rd Foot was one of the fortunate ones. Hit in the thigh by a musket ball towards the end of the action, he

hobbled about half a mile to the rear, when I met our Sergeant Sutler who, with the feelings and foresight of an old soldier, had brought a horse for the relief of his comrades and conveyed me about half a mile to the rear where their baggage was then standing, where I was glad to lay down. It was now between one and two [P.M.], and commenced raining hard and never ceased the whole evening. ...... Having laid in this state for nearly four hours, and seeing no chances of conveyance except my horse, there not being more than two or three wagons employed, which were obliged to attend to those in greater distress, and not admiring my berth for the night, I summed up resolution and proposed to Castle [his soldier servant] to accompany me on a mule which he consented. With some difficulty and much pain I was mounted and we set off for Valverde.

The road presented a shocking scene, numbers exerting themselves to avoid the inclemency of the night from which numbers lost their lives. Not being more than two leagues [6 miles] we reached Valverde soon after ten. I had previously sent my servant on to endeavour to get us an empty hovel, but this was out of the question, and we pigged in with some soldiers of the Buffs. Still no "Pill" [surgeon] was to be procured, being few in number and having many subjects. ...... I refreshed myself with a little tea and bread, which was all the sustenance I had that day, but not withstanding slept pretty well on a little straw until morning.[8]

Harrison was lucky to be evacuated; many others were not, among them Ensign Hay of the 66th Foot, who had taken a lance thrust through his lung. In the evening, Lieutenant John Clarke went to look for Hay and found him "quite cool and collected" but "sitting up to his hips in mud and water."[9] Hay told his comrade not to bother with him as "there were many worse" who required immediate attention. *Schütze* Lindau encountered another unfortunate when he was posted that evening in a position just outside Albuera. A veteran soldier, Lindau immediately found himself a soft place and lay down, but I did not sleep all night on account of the cold and stormy rain, and an abominable stench close beside me. So I crept stealthily into the village to try and find food; and there heard all at once a soft whimpering. I went in search of it and recognized an officer from our battalion, *Hauptmann* Heise, who, with his face full of blood, told me in a feeble voice to shoot him dead. I shuddered at his distress and comforted him, for I liked him, he was a real friend to the soldiers. With kindly words I told him he should be patient and that he would soon feel better, then I put some hay under his head, hurried back to my picquet and lay down once more.[10]

Hauptmann Arnold Heise later died from his wounds.

It was a terrible night. There being no wood available, Schepeler recalled, "miserable fires were kindled from damp herbage and sedge, fed with the butts of thousands of broken muskets which lay around."[11] Most of the wounded remained, untended, on the field through the night and Cooper remembered lying "among the mire and dead men," being unable to sleep because of hunger and cold, but seeing "a poor wounded man stark naked, crawling about, I suppose, for shelter."[12] Sherer of the 34th recalled that the French wounded would grasp at the coats of the British soldiers to beg for protection from "the exasperated and revengeful" Spaniards because they knew what was coming.[13] Serving with the Spanish, Schepeler had a somewhat different opinion:

As I was riding about the place where the French first line had stood, I heard many of their wounded asking for protection, generally inquiring for an English officer, in fear of being killed off by the Spaniards. Some of the English narrators of the fight take this as a proof of the chivalry with which they always conducted war. But remember – the French had never been wasting and burning the English countryside! Would British soldiers have been so humane if the struggle had been waged in their own land? I doubt it. If so, their cold-bloodedness would have approached insensibility.[14]

When darkness fell, local civilians, camp followers and even soldiers crept among the human wreckage, looting and stripping the dead and wounded of all nations without discrimination and sometimes killing any wounded who had the strength to resist. A group of soldiers' wives of the 1/48th Foot went out to guard their regiment's wounded against marauding Spanish and Portuguese women, many of whom were armed with hammers or rocks to end any resistance on the part of their victims. As the survivors, sitting or lying on ground trampled

Stripping the dead
In this graphic drawing by the Spanish artist Goya, the dead and wounded are stripped
of their clothes, money and possessions. Several eyewitnesses recorded similar scenes at
Albuera and the ghouls who carried out this awful work were not above killing the wounded
if they resisted such treament. (Print after Goya, "The Horrors of War")

by the opposing armies and slick with blood, clustered around fires fuelled by
abandoned muskets, near them in the dark the wounded crawled, moaned or
implored while shadowy figures moved about carrying out their ghastly work.
What made that awful night worse, one survivor remembered, was the incessant
howling of the wolves in the distance.

When morning came, both armies stood to their arms and formed for battle. Neither was in any condition to renew the fight and, if anything, the scene
was worse by daylight. When Kemmis's brigade of the 4th Division, 30 hours
on their march from Badajoz, arrived at Albuera at about 6 A.M. on 17 May it
piled its arms and, as a man of the 27th Foot remembered, "gazed on the terrific
scene before us; a total suspension took place of that noisy gaiety so characteristic of Irish soldiers."[15] Before them

> lay the appalling sight of upwards of 6000 men, dead, and mostly stark-naked,
> having, as we were informed, been stripped by the Spaniards, during the night;
> their bodies disfigured with dirt and clotted blood, and torn with deadly gash-
> es inflicted by the bullet, bayonet, sword, or lance, that had terminated their
> existence. Those who had been killed outright, appeared merely in the pallid

Burying the dead
In the days after the battle, the allied army had to dispose of thousands of corpses. The allied dead were buried in mass graves as shown in this drawing by George Jones, and the French were heaped on pyres and burned. The work was apparently done carelessly and the battlefield remained a ghastly sight for months. (From George Jones, *The Battle of Waterloo,* 1852)

sleep of death, while others, whose wounds had been less suddenly fatal, from the agonies of their last struggle, exhibited a fearful distortion of features.

Near our arms was a small stream almost choked with the bodies of the dead, and from the deep traces of blood on its miry margin, it was evident that many of them had crawled thither to allay their last thirst. The waters of this oozing stream were so deeply tinged, that it seemed actually to run blood.

A few perches* distant was a draw-well, about which were collected several hundreds of those severely wounded, who had crept or been carried thither. They were sitting, or lying, in the puddle, and each time the bucket reached the surface with its scanty supply, there was a clamorous and heart-rending confusion; the cries for water resounding in at least ten languages, while a kindness of feeling was visible in the manner this beverage was passed to each other.[16]

For three days, the survivors of the 4th Division, assisted by 1,500 Spanish infantry that Blake grudgingly but finally provided, collected and transported the wounded from the battlefield. The majority of the British wounded were

---

* A perch equals a rod which is 5.5 yards or 16.5 feet.

removed to Valverde and ultimately to Elvas, where medical personnel such as Surgeon George Guthrie laboured 18 hours a day for three weeks in hastily-created operating rooms. For serious wounds of the limbs, military surgeons resorted to amputation because it converted a complicated wound into one simpler to tend and because it was the best way to counteract the inevitable gangrene. If alcohol or opium was available, the patient might receive some before the procedure, but more commonlythe surgeons resorted to straps and strong assistants to hold down the afflicted while the procedure was carried out. Thousands of men lay in makeshift hospitals for weeks after the battle and their situation was truly heart-rending, Among them was Sir George Prevost's nephew, Lieutenant Henry Prevost of the 1/7th Foot, who was mortally wounded but who "bore his sufferings afterwards with equal manfulness, indeed the surgeons declare this as a strong instance of what we mortals can bear when dire and painful necessity requires it."[17]

Surgeon George Guthrie, one of more eminent members of his profession attached to the Peninsular army, treated the wounded after Albuera and his case notes provide some details of the wounds inflicted and their treatment. Captain Wade, one of Cole's aides de camp was hit in the side by a musket ball which Guthrie could not extract but Wade "gradually recovered his health" although a "small funguous protrusion and discharge continued … for several years, with a certain degree of pain, and occasional lameness in the leg and thigh."[18] Wade survived until 1847 when he had an appointment with Guthrie for an examination, which he missed because he was "suddenly cut off by apoplexy." Sergeant Baptiste Ponheit of the 64th *Ligne* was hit by a musket ball in the upper thigh near the femoral artery and lost a great deal of blood but was in fairly stable condition until ten days after the battle when the wound opened and bled copiously. Guthrie placed a screw tourniquet above it and instructed the sergeant how to use it and things seemed to be going well for the man, until the circulation in his bad leg became restricted and the limb became so swollen and discoloured that there was no doubt that "mortification" or gangrene had set in. By the time Ponheit died, the leg up to the location of the wound was "nearly all in a gangrenous state."[19] Guthrie was interested to discover that lance wounds tended to heal more quickly than bayonet wounds, a fact he attributed to the larger puncture which "does not afford so great an obstacle to the discharge of fluids poured out or secreted as when the opening is small" and his conclusion was that lance wounds were actually less dangerous than those inflicted by the bayonet.[20]

In the weeks that followed, as transport became available, the wounded were

Caring for the wounded
For weeks following the battle medical personnel laboured ceaselessly to treat the wounded. Neither army was prepared for the heavy numbers of wounded and Albuera proved to be a medical catastrophe. (Drawing by George Balbar reproduced with permission from Robert Foley, *The War of 1812*)

moved from Elvas back to Lisbon, a 75-mile journey. Conditions on the road were terrible and many did not survive the trip. A British dragoon moving forward nearly a month after Albuera recalled that his regiment encountered a convoy of 700 wounded men from the battle being transported to Lisbon on carts. Their wounds had not been dressed since they had left Elvas and the dragoons tried to assist these poor unfortunates by sheltering them in houses, which they hastily cleaned. They also tried to dress their wounds but repeatedly had to "quit the miserable patients in a hurry, and run out into the open air, to save ourselves from fainting" from the smell. This same witness recorded that on one cart lay a French soldier and an Irish soldier, both of whom had lost their legs but "who ceased not to abuse and revile one another from morning till night" in "their respective tongues, and threatening one another in a manner strikingly characteristic of their two nations." The dragoon was so affected by his experience that for days he "could neither sleep nor eat, for everything seemed to be tainted with effluvia from these cankered wounds."[21]

The plight of the French wounded was worse. *Maréchal* Soult abandoned many on the battlefield and the allied troops eventually carried them to Albuera. When Soult retreated on 18 May, he left hundreds of seriously wounded on the east side of the river. Already dealing with his own medical crisis, Beresford sent a flag of truce into Badajoz on 21 May "demanding Medical Assistance, clothing, &c. for the French Wounded. We have none for them. We have fed and dressed and attended them, but we can't recover or remove them."[22] The governor, *Général de brigade* Armand Philippon, replied that he could do nothing and, D'Urban recorded, "thus they must perish." In actual fact, though their chances of survival were worse than the allied wounded, these Frenchmen were ultimately evacuated through the British medical system.

Even those of his wounded whom Soult was able to transport faced a grim journey to Seville, piled in supply and ammunition wagons whose contents had been hastily dumped. Under the command of *Général* Gazan, this hospital convoy moved ahead of the main body of the Army of the South, which acted as a rear guard. Conditions on this march were terrible: Gazan complained that he had only five surgeons to treat 4,000 afflicted men. Major William Brooke of the 48th Foot, who had been captured during the battle, recalled that, with almost no medical attention available, between 600 and 700 men in the hospital convoy died during an awful journey in unsprung wagons in savage heat.[23]

There was also the problem of disposing of more than 2,000 bodies lying about the battlefield. Although the evidence is not conclusive it appears that this task was left to Spanish civilians working under military supervision who buried the allied dead in large trenches and burned the French on funeral pyres. Because of the heat, this work was done quickly and, it appears, carelessly as a British officer who visited Albuera a month after the battle was shocked to find corpses lying "half roasted in every direction" and the trees covered "with eagles and birds of prey" waiting to resume their feeding which he had interrupted.[24] In May 1812, a full year after the battle, a British regiment which camped at Albuera found a trench 40 yards long "nearly half filled with human skeletons, without so much as one handful of mould sprinkled over them, to screen them from the eye of the eagle, the vulture, or carrion crow."[25] It was dreadful scenes like these that created in Surgeon Charles Boutflower of the 40th Foot, a veteran soldier, "a disgust for the army I never before entertained."[26]

Marshal William Beresford was not a popular man after the battle. Harrison of the 23rd believed that "every soldier did his duty, but there is not much doubt a great want of Generalship was evinced throughout the whole affair, otherwise our success must have been more complete."[27] Some of Harrison's discontented comrades "complained bitterly that the army had been sacrificed by a series of blunders" and feeling against Beresford was widespread, not only among those under his immediate command but also throughout the Peninsular army. Brigadier-General Robert Long, no friend of the marshal, noted that "I have never said half as much against him as I hear from others."[28] Lieutenant William Tomkinson of the 16th Light Dragoons recalled that among his comrades considerable blame "was attached to Beresford for the way he fought, having neglected to occupy the key to the position" and for having "lost his head when the enemy gained the hill" after which "he was for an immediate retreat."[29] Although not present at the battle, Lieutenant John Mills of the Guards was scathing: "Beresford is the most noted bungler that ever played at the game of soldiers, and at Albuera he out-bungled himself."[30] A common refrain was that, if Wellington had been present, the losses would have been less and the outcome more decisive. One officer noted that the complaints about Beresford often "ended with some expressions of deep regret for the absence of him … whose presence gave us additional courage, and under whom we deemed ourselves invincible and certain of success."[31]

Wellington, who had ridden hard for the south as soon as he had learned of Soult's advance from Seville, arrived at Albuera on 21 May 1811. Publicly, he supported Beresford, particularly because, appalled by his heavy losses, that officer was in a state of near shock and confessed to Wellington that he was unable to forgive himself "for risking this battle" as it was "unwise" and "I ought

Spanish memorial at Albuera
In the years after the war the Spanish government erected a memorial in the village of Albuera which can be seen today. Although it gives much credit to the Spanish commanders, it acknowledges that they fought under Beresford's command. (From James Grant, *British Battles on Land and Sea*)

not to have done it."[32] His superior delivered the realistic advice to Beresford that no general could win "such an action without a large loss; and we must make up our minds to affairs of this kind sometimes, or give up the game."[33] That being said, Wellington was not happy with Beresford's report on the battle, written "quite in a desponding tone," and, telling him that "this won't do," directed the marshal to "write me down a victory."[34] The wording was accordingly changed to a more positive account of a resounding but bloody success in which Beresford paid full credit to the men who had earned it:

It is impossible, by any description, to do justice to the distinguished gallantry of the troops; but every individual most nobly did his duty, and which will be well proved by the great loss we have suffered, though repulsing the enemy; and it is observed that our dead, particularly of the 57th regiment, were lying, as they had fought, in ranks, and every wound was in the front.[35]

Beresford's report of the battle, written to Wellington, was taken to England by Major Robert Arbuthnot, his military secretary. Arbuthnot reached London at about 5 P.M. on 2 June 1811 and "the Park and Tower guns were fired late the same evening" in celebration.[36] By this time many Britons knew that a bloody battle had taken place in Spain as many of the survivors, and Pearson was probably among them, had written short notes soon after the engagement to reassure their families and loved ones that they were unharmed. Beresford received a Vote of Thanks from parliament, which did not please many serving in the Peninsula – as one officer remarked, "Good John Bull, how easily art thou duped."[37]

In private, Wellington was much less supportive of his subordinate. A commander who husbanded the lives of his troops, he was angered by the losses and, having ridden over the ground, not pleased with Beresford's dispositions, remarking that "his right seems to have been where his left should have been."[38] Writing to a friend in England, he summed up the "strange concern" of Albuera, using the term "they" to mean Beresford and his staff:

They were never determined to fight it; they did not occupy the ground as they ought; they were ready to run away at every moment from the time it commenced till the French retired, and if it had not been for me, who am suffering from the loss and disorganization occasioned by the battle, they would have written a whining report upon it, which would have driven the people in England mad.[39]

On 27 May, 11 days after the battle, Wellington sent Beresford back to Lisbon on the pretext that the marshal's services were needed there to supervise the administration of the Portuguese army. Beresford made no complaint and actually seems to have suffered a mild nervous collapse which kept him from active duty. D'Urban described his superior's problems as "a lingering Feverish affection and great debility."[40] Captain William Warre, one of Beresford's staff, noted in June 1811 that the marshal needed "some time of quiet body and mind to put him quite right again."[41] It would actually take Beresford more than six months to recover and he did not rejoin the army until early 1812. Although he held important commands in 1813 and 1814, he was never again given the independence he had enjoyed in the spring of 1811. Unfortunately for Beresford, Albuera would continue to haunt him decades after it was fought.[42]

For his part Soult was disingenuous rather than generous. Reporting to Paris, he tried to claim Albuera as a victory because, as we shall see, the siege of Badajoz was lifted a second time in June. This claim of success did not withstand the close scrutiny of his imperial master, who, having examined the returns of Soult's forces, acidly informed the marshal that,

> It seemed to His Majesty that the battle of 16 May should have gone in your favour, had you remained in your position; according to news from London, it is clear that the English wanted to withdraw. The Emperor found that you had not assembled enough troops for this battle, that you ought to have been able to get 8,000 to 10,000 more men; for, after all the fuss of placing the troops, there were plenty of them scattered beside Cordova, Jaen, etc. etc.[43]

"When one decides to wage battle, one must assemble as far as possible, all one's forces," was the Napoleon's advice to Soult, and the emperor added that he was "upset to see that this principle is, as a rule, not practiced enough." As for his British opponents, Soult was apparently heard to complain that there was

> no beating these fellows, in spite of their Generals. I always thought them bad soldiers, and now I am sure of it; for I turned their right flank, penetrated their centre; they were completely beat and the day mine, but yet they would not run."[44]

In the weeks following the battle, Pearson commanded the Fusilier Brigade, which was temporarily attached to Stewart's 2nd Division. In his absence from the 23rd Foot, Captain Jack Hill, the sole officer survivor of the 1799 *Valk* disaster and commander of the Welch Fusilier light company, took over the battalion. It was universally acknowledged in Beresford's army that the Fusilier Brigade had played a decisive part in the battle. As Major Henry Hardinge wrote to Cole: "The Fuziliers exceeded anything the usual word gallantry can convey, and your movement on the left flank of the enemy unquestionably saved the day and decided the victory."[45] "Auld Grog Willie" Stewart agreed that the conduct of the brigade was not only "admirable" but "effectually secured the victory of the day" and he was instrumental in getting a deserving NCO from each of the three Fusilier battalions a field commission as an ensign.[46] As was normal after a victory – even a disputed victory – officers who had commanded corps or units during the action were eligible for field officer's gold medals and, at Stewart's request, Pearson forwarded the names of those who had commanded either the Fusilier Brigade or one of its battalions on 16 May 1811. In passing these names on to Beresford for consideration, Stewart noted that they had been furnished by Pearson, "the officer now in command of the Fusilier Brigade, and who commanded the same in action, after the successive incapacity from wounds of his four senior officers."[47]* Stewart apparently took a personal interest in Pearson, who received not only a gold medal but also a promotion to brevet lieutenant-colonel with seniority as of 4 June 1811.[48]

This promotion was "in the army" and not in the 23rd Foot so until employment could be found in his new rank, Pearson continued to serve with the Welch Fusiliers. In career terms, however, it was an important step as, after an officer reached the rank of either substantive or brevet lieutenant-colonel, promotion was based on seniority, so that if Pearson lived long enough and minded his behaviour, he could expect to eventually reach general officer rank. For a man who had spent nearly seven years as a major and had a wife and young child to support, reaching the rank of lieutenant-colonel was an important professional milestone. In the meantime Pearson continued to command the Fusilier Brigade until the middle of June 1811, when Major-General Edward Stopford was appointed to that formation, which had changed as the 48th Foot

---

* In fact, only three of Pearson's senior officers were incapacitated – Myers commanding the Fusilier Brigade, Ellis commanding the 1/23rd and Blakeney commanding the 2/27 – as Pearson was the fourth field officer in seniority, ranking above Nooth, who commanded the 1/7th during the battle.

was added to it while the two battalions of the 7th Foot were amalgamated. Lieutenant-Colonel Henry Ellis of the Welch Fusiliers was some time in recovering from the wounds he had suffered at Albuera, and after Stopford took over the brigade, Pearson appears to have remained in command of the 1/23rd Foot through much of the following summer.[49]

The pace of operations was slower that summer. After Soult withdrew from the immediate vicinity of Albuera on 18 May, Beresford, still in command, dispatched Major-General William Lumley's cavalry to follow him. Because he was outnumbered, Lumley did not press the retreating enemy too closely but more or less trailed the French as they marched southeast. It was four more days before Beresford's two battered British infantry divisions – having cleaned up the battlefield, recovered their transport, rested and reorganized – followed them. On 22 May the Fusilier Brigade marched east to Solana de los Barrios, but by now the main body of the French army was 30 miles ahead. Three days later Soult, feeling that the allies were pressing a little too hard on his heels, ordered La Tour-Maubourg to attack the allied advance guard to ascertain whether there was any infantry with them. La Tour-Maubourg led four cavalry brigades against Lumley at the town of Usagre and was soundly trounced for his troubles, but after this successful little action Wellington ordered a halt as he had no intention of invading Andaluzia, nor did he want to bring on another major action until Badajoz had fallen. Beresford thereupon formed a cavalry screen in his front and pulled his infantry farther back, the 4th Division being stationed in and around Solana and Almendral. On 30 May, most of Beresford's officers and men rejoiced when Lieutenant-General Rowland Hill replaced the marshal.

Wellington, meanwhile, turned to Badajoz. It had been invested for a second time immediately following Albuera, but this second siege proved no more successful than that of a month earlier. Mistakes were made in the placement of batteries and the wrong side of the city was again chosen as an objective, but the worst problem was the lack of proper siege artillery. Wellington's intrepid artillery commander, Major Alexander Dickson, was reduced to using ancient Portuguese pieces from "the Elvas Museum of artillery antiquities" with corresponding miserable results.[50] Despite the difficulties, the gunners were able to make a breach in an outer work of the fortress and an assault was made on the night of 6 June, but it failed with heavy losses as did a second assault three days later. On 10 June, convinced that an attack on Badajoz from the north side of the Guadiana was impossible, and concerned about a possible enemy advance to succour the garrison, Wellington ordered the siege raised a second time.

Badajoz was vital to the interests of both sides and the British commander had been sure any attempt he made against it would elicit a response from the French. This time it came in the form of a junction of the forces led by *Maréchal* Auguste Marmont, who had replaced Masséna as commander of the Army of Portugal, with the troops commanded by Soult. This was an unpleasant turn of affairs and when Wellington learned that the two marshals had joined forces at Mérida with a total of 60,000 men, he decided to pull back as he did not want to fight on the south side of the Guadiana. He carried out a skilful withdrawal of his forces to the north side of the river, where he was joined by the greater part of the forces he had left in the north covering Ciudad Rodrigo. The Fusilier Brigade under the command of Stopford, now back with the 4th Division, crossed the Guadiana on 18 June and was posted at Estremoz, west of Elvas, which formed the right flank of a defensive position that ran behind the Guadiana and Caya Rivers from Elvas to Campo Major.

On 20 June Marmont and Soult entered Badajoz and then pushed on to the Guadiana. After reconnoitring the Anglo-Portuguese position they decided that, even with their combined force, it was too strong for them risk an attack. Neither marshal was overly eager to cross the Guadiana, and while admitting it was "vexatious" that "no general action could take place" as French success "would not be doubtful," the best they could do was to boast to their emperor that they had relieved Badajoz.[51] They also had other problems. Both French commanders had stripped the garrisons of their respective commands to take the field and it was not long before Spanish guerilla and regular forces began to threaten their rear areas. In addition, given the French supply system and the perpetual guerilla threat to their communications, the two marshals could not feed their combined army for any great length of time. Soult was the first to turn back and on 25 June, after leaving much of his army with Marmont, he withdrew to Seville. Marmont hung on for another three weeks, during which time he gathered enough food to provide the garrison of Badajoz with a six-month supply of provisions and then, on 15 July, withdrew to the north.

Wellington, however, decided not to make a third attempt against Badajoz until he had proper siege artillery. For three weeks, until mid-July 1811, his army therefore experienced a quiet period on the banks of the Guadiana. After Marmont withdrew, Wellington moved his forces out of the river valley as it was an unhealthy fever-ridden area and the number of sick was on the rise, pulling them back to higher and healthier country around Portalegre and Castello Branco. Here they would be in a position to both watch the frontier between

Maréchal Auguste-Fréderic Marmont (1774-1852)
An artillery officer, Marmont was closely associated with Napoleon in his Italian and Egyptian campaigns. Named a *maréchal* in 1809 after outstanding service in the war against Austria, Marmont was sent to Spain in 1811 to relieve Masséna, and although he threatened Wellington in 1811, the British commander beat him decisively at Salamanca in 1812. (From *Portraits des généraux français faisant suite aux victoires et conquêtes des Français,* 1818)

Portugal and Spain and, if necessary, move on either Badajoz or Ciudad Rodrigo. The Fusilier Brigade, however, remained at Estremoz where it had gone into summer camp on 24 June.

During this time, officers and soldiers lived in huts they built for themselves. When drill and duty permitted, the officers passed their leisure time playing cricket or cards, smoking "seegars," or reading newspapers – but not the *Morning Chronicle*, brewer Samuel Whitbread's effort, which was disliked because of its perceived republican and pro-French views. An officer of the 4th Division remembered that his comrades held

dinner parties, and evening parties, and dancing parties, and horse-racing parties all very simple in their way, and not attended with any expense; for instance, "Come to dinner tomorrow in camp fashion", that means, send your rations, your servant, chair, knife, fork, spoon and plate (not plates); three or four rations of beef made better soup than three-quarters of a pound with a bone in it; then there might be a bit of liver and bacon, and some roast tatties, and roars of laughter and fun ……

Those who could afford an evening party had brandy and cigars, or wine and crackers for their guests, plenty of chat about the past, the present, and the future, and some comic songs. The bottles being all drained, the evening closed, and good night was said; some one of the guests adding, "You will come to me tomorrow night."[52]

The biggest complaint was the heat – the Estremadura plain was a bake oven and it rained only once between 20 May and 20 August 1811. It was so hot that bacon fat left in the sun would melt and grass fires were a constant danger, some units being burnt out of their cantonments. One officer recalled that

The whole atmosphere was black with heat, and a distressing sirocco wind prevailed, which passing over the burning fallow ground felt to the hand, when extended, like burning steam. The hilt of my sword became so hot, that I literally could not grasp it for any length of time, and the heat of the stirrup irons was not less annoying. Such weather you may well conceive is ill adapted to taking or keeping the field, and the scarcity of water completes the quantum of suffering.[53]

Heat aside, life was actually rather pleasant that summer, but of course the idyll did not last. The indefatigable Dickson had finally assembled a proper siege train of 68 modern guns, howitzers and mortars landed from Britain at Oporto, which he then transported by water up the Douro River to Lamego, 85 miles northwest of Ciudad Rodrigo. It had been reported that the French garrison of that place was running low on provisions and it was Wellington's intention to direct his army, rested and reinforced, against it. He decided to mount a blockade that would starve the defenders into submission and if that did not succeed, he was prepared to mount a formal siege using Dickson's artillery. The orders were issued and on 30 July 1811 the Fusilier Brigade, with the remainder of the 4th Division, marched for the north. On 1 August they crossed the Tagus and all officers and men rejoiced when it was announced that the popular Colonel Edward Pakenham would resume command of the brigade. That day's journey was so hot, Cooper of the 7th remembered, that six men died from heat stroke on the dusty roads.

Marches in the Peninsular army were strictly regulated. They usually began at daybreak and the troops, who had been awakened 90 minutes before by the drummers beating "Reveille" to the rhythm of "Hey, Johnnie Cope, are ye waukin' yet?", were "dressed, with blankets rolled, packed, equipped, squadded, paraded in companies" and ready to move off when the order was given. Each enlisted man was carrying between 60 and 65 pounds, including his weapons and rations, and Corporal Cooper later complained that "the Government should also have sent us new backbones to bear the extra weight."[54] If the march was "tactical" – that is to say, if enemy action might take place – an advance guard would precede the main column of the Fusilier Brigade, in which case it would probably have been commanded by Pearson with one or more of the brigade's light companies. More often than not in August 1811, however, the marches were routine.[55]

The first halt was usually made 30 minutes after the march started and breakfast was eaten at this time. Thereafter halts were made every hour, usually for about five minutes. These breaks not only let the soldiers rest but also provided an opportunity for those men who had obtained a "ticket" from their company commander to fall out, attend a call of nature and catch up. At the rear of the column, following the soldiers, were the baggage and supply trains and attendant civilian camp followers including the soldiers' wives. These independent souls, however, displayed resourceful cunning and, although it was strictly against orders, often went ahead of their battalions to forage for and prepare the evening meal. They did this so that, as one army wife (clearly from the Emerald Isle) put it, to have "the fire an' a dhrop of tay ready for the poor crathers after their load an' their labour."[56] Behind the column of march came a Provost officer and escort who would arrest any soldier found without a ticket. If the enemy was not near, each battalion sent an advance party ahead consisting of an officer with the "camp colour men" from each company, who would arrange billeting on civilians if the unit was to stop in a village, or lay out their battalion's camp site so that there would be no confusion when the main body arrived.

Camps were generally sited, if circumstances permitted, on the edge of a wood or near a river or stream. When a battalion arrived in its camp site, one officer remembered, all was activity:

> The troops are halted in open columns, arms piled, picquets and guards paraded and posted, and, in two minutes, all appear at home. Some fetch large stones to form fire places; others hurry off with canteens and kettles for water, while the wood resounds with the sound of the bill-hook. Dispersed, under the more distant trees, you see the officers; some dressing, some arranging a few boughs to shelter them by night; others kindling their own fires; while the most active are seen returning from the village, laden with bread, or, from some flock of goats, feeding near us, with a supply of new milk. How often, under a spreading cork-tree, which offered shade, shelter and fuel, have I taken up my lodging for the night; and here, or by some gurgling stream, my bosom fanned by whatever air was stirring, made my careless toilet, and sat down with men I both liked and esteemed, to a coarse, but wholesome meal, seasoned by hunger and by cheerfulness. The rude simplicity of this life I found most pleasing.[57]

On 7 August the Fusilier Brigade reached Castello Branco where it paused for a few days before moving on to Castellojo, southeast of Ciudad Rodrigo. Here they were stationed for some weeks to await the outcome of Wellington's manoeuvres around that fortress.

The intelligence that the garrison of Ciudad Rodrigo was low on provisions turned out be false. For nearly a month in late August and early September 1811, Wellington blockaded and threatened the fortress, certain any move he made would provoke a French response. It took the opposing French commanders, *Maréchal* Marmont of the Army of Portugal and *Général de division* Jean Dorsenne of the Army of the North, some time to react, but in mid-September they joined forces and, with 60,000 troops and a convoy of more than a thousand wagons carrying supplies, moved toward Ciudad Rodrigo. Having watched Marmont refrain from attacking on the Caya in June, Wellington was convinced that at best the marshal would reprovision Ciudad Rodrigo and then inevitably be forced by the depredations of the guerillas in his rear and the perpetual French supply shortage to withdraw. For this reason he left only a thin screen, consisting of Major-General Thomas Picton's 3rd Division and Major-General Robert Craufurd's Light Division, immediately west of Cuidad Rodrigo while he moved the remainder of his army back to the hill country farther west, with the 4th Division being stationed at Fuente Guinaldo.

This proved to be an error. After reprovisioning Ciudad Rodrigo, Marmont mounted a strong reconnaissance in force to the west and, when it reported that the British were not concentrated, he advanced in strength on 25 September, catching Wellington off guard. In the face of 3,000 French cavalry with 8,000 infantry in support, Picton was forced to retreat with the 5,000 infantry of his 3rd Division and some cavalry across a nearly flat plain around the village of El Bodon to reach the safety of Fuente Guinaldo. Forming and moving in square, Picton's infantry fought off repeated cavalry attacks throughout a very long day as they moved back. The latter part of this action was witnessed by the British troops at Fuente Guinaldo and Cooper of the 7th Foot thought the conduct of Picton's infantry "in squares, marching as steadily as in a field day, was splendid."[58] By mid-afternoon the 3rd Division was nearing Fuente Guinaldo but Wellington, seeing the French cavalry massing for a final charge, ordered Pakenham to take his brigade and the 3rd Dragoon Guards, and "advance with all haste" to cover the final movement of Picton's weary men.[59]

Pakenham formed the 7th Foot in line, placed the 23rd and 48th Foot in column on either side and, preceded by the Dragoon Guards, approached within 300 yards of the enemy cavalry. He then halted, formed his three infantry battalions in regimental squares and waited for the French to make the next move. At that moment, Cooper recorded, "a French officer, perhaps a General, came cantering to within fifty or sixty yards of our front, and having satisfied his curiosity or impudence," fired his pistol at Pakenham and then "galloped off like an Arab."[60] This was rather unsporting and Pakenham turned to a nearby sergeant of the rifle company of Brunswick Oels attached to his brigade and said "Brunswick, give him a shot." The sergeant "ran forward eight or ten paces, kneeled and fired, but missed his lordship." It was at this tense moment, with both forces staring at each other, waiting for the game to begin, that an officer of the 7th Foot rode up and reported to Pakenham that he had just arrived from England with 400 men, mostly recruits, and asked if he should bring them forward. "No, no," responded the distracted Pakenham, "Take them away; take them away."[61] As he had achieved Wellington's purpose – to protect the entry of Picton's units into the position at Fuente Guinaldo – Pakenham ordered his brigade to fall back and they retired slowly under the cover of their own artillery.

The fight at El Bodon had been close but the 3rd Division got away without serious damage and late the following day Craufurd's Light Division also appeared after a rather tardy withdrawal of its own. Much of Wellington's army, however, had still to be concentrated and at Fuente Guinaldo he had only 15,000 troops to face the greater part of Marmont and Dorsenne's combined forces, about 40,000 men. Lieutenant Robert Knowles of the 7th Foot, just arrived from England, remembered that the allied commander was often in the position of the Fusilier Brigade, observing the enemy "amusing us by manoeuvring in our front and bringing up their numerous reinforcements."[62] To Knowles, a newcomer, it was all most exciting but to the veteran Corporal Cooper, it was not nearly as amusing, particularly after he overheard a staff officer ask a colleague how many enemy he thought were in front, only to receive the reply, "about 60,000," words that made Cooper uneasy for he "could see no more than 5,000 or 6,000 of our own troops."[63]

The French, however, did not attack although both Marmont and Dorsenne spent considerable time examining the British position and debating what to do. *Général de division* Paul Thiébault, one of Dorsenne's senior officers, has left a rather wicked pen portrait of the French commanders' deliberations:

Finally Marshal Marmont and General Dorsenne appeared at the head of their showy staff officers … but hardly had these gentlemen arrived than they dismounted from their horses and, having trained their telescopes, they began to study the English camp which covered Fuenteguinaldo, a camp I had known by heart for two hours …… "Yes," said the marshal, endeavouring to see that which wasn't, through his telescope leaning on the shoulder of one of his aides de camp, "yes, my reports are spot-on, the right of the English line is shored up on a difficult escarpment." Hearing this, I took my own telescope which was excellent and, like General Dorsenne, I could discover nothing that indicated this escarpment. When the general [Dorsenne] announced this, the marshal, without replying, continued: "This camp is covered in reveted fortifications," and …… completed his investigation, adding "And, just as I was informed, these reveted fortifications are armed with large-calibre guns brought forward from Almeida, so there's nothing can be done." And so saying, he requested his horse and made no reply to General Dorsenne who stated that he did not share the marshal's opinion.[64]

According to Thiébault, Dorsenne then invited all his divisional commanders to dinner at his bivouac to discuss the matter. The meal was held on "a magnificent tablecloth the size of fifteen blankets" upon which were "pies and other very fine cold dishes served on silver platters" and "bordered with plates and goblets with silver covers; the soup and the wines, the coffee and liqueurs were served separately." Following this repast, Dorsenne put the question to his subordinates on whether to attack the British position or not, and received the unanimous reply that an attack should be made. Confessing himself delighted, Dorsenne then went to Marmont's tent to remonstrate with the marshal. A few minutes later *Général de division* Louis Montbrun, Marmont's cavalry commander, emerged from the tent and approached Dorsenne's officers to ask them why they were gathered together as they looked like "conspirators." "In fact," Thiébault replied, "we are conspiring, but it's for the honour of our arms." "Bah," Montbrun responded, "after so many campaigns, so many years of combat and glory, the honour of our arms doesn't depend on an action at Fuenteguinaldo." "The vital thing," he continued, "is not to get exposed to skirmishing" because the British position "is unassailable and what stymies any attempt to prove it is the fact that Wellington is waiting for us there; and what's needed to finish him won't be a head-long [attack] with no result." To the officers' disappointment, a few minutes later Dorsenne joined them and said simply, "we beat the retreat."[65]

The French had been stymied not by Wellington but by his reputation – and perhaps the recent lesson of Albuera. Having had experience of the British commander's ability to fight defensive battles on ground of his own choosing, Bussaco being the classic example, they passed up an excellent opportunity to inflict serious harm on Wellington during one of the few times that he was

Général de division Paul-Charles Thiébault (1769-1846)
Thiébault was a veteran soldier who had reached the rank of *général de division* by 1807. Highly intelligent, he was the author of a useful staff manual but he was also a vain and quarrelsome individual, traits that are evident in his lengthy memoirs. (From Paul Thiébault, *Mémoires du Général Baron Thiébault*, Paris, 1896-1913)

caught off balance. Although by now Marmont and Dorsenne had assembled nearly all 60,000 men of their combined armies, they gave orders for a withdrawal to commence that night. For his part, not wishing to tempt fate any further, Wellington waited until dark and, after leaving behind a small force to keep the allied bivouac fires burning to fool the enemy, withdrew from Fuente Guinaldo. His troops marched all night through a heavy fog to a new position in front of Alfayates, where during the day the greater part of the army joined him.

Cole's 4th Division provided the rearguard for this movement and Pakenham's brigade the rearguard for the division. The brigade left camp at about 11 P.M. on 26 September and marched 12 hours to reach the hamlet of Aldea de Ponte de Lima northeast of Alfayates. There being no sign of the French, rations were issued in the late morning and the men ordered to cook their dinner. "Scarcely had we got our stinking messes of meat half boiled," remembered Cooper, "when an order was given to fall in immediately."[66] The pickets had reported that French cavalry were in sight and Pakenham immediately put his brigade under arms.

The French cavalry were commanded by *Général de brigade* Pierre Watier, who was acting under Thiébault's orders. The previous night Thiébault had noticed that the British campfires seemed fewer than usual and he became suspicious when his sentries reported that they had lost touch with their British counterparts. After patrols confirmed his suspicions, Thiébault reported to Marmont that Wellington had withdrawn and the marshal ordered two infantry divisions, commanded by Thiébault and *Général de division* Joseph Souham, and two cavalry brigades to follow them. Thiébault and Souham were not to attack but simply maintain contact with the British so that Marmont would not get any unpleasant surprises. The two divisions moved along separate roads with Thiébault's infantry and Watier's cavalry brigade using a route that led to Aldea de Ponte, which they approached at about noon on 27

September 1811. Aldea was outside Wellington's main defensive line but since it was a useful location at the junction of several roads, he had ordered it to be defended and on 27 September 1811 it was held by the light companies of the Fusilier Brigade under the command of Pearson.

The village was located in a narrow gorge with a stream running through it and was flanked on its south by a rocky hillside and on its north by wooded slopes. Pearson, with the light companies of the 7th, 23rd and 48th Foot and the brigade rifle company of Brunswick Oels, only had enough men (probably between 150 and 200 bayonets) to secure the road junctions in the village itself and not the surrounding area. As the British cavalry screen, consisting of Brigadier-General John Slade's brigade (1st and 12th Dragoons) which had been posted to the northeast of Aldea, fell back through the village, Pearson prepared to meet the enemy.

Watier, however, perceiving that the village was held by British infantry, did not enter it but waited for Thiébault's division to come up. That officer was with his advance guard and, after a quick reconnaissance, ordered his lead regiment, the 34th *Léger*, to attack with one battalion while the other two moved around the village on either side. This attack went in and Pearson, badly outnumbered, withdrew in good order southwest toward the main British position. Seeing this, Thiébault exalted that he had routed "two English battalions" who, "for fear of being surrounded, retreated promptly." Watier's mounted troops now passed through Aldea and trotted toward Alfayates.

Wellington had been alerted to the approach of the French and had ridden to the high ground of the Alfayates ridge just west of Aldea. Watching Pearson's light infantry fall back in good order, guarded on their flanks by Slade's cavalry, he concluded correctly that, at worst, only the lead elements of one French division were in his front. Deciding he was not going to be pushed out of useful Aldea so easily, he ordered Pakenham to advance with his brigade, supported by Collins's Portuguese brigade and Slade's cavalry, and retake the village. As the Fusilier Brigade formed, Lieutenant Knowles of the 7th Foot, about to experience his first action, thought it "a beautiful sight to see our Cavalry skirmishing with them, but before their superior numbers they gradually retired on us."[67] In the face of Watier's cavalry, Pakenham deployed in three regimental squares, the 7th, 23rd and 48th from left to right, and placed Collins's Portuguese brigade (11th and 23rd Regiments and the 7th *Caçadores*) in line on some rising ground to his rear, while Slade's dragoons were placed to his left. Pearson's light infantry remained in front to provide a skirmishing screen for the squares and, as the brigade slowly moved forward, Knowles recalled that they "gave a good account of the enemy's Cavalry, which retired in confusion."[68]

Behind the French cavalry were Thiébault's infantry, consisting of the three battalions of the 34th *Léger*, a Swiss battalion and a battalion of grenadiers, all moving in column. Thiébault, seeing the Fusilier Brigade bearing down on him with supporting infantry and cavalry, thought he was facing 6,000 men personally commanded by Wellington but kept advancing himself. While an excited Knowles watched,

> Several columns of [French] Infantry continued to advance rapidly when we were suddenly ordered to form line. …… We advanced steadily against a heavy column of Imperial Guards [actually Thiébault's grenadier battalion], but they perceiving our intention, retired in double quick time. Our Light Infantry poured in a dreadful fire amongst them, and numbers of them lay dead and dying on the field. They attempted to form on a rising ground opposite, where our Artillery did great execution. Our Cavalry and Light Infantry pursued them several miles, and were supported by a Regiment of Portuguese Cacadores.[69]

Although he would not admit it in his postwar memoirs, Thiébault was thrown out of Aldea de Ponte, which was once more in British hands. Pearson reoccupied the village with his light companies while Pakenham stationed the Fusilier Brigade in immediate support behind it.

Thiébault, however, was "very proud to have shown these English to what extent they had ignored the advantages that Aldea de Ponte could offer in terms of defence."[70] As all "signs being that the fighting was at an end, I reformed my lines after which I gave permission for the troops in my division to make soup." While his men cooked, the lead elements of the second French infantry

Général de division Joseph Souham (1760-1837)
A veteran of the Bourbon Royal Army, Souham was a cavalryman who had a distinguished career in the 1790s but was proscribed for a number of years after he joined in a plot against Napoleon. He was called back to active service in 1807. He was badly wounded in Spain in 1810 but returned the following year as a divisional commander. Souham and Thiébault's divisions pursued Wellington's rearguard in 1811. (From *Portraits des généraux français faisant suite aux victoires et conquêtes des Français,* 1818)

division, commanded by Souham, arrived. Although Souham was senior to Thiébault, the latter was not under his command and indeed there was little love lost between the two men. When Souham suggested that Thiébault mount a second attack on Aldea, Thiébault was suspicious of his motives:

"My dear general," he [Souham] stammered from the height of his full six foot, one or two inches, and the natural self-assurance needed by a man who for eighteen years has been an aide de camp, "have your division quickly take up arms and attack the enemy again." I guessed his motives. The oldest divisional general in our army [Souham was 51], nowhere could he serve without playing an active role as he was still rising from a state of disgrace and, to get the favours [promotions] that he lusted after, it was necessary for him to pull off a few cannon shots. But these considerations, which were very powerful for him, were of no consequences whatsoever as far as my own duties were concerned. ......

I replied: "Night is approaching; the enemy is retreating through the mountains where we cannot hope for success except by flanking movements that cannot be judged and executed except by day. Thus, there is nothing more to be done. My troops are tired. They have just fought for five hours and have been marching for nineteen; they are very hungry and are going to cook the last meat that they will eat between here and Salamanca; so they will go no farther."[71]

At this, Thiébault more or less turned his back on Souham, who then attempted to obtain troops from Watier only to meet with a firm refusal. Frustrated, he decided to attack Aldea with four infantry battalions and two artillery pieces from his own division and, as Thiébault sneered, Souham "marched on the rear scouts of the enemy, sent them five or six roundshot, followed them for a quarter of league [about three-quarters of a mile], all the while blazing away at them in a most useless manner, and then returned to bivouac, God knows where."[72]

Actually, Souham's attack against Aldea was somewhat more serious. Under the covering fire of his artillery Souham sent his four battalions of infantry either directly at Aldea or through the flanking woods, forcing Pearson's four companies to again pull out of the village back to the main brigade position. Pakenham immediately advanced to their support and, as Lieutenant Knowles of the 7th Foot recorded,

About six o'clock we heard our Light Infantry very warmly engaged with them. General Packenham [sic] ordered the Fusiliers to fall in, and immediately marched us in the direction of the fire. My Captain was just gone on picket, so that I had the honor of commanding a company in action. We advanced in double quick time, and arrived when they had nearly surrounded the Light Infantry. Our right wing was ordered to charge, and to describe the eagerness of the men to close with them is impossible. General Packenham led us on (… under such a man cowards would fight). Balls were flying about our ears like a hail-storm. He took off his hat, waved it in the air, and cried out "Lads! Remember the Fusiliers!" The huzza that followed intimidated the French, and they ran too fast for our bayonets, but our fire mowed them down by the dozens. We pursued them to the skirts of a wood when we were ordered to retire.[73]

In what one eyewitness termed "a brilliant charge" done "in gallant style," the Fusilier Brigade cleared Aldea de Ponte of Frenchmen for the second time.[74] Pakenham, however, ordered it to retire from the village. This decision met with Wellington's approval for, as he reported to London, "night having come on, and as Gen. Pakenham was not certain what was passing on his flanks, or of the numbers of the Enemy, and he knew that the army were to fall back still farther, he evacuated the village, which the Enemy held during the night."[75] While the wounded were brought in, the brigade made camp near their original position. "The night was cold," recalled Cooper, "and what was worse, eatables were short."[76] Worse still, around midnight the brigade was ordered to march to a new position at Boucafarinha near the Coa River and "stumbled on in bad roads till daybreak." As Pakenham's brigade formed the rearguard of the army, Wellington asked him to provide a "stop-gap regiment" to cover its withdrawal. Pakenham replied that "he had already placed the Royal Welch Fusiliers there." "Ah," responded Wellington, "that is the very thing."[77]

The action at Aldea de Ponte, fought on 27 September 1811, was one of the many minor affairs that took place in the Peninsula and rated only a paragraph in the dispatch Wellington wrote to London two days later.[78] It is of greater interest to our story, however, because in the list of wounded officers appended to that dispatch, there appears an ominous entry: "23rd Foot, Major and Brevet Lieut-col. Pearson … severely."[79]

PART III

MASTER OF THE TRADE,
1812–1815

United States Infantry, 1813
Having fought the Danes, the Dutch and the French on three continents, Pearson encountered a new enemy in 1812 – the American army. At the battle of Crysler's Farm in 1813, he
admired the courage of American soldiers but thought their officers were ignorant of their
profession. In this painting H.C. McBarron a platoon of United States infantry wears the
regulation uniform of 1813. (Courtesy, Parks Canada)

Tyendinaga Mohawk warrior, autumn 1813

The little Mohawk community at Tyendinaga, west of Kingston, were staunch supporters of the Crown and, although only numbering about 200-250 souls, routinely sent 30-50 warriors into the field. Throughout most of his time at Prescott, Pearson had a small group of Tyendinaga Mohawk warriors under his command but traditional methods of discipline could not be used with these free spirits. This warrior, dressed for cold weather, wears a mixture of white and aboriginal clothing and is armed with a trade musket, a tomahawk and a scalping knife. (Painting by Ron Volstad, courtesy of the Department of National Defence, Canada)

CHAPTER NINE

"AS YOU WERE! AS YOU WERE?"

PORTUGAL, BRITAIN AND NORTH AMERICA, OCTOBER 1811 – AUGUST 1813

The drums are beating to alarm them,
We wish to stay still in your arms.
But we must go and cross the ocean,
The Americans keep us all in motion.
*   A long farewell.*

I think I hear my brother crying,
"March, my lads, the colours flying.
Our cause is just, we'll be victorious,
If we're killed, our death is glorious."
*   A long farewell.*

Dear Mothers, weep not for us,
We going to fight for Britain's glory.
Our country calls, our courage to display.
The drums are beating, there's no delay.
*   A long farewell.[1]*

Pearson's wound, the third he had suffered in his career, was serious. He had been struck in the thigh by either a spent roundshot or canister bullet which broke one his femur bones. In such a case, if the bone was shattered, the normal period medical procedure was immediate amputation but this was not done in Pearson's case, either because the injury was too close to the hip joint for such an operation or because the bone was only fractured, not shattered. The surgeons immobilized Pearson's upper leg, hoping the breaks would heal more or less properly and evacuated him by unsprung ox cart nearly 30 miles to the military hospital at Sabugal, a journey that must have been frightful. Given the nature of his injuries, the result would almost

Captain James Prevost (1786-1811)
Captain James Prevost was a nephew of Lieutenant-General Sir George Prevost. An American by birth, he was commissioned in the British army, as were three of his brothers. His younger brother, Henry, was killed at Albuera while serving with the 7th Foot and a third brother also died in service. Pearson knew James Prevost as he had been with him in Halifax in 1809 and Prevost's company of the 5/60th Foot was attached to Cole's 4th Division. James Prevost was serving on Pakenham's staff when he was mortally wounded at Aldea de Ponte. (Courtesy of Sir Christopher Prevost)

certainly have been that Pearson's afflicted leg would be an inch to two shorter than his good leg and that the foot of the injured limb would turn outwards slightly. This meant that, even if he recovered the use of the leg, Pearson would limp or hobble for the remainder of his life and there was a strong possibility that he would never again be fit for active service.

As bad as this was, Pearson was more fortunate than others who had fought at Aldea de Ponte. The 23rd Foot lost one officer and 14 enlisted men wounded or missing, and one officer killed. That unfortunate officer was 34-year-old Captain John van Courtland, who had been with the Welch Fusiliers as long as Pearson. Courtland had been hit in the stomach by a spent roundshot which caused fatal internal injuries but "retained his perfect sense for an hour," asking Lieutenant-Colonel Ellis "to tell his wife his last thoughts were of her and the dear children."[2] There being no cleric to preside at Courtland's funeral, Lieutenant George Browne, younger brother of the diarist, Thomas Browne, recited from memory the complete burial service from the Book of Common Prayer of the Church of England, a useful talent for a junior officer to possess.

Among the mortally wounded was another nephew of Sir George Prevost, 27-year-old Captain James Prevost of the 60th Foot, who had been hit by a musket ball while acting as an aide de camp to Pakenham. The round entered Prevost's left side, "pierced the lung of that side and came out above the navel."[3] In 1811 such a wound was nearly always mortal but James Prevost lingered in pain for some weeks. His case was interesting enough to attract the attention of Surgeon George Guthrie, who recorded in his notes that

A good deal of blood was lost from the posterior wound, but he did not spit up any. He was carried to Alfaiates, and there he threw up a small quantity of bloody matter by vomiting. The posterior wound was enlarged and continued to discharge some blood, the intercostal artery being in all probability wounded. Sixteen ounces of blood were taken from the arm, giving great relief, and the bowels were opened by sulphate of magnesia.

Sept 29th. Bleeding up to eighteen ounces; on the 30th he was [bled] again to thirty-two ounces, for which great relief was obtained; he fainted however, on making a trifling exertion to relieve his bowels.

Oct 1st. Accession of symptoms as yesterday, relieved of bleeding in a similar manner; bowels open.

3d. The inflammatory symptoms recurred this morning and were again removed by abstraction of sixteen ounces of blood. Beef-tea.

5th. Passed a sleepless night, and was evidently suffering from considerable internal mischief; wandered [in his mind] occasionally; pulse quick, 120 and small; felt very weak and disponding. A little light, red wine given, with beef tea and bread; opium night and morning.

6th and 7th. Much the same; pulse very quick, with much general irritability.

15th. The wound discharged considerably, particularly the posterior one; has a little cough; pulse continues very quick; spasms of the diaphragm

Ox cart, Portugal, 1811
In this Rowlandson illustration a British officer is evacuated to the rear in an ox cart, unsprung and with rough wooden wheels affixed to ungreased wooden axles. This is probably the means of transportation that took Pearson to hospital in the rear after his thigh bone was broken when he was wounded at Aldea de Ponte in September 1811. (From *Johnny Newcome*)

troubled him for the first time, and caused great pain and uneasiness; they were relieved by opium in large and repeated doses.

On the 18th the spasmodic affection of the diaphragm and the pain returned with great violence, so as to threaten his dissolution, which took place on the 20th [of October 1811].[4]

From Sabugal to Lisbon, where he was reported as being in hospital on 25 October 1811, Pearson would have had a much easier journey as much of it could be accomplished by water on the Zezere and Tagus Rivers. From Lisbon it was a ship to Plymouth or Portsmouth and from there by carriage to Somerset. Pearson probably recuperated either at his parents' home at Queen Camel or at some property at Corton Denham, a few miles away, which he had purchased some five years earlier. He was certainly back in England by early December but then came long months of recovery.

The winter of 1811-1812 must have been a frustrating time for Thomas Pearson as, it not being entirely clear that he would again be fit for service, at the age of 31 he faced the prospect of supporting his Ann and infant son on the half-pay of his rank, £155.2.6 per year, about the same income as a thriving shopkeeper, minor clergyman or small farmer. Although, being the eldest son, he stood to inherit much of his father's property, a sedentary life in rural Somerset would not have appealed to a fighting soldier like Pearson, particularly as the war with France was still raging. At this point, however, the future must have looked rather bleak.

Fortunately, Sir George Prevost, his old commander from Halifax and Martinique, now the governor-general of British North America, had not forgotten him. On learning that Pearson was recovering from a serious wound that might preclude his return to active service, Prevost requested the War Office to appoint him an inspecting field officer of militia in British North America. This was a staff job but it was better than the alternatives, and there was also the attraction that Ann could be closer to her family in New Brunswick. Pearson was therefore quick to accept the appointment, which was officially gazetted on 28 February 1812.[5]

In the spring of 1812, Lieutenant-General Sir George Prevost had need of all the competent officers he could get because he was facing active war with the United States. Prevost had been appointed governor-general and captain-general of British North America late in 1811, just as the long simmering tension between Britain and the United States, caused by the question of maritime rights and seemingly interminable problems with the aboriginal peoples on the American northwest frontier, had boiled over into outright hostility. When the Twelfth Congress met in Washington in November 1811 President James Madison issued a call to "put the nation in armour" and the United States actively began to prepare for war.[6] Early in 1812 the establishment of the American regular army was tripled, a call was issued for 50,000 volunteers to conquer the British possessions to the north and the small but highly professional American navy was put on a wartime footing.

In Washington there was supreme confidence that a campaign to seize Britain's North American provinces would be short, relatively bloodless and victorious. There was reason for that confidence because, on paper, the odds were much in favour of the republic, which with a population of over six million stood against a Canadian population that numbered about half a million people, most of whom resided along the international border. Madison's government was fully aware that Britain had extensive naval and military commitments in Europe, and even if she sent aid and reinforcements to her North American possessions, they probably would not reach their destination until after the war had been brought to a satisfactory conclusion in favour of the United States.

For his part, Prevost had fewer than 8,500 British and Canadian regulars, spread from Halifax to the upper Great Lakes, a distance of more than a thousand airline miles. With the exception of Halifax and Quebec, there were no permanent fortifications in the European sense, only a series of small posts that were more supply depots than military defence works. Prevost did have some advantages. Ironically he had almost as many regular troops as the United States army and they were well-trained professionals. He also possessed a miniature fleet, the Provincial Marine, on the Great Lakes which would allow him to use waterborne communication to shift forces rapidly from one threatened area to another. Under orders from London to fight a defensive war, Prevost's plan was to abandon no part of British North America but only to vigorously defend the province of Lower Canada, particularly Quebec, until help could arrive from Britain. He was prepared to give up the province of Upper Canada, surrounded on three sides by American territory, and placed the greater part of his regular troops around Montreal in Lower Canada, as an invader trying to attack Quebec City could not afford to bypass that place. This plan did not meet the approval of his subordinate in Upper Canada, Ma-

The Niagara Peninsula

jor-General Isaac Brock, who was convinced that the upper province could be successfully defended.

In London, Prime Minister Spencer Perceval's government, preoccupied with Europe, had more or less ignored the increasingly dangerous situation developing in North America. When it became apparent in 1812 that the United

States meant business, the British government took long-overdue steps to ame-
liorate the tensions between the two nations. Foremost among them was re-
pealing the Orders-in-Council and eliminating the maritime restrictions that
were the major source of American resentment. Unfortunately, it was too late
and on 18 June the United States declared war on Great Britain.

Montreal

This view, done in the 1830s, shows Montreal, the largest and wealthiest city in British North America, and the commercial centre. It was only seriously threatened once during the war, in the autumn of 1813 when two American armies advanced toward it. Both were defeated. Pearson's wife, Ann, and his son, Thomas Aylmer, spent most of the war here. (Ink sketch by R.A. Sproule, National Archives of Canada, C-100559)

As the shipping season to British North America was restricted by weather to about a six-month period from April to September, it took some time for Pearson, with Ann and their son, Thomas Aylmer, to obtain a passage and they did not arrive in Halifax until July 1812. The Pearsons only stayed there for a few days before sailing on 18 July for Quebec on the schooner *Mary Ann*, Hilarion Dugas master, laden with 350 barrels of tar. Unfortunately, although the United States Navy did not pose a threat to travel, American privateers did: in the month that followed the declaration of war, no fewer than 65 privateers were cruising in the waters off Nova Scotia, among them the schooner *Buckskin* from Salem, Massachusetts, commanded by Israel Bray. *Buckskin* had already taken five prizes when Bray overtook the *Mary Ann* on 19 July, which, being unarmed, immediately hauled down her colours. Bray put a prize crew on board and the *Mary Ann* made for Salem.[7]

Things were not looking good for Pearson and he must have regretted not obtaining passage on a warship. Although he had no fear for the safety of Ann and little Thomas, who were treated kindly, it would be many months before his superiors would be able to arrange an exchange that would permit his return to British territory. On 23 July, however, Pearson's luck took a change for the better when the *Mary Ann* sighted a strange sail which turned out to be His Britannic Majesty's Frigate *Maidstone*, 32 guns, commanded by Captain George Burdett. A British prize crew now went aboard the schooner, which sailed for Halifax, while the Pearsons and the Americans were transferred to the frigate. The *Maidstone* then made for the same place, the colonel being bound for his new appointment and the American privateersmen for the prison on Melville Island, where they would shortly be joined by Isaac Bray and the remainder of his crew, who were captured a few days later.[8]

Pearson and his family were reported safely back at Halifax on 25 July 1812. Lieutenant-General Sir John Cope Sherbrooke, commander-in-chief in the Atlantic provinces, co-opted him to sit on a court martial, but Prevost, anxious to obtain his services, ordered him released from that duty and with his wife and son he sailed for Quebec in the sloop-of-war HMS *Prometheus* in early September. This time the Pearson family arrived safely and from Quebec to Montreal they went by boat – possibly the new-fangled steamboat *Swiftsure* operated by Hiram Molson – because Pearson was at the latter place by the end of September 1812. On the 30th of that month, Pearson was appointed the garrison commander of Montreal, but he did not hold that position long as nine days later he was ordered to Prescott in Upper Canada to assume the command of that post and the surrounding area.

Prescott, a hamlet on the north bank of the St. Lawrence River a hundred or so miles west of Montreal, occupied a strategic position. The St. Lawrence River and the Great Lakes form one of the major waterways of the world and provide a waterborne communications system some 2,200 miles long from the Atlantic Ocean to the interior of the North American continent. From Prevost's point of view, this system was both a blessing and a curse, for although it could be utilized to move forces as required, he was concerned about its vulnerability, particularly the 150-mile stretch between Kingston and Montreal where the river acted as the border between the United States and British North America. The St. Lawrence was also the vital link between Upper and Lower Canada. It was deep enough from Kingston to Prescott to permit larger vessels from Lake Ontario to reach the latter place, but below Prescott five rapids dropped the river nearly 200 feet before it reached Montreal. This stretch of the river could only be navigated by small boats manned by skilled river men, and Prescott's major function was to act as a "forwarding centre" where cargo and passengers were transferred from the larger lake vessels to smaller craft which ran the rapids.

Fortunately for Prevost, the United States did not attempt to cut the St. Lawrence in the opening months of the war. Instead, the major American military effort was directed farther west, along the Detroit River, and an enemy incursion into Upper Canada was decisively halted by the aggressive Major-General Brock, who not only shepherded the invaders back to American territory in August, but also convinced the American commander, Brigadier-General William Hull, to surrender his entire army at Detroit. A second American attempt to invade the Niagara area of Upper Canada in early October was decisively rebuffed at the battle of Queenston Heights, a victory that cost Brock's life but brought an end to military operations until the following spring. The people of Upper Canada, formerly convinced that the province would fall within a few months of war being declared, now took heart while the British and Canadian regulars and militia made jokes about the military ineptitude of "Cousin Jonathan Yankee," their term of derision for the citizens of the republic to the south.

During this period, the St. Lawrence corridor was relatively quiet. The provincial militia was called out to guard vital points and a boat service was organized between Montreal and Prescott, where primitive defence works were constructed. It was ironical that although the population of the United States far outnumbered that of the Canadas, there were fewer people on the south bank of the St. Lawrence than on the north and communication between these sparse settlements and the government in Washington was long and difficult. For good reasons, the American population along the St. Lawrence largely decided to remain neutral during the conflict.

This quiet period ended in September 1812 when Captain Benjamin Forsyth was sent with a company of the United States Rifle Regiment to Ogdensburg, across the river from Prescott. An aggressive officer, Forsyth began to harass the British boat traffic from the south bank and on 21 September mounted a successful raid on the Canadian village of Gananoque 40 miles west of Prescott. This prompted Colonel Robert Lethbridge, an elderly half-pay officer who had been assigned the command at Prescott with instructions "to preserve the tranquillity of that part of the province," to mount a retaliatory raid on Ogdensburg.[9] The attack, made early in the morning of 4 October 1812 by some 700 British regulars and Canadian militia, was an unmitigated disaster. As an eyewitness remarked, the whole force there [at Prescott] Embarked in batteaux [sic] at the wharf and proceeded about a mile up the river before pulling accross [sic]. It was an ill managed business for the current carried them down in front of the Enemies [sic] batteries, whilst yet some hundred yards from the Shore and there exposed to the fire of grape and round shot, the batteaux cheifly [sic] pulled by the Militia got into confusion and rowed back to Prescott. This was not a cheering commencement but we lived on hopes of better luck next time.[10]

Ogdensburg had been ably defended not only by Forsyth but also by a New York state militia officer, Brigadier-General Jacob Brown, of whom we shall hear more. This badly-planned and abortive operation, which clearly exceeded Lethbridge's orders, infuriated Prevost who, "having had repeatedly cause to mistrust the judgement in command" of Lethbridge, replaced him with Lieutenant-Colonel Thomas Pearson, "whose zeal & talents as a Soldier" the commander-in-chief had "frequently witnessed."[11]

Leaving Ann and young Thomas in Montreal, Pearson travelled to Prescott in late October 1812 to find a straggling little village huddling on the bank of the St. Lawrence. There had been white settlement in the Prescott area since 1785 when Major Edward Jessup, a Loyalist officer from the American Revolutionary War, had received a grant of 1,200 acres in compensation for his property losses in that conflict. Jessup gradually cleared the land and created what was, for Upper Canada, a fairly prosperous farm, which in 1811 he began to turn into a town site. The first house was built that year by William Gilkinson, a merchant intent on developing the forwarding trade on the river, and he was followed by others so that, by the outbreak of war, there were about 20 buildings of all types in the hamlet and three wharves on the river bank. Many of the houses were still under construction, causing one British officer who served at Prescott to quip that it consisted "of five houses, three of which were unfinished."[12]

Pearson was less concerned with the appearance of the place than he was with its military defences and these were nearly as primitive. In the preceding months, Colonel William Fraser of the 1st Stormont Regiment of militia had erected an earthwork battery containing two 9-pdr. guns on the river bank and a wooden stockade fort somewhat back from the water. Civilian buildings had been taken over to serve as a powder magazine, a hospital and barracks,

View of Prescott from Ogdensburg
This view, done in the 1840s, from Ogdensburg on the American bank of the St. Lawrence, shows Prescott across the river. In 1812-1814, Pearson was the garrison commander at Prescott and Ogdensburg was in range of his artillery and he used it against that village on a number of occasions. During the War of 1812, however, Prescott consisted of not more than a dozen buildings. (Print by W.H. Bartlett, author's collection)

although the majority of the militia garrison lived in crude stone and plank shanties that they themselves constructed. Things began to improve after Pearson arrived, as Prevost had decided to make Prescott the major defence point between Kingston and Cornwall. The garrison was increased in strength and over the winter of 1812-1813 Pearson commanded 300 regulars drawn from the 8th Foot, the Royal Newfoundland Regiment and the Glengarry Light Infantry, as well as a detachment of gunners from the Royal Artillery. The Royal Newfoundland Regiment and the Glengarry Light Infantry were fencibles, regular units recruited in British North America but not required to serve outside of it. The Newfoundlanders, skilled boatmen, were usually employed on the boat convoys that steadily made their way up and down the river, while the Glengarries were a light infantry battalion whose dark green uniforms had earned them the nickname of "black stumps" from the aboriginal peoples.[13] Also attached to Pearson was a small band of 30-40 Mohawk warriors from their settlement at Tyendinaga west of Kingston.

After Pearson's arrival, a flurry of military construction began to trans-

Boats on the St. Lawrence
The St. Lawrence River system provided a waterborne communications system from the Atlantic into the interior of North America. Pearson's main duty in 1812-1814 was to protect this vital route by which supplies reached British troops and the Royal Navy squadrons farther to the west, and he was successful in this task. Here, reconstructed bateaus or river boats move on the St. Lawrence today. (Photograph by René Schoemaker)

form Prescott. Work started on additional barracks and storehouses but the major project was a large blockhouse set on high ground back from the river bank. This project originated from a visit made to the post in January 1813 by Lieutenant-Colonel Ralph Bruyeres, RE, who was under orders to survey the St. Lawrence and recommend appropriate defence works to be built. Bruyeres ordered Lieutenant Frederick de Gaugreben, an officer of the King's German Legion, "to erect without delay a Block House on a small commanding spot in the rear of the present [earthwork] Battery which it will completely protect."[14] This order for a relatively simple structure became transformed into the construction of not only a strong blockhouse but a massive earthwork surrounding it, which was to take nearly 14 months to complete. As much of the labour force for the construction was drawn from Pearson's troops, the slow progress made on this structure was a continual source of frustration for him and on occasion he refused de Gaugreben the use of military assistance to build what another Royal Engineer termed "a great mass of earth badly put together."[15]

Pearson took steps to control river traffic on the St. Lawrence and increase the security of Prescott. All troops in garrison were ordered to sleep fully dressed and accoutred to prevent surprises. All boats not under guard or in military service were destroyed and any boats seen on the river whose crews could not produce the proper permission were brought into the garrison for questioning. When the St. Lawrence froze in late December, this order was extended to include sleigh traffic. No persons, military or civilian, could enter or leave the garrison without a pass signed by Pearson, and no persons could communicate or travel to the American bank without his authorization. He was quick to observe and apprehend any Canadian who had illegal communication with the American side of the river and, as he reported to Prevost, there were "but too many" Canadians "whose characters created much suspicion and whose movements occasion me as much anxiety as those of the Enemy."[16] If such persons came to his attention, he arrested them and sent them to Montreal for examination by the authorities.

Pearson did not, however, mount any attacks across the river although he occasionally chased deserters into American territory. Prevost had forbidden offensive action because he wanted to keep on good terms with the inhabitants of the border states for the simple reason that, through widespread smuggling, they were providing a considerable portion of the provisions for the British army in North America. "It is incredible," a resident of Ogdensburg remarked, "what quantities of cattle and sheep are driven into Canada. We hardly get any for love or money; the day before 100 Oxen went through [across to] Prescott, yesterday about 200."[17] For this reason, Pearson did not unduly restrict civilian movement across the river and the inhabitants of both villages regularly visited each other, with many Canadians shopping at David Parrish's store on the American side.

We get a glimpse of this aspect of Pearson's duties from the memoir of Lydia Hayward, an American woman who had resided in the Kingston area before the war. Her husband had returned to the United States shortly after hostilities began as he did not want to be called up for service in the Canadian militia and, wishing to join him, Lydia had applied and received the necessary passport to leave the province. Having been informed that she could only exit at Prescott, she travelled with her children under the protection of another American, a Mr. Skinner, in late December 1812. As soon as they reached their destination, Lydia recalled,

Mr. Skinner carried my pass with his to Col. Pierson's [sic] office, but the Col. sent mine back, saying the woman must herself appear. Accordingly I took my pass and Mr. S. conducted me to the office. We passed the sentinel and walked to the Col. He was standing upon a platform about breast high in front of a building. He accepted my pass, then …… observed it was rather a cold day to stand outdoors – that by passing round the corner of the house I would find a passage for entrance, which I did and sat down to wait for the return of Mr. Skinner with his wife and children. The revolving thoughts and feeling that alternately occupied this little pause of time, I cannot describe. A stranger in a land of strangers; a lone female seated in the office of a British garrison; my heart trembled at the reflection, my blood chilled in my veins, my only consolation was tears and sighs.[18]

Fortunately for Lydia, Thomas Pearson did not make war on women and children – or maybe he was just in a good mood that day. After some routine questions he approved her pass and sent her with her children to a boat waiting to put off for Ogdensburg. The emotional Lydia was delirious with happiness when she saw a company of American soldiers drawn up on the south bank of St. Lawrence to receive the boat and felt "they appeared like friends and neighbours, while prejudice against the British was so great, I thought their soldiers appeared like savages."[19]

Not all Pearson's relations with Americans were so benign. Aware that the security of his stretch of the St. Lawrence depended on his having good information, he created an intelligence network. His main informant was Samuel Steacy, an American Pearson engaged in February 1813 for £100 to spy on the enemy naval base at Sacket's Harbor across Lake Ontario. Steacy made regular trips to that place and then travelled to Ogdensburg, where he passed information to two enterprising Canadian militia officers who crossed the river to debrief him. One of them was Captain Reuben Sherwood from Brockville, 12 miles to the west of Prescott, a peacetime surveyor who had worked in northern New York state before the war, and whom Pearson appointed his "Captain of Guides." Pearson thought highly of Sherwood and wrote to Prevost that he "appears, of all the men I have met with in this country the best qualified for an appointment which I would strongly recommend … for superintending and organizing the procuring of secret intelligence."[20] The other intelligence officer was Captain William Gilkinson, the Prescott merchant, who had extensive business and personal connections in New York state. The creation of this

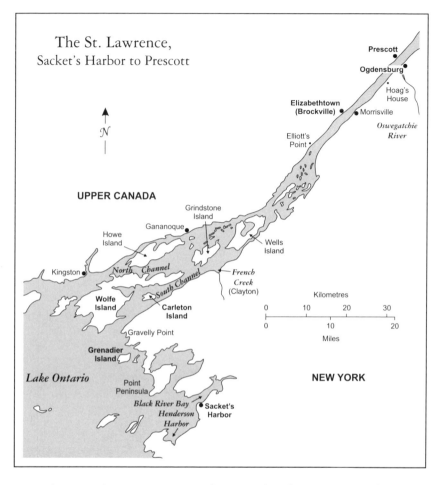

The St. Lawrence,
Sacket's Harbor to Prescott

network was a wise move on Pearson's part and in the coming months would
pay enormous dividends.[21]

Although his main concern was the security of the St. Lawrence corridor
from Cornwall to Kingston, Pearson did not neglect the duties attendant on
his position as inspecting field officer of militia. The militia organization in the
Canada differed considerably from its British counterpart, which was composed
of uniformed regiments raised from men "balloted" or drafted, who served for
long periods. There were numerous exceptions to militia service in Britain and
much of the male population was not required to serve – and even if a man was
so unfortunate as to be drafted, he could, if he possessed the requisite funds,
obtain a substitute to take his place. In British North America, service in the militia was, with few exceptions, incumbent on every male of military age and was
really a form of feudal levy (which, in fact, is where it originated). In peacetime

Upper Canada, the greater part of this force, commonly called the "sedentary" militia, was organized by counties and mustered once a year for training, usually on 4 June, the King's birthday, and a day marked by little drill and much alcoholic good cheer. As war approached, however, the capable Major-General Isaac Brock formed "flank companies" from the younger men in each of the county regiments, who received better arms and more training and, in the opening months of the conflict, these "flankers" proved to be a valuable support for the small number of regular troops defending Upper Canada and fought better than expected at Detroit and Queenston Heights. It should always be remembered, however, that in the Canadas, unlike the United States, the militia was never regarded as the first line of defence, only as an auxiliary to the regular army. Regular officers enjoyed precedence over militia officers of the same rank and it was rare to find militia officers commanding regular troops. The defence of British North America was conducted by professional soldiers, many of them, like Pearson, relatively young but possessing considerable combat experience – another advantage that offset American numerical superiority.

Inspecting field officers did not actively command the militia units in their districts; they only supervised their training and acted as a channel of communication between them and the regular army. It was a job that required "active and intelligent" officers, which Pearson most certainly was, because their primary function was to bring the militia close to the standards of regular troops, but it was also a thankless task as it meant trying to transform an undisciplined mob of what were essentially civilians, possessing limited arms and equipment, into something approximating soldiers.[22] Assisted by his staff adjutant, Lieutenant George Ridge of the 8th Foot, Pearson set about this task with a will in the winter of 1812-1813, and it is in connection with this activity, more than any other, that Thomas Pearson emerges from being a vague figure outlined in official correspondence to assume a definite, indeed colourful, personality. Unfortunately, it was not an attractive personality, as Pearson quickly acquired a reputation among the Canadian militia as a bloody-minded tyrant and a ferocious-tempered martinet.

The bad temper may have been caused by the wound he had received at Aldea de Ponte or it may just have been his personality as Pearson was not a man who suffered fools gladly. As for being a martinet, there was no doubt about it. Thomas Pearson was a professional soldier who had been at war with the King's enemies for much of his adult life and, if ordered, would cheerfully and efficiently dispatch those enemies, be they Frenchmen, Danes, Dutch or

Americans, it really didn't matter much. His duty, as he saw it, was to turn the Upper Canada militia into a pale replica (because they would never come up to the real thing) of his beloved Royal Welch Fusiliers, and he trampled over anyone or anything that stood in his path. It should therefore come as no surprise that a British officer who came to know Pearson well during the War of 1812 summed him up as "singularly intemperate but a first rate Soldier."[23]

Frankly, he terrified the Upper Canada militia. Pearson had absolutely no patience or respect for the professional pretensions, social position or political connections of senior militia officers, many of whom were among the leading citizens of the province. At an inspection in Kingston of the 1st Frontenac Regiment, commanded by Colonel Richard Cartwright, one of the most prominent businessmen and landowners in Upper Canada and a confidant of the lieutenant-governor of the province, Pearson lost patience with Cartwright's inept handling of his unit. To the horror of another British officer who, being the son of a general, was more closely attuned to the niceties of rank and station, Pearson proceeded to tear a very wide strip off Cartwright's back by abusing him "for not performing some movement which a Militia officer could not be expected to know."[24] The point was that, if the movement was in the simplified militia manual, which it probably was, Cartwright should not only have known it, but should have been able to execute it.

Pearson was fanatical about training, and a militiaman who served at Prescott in the winter of 1812-1813 remembered that on Pearson's orders his regiment was "subjected to hard drilling."[25] But then Pearson well knew the importance of such training as he had been at Albuera when 5,000 men of the 4th Division had advanced in echelon of battalion columns under heavy artillery fire, a feat that would have made any drillmaster proud, and he saw no reason why a Canadian militia officer could not carry out a simpler evolution with a smaller number of men. The key to Pearson's attitude was that there was no difference to him between the regulars of Major-General Lowry Cole's 4th Division and the militiamen of Colonel Richard Cartwright's 1st Frontenac Regiment. He regarded the militia as soldiers in the King's service, there was an enemy to fight and a war to be won, and he simply would not tolerate any slackness.

This was not an attitude calculated to make him many friends, not that Pearson cared a farthing. Although the rather sensitive and religious Cartwright gently complained that Pearson "little knew what a zealous and anxious man He was reproving, and that He offended my Regiment more than He did me," it was certain the next time the inspecting field officer came round to have a look at the 1st Frontenac, it would know its drill.[26] As it was, Cartwright got off lightly. At an inspection of an unidentified militia regiment, the commanding officer became totally confused while drilling his unit and constantly brought them to a halt by calling, "as you were! as you were!" Pearson put up with this for some time before exploding at the wretched man: "As you were? As you were! I'll be damned if you are as you were, for you are not half as good as the last time I saw you."[27]

There was, however, a softer side to "Tartar" Pearson, as he was called by those who served with him, although he took great pains to conceal it. We have seen it above in connection with the emotional Lydia Hayward, but Pearson always respected anyone who had the courage to stand up to him, if that person had good reason. The story is told that

Pearson being applied to personally by a Militiaman for leave of absence, the Colonel who was in a moody humour answered: "Go to hell!" The man quietly said: "Has your honour any orders for the devil?" Pearson looked at Him, smiled [and said]: "What leave do you want? Six days!!!" He doubled his leave and gave Him a pound to take home![28]

After several months at Prescott, Pearson believed he had the solution to the problems of the Upper Canada militia. Writing to Colonel Aeneas Shaw, adjutant-general of that force, on 19 January 1813, Pearson told Shaw bluntly that

I have no hesitation in asserting that this force will never be brought to meet the expectations of the country. In the first place from the constant and numerous desertions of the militia, it is next to an impossibility ever to calculate on the force you can bring to action. This I principally attribute to the incapacity of the generality of the officers who have been for the most part selected from family connections without reference to capacity or respectability.

The advantage accruing of having young men of local interest placed at the head of the companies has never been made a subject of consideration, on the contrary, men are placed in the responsible and important situations, who instead of benefitting Government by their zeal and alacrity, have in many instances irreparably injured the service by their imbecility and precept.[29]

As Pearson saw it, the solution was clear. The province should form two battalions of 500 R[ank]. & F[ile]. each from the flankers of the District, and such others that might choose to extend their services from the Sedentary Militia. These corps I propose being commanded by militia Lt. Colonels with a captain of the line [regular army] appointed as a major, with two lieutenants of the regulars as captains to each of the Battns., the remaining officers to be militia and to be selected by the Lt. Colonels subject to the approval of the Inspecting Field Officer [Pearson]. Their pay and allowances as at present, but the men to be clothed at the expense of the Government, and to be embodied for the continuance of the American war.

Should his proposal be approved, Pearson confessed he would "feel happy in being the instrument of putting it into execution and of taking the superintendence of their formation under my immediate charge" and he ended his missive by stating that "these measures are the only ones by which the [militia] force of this country can ever be brought to be of real utility to the Province."

One should always be careful about what one asks for because, as we shall see, Pearson's wish was granted but he would not "feel happy" about the result.

During the four months that followed the abortive British attack on Ogdensburg, relative calm reigned on the St. Lawrence. In the early morning of 7 February 1813, however, the war came alive again when the aggressive Forsyth attacked the village of Brockville, west of Prescott, capturing the small militia garrison and terrifying the civilian inhabitants, who were awakened by the sound of gunfire and Yankee feet running in the streets. Reporting to his immediate superior, Major-General Francis de Rottenburg at Montreal, Pearson attributed "this disaster chiefly to the incautious conduct of the Comm[andin]g. Officer of the Post, a Captn. of the Leeds [County] Militia who it appears was surprized in his bed as well as the rest of the Garrison" but Pearson did not think it worthwhile stationing regular troops at Brockville because it was "of no consequence in a Military View." Since the best defence is a good offence, he instead suggested that "the destruction of Ogdensburg could be easily effected, provided a Party of Regulars were sent for that Purpose" as "with two hundred in addition to my present Force, I have no doubt but I could succeed in effectually destroying this Post."[30] In response, de Rottenburg sent militia reinforcements and two 12-pdr. field pieces but did not give Pearson permission to attack across the river.

Pearson was further annoyed some weeks after the Brockville raid when

Major ("Red") George Macdonell (1780-1870)
A veteran of the Egyptian campaign of 1801 and one of the senior officers of the Glengarry Light Infantry, Macdonell was serving as Pearson's second-in-command at Prescott in the winter of 1812-1813. When Pearson was transferred to Kingston in February 1813, this Scotsman executed a successful attack on Ogdensburg using a plan that Pearson had devised. (National Library and Archives of Canada, C-19719)

the newly-promoted Major Forsyth sent a patrol over the St. Lawrence, which snatched three Canadian farmers and a team of horses. Pearson's second-in-command, Major George Macdonell of the Glengarry Light Infantry (like Pearson a veteran of the Egyptian campaign) was dispatched to Ogdensburg under a flag of truce to remonstrate about such needless depredation. Forsyth met him halfway across the frozen river and "in conversation expressed his desire to meet Col. Pearson with his force on the ice," whereupon Macdonell gave the American to understand that, should the command of Prescott devolve upon him, "he certainly would have no objection to gratify his wish."[31]

On 21 February 1813, when Sir George Prevost arrived at Prescott with his staff on his way west to undertake a tour of inspection, Pearson again asked for permission to attack Ogdensburg. He stressed that the time was opportune because a strong detachment of regular troops had just arrived at Prescott and he now had the men needed to accomplish a plan of attack that he had formulated. Its success hinged on the fact that the Americans had grown accustomed to seeing Pearson's staff adjutant, Lieutenant Ridge, drilling troops from the garrison on the frozen river near the Canadian shore. It was Pearson's intention to make these troops the spearhead of an attack as, moving swiftly, they would be able to cross most of the 1,800 yards of frozen river before the Americans could react. Once this advance element was in motion, he intended to follow them with every regular soldier and militiaman he could muster. With the element of surprise and some luck, his men would be able to take the batteries that defended the American side and after that, it would be a matter of simple bayonet work.

Prevost listened to the plan but not only refused permission for Pearson to carry it out, he also told him to pack his belongings because he was going to be

Canadian militiaman

Although this painting by Douglas Anderson shows a Canadian militiaman as
he might have appeared in the 1830s,
the sedentary militia of the War of 1812
would have looked much the same – under arms but still wearing civilian clothing. All males in the Canadas were, with
few exceptions, subject to call out for
militia service. Their combat record was
variable but they proved an essential
and useful auxiliary to regular units and
long-service provincial units. (Painting by
Douglas Anderson, courtesy Parks Canada)

transferred temporarily to Kingston. Major-General Sir Roger Hale
Sheaffe, the commander in Upper
Canada (and Pearson's brother-in-
law as he was married to Ann's older
sister), had fallen ill. Pearson was to replace Colonel John Vincent at Kingston, who was being sent to the provincial capital at York to take over Sheaffe's
duties. As he was somewhat concerned about the Americans learning of his
journey, the cautious Prevost did, however, give Macdonell, who now assumed
command at Prescott, permission to make a "demonstration" the following
morning to cover the commander-in-chief's departure for Kingston.[32]

Prevost, Pearson and party left for Kingston by sleigh before dawn on 22
February 1813, and once they were out of earshot Macdonell promptly launched
a full-scale attack on Ogdensburg. As an eyewitness recalled,

> about half past six, the garrison was under Arms. The force disposable for
> attack was less than five hundred men and was divided into two columns,
> one of these under the command of Captain Jenkins consisted of his Com-
> pany of Glengarry Light Infantry and two companies of Militia, one from
> the County of Glengarry commanded by Captain McMillan the other from
> the county of Dundas under Captain Ault – a six pounder gun was attached
> to this column but there were only two Royal Artillery men with it. The oth-
> er column consisted of about one hundred men of the 8th Regiment – fifty
> of the Royal Newfoundland and two hundred Militia, the latter column at

the hour named was formed in the main street of the village [of Prescott], the former on the road a short distance above the village.

At peep of day the major [Macdonell] came to the Parade in the street and by this time Every man knew then intention was a visit to Ogdensburg. But a short time elapsed after the Majors [sic] appearance before the word was given "Forward" [and] both Columns were in motion and soon on the ice.[33]

Legend has it that when the American sentries alerted Forsyth that his enemy was crossing the river, he replied that they were mistaken, the British were only drilling on the ice as they had done for much of the winter. Forsyth was soon disabused of that notion and immediately ordered his gunners to open fire, and they concentrated on Jenkins's column:

Almost the first Cannon shot upset the six pounder Jenkins had with him, killing the only two royal Artillery men with it – this happened when half-way over the river however on went the column and reached the shore, where an unforseen obstacle presented itself, the snow drift on the shore had accumulated, to flounder through it – up to their middle was no easy task and Jenkins gave the Word to keep to the ice along the bank. Owing to this circumstance the men were much more exposed and the plan of operations to some extent defeated for it had been intended that the left column should get across at some distance from the Fort and attack it from above or not attacking intercept the retreat of the Enemy as circumstances might decide. As it was Jenkins moved directly towards the fort. When within pistol shot of it he was knocked over by a grape shot which shattered his left arm, on his legs again in a minute (seeing his men put out by his fall) he shouted "never mind me," and ran on a few steps farther when down he went again, the right arm now shattered like its fellow. Rise again, he could not, what with this second mischance and long exposure on so open a surface, as the ice, the men in confusion began to turn back. Lieut. Macauley endeavoured to restore confidence but was unsuccessful and the left column found its way back to the British shore all the time under fire of the Enemy's cannon. They carried their gallant young leader with them however.[34]

When Jenkins's men arrived back at the Canadian bank, Father Alexander Macdonell of Glengarry County was waiting. A devout believer in the church militant, the good father promptly re-formed them and ordered them back over the St. Lawrence to join Macdonell's column. As they moved again out on the ice, the priest marched behind, encouraging any laggards with a blow from a large and heavy crucifix he swung in one hand, and legend has it that after one man disobeyed several divine orders to "keep moving," Father Macdonell excommunicated him on the spot.

Major Macdonell (no relation to the priest), seeing the rebuff of Jenkins's column,

> sent forward. Lieut MacLean … of the militia to overtake Lieut. Ridge who was at the head of the column with his Newfoundlanders and Selected Militia Men and direct him to hasten on with all speed to divert some of the Enemy's fire …… The Newfoundlanders had no officer of their own corps with them being under the command of Ridge of the 8th or Kings Regiment. The officers of the half hundred Stormont and Dundas Militia attached to the Newfoundlanders were Lieut Burritt and Peter Fraser. McLean came up with Ridge just as the advance approached the deep snow bank on the south side of the river And having delivered Major Macdonells [sic] orders the men pushed on with all speed but such was the depth of snow that before the men got to the road on shore they were all completely out of wind. It was necessary to call halt for a few minutes the men were got together behind a slaughter house; while in that position, two or three of the enemy's militia armed with rifles came round the corner and were made prisoners.
>
> After taking breath – the advance was resumed. Along the river bank two abreast a fine young fellow of the Dundas Militia and McLean were the leading files. A man issued from a house ahead and taking deliberate aim fired and young Ondereack pitched forward dead, his slayer was soon rolled over in the snow well perforated and the death avenged. On reaching the street leading to [David] Parish's [sic] house, a number of men were seen collected at a corner and it was observed they had three pieces of artillery with them, these had been placed at that point to command different approaches. These they were endeavouring to wheel round upon the advancing British but the snow was so deep and the guns so heavy (two twelve, and one six pounder) they were slow in doing it. Lieut Ridge was now leading and perceiving their intentions shouted to increase speed, on they rushed like the wind for had the guns been fired they would have cleared the street – and every muscle was strained to reach them. The Enemy seemed daunted by the speed and

ardour of the advance for only the six pounder was discharged its contents was only one round shot and its only damage was leaving its mark on
McLeans left thigh, the guns were captured, and the on [sic] that had not
been fired were turned on the retreating Enemy with effect. After which
they were spiked by breaking the points of bayonets in the touch holes and
hammering them down with the butts of firelocks.[35]

The various columns now converged on the village but the enemy gunners
in the "Green Battery," as it was called,

directed its fire on the main body. The advance rushed on with the intention of storming the Battery East of Parish's Store when they observed a
company of the Osnabruck Militia from the main body commanded by
Capt Morgan advancing to storm it, which they did successfully. The enemy
in the Green Battery, perceiving it had fallen into the hands of the British
turned their guns upon it and compelled the Osnabruck people to abandon
it. Lieut. Empey and a private named Servos had their legs carried away in
the battery by round shot. The main body by this time had come up with
the field pieces, and a few shots directed at the Green Battery compelled
the enemy to abandon it. Major Macdonell then dispatched an officer to
summon the fort but ere he reached it, the enemy was in full retreat, over a
distant eminence.[36]

Thus fell Ogdensburg. The British and Canadians burned two schooners,
the *Niagara* and *Dolphin*, trapped in the ice and took 11 pieces of artillery,
including two 12-pdr. guns engraved "as having fallen into the hands of the
rebels, at the surrender to General Burgoyne, in 1777," which made everyone
happy.[37] They also picked up 672 stand of arms and a considerable amount
of ammunition, provisions and useful stores. Forsyth reported 26 men killed
and 60 taken prisoner and was admonished by his superiors, who had given
him "repeated cautions" about his raids as they "would probably produce such
retaliating strokes as he would be unable to resist," as was clearly the case.[38]
Nothing more was heard of Forsyth or his riflemen along the St. Lawrence and,
as the village magistrates pledged themselves to keep the peace, there "was no
further annoyance from Ogdensburg, after this visit."[39]
Macdonell's losses were 8 killed and 52 wounded, who were cared for by Father Macdonell, who had them carried to a tavern in Prescott. When the good

father, seeing that the wounded were as "in need of stimulants as of priestly counsel," asked for some brandy, he was told by the owners, suspected American sympathizers, that the tap room door was locked. He promptly kicked it off its hinges and distributed brandy not only to the wounded, but to all present.[40]

Prevost and Pearson had arrived at Kingston before news of Major Macdonell's attack reached them. Since the venture had ended well, the commander-in-chief overlooked his subordinate's disobedience and actually altered his report to take some personal credit for the victory. Macdonell, however, believed he did not receive enough praise or reward for his success and tried for many years, unsuccessfully, to get extra distinction. While he would have been generous enough to praise his subordinate's initiative, it must have been galling to Pearson to learn that an attack, which he had carefully planned and was refused permission to execute, was carried out with good results by another officer. On the other hand, Pearson knew only too well that such is life in the service.

Pearson was at Kingston for just under two months. As this town was the major British naval base on Lake Ontario, his main concern was to improve its defences by erecting blockhouses to protect the shipyard on Point Frederick, across from the town. Although an army officer, Pearson's duties as garrison commander also involved him in the affairs of the Provincial Marine, the British naval service on the Great Lakes that had been created to provide transport for troops and supplies in the western part of British North America. The Marine was actually under control of the Quartermaster General's Department, service in it was a sinecure and most of the captains were superannuates of the Revolutionary War. Nonetheless, its four vessels dominated Lake Ontario in the opening months of the war as there was only one American warship on that body of water. Trying to overcome this initial disadvantage, the United States Navy established shipyards at Sacket's Harbor on Lake Ontario and at Presque Isle on Lake Erie, and a shipbuilding race commenced as both sides launched progressively larger warships to gain control of the lakes, as whoever controlled the water dominated movement. The Admiralty had realized that the matter of the naval service on the lakes was too important to be left to the army and a strong force of Royal Navy officers and seamen was already on its way to take over the rather shaky Provincial Marine.

It was not long before Pearson was forced to take steps with regard to this service. When he arrived at Kingston the shipyard was under the supervision of one Daniel Allen, who was not only inefficient but also dangerous as he tried

Kingston, Upper Canada, during the War of 1812
The major British naval base and shipyard on Lake Ontario, Kingston was an important part of the defence of Upper Canada. Pearson commanded the garrison for two months in the spring of 1813 and was involved not only in improving the defences of the town but also in naval construction and training. Kingston was attacked once by American naval forces but remained safely in British hands throughout the war. (Print from *Canadian Geographical Magazine,* 1961)

to instigate a strike for higher wages among his own workers. On 11 March 1813 Pearson dismissed Allen from his post and, on the advice of Captain Andrew Gray, who oversaw the marine service, replaced him with George Record, a more experienced and productive man. Pearson then conducted an inspection of the largest vessels of the Provincial Marine, the ship *Earl of Moira*, 14 guns, and the corvette *Royal George*, 22 guns, making sure that the crews carried out gun drill with live rounds under his critical eye and he was, perhaps reluctantly, forced to confess that they proved "more expert at their guns than I had reason to believe."[41] The main problem with the *Moira* was her captain, Lieutenant Theophilus Sampson, who proved so lazy, insubordinate and disobedient that Pearson and Gray removed him from command and placed him under arrest. Between them, the two army officers were able to improve the productivity of the shipyard and the efficiency of the squadron on Lake Ontario.

The sight of these warships more than a thousand miles from the ocean was a never-ending source of amazement for newcomers to Kingston. When the 104th Regiment of Foot entered that town on 12 April to be billetted by Pearson after an epic 700-mile march from New Brunswick, one officer remembered that

The war of the carpenters

During the War of 1812, the opponents built powerful squadrons on the inland lakes, each side in turn launching larger and larger warships. In 1812, the largest warship on Lake Ontario carried 20 guns; two years later the Royal Navy commissioned a 102-gun ship of the line that was larger than Nelson's *Victory*. As one British officer termed it, this shipbuilding race was "a war of carpenters." (Drawing by George Balbar reproduced with permission from Robert Foley, *The War of 1812*)

there was a general exclamation of "The sea, the sea – the ships, the ships!" The whole of us spontaneously broke and ran to witness the novel and interesting sight. Some of us had been marching between eight hundred and a thousand miles in six weeks, with only ten days' halt, during which time we had never lost sight of a forest, when suddenly there lay before our astonished and delighted view the town of Kingston, the magnificent Lake Ontario, and what was far more surprising still, a squadron of ships-of-war frozen on its bosom. It produced a striking and indescribable sensation, as none of us Europeans appeared to have reflected on the circumstance of being sure to find a fleet of men of war on a fresh water lake.[42]

The arrival of the 104th ended Pearson's spell of duty at Kingston as on 17 April 1813 he was replaced in command by Colonel Alexander Halkett, that regiment's commanding officer, and ordered to Montreal. Ann and young Thomas had been living there since the previous September as a shortage of provisions had led to the presence of military dependants being discouraged in Upper Canada. Ann had friends and family in Montreal and she was probably more comfortable in the largest city in British North America but, as it was, Pearson was only in Montreal for a few weeks when he was ordered back to Prescott.

When Pearson returned in the second week of May 1813, he found a new unit, the Incorporated Militia Battalion of Upper Canada, waiting for him at Prescott. The title of this unit is somewhat misleading as it was not a militia regiment in the traditional Canadian sense but was composed of soldiers enlisted for the duration of the war and in fact originated from Pearson's suggestions made the previous January. The authorities had taken time to mull over the matter but, in late March 1813, beating orders had been issued to recruit strong and healthy men, aged 16 to 45, for an infantry battalion that would be armed, uniformed and equipped, as were British and Canadian regular units, with each man to receive $18 bounty and a land grant at the completion of his service. The strongest response came in the eastern part of the province and in late April 1813 six companies of the Incorporated Militia, 339 officers and men, were concentrated at Prescott under the command of Lieutenant-Colonel Justus Sherwood, the father of Reuben Sherwood, Pearson's "Captain of Guides." At the same time the infantry battalion was raised, recruits were enlisted for two troops of Incorporated Militia Cavalry, or Provincial Light Dragoons, which also assembled at Prescott under the command of Captains Richard Fraser and Andrew Adams.[43]

Pearson probably got his first look at the Incorporated Militia on or about 12 May 1813, and he did not like what he saw. It shortly became apparent that many of the officers were incapable of their duties, as the authorities had not only disregarded his suggestion that he approve potential officers, but had commissioned them according to the number of men they recruited. Most had no military experience whatsoever and not a few were completely useless. Disappointed, Pearson immediately set out to beat the Incorporated Militia into shape. On 13 May he announced that he would inspect the battalion and expected that "their arms, accoutrements, ammunition" be "in perfect order" and that the officers would "be properly dressed in their uniforms immediately."[44] This apparently did not have the desired result so, in an order dated 26 May, Pearson was forced to confess himself "much surprised" that any officer "should appear in the dress of an American Riflemen as some have lately presumed to do, and most positively forbids it."[45] Three days later he ordered all officers off duty to parade with their men and, still annoyed about their appearance, again emphasized that they "be dressed agreeably to His Majesty's Regulations."[46]

When he finally seems to have got the officers of the Incorporated Militia in correct uniform, Pearson began to instruct them in their duties. In the spring of 1813 the new battalion had two functions – it was undergoing basic training at the hands of Lieutenant Ridge and it was providing labour for the construction of the blockhouse and the earthwork surrounding it. This latter activity was very unpopular with the new soldiers, who felt they had enlisted to fight, not dig, and their officers seem to have agreed with them. Very shortly, Pearson promulgated an order directing that every officer and NCO was "to carry a roll

Fort Wellington, Prescott, 1814
This defence work, which was begun in early 1813, took over a year to complete and was the source of much irritation for Pearson. He did not get along with the engineer in charge of its construction, who he believed was not moving fast enough, and often refused to let him use troops to work on the fort. It was finally completed early in 1814, well behind schedule. (Painting by Thomas Burrowes, Archives of Ontario)

The Incorporated Militia Battalion of Upper Canada
Created at Pearson's suggestion, this unit was, despite its title, a long-service unit enlisted
for the duration of the war and was uniformed, armed and equipped like regular units. Although he was the unit's "father," the Incorporated Militia Battalion gave Pearson endless
trouble in 1813 until he had whipped it into shape. During the Niagara campaign of 1814,
it was under his command for a lengthy period of time and performed well in combat. The
officer on the left wears the broad-brimmed, low-crowned hat which was popular summer
wear in the Canadas. A shortage of red cloth in North America meant that the unit's first issue of uniforms consisted of green coatees, as shown on the private soldier, but they later
received the standard red garment. (Paintings by G.A. Embleton, courtesy Department of
National Defence, Canada)

of his company in his pocket and to be able to account for the whereabouts of
any man in the company at all time" and that no man "was to be absent from
work details" and, if they were, officers were to pursue any absentees.[47] Pearson
followed this with orders instructing officers to inspect barracks daily to make
sure they were clean, to make sure that their men were familiar with their posts
if an alarm was given, and to read daily orders to their subordinates and verify

that they understood them. All this was the standard military routine but with the Incorporated Militia Pearson had to start at the very beginning and work his way forward. In doing so, he could not make use of the threat of flogging as, under the terms of their enlistment, the men of the Incorporated Militia were not subject to this punishment.

These orders did not have the intended effect as it appears there were still some officers of the battalion who did not get the message Pearson had spelled out many times. The upshot was that on 5 July 1813 he issued a garrison order reporting that, with "sincere regret," he was under "the painful necessity of publicly exposing his displeasure at the conduct of the following officers of the Incorporated Militia" and the names of four captains, three lieutenants and five ensigns followed, who were "not attending their respective stations."[48] Having opened fire, Pearson then let loose a full volley:

It is but too obvious from the behaviour of many of the Militia Officers in the Garrison that the emoluments arising from their commissions are to be the only objects of their attention, and their services on behalf of their country are but objects of a secondary consideration expressed with imputation of men whose properties, families and connections are all dependent on their exertions [but who] will most cheerfully come forward and defend their fireside.

What can they expect from others – who have not these inducements – but who are instigated solely by the impulsion of honour which is the proud characteristic of every British soldier who labours unceasingly on the work at Prescott so that it might immediately prove the safeguard of the Province. How pleasing is the satisfaction of the thinking man that his personal exertions contributed to the discomfiture of his countries Enemy and the situation of his own property. Not so will be the reflection of those whose lukewarm aid in the hour of threatening danger will scarcely allow them to be ranked among the gallant defenders of this country.[49]

It is unlikely that Thomas Pearson would ever have enjoyed success as an author but in his orotund fashion he had tried to get the point across. Unfortunately, it does not seem to have worked as, on 27 July, we find him issuing an order that, in "consequence of the reluctance manifested by some of the officers particularly of the Incorporated Militia to perform the duties required of them as officers in His Majesty's Service," they would in future "parade with their men at fatigues."[50] In other words, the officers of the battalion were going to have to pick up shovels and dig.

In fairness to the Incorporated Militia, it was not the only unit in the Prescott garrison that incurred Pearson's wrath. All received their share, although the new battalion seems to have been the worst offender. As Prescott was a staging point for military movement between the Canadas, units were rotating through the garrison about every two weeks, which meant that Pearson was forever having to break in new arrivals to his tightly regulated manner of command. Soldiers stationed at Prescott were not "to put off their clothes at night but every person belonging to the garrison to hold himself in readiness to turn out a moment's warning."[51] Day and night patrols were sent out around the surrounding area and deer hunting near the post was prohibited lest the shots alarm the garrison. Reveillee was at 5.30 A.M. in summer and 6 A.M. in winter but punishment parades, called to witness floggings, were held at 5.30 A.M. – a pleasant way to start the day which included two garrison parades in full marching order. Sick call came at 6 A.M., and all patients who could stand paraded in front of their barracks or tents, and those who could walk were marched by a sergeant to the surgeon. Barracks were cleaned and washed daily, blankets weekly, and wives and children were expected to assist in this labour.[52]

Pearson even tried to organize the small group of Tyendinaga Mohawk warriors attached to his command. He ordered Lieutenant Charles Anderson, their Indian Department interpreter, to assemble them "evening and morning at parade to show they are present and ready to fight."[53] It is doubtful that warriors like Shagaunnahquodwaby ("Captain James") or Pahguahjenemy ("Old Peter") paid much attention to this fuss so typical of the whites and probably did just what they wanted to do. It is fascinating to speculate what the Mohawks may have called Pearson – possibly a long and unpronounceable moniker which, translated, meant "Yingees-officer-who-limps-and-shouts-much."

"Jack, drop cooking!" – the morning of the battle
When Morrison ordered his troops to form for battle, Lieutenant John
Sewell of the 49th Foot was using his sword to cook a piece of pork over
a campfire. Reluctantly he had to leave his breakfast and fall in with his
company. It had been a cold, wet night with rain, sleet and hail and the
day of the battle was not much better. (Drawing by George Balbar reproduced with permission from Robert Foley, *The War of 1812*)

CHAPTER TEN

"THE BRAVEST MEN
I HAVE EVER SEEN"

ON THE ST. LAWRENCE,
JULY 1813 – APRIL 1814

The Yankees did invade us,
To kill and to destroy,
And to distress our country,
Our peace for to annoy,
Our countrymen were filled
With sorrow, grief and woe,
To think that they should fall,
To such an unnatural foe.

Come all ye bold Canadians
Enlisted in the cause,
To defend your country,
And to maintain your laws;
Being all united,
This is the song we'll sing;
Success unto Great Britain
And God save the King![1]

In the late spring of 1813, the United States resumed its offensive against British North America. American leaders, having learned from the mistakes of the previous year and over the winter, had put tremendous energy into building up naval squadrons on Lakes Ontario and Erie. Despite the best efforts of Pearson and Gray at Kingston, when the ice melted from Lake Ontario in early April 1813, the American naval commander, Commodore Isaac Chauncey, had superiority on that body of water. Although Secretary of War John Armstrong wanted Chauncey and the senior military commander in the north, Major-General Henry Dearborn, to attack Kingston, they instead directed their efforts against York (modern Toronto), the capital of Upper Canada, which they took on 27 April 1813. Following a brief occupation, Chauncey's squadron then transported Dearborn's army to the Niagara Peninsula, where it again invaded Canada at the end of May, capturing Fort George at the mouth of the Niagara River and driving outnumbered British forces back to their supply depots at Burlington Bay, some 40 miles west. Thereafter, the impetus went out of the American offensive and the campaign degenerated into a loose British blockade of the American position at Fort George, which lasted nearly the entire summer. Disappointed, Secretary of War Armstrong removed Dearborn from command and replaced him with Major-General James Wilkinson, but it took that officer nearly two months to reach the frontier and he did not arrive at Fort George until early August.

Pearson was only indirectly connected with these events, which took place some 250 miles to the west of Prescott. As his area of the St. Lawrence was quiet after the attack on Ogdensburg the previous February, his energies were directed toward finishing the blockhouse and earthwork, overseeing the security of the river and, above all, ensuring that there was no interference with numerous military boat convoys moving up and down it. This duty became all the more important in May 1813 when Commodore Sir James Lucas Yeo and a strong detachment of Royal Navy personnel took over the Provincial Marine and began to transform that somewhat backward force into an efficient naval service. Yeo stepped up the building effort at Kingston and this resulted in an increase in the supplies, ordnance and war materiel transported up the vulnerable St. Lawrence. The Americans made no serious attempt to interdict this vital communications route, a matter that puzzled the British commanders because, as one officer who served with Pearson remarked:

Canada, so far from being able to supply an army and navy with the provisions required, was (as a great many of her effective population were employed in the transport of military and naval stores) not fit to supply her own wants, and it was essential to secure supplies from wherever they could be got soonest and cheapest. Troops acting on the Niagara frontiers, 1,000 miles from the ocean, were fed with flour the produce of England, and pork and beef from Cork, which, with the waste inseparable from a state of war, the expense and accidents to which a long voyage expose them, and the enormous cost of internal conveyance, at least doubled the quantity required, and rendered the price of them at least ten times their original cost.

Not only provisions, but every rope yarn, as well as the heavier articles of guns, shot, cables, anchors, and all the numerous etceteras for furnishing a large squadron, arming forts, supplying arms for the militia and the line, had to be brought from Montreal to Kingston, a distance of nearly 200 miles, by land in winter, and in summer by flat-bottomed boats, which had to tow up the rapids, and sail up the still parts of the river (and in many places, not a mile in breadth, between the British and American shores) exposed to the shot of the enemy without any protection; for with the small body of troops we had in the country, it was utterly impossible that we could detach a force sufficient to protect the numerous *brigades* of boats that were daily proceeding up the river, and we must have been utterly undone, had not the ignorance and inertness of the enemy saved us.

Had they stationed four field guns, covered by a corps of riflemen, on the banks of the St. Lawrence, they could have cut off our supplies without risking a man. As it was we only had to station a small party at every fifty miles, to be ready to act in case of alarm; but fortunately for us, they rarely or never troubled us. If they had done so with any kind of spirit, we must have abandoned Upper Canada, Kingston and the fleet on Ontario included, and leaving it to its fate, confined ourselves to the defence of such part of the Lower Provinces as came within the range of our own empire, the sea.[2]

As we have seen, however, whenever the enemy did attempt to interfere with the St. Lawrence, British officers such as Thomas Pearson, who commanded posts along the river, were quick to respond.

Given the crucial importance of the St. Lawrence, there was always concern when even the slightest threat was made to that lifeline. In late July 1813, two American privateer vessels – actually longboats each carrying a 6-pdr. gun and about 25 crew – attacked a British provisions convoy on the river west of Prescott and captured 15 boats, their supplies and crews. When word of this reached Kingston, three gunboats were dispatched with a detachment of the 100th Foot to recover boats and cargo. This force attacked the privateer encampment at Goose Creek, on the American bank about 40 miles above Ogdensburg, but the privateers, who had built a rough log fort, fought off the attackers and forced them to retire with some loss. Learning of this incident, Pearson used his intelligence network to find out more about these new and dangerous arrivals on the river. Unfortunately he could not use his chief spy, Samuel Steacy, as that agent had been arrested and imprisoned by Commodore Chauncey, only to be later released by Secretary of War Armstrong on the rather dubious grounds that "a citizen cannot be considered a spy."[3] Pearson's intelligence officers, Captains Sherwood and Gilkinson, were able to ascertain that the privateers were volunteers "who have been permitted to engage from the troops at Sackett's Harbour, a proportion being seamen."[4] Pearson then dispatched his staff adjutant, Lieutenant George Ridge, and one of the intelligence officers over the St. Lawrence to locate the privateers' base, and when that was done he mounted an amphibious expedition using gunboats from Prescott and thoroughly examined the area around Goose Creek but could find no sign of the privateers.

It was about this time that Ann and infant Thomas joined Pearson at Prescott, and the family lived in the one-storey weatherboarded house that served as the garrison commander's quarters. Work on the blockhouse and its attendant earthwork had continued throughout the spring and summer, but Pearson's relations with the engineer of the project, Lieutenant Frederick de Gaugreben, were often not the best, the engineer complaining that Pearson would not provide enough military labour. For his part, Pearson, wondering like many others when this interminable construction project would be finished, reported in the late summer of 1813 that, although his men were working hard, he doubted it would be ready to house a garrison until October while, "as for finishing the work this Year it is out of the Question, all I dare hope is to secure what we have done."[5]

Construction of the blockhouse, which would be named Fort Wellington in 1814, was advanced enough by early August for it to be used for a ball arranged by Pearson's commissary officer to honour the visit of the wife an officer of a unit in transit through the post. One of Ann Pearson's sisters – possibly the spirited Sophia of boat and bear fame – was also visiting, and a good time seems to have been had by all. Unfortunately, later that month Ann, was taken so "alarmingly ill" as to be "incapable of being moved."[6] When she had recovered somewhat, Pearson received permission to take her and Thomas back to Montreal.

By the time he returned in early September, the war on the St. Lawrence had started to heat up. Major-General James Wilkinson, the new American commander, had finally reached the northern theatre and began to carry out Armstrong's plan to mount a major offensive against Montreal before the onset of winter. This operation envisaged a two-pronged attack: Major-General Wade Hampton would move northwest with his division from Lake Champlain directly against the objective while Wilkinson with a larger force would move

Major-General James Wilkinson, U.S. Army (1757-1826)
A veteran of the War of Independence, Wilkinson was a disaster as a field commander in 1813. He was old and sick and proved to be a complete incompetent although he survived the resulting court martial unscathed. His men fought bravely but deserved a better leader. (Courtesy of the National Portrait Gallery, Washington, NPG 75.15)

down the St. Lawrence in a flotilla of small boats and, joining with Hampton, their combined forces would take Montreal. It was a good plan but it almost immediately began to unravel. Hampton hated Wilkinson and was unwilling to co-operate, although he was technically under Wilkinson's command. Wilkinson not only reciprocated the animosity but also proved a reluctant warrior and began to suggest that perhaps Kingston, rather than Montreal, should be the objective. When Armstrong came north to Sacket's Harbor to straighten out the uncertainty, the two men wasted weeks of crucial time arguing over the objective, both changing their minds several times. Meanwhile, the greater part of the American army at Fort George in the Niagara was transferred to Sacket's Harbor, where an intense building programme, supervised by that active officer, Brigadier-General Jacob Brown, now commissioned in the regular army, was under way to construct the armada of small boats necessary for Wilkinson's movement.

The American build-up at Sacket's Harbor was obvious to senior British commanders but they were puzzled as to where the enemy would attack. In British eyes, the main targets were either Montreal or Kingston, but there were also suspicions that either Prescott or York might be the enemy objective. In the meantime, until the matter became more clear, a corresponding movement of troops was made from the Niagara to Kingston and security generally tightened along the St. Lawrence corridor. Pearson prohibited visits to Ogdensburg and further increased the state of alert for the troops under his command, which at this time consisted of about 1,000 men. He received a steady stream of information from his intelligence sources and, as September turned to October, became convinced that either Prescott or Montreal would come under attack. He informed Prevost that,

In consequence of which it is my intention to be prepared with all my disposable force to act accordingly to the movements of the enemy. If they proceed downwards without noticing me at Prescott, I will instantly follow them with my light artillery and part of my regulars and militia, and by means of waggons occupy such positions as may considerably annoy his descent down the river. Whenever the enemy does appear I hope to God we shall be able to give some account of him.[7]

And he was ready to do just that. On the same day, 12 October 1813, that Pearson penned this letter, a force of American cavalry was observed entering Ogdensburg. As the inhabitants of that village had been asserting their neutrality since the previous February, Pearson was unhappy to see blue-uniformed enemy dragoons riding through their streets and ordered his artillery commander, Captain Henry Jackson, RA, to open fire on Ogdensburg with two long range 24-pdr. guns. The noise of the gunfire caused Judge Benjamin Raymond of Ogdensburg, presiding over county court that day, to hastily adjourn, and it was well he did so because minutes after the courtroom was vacated a 24-pdr. round shot penetrated the wall and cut obliquely through the jury seats. The enemy cavalry hastily vacated the village but returned the next day, evidently trying to draw fire so as to estimate the number and types of ordnance at Prescott. This time, Pearson sent over several heavy mortar shells, "the effect of which was to make" the enemy dragoons "leave the village hastily, when the firing ceased immediately."[8]

Prescott's commander was ever vigilant and any military movement on the American side of the river was sure to attract his attention. When he observed mounted groups of what were obviously enemy staff officers moving along the American bank, he dispatched Sherwood and a few of his militia across the river to harass them. The staff officers were actually Colonel Joseph Swift, Wilkinson's chief engineer, and his assistants, who had been dispatched to survey the American shore for landing places, and Sherwood was successful in interfering and delaying their work. A few days later, Pearson became aware that the enemy had established cavalry vedettes on the American shore below Ogdensburg and began to plan a raid across the river. It was put into effect on the night of 16 October when Major Francis Cockburn of the Canadian Fencibles, then under Pearson's command, moved quietly over the St. Lawrence with a strong detachment from his regiment. Cockburn cut off the vedette at Red Mills, about eight miles below Ogdensburg, killing three Americans and capturing an officer and seven dragoons.

Rough passage on the Great Lakes waterways
In October 1813, Major-General James Wilkinson's army, more than 7,000 men, boarded a fleet of 328 boats, scows, skiffs and small schooners to commence a journey down the St. Lawrence. Delayed by bad weather, they did not reach Prescott until 6 November and five days later were defeated at the battle of Crysler's Farm. (Sketch by Peter Rindlisbacher from Donald E. Graves, *Field of Glory: The Battle of Crysler's Farm*)

One week later, Wilkinson's army left Sacket's Harbor in an armada of more than 300 boats, schooners and gunboats and sailed to Grenadier Island, at the mouth of the St. Lawrence River, directly across from Kingston. Consisting of five brigades of infantry, some 7,300 men with 22 pieces of field artillery and 17 siege pieces, this was the largest force of regular troops to be assembled by the United States prior to 1861. Unfortunately for Wilkinson, he had delayed so long that the autumn gales had arrived and he lost a number of boats and nearly half his provisions in a very rough passage to the island. His movement, however, was no more enlightening to the watchful British commanders as Grenadier Island could serve as a staging point for an attack on either Kingston or Montreal; all they could do was make ready and wait on events.

On 3 November 1813, Wilkinson ended British uncertainty when, under the protection of the warships of Commodore Chauncey's Lake Ontario squadron, his troops embarked on their boats and moved into the St. Lawrence to commence a 200-mile water journey to attack one of the most strongly defended cities in British North America at the onset of the ferocious Canadian winter. When the flotilla bypassed Kingston, it became clear that Montreal was the enemy objective and British commanders took the necessary steps. For his part, Pearson called out the militia in his district and sent officers to selected posts up river from Prescott to warn of the enemy's approach. One of them was Lieutenant Duncan Clarke of the Incorporated Militia, who was ordered to a point five miles above Brockville. Clarke unfortunately did not own a horse so when he saw the leading boats of the American flotilla approaching him on 5 November, he commandeered a slow and cumbersome ploughhorse from a nearby farmer and, moving at the fastest plod possible, spread the alarm down the Canadian bank to Prescott.

Another of Pearson's officers behaved less creditably. Captain Richard Fraser, commanding the troop of Provincial Light Dragoons attached to Pearson's command, was dispatched to Brockville to report on the enemy and to order to Prescott any militiaman who had not answered the call to arms. When Fraser encountered Hiram Spafford, a militia officer and local merchant – and a suspected American sympathizer – he ordered him to go to Prescott, but Spafford refused, pleading that he had property to protect. Fraser immediately placed him under arrest but permitted Spafford to go to his house to collect his horse. When the miscreant did not return in due course, Fraser and a fellow militia officer, who had meanwhile been fortifying themselves in a local tavern, went to Spafford's residence, "in a rage and much intoxicated," according to a witness, and finding that the man had fled, attempted to set fire to his house but were prevented by neighbours.[9] Spafford later sued the two officers in civilian court for property damage, and although Pearson admitted they were "delinquents," he defended them by stressing that they "meant and intended well."[10] When the court found against Fraser and his companion, Pearson retaliated by cancelling Spafford's trading licence and removing him from his militia appointment.

By 5 November 1813, the American army had reached a point just below Morrisville, New York. Wilkinson now faced the task of getting past Prescott, where Pearson was eagerly waiting, actually itching to get at him. The American commander wisely disembarked his troops, stores and artillery to move overland while skeleton crews, commanded by the capable Brigadier-General Jacob Brown, rowed the flotilla past Prescott under cover of darkness. By the late afternoon of 6 November all was ready, and although it was a full moon, providentially for Brown a thick fog settled on the river to provide cover. Unfortunately, just as the lead boats came within British artillery range it lifted,

The passage of Prescott, 6 November 1813
During the night of 6 November 1813, Wilkinson's army successfully made a perilous night-time passage on the river past the obstacle of Pearson's batteries at Prescott. The St. Lawrence was nearly a mile wide at this point and despite being under fire for several hours, only one boat was hit and there were no serious casualties. (Sketch by Peter Rindlisbacher from Donald E. Graves, *Field of Glory: The Battle of Crysler's Farm, 1813*)

and Captain Henry Jackson, Pearson's artillery commander, opened up with the 17 pieces of artillery positioned in the batteries at Prescott. An American officer and some comrades, who had taken the opportunity to order a steak dinner in a tavern in Ogdensburg, were just sitting down to enjoy it when, "bang! bang! and bang!" and a round shot "passed right through the upper storey of the hotel, crashing and splintering its way through walls, partitions, and such articles of furniture as stood in its path."[11] Hastily rising from their meal, the officers paid their bill and departed for safer pastures.

As soon as the fog lifted, Brown ordered the boats to move in close to the American shore until the moon had set, before trying again. When he did, Jackson resumed fire and one American in the boats recorded that "the roar of cannon was unremitting" and the night sky "rendered visible by the whizzing and bursting of shells."[12] The St. Lawrence, however, was 1,800 yards wide at this point, and although Jackson's gunners fired for more than three hours at the hundreds of watercraft, they only hit one boat and killed one man. By dawn, when the armada was safely past Lieutenant-Colonel Thomas Pearson, the "Cyclops" of the St. Lawrence, Wilkinson's troops then re-embarked and the American army continued on its journey.

Angry that his enemy had escaped almost untouched, Pearson decided to continue the battle. He dispatched Fraser's dragoons and some militia to trail the American flotilla down the river and also sent Jackson with two 6-pdr. field guns to snipe at it. As he could see enemy troops moving in the streets of Ogdensburg, Pearson continued to fire at the village throughout 6 November and after they had disappeared, he sent an officer over under a flag of truce to demand the surrender of any public stores left by Wilkinson's army. The people of Ogdensburg, themselves annoyed by the intrusion of war into their peaceful pursuits, cheerfully turned over two siege mortars, 30 barrels of pork and 20 barrels of whisky before giving firm guarantees of neutrality in the future. Pearson remained unmollified, as he still very much wanted "to get some account" of Wilkinson's army.

He was therefore pleased when Lieutenant-Colonel Joseph Morrison arrived in Prescott that evening (8 November) by boat from Kingston with an amphibious "Corps of Observation," which had been sent to follow the Americans down the river and harass them at every opportunity. Morrison's command consisted of the 89th and 49th Foot, a total of about 850 officers and men, which was not a strong force to tackle an enemy army of 7,000, and when Pearson proposed joining him with a detachment from the Prescott garrison, Morrison was only too delighted. Pearson chose his best units, taking with him the two flank companies of the 49th, three companies of the Canadian Fencibles and three companies of the *Voltigeurs Canadiens,* provincial regulars from Lower Canada who were light infantry specialists. He also contributed Captain Jackson and an RA detachment and his small force of Mohawk warriors, but significantly left the Incorporated Militia Battalion behind to defend Prescott. When the newly-augmented "Corps of Observations" departed by boat early on the morning of 9 November, Morrison was commanding just under 1,200 men with three 6-pdr. guns

Morrison's troops caught up with the enemy the next day. After leaving Ogdensburg, Wilkinson had moved along the Canadian bank of the river, the infantry and cavalry marching, while the artillery remained on the boats which followed the army's progress. Morrison therefore disembarked on the Canadian bank and hastened forward to make contact, but his progress was slowed by the fact that rain had made the primitive King's Highway that paralleled the St. Lawrence a morass, and the American rearguard had destroyed the bridges crossing the many creeks that flowed into the river. During the march, a British officer approached a Canadian farmer who was curiously watching the mud-

Canadian *Voltigeurs* and aboriginal ally, 1813
The Canadian *Voltigeurs* or Provincial Corps of Light Infantry were a long-service unit raised in April 1812 for the duration of the war. They were commanded by Lieutenant-Colonel Charles de Salaberry, an officer of the 60th Foot, and saw considerable action. They wore grey uniforms trimmed with black and bearskin caps as shown here, while their officers wore green uniforms very similar to those of the 95th Rifles. (Painting by G.A. Embleton, courtesy Parks Canada)

spattered column pass by to ask him if he had seen the enemy and the man replied that he had, but not to "follow them for they are ten to your one."[13] "Never mind that," the officer retorted, "we are not asking your opinion."

Near midday, the British and Canadians came close to the enemy rearguard, which halted and faced them. As both Wilkinson and his second in command, Major-General Morgan Lewis, were sick on their boats from dysentery, command in the American army had devolved on Brigadier-General John P. Boyd, who decided to keep the pursuers at a safe distance. What followed was a very long and wet afternoon for both armies as they lunged and parried at each other without really getting to grips. Morrison was reluctant to bring on a major action because, given the disparity in numbers, it would have to be a defensive action on his part and he wanted better ground than his current position. He therefore kept his distance and simply annoyed the enemy with long range artillery fire. When the Americans withdrew late in the day to rendezvous with their boats, anchored in a cove about two miles downriver, he followed in their footsteps.

After marching about a mile, Morrison found the fine defensive ground he was looking for – a low-lying ridge running north and south, called Bush's Hill after a local farmer. At its southern extremity this ridge ended at the St. Lawrence, while to the north it terminated in swampy pine woods much ob-

Lieutenant-Colonel Joseph W. Morrison (1783-1826)
The American-born British commander at the battle of
Crysler's Farm, fought on 11 November 1813, Morrison
used ground and the superior training of his troops to
fight a near-perfect defensive battle. Amazingly enough,
it was his first major engagement since being commissioned in 1799 but he had capable subordinates in
Lieutenant-Colonels Thomas Pearson and John Harvey,
both veterans of the 1801 Egyptian campaign. (Courtesy
of the McCord Museum, Montreal, M 401)

structed by undergrowth. To the east, in the direction of the enemy, was a series
of open, muddy farm fields, about half a mile wide, bounded by a wood that
masked the two armies from each other's view. If Morrison placed his army
along this ridge with its flanks protected by terrain features, the enemy would
have to cross these fields, which were cut across by a large ravine and two gul-
lies running down to the St. Lawrence that made the movement of formed
troops very difficult. Satisfied that he had a good position, Morrison set up
his headquarters at the nearby residence of John Crysler, the most prominent
landowner in the area, placed a skirmish line of about 200 *Voltigeurs* and Mohawks in the woods separating the two armies, posted pickets and bivouacked
the remainder of his troops in the nearby fields. Everyone then tried to make
themselves as comfortable as they could under a steady downpour of rain.

When dawn came on Thursday, 11 November 1813, it brought a grey and
overcast sky. As soon as it was light, scattered shooting broke out between the American pickets and the *Voltigeurs* and Mohawks in the woods.
Facing an enemy estimated to be more than six times his number, Morrison
took no chances and immediately formed to meet an attack. Lieutenant John
Sewell of the 49th Foot was cooking breakfast by toasting a piece of pork on
the tip of his sword when a call from his company commander, "Jack, drop
cooking, the enemy is advancing!", brought him hastily to his feet.[14] Morrison
formed his main line, which consisted of the 49th Foot less its flank companies,
and seven companies of the 89th Foot, on a farm lane that led north along the
ridge from the King's Highway by the river bank. That wet day, the 89th Foot
were wearing only their red coatees but the wiser 49th, which had served in
Canada for more than a decade and knew the perversity of the weather, were in
their grey greatcoats. Pearson took post with the flank companies of the 49th,

three companies of the 89th and the three Canadian Fencibles companies at an advanced position on the King's Highway about one thousand yards east of the main line, while Jackson placed one of his 6-pdrs. with Pearson and the other two on the right flank of the main line. This done, everyone waited for an attack but when there was no sign of the enemy, shortly after noon Morrison ordered the *Voltigeurs* and Mohawks to push closer to the Americans to try to get something going.

The absence of the enemy was due to widespread confusion in the American command. Two days before, Wilkinson had dispatched Brown with two of his five infantry brigades ahead of the main army to take Cornwall but the remaining brigades were lined up on the road under the command of Brigadier-General Boyd, ready to resume their march, which they commenced at 8.30 A.M. Almost immediately, the column was halted by order of Wilkinson who, although sick on his boat and having officially turned over command to Lewis, still persisted in issuing orders. Around 10 A.M., seven British gunboats came down the river and bombarded the American camp for an hour, inflicting little damage and few casualties but causing a near panic among the civilian boatmen of the flotilla, many of whom hastily departed the scene with their craft.

It took some time to regain control and by 1.30 P.M. Boyd, whose men had been standing patiently for several hours in drizzling rain, finally rode to

U.S. infantry soldier, 1813
As they were poorly trained in contrast to their British and Canadian counterparts, the courage of the American soldiers at Crysler's Farm could not overcome the ineptitude of their generals and the result was that they were soundly beaten. Thomas Pearson, who was not an officer generous with his praise, admired his enemy, however, and once termed American soldiers "the bravest men I have ever seen." (Painting by Charles McBarron, courtesy Parks Canada)

Crysler's Farm – 11 November 1813
Phase 1: c. 1:30 – 2:00 PM

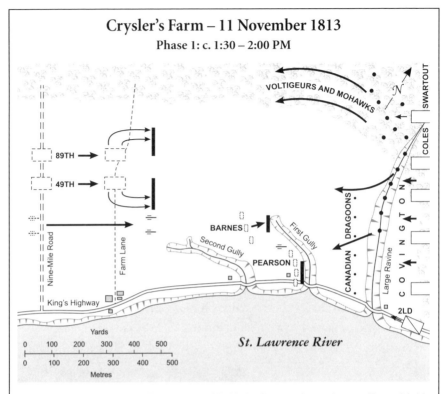

St. Lawrence River

Morrison deploys on good defensive ground behind a large ravine and two gulleys with his right flank guarded by the river, his left by woods and swamps. Pearson occupies a forward position on the river bank with one 6-pdr. gun in support. Barnes with three companies of the 89th Foot connects Pearson with the main British line. As the Americans advance, the *Voltigeurs*, Mohawks and Canadian dragoons fall back before them.

the river bank and shouted across to the commanders' boats, asking for orders. After a lengthy wait, he received one from Lewis to resume the march but, if the enemy pressed too closely on the rear, he was to "turn and beat him back."[15] A few minutes later, word came from the rearguard that British skirmishers and warriors were advancing through the woods and this was enough for Boyd, who was not a markedly intelligent officer, to decide to attack. He ordered his infantry to turn in their tracks and they began to advance west through the woods, pushing the *Voltigeurs* and warriors before them.

In the British position, the noise of increased firing in the woods made it clear that, at long last, the ball was rolling. From time to time they could see men moving through the trees, which had been stripped of their foliage by the autumn rains. At about 2 P.M., the grey-uniformed *Voltigeurs* dashed back to

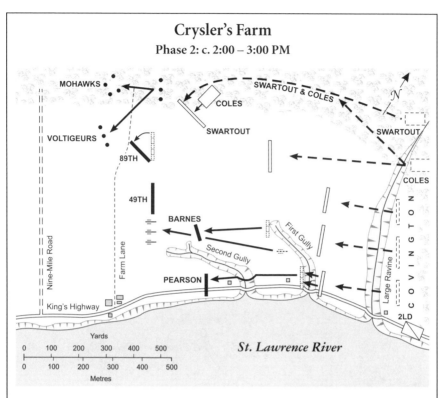

Crysler's Farm

Phase 2: c. 2:00 – 3:00 PM

Boyd attempts to outflank Morrison's main position using the brigades of Swartout and Coles but is stopped cold by disciplined British musketry. At the same time, however, Covington advances his brigade against Pearson and forces him to withdraw behind the second gully. Barnes and the 6-pdr. gun supporting Pearson move back in tandem.

the main position and, a few minutes later, three heavy columns of blue-uniformed American infantry emerged from the tree line. Trooper John Loucks of Fraser's Provincial Light Dragoons, all of 17 years of age and very excited, galloped back to Pearson to give him the somewhat redundant information that the Americans were coming, only to be told that when "falling back" it "was not good form to ride so fast in the face of the enemy."[16] As Boyd's three brigades emerged onto the cleared fields, British observers estimated their numbers at between three and four thousand. They were actually about 2,200 strong but their appearance was impressive and a sergeant of the 49th Foot, losing his composure, cried out that "there are too many, we shall all be slaughtered."[17] Standing nearby, Lieutenant Sewell coldly told the man that "it will be better for you to die doing your duty, than to be shot for mutiny." A few minutes

Crysler's Farm
Phase 3: c. 3:00 – 3:30 PM

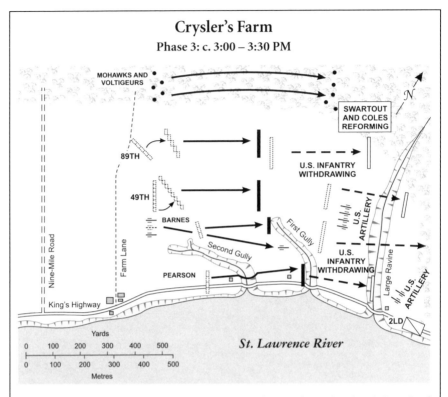

As Swartout and Coles withdraw to re-form, Morrison advances the 49th and 89th Foot. Boyd then withdraws his three brigades behind the ravine to re-ammunition just as the American artillery enters the battle. Two 6-pdr. guns are deployed on the river road while four 6-pdr. guns are advanced across the ravine in the middle of the battlefield. At this point Pearson reoccupies his former position and Barnes moves up to support him.

later, Jackson's guns took the Americans under fire to open an engagement that would later come to be known as the battle of Crysler's Farm.*

Jackson's gunners quickly found the correct range and began to torment the enemy with roundshot and shrapnel. The American advance faltered and some units fell back, leading one British officer to quip that "the enemy came on in a *pas de charge à la française* which was quickly changed by a well directed fire from our Field Artillery into one more comporting with the dignity of the American Nation."[18] For his part, Boyd was somewhat astonished by the course of events: he had advanced to push back a threatening but small enemy force and now found himself engaged with a stronger force posted on every good

---

* Complete Orders of Battle for the opposing forces at the battle of Crysler's Farm, 1813, will be found below in Appendix F.

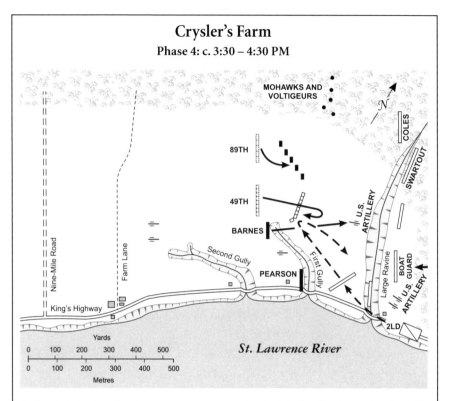

Crysler's Farm
Phase 4: c. 3:30 – 4:30 PM

MOHAWKS AND VOLTIGEURS

89TH

49TH

BARNES

PEARSON

Second Gully

First Gully

Nine-Mile Road

Farm Lane

King's Highway

U.S. ARTILLERY

COLES

SWARTOUT

Large Ravine

BOAT GUARD

U.S. ARTILLERY

2LD

St. Lawrence River

Yards
0   100   200   300   400   500

0   100   200   300   400   500
Metres

Seeing that the four American guns are not supported by infantry, Morrison orders the 49th Foot to advance in line against them, covered by the 89th Foot in echelon of companies. The 49th, under heavy fire, fails to take the American guns and is forced back.

Realizing that his guns are isolated, the American artillery commander begins to withdraw them across the ravine and, in an effort to protect them, a squadron of the 2nd U.S. Light Dragoons mounts a charge against the right flank of the 49th. This is beaten off by firepower but it permits three of the four guns get safely away. The fourth gun is captured by Barnes.

At this point, Boyd decides to break off the engagement and his three brigades and guns retreat, covered by the 600-strong boat guard which has just arrived on the battlefield. Morrison orders Pearson to maintain contact with the retreating Americans and, assuming command of all the light troops and warriors, Pearson does so.

defensive ground of their own choosing. Given the terrain, a direct movement against the grey and red British line on the ridge was going to be very difficult and, worse, his artillery was still being disembarked from the boats and it would be some time before it would be on the battlefield. Any offensive movement that Boyd made, therefore, would have to be done without artillery support. Perhaps his wisest move would have been to stand his ground and permit the

Brigadier-General John Boyd, U.S. Army (1764-1830)
In tactical command of the American army at Crysler's Farm, Boyd committed a series of fatal blunders, throwing his superior forces piecemeal against British regulars positioned on good defensive ground. What little glory that accrued to the U.S. Army on that day resulted from the work of his subordinates as Boyd was aggressive but not terribly intelligent – a fatal combination in a general. (From Benson Lossing, *Pictorial Field-Book of the War of 1812*)

flotilla to continue on its course while guarding its rear, but common sense was not John Boyd's forte. He decided to make a flank attack through the woods to the north and ordered Brigadier-Generals Robert Swartout and Isaac Coles to take their brigades through the pine trees and attack the British left flank. Boyd more or less ignored his third brigade, commanded by Brigadier-General Leonard Covington, which was deployed in line behind the large ravine opposite Pearson's position on the river bank.

It took Coles and Swartout some time to get under way in the woods and their intentions were obvious to the British. As the 1,300 Americans crashed through the undergrowth, they were hit by aimed fire from the Mohawks and *Voltigeurs,* who fell back slowly before them, the warriors, as was their custom in battle, screeching war whoops and shouting threats and insults. Morrison could follow the progress of the enemy columns by the smoke and the noise, and when the *Voltigeurs Canadiens* came, as one participant recalled, "bursting out of the woods on the left of our line like greyhounds," he ordered Major Miller Clifford, commanding the 89th Foot on that flank, to wheel back his left four companies so that they were at a rough 45-degree angle to the remaining companies of that regiment.[19] A few minutes later, the head of Swartout's brigade emerged from the woods and began to deploy into line, where some of its men commenced a ragged individual fire. In response, Clifford fired a single devastating volley by wings into the Americans, who fell back in confusion, and then followed it with a series of rolling platoon volleys from right to left. Swartout's brigade disintegrated, and his men ran back into the woods where they became tangled with Coles's brigade coming behind and both formations retreated in great confusion. Seeing this, Morrison ordered both the 49th and 89th Foot to advance in echelon of battalions to the right to bring the fleeing enemy within close range. This order was carried out as smoothly as possible, given the mud, the split rail fences which had to be torn down, and the occasional casualty from long-range fire.

Pearson had no time to watch this display of disciplined firepower as he had been having troubles of his own. Brigadier-General Covington, seeing the main British line engaged with Coles and Swartout, decided to attack the smaller enemy force facing him and ordered his brigade to advance in line across the large ravine, which was accomplished with some difficulty. Now within musket range, Covington opened fire with his three regiments, about 900 men strong, on Pearson's detachment, which only numbered about 200. Pearson returned fire but the British and Canadians got the worst of it and Pearson was thrown to the ground when his horse was shot out from under him. Confusion broke out among his men, possibly because their commander needed time to recover his senses from the fall, and Covington, seeing this, ordered an advance with the bayonet. Realizing he was outgunned and outnumbered, Pearson ordered a withdrawal behind the second gulley but the lead enemy elements were close enough to take prisoners and he lost a number of men.

Morrison, observing this attack on his right, opted to meet it with his main line and moved forward until his right flank unit, the 49th, was parallel to Pearson's new position. While that officer struggled to regain control of his men and redeploy them to meet Covington, every company in the British line that could bring its muskets to bear opened a steady fire on Covington's regiments. The intrepid Covington was mortally wounded by a musket ball in the stomach and command of his brigade devolved on Colonel Cromwell Pearce of the Sixteenth Infantry Regiment. Pearce replied to the British fire as did the brigades of Coles and Swartout, which had managed to reform on his right, and a musketry duel ensued with casualties on both sides. The Americans soon began to run out of cartridges because Boyd, never expecting a hard fight, had not thought to bring up a proper reserve of ammunition. The result was that

Brigadier-General Leonard Covington, U.S. Army (1768-1813)
Covington was a member of the younger generation of American officers who were saddled throughout the 1813 campaign with incompetent superiors. At Crysler's Farm, at the cost of a mortal wound, he gave Thomas Pearson a very hard time, forcing him to retreat, but this was one of the few bright spots in an otherwise dismal day for the United States Army. (From *Memoir of Leonard Covington*, 1928)

all three American brigades were withdrawn in good order to the edge of the woods to await a new supply of cartridges, and the duel ended. It was now about 3.30 P.M. and there was a brief lull.

It was broken when the American artillery appeared on the battlefield. It had taken some time for the field pieces to be landed from the boats and there was a further delay caused by the need to find draught animals and harness, as the previous day some fool had sent all the gun teams downriver. In the end, the horses of the squadron of light dragoons attached to the army were impressed into service and harness extemporized from whatever was available. It took nearly two hours for the first American artillery to reach the battlefield – two 6-pdr. guns that went into action on the King's Highway. With great difficulty, Lieutenant Henry Craig of the U.S. Artillery took four more 6-pdrs. across the ravine and deployed in front of the centre of the American line, about 300 yards from the British. He immediately brought the 49th Foot, directly opposite, under a heavy and accurate fire of canister, to which it could not make an effective reply as Craig was outside good musket range.

At this point, Lieutenant-Colonel Joseph Morrison made his first and only mistake of the day. He ordered Lieutenant-Colonel Charles Plenderleath, commanding the 49th, to advance and capture the enemy battery and in response the 49th, known as the "Green Tigers" from the colour of the facings or trim on their red coatees, moved forward. Whatever the problems with the other arms of the American army on this overcast Thursday afternoon in November, once it got into action, the United States Artillery functioned with professional efficiency. Craig's gunners devastated the oncoming regiment, killing or wounding 11 of its 18 officers, including Sewell's company commander, who died when a canister bullet "entered his head above the left Ear & passed thro' on the other Side" causing him to fall "lifeless in the same moment."[20] The senior lieutenant took over, only to be wounded minutes later, and command devolved on Sewell. The 49th began to falter but Plenderleath, an experienced officer, pulled them back to a safe distance, a manoeuvre made, as Sewell remarked, under a heavy fire of "grape and canister from the enemies' guns to which we were in close proximity."[21] Once in their new position the 49th opened up with long-range musketry while Captain George Barnes, commanding three companies of the 89th Foot on their right flank, moved closer to take the enemy gunners under fire.

As he had no infantry support of his own, Craig decided it was time to depart. He left one gun in position to cover his withdrawal while he commenced the onerous job of getting his other three 6-pdrs. back over the ravine. Barnes of the 89th, seeing the enemy start to withdraw, moved his three companies closer and brought this piece and its detachment under fire, hoping not only to capture it but also the other three weapons being dragged over the ravine by straining and unwilling cavalry horses, and pushed and pulled by mud-spattered gunners. Wilkinson's adjutant-general, Colonel John de Barth Walbach, a German who had once served in the French royal army before joining the American service, saw the peril and rode to Major John T. Woodford, commanding a squadron of the Second Regiment of United States Light Dragoons. With a heavy German accent, Walbach ordered Woodford to "Charge mit de dragoons!"[22]

Woodford led forward his squadron, 150 sabres strong, directly at the right flank of the 49th Foot. As the dragoons moved across the front of both Pearson and Barnes, their men fired a volley into them which emptied many saddles, while Jackson's gunners contributed some canister. Woodford's formation began to break up but the survivors, now picking up speed, continued straight at the 49th Foot and for a moment it looked as though there might be a replay on a smaller scale of the destruction of Colborne's brigade at Albuera. However, Lieutenant Dixie Ellis, the officer commanding the right flank company of the 49th, kept his head. As Sewell watched with admiration, Ellis waited until exactly the right moment before

United States light dragoon, 1813
Cavalry did not play a major role in the war in North America as the terrain was too wooded and forage for the horses difficult to procure. Even the cavalry's traditional task of reconnaissance was generally assumed by light infantry and aboriginal warriors. On 11 November 1813, however, the 2nd Regiment of Light Dragoons mounted one of the few cavalry charges of the War of 1812. (Painting by H.C. McBarron, courtesy Parks Canada)

The climax of the battle of Crysler's Farm, 1813
In this panoramic painting by Adam Sherriff-Scott, the American forces begin to withdraw
from the action. Throughout the grey and rainy afternoon of 11 November 1813, British and
Canadian regulars, using superior training, tactics and disciplined fire power, doomed American ambitions to take Montreal. (Courtesy, The St. Lawrence Parks Commission)

wheeling his company a few paces back to the right and pouring a concentrated
volley into the dragoons. At the same time, Barnes's three companies of the
89th, having reloaded, delivered another volley into their rear and Woodford's
squadron fell apart, scattering in all directions. The Virginian Woodford kept
going. Sewell watched him leap a split rail fence with his horse and ride toward Ellis's company, where "some of the men rushed out to attack him with
their bayonets," but Woodford, suddenly realizing he was alone, wheeled his
horse, "took the fence again in good hunting style" and followed his retreating
men.[23] The American cavalry had suffered heavy casualties but had protected
the withdrawal of the artillery. Craig managed to get all his guns away but the
one on the east side of the ravine, which was triumphantly captured by Barnes
at the point of the bayonet.

Boyd, whose nerve had been somewhat shaky all afternoon, now decided
things could only get worse and ordered a general withdrawal to the boats. Seeing his enemy giving up the action, Morrison ordered a general advance and,

as one of his staff officers remembered, "the fire of our Platoons and Guns and above all the steady countenance of the troops finally drove the enemy out of the field and about half past four o'Clock he gave up the contest and retreated rapidly through the woods covered by his light troops."[24]

Morrison directed Pearson to maintain contact and his subordinate took the flank companies of the 49th and the *Voltigeurs* forward in a style that the British commander thought most "judicious."[25] On his part, Wilkinson ordered his army to cross to the American bank of the St. Lawrence and by late that evening, his army, with the exception of Brown's two brigades at Cornwall, had left Canadian soil. The battle had cost the American commander just over 400 killed, wounded and missing, while Morrison reported his losses as being 179 of all types.

The next day, Wilkinson moved down the American side of the river to the area of Cornwall. Here he picked up Brown's two brigades and then took his entire army six miles up the Salmon River, across from Cornwall, to the little settlement of French Mills, New York, where he prepared to go into winter quarters.

During his journey down the St. Lawrence, Wilkinson had learned of the defeat of Major-General Wade Hampton, who had moved directly from Lake

Champlain toward Montreal, at the battle of Châteauguay fought on 25 October, but he had still been expecting Hampton to join him on the St. Lawrence. When he now learned that Hampton, contrary to orders, had retreated back to Lake Champlain, Wilkinson, a skilled hand at the politics of high command, immediately made Hampton the scapegoat for the failure of the offensive and ordered his arrest. Hampton managed to escape to Washington before the arresting officer arrived, and demanded a court of inquiry. As such a proceeding would be as detrimental to Secretary of War Armstrong, who bore no small responsibility for the fiasco, Armstrong wisely let Hampton retire from the army without penalty. Wilkinson lasted until the following spring when he too was relieved of command, as was almost every other senior officer in his army. They were replaced by younger, more capable men who had proved themselves in action, among them Jacob Brown, who was promoted major-general and placed in command at French Mills when Wilkinson, pleading illness, withdrew to more hospitable quarters for the winter.

After the battle, Pearson returned to Prescott but did not remain there more than two weeks, as on 25 November 1813 he was ordered to assume command at Cornwall. His intelligence network continued to function well and he soon began to receive accurate information about the state of the American army at French Mills, which not suprisingly was said to be sickly and demoralized. The ubiquitous Reuben Sherwood was dispatched to scout the American position and returned with a detailed and accurate plan of its defences. With this in hand, Pearson suggested to Prevost that, with some reinforcements, he could attack French Mills and bring to a successful conclusion, once and for all, this most serious American attempt to cut the St. Lawrence. The British commander-in-chief, always cautious about incurring casualties, which were nearly impossible to replace, refused and Pearson contented himself with keeping a vigilant eye on the enemy. This was not difficult to do as Wilkinson had nicely bottled himself up in a place where there was only one exit by water to the St. Lawrence, but which was extremely difficult to supply by land. American problems increased when the St. Lawrence froze in late December, bringing an end to water movement.

In the meantime, Pearson maintained some communication with the enemy and the officers of both armies under flags of truce met at the appointed place, a tavern about three miles downriver from Cornwall. It was during one such meeting that Pearson made one of the few gracious public comments ever attributed to him. It seems that he had been rather impressed by the performance of his enemy at Crysler's Farm; the American regulars were perhaps not yet up to the standards of the French 5th Corps at Albuera but Covington's brigade had been one of the few opponents who had not only forced Pearson to retreat, but had also put him in a rather sticky position for some time. Pearson rated soldiers by their performance in battle, and although it was clear that, while many American senior commanders were thoroughly incompetent – "imbeciles" and "stupid asses" were among the kinder epithets applied to Wilkinson and his generals by their own subordinates after the campaign was over – it was also clear that they were commanding some very good human materiel.[26] Having thought the matter over, Pearson issued a judgement on the soldierly qualities of Cousin Jonathan to a visiting American: "Ah!, Sir, your troops are the bravest men I have ever seen, but your officers know little of service."[27]

Pearson was only at Cornwall for about two months but, as usual when he commanded any garrison, he subjected it to an intense course of improvement. Wearing his other hat as inspecting field officer, he took steps to whip the local militia, a rather slack bunch in his opinion – into shape and they were soon the recipients of a series of orders concerning their dress, deportment, drill and just about every other aspect of military life. Discipline was increased, punishments were doubled and every officer and soldier walked about looking warily over their shoulder for the unmistakable presence of their hawk-eyed and limping commanding officer. It was in connection with this duty that Pearson ran afoul of one of Cornwall's characters – Peggy Bruce, proprietress of the St. Patrick's and St. Andrew's hotel.

In Cornwall, irrepressible Peggy was known for two things: her caustic wit and her care of the sick of the village. An Irish lass who had run away from her family to marry a Scots soldier during the American Revolutionary War, the widowed Peggy respected few who did not wear a uniform and "a scarlet coat was the best recommendation to her good offices," whereas civilians of "whatever rank she deemed an inferior class of the human race."[28] Peggy had no time for pomp and pomposity. Hearing a militia officer, who had once served as a corporal with her husband, berate his men with a great deal of profanity, she took him to task: "Och! John, dear, don't let the devil get so great a hould of ye as to be blaspheming like a heathen in that fearful way; things are not so bad with you yet, sure you have twice as many men under your command as you had when I knew you first."[29]

Surgeon William Dunlop of the 89th Foot, stationed in Cornwall that winter, tells the tale of an encounter between Peggy and Pearson in early February 1814, just after Pearson had been ordered to return to Prescott. As Dunlop described it: "Peggy, who respected his [Pearson's] military talents at least as much as she disliked his hauteur, meeting him on the day before his departure addressed him with – 'Och! Colonel dear, and are you going to lave us – sure there will be many a dry eye in the town the day you quit it.'"[30] History does not record Pearson's reply, if indeed he made one. Probably the best he could manage was a dignified "harrumph" before limping on about his business.

Pearson was back in Prescott by 6 February 1814. This can be said with some assurance as on that day he issued an order informing the garrison of his return and stressing that they should pay "every attention" to "the performance of all duties" and "constantly be vigilant and alert."[31] There was, however, now no serious threat to Prescott as Wilkinson's army broke up its camp at French Mills in the first days of February and split into two divisions, one marching for Lake Champlain and the other for Sacket's Harbor. As soon as Sherwood reported this movement, the British commanders on the north shore of the St. Lawrence – Pearson at Prescott and Morrison at Cornwall – carried out a series of raids into American territory that penetrated as far as Malone in New York state, 30 miles south of the river. Except for local militia, who were easily swept aside, there was almost no resistance, as the enemy's regular army had more or less abandoned the area. The American offensive of 1813, intended to cut the lifeline of Upper Canada, had not only disastrously failed but had left the St. Lawrence firmly under British control and it was to remain so until the end of the war.

By the spring of 1814, therefore, one of Pearson's major problems – the United States Army – had disappeared from view but he still had other headaches. Throughout the lengthy term of his command at Prescott, he had been forced to deal with a widespread variety of civilian matters, including the issue of authorizations to travel to American soil, the approval of licences to trade with the United States, the curtailment of the smuggling of luxury goods into Upper Canada, prevention of the counterfeiting of army bills (which had replaced specie as currency) and negotiations with farmers to supply provisions. Yet, with the exception of the acquisition of provisions for the army, civil law continued to prevail in Upper Canada during the war, despite the fact that the province was actively threatened with foreign invasion. The civilian population, which had enjoyed harmonious relations with their American neighbours across the river before the war, saw no reason why these relations should not continue during hostilities, particularly if there was a handsome profit in it. Pearson's attitude, of course, was different and he was the subject of a number of civilian complaints because, as one historian remarked, he "sometimes acted precipitously in his dealings with civilians and tended to view disagreements from a black and white adversary stance."[32]

This should come as no surprise because Pearson had a different benchmark by which to measure the effect of war on civilians. He had seen at first hand the horrors inflicted on an unoffending population by the French in Portugal in 1811, and compared to that the Canadians were not suffering at all – in fact they were doing very well indeed. Another accusation made against Pearson was that, in the matter of trading licenses and other permissions, he tended to favour the merchants of Prescott over those in neighbouring Brockville. This too is not surprising as many of the men he associated with in Prescott were also military men, notably Captain William Gilkinson, one of his intelligence officers, and he probably preferred dealing with men he knew and trusted. Unwittingly, Pearson had become caught up in the intense rivalry between the two communities, a rivalry that continues unabated to this day. Discovering, as have many good soldiers before and since, that civilians are essentially difficult to deal with, there were undoubtedly many days when Pearson must have longed for the imposition of martial law, which would have permitted him to resolve many of his civilian problems by a court martial, with serious offenders facing a lengthy term in a military prison or suspension by the neck from a goodly length of Board of Ordnance hemp.

An additional frustration was that Pearson wanted more active military employment. It was clear to him that the St. Lawrence was becoming a secondary theatre and that the real action was farther west. Even the humble Incorporated Militia Battalion of Upper Canada, which had suffered at his hands for nearly a year, left Prescott for York in early March 1814. Despite all his problems with them, Pearson praised the unit in a daily order when they departed, promising to "give a positive report to their future commanders."[33] But he must have asked himself when his turn would come. The previous summer he had requested a transfer to command "of a line battalion or a fencible regiment in North America" and Prevost, in passing this request along to the Duke of York at the Horse Guards, had added the endorsement that Pearson was "an Officer well qualified and deserving of the Indulgence he solicits."[34] The Horse Guards' reply was that, although the applicant was deserving of consideration, given the few available vacancies, it would be some time before there would be a suitable opening for an officer of his rank.

There was nothing to do but wait, and what made that all the more difficult was that Pearson's beloved Welch Fusiliers had been carving out a splendid record in Europe. He could follow their activities as both Canadian and American newspapers regularly printed news of the war in Europe, including many of Wellington's dispatches. Pearson would have known that, when that general had finally taken Badajoz in April 1812, the 23rd Foot had suffered 151 killed and wounded assaulting the main breach so ably defended by *Général de brigade* Phillipon. He would have read how Lieutenant-Colonel Henry Ellis of the 23rd had commanded the Fusilier Brigade at Salamanca the following July when, still part of Cole's 4th Division, they had launched the main attack against Marmont's centre. He would have read of their presence during Wellington's great victory at Vittoria in June 1813, the battle that broke the back of the French armies in Spain, and would have followed them as they crossed the Pyrenees into France during the following autumn and read about the battles they had fought at Sorauen, the Nivelle and Orthes. In the spring of 1814, the 23rd Foot, still under Ellis's command, was now approaching Toulouse, defended by their old enemy, *Maréchal* Soult. It would have galled Pearson to examine the current Army List and see he was no longer listed as an officer with his regiment but "on the staff" in North America, and that Jack Hill, who had fought as a captain under his command at Albuera in 1811, was now a lieutenant-colonel.*

Pearson would also have learned of Napoleon's disastrous invasion of Russia in June 1812 and the creation of a Fifth Coalition against him by Austria, Britain, Prussia, Russia and Sweden in 1813, which had driven the French back to their own borders by the end of that year. Even as he was dealing with smugglers, counterfeiters, irate merchants, whining civilians and miscreant militiamen in the spring of 1814, the allied armies were closing in on Paris and Napoleon Bonaparte's ramshackle empire was entering its death throes. On 30 March 1814 Paris surrendered; on 3 April the French senate declared Napoleon dethroned and eight days later the "great thief of Europe" abdicated to go into exile on the small Mediterranean island of Elba. When Wellington heard the news outside Toulouse on 11 April, he was delighted: "How, abdicated? Ay, 'tis

---

* Pearson received the local rank of colonel in 1813 but it does not seem to have mattered much as even in official correspondence and orders, he was referred to as a lieutenant-colonel.

time indeed. You don't say so, upon my honour. Hurrah!"[35] It took some time for this epic news to reach Prescott in far-off Upper Canada, but when it did Pearson must have wondered what it meant for him, as it appeared his active service career was about to end in an obscure colonial garrison fighting a rather strange war against an enemy who, although brave, was not particularly professional.

Pearson need not have worried, however, as fate had more fighting in store for him. In early April 1814 he finally received a transfer to an active appointment in the field. It resulted from the fact that Lieutenant-Colonel Joseph Morrison was ordered to move his 89th Foot to Prescott, which created a problem because, as a lieutenant-colonel, Morrison was senior to Pearson and it would not be proper for him to take orders from a post commander who was his junior. The solution was to appoint Morrison as the post commander (which probably did not please that fighting officer) and transfer Pearson. It was Lieutenant-General Sir Gordon Drummond, commanding in Upper Canada, who pointed out the problem to Prevost and there is little doubt that Drummond, who had led the 8th Foot in Egypt under Abercromby, had a job in mind for Pearson because he was quick to suggest that "an Officer of Lieutenant Colonel Pearson's intelligence, zeal and ability" was "very particularly wanting" in the Right Division, the westernmost formation of the British army in Upper Canada.[36] Drummond's suggestion was accepted and, when informing Pearson of the good news of his impending transfer, Captain Noah Freer, Prevost's military secretary, enquired if the change was "what you asked and sought for?"[37]

It certainly was because an appointment to the Right Division meant service in the Niagara Peninsula, the most active theatre of war in North America.

The Royal Marines
In the spring of 1813 two battalions of Royal Marines, each a thousand bayonets strong with an attached company of Royal Marine Artillery, were sent to North America. One battalion was transferred to the Lake Ontario squadron the following year and its artillery company served in the Niagara campaign of 1814, providing the Congreve rocket section that participated in the battle of Lundy's Lane. Throughout the Great War with France, the Marines were able to attract the best class of recruits because they offered better conditions of service than the army and a greater chance of prize money.
(From C.H. Smith, *Costume of the Army of the British Empire*, 1814)

CHAPTER ELEVEN

"A FAIR TRIAL OF NERVE AND DISCIPLINE"

THE BLOODY SUMMER OF 1814 (1): OSWEGO AND CHIPPAWA

Great guns have shot and shell, boys,
Dragoons have sabres bright.
Th' artillery's fire's like hell, boys,
And the horse like devils fight.
But neither light nor heavy horse,
Nor thundering cannoneers,
Can stem the tide of the foeman's pride,
Like the British Bayoneteers

The English arm is strong, boys,
The Irish arm is tough.
The Scotman's blow the Yanks well know
Is struck by sterling stuff.
And when before the enemy
Their shining steel appears,
Goodbye, goodbye, how they run, how they run,
From the British Bayoneteers.[1]

P earson wasted no time in taking up his new post, arriving at Kingston in the first few days of May 1814. It was an opportune time to be at the naval base as Commodore Sir James Lucas Yeo, the Royal Navy commander on the Great Lakes, had just launched two large frigates, the 58-gun *Prince Regent* and the 40-gun *Princess Charlotte*, which gave him naval superiority on Lake Ontario. His American counterpart, Commodore Isaac Chauncey, had accordingly removed himself and his squadron into Sacket's Harbor. Chauncey would emerge again after he had completed larger warships which would put him ahead in this naval "war of carpenters" on the Great Lakes.[2] Yeo and Drummond planned a major attack on Sackets Harbor but Prevost, who always disliked risking too much on one throw of the dice, would not give them the troops they needed, so they contented themselves with a raiding cruise along the American shore of Lake Ontario.

Their main target was Oswego, a small port that was the transfer point for naval stores and ordnance coming to Sacket's Harbor from the eastern seaboard of the United States. The thought was that if they could seize this materiel on its way to Chauncey, they could delay his shipbuilding programme, and on 3 May, Yeo's squadron therefore embarked the 2nd Battalion of Royal Marines, De Watteville's Regiment, a company of Glengarry Light Infantry and some gunners, 980 all ranks, and set sail from Kingston. Pearson, never a man to shrink from an opportunity for action, volunteered his services as a staff officer to Drummond and accompanied him on board the *Prince Regent*, Yeo's flagship.

The British squadron, consisting of two frigates, two corvettes, three brigs and several gunboats, set sail the following day. The winds were so weak that it took Yeo's vessels nearly a day and a half to cover the 60 miles to Oswego and it was not until the afternoon of 5 May that they were off the little port at the mouth of the Onondaga River, which was protected by a fort perched on the 50-foot cliff that overlooked the village. The greater part of De Watteville's Regiment, a nominally Swiss unit that had been brought onto the British establishment, was in the flagship with Drummond and Pearson, and Lieutenant Joseph Mermet of that unit, a literary officer, has left a colourful account of operations against Oswego that is worth quoting at length:

At twelve-thirty P.M. [on 5 May 1814] we dropped anchor a mile and a half from the fort, which the *Prince Regent* weakly saluted with six shots. The fort and the position of the enemy were examined and the order was given to

Commodore Sir James Lucas Yeo (1782-1818)
Yeo assumed command of the Royal Navy on the inland lakes in the spring of 1813. He energetically constructed a powerful squadron on Lake Ontario but became hesitant about committing it to action. The relationship between the Royal Navy and the army in North America was always difficult and on some occasions the navy failed to render proper logistical support to the army. (Print after painting by A. Buck, courtesy, Toronto Reference Library, T-15241)

Lieutenant-General Gordon Drummond (1771-1854)

Drummond, another veteran of the Egyptian campaign, commanded British forces in Upper Canada in 1814. He planned an aggressive strategy of pre-emptive attacks to offset American superiority in numbers, but when Prevost refused him the troops he needed, he reverted to a defensive strategy. Drummond commanded at Lundy's Lane, where he was wounded, and during the siege of Fort Erie. A good if somewhat conservative soldier, he was instrumental in containing the American offensive in the Niagara during the summer of 1814. It was Drummond who procured Pearson an active command, releasing him from garrison duty at Prescott. (McCord Museum, Montreal, M400)

disembark as the brigs and schooners were already moving under the fort, and the [American] artillery was firing without success. The fort mounted only three guns in a battery and the Americans moved onto their glacis and onto the beach; countermarching, they formed themselves in a single rank.

All was ready and we were in the boats. It was three o'clock. A light wind [sprang up] from the south. The disembarkation was stopped, the brigs and schooners pulled back along the shore. At five o'clock [it was] calm and hot [with] a cloudy sky. The troops left the boats and re-embarked on board the warships.

At 6 o'clock P.M. we dined amid confused shouts, whistles [and] a thousand "God-damns." "All hands, all Royal Marines on deck, God-damn! All foreigners below; God-damn! Up and run; be quick, be quick!" At eight o'clock the hurricane suddenly appeared ...... The wind was from the northwest and the enemy coast was left behind. We cruised until four A.M. on the 6th [May]. The wind blew from the southeast until nine and from the east at ten. The anchor was let go again before Oswego at eleven [A.M., 6 May 1814].

The *Princess Charlotte*, the *Wolfe* and *Royal George* fired at the fort. The order to disembark was given. The enemy placed two more guns in the battery. The[ir] fire was more brisk. We were packed into the boats. The fifty men of the Glengarries and most of our light infantry were in a flat[-bottomed] boat with twenty-four oars. Colonel Fischer [commanding De Watteville's Regiment], Mermet [the narrator], [Captain] De Bersy and his grenadiers, and the light infantry under [Lieutenant] V[ictor]. May were in the *Cleopatra*, gun boat. ...... The artillery detachment and our centre companies, commanded by Major De Courten, were in a reserve behind the large ships. We rowed. Three hundred Marines under the orders of Lieutenant-Colonel

Malcolm moved with us while the brigs and schooners cover our landing.

We landed on the beach. The enemy showered us with his murderous shells and smaller shot – we answered with the triple cry of victory. "Gentlemen, let us set an example!" We landed ...... on the beach, helping one another and formed. Our [cartridge] pouches were full of water – what did that matter – we had bayonets!

The Royal Marines formed twenty paces to our right. The Glengarries extended themselves into the woods on our left. Colonel Fischer commanded: "Forward." The drum beat [and] the two columns advanced at the charge. The enemy, formed on the glacis of the fort, continued to fire at us. We arrived at the foot of the glacis; the enemy retreated into the fort and their fire increased. Although the dead and wounded fell, we continued to charge to the top of the glacis. The enemy fled in disorder and we pursued them a distance of thirty or forty paces. They ran faster – a volley would have decimated them, but we could not fire our muskets. The Royal Marines entered the fort and the British flag replaced the American. The trumpet sounded [and] we halted. It was six minutes past one P.M., and it was ten to one when Colonel Fischer commanded "Forward."[3]

The attack on Oswego, 6 May 1814
In this aquatint based on a drawing published in London in 1815 by Royal Marine Lieutenant John Hewett, who participated in the attack, the British Lake Ontario squadron bombards the American fort on the heights overlooking Oswego. In the foreground are the powerful new frigate HMS *Prince Regent* (front left) and HMS *Princess Charlotte*. Pearson participated in this action as a volunteer. (National Library and Archives of Canada, C-794)

The small American garrison at Oswego, just 325 regular military and naval personnel as well as some militia, had resisted only for a short period before withdrawing into the interior. The victory, however, did not come cheaply as 20 British soldiers or sailors were killed and 71 wounded, and although the fort and the village were now in British hands and some naval stores, including 16 guns, and foodstuffs seized, the Americans had used the 16 hours of grace granted to them after the first landing attempt had been stopped, to remove and conceal most of the vital war materiel. Pearson, who had accompanied Drummond and Yeo when they went ashore just after the first wave of troops, participating in what was the fifth amphibious landing of his career, had shared in the adventures of the day and was mentioned in the dispatch Drummond sent Prevost to report his victory.

Having shipped what they could, and destroyed what they could not, the squadron sailed on 7 May for Kingston. Pearson would certainly have been present during the victory party held that afternoon in the great cabin of the *Prince Regent* where, as Mermet recorded, about 40 officers sat "at their ease," all the while "babbling a Franco-Anglo-Italian patois (for all naval officers have travelled around the world), … and how they listened, and how they sang – and how they drank! 'Gentlemen, a toast: Colonel Fischer and De Watteville's Regt. – Colonel Malcolm and 2nd B[attalio]n. R[oya]l. Marines! Our victory! Gen[era]l Drummond! Sir James Yeo etc., etc., etc.'"⁴

U nfortunately, Yeo and Drummond's offensive, which had begun well, soon went sour. At the end of May 1814, most of the boats of Yeo's squadron were lost when they were ambushed after chasing an American boat convoy into Sandy Creek near Sacket's Harbor. A few days later, Yeo lifted the loose blockade he had been maintaining on the American base, leaving Chauncey free to complete the large warship he had on the stocks. The initiative was slowly but surely passing to the enemy who, Drummond and Prevost suspected, would mount a major offensive before Britain, with troops at her disposal since the end of the war in Europe, could send reinforcements across the Atlantic. Drummond was convinced that such an attack would come in the Niagara area but Prevost was just as certain that it would be made against Montreal and refused to give the commander in Upper Canada the reinforcements he requested.

Responsibility for the defence of the Niagara was vested in Major-General Phineas Riall and his Right Division. An Anglo-Irishman, the 38-year-old Riall had joined the army in 1794 but had spent long periods on half pay and had not actually seen much active service. Most of it had been in the West Indies, where he had served on and off with his regiment, the 15th Foot, between 1805 and 1810. In June 1813 Riall was promoted a major-general and sent to Canada where – in response to the enemy burning the Canadian village of Newark – he had led a British campaign of retribution against the American side of the Niagara in December of that year. Riall probably knew Pearson, as they had both participated in the Martinique campaign of 1809, and he was glad to have him under his command because the Niagara, one of the most fertile and heavily-populated regions of Upper Canada, was a difficult area to defend.

The basic problem was that Riall's main line of defence, the 30-mile-long Niagara River, was easily crossed nearly everywhere along its length except for the 8-mile gorge below the great falls. His Right Division was a division in name only; it was actually an administrative and geographical district rather than a mobile, field formation of all arms, and, worse still, Drummond would not give Riall enough troops to adequately defend the entire length of the river but would not permit him to concentrate his forces at some central position to be able to move quickly to any threatened point. The best Riall could do was to place most of his strength in the three mutually-supporting forts – Forts George, Mississaga and Niagara – at the mouth of the river, and position small garrisons along it at Queenston, Chippawa and Fort Erie. It was the 16 miles of the Niagara between Chippawa and Fort Erie that worried Riall because the river was easily crossed at any point along that stretch and the small stone Fort Erie at the southern extremity was almost indefensible. When he learned that Pearson would be joining him, Riall placed him in command of a small but elite force at Chippawa that could react quickly to any enemy crossing of the vulnerable upper river.

In fact, the Americans were preparing just such a movement. In Washington that spring, President James Madison's government had been pondering their options because it was imperative that, with the war in Europe ended and peace negotiations about to begin to end the conflict in North America, the United States must have a military success to provide it with a stronger hand at the negotiating table. It was also important that such a success be gained before Britain sent reinforcements across the Atlantic but Madison, possibly one of the worst war leaders in the history of the United States, and his cabinet kept vacillating and it was not until early June that they decided the offensive should be undertaken in the west. A strong force would be sent to recapture Mackinac

Major-General Phineas Riall (1775-1851)

The commander of the British Right Division defending the Niagara in 1814, Riall was an aggressive but somewhat rash officer. He had defeated American militia in a winter campaign the previous December but at Chippawa on 5 July 1814 he encountered well-trained American regular troops and the result was not good. Pearson had fought alongside Riall in Martinique in 1809 and the general was glad to have Pearson with him 1814, appointing him to command his elite light infantry brigade. (Courtesy, Riall family)

Island in the upper Great Lakes while Major-General Jacob Brown and his Left Division, concentrated at Buffalo, would invade Canada, march to Burlington Bay on Lake Ontario and then, with the co-operation of Chauncey's squadron on that body of water, successively capture York and Kingston. It was an ambitious plan that depended on Chauncey having naval superiority on Lake Ontario. Since that would not be before the end of June at the earliest, Secretary of War Armstrong suggested to Brown that, while he was waiting, to "give immediate occupation to your troops and prevent their blood from stagnating," Brown should think about taking Fort Erie and seizing the bridge over the Chippawa River and then "be governed by circumstances either in stopping there or going further."[5] These fateful words were the origin of the longest, most hard-fought and bloodiest campaign of the War of 1812.

Brown was confident that he could carry out his government's orders (or even its suggestions) because his Left Division* was the best-trained formation in the United States Army. Under his command were about 5,000 officers and men, organized in two regular brigades, composed mainly of veterans, and one volunteer or militia brigade. He also had a small force of cavalry and about 30 pieces of artillery. Brown's biggest problem was Commodore Isaac Chauncey, who kept equivocating about a date when he would take his squadron out of Sacket's Harbor to co-operate with him. Chauncey insisted that his movements must depend on those of Yeo's squadron and the best Brown could get out of the sailor was a statement that he would sail on or about 10 July 1814, "but I shall not leave this vicinity unless the Enemy's fleet leads me up the Lake."[6] Brown interpreted this to mean that Chauncey would meet him on or about

---

* The British called their westernmost formation in North America the Right Division while the Americans called theirs the Left Division. The titles came from the way they faced on the map, the west being the British right flank but the American left flank. There was also a British Left Division and an American Right Division at the other end of the theatre of war.

Major-General Jacob Brown, U.S. Army (1774-1828) Almost forgotten today, Brown was the best field commander in the American army during the War of 1812, fighting and winning more engagements against British regular troops than any of his contemporaries, including Andrew Jackson. Brown commanded the army that invaded the Niagara in the early summer of 1814 to begin the longest, most hard-fought and bloodiest campaign of the war. (From Benson Lossing, *Pictorial Field-Book of the War of 1812*)

10 July on the Lake Ontario shore of Upper Canada and, although not entirely convinced he would get the necessary naval support, he decided to attack.

The invasion began on the night of 2 July 1814 when Brown's two regular brigades rowed across the Niagara, landed on either side of Fort Erie and invested that small defence work. Before that happened, Major Thomas Buck, the British commandant of Fort Erie, managed to get an express rider off to warn Riall of the enemy landing. All through the morning of 3 July, Buck watched as more and more American infantry and then artillery were transported across from Buffalo. Buck commanded only a single company of the 100th Foot and an artillery detachment, 137 officers and men in total, and his fort mounted only three guns. Although some of his officers wanted to resist to buy time for Riall, Buck decided it was hopeless, and early in the afternoon of 3 July sent a flag of truce out to propose a surrender. The formalities were completed by 5 P.M., at which time the British garrison marched out of Fort Erie and the American fifers and drummers played "Yankee Doodle" as the Stars and Stripes was raised over the fort.

Riall received news of the invasion at 8 A.M. on the morning of 3 July at his headquarters at Fort George and immediately issued orders for all the regular troops and militia available to march to Chippawa, which offered a good defensive position. At that place, meanwhile, Pearson had learned about the landing somewhat earlier and mounted a reconnaissance in force to ascertain the enemy's strength and position. He had only the two flank companies of the 100th Foot to spare for this task but was able to call on the services of Teyoninhokarawen or the "Snipe", the half-Scot and half-Cherokee war chief of the Mohawks and a man whom British officers usually called (with some gratitude as nobody could pronounce his aboriginal name) Major John Norton. Norton was camped near the falls of Niagara with a force of warriors when he received

354

Major John Norton, or the Snipe
Half Scot, half Cherokee, Norton was the war chief of the Grand River Mohawk people during the war and served throughout the conflict. One of the most effective aboriginal leaders, he fought alongside Pearson in several of the major battles of the bloody Niagara campaign of 1814, for which Norton's postwar journal is a major source. (Print after painting by Thomas Philips, National Library and Archives of Canada)

Pearson's request to come to Chippawa and moved quickly south down the Portage Road which paralleled the Niagara River bank along the Canadian shore.

He reported to Pearson with about 200 warriors and, with the flank companies of the 100th Foot, they then proceeded south on the River Road as far as Frenchman's Creek, about four miles north of Fort Erie.* Along the way, Pearson stopped and questioned the local civilians, and as Norton remembered, he learned that "one Division of the Enemy was proceeding by a back Road from Point Abenau [Abino] to the Mouth of Chippawa" while "another was to cross [the Niagara] in our Rear at the Lower End of Grand Island [near Chippawa]".[7] Pearson was not unduly worried by this information as he suspected – quite rightly as it turned out – that it was exaggerated. It became clear, however, after some of the warriors scouted south of Frenchman's Creek toward the ferry crossing just north of Fort Erie, that the Americans had landed in considerable strength. As there was nothing Pearson could do with his small force, he posted pickets at Frenchman's Creek and withdrew to Chippawa that same evening.

There he found Riall, who had arrived from Fort George with a force of regular cavalry, infantry and artillery. The two officers discussed the situation. Riall wanted to relieve the garrison of Fort Erie, which he believed was still holding out, but having only two weak regular battalions with him, decided to stand on the line of the Chippawa River until further reinforcements arrived. It was agreed, however, that next day Pearson would take a small force toward Fort Erie to observe the enemy. Early on 4 July 1814 Pearson marched south

---

* The road that paralleled the Canadian bank of the Niagara from Fort Erie to Fort George was known from Fort Erie to Chippawa as the River Road but as the Portage Road from Chippawa to Queenston as it was the route around the barrier to water traffic posed by the falls of Niagara and the river gorge below them. From Queenston to Fort George and Lake Ontario, it was again known as the River Road.

on the River Road with a weak troop of the 19th Light Dragoons, the flank companies of the 100th Foot, the light company of the 1st Foot and an artillery detachment with two brass 24-pdr. field pieces.[8] Although he sent a messenger for Norton to join him, the war chief did not appear before Pearson departed.

Late in the morning Pearson's troops reached Frenchman's Creek, eight miles south of Chippawa. There he deployed for action on the north bank of the creek, which had been swollen by recent rains and was not fordable near its junction with the Niagara River. The 19th Light Dragoon troop, under the command of Lieutenant William Horton, was posted upstream to prevent a flanking move while the three infantry companies formed line on the north side of the creek and the two field pieces were positioned to bring the southern approaches to the bridge under fire. Thinking to destroy it, Pearson then turned his attention to the bridge but wooden bridges, particularly wooden bridges thoroughly soaked by rain, are much harder to set on fire that might be supposed, and since there was no large amount of powder to spare, Pearson contented himself by ordering his men to tear up the planks of its flooring and throw them in the river.

These preparations were no sooner complete than the pickets posted south of the bridge came running in with information that enemy cavalry was coming up the River Road. While Lieutenant Richard Armstrong, RA, loaded his 24-pdr. guns, the pickets either swam across the creek or carefully crossed on the remaining beams of the bridge. In a few minutes, blue-uniformed American dragoons appeared around a bend in the road to the south and, since they were at extreme range, Armstrong gave them a round from each of his guns. This caused some excitement and the horsemen disappeared, to be replaced by a strong force of infantry wearing black leather shakos, grey jackets and white trousers. This force, easily a brigade or more, deployed quickly and smoothly just beyond Armstrong's range and a few minutes later American artillery appeared, unlimbered and prepared to fire. Pearson, watching these moves with interest through his telescope, would have noted that the Jonathans were moving in a much more disciplined manner than the enemy he had faced at Crysler's Farm the previous autumn. Despite the fact that they were wearing grey like the homespun cloth of the militia of both Canada and the United States, these Yankees moved like well-trained soldiers.

And that they most certainly were, for these men belonged to Brigadier-General Winfield Scott's First Brigade of the Left Division. The 28-year-old Scott had fought in almost every major engagement along the northern frontier during the war, and was a fighter from the soles of his boots to the top of his 6 foot, 5 inch frame. He had just finished putting Brown's regular units through an intensive eight-week training programme at Flint Hill camp near Buffalo, working from dawn to dusk, and the result was that he had produced the best-trained American regulars of the war.

Scott was particularly proud of his own brigade and that morning he had jumped at the opportunity when Brown had ordered him to take it and some cavalry and artillery and move north to the Chippawa River. Scott was, in that immortal phrase much loved by American military leaders, "to be governed by circumstances" but was to be sure "to secure a military position" or camp site for the night.[9] Always happy when in independent command, the aggressive Scott was in a good mood as he stared back through his telescope at the redcoats north of Frenchman's Creek and decided they would not hold him up long. Unfortunately for the firebreathing young American general, he had just met Thomas Pearson, the living soul of obstinacy, who was about to give him an object lesson in the proper way to carry out a delaying action with light troops, a lesson likely not contained in the library of military texts, mostly French, kept in the large portable bookshelf that accompanied Scott on campaign.

And it was important that the American advance be delayed because it would be evening before Riall had assembled enough regular troops at Chippawa to

Grey jackets, 1814

A shortage of indigo blue dye caused by the British blockade forced Scott to issue the troops of his brigade grey jackets in lieu of the regulation blue wool coatees. They would make this simple garment famous during the Niagara campaign of 1814, and though Scott later claimed this makeshift uniform was the origin of the grey cadet uniforms still worn at the United States Military Academy today, recent research has revealed this claim to be false. Regardless of the colour of their uniforms, the American regulars of 1814 were a far cry from the badly led amateurs of 1812, as two years of war had turned them into hard-biting and professional soldiers. Thomas Pearson faced these tough opponents throughout the summer of 1814. (Drawing by R.J. Marrion, author's collection)

Brigadier-General Winfield Scott, U.S. Army (1786-1866)
A professional and aggressive officer who had seen much combat during the war, Scott was responsible for the high state of training of Major-General Jacob Brown's army which invaded Canada in the summer of 1814. On 4 July 1814, however, Scott got an object lesson from Pearson on the proper way to conduct a delaying action. Scott went on to dominate the postwar American army and was still in service when the Civil War broke out in 1861. (From *Portfolio Magazine,* 1816)

properly defend the north bank of the river. Therefore, as soon as Pearson was sure that Scott had fully deployed and was about to attack under the cover of his artillery, he swung into action. While Armstrong fired a few more shots from one of his guns, the other gun and half of the infantry departed for the next creek, a few miles to the north. When the enemy artillery opened fire to cover the advance of their infantry up to Frenchman's Creek, Pearson put Armstrong's second gun and the remainder of his infantry on the road north, while Horton's dragoons acted as a rear guard. By the time Scott's men got up to the damaged bridge there was no sign of the British, and they now faced the laborious task of either fishing the floor planks out of the water or cutting down trees so that the bridge could be improved enough to allow them to cross the creek. This took time but finally Scott resumed his advance, only to find Pearson waiting for him, two miles up the road, on the north side of Winterhute's Creek.

So it went, creek after creek – Frenchman's, Winterhute's, Halfway and Black's – during what turned out be a long afternoon for the First Brigade and their tall general.

It was late, probably approaching 6.00 P.M., when the Americans came up to Street's Creek, a mile and a half south of the Chippawa River. Armstrong greeted them with his usual salutation, a 24-pdr. roundshot or two, and, possibly, if Pearson permitted it, the men of the 1st and 100th Foot waved their shakos and shouted loud insults at their grey-uniformed opponents – insults relating to their intelligence, legitimacy and virility as, after all, they were by now old friends. The British, however, should not have been too cocky as, to give Cousin Jonathan credit, he is a fast learner and Captain Turner Crooker of the Ninth United States Infantry had a surprise in store for the redcoats. As soon as his company had crossed Black Creek, the previous obstacle, Crooker had got Scott's permission to leave the brigade and strike directly northwest, cutting out the long bend in the river and the road that bordered it, thus ar-

riving at Street's Creek upstream of Horton's dragoons and considerably before Scott's main column reached the bridge spanning it. Crooker's men then
waded across through chest-deep water and, unknown to Pearson or anyone
under his command, were now on the north side of Street's Creek.

Turner Crooker was no fool. He waited until the usual charade at the bridge
had been played out and then, as the British withdrew, advanced at a half jog
across the open fields of Canadian farmer Samuel Street towards one of Armstrong's guns, which was following Pearson's infantry up the River Road. In his
haste, Crooker failed to spot the British dragoons bringing up the tail of the
column, while Lieutenant William Horton, seeing a small company of grey-
clad enemy infantry moving across an open field, did what any red-blooded
British cavalry officer would have done – he ordered his men to draw sabres
and charge. It might have turned out rather badly but Crooker, a wily son of
Massachusetts (and thus a true Yankee), kept his head, told his men to fire one
volley at the oncoming horsemen and then run to a nearby farmhouse. They
reached it just before the 19th Light Dragoons reached them and then fired

Vedette, 19th Light Dragoons, 1814
The 19th Light Dragoons were the only British regular cavalry regiment to fight in the Canadas during the war. In the northern theatre, cavalry were very much a secondary arm and
there were few opportunities to engage in their most favoured tactic – the charge. This was
just as well as the American opponents were very good marksmen. Pearson had elements
of two squadrons of this regiment under his command at various times during the Niagara
campaign. (Drawing by A. Robinson Sager, courtesy Parks Canada)

out of its windows, killing eight horses and wounding four dragoons. It was nicely done, indeed, and Scott, who had watched the entire episode from the south bank of Street's Creek, later reported that he had "witnessed nothing more gallant in partizan warfare" than the "conduct of Captain Crooker and his company."[10]

Having delayed Winfield Scott's advance for nearly six hours – and on the 4th of July of all days – Pearson's men crossed to the north bank of the Chippawa River on the long King's Bridge. When Scott and his weary men finally reached the Chippawa after nearly 17 miles on their feet, they came under heavy fire from the British batteries on the north bank just as Riall's sappers dropped a span of the bridge into the river. Seeing this, Scott wisely decided his day was done and withdrew to a camp site just south of Street's Creek, where late in the evening he was joined by Brown and Brigadier-General Eleazar Ripley's Second Brigade of regulars.

During the night of 4 July and morning of 5 July, Riall pondered his options. Reinforcements had arrived and he now had 1,500 regular troops under command, including the 1st and 100th Foot, a squadron of the 19th Light Dragoons and Captain James Maclachlan's battery of artillery, with five guns and a light howitzer. He expected the 8th Foot to arrive at any moment and his strength was also augmented by the 2nd Lincoln Regiment of militia and about 300 aboriginal warriors led by Norton. Still convinced Fort Erie was holding out, on the morning of 5 July Riall dispatched a number of scouting parties of militia and warriors "who got close to them [the American camp] and climbed Trees to overlook their Position."[11] Unfortunately, although they were not supposed to shoot, these parties "became a Band of Skirmishers, who began firing at the Sentries" and this firing, once started, continued throughout the morning. Norton, who crossed the Chippawa with a few of his warriors but did not get involved in any shooting, was able to interrogate a civilian who informed him that "only one Division of the Enemy's army was now before us, and that the other Division which had not yet joined was the most numerous."[12]

Not entirely convinced of the reliability of this intelligence, Riall decided to see for himself and, taking Pearson, they made a personal reconnaissance late in the morning. Encountering Norton, the three discussed the situation and Riall, convinced he was facing at most about 2,000 enemy troops, decided to attack as soon as the bridge was repaired, which would take three to four hours. The three men agreed that the surest mode of attack as soon as the Bridge could be repaired, and the Troops had passed over, that my Party of about 250 men, followed by 100 men [warriors] of the Western Dept. – the same number of Militia, and supported by the flank companies, – should pass through the Woods in such a manner as to arrive imperceptibly upon the flank of the Enemy, and from the covert of the Wood open a heavy fire upon it, – his attention thus engaged, – the main Body of our troops might advance and attack him in front.[13]

The little village of Chippawa was shortly a scene of activity as the troops made ready and Riall's engineers hammered away on the bridge.

A few miles to the south Major-General Jacob Brown was also planning an attack. Annoyed by the sniping that had continued through the morning, he ordered Brigadier-General Peter B. Porter, whose brigade of volunteers had just arrived from Fort Erie, to clear the woods around the camp. Porter only had about half his brigade with him – the remainder were still crossing the

The bridge over the Chippawa River
The Chippawa River constituted the best defensive position in the Niagara against an enemy moving north from Fort Erie. In July 1814 Riall concentrated his troops to defend this waterway but then decided to cross it and engage in open battle against his enemy. He would have been wiser to stay put in this strong position as he was soundly drubbed for his troubles at the resulting battle of Chippawa, 5 July 1814. (National Archives of Canada)

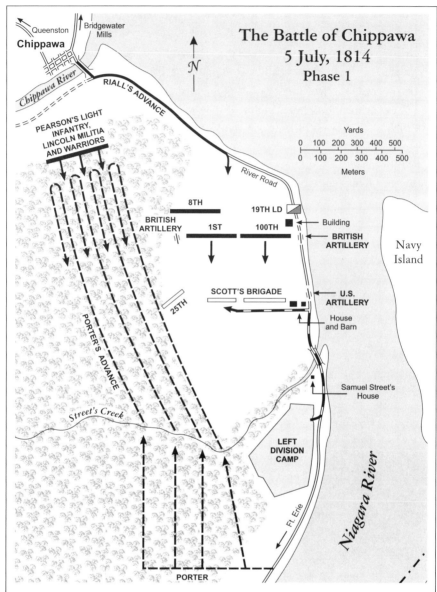

The Battle of Chippawa
5 July, 1814
Phase 1

Annoyed by British snipers, Brown orders Porter to take his brigade and clear them out. Porter does so and then advances north to encounter Pearson's troops and is in turn pushed back. At the same time Riall deploys his three regular battalions on the north end of "the plain." Brown orders Scott to deploy his brigade at the southern end. Scott does so and detaches Jesup and his 25th Infantry to counter Pearson.

Niagara – but he also had a large force of warriors, at least 300, drawn from a variety of nations but mainly Seneca, Onondaga, Tuscarora and Delaware. His men being tired from their long march of the morning, Porter permitted them to cook their dinner before calling for volunteers to help drive away the enemy snipers – he got about 200 volunteers and most of the warriors. He told the volunteers to leave their hats behind so that they could recognize each other in the woods, and ordered the warriors to wrap strips of white cloth around their heads or arms as a means of identification. This done, he led his force into the woods southwest of the American camp at about 2 P.M. and formed it into a long skirmish line. On his command, and preceded by aboriginal scouts, Porter's men began to cautiously and quietly move north.

Near the area of the American camp the volunteers and American warriors made contact with the British scouting parties. They let their opponents fire first, and then rushed upon them "with the warwhoop" to "pursue, capture and slaughter as many of them as practicable."[14] A bloody and vicious running fight ensued with muskets, tomahawks, clubs and scalping knives creating "scenes of indescribable horror."[15] Few from the outnumbered British scouting parties tried to surrender; most tried to escape but they were "overtaken and cut down with the tomahawk, or turned upon their pursuers and fought to the last." Those that survived were pursued by Porter's volunteers and warriors with the latter, more at ease in such bush, gradually drawing ahead of the whites. Porter remembered that there was suddenly a "tremendous discharge of musketry" and the American warriors came running back through the volunteers. While their war chiefs tried to steady them, Porter advanced to the edge of the wood only to find himself "within a few yards of the British army formed in line of battle."[16]*

It took until 3 P.M. before the engineers had finished repairs on the bridge and Riall's troops could cross the Chippawa. While the three battalions of regular infantry (the 8th Foot having just arrived), the artillery and dragoons formed on the road behind a belt of woods that blocked the view of the American pickets, Pearson, who was acting as Riall's second-in-command, led the light companies of the 1st, 8th and 100th Foot, the 2nd Lincolns and a strong force of British warriors – perhaps 750 men in total – into an area of cleared fields north of those woods. Scattered firing, which appeared to be coming closer,

---

* Orders of battle for the opposing forces at the battle of Chippawa, 5 July 1814, will be found below in Appendix G.

could be heard and Norton took two hundred of his people westward, hoping to outflank and attack an advancing enemy. In a few minutes, British warriors, shouting, "Yankee too strong! too many!" burst out of the treeline and Pearson ordered the 2nd Lincolns and his remaining aboriginal allies into the woods, where they collided head-on with the excited American warriors intent on their prey.[17] A confused firefight ensued in which the American aboriginals got the worst of it and fell back, but it was not long before they returned, this time supported by Porter's volunteers.

A second firefight occurred and it did not go as well for the Lincolns and their allies. A number of war chiefs and nearly all the Lincoln officers were killed or wounded, and both groups fell back in confusion. Seeing this, Pearson deployed his three companies in line and advanced in open order to the tree line, permitting the fugitives to run through his files and rally in safety. He then halted, closed his files and waited. When the Americans and enemy warriors came in view in the undergrowth, he fired three or four measured volleys into them and when they broke, ordered an advance with the bayonet. Norton, who witnessed this action, thought that the Lincolns and their warrior allies "were only saved by the simultaneous attack of the Flank companies upon those who immediately pursued them," an attack pressed "with such vigour as to rescue many that were just overtaken by the exulting enemy."[18] The Lincolns and British warriors, seeing the enemy now in flight, took heart and chased after them, passing the light companies who moved forward in open order at a slower pace through the undergrowth. Another deadly race now took place as the Canadian militia and their allies pursued Porter's volunteers and warriors, killing without mercy anyone they overtook. John Norton remembered that his men

proceeded in as good order as it was possible, – advancing in separate files; – we had gone perhaps something more than half way to the point of our destination, when a firing commenced on our left, – we hastened forward and soon came in contact with the Enemy; – ascending a gentle rise, we received their fire, – they were concealed behind trees and fallen timber, – We shouted and closed with them without firing till we reached them; – they had not reloaded their pieces, – they ran, many of them falling before us. We received several volleys from other parties of the same Division, but we constantly advanced, driving one part into the field … the other dispersing through the Woods.[19]

The fight in the woods, 5 July 1814
While historians have paid more attention to the main infantry battle between the American and British regulars, there was a separate battle in the woods between American volunteers and warriors and British light infantry, Canadian militia and British-allied warriors, all under Pearson's command. It was a vicious seesaw engagement with little quarter asked and not much given. (Drawing by George Balbar, reproduced with permission from Robert Foley, *The War of 1812*)

As Norton's men approached the eastern edge of the woods and looked out on the open farm fields beside the Niagara River, their leader was surprised to see enemy infantry "advancing through the field with colours flying." It was clear that the regular American army was about to join the battle.

Earlier, Brown and his staff had ridden north of Street's Creek to observe the progress of Porter's attack. When they heard the disciplined volleys of Pearson's light infantry and saw dust clouds behind the woods to the north, they concluded British regulars were south of the Chippawa and about to attack. Brown sent a staff officer to Scott to order him to bring up his brigade and deploy on the open fields, called "the plain" in most accounts of the battle,

365

north of Street's Creek. The First Brigade had just assembled for drill and Scott immediately put them in motion north on the River Road. As they neared the bridge over Street's Creek, Brown rode up and shouted, "You will have a battle!" before moving on to bring up his Second Brigade.[20] At almost the same moment, Scott's brigade came under British artillery fire and he hastily led it over the defile of the bridge and began to deploy.

While Pearson was occupied in clearing the enemy out of the woods to the west, Riall had marched down the River Road and formed on the northern end of the "plain." The troop of 19th Light Dragoons, 70 odd sabres, two 24-pdr. guns and a 5.5-inch howitzer took position on the road while the 1st and 100th Foot formed in line, with the 1st Foot near the River Road. Three 6-pdr. guns were brought into action on the right of the 100th Foot and, there not being enough room for the 8th Foot, Riall placed it in line to the rear of the other two battalions. Riall was supremely confident. The only time he had been in action against Americans was during the previous winter when he had brushed aside a force of New York militia and burned Buffalo. Having no respect for Cousin Jonathan as an opponent, he was not at all impressed when one of his staff pointed out how steady the grey-uniformed American infantry were moving while under artillery fire and is said to have exclaimed, "O, they are a set of cowardly, untrained men – scape gallows or state prison men who will not stand the bayonet."[21] Although the five British guns and one

Private soldier, 1st (or the Royal Scots) Regiment of Foot, 1814

The 1st Battalion of this regiment fought throughout the War of 1812 in the northern theatre of operations, suffering 650 casualties, of which 400 fell in the Niagara battles. The British redcoats and their Canadian regular counterparts performed well during the conflict and did the greater part of the fighting and suffered the greater part of the casualties. The one disadvantage of British regulars was that they were not as adept at fighting in the heavily wooded terrain, a disadvantage that was offset by Canadian regular and long-service militia units, and their aboriginal allies. The main engagements of the war, however, were fought using European tactical methods and in such battles the regulars always performed well. (Painting by G.A. Embleton, courtesy Parks Canada)

Major Thomas S. Jesup, U.S. Army (1788-1860)
A good soldier and a leading member of the wartime generation of young American officers who had
learned their profession the hard way, Jesup played
a prominent role in the battles of Chippawa and Lundy's Lane. Pearson faced Jesup's Twenty-Fifth Infantry Regiment at the former action and the result was
about even, although Jesup managed to upset British
offensive plans. (With permission of the Washington
National Cathedral)

howitzer fired steadily at Scott's infantry opposite, inflicting heavy casualties, the Ameri-
cans did not flinch and within a few minutes Scott's artillery unlimbered on
the road north of the bridge to reply.

Since the number of enemy troops he could see accorded with his belief that
he was only facing part of Brown's army, Riall decided to attack. He ordered
Lieutenant-Colonel John Gordon's 1st Foot and Lieutenant-Colonel George
Hay's 100th Foot forward in line while the 8th Foot commanded by Lieutenant-Colonel Thomas Evans (whom we have met before as a young lieutenant in
Egypt) moved in their right rear. All three commanders had the same plan: they
would advance within musket range, halt, fire a couple of quick and devastating volleys, then push home with the bayonet. It was a tactic that had worked
against the Jonathans before and no one doubted that it would work this day.

It was about 4.30 P.M. when the three battalions went forward. Winfield
Scott was prepared to meet them. He had deployed most of his brigade along
a farm lane running west from the River Road but had detached the Twenty-
Fifth Infantry under Major Thomas S. Jesup farther west to counter the British
warriors and light infantry that could be seen moving in the woods. As the
British battalions moved steadily toward him, Scott realized that when they
entered the wider southern part of the plain, the 1st and 100th Foot in the lead
would be flanked by his left. He therefore ordered the commanding officer of
the Eleventh Infantry on that flank to throw forward his left companies.

When the 1st and 100th Foot were between 150 and 200 feet distant, Scott gave
the order and his brigade fired a properly-loaded and devastating first volley into
the British line, while the American artillery on the River Road added canister to
increase the effect. As men fell, the two battalions shuddered and came to a halt
but quickly reformed their ranks. Hay and Gordon ordered their men to return
fire and "the action became general" as the opposing lines exchanged fire at close

range.[22] The fire of the Eleventh Infantry, which enfiladed the British right flank, was "most effective" and inflicted heavy British casualties.[23] The American artillery, according to a witness, blew "breaches" through the British line but they "were soon filled up" as the two battalions closed in to their centres.[24]

The British infantry maintained their ground and returned the fire. It was somewhat ironic that this action was being fought between the infantry of possibly the only two armies in the world that emphasized effective musketry and trained their men to carry it out. Both sides suffered but the British had the worst of it. Private George Ferguson of the 100th Foot remembered that the "slaughter was great" as men "fell on my right and left."[25] Lieutenant John Stevenson of the same regiment recalled that it was a "scene of carnage" as officers and men dropped "like hail."[26]

While this firefight was in progress, Brown ordered Brigadier-General Eleazar Ripley's Second Brigade to cross Street's Creek upstream of the bridge and take position on Scott's left. Meanwhile, Major Jacob Hindman, the American artillery commander, dispatched four more pieces to support Scott and, finally, Porter managed to rally his volunteers and warriors and hold off the Canadians and British warriors.

It was at this point that Pearson became involved in the battle on the plain. When his militia and warriors had disappeared after the Americans through the underbrush, Pearson had held his three light companies firmly in hand. As soon as he saw the British line advancing on the "plain," he paralleled it by moving along the skirt of the woods to a point where his troops were behind a split rail fence about 150 yards from Jesup's Twenty-Fifth Infantry. As the American unit was in column, it presented a fine target and Pearson immediately opened up at it.

Jesup, realizing that engaging in a duel with an enemy behind good cover was not productive, ordered his men to form line, shoulder arms and advance toward Pearson's position. When they were "within grinning distance," one of his officers recalled, Jesup gave the orders: "halt: ready: fire three rounds and charge!"[27] The volleys did not have much effect but, as the Americans moved forward with the bayonet, Pearson pulled his outnumbered command back into the woods. It was not his job to get involved in heavy fighting; his task was to screen the flank of the British line.

Delighted, Jesup ordered his men to pull down the split rail fence and reform in the skirt of the wood.[28] He then moved north to pursue Pearson and

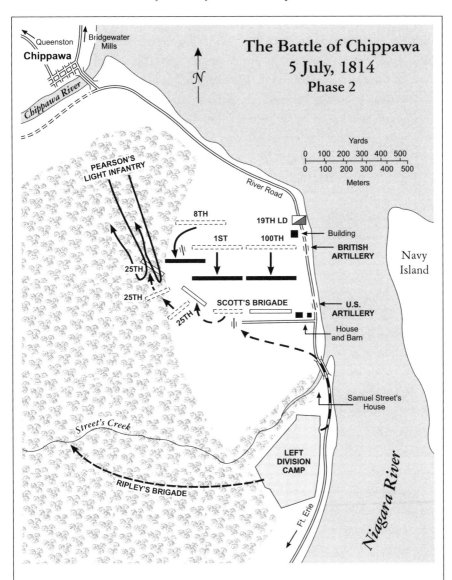

The Battle of Chippawa
5 July, 1814
Phase 2

Riall orders the 1st and 100th Foot forward and they move with the 8th in their right rear. As they approach. Scott throws forward his left flank unit to provide enfilade fire. A musketry duel ensues between the two lines. Brown steadily augments Scott with artillery and orders Ripley's brigade to undertake a flanking movement.

Meanwhile, Jesup forces Pearson back and then flanks the 8th Foot, preventing it from supporting the 1st and 100th. When it becomes clear to Riall that he cannot break the American line, he orders a retreat and his troops withdraw in good order to Chippawa, dropping the bridge behind them.

almost "gained the flank of a strong [British] detachment posted in a field on our right" – this was Evans's 8th Foot advancing to support the 1st and 100th Foot.[29] Jesup detached one company to keep the British light infantry occupied, changed front and fired into Evans's flank. Evans in turn withdrew north to a new position and Jesup pursued him under cover of the fence, constantly attacking and forcing him back. Things were looking good when Jesup received an urgent request for help from his detached company as, sensing that there were fewer enemy pursuing him, Pearson had halted and counter-attacked, forcing the now outnumbered Americans back. When Jesup came up with his entire regiment, Pearson in turn withdrew, a movement which, as Jesup reported, "terminated the action."[30] Jesup had, however, prevented Evans's 8th Foot from supporting the 1st and 100th Foot in their musketry battle with Scott's brigade – and he had also outfought Thomas Pearson.

On the plain, meanwhile, Hay and Gordon were in trouble. Despite the heavy exchange of musketry, which by now had continued nearly 20 minutes, the American line had not wavered and both battalion commanders realized that they would have to close with the bayonet. Yet, despite all their efforts, they were unable to get their men to advance. Partly it was the old problem of making soldiers who had stopped to fire move again, and partly it was the high number of officer casualties. Seventeen of the 21 officers in the 100th Foot were killed or wounded during this action, including the captain, lieutenant and ensign of the grenadier company who were hit in succession as Hay tried to get that company to lead a charge. Things were no better in the 1st Foot, which lost ten officers during the duel. When Gordon took a musket ball in the mouth, he was unable to give orders and had to leave the field and was shortly followed by Hay, whose achilles tendon was severed by another round. This brought to an end all attempts to advance and the two battalions, reluctant to retreat, stood their ground, fired, and took their casualties. When Hindman's four guns came into action, firing canister, those casualties increased until Scott thought that it "was not in human nature that a conflict like this should last many seconds," and first the flanks and then the centre of the British line began to waver.[31] Seeing this, Riall ordered a withdrawal and the 1st and 100th Foot steadily moved back in good order north up the plain. Here they reformed in column of march before crossing with the artillery over the bridge to the village of Chippawa, leaving the 8th Foot and the 19th Light Dragoons as a rearguard.

In the woods to the west, meanwhile, Pearson withdrew his light infantry and militia. Some of the British warriors had pursued Porter's men so far that

Scott's brigade, Chippawa, 5 July 1814
The American victory at Chippawa was an important event in the history of the United
States Army. It marked the professional coming of age of that service and is justly cele-
brated in this painting by H.C. McBarron – which actually shows Colonel Hugh Brady's 22nd
Infantry during the battle. (Courtesy, U.S. Army Center of Military History)

they had difficulty breaking off the action and getting away. Norton's detachment had the longest distance to cover and were horrified to find, when they
reached the Chippawa, that the bridge had been "demolished, excepting a Log
or two which yet remained."[32] Fortunately, he was able to get his men to safety
on the remaining pilings just as the head of Scott's First Brigade appeared on
the River Road.

When Riall pulled back, Scott ordered an immediate advance but when his
leading elements approached the Chippawa, they came under heavy artillery
fire from the north bank. Scott told his men to lie down in their ranks and
waited for Brown and the other two brigades. When Brown arrived, the American commander contemplated bringing up all his artillery and forcing a crossing "by a direct attack" but concerned about "the lateness of the hour," it being
about 6.30 P.M., Brown decided to retire.[33] The battle of Chippawa was over.*

---

* The battle is known today in Canada by the spelling used in the text. The Chippawa were an
aboriginal nation allied to Britain and both the river and the village took their name from these
people. In the United States, the battle is spelled Chippewa.

There was naturally little cheer in the British camp that evening. "The Loss of our friends," remembered Norton, "gave us all a gloomy appearance" and "in ev'ry division they seemed to think that they alone had more particularly fallen a sacrifice to the misfortune of the Day."[34] The British and Canadian casualties in this hardfought little action were 149 killed, 316 wounded and 46 missing for a total of 515, while Brown reported 58 killed, 241 wounded and 19 missing for a total of 328 American casualties. The most striking fact was the number killed, Riall losing nearly three times as many as Brown, and what is even more striking is the difference between the total number of fatal casualties of Scott's brigade and the three British infantry battalions that opposed him – Scott lost 41 men killed in action against 135 in the 1st, 8th and 100th Foot.

In his report on an action "not attended with the success which I had hoped for," Riall blamed superior enemy numbers for his defeat, claiming that, with no more than 1,800 men he had fought 6,000 Americans.[35] Drummond echoed this excuse by reporting to Prevost that only superior numbers "could have prevented the attack from being covered with complete success."[36] But the British commander-in-chief would have none of it, particularly as he had been having doubts about Riall for some time and had considered removing him from command. To Prevost, the reason for the British defeat was the "improvement in discipline and the increased experience of the Enemy," who had "evinced judgement in the position selected."[37] Privately, he was angry with Riall's performance and later remarked that "neither the Union of Science, organization or force will give" the battle of Chippawa "any éclat."[38]

British claims that they were defeated by superior numbers have no basis in fact as much of Brown's Left Division never saw action, and the main engagement on "the plain" matched 1,200 British regulars with six artillery pieces against 1,350 American regulars with seven pieces of artillery, nearly equal odds. In the words of one observer, the battle of Chippawa was "a fair trial of nerve and discipline" and the American soldier won that trial.[39] Brown exalted to Washington that his victory was "gained over the enemy on a plain" and it marked the professional coming of age of the United States Army.[40] In the future there would be much less British and Canadian sneering about bumbling Cousin Jonathan.

For three days after the battle there was a lull as the two opponents stared at each other across the Chippawa. Since the British did not withdraw, Brown now faced the task of carrying out an assault crossing of a fairly deep and swift-flowing river about 100 feet wide. There was no way of flanking it on the right using the Niagara, because the current of that river was so strong below its junction with the Chippawa that inexperienced boatmen were not uncommonly caught in it and swept over the falls. Brown pondered his problem for a few days and then fortune smiled on him when a local inhabitant told of him of a disused logging road that led to a crossing place upstream of Riall's position. On the morning of 8 July his engineers supervised the clearing of this road and the gathering of lumber for a pontoon bridge. By noon all was ready and two companies of artillery were posted to sweep the north bank opposite the bridging point if the British should attempt to interfere. The noise of the American work parties alerted a vedette of the 19th Light Dragoons, who discovered the enemy activity and reported it to Riall.

The British commander ordered Pearson to take the flank companies of the 1st Foot and three 6-pdr. guns upstream to stop the Americans. He did so, but as soon as he approached the bridging site on the opposite bank his troops came under heavy canister fire from three 12-pdr. and three 18-pdr. guns on the American bank. Stymied, he requested reinforcements and Riall was just about to send them when he was pinned in place by Winfield Scott's brigade, which made a strong demonstration opposite Chippawa. Deciding that he could not be strong everywhere along the river and that ultimately he would be overwhelmed by superior American numbers, Riall ordered a withdrawal to the forts at the mouth of the Niagara River. As the British and Canadian troops and their aboriginal allies made their way north up the Portage Road on the afternoon of 8 July, Pearson commanded the rearguard, which consisted of the light companies of the regular battalions and detachments of dragoons.

As his men approached the falls of Niagara, he encountered some old friends – the 379-strong Incorporated Militia of Upper Canada – just arrived in the Niagara after three months of garrison duty and training at York. The battalion stood aside while Riall's retreating army passed by, and then Pearson took them under command (which must have made them truly happy) and they trudged north to Fort George under his stern and watchful eye.[41]

Night battle

The battle of Lundy's Lane, the bloodiest single engagement of the War of 1812, was unique in that it continued after darkness had fallen. Since both armies wore a similar uniform and spoke the same language, mistakes in identification were common and often fatal. Casualties were increased by the fact that the opposing sides fought at ranges that would not be attempted in a daylight engagement and both armies displayed uncommon valour and obstinacy as neither would give way. In this drawing by George Balbar, British troops await an American attack. (Drawing by George Balbar, reproduced with permission from Robert Foley, *The War of 1812*)

CHAPTER TWELVE

"FULL BLOODED EATERS OF THE PUMPKIN"

THE BLOODY SUMMER OF 1814 (2): LUNDY'S LANE AND FORT ERIE

Eyes right, my jolly field boys,
Who British bayonets bear,
To teach your foes to yield, boys,
When British steel they dare!
Now fill the glass, for the toast of toasts
Shall be drunk with the cheer of cheers,
Hurrah, hurrah, hurrah, hurrah!
For the British bayoneteers.[1]

Brown did not immediately pursue the British. He had first to repair the bridge over the Chippawa River and, as it was approaching the time he thought that Commodore Isaac Chauncey would appear with his squadron on Lake Ontario, Brown took his time moving north to Queenston Heights, where he camped at the bottom of that prominent terrain feature. This puzzled Riall and when there was no sign of the Americans four days after Riall's arrival at Fort George, on 12 July he ordered Pearson to carry out a reconnaissance in force to locate the enemy position. Pearson found the Americans in and around the village of Queenston, but not showing any signs of preparing to advance farther. With this information, Riall correctly assumed that his opponent was waiting for naval support and, not wanting to be trapped between two forces, decided to leave a strong garrison in the three forts at the mouth of the Niagara River while he pulled the remainder of his army to the west, closer to his supply depots at Burlington Bay.

The British withdrawal to Twelve-Mile Creek, which was that distance from Fort George, took place on the night of 13 July and was unhindered by the

Americans. Riall established his headquarters at the Twenty-Mile Creek and positioned troops there and as far forward as the Twelve and Four-Mile Creeks. By this time, Lieutenant-General Gordon Drummond at York was forwarding every regular unit he could to the Niagara, calling out the militia and requesting Norton to assemble as many warriors as possible. As his strength grew, Riall reorganized the Right Division into two regular and two militia brigades to make it more flexible for field service. Drummond had previously advised Riall to employ Pearson as a leader of light infantry and Riall, taking this advice, gave Pearson a plum appointment – command of his 2nd or Light Brigade.

This formation consisted of two Canadian infantry units, the Glengarry Light Infantry and the Incorporated Militia, an attached half-battery (two 6-pdr. guns and a 5.5-inch howitzer) of artillery and a troop of the 19th Light Dragoons. The Glengarries were commanded by Lieutenant-Colonel Francis Battersby, an Irishman from County Meath, major in the 8th Foot and veteran of Egypt, who had seen much service during the American war and had achieved a notable combat record. The Incorporated Militia were, of course, old acquaintances to Pearson and, having supervised their early military training, he was perhaps pleased that he would be able to put the final polish on them – whether they reciprocated that feeling is quite another matter. In any case, the Incorporated Battalion had improved immeasurably from the previous year, particularly after it came under the command of acting Lieutenant-Colonel William ("Billy") Robinson, a brevet major in the 8th Foot and a jovial Irishman who knew exactly how to get the best out of raw soldiers. Pearson knew both Battersby and Robinson as he

Private, Glengarry Light Infantry, 1813
A fencible unit raised in 1812, the Glengarry Light Infantry were uniformed as a rifle regiment and trained as light infantry specialists. They saw considerable action during the war and Pearson had them under his command not only at Prescott but also in the Niagara Peninsula during the summer of 1814. (Painting by G.A. Embleton, courtesy of Parks Canada)

had served alongside them in Egypt in 1801, Copenhagen in 1807 and Halifax in 1808-1810. Pearson's brigade was not strong – he only had a total of 825 all ranks, barely a strong battalion by European standards – but it was composed of very good materiel and commanded by veteran officers.

Pearson being Pearson, he wasted no time in whipping it into shape according to his lights. It is notable, however, that he issued remarkably fewer orders than when stationed at Prescott these troops did not need so many admonishments, although there were always a few things to be tightened up:

Light Brigade Orders, 21st July 1814
Staff Adjutant Gregg will do duty of Brigade Major to the light Brigade. A Sergeant or steady Corporal will be selected from the Brigade for the purpose of copying all division and Brigade orders, an orderly Bugle to attend at the quarters of the Staff Adjutant.

The Commanding officers of Corps & detachments will send in at 8 o'clock every morning while the Brigade is stationary field returns of their respective commands noting any detached parties & Casualties of the preceding 24 hours.

All Picquets and Guards furnished by the Light Brigade will be mounted at 6 o'clock in the morning, a return of the same to be furnished the Staff Adjutants by the Brigade Adjutants of the day for Lieutenant-Colonel Pearson's information.

No Parties from the Light Brigade to be placed in any detached duty without acquainting Lieutenant-Colonel Pearson or in his absence Lieutenant Colonel Battersby.

Commanding officers of Corps will be particularly attentive to the division order of the day which relates to the Provisioning of their men.
Pearson
Lieutenant-Colonel commanding[2]

During this time, while the Americans were camped at Queenston, Riall's troops moved between the Four-Mile, Twelve-Mile and Twenty-Mile Creeks. It was a period of heavy rain and, as there were no tents, they often had to shelter in barns and houses – in fact the weather was so bad that Riall authorized an extra ration of rum. Reinforcements gradually began to arrive as more militia were called out and Norton came up with a large force of warriors. As usual, the aboriginals were a remarkable sight: Ensign Benjamin Warffe of the Incor-

The Falls of Niagara, 1814
The battle of Lundy's Lane, 25 July 1814, was fought within two miles of this great natural wonder. Although it formed a scenic attraction, the falls also created a logistical problem for the armies as it restricted the use of the Niagara River as a communications route. (Painting by George Heriot, National Library and Archives of Canada, C-12797)

porated Militia recorded in his diary on 18 July that "800 Indians passed us that day, frightful beasts."[3] On 20 July Brown finally advanced north to Fort George. As Chauncey's squadron had still not appeared on Lake Ontario, he could do nothing without the heavy guns of the fleet and contented himself with demonstrations, hoping in vain to lure the British into the open to bring on a general engagement. That day, Pearson's brigade was holding the forward position at Four-Mile Creek and his men could hear artillery fire from the direction of the forts. Riall, however, did nothing to assist Fort George, because he had been told that Drummond was coming to the Niagara to assume command, and he was therefore relieved when Brown, frustrated in his attempts to lure the Right Division into open battle, withdrew to Queenston on 22 July. But Riall was also worried because he had learned that the enemy were building new batteries on the American side of the Niagara River that would threaten Fort George.

He informed Drummond of this fact, and although the information was actually false, it spurred Drummond into planning an offensive in the Niagara. As Chauncey had not yet emerged from Sacket's Harbor, the British commander could send reinforcements by water from York to Fort Niagara on

23 July and he planned to cross himself the following day and with every available man push south along the American side of the Niagara on 25 July, taking the batteries that so worried Riall. Riall, for his part, was ordered to mount a demonstration against Queenston to hold Brown in place. Once the batteries had been destroyed, Drummond intended to recross to the Canadian bank and then drive Brown and his army out of Canada before the American naval squadron emerged on Lake Ontario to interdict his waterborne supply line. Pearson's light brigade was chosen as the vanguard of Riall's demonstration and in anticipation it was concentrated at Twelve-Mile Creek on 23 July since this was a better position from which to move against Queenston. Pearson's men were ordered to cook two days rations in advance and "to be in readiness to march at a moment's warning."[4] These precautions possibly caused some grumbling but it was well that they were made because the situation was about to change.

During the afternoon of 24 July John Norton, scouting down the Portage Road, discovered that Brown's army had withdrawn from Queenston to a position near the falls of Niagara. Late in the evening, Riall therefore ordered Pearson to take his own and the 1st Militia Brigade (1st, 2nd, 4th and 5th Lincoln Regiments and 2nd York) forward to locate and maintain contact with the enemy. Pearson's command moved out at 10 P.M. and, guided by Captain William Merritt's Provincial Light Dragoons, marched slowly but steadily through the night, arriving at the village of St. David's, a few miles west of Queenston, just as dawn broke on the morning of 25 July 1814. By 2 A.M., Pearson had reached the junction of the Portage Road and a tree-shrouded, sunken county route called Lundy's Lane after a prominent local farmer. His troops were now about a mile from the falls of Niagara, where, according to Norton, the Americans were camped, but there was no sign of the Yankees. When Norton arrived with his warriors, Pearson dispatched him and Merritt with some of the Canadian dragoons south down the Portage Road to locate the enemy and they soon returned to report that the American camp was at Chippawa.

Having accomplished his mission, which was to locate the enemy, Pearson took due precautions. He posted a dragoon vedette at a tavern halfway between Chippawa and his position, and placed a couple of Glengarry Light Infantry companies in the woods around it to prevent unwanted surprises. He positioned the remainder of his two brigades along a low hill, actually a sandy ridge traversed by Lundy's Lane, that ran west from the Portage Road. This ridge possessed not only good lateral communications but an excellent field of fire to the south across open wheat fields and it constituted the best defensive position between Chippawa and Fort George – which is exactly why Pearson chose it. This done, he told his men to get some sleep and sat down to await events.[5]

It was a beautiful day, sunny but not hot, and the mist from the falls of Niagara, roiling up hundreds of feet above the great cataract, hung in the air. In the early afternoon, Riall arrived to tell Pearson that he was concentrating the Right Division at this forward position and that orders had been sent for the 1st Regular Brigade under Colonel Hercules Scott, the reserve under Lieutenant-Colonel John Gordon and the 2nd Militia Brigade, to march towards it. In addition, Riall also had the interesting news that Drummond, who had sailed across the lake to the Niagara from York on the previous night, would soon be coming up with considerable reinforcements and would assume command.

It looked as though it was going to be a quiet evening but at about 5.30 P.M., just as everyone was thinking of cooking a meal, dragoons came galloping along the Portage Road to report that Brown's entire division, 5,000 strong, was moving on Lundy's Lane. At almost the same moment, scattered firing broke out in the woods to the south, indicating that the Glengarries were in action. It was all rather worrying to Riall, who had become somewhat wary

Canadian light dragoon, 1814
During the War of 1812, two small cavalry units were raised in British North America: the Canadian Light Dragoons and the Niagara Dragoons. They wore similar uniforms, which included the Tarleton helmet, as shown in this painting of a Canadian Light Dragoon. The primary purpose of these units was to serve as dispatch riders and scouts. When he commanded the Light Brigade of the British Right Division, Pearson had elements of the Niagara Dragoons under his command. (Painting by G.A. Embleton, courtesy Department of National Defence, Canada)

of American regulars after the drubbing they had given him at Chippawa. He decided that the odds were too great and ordered a retreat north to Queenston, where he could meet up with the remainder of his division, Drummond and his reinforcements, and make a stand. In a few minutes, the militia and the artillery, followed by the Incorporated Militia, were on the road north while Pearson was left with a rearguard consisting of the Glengarries and dragoons to cover the withdrawal.

It was not long before the troops returned. Drummond had encountered the retreating columns and had ordered them to turn in their tracks and re-trace their steps back to Lundy's Lane. He and Riall then rode onto the hill and Drummond, appreciating at a glance that it was good ground, began to position his units as they arrived, on and around the hill. The British commander had about 2,000 troops and five pieces of artillery so he positioned his regulars, about 750 men drawn mainly from the 89th Foot with detached companies from three other regular British battalions, on the ridge along Lundy's Lane behind his artillery. Pearson was sent to the right flank with the Glengarries and 1st Militia Brigade but lost the Incorporated Militia, who were removed from his direct orders and positioned on the left flank. To Drummond, who thought Brown's strength was about 5,000, it appeared to be a question of holding on until the arrival of the 1,400 regulars and 250 militia currently on the march to join him. The last British troops were just getting in place at about 7 P.M. when a squadron of American cavalry appeared and halted on the Portage Road where it traversed a belt of chestnut woods about 700 yards south of the ridge. A few minutes later, a column of infantry came into view, their grey jackets identify-ing them as Scott's First Brigade.

Winfield Scott was somewhat surprised when he emerged from the trees. When Brown had learned earlier that afternoon that his supply depot at Fort Schlosser on the American side of the Niagara was being threatened by British troops advancing from Fort Niagara, he had decided that the best defence was a retaliatory strike on the British side of the river. He had therefore ordered Scott to take his brigade and detachments of artillery and cavalry, some 1,250 men in total, and move north up the Portage Road. Scott marched out of Chippawa some time after 5 P.M. and it was his column that had been incorrectly reported to Riall as Brown's entire division. Stopping at a tavern on his route, Scott had obtained from the woman proprietor information about the strength of Pear-son's force ahead of him but it was out of date. Therefore, when he emerged from the chestnut woods at about 7.15 P.M. he found, not the 1,100 men and two artillery pieces he had been told were waiting for him, but a far superior force posted on very good ground. Scott sent messengers back to Brown but as he was too far from Chippawa to receive immediate help, he faced the choice of either waiting until reinforcements arrived or attacking.

The ever-aggressive Scott, possibly buoyed by the recent success at Chippawa, seems never to have seriously considered anything other than an attack. Detaching Major Thomas S. Jesup and his Twenty-Fifth Infantry down a lane leading northeast from the Portage Road, he ordered his three remaining regiments to deploy in line at the southern extremity of the area of cleared fields. Seeing this, Drummond gave the order and the British gunners opened fire to commence the bloodiest battle of the War of 1812.[6]*

The opening phases of this engagement did not go well for Winfield Scott. His brigade was deployed between 500 and 600 yards from the British guns, well out of musket range, but well within artillery range and Captain James Maclachlan, RA, Drummond's artillery commander, immediately took full advantage of the disparity to pour roundshot from his two 24-pdr. and two 6-pdr. guns and shells from his single 5.5-inch howitzer into the grey-uniformed ranks. His aiming points were the blue and buff colours at the centre of the Ninth, Eleventh and Twenty-Second Infantry Regiments and the result was heavy casualties among the colour bearers and the commanding officers who took post near the colours. Within minutes only the commanding officer of the Ninth Infantry remained unwounded. The American artillery tried to return the fire of the British gunners with interest but found it difficult, given the difference in elevations, to put down accurate fire on the hill and finally ceased fire to conserve ammunition. There was nothing wrong with the position of the Royal Artillery, however, and they inflicted heavy losses on the First Brigade. "We were completely cut up," an officer of the Twenty-Second Infantry later wrote, "more than half the officers and men being killed or wounded."[7] The grey-jacketed infantry did not waver under this torment, however, but responded with almost useless volleys of long-range musketry, closed in to their centres as casualties were taken and held their ground. A British officer watching from the hill thought that the American enemy "remained firm in their position which he had at first assumed," as "Dread seemed to forbid his advance, and Shame to restrain his flight."[8]

* Orders of battle for the opposing forces at the battle of Lundy's Lane, 25 July 1814, will be found in Appendix H below.

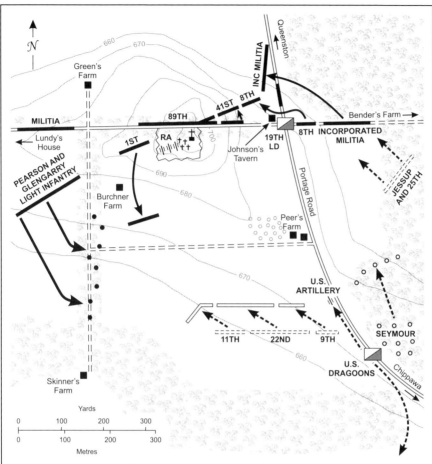

Lundy's Lane – 25 July 1814
1st Phase: c. 7:15 – 8:45 PM

Drummond deploys along Lundy's Lane with his artillery on the hill near a meeting house and cemetery (building with a cross and group of crosses). Scott forms his brigade west of the Portage Road while his artillery unlimbers on the road itself.

Coming under heavy fire, Scott orders an advance on the hill but later countermands the order. Pearson, seeing an opportunity, attacks Scott's left flank with the Glengarry Light Infantry and militia. The 1st Foot advances to support this attack.

Meanwhile, Jesup of the 25th Infantry, having left a company under Seymour to cover his position, attacks the British left flank and forces the Incorporated Militia to retreat.

After about 45 minutes, Scott decided that something had to be done and ordered an advance "upon the enemy with a view to charge him."⁹ His three regiments moved forward but had only gone about a hundred yards when Scott ordered a halt. They were now about 400 yards from Maclachlan's artillery – extreme canister range but Maclachlan, presented with such a tempting target, might just have used that projectile as it was more effective against infantry in line than round shot. Just to add to Scott's problems, the Royal Marine Artillery Congreve rocket detachment with Maclachlan fired some of their 12-pdr. rockets at his line. The use of rockets at Lundy's Lane was noted by several eyewitnesses but the historical record is silent as to whether they actually hit anything.

Pearson now entered the battle. Scott's advance had brought his left flank out from the cover of the chestnut woods and it presented an attractive target for Pearson, who had been watching the shooting gallery from his position on the British right flank. He ordered the Glengarries to form a skirmish line and advance on the enemy flank, followed by the five weak regiments of the 2nd Militia Brigade. Drummond, seeing this movement, sent three companies of the 100th Foot, positioned at the base of the hill, forward to join the party. As soon as they were within range, the British and Canadians began to fire at the

Eleventh Infantry, the left flank unit of Scott's brigade and, to that unit's commanding officer, Major Henry Leavenworth, it seemed as though his enemy "was pressing

Gunner, United States Artillery, 1813
Throughout the War of 1812, the artillery was the most effective branch of the American army as it benefited from a higher proportion of professional officers, many of them graduates of the Military Academy at West Point. Such was the quality of American gunners that a British officer who fought in the Niagara campaign of 1814 rendered an American artillery officer the supreme accolade: "We thought you were French." (Painting by Charles H. McBarron, courtesy of Parks Canada)

very hard" on him.[10] On Scott's command Leavenworth threw back his own left flank and returned the fire with volleys, which had little effect as the targets "were scattered according to the practice of irregular Warfare, taking ev'ry advantage of which the open nature of the ground would admit."[11] Neither side pressed the matter but Pearson's advance seems to have finished any idea Scott had about making a charge.

By this time, about 8.30 P.M., the American commander's situation was nothing short of desperate. The three regiments in his line had suffered very heavy casualties for absolutely no profit and the only thing that prevented their utter destruction was the coming of darkness, which caused the British gunners to cease fire as their targets disappeared in the twilight. The one bright spot was that Jesup's Twenty-Fifth Infantry, operating independently, had managed to launch a devastating flank attack on the Incorporated Militia and push them back from their original position to a new position north of the Portage Road. Lieutenant-Colonel William Robinson managed to reform the battalion but was himself seriously wounded. As he was carried to the rear, the Irish Robinson called out to his men advising them that "a stump or a log will stand a leaden bullet better than the best of yees, and therefore give them the honour to be your front rank man."[12]

The presence of American troops in the junction of the Portage Road and Lundy's Lane, combined with the growing darkness, inevitably led to mistakes in identification. Jesup captured a number of British officers, including Major-General Phineas Riall who was riding to the rear to seek medical attention for a wounded arm. Having disrupted the British flank, Jesup now opted to withdraw south by stages in the fields east of the Portage Road and was doing so when he encountered the leading elements of American reinforcements coming from the camp at Chippawa.

As soon as Scott's messengers had arrived, Brown had put much of the remainder of his division on the road north. Consisting of Brigadier-General Eleazar W. Ripley's Second Brigade, Brigadier-General Peter B. Porter's volunteer brigade, an unbrigaded regiment of regulars and two companies of artillery, their numbers amounted to about 1,600 effectives. Riding ahead, Brown found Scott and the remnants of his units just as darkness fell and the British artillery ceased firing. The noise made by some of the arriving units drew the occasional round from Maclachlan's gunners but it was only random fire as the fields and woods south of the hill were shrouded in darkness.

The battle of Lundy's Lane, 1814
This period print, which was produced in 1815, is one of the few contemporary illustrations of the bloody nighttime battle fought on 25 July 1814. It shows the Twenty-First Infantry capturing the British artillery and the small church or meeting house that was on top of the hill. (Engraving by William Strickland, based on a sketch by Major Thomas Riddle first published in the *Portfolio*, National Library and Archives of Canada, C-4071)

Brown heard Scott's report, and after some of his staff carefully scouted the British lines, decided to renew the battle by attacking the hill, the key to Drummond's position. His plan was to mount a demonstration in front to distract the British gunners, while Ripley's brigade moved up the hill by way of Lundy's Lane and the slope itself, directly at the British artillery.

On his side, Drummond had reason to be satisfied with events. Although his left flank had been pushed back, the Americans had not pressed the advantage and, moreover, Colonel Hercules Scott had just arrived with 1,600 reinforcements after a 20-mile march, including 1,250 regulars from the 1st, 8th, 103rd and 104th Foot and 250 militia with three 6-pdr. guns. The British commander, however, was taking no chances and carried out a cautious re-alignment of his forces, pulling Pearson's units back from their advanced position on the right and placing his regular infantry along the hill, beside and behind his artillery, but not in front of it. Drummond then waited for the Americans to make the next move. He knew they must either attack – a very tricky thing in the dark – or withdraw and, if the action was going to be renewed, Drummond preferred to fight on the defensive rather than to try and co-ordinate a night attack.

Major-General Jacob Brown decided to fight. The first warning the British

had of this was when the First U.S. Infantry, ordered to make a musketry demonstration to distract the British artillery, instead advanced directly at them.
Maclachlan's gunners opened a furious fire of canister at the Americans, whose
commanding officer wisely withdrew into the darkness at the bottom of the
hill. Unfortunately for Maclachlan, his attention had been distracted from the
approach of Colonel James Miller and his Twenty-First Infantry from Ripley's
brigade as they climbed the dark southeast slope of the sandy ridge. There
being no screen of British light infantry in front of the guns, Miller was able
to get within decent musket range before being noticed. John Norton, who
was beside the gun position talking to some officers, suddenly saw a group
of soldiers appear out of the darkness and "enquired what Body of men it
might be that were approaching" but almost immediately recognized them as
Americans from the shape of their shako plates.[13] On Miller's command the
Twenty-First Infantry fired a volley and then advanced on Maclachlan's gunners with charged bayonets. Before the British infantry, posted behind their
artillery position, could intervene, the Americans were in among the guns with
the bayonet and those gunners who did not flee were taken prisoner.

Lieutenant-Colonel Joseph Wanton Morrison, victor of Crysler's Farm, had
deployed his 89th Foot in line along Lundy's Lane, directly behind the British
artillery. As soon as he saw the Americans among the guns he mounted an
immediate counterattack in line but his advance was hampered by caissons,
gun carriages, wagons and general confusion. Miller steadfastly refused to give
up his trophies and the British attack deteriorated into a firefight across the
captured ordnance, with the opposing lines so close that the muzzle blazes
from their weapons, clearly visible in the dark, "crossed each other."[14] Morrison fell back, re-formed and then returned again with three companies of
the 1st Foot on his right and the light company of the 41st Foot on his left.
Again, a close-range musketry duel took place and casualties were heavy on
both sides, including Morrison and Drummond, who had joined in the action.
For a second time the British withdrew to re-form but soon advanced again
and this time the fighting was even more obstinate. For a few minutes, some of
the guns were in the possession of the light company of the 41st Foot but they
were recaptured at the point of the bayonet, when the British fell back and this
time they did not return.

Contact was now broken between the two armies and a lull ensued as Miller
was joined on the hill by Brown and the rest of the Left Division. The First Infantry formed along Lundy's Lane on Miller's left while the Twenty-Third and

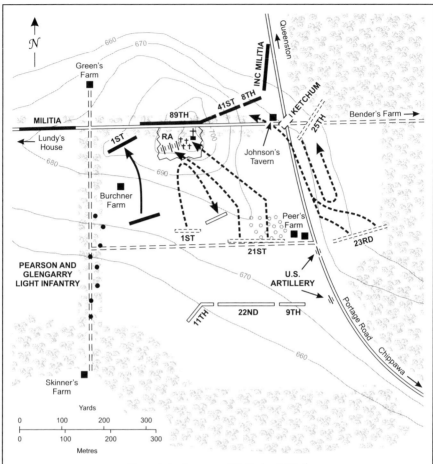

Lundy's Lane – 25 July 1814
2nd Phase: c. 8:45 – 9:45 PM

Pearson skirmishes against Scott's left flank with the Glengarry Light Infantry and York militia. Ketchum's company of the 25th scoops up prisoners in the road before Jesup withdraws.

Brown now arrives on the battlefield with Ripley and Porter's brigades. Ripley's brigade captures the hill and the British artillery and successfully fends off counterattacks mounted by Drummond with 1st, 41st and 89th Foot.

Twenty-Fifth Infantry took position on his right. Porter's volunteer brigade came up on the far left flank while the remnants of Scott's brigade, less the Twenty-Fifth Infantry, took a position in column behind the main infantry line. Brown and his officers admired the captured artillery; Lieutenant David Douglass of the engineers enjoyed "the satisfaction of seeing and handling brass guns of the most beautiful model, of different calibers, from six to twenty-four pounders" and it was decided to bring the American guns up to the top of the hill to form a formidable battery against the British counterattack that was inevitable.[15] As they moved about, the Americans could hear commands shouted in the darkness below the hill's northern slope and the sounds of troops moving about in the dark. In addition, the occasional glimpse of a lantern made it clear that the British would shortly be returning.

Immediately after he had withdrawn from the hill, Drummond made preparations to retake both it and his artillery. It was absolutely essential that the ordnance be repossessed; otherwise he would not be able to campaign in the field until replacement weapons were procured from Kingston or even Lower Canada, which could take weeks. He therefore organized for a counterattack but, owing to the dark, confusion, the loss of officers and the inevitable confusion, it was nearly half an hour before his units were formed and ready. As the Canadian militia would be of no use in what promised to be a very tough business, their ammunition was stripped from them and given to the regulars, and they were assigned such secondary tasks as knocking down the split rail fences which cut across the battlefield rendering movement difficult, and transporting the wounded to the rear. Despite precautions being taken, mistakes did happen – Battersby's Glengarries were pulling back from their advanced position when they were fired on by the 103rd and 104th Foot. The fire was only stopped after Battersby rode between the lines "in the most daring manner" to cry out that the Glengarries were friendly and to cease fire.[16] It took officers and sergeants considerable effort to get their men formed and ready but finally at about 10 P.M. Drummond, a neck wound he had suffered during the fight over the guns heavily bandaged, gave the order and the British line climbed the north slope of the hill.

The Americans, who could hear them coming, were waiting and saw "a dark line" approaching, at a distance "of perhaps sixty paces."[17] The British halted, dressed their line and then fired a volley which was returned by the Americans, and a vicious exchange of fire ensued as the two lines engaged in what a British participant later described as a contest "obstinate beyond description."[18] There was so much light from the muzzle blaze that the men of both armies could see the faces and buttons of their opposite numbers. Almost all the American gunners were cut down by musketry, which brought an end to Brown's attempts to bring artillery into action on the hill. Heavy casualties were suffered by both sides but neither wavered and both lines were so "cut to pieces that neither side could effect a charge."[19] The duel continued for approximately 20 minutes and then the British withdrew to re-form in the darkness.

A few minutes later they were back, "undismayed and in good order."[20] A second musketry contest, longer and more intense than the first, followed, although this time the British line did not approach as close before opening fire. Their fire was so heavy, however, that some of the American units began to waver. On the left, Porter's non-regular volunteers fell back some distance down the south slope of the hill before Porter and his officers got a grip and re-formed them. In the centre, the Twenty-Third and part of the Twenty-First began to drift to the rear away from the fire, but were stopped by their officers and steadied. On the right, Jesup of the Twenty-Fifth Infantry, already wounded, was hit twice during this attack but remained on his feet and continued to lead his regiment.

What made the second British attack even more confusing is that Winfield Scott, determined to get back into the battle, led the remnants of his brigade in column north along Lundy's Lane *between* the two opposing lines, only to be fired on by both sides. The weary men of the First Brigade broke and fled behind the American line where Scott managed to re-form them, a tribute to their bravery and training.

The second musketry exchange continued but the British did not press home with the bayonet and after about 25 minutes Drummond broke off and withdrew.

At this point in the battle, after more than four hours of fighting, the men of both armies were in a bad way, tired, thirsty and low on ammunition. Some had been in action or marching for nearly 12 hours and did not have much more to give, but Drummond, reasoning that if his troops were in poor condition, the Americans must be as bad, decided to make one last effort. The orders were given and at about 11.30 P.M. a weary two-rank line of British and Canadian regulars again ascended that dark hill. They halted within musket range and, on command, began firing volleys into the Americans opposite, who returned the fire.

Just after this attack began, Scott returned yet again to the battle. He had reformed the remnants of the Ninth, Eleventh and Twenty-Second Infantry in column along a farm lane that ran north and south beside the left flank of the American line. He then led them north in column in an apparent attempt to break through the British line but, unfortunately for his men, they came within range of the 103rd, 104th Foot and the Glengarries, who promptly fired a volley into the First Brigade's crowded ranks. The Americans tried to return it, a lot of wild shooting ensued and it was probably during this scrap that Pearson, positioned with Batterby's Glengarries, was hit in the arm by a musket ball but had it bound it up and continued in action. After a few rounds, the men of the First Brigade gave up the contest as hopeless and fell back behind their own line. As their day was clearly done, Scott now left them and moved to the position of the Twenty-Fifth Infantry on the American right flank.

On the hill, meanwhile, the opposing lines exchanged fire across Lundy's Lane. It was during this action that both Brown and Scott were seriously wounded. Brown remained in the saddle but was forced to give up command while Scott was carried to the rear, having fought his last battle in this war. On the American left flank, the volunteers of Porter's brigade and the First Infantry made a short charge and actually crossed bayonets with the British before falling back. On the American right flank, the indefatigable Jesup suffered his fourth wound but continued in action. By now his Twenty-Fifth Infantry had taken so many casualties that he had formed it in a single rank and Jesup had put his file closers – the junior officers and sergeants – in that rank. But it was in the centre around the artillery where Drummond made the greatest effort and here the 1st Foot and the 89th Foot got into the gun position. Brigadier-General Eleazar Ripley, who had assumed command of the Left Division on Brown's wounding, led the First and Twenty-First United States Infantry in a counterattack and there was vicious fighting in and around the gun carriages, caissons and wagons on the hill as men fought with bayonets, clubbed muskets or fired at short range. The Americans refused to break – as an officer of the Left Division later put it, the redcoats could not overcome "the obstinate desperation of the Yankees" and "every charge with the bayonet" showed "how idle and how vain the boasting of the British infantry is when opposed to full blooded eaters of the pumpkin."[21]

And it was true. The tactics of disciplined volley fire followed by a vicious bayonet charge, which had worked against the French on a score of European battlefields, did not work against well-trained American regulars, whose fire

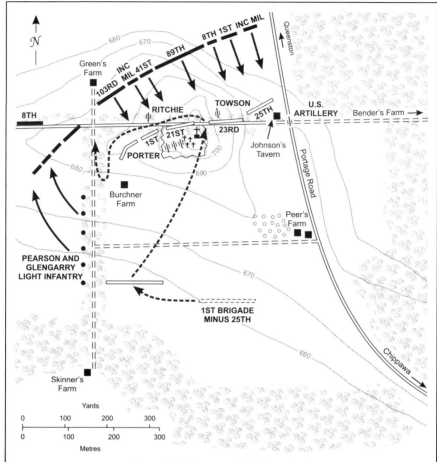

Lundy's Lane – 25 July 1814
3rd Phase: c. 9:45 – 12:00 PM

Drummond re-forms his troops, including recent reinforcements, into line. When Pearson withdraws to re-ammunition, his men are fired upon by their own side.

Brown deploys on the hill with Porter's brigade on the left and Ripley's brigade on the right, and his artillery. Drummond mounts several attacks to recapture his artillery but they are repulsed by the Americans. Scott moves the remnants of his brigade along Lundy's Lane and is fired on by both sides. In a subsequent action, Scott encounters Pearson and the Glengarries and Pearson is wounded in an exchange of fire.

When the last British attack fails, Brown remains in possession of the hill and Drummond's artillery.

was just as effective, if not more. Drummond's troops had met their match, and when the British bugles sounded a recall shortly before midnight and they withdrew in good order down the northern slope of the hill, the guns remained in possession of Major-General Jacob Brown's Left Division.

Unfortunately for an American claim of victory in this desperately-fought battle, only one of these trophies was removed from the battlefield. When the firing died away, Brown, in pain but still gamely trying to stay in the saddle, ordered Ripley to get the captured ordnance away, collect and transport the wounded, and return to the camp at Chippawa to make ready to fight again the next day. Ripley sent working parties to collect the captured guns but they were hampered by a shortage of transport animals and harness and ended up simply rolling them down the southern slope of the hill where they could be retrieved the next morning, apart from one brass 6-pdr. gun which was taken away by an artillery officer who managed to hitch it to one of his limbers.[22] The remaining seven pieces were left. The working parties then followed the Left Division as it made an orderly withdrawal to its camp at Chippawa.

During the night that followed, British patrols found that their enemy had abandoned the top of the hill but it was only when daylight came on 26 July that they found that their artillery, less the one 6-pdr. gun, was still on the battlefield. Drummond promptly moved his troops forward to occupy the high ground and they commenced cleaning up the battlefield, locating and transporting the wounded of both sides (many of the American wounded had been left behind because their comrades could not find them in the dark) and burying or burning the dead. His men were involved in this activity when the pickets sent word that the enemy was advancing.

Most reluctantly, but at Brown's insistence, Ripley had paraded the Left Division that morning and set out to either reoccupy the battlefield or re-new the action. His heart was not in it and, as his lead elements came within view of the tavern midway between the camps of the two armies, he halted and called a conference of his senior officers. Telling them that the scouts had reported that Drummond's army was formed for battle and had clearly been reinforced, he proposed withdrawing the division across the Niagara to American soil. Although none of the senior officers wished to renew the fight-ing, all of them protested against any retreat to the United States and in the end a compromise was made – the Left Division would withdraw to Fort Erie and entrench. At this, the grey- and blue-uniformed columns turned in their tracks and marched down the River Road to Fort Erie, which they reached late that night.

Lieutenant-General Gordon Drummond was not unhappy to see them go as his Right Division was also in no condition to renew the fighting. The casualties in the battle of Lundy's Lane, as the engagement fought during the evening and night of 25 July 1814 not more than a mile from the great falls of Niagara came to be known, were very heavy. Drummond reported 878 officers and men killed, wounded or missing, approximately a quarter of his effectives, with the 1st, 8th and 89th Foot paying the highest cost, the 89th losing 60% of its strength. The Incorporated Militia and Glengarry Light Infantry from Pearson's brigade lost 61 and 56 respectively. Major-General Jacob Brown's Left Division listed 860 casualties of all types with the worst losses being in Scott's First Brigade, which suffered 416 casualties from an engaged strength of between 1,100 and 1,200 troops. Miller's Twenty-First Infantry, which had played such a prominent role in the battle, reported 104 casualties, about a quarter of its strength.

Given the price they had paid and the duration, intensity and confusion of the fighting, it was not surprising that both commanders believed they had won the battle. Brown had a good claim for a tactical victory as he had taken and held the crucial position on the battlefield, the hill, against repeated counterattacks, and had also captured the British artillery. But his success had been diminished by the fact that the captured ordnance, the proof of his triumph, had been left on the battlefield. In operational terms, the Left Division was defeated at Lundy's Lane because it withdrew to Fort Erie following the engagement and advanced no further into Upper Canada. Drummond could therefore lay claim to a success at Lundy's Lane because he had stopped a major American invasion and had some cause to claim a tactical victory because he remained in possession of the battlefield – although only because it was relinquished by the enemy.

Instead of vigorously pursuing the enemy, however, Drummond gave up the battlefield on 26 July and withdrew north to Queenston. He then did nothing for four days except to send Norton on 27 July as far as Bridgewater Mills to maintain contact. This rather weak response may have been due to the fact that his army needed time to rest and reorganize, or it may have been due to his wound, which was to plague the British commander for the rest of the campaign. Whatever the cause, Drummond's failure to actively pursue the enemy after Lundy's Lane gave the Americans nearly a week of heaven-sent grace and they put it to good effect by entrenching around Fort Erie.

The result was, that by the time British and Canadian troops arrived at that place in the first few days of August 1814 they found the enemy in a very strong position. The original small stone fort had been extended by an earthwork, protected in part by ditches and *abbatis* constructed of fallen timbers and bristling with gun emplacements. Even worse, Chauncey had at last emerged on Lake Ontario with a new, large warship, sending Yeo scurrying into Kingston until he could emerge with something even bigger. Drummond would now have to depend on a logistical line running along more than 200 miles of wretched roads back to Kingston, which could be interdicted easily by enemy naval forces anywhere along its length. To make matters even more disagreeable, Drummond possessed neither siege artillery nor enough troops to completely invest the American position at Fort Erie, nor could he cut it off as the United States Navy controlled Lake Erie. The best the British commander could do was to position himself on the north end of the enemy defences, and skirmish for control of the "no-man's land" around the middle and southern parts. What Drummond had on his hands was not a typical siege operation – the investure of a position that could be isolated and attacked at leisure. He faced a heavily-fortified and well-supplied bridgehead with clear and short communications to its own supply depots in Buffalo just across the river.

Not surprisingly, Drummond decided that the weakest part of the enemy defences were these same depots. If they could be destroyed or captured, then the Americans might be forced to retire to their own soil or, at the least they would be much weakened. He therefore planned an attack across the Niagara and assembled a fairly elite force consisting of 600 men drawn from six flank companies of the 41st, 89th, 100th and 104th Foot, and four battalion companies from the 41st Foot. Pearson would have been the logical choice to command this expedition but it seems his wound kept him out of action for eight or nine days after Lundy's Lane, and in his absence the operation was placed under Lieutenant-Colonel John Goulston Price Tucker of the 41st Foot. Tucker was not very experienced. He had seen some service in India and the Cape of Good Hope before transferring as a major to a garrison battalion in 1808 and had spent the next four years on half-pay before returning to active service in early 1814 as a lieutenant-colonel in the 41st Foot. Nor was Tucker a well-respected officer. His army nickname was "Brigadier Shindy," which was a combined slight on his rank, his relative lack of experience and his intelligence. A "shindy" was period slang for a dance and the implication was that Tucker was an officer good for nothing better than being a dancing master – in short, he was useless. The rules of seniority were the rules, however, and it did not matter that there were other officers with considerable light infantry experience available such as Lieutenant-Colonels William Drummond of the 104th or Francis Battersby of the Glengarry Light Infantry – Tucker ranked them. Drummond, a stickler for following the rules of the military hierarchy, therefore placed him in command of the expedition across the Niagara River.

The result was predictable. Tucker got his men over the river on the night of 2/3 August without a problem but then, although he was supposed to attack his objective at dawn, he did nothing for four hours and when he finally did move without an advance guard, it was well into the morning. By this time the enemy was forewarned and a battalion of regular American riflemen, which had hastily entrenched behind a wide creek, shot up Tucker's lead elements and they fell back in confusion. Rather than trying to flank the enemy position upstream where there was a ford, Tucker opted to skirmish with the riflemen for several hours, a useless and costly exercise given the disparity in weapons between the two opposing sides – rifles behind cover being infinitely superior to muskets in the open – before finally recrossing the Niagara.

His attempt to lever the Americans out of their position having failed, Drummond now had to contemplate an attack directly on Fort Erie. On the morning of 3 August 1814 Pearson was back with his brigade when it drove in the enemy pickets outside Fort Erie to permit the British commander to make a closer examination of the defences. He did not like what he saw, as he faced a very strong position held by a defending force that had as many or more troops than were under his command, with 18 guns in position plus batteries on the American side of the Niagara and naval support on Lake Erie.

For the next nine days, from 4 August to 13 August, British fatigue parties worked hard to construct a battery for heavy ordnance which, with great difficulty, was brought up from the forts at the river mouth. In the meantime Pearson's "Light Demi-Brigade," as it was now officially termed, tried to get control of the "no man's land" between the batteries and the American defences. Pearson's command consisted of the flank companies of the 104th Foot (a regiment of the line recruited in Canada), the Glengarry Light Infantry and the Incorporated Militia, the latter being under the command of Major James Kerby in the absence of the wounded Robinson. It is interesting to note that Pearson's troops were all Canadians. There was considerable skirmishing outside the fort between his men and their American counterparts – a regular rifle battalion that frequently tried to attack the battery site to slow down the rate of construction.

"The enemy makes daily efforts with his riflemen to dislodge our advanced picquets and to obtain a reconnaissance of what we are doing," reported Drummond to Prevost, adding that these attacks, "tho' feeble and invariably repulsed, yet harass our troops and occasion us some loss."[23] Drummond also rendered Pearson a compliment when he praised the "good conduct" of the Glengarries and Incorporated Militia during these actions.[24] War chief John Norton, whose warriors often joined in this bush fighting, thought they were "trifling Encounters" but noted that the friendly casualties "were not inconsiderable."[25]

But there were lighter moments and Surgeon William Dunlop of the 89th Foot, last met at Cornwall during the previous winter, remembered one misadventure involving Pearson. Dunlop, who spent much of his four years in the army avoiding his medical duties in favour of trying to get into combat, was delighted to be appointed surgeon of the light demi-brigade. Dunlop knew Pearson and his temper well enough to know it was not a good idea to get on his brigade commander's bad side and managed to avoid problems until one day, by accident, he rubbed Pearson the wrong way and paid the price. But it is a story best told in Dunlop's own words as the good doctor was a famous raconteur:

One day, when relieved from picquet, I announced to Col. P[earson]., who commanded our brigade, that I had discovered a short way through the woods to the camp, and I accordingly led the way, he and Captain F[itzgibbon] of the Glengarries, following. By some fatality I mistook the path, and took a wrong turn, so that instead of finding the camp we came right on the top of an American picquet, which opened fire upon us at about fifty yards distance. Being used to this we were behind trees in a moment, and the next were scampering in different directions at greater or lesser angles to the enemy.

Major James Kerby, Incorporated Militia, 1814 (1785-1854)
Kerby commanded the Incorporated Militia in Pearson's light demi-brigade during the siege of Fort Erie. He was badly wounded during the siege but recovered and lived to become the collector of customs in Fort Erie, the town that grew up around the old battlefield. (National Library and Archives of Canada, C-130537)

It may be well supposed that I did not wait on our brigadier [Pearson], during the time we were off duty, to receive thanks for my services as a guide, nor when we did go on duty again was I at all anxious to obtrude myself upon him; indeed I kept as far from him as I could, but in going his rounds at daylight he came up with me seated by a picquet fire at the extreme left of our line. He saluted me most graciously, alluded to our late exploit as a good joke, and asked me to breakfast with him. "Ho, ho," thinks I, "he has forgotten it all, and I'm forgiven – this is as it should be."

Lounging about after breakfast, and talking over indifferent matters, a sputtering fire began a little to our left, and the Colonel ordering a look out on the right, proceeded, followed by me, to the scene of action. We soon saw that it was the point of attack, so he sent me to order up the reserve.

This done I rejoined him, and found him standing coolly giving his orders in the middle of a whistling of bullets, far too thick to be pleasant. I stood by his side for a few minutes, thankful that none of these missiles had a billet on us, when on a sudden I felt a severe sharp pain from my brow to the back of my head at the same moment the Colonel exclaimed: "By G-d, you're shot through the head."

I sunk upon one knee, and taking off my forage cap felt along my head for blood, but none was to be found. "It is only a graze," said I, "Colonel, is there any mark?" "Yes," said he, "there is a red mark, but not from a ball, it came from my switch. You gave me a d___l of a fright the other day – now I have given you one, so we are quits."[26]

AUTHOR OF SKETCHES OF UPPER CANADA

Surgeon William ("Tiger") Dunlop (1792-1848)

William Dunlop, a surgeon with the 89th Foot, spent most of his four years in the army trying to get out of his medical duties and into a combat role. He was delighted to be appointed medical officer of Pearson's light demi-brigade at Fort Erie as he would be sure to see more action with that formation than any other. A noted raconteur, Dunlop published a memoir of his wartime experiences which is notable both for its humility and humour, and which contains some anecdotes about his bad-tempered commanding officer. (Archives of Ontario, S-17142)

Pearson would probably have forgiven Dunlop by 13 August 1814, the day
the siege battery was ready and the heavy ordnance – three 24-pdr. guns, a
24-pdr. carronade and an 8-inch mortar – opened fire. It immediately became
obvious that the battery was situated too far from Fort Erie to have any real
effect on its earthen ramparts, and even those rounds that hit the two stone
buildings in the fort rebounded from them "as innocuous as tennis balls."[27]
This ineffectual bombardment continued throughout 13 and 14 August and
the gunners had little to show for their work until late in the afternoon of
the latter day a shell exploded a small expense magazine inside the fort. This
convinced Drummond that the bombardment had shaken the defenders' will
even if it had not shaken their walls. His chief engineer disagreed with him,
recording in his diary that the effect of the bombardment had been "very trifling."[28] Nonetheless, perhaps thinking of a similar assault he had successfully
carried out against Fort Niagara the previous December, Drummond decided
to attack that night.

His plan was a complicated business. First, a party of Norton's warriors
would mount a demonstration midway between the stone fort and the end
of the American earthwork to distract the defenders' attention. Next, a column composed of De Watteville's Regiment and the 8th Foot would assault the
Snake Hill battery, the cornerstone of the southern end of the defences. After
Snake Hill had fallen and the result was signalled by a rocket, two more columns would move in from the north. The first, under Lieutenant-Colonel William Drummond of the 104th Foot, would hit the stone fort while the second,
under Colonel Hercules Scott, would attack the defence line between the fort
and the shore of the lake. Drummond urged his subordinate commanders to
make "a free use of the bayonet" and to remove the flints from their men's muskets, but only Colonel Victor Fischer, commanding De Watteville's Regiment,
followed this suggestion.[29] Overall, it was a complex operation that required the
co-ordination of four separate forces with split-second timing.

Unfortunately it did not work – in fact it was disastrous. A heavy downpour of rain hampered and slowed movement and Norton's warriors were
unable to get to the right point in time to mount the demonstration before
the southern column assaulted Snake Hill. The men of that force cleared the
outerworks with the bayonet, but when they threw their scaling ladders against
the main rampart, they found the ladders were too short and, having no flints
to fire, milled around in confusion while the delighted Americans shot them
down "like so many sheep."[30] Although they did not see the signal rocket, the

northern columns went forward anyway but were repulsed and Hercules Scott was killed.

The survivors of these two columns mixed together in confusion in the ditch of the small stone fort until Lieutenant-Colonel William Drummond, using the cover provided by darkness, mist and smoke, got a scaling ladder against the northeast bastion of the fort and took it at the point of sword and bayonet. His men and those of Hercules Scott then poured into the bastion but found that it was easier to get into that place than out of it, as the only exit to the interior of the fort was a narrow passageway which was quickly blocked by a formed body of defenders. Drummond led numerous attempts to break out but all were rebuffed while at the same time the defenders fired down into the bastion from a stone building that overlooked it. Dawn was approaching and the attacker's situation was getting critical. The brave William Drummond was killed leading an attack and, worse still, an expense magazine located under the floor of the bastion exploded, sending timber, guns, gun carriages and men into the air, all of which came down on top of the men in the ditch, killing or injuring many. When the Americans turned a 6-pdr. gun on the ditch and swept it with canister, it was too much and the attackers fled to the safety of their own lines.

Norton, who witnessed the explosion and the retreat of the attackers, was "enraged by their misfortune."[31] Many of the weary survivors were in a state of shock from their ordeal. One young officer threw down his sword and burst into tears after he reached safety, but Pearson, whose demi-brigade had been held back as part of the covering force for the assault, immediately took him in hand, giving him duties to perform to keep his mind occupied and the man shortly recovered himself. The failed night assault on Fort Erie, according to Captain William Merritt of the provincial dragoons, was the most "unfortunate business that happened" during the war to the soldiers of the King, and the losses were appalling.[32] Out of an attacking force of about 2,500 men, Drummond lost 905 killed wounded or missing, a casualty rate of 36%, and most were from the northern columns, with the 103rd and 104th Foot losing two-thirds their number.

Lieutenant-General Gordon Drummond's second attempt at a *coup de main* having failed, he had no choice but to continue the siege.

Although many expected the Americans to mount a sortie after this disastrous failure, it was actually quiet for some days. On 20 August, however, the defenders made a determined attempt to cut off a British picket but were repulsed by Pearson's light troops and Norton's warriors. Lieutenant John Le Couteur of the 104th Foot recorded that

> We had a very sharp skirmish with them. Our men got ten of their rifles, of which I obtained one. No sooner had we driven them off, then the Fort opened and pelted us with shot and shell the whole afternoon. We kept quietly in the ditch, nevertheless got one man wounded.[33]

That there were perils in North American warfare not found in Europe is clear from Drummond's report on this action: "From the number of scalps that were taken by the Indians and the number of dead and wounded," which were seen being carried into the fort, "the enemy must have lost 40 to 50 men in this affair."[34]

The British commander now began the construction of new and better-sited batteries. His problems, however, kept increasing as the American squadron on Lake Ontario actively interdicted his supply lines, causing him to run low on ammunition and food – and what was worse, it rained almost incessantly. In vain he implored Commodore James Yeo "that nothing but the assistance of the whole of H.M. squadron on Lake Ontario" could enable his Right Division "to continue its operations against the enemy or even to retain its present position on this frontier."[35] But Yeo would not emerge from Kingston until he had completed his latest and largest warship and it was not yet ready. Three weeks after his failed assault, Drummond warned Prevost that although he would make every effort, his situation was such that he might have to withdraw north behind the Chippawa River. The two new batteries were ready to fire by 15 September but such was the state of the ammunition supply that they were restricted to one round an hour.

By now, Drummond was losing faith in his ability to take the fort and many of his senior subordinates, including Lieutenant-Colonel John Harvey, his chief of staff and another veteran of the Egyptian campaign, agreed with him. Major-General Louis De Watteville, Drummond's new second-in-command and a Swiss officer with two decades of active service in Europe, publicly voiced what most of the army already knew when he told the British commander on 16 September that the situation was hopeless and that he should abandon the siege. Disheartened, Drummond ordered the heavy guns to be removed from the batteries the following day in preparation for a retreat and the engineers and gunners were engaged on this task on 17 September when the Americans mounted a major sortie.

This attack was the brainchild of Major-General Jacob Brown, who had resumed command of the Left Division in early September. The American commander had no idea of Drummond's problems or that his opponent was preparing to withdraw; what he did know was that the American Right Division, under the command of Major-General George Izard, was moving slowly from Lake Champlain to his assistance. Fearing that Fort Erie would fall before this help arrived, Brown was very glad in early September when 1,500 New York volunteers crossed over from Buffalo and with this reinforcement, he began to plan a sortie. His object was "to storm the batteries, destroy the cannon, and roughly handle the [British] brigade on duty" before the remainder of the besiegers recovered.[36]

Early in the morning of 17 September 1814, mist and a drizzling rain covered the mile-long movement of a force under Brigadier-General Peter B. Porter which made a circuitous approach that brought them abreast of the right flank of the British lines. Another assault force, under the command of the newly-promoted Brigadier-General James Miller, moved directly into a ditch just outside the fort. At 2.30 P.M., under a downpour of rain, Porter's force attacked the right end of Drummond's line and when Miller heard the noise of the firing, he went straight for the centre. The regiments on duty, the 8th Foot and De Watteville's regiment, taken by surprise, suffered heavy casualties and retreated in confusion, leaving Battery No. 3 in Porter's hands and Battery No. 2 in those of Miller. Their soldiers immediately began to destroy the gun carriages and spike the weapons.

The Americans had just begun this work when the British and Canadians counterattacked under De Watteville's command. This attack was led by two companies of the 82nd Foot, a veteran unit from Wellington's army, followed by Pearson with Battersby's Glengarries and a party of Norton's warriors. De Watteville reported that "Pearson with the Glengarry Light Infantry under Lieut-Colonel Battersby, pushed forward by the centre road and carried with great gallantry the new entrenchment, then in full possession of the enemy."[37] The Americans in Battery No. 2, taken by surprise, surrendered, but just as the victors were about to disarm them, firing broke out again and a vicious close-quarter battle ensued in the battery position. Drummond himself "witnessed the good order and spirit with which the Glengarry Light Infantry" of Pearson's demi-brigade "pushed into the wood, and by their superior fire drove back the enemy's light troops."[38] It was during this action that Pearson, at the head of the Glengarries, was hit over his right eye by a rifle bullet. Bat-

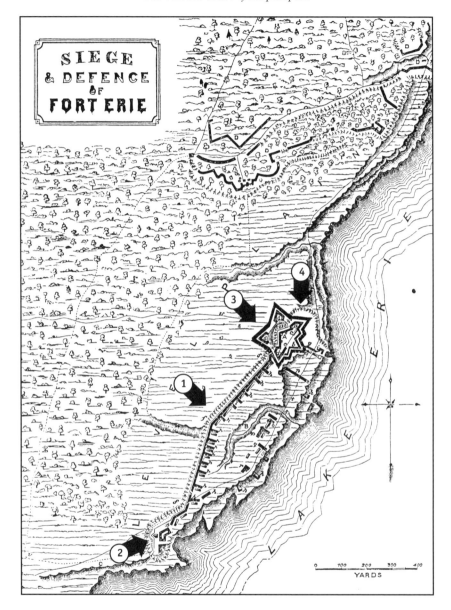

The assault on Fort Erie, 15 August 1814

1. Indian deception attack force
2. Snake Hill assault force (De Watteville's Regiment, 8th Foot and attachments) commanded by Lt. Col. Viktor Fisher, De Watteville's Regiment
3. Fort Erie assault force (104th Foot, light infantry attachments, Royal Marines and Royal Navy sailors) commanded by Lt. Col. William Drummond, 104th Foot
4. Northern assault force (103rd Foot) commanded by Col. Hercules Scott, 103rd Foot

tersby assumed command of the demi-brigade, and joined by the 6th Foot, another veteran Peninsula unit, and the remainder of the 82nd, engaged in a bloody and confusing battle with the attackers in the batteries and surrounding woods. Miller and Porter, who had joined forces, were able to make no progress toward Battery No. 1, and were forced to fall back to the fort, supported by the American reserve which came to their assistance.

The losses in this action, which lasted no more than three hours, were almost equal. Brown listed 511 men killed, wounded or taken prisoner while Drummond suffered 516 British, Canadian and aboriginal casualties. As Drummond was actively preparing to withdraw, it was an unnecessary action – although Brown could not know that – and when the British commander pulled back to a position around Chippawa on 21 September, it was with some credence that Brown believed his sortie had forced his opponent to lift the siege.

Pearson's wound, Drummond reported to Prevost, was severe but hopefully not dangerous. After the army withdrew north to the Chippawa, Pearson was given leave to go to New Brunswick where Ann and their son were residing at Alwington Manor, the home of her father, to recover. He travelled there by water as much as possible, and with the assistance of his staff adjutant, Lieutenant Alexander Greig of the 8th Foot, reached Saint John on 18 November 1814. The mayor and municipal council of the town, wishing to honour him, unanimously granted Pearson the freedom of the city for "his long and gallant services in the armies of his country, particularly of the skill and bravery he has so conspicuously displayed in the late campaigns in Upper Canada."[39] While Pearson made his way up the St. John River by boat to Alwington Manor, the mayor and council then returned to debating and ultimately passing a motion that resulted in a bylaw prohibiting the smoking of "seegars" on the streets of Saint John, at the pain of a 10 shilling fine.[40]

Under Ann's care, Pearson slowly but gradually recovered from his wound over the winter of 1814-1815. It was a long convalescence – he had no vision in his right eye for some time, permanently lost the hearing in his right ear and suffered "several exfoliations of the skull."[41] The cold of a Canadian winter would have irritated such a wound and Pearson was probably forced to remain indoors until the coming of spring, but he would have followed military events through the newspapers and learned that a British army under Major-General Robert Ross had captured Washington the previous August but had been rebuffed at Baltimore in September. While diplomatic negotiations to end the

The Emperor of the French, 1814-1815

After his invasion of Russia failed disastrously in 1812, Napoleon fought desperately to defend France from superior allied forces. In the spring of 1814 he was forced to abdicate and sent to exile in the little Mediterranean island of Elba. The Great War was not over, however, as in the spring of 1815 Napoleon landed in France and regained his throne for a period of 100 days, which ended with his final defeat at the battle of Waterloo in June 1815. Throwing himself on the mercy of Britain, he was imprisoned on the island of St. Helena, where he died in 1821. (From *Portraits des généraux français faisant suite aux victoires et conquêtes des Français,* 1818)

war were taking place in Europe, Sir George Prevost had then invaded the Lake Champlain area with a large army, an incursion that ended in an ignominious retreat after the British naval squadron on that body of water was captured in a disastrous engagement at Plattsburgh on 11 September.

Pearson would have taken keen interest in the final events of the Niagara campaign. Late in September, Major-General George Izard's American Right Division joined Brown's Left Division at Fort Erie and advanced on Drummond's position north of the Chippawa River in October. Izard, who assumed command of the American forces in the Niagara, demonstrated a marked reluctance to assault the strong British position and, after some skirmishing and demonstrations, withdrew his army from Canadian soil in early November, blowing up the blood-soaked ruins of Fort Erie as a final gesture.

But the fighting had not yet ended and Pearson would have read how a British army invaded Louisiana in December under the command of Major-General Sir Edward Pakenham, the former commander of the Fusilier Brigade in Spain. Unfortunately, that gallant soldier was killed in this last major battle of the War of 1812, an unmitigated defeat for the British army, fought at New Orleans on 8 January 1815. Peace between Britain and the United States was officially concluded at Ghent on Christmas Eve 1814 but it was not until February 1815 that news of the end of the war reached North America. As the causes of the conflict had been a direct outcome of Britain's war with France, which had commenced in early 1793, it was now felt with some assurance that the long decades of warfare had blessedly come to an end.

Victory for the British army, 1815

In this contemporary print, a victorious Britannia sits atop a monument inscribed with the victories of the army between 1793 and 1815 while a winged angel places the laurel of victory on her head. Captured French trophies are placed at the foot of the memorial along with the triumphant flags of Britannia and her regiments. After more than two decades of almost unceasing warfare, the British army recovered from its early weaknesses to become a very professional fighting service. (From Charles H. Smith, *Costume of the Army of the British Empire,* 1814)

Unfortunately, they had not. On 1 March 1815 Napoleon escaped from Elba with about a thousand soldiers and landed in France to popular acclamation – three weeks later he was in Paris and actively planning the restoration of his empire. The allied powers immediately declared the French leader beyond the law and mobilized their armies against him and the 1st Battalion of the 23rd Foot, under the command of Colonel Sir Henry Ellis, joined the Duke of Wellington's army in Belgium. The duke was glad to have the Royal Welch Fusiliers under his command, remarking soon after the unit joined his army at Brussels: "I saw the 23rd the other day and I never saw a regiment in such order … it was the most complete and handsome military body I ever looked at."[42]

On 18 June 1815 Wellington met Napoleon in battle for the first time near the Belgian village of Waterloo. Throughout that long and bloody day, the 23rd Foot served on the British right flank, somewhat outside the area of the heaviest action in an engagement that, in its intensity of fighting and heavy losses, reminded many veterans of Albuera. The casualties of the Welch Fusiliers at Waterloo, 15 officers and men killed and 86 wounded, were considerably less than many other regiments but among them was 32-year-old Colonel Henry Ellis, Pearson's commanding officer for many years, who was mortally wounded in this last great battle against the French.

Napoleon's gamble having failed, he took refuge on a British warship and was soon on his way to Saint Helena to spend the remainder of his life in exile. The Great War with France, which had raged almost ceaselessly since 1793, had finally ended.

Great with honours: Lieutenant-General Sir Thomas Pearson

In this portrait, which dates to the early 1840s, Thomas Pearson is seen in the uniform of a lieutenant-general and is wearing all his decorations. Suspended by a ribbon around his neck is the badge of a Knight-Commander of the Royal Guelphic and Hanoverian Order (KCH). Immediate to the right is the badge of a Companion of the Bath (CB), Military Division. Beside that is the Maltese Cross badge of a Knight-Commander of the Hanoverian Order while immediately beneath is the Field Officer's Gold Medal he received for Albuera in 1811 with a clasp indicating a second award earned for Crysler's Farm in 1813. The small medal to the right of the Gold Medal is the Khedive's Medal for the Egyptian Campaign of 1801. Thomas Pearson unfortunately died just before the issue of the Military General Service Medal, 1793-1814, which took place in 1847. He would have been eligible for this medal and four battle/campaign clasps (Egypt 1801; Martinique 1809; Albuera 1811; and Crysler's Farm 1813). Curiously enough, he was also present at an action for which a clasp was issued for the Naval General Service Medal and that was the attack on Oswego in May 1814. As portrayed by the artist, the wound Pearson received at Fort Erie is visible near his right eyebrow but his drooping left eyelid may also be the result of an injury, indicating that his fifth wound was fairly extensive in nature. (Courtesy, Royal Welch Fusiliers Museum)

408

EPILOGUE

"THE SODGER'S WEALTH
IS HONOUR."

THE LATER YEARS, 1815–1847

When wild war's deadly blast was blawn,
And gentle peace returning,
Wi' mony a sweet babe fatherless,
And mony a widow mourning,
I left the line and tented field,
Where lang I'd been a lodger,
My humble knapsack a' my wealth,
A poor and honest sodger.

For gold the merchant ploughs the main,
The farmer ploughs the manor;
But glory is the sodger's prize;
The sodger's wealth is honour;
The poor brave sodger ne'er despise,
Nor count him as a stranger;
Remember he's his country's stay
In day and hour o' danger.[1]

In the summer of 1815 Lieutenant-Colonel Thomas Pearson, still recovering from his wound, returned to Britain with Ann and their four-year-old son, Thomas Aylmer. The couple probably resided at Corton Denham in Somerset, living on Pearson's half pay of £155.2.0 a year. Pearson would have been pleased to learn that on 4 June 1815 he had been made a Companion of the Bath but what he really sought was a military appointment. There were not many to be found as within a year of Waterloo the army was reduced to 225,000 men, half its 1815 strength. First, the foreign regiments such as the King's German Legion and De Watteville's Regiment were disbanded, then the colonial units such as

409

the fencibles in Canada, then the second battalions of the line regiments raised during the war and, finally, ten infantry and seven cavalry regiments were cut from the order of battle. Four years after Waterloo, the army consisted of just 100,000 infantry and cavalry. As the artillery, engineers and navy were cut in proportion, Britain was flooded with ex-servicemen, including thousands of unemployed officers on half pay, looking for gainful employment.

Given this climate of severe cutbacks, Pearson was fortunate to be appointed commanding officer of the 2nd Battalion of the 43rd (Monmouthshire Light Infantry) Regiment in late 1815. The 43rd had been one of Sir John Moore's Shorncliffe units and the 1st Battalion of that regiment had been a mainstay of the famous Light Division during the Peninsular War although the junior battalion of the 43rd had only once served outside Britain when it participated in the Walcheren campaign of 1809. Pearson, however, only held this appointment for just over a year as the 2/43rd was disbanded in February 1817 and he was back on half pay. Fortune, however, greatly smiled on him when Lieutenant-Colonel Thomas Dalmer, commanding the 23rd Foot, agreed to an exchange and so Dalmer went on the half pay of the 43rd while Pearson attained what was probably his life's ambition – command of the Royal Welch Fusiliers.

He joined the regiment, which now consisted of a single battalion, at Valenciennes, France, in late August 1817. It was there serving in the occupation army as part of a brigade commanded by Major-General Sir James Kempt, which also included the 7th or Royal Fusiliers and the 43rd Light Infantry. Pearson quickly put his stamp on the 23rd and the general officer who carried out its first inspection after he took command not only praised the Welch Fusiliers as a "very excellent body of men with a very healthy and clean appearance," but added that it was "impossible for any officer to evince more ability, zeal, and attention than Lieut.-Colonel Pearson has employed in his command of the 23rd."[2] In November 1818, the occupation army was broken up and the Welch Fusiliers embarked for Ireland, where they served for five years before being transferred to Gibraltar in 1823. Here they remained for 11 years, except for a brief nostalgic deployment to Portugal in 1826-1828 as part of a 5,000-strong British force sent at that nation's request to provide some stability during a period of internal disturbances. It was at Gibraltar on 1 December 1826 that, following their consecration, Ann Pearson presented the Royal Welch Fusiliers with new Colours which bore many of the Battle Honours they had earned between 1793 and 1815. "MARTINIQUE," "WATERLOO," "BADAJOZ" and, of course,

Royal Welch Fusilier Colours

The Colours presented by Ann Pearson to the Royal Welch Fusiliers at Gibraltar in 1826 were emblazoned with the many Battle Honours they had gained during the Great War with France. These Colours are now in the Royal Welch Fusiliers Museum in Caernarfon Castle. The Colours illustrated here were those presented to the regiment in 1849.

The Welch Fusiliers were awarded 12 Battle Honours from 1793 to 1815: CORUNNA 1809, MARTINIQUE 1809, ALBUHERA 1811, BADAJOZ 1812, SALAMANCA 1812, VITTORIA 1813, PYRENEES 1813, NIVELLE 1813, ORTHES 1813, TOULOUSE 1814, PENINSULA 1808-1813, WATERLOO 1815 and also the "Sphinx" badge for the Egyptian Campaign. The incorrect spelling, "Albuhera" instead of "Albuera," apparently resulted from a mistake by a clerk at the War Office, but once it had entered the traditional lexicon of the army and was emblazoned on a Colour, "Albuhera" became sacred, even if incorrect, and remains so today. (From Richard Cannon, *Historical Record of the Twenty-Third Foot or The Royal Welsh Fusiliers*, 1850)

QUEEN'S COLOUR.

REGIMENTAL COLOUR.

XXIII
THE ROYAL WELSH FUSILIERS.

For Cannon's Military Records.

411

"ALBUHERA" were chosen, among others, as signal honours to be placed on the Regimental Colour.

It will come as no surprise that Pearson, who was promoted colonel in July 1819, was an outstanding regimental commander. In this respect, his qualities are demonstrated by the inspection reports during his time with the Welch Fusiliers, which were, without exception, highly commendatory:

[October 1818]
The regiment is in the most efficient state in every respect. ......

[May 1819]
Major-General O'Loghlin feels much gratification in expressing to Lieu-tenant-Colonel Pearson and the Officers of the Royal Welsh Fusiliers his unqualified approbation of the very soldierlike and steady appearance of that corps .... as may naturally have been expected from so distinguished a corps under an officer of Lieutenant-Colonel Pearson's capability and ex-perience. ......

[October 1819]
Major-General Gordon is very much pleased with the appearance of the 23rd Regiment on parade. It is a very steady corps and performs the ma-noeuvres according to His Majesty's Regulations with much precision and celerity. ......

[May 1822]
This corps is in a high state of discipline, perfectly equipped, and in every respect fit for service. ......

[June 1823]
Colonel Pearson is a most valuable Regimental Officer. A most exact and strictly enforced discipline is maintained in this excellent Corps, which in parade appearance, and field manoeuvre, is not perhaps to be surpassed by any Battalion in the British service. ...... I have seen no corps surpass and scarcely any equal the Fusiliers, in appearance, movement, and discipline. ......

[May 1827]
I can say nothing that can add to the well-earned renown of the Royal Welch Fusiliers. Their interior arrangements, appearance under arms, and steady discipline in the field are all of the most perfect description.[3]

These long years of garrison duty at home and abroad were marked by a change of monarchs. In 1820 King George III, mad and blind, died and was succeeded by the Prince Regent, who took the throne as George IV. Overweight, dissolute, debt-ridden and irresponsible, the new monarch was not popular with his subjects, who tended to agree with Charles Lamb's verses which had earlier harpooned him:

> Not a fatter fish than he
> Flounders round the polar sea.
> See his blubbers – at his gills
> What a world of drink he swills ......
> Name or title what has he? ......
> Is he Regent of the Sea?
> By his bulk and by his size,
> By his oily qualities,
> This (or else my eyesight fails),
> This should be the Prince of Whales.[4]

The 1821 coronation of George IV cost the taxpayer £243,000, of which £24,000 was spent on robes that included a velvet train 27 feet long.

Six years later, the Duke of York, the king's admired younger brother and the best of the nine sons of George III, died at the age of 63. Commander-in-Chief of the army for nearly 30 years, it was fitting that one of the last official acts of this outstanding administrator, known rightfully as "The Soldier's Friend," was to arrange for the relief of old and deserving lieutenants who were too poor to obtain promotion by purchase.

In 1830, George IV succumbed to excessive drinking and eating and was succeeded by William IV, who, as a young frigate captain, used to make lively runs ashore in Halifax. In July of that year, after 17 years in command of the Welch Fusiliers, Colonel Thomas Pearson was promoted by seniority to major-general and given the command of a district in Ireland. Now came the time Pearson must have dreaded as he had to part from a regiment in which he had served his entire military career – with the exception of the six years between 1811 and 1817. Pearson's farewell letter to the officers of the 23rd was somewhat emotional in tone and contained just a hint of an apology – just a hint, mind – to his subordinates for any harsh treatment he may have meted out:

The most painful moment of my life has at length arrived when I am obliged to take a final leave of the Royal Welch Fusiliers, in which distinguished corps I have served Twenty-seven years. To separate myself from a Regiment with which my best interests have been identified, and in which I have passed the best and happiest days of my life, is an event of so trying a nature, that I find myself utterly at a loss for expression to describe my feelings on the occasion. The only sad duty left me to perform is to pronounce a sorrowing farewell to all. ......

Human interest is ever liable to err and in no situation more so than in the exercise of command; be assured that in those instances when in the execution of public duty I may unintentionally have given pain, the fault has proceeded from the head, and not from the heart, and it is now only permitted me to hope that the sentiments of affectionate regard which I have ever entertained for every member of the Royal Welch, will enable me to cherish the idea that when remembered it will not be with other feelings than those with which I now in the full sincerity of an overflowing heart subscribe myself your ever attached and truly affectionate friend.

T. Pearson
Major-General; Late Lt.-Col. R.W.F.[5]

In responding, Major William Ross of the 23rd assured his former commanding officer that, speaking for all the members of the regiment, "nothing would afford us greater pleasure than to see you again in the full exercise of your profession with the Old Welch under your command."

Pearson's successor was Lieutenant-Colonel John Harrison, who had served in the 23rd since 1806 and whom we have met before as a young lieutenant at Albuera. Pearson had always encouraged the wearing of the "flash" or black ribbons that had adorned the collars of the Welch Fusiliers since 1809. Harrison followed suit, but soon after he assumed command, higher authority took exception to a practice that seems to have escaped official notice for nearly three decades. In 1834 an inspecting officer complained about this "superfluous decoration" on the officers' collars and urged its "immediate abolition."[6] Harrison appealed to the Colonel of the Regiment, Lieutenant-General Sir James Willoughby Gordon, for assistance and Gordon, a former secretary to the Duke of York and the Army Quartermaster-General, not only had connections but knew how to use them. The result was that William IV announced that he was "graciously pleased to approve of the 'Flashes' now worn by the officers of the Twenty-Third Foot, or Royal Welch Fusiliers being henceforth worn and established as a peculiarity whereby to mark the dress of that distinguished Regiment."[7]

One would think that this would have put an end to higher authority's discontent with the "flash" which, by the first decade of the 20th century, had been adopted by all ranks of the Welch Fusiliers. In fact, the matter was not finally laid to rest until 1915 when the War Office ordered the Welch Fusiliers to stop wearing it while serving in the trenches of the Western Front, as it might serve as an aiming point for German snipers. The regiment appealed to its Colonel-in-Chief, King George V, and he told the authorities to cease their carping because "the enemy would never see the Flashes on the backs of the Royal Welch" because they never retreated.[8] That more or less settled the business and five years later, after more than a century and a half of agitation, the regiment was permitted the right officially to use the older spelling "Welch" in their title although, unofficially, they had been doing so since the mid-18th century.

From 1830 to 1843, Pearson commanded various districts in Ireland, years marked by some discontent in that unfortunate land but no outbreaks of violence similar to the 1798 rebellion. During this time, additional honours came his way. In 1835 he was made both a Knight Bachelor and a Knight Grand Cross of the Royal Hanoverian Order, becoming Sir Thomas Pearson, while Ann became Lady Pearson. In 1841 he was promoted lieutenant-general by seniority and could now style himself Lieutenant-General Sir Thomas Pearson, CB, KCH. In 1843 he was named Colonel of the 85th (Bucks Volunteers) (The King's Light Infantry). At one time, such an officer was the proprietary colonel of a regiment who, while he did not command it in the field, was responsible for its pay, clothing, accounts, and choice of officers. By the mid-19th century the appointment was honorary, although remunerated, and was usually given as a reward to distinguished senior officers for their services, although they were still expected to look after their regiment's well-being and, above all, represent it with higher authority, be it the Horse Guards or the Sovereign. The 85th was a good solid unit, perhaps not quite up to the standards of Pearson's beloved "Old Welch," but still very respectable, and it is noteworthy that other than the 23rd, the two units that Pearson was connected with during his career, the 43rd and 85th, were both light infantry. Pearson was now at the pinnacle of his profession and the only higher honour to which he could aspire was to become Colonel of the Royal Welch Fusiliers. In this he was to be disappointed as Lieutenant- General Sir James Willoughby Gordon, appointed Colonel of the 23rd in 1823, proved to be remarkably long-lived and retained that appointment until his death in 1851.

In 1843 Lieutenant-General Sir Thomas Pearson, aged 62, retired from active service but not from the army as, being a general officer, he was still liable to be called out if required to assume a new appointment. He chose to spend his retirement in his native Somerset near the little village of Sandford Orcas, about three miles north of Sherborne and ten miles east of his childhood home at Queen Camel. He had inherited this property from his father, the Reverend Thomas Horner Pearson, who had died at Queen Camel in 1832, aged 81, having served that parish for 45 years. The reverend is commemorated by a stone tablet in St. Barnabas Church at Queen Camel which states that, "To great firmness of mind he added an ardent love of truth and a punctual discharge of his various duties," words that in many ways also apply to his eldest son.

Mention of the Reverend Pearson brings up the subject of Pearson's family and how they had fared over the years. Of his three younger brothers, Charles, Robert and George, only Charles was still living in 1843. Robert had died from illness in 1812 at the age of 22 while George, who had joined the Royal Navy and been wounded at Trafalgar, died at Plymouth as a 24-year-old lieutenant on his return from India in 1816. Charles, the second son of the Reverend Pearson, had entered the navy at the age of 13 as a volunteer in the ship of the line HMS *St. George,* commanded by Captain Thomas Hardy, and had fought as a midshipman in the West Indies in 1806 and Copenhagen in 1807. He was appointed a lieutenant in the bombship HMS *Thunder* and participated in a notable action against Danish gunboats in 1809 before serving in Java and the East Indies. He returned to European waters as a lieutenant in the ex-American frigate HMS *President* and retired on half pay in 1815 to reside at Thorne Manor in the Somerset village of Thorne Coffin, which he inherited from his father. Of Pearson's two sisters, Anne and Frances, Anne had not married by the time her father died when she inherited money and property, while Frances had married Vice-Admiral John Aylmer in 1809.

Thomas Aylmer Pearson, the only child of Thomas and Ann Pearson, born in 1811 while his father was campaigning under Beresford in Spain, followed in his father's footsteps. Thomas Aylmer was commissioned as an ensign in the 90th Perthshire Light Infantry and transferred to the 43rd Foot in 1828. He served briefly as an ADC to his father in Ireland before his regiment was transferred to Canada, where it became involved in operations to suppress putative uprisings by political dissidents in 1837-1838. Thomas Aylmer had reached the rank of captain by December 1841, when he resigned from the army shortly after marrying Frances Armstrong. He and his wife had only one child, a daughter.

"The sodger's wealth is honour."

Country life in Sandford Orcas apparently did not suit Lady Ann, who preferred to reside in Bath, 50 miles to the north, in a house at No. 2, Edgar Buildings, which the general rented for her. The social life in this popular spa, with
its assemblies, concerts, balls, lectures, theatre, tea and card parties and, of
course, the famous Grand Pump Room, or hot springs – not to forget the annual Cherry Fair – was more to her liking than the variety found in rural Somerset. There was also the attraction that her son, daughter-in-law and grand-
daughter resided in or around Bath and that her sister Amelia and husband
had a house near the town. While there appears to be no evidence that Lady
Ann travelled to Sandford Orcas, there is clear evidence that Pearson visited
Bath. Every spring, just as the social season began, the Bath newspapers would
duly note his arrival on the mail coach, and thus he appeared in the resort on
11 May 1844, 8 May 1845, 25 April 1846 and 15 May 1847.[9] The newspapers also
noted that Pearson usually chose to stay at the famous White Hart Hotel rather
than at No. 2, Edgar Buildings, which might indicate that he was not on the
best terms with Lady Ann, but on the other hand after more than three decades
with Pearson, perhaps she deserved a rest.

The Edgar Buildings, Bath, Somerset
Lady Ann Pearson resided at No. 2, marked by arrow, and Pearson died in that house in May
1847. (Photograph by Dianne Graves)

Assembly rooms, Bath
This was the centre of social activity in Bath and Pearson may have reluctantly spent several evenings in this building during his annual visits to the popular spa city. (Photograph by Dianne Graves)

Her husband, as we have seen, was never known for his patience toward fools. It is entirely possible that Pearson would have preferred to again ascend the hill at Albuera while under fire from Ruty's gunners than to suffer the posturing, pomposity and persiflage of Bath high society. But Pearson always did his duty and, if duty called for a yearly "march" to Bath, he would undertake it. A good idea of what he would have had to put up with during an evening at the Assembly Room in Bath has been described by a better writer than the present author:

> Lounging near the doors, and in remote corners were various knots of silly young men, displaying various varieties of puppyism and stupidity; amusing all people near them with their folly and conceit, and happily thinking themselves the object of general admiration – a wise and merciful dispensation which no good man will quarrel with.
>
> And lastly, seated on some of the back benches where they had already taken up their positions for the evening, were divers unmarried ladies past their grand climacteric, who, not dancing because there were no partners for them, and not playing cards lest they should be thought irretrievably

single, were in the favourable situation of being able to abuse everybody without reflecting on themselves. In short, they could abuse everybody, because everybody was there. It was a scene of gaiety, glitter, and show; of richly-dressed people, handsome mirrors, chalked floors, girandoles and wax candles …[10]

Evenings like this would have been excruciating to Pearson, but at least he got into town a few weeks too late in 1845 to attend the "Grand Fairey Ball" with 800 of the town's fashionable elite.[11] We do not know what Bath society thought of the limping older man who threaded his way carefully through the crowded Assembly Rooms with his cane (as Pearson would have been using one by now), but if they did not know him, the more observant would quickly have identified Pearson for what he was – a veteran of the Great War with France. His age, his trim figure, erect posture, the well-tailored frock coat, the limp, the cane, the sunburned face, the obvious damage over his eye inflicted by the rifle bullet at Fort Erie and the curt manner of speech stamped him immediately as a soldier.

There were thousands like him in Britain in the 1840s and the younger postwar generation, living in a time of prosperity with railways crossing the land and steamships the ocean, and the word "progress" on everyone's lips, had grown somewhat impatient of these ancients from the hard riding, fighting and drinking Georgian and Regency days. Things had changed and society now took its cue from its young queen, Victoria, who had ascended the throne in 1837 and, at least outwardly, was more moral, more mannerly and devoted to family life and hard work. In their turn, the veterans didn't think much of this well-behaved (but soft) younger generation, particularly those who wore uniform. Surgeon William Dunlop, who had served with Pearson in Upper Canada, probably summed up their attitude best when, at about the same time the general was suffering from Bath society, he commented that

The Army is a very different thing from what was in my day – sadly changed indeed! It will hardly be believed, but I have dined with officers, who, after drinking a few glasses of wine, called for their coffee. If Waterloo was to fight over again, no rational man can suppose that we would gain it after such symptoms of degeneracy. Such lady-like gentlemen would certainly take out vinaigrettes and scream at a charge of the Old Guard, and be horrified at the sign of a set of grim-looking Frenchmen, all grin and gash, whisker and moustache.[12]

If Lieutenant-General Sir Thomas Pearson, CB, KCH, was annoyed with the younger generation he sadly did not have to put up with them for long. In mid-May 1847 he made his last coach journey to Bath, where, on the 21st of that month, he died, aged 66, at No. 2, Edgar Buildings. He was commemorated in a not entirely accurate obituary published in the *United Service Journal*, which noted that

> Sir Thomas Pearson served on the expedition to Ostend, in 1798, under Sir Eyre Coote; at the Helder in 1799, including the actions of 27th August, 2nd and 6th October [1799]; with the expedition to Ferrol in 1800; the Egyptian campaign of 1801, including the storming of the heights of Aboukir (severely wounded in the thigh), and actions of 13th and 21st March. Siege and capture of Copenhagen, in 1807; expedition to Martinique, in 1809; succeeded to the command of the Light Battalion, and held it till the surrender of the Island, when he received the public thanks of the Commander of the Forces for his surprise of a French picquet under the walls of Fort Bourbon [Desaix], where he was wounded in the leg by a grape-shot. Peninsular campaigns during the latter part of 1810, and 1811, including the occupation of Torres Vedres [sic], first siege of Badajoz, battle of Albuhera – succeeded to the command of the Fusilier Brigade; action at Fuentes Guinaldo and siege of Olivenca, at which last he received a severe wound which shattered the thigh bone. Served afterwards throughout the American war, including the action at Chrystler's Farm [sic] (horse shot under him); attack and capture of Oswego, actions at Chippawa (as second in command) and Lundy's Lane (wounded in the arm), siege of Fort Erie, where he was dangerous wounded by a rifle-ball in the head in an attack made by the Americans on the British position.[13]

Unfortunately, despite a lengthy and distinguished career, it seems that Pearson had never been particularly competent with money matters and he died – as the song has it – a truly "poor but honest sodger" whose only "wealth was honour." Although he left all his property and possessions (including a rather good wine cellar) to Ann, by the time his debts and the expenses for his burial in the crypt of St. Swithin's Church in Bath were paid, there was little remaining. Two months after his death, when Lady Pearson petitioned the War Office for a pension, she stated she had only £30 a year to live on, not much more than a farm labourer, and it was fortunate that the Horse Guards granted her an annual stipend of £120.[14] Ann spent the remaining years of her life living with her sister Amelia and brother-in-law, Lieutenant-Colonel Tobias Kirkwood, in Bath and died at the age of 70 in December 1859. She was laid to rest alongside her husband in St. Swithin's, where their son, Thomas Aylmer Pearson, placed a wall tablet commemorating his parents that can be seen to this day.

This is the only visible memorial to a soldier who, in the Great War with the France, fought in 12 major battles or sieges on three continents as well as many minor actions, received five wounds, a battlefield promotion, two field officers' gold medals, a knighthood and other rewards, honours and distinctions.* During his career, Thomas Pearson was associated with some of the

most prominent British military leaders of his time and with the four officers primarily responsible for the British army's superb performance in the latter years of the conflict: Lieutenant-General Sir Ralph Abercromby, Lieutenant-General Sir John Moore, the Duke of Wellington and the Duke of York. The lessons Pearson learned in Egypt, Martinique and the Peninsula served him

St. Swithin's Church, Bath
Lieutenant-General Sir Thomas Pearson and Lady Ann Pearson were laid to rest in this church. They are commemorated in the memorial tablet below, erected by their son. (Photographs by Dianne Graves)

SACRED TO THE MEMORIES OF
LIEU: GEN! SIR THO: PEARSON, C.B.& K.C.H.
WHO DIED MAY 21ST 1847,
AGED 66 YEARS.
AND OF ANN ELIZA. HIS WIFE
WHO DEPARTED THIS LIFE NOV: 26TH 1859,
AGED 70 YEARS.
THEIR MORTAL BODIES REPOSE IN THE CRYPT OF THIS
CHURCH AWAITING THE DAY OF RESURRECTION.
"For as in Adam all die, even so in Christ shall
all be made alive."

well in North America, where he played an important role in events that shaped Canada's history. In that nation today, however, Thomas Pearson is all but forgotten although many of his contemporaries, including Colborne, Drummond, Kempt, Maitland, Picton and Wellington among others, are commemorated by place names.** One can conjecture that this lack of attention would not bother Pearson in the slightest as he would be certain to regard his greatest achievement as commanding and preserving the regiment he was so proud to serve for much of his life – the Royal Welch Fusiliers.

In the 159 years since his death, the Royal Welch Fusiliers have established a magnificent military record in the Crimean War, various 19th-century colonial campaigns including the relief of Peking, the South African war, the two world wars of the 20th century, Korea, Malaya, Northern Ireland, the Balkans and, most recently Iraq in 2004, earning more than 120 new Battle Honours. When the Victoria Cross, the highest award for valour in the British armed forces, was instituted in the 1850s, two Welch Fusiliers were among the first dozen recipients and ten other Fusiliers have since received the medal. The regiment retains the customs and traditions of Pearson's time: the leek is still eaten on St. David's Day, the "Flash" is still worn and the Regimental Goat, attended by the Goat Major, still precedes the regiment on ceremonial occasions.[15] More than three centuries after first being raised, the Royal Welch Fusiliers continue to serve Queen and Commonwealth.

For Lieutenant-General Sir Thomas Pearson, CB, KCH, this would be memorial enough.

THE END

---

* A summary of Lieutenant-General Sir Thomas Pearson's military career will be found in Appendix A.

** The only memorial in Canada mentioning Thomas Pearson that the author has seen is a brass plaque at Fort Wellington National Historic Site in Prescott, Ontario, that notes that he was the first commandant of the fort.

Pearson, despite his services during the War of 1812 and his Canadian connection by marriage, was not accorded the honour of an entry in the *Dictionary of Canadian Biography* although many of his contemporaries who did considerably less during that conflict have entries.

APPENDIX A

LIFE AND CAREER
OF LIEUTENANT-GENERAL
SIR THOMAS PEARSON,
CB, KCH, 1781–1847

1781

Born, Podimore Milton, Somerset, England.

1796

Commissioned **second lieutenant** by purchase, 23rd Foot, 2 October 1796.

1798

First Lieutenant by purchase, 23rd Foot, 25 April. Participates in **raid on Ostend** in May but sees no action.

1799

Participates in **Helder campaign**, August to October. Fights in **landing on 27 August, battle of Bergen**, 18 September, **battle of Egmont-op-Zee**, 2 October and **battle of Kastricum**, 6 October.

1800

Captain by purchase, 23rd Foot, 7 August. Sails with 23rd Foot as part of Ferrol expedition in August and then to Marmoris Bay in Turkey in December as part of Egyptian expedition.

1801

Serves in Egyptian campaign and participates in **landing at Aboukir Bay**, 7 March, where he receives **first wound** (by musket ball in thigh). Fights in **battle of Mandara**, 12 March and **battle of Al-**

exandria, 26 March. **Awarded Khedive's medal** for campaign.

Sails to Gibraltar with 23rd Foot, December.

1802

Granted six months leave in England.

1803

On recruiting service in England.

1804

Serves on recruiting service in England and is promoted **major** (non-purchase) in 2nd Battalion, 23rd Foot on 8 December.

1805

Commanding 2nd Battalion, 23rd Foot, in England for part of the year.

1806

Serving with 2nd Battalion, 23rd Foot, in England.

1807

Joins 1st Battalion, 23rd Foot, February 1807 and participates in **Copenhagen expedition**, August to October, where he commands light companies of brigade during advance on Copenhagen.

Commands 1/23rd Foot at Colchester in December.

1808

Commands 1/23rd Foot at Colchester in January and transfers with battalion to Halifax in April where he commands outposts until October. In November, sails with 1/23rd Foot to West Indies.

1809

Participates in **Martinique campaign**, January to March. In action at **Morne Bruneau** and **siege of Fort Desaix**, commands light battalion of Prevost's division, receives **second wound** (canister bullet in leg) before Fort Desaix in February.

Returns to Halifax with 1/23rd Foot in April and in September, assumes command of military forces in New Brunswick.

1810

July, **marries** Ann Eliza Coffin and returns to Halifax.

Transfers with 1/23rd Foot to Portugal in October and spends winter in cantonments of 4th Division.

1811

Participates in **battle of Redinha**, 12 March, where he commands light companies of Fusilier Brigade, and **siege of Olivenza** and **first siege of Badajoz** in May.

Participates in **battle of Albuera**, 16 May 1811 and assumes command of Fusilier Brigade, 4th Division, in action. Promoted **brevet lieutenant-colonel**, 4 June. Receives **Field Officer's Gold Medal** for this action.

Commands 1/23rd Foot, May to July, and then participates in the **action at El Bodon**, 25 September, and the **action at Aldea de Ponte**, 27 September, where

he receives **third wound** (canister ball in thigh) and is invalided to England in November.

1812

Appointed Inspecting Field Officer of Militia, British North America, 28 Februrary.

Arrives in Halifax in July. **Captured by American privateer *Buckskin*** on 19 July while on passage to Quebec but on 23 July is **recaptured by British frigate *Maidstone*.**

Appointed garrison commander, Montreal, 30 September, and then commander, Prescott and area, in October.

1813

Appointed commander, Kingston, February to April, before returning to command at Prescott in April.

Participates in **expedition on St. Lawrence in July** and attempts to block **passage of American army** past Prescott on 5 November.

Commands advance guard of British force which fights at the **battle of Crysler's Farm** on 11 November in which he has his horse shot from under him but for which he receives his second **Field Officer's Gold Medal**. Appointed commander at Cornwall in November and conducts **raids on northern New York** state in December.

1814

Conducts **raids on northern New York** state in January before being appointed commander at Prescott in February.

In May, transferred to staff of the Right Division, British Army in North America, and participates as volunteer in amphibious **attack on Oswego**, New York, on 5 May.

Appointed commander at Chippawa and serves as second-in-command at **battle of Chippawa, 5 July 1814**.

Appointed commander of Light Brigade, Right Division in July. Commands brigade at **battle of Lundy's Lane**, 25 July 1814, **receives fourth wound** (musket ball in arm).

Commands light demi-brigade at **siege of Fort Erie** in August and September and **receives fifth wound** (rifle bullet in forehead) while repulsing American sortie from Fort Erie on 17 September.

Permission given to travel to New Brunswick for recovery of health and granted Freedom of City of Saint John, New Brunswick, in November.

1815

Returns to England on half pay and is made a **Companion of the Order of the Bath** on 4 June and appointed **commanding officer of 2/43rd Foot** on 16 November.

1817

Half pay on reduction of 2/43rd in February, but appointed **commanding officer of the 23rd Foot** on 24 July.

1821

Promoted **colonel** 19 July.

1830

Promoted **major-general** in July, assumes command of district in Ireland.

1835

Made a **Knight Bachelor** and a **Knight Grand Cross of the Royal Hanoverian Order**.

1841

Promoted **lieutenant-general** by seniority, 23 November.

1843

Retires from active service to reside at Sandford Orcas, Somerset, England.

Appointed **Colonel of the 85th** (Bucks Volunteers) (King's Light Infantry) on 21 November.

1847

Dies at Bath, 21 May, and is buried in the crypt of St. Swithin's Church, Bath.

Sources

Primary
National Archives, Kew, Surrey: War Office 25, vol 747, Statement of Major Thomas Pearson; War Office 42, bundle 37, Form of an oath, Lady Anne Pearson, 1847; National Library and Archives of Canada, Ottawa: correspondence in Record Group 8 I, British military records in Canada.

Secondary
John Phillipart, ed., *The Royal Military Calendar, or Army Service and Commission Book* ... (5 vols, London, 1820), vol 4, 339-41; Stewart Sutherland, *His Majesty's Gentlemen: A Directory of British Regular Army Officers of the War of 1812* (Toronto, 2000), 295: *United Service Journal* (1847), pt 2, 479.

ORDER OF BATTLE, STRENGTH AND CASUALTIES, ALLIED ARMY, ALBUERA, 16 MAY 1811

PART I: ORDER OF BATTLE

BRITISH AND PORTUGUESE ARMIES

Staff

Commander-in-Chief, Allied Army: Marshal/*Marechal do Exército*[1] William Carr Beresford

Quartermaster-General: Colonel Benjamin D'Urban

Adjutant-General, Portuguese Forces: *Brigadeiro* Manuel de Brito Mozinho

Adjutant-General, British Forces: Lieutenant-Colonel John Rooke

Adjutant-General, British Forces: Lieutenant-Colonel Henry Wade

Deputy Quartermaster-General: Lieutenant-Colonel Henry Hardinge

Military Secretary to Beresford: Major Robert Arbuthnot

Cavalry

Cavalry Commander: Major-General William Lumley

Second in Command: Brigadier-General Robert B. Long

> **Heavy Brigade**
>
> Commander: Colonel George De Grey
>
> > 3rd (or the Prince of Wales's) Regiment of Dragoon Guards
> > Lieutenant-Colonel Granby T. Calcraft
> >
> > 4th (or the Queen's Own) Regiment of Dragoons
> > Major Burgh Leighton
>
> **Unbrigaded**
>
> > 13th Light Dragoons
> > Lieutenant-Colonel Michael Head
>
> **Otway's Portuguese Brigade**
>
> Commander: Colonel Loftus Otway
>
> > *Regimento de Cavalaria nº.1* (Alcântara)
> > *Tenente-Coronel* Manoel Paes do Amoral
> >
> > *Regimento de Cavalaria nº. 7* (Cais)
> > Lieutenant-Colonel Henry Watson
>
> **Madden's Portuguese Brigade**
>
> Commander: Brigadier-General George Madden

+ Indicates killed in action or died of wounds

* Indicates wounded in action

1 squadron, *Regimento de Cavalaria nº. 5* (Evora)
Captain Frederick Watson

1 squadron, *Regimento de Cavalaria nº. 8* (Elvas)
Captain Henry Wyndham*.

Infantry

2nd Division
Commander: Major-General William Stewart*
Divisional Light Companies: Three companies of the 5/60th Foot (Royal Americans)[2]

1st Brigade
Commander: Lieutenant-Colonel John Colborne

1st Battalion, 3rd (or East Kent) Regiment of Foot, or the Buffs
Lieutenant-Colonel William Stewart

2nd Battalion, 31st (or the Huntingdonshire) Regiment of Foot
Major Guy L'Estrange

2nd Battalion, 48th (or the Northamptonshire) Regiment of Foot
Major William Brooke*

2nd Battalion, 66th (or the Berkshire) Regiment of Foot
Captain Conway Benning+

2nd Brigade
Commander: Major-General Daniel Hoghton+

1st Battalion, 29th (or the Worcestershire) Regiment of Foot
Lieutenant-Colonel Daniel White+

1st Battalion, 48th (or the Northamptonshire) Regiment of Foot
Lieutenant-Colonel George Henry Duckworth+

1st Battalion, 57th (or the West Middlesex) Regiment of Foot
Lieutenant-Colonel William Inglis*

3rd Brigade
Commander: Lieutenant-Colonel Alexander Abercromby

2nd Battalion, 28th (or the North Gloucestershire) Regiment of Foot
Major Charles Paterson

2nd Battalion, 34th (or the Cumberland) Regiment of Foot
Lieutenant-Colonel William Fenwick

2nd Battalion, 39th (or the Dorsetshire) Regiment of Foot
Major Patrick Lindsay

4th Division
Commander: Major-General Galbraith Lowry Cole*

Divisional Light Companies: 1 company of the 5/60th and 1 company of Brunswick Oels[3]

Fusilier Brigade
Commander: Lieutenant-Colonel William Myers+

1st Battalion, 7th Regiment of Foot (or Royal Fuzileers)
Major John M. Nooth

2nd Battalion, 7th Regiment of Foot (or Royal Fuzileers)
Lieutenant-Colonel Edward Blakeney*

1st Battalion, 23rd Regiment of Foot (or Royal Welsh Fuzileers)
Lieutenant-Colonel Henry W. Ellis*

Kemmis's Brigade

Light companies of the 2/27th, 1/40th and 97th Foot attached to Fusilier Brigade

Harvey's Portuguese Brigade

Commander: Brigadier-General William M. Harvey

Regimento Infantaria nº. 11 (Regimento de Penamacor)
Lieutenant-Colonel Donald MacDonald

Regimento Infantaria nº. 23 (2nd Regimento de Almeida)
Lieutenant-Colonel William Stubbs

1st *Batalhão, Leal Legião Lusitana*
Major Edward Hawkshaw*

Hamilton's Division

Commander: Major-General John Hamilton

Fonseca's Brigade

Commander: *Brigadeiro* Agostinho Luiz da Fonseca

Regimiento Infantaria nº. 2 (Regimento de Lagos)
Coronel António Hypolito da Costa

Regimiento Infantaria nº. 14 (Regimento de Tavira)
Lieutenant-Colonel James Oliver

Campbell's Brigade

Commander: Brigadier-General Archibald Campbell

Regimiento Infantaria nº. 4 (Regimento de Freire-Lisbon)
Lieutenant-Colonel Allan Campbell

Regimiento Infantaria nº. 10 (Regimento de Lisboa)
Coronel Luiz Benedicto de Castro

Collins's Brigade[4]

Commander: Colonel Richard Collins

Regimiento Infantaria nº. 5 (1st Regimento de Elvas)
Tenente-Coronel Francisco da Silva Pereira

Batalhão de Caçadores nº. 5. (Campo-Major)
Lieutenant-Colonel Michael McCreagh

King's German Legion Brigade (42/1,056)

Commander: Major-General Charles von Alten

1st Light Battalion, King's German Legion
Lieutenant-Colonel Ernest Leonhart

2nd Light Battalion, King's German Legion
Lieutenant-Colonel Colin Halkett

Artillery

British and King's German Legion Artillery
Commander: Major Julius Georg Hartmann, KGL

Captain George Lefebvre's Troop, Royal Horse Artillery
4 x 6-pdr. guns

Captain James Hawker's* Brigade, Royal Artillery
4 x 9-pdr. guns

No. 2 Company, King's German Legion Artillery
Captain Andrew Cleeves
5 x 6-pdr. guns
1 x 5.5 inch howitzer

No. 4 Company, King's German Legion Artillery
Captain Frederick Sympher
5 x 6-pdr. guns
1 x 5.5 inch howitzer

Portuguese Artillery
Commander: Major Alexander Dickson, Royal Artillery

Companhia de artilharia, Capitão José Sebastião de Arriaga
5 x 6-pdr. guns
1 x 5.5 inch howitzer

Companhia de artilharia, Capitão Wilhelm Braun
4 x 9-pdr. guns

SPANISH ARMY

Staff
Commanding General, 4th *Ejercito* (Army): *Teniente-General* Joaquin Blake
Commanding General, 5th *Ejercito: Capitán-General* Francisco J. Castaños
Chief of Staff, 4th *Ejercito: Teniente-Coronel* Antonio Burriel
Chief of Staff, 5th *Ejercito: Mariscal de Campo* Martin de la Carrera

Cavalry

4th *Ejercito*
Commander: *Teniente-General* Alfredo Loy

Regimiento de Santiago
Húsares de Castilla
Escuadrón de Granaderos Montados
Escuadrónes de Instrucción

5th *Ejercito*
Commander: *Mayor-General* Conde Penne Villemur

Caballeria de Loyola-Este, 4 weak squadrons
Caballeria de Carvajal, 3 weak squadrons

Infantry

4th Ejercito

Vanguardia
Commander: *Mariscal de Campo* José Lardizábal

Regimiento de Murcia
Regimiento de Canarias
2nd *Battalón, Regimiento de León*
Regimiento de Campo Mayor

3rd *División*
Commander: *Teniente-General* Francisco Ballesteros

1st *Batallón, Regimiento de Cataluña*[5]
Regimiento de Barbastro
Regimiento de Pravia
Regimiento de Lena
Regimiento de Castropol
1st *Batallón, Regimiento de Cangas de Tineo*
Regimiento de Infiesto

4th *División*
Commander: *Mariscal de Campo* José de Zayas
Divisional Troops: Company of *Zapadores*

2nd *Batallón, Regimiento de Reales Guardias Españoles*
4th *Batallón, Regimiento de Reales Guardias Españoles*
Regimiento de Reales Guardias Walonas
Regimiento de Irlanda
Legión Extranjera
Regimiento de Patria
Regimiento de Toledo
Regimiento de Ciudad Rodrigo

5th *Ejercito*

1st *División*
Commander: *Brigadier-General* Carlos España

Regimiento del Rey
Regimiento de Zamora
Voluntarios de Navarra
Zapadores

Artillery[6]

4th *Ejercito*
One battery, 8 x 4-pdr. guns

5th *Ejercito*
One battery, 6 x 4-dpr or 6-pdr. guns

PART II: STRENGTHS AND LOSSES

	Strength (Officers/Men)	Losses (All Types)
BRITISH AND PORTUGUESE ARMIES		
Heavy Cavalry Brigade (De Gray)		
3rd Dragoon Guards	374	20
4th Dragoons	387	27
Total	761	47
13th Light Dragoons	403	1
Otway's Brigade		
Regimento nº. 1	317	-
Regimento nº. 7	324	2
Total	651	2
Madden's Portuguese Brigade		
Sqdn, *Regimento nº. 5*	104	-
Sqdn, *Regimento nº. 8*	104	-
Total	208	-
2nd Division Light Companies	146	21
1st Brigade		
1/3rd Foot	755	643
2/31st Foot	418	155
2/48th Foot	452	343
2/66th Foot	441	272
Total	2066	1413
2nd Brigade		
1/29th Foot	507	336
1/48th Foot	497	280
1/57th Foot	647	428
Total	1651	1044
3rd Brigade		
2/28th Foot	519	164
2/34th Foot	596	128
2/39th Foot	482	98
Total	1597	390
Fusilier Brigade		
1/7th Foot	714	357
2/7th Foot	568	349
1/23rd Foot	733	339
Total:	2015	1045
Kemmis's Brigade		
Coys, 27th, 40th and 97th Foot	165	20

Harvey's Portuguese Brigade		
Regimento Inf. nº. 11[7]	1154	13
Regimento Inf. nº. 23 1201	19	
Legião Lusitana	572	171
Total	2927	203
Fonseca's Brigade		
Regimento Inf. nº. 2 1225	8	
Regimento Inf. nº. 14 1204	2	
Total	2429	10
Campbell's Brigade		
Regimento Inf. nº. 4 1271	60	
Regimento Inf. nº. 10 1119	11	
Total	2390	71
Collins's Brigade		
Regimento Inf nº. 5	985	60
Batalho. Caçad. nº. 5.	400	31
Total	1385	91
King's German Legion Brigade		
1st Light Battalion	588	69
2nd Light Battalion	510	37
Total	1098	106
Artillery		
British (RHA and RA)	255	15
KGL	292	49
Portuguese Artillery	221	10
Total	768	74
Staff	Number unknown	12

SPANISH ARMY

Brigada del Loy		
Regimiento Santiago	338	7
Húsares de Castilla	412	3
Granaderos Montades	284	17
Escadrones de Instruccion	132	13
Total	1165	40
Brigada del Penne Villemur		
Caballeria de Loyola-Este		
Caballeria de Carvajal		
Total	721	28
Vanguardia		
Cazadores[8]		10
Regimiento de Murcia	706	91
Regimiento de Canarias	433	86
1st *Bn, Regimiento León*	586	58
Regimiento de Campo Mayor	673	44
Total	2398	279

3rd *División*

Zapadores[9]	40	11
1st *Bn, Regimiento Cataluña*	227	1
Regimiento de Barbastro	563	30
Regimiento de Pravia	573	57
Regimiento de Lena	527	42
Regimiento de Castropol	588	41
1st *Bn, Cangas de Tineo*	580	20
Regimiento de Infiesto	467	27
Total	3525	130

4th *División*

Zapadores	49	13
2nd *Bn, Guardias Esp.*	630	174
4th *Bn, Guardias Esp.*	647	169
Reales Guardias Walonas	623	8
Regimiento de Irlanda	748	272
Legión Extranjera	547	19
Regimiento de Patria	594	3
Regimiento de Toledo	577	21
Regimiento de Ciudad Rodrigo	445	13
Total	4852	291

1st *División*

Regimiento del Rey	594	8
Regimiento de Zamora	343	3
Voluntarios de Navarra	445	19
Zapadores	70	-
Total	1777	30

Artillery

4th *Ejercito*	103	
5th *Ejercito*	64	
Total	167	11

Engineers	6	-
Staff	Number unknown	11

RECAPITULATION

	Strength	Losses
British Army (including King's German Legion)		
Cavalry	1164	48
Infantry	8738	4018
Artillery	637	64
Staff	Number unknown	2
Total British troops and losses	10539	4132
Portuguese Army		
Cavalry	849	2
Infantry	9131	375
Artillery	221	10
Staff	Number unknown	2
Total Portuguese troops and losses	10201	389

Spanish Army

Cavalry	1886	68
Infantry	12,553	1276
Artillery	165	20
Engineers	6	–
Staff	Number unknown	11
Total	14,604	1374
Total of allied strength and losses	35,344	5895

Notes

1. All British officers in Portuguese service had Portuguese ranks and used their Portuguese rank titles in all official correspondence having to do with the Portuguese army. For purposes of clarity and concision, however, in both the main text and this appendix, Portuguese ranks will only be used for Portuguese officers while British officers in the Portuguese service will have the British version of their ranks.

2. National Archives of Britain, WO 17, vol 180, Monthly Return of the 5th Battalion, 60th Foot for May 1811 shows that three comapnies of this unit commanded by Captains Peter Blassiere, John McMahon and Lieutenant John Franchini were attached to the 2nd Division, probably one to each of the three brigades.

3. NAB, WO 17, vol 803, Monthly Return of the Brunswick Oels for May 1811 shows that Captain Friedrich Wachholtz's company was attached to the Fusilier Brigade but it is unclear from this document whether the company was at the battle. As the return give few casualties for the month of May 1811 and no indication only when they occurred, it is probable that this company did no participate in the battle.

    NAB, WO 17, Monthly Return of the 5th Battalion/60th Foot for May 1811 shows that Captain Jame Prevost's company was attached to Kemmis's Brigade of the 4th Division but it is not clear whether this company was present during the battle.

4. An independent brigade that usually marched with Hamilton's division.

5. This unit was part of España's division of the 5th *Ejercito* but during the battle was attached to this formation.

6. In T.H. McGuffie, ed., *Peninsula Cavalry General* (London, 1951), 89, Long to brother, 12 April 1811, Long mentions that his cavalry was augmented by two Spanish guns drawn by mules but it is unclear whether this detachment was present at the battle.

7. Note that each of the Portuguese infantry regiments had two battalion, which accounts for their higher strength.

8. In the Spanish strength return on p. 521 of Arteche y Moro, *Guerra de la Independencia*, the numbers of the *cazadores* or light companies in Lardazibal's division are included in those for their parent regiments. In the casualty return on p. 524 the casualty figures for the *cazadores* are listed separately.

9. Sappers which were in the Spanish army, a form of elite infantry.

Sources

British Army Sources

The main source for the strengths of British units and their organization are: Appendix XV of Charles Oman, *A History of the Peninsula War*, vol 4, 631-632; and Benjamin D'Urban, "Report on the Operation of the Right Wing of the Allied Army … During the Campaign of 1811" contained in *Further Strictures on those Parts of Col. Napier's History of the Peninsular War which relate to the Military Opinions and Conduct of General Lord Viscount Beresford* (London, 1832).

Information on British officer casualties is from Beresford's dispatch to Wellesley dated 18 May 1811, contained in John Gurwood, ed., *The Dispatches of Field Marshal the Duke of Wellington, 1799-1818* (London, 1834-1839) vol 7, 588; and John A. Hall, ed., *The Biographical Dictionary of British Officers Killed and Wounded, 1808-1814* (London, 1998).

British regimental titles and the spelling of British officers' names are from the 1811 *Army List*.

Information was also extracted from the following personal accounts and memoirs: William

Brooke, "A Prisoner of Albuera. The Journal of Major William Brooke from May 16th to September 28th, 1811," *Blackwood's Magazine* (October 1908); C.D. Hall, ed., "Albuera and Vittoria: Letters from Lt. Col. J. Hill," *JSAHR*, vol 66 (1988); William Inglis, letter in *USJ*, June 1832; Charles Leslie, *Military Journal of Colonel Leslie, D.H., of Balquhain: Whilst Serving with the 29th Regt. in the Peninsula, and the 60th Rifles in Canada* (Aberdeen, 1887); Charles Madden, "The Diary of Charles Dudley Madden, Lieutenant, 4th Dragoons, Peninsular War, 1809-1811," *Journal of the Royal United Services Institute*, vol 58 (1914); T.H. McGuffie, ed., *Peninsular Cavalry General, 1811-1813: The Correspondence of Lieutenant-General Robert Ballard Long* (London, 1951); Moyle Sherer, *Recollections of the Peninsula* (Spellmount, 1996); and Charles B. Vere, *Marches, Movements, and Operations of the 4th Division of the Allied Army in Spain and Portugal in the Years 1810, 1811 & 1812* (1812, reprinted London, 2003).

Finally, the following regimental histories provided information on strengths and casualties: N. Ludlow Beamish, *History of the King's German Legion* (1831-1832, reprinted London, 1997); Rowland Broughton-Mainwaring, *Historical Record of the Royal Welch Fusiliers, late the Twenty-Third Foot* (London, 1889); Richard Cannon, *Historical Records of the Seventh Regiment or The Royal Fusiliers* (London, 1847) and *Historical Record of the Twenty-Third Foot or The Royal Welsh Fusiliers* (London, 1851); A.D.L. Cary and Stouppe McCance. *Regimental Records of the Royal Welch Fusiliers (Late the 23rd Foot)* (London, 2 vols, 1921); H. Everard, *History of Thos. Farrington's Regiment ... The 29th (Worcestershire) Foot* (Worcester, 1891); Franz von Gottberg, *Geschichte des Hannoverischen Jäger-Bataillons Nr. 10. Vol. 1 (1803 bis 1866)* (Berlin, 1913); J.P. Groves, *The 66th Berkshire Regiment* (Reading, 1887); Russell Gurney, *History of the Northamptonshire Regiment. 1742-1914* (Aldershot, 1935); Charles Kingsford, *The Story of The Duke of Cambridge's Own (Middlesex) Regiment* (London, 1916); C.R.B. Knight, *Historical Records of the Buffs ... Volume I: 1704-1814* (London, 1935); Hugh Pearse, *History of the 31st Foot and 70th Foot subsequently ... The East Surrey Regiment. Volume I: 1702-1914* (London, 2 vols, 1916).

Portuguese Army Sources

The strengths and organization of Portuguese units are from Oman, vol 4, and D'Urban as noted above. Titles, ranks and the spelling of Portuguese officers' names are from João Centeno's two-volume work on the Portuguese army which will shortly see publication. Additional information came from Andrew Halliday, *The Present State of Portugal and of the Portuguese Army* (Edinburgh, 1812). Ranks and spelling of British officers serving with the Portuguese army are from the 1811 *Army List*.

Spanish Army Sources

The strengths and organization of Spanish army units are from the tables contained in José Arteche y Moro, *Guerra de la Independencia: Historia Militar de España de 1808 a 1814* (Madrid, 1896). As Oman notes in his Appendix, however, there are some problems with Arteche's casualty figures and the present author found other mistake in addition which have been corrected above. Information on officer casualties was found in Antonio Burriel, ed., *Battle of Albuera* (Cadiz, 1811) and Andreas von Schepeler's edited Charles Oman as "Albuera Once More," *Army Quarterly*, vol 24, April, 1932.

ORDER OF BATTLE, STRENGTH AND CASUALTIES, FRENCH ARMY, ALBUERA, 16 MAY 1811

PART I: ORDER OF BATTLE

GdD = *Général de division*

GdB = *Général de brigade*

Staff

Commander-in-Chief: *Maréchal* Jean-de-Dieu Soult

Chief of Staff: *GdD* Honoré Gazan de la Peyrière*

Deputy Chief of Staff: *GdB* Jean-Dominique Bourgeat

Cavalry

Commander: *GdD* Marie-Victor-Nicolas La Tour-Maubourg

Brigade Briche

GdB André Briche

2nd *Régiment de Hussards*
Colonel Gilbert-Julian Vinot

10th *Régiment de Hussards*
Colonel François-Marie De Laval

21st *Régiment de Chasseurs à Cheval*
Colonel Charles-François-Antoine Steenhardt

Brigade Bron

GdB André-François Bron de Bailly

4th *Régiment de Dragons*
Colonel Pierre-Joseph Farine

20th *Régiment de Dragons*
Major *Dejean*

26th *Régiment de Dragons*
Colonel Gabriel Montlegier

Brigade Bouvier

GdB Joseph Bouvier des Eclaz

14th *Régiment de Dragons*
Major Hambersand

+ Indicates killed in action or died of wounds

* Indicates wounded in action

Strength figures include both officers and enlisted men

17th *Régiment de Dragons*
Colonel Albert-François Larcher

27th *Régiment de Dragons*
Colonel François-Antoine Lallemand

Unbrigaded

1st *Régiment des Lanciers de Vistule*
Colonel Jan Konopka

27th *Régiment de Chasseurs à Cheval*
Colonel Prosper-Louis d'Arenberg [Arembourg]

4th *Régiment de Chasseurs à Cheval de l'Espagne*
Colonel Foivin

Infantry

5th Corps
Commander: *GdD* Jean-Baptiste Girard

1st Division
Commander: *GdD* Jean-Baptiste Girard but division probably commanded during the battle by *GdB* Michel-Sylvestre Brayer*

1st Brigade
Commander: *GdB* Michel-Sylvestre Brayer but brigade probably commanded during the battle by *Colonel* Charles-François Remond

34th *Régiment d'Infanterie de Ligne* (2 battalions)
Colonel Charles-François Remond

40th *Régiment d'Infanterie de Ligne* (2 battalions)
Colonel Theodore Millet

2nd Brigade
Commander: *GdB* Michel Vielande

64th *Régiment d'Infanterie de Ligne* (3 battalions)
Commmand vacant but possibly led by *Lieutenant-Colonel* Pierre Aulard

88th *Régiment d'Infanterie de Ligne* (3 battalions)
Colonel François-Josephe-Alexandre Letourneur

2nd Division
Commander: *GdD* Honoré Gazan but probably commanded during the battle by *GdB* Jean-Pierre Maransin.*

1st Brigade
Commander: *GdB* Joseph Pépin+

21st *Régiment d'Infanterie Légère* (2 battalions)
Colonel Henri-Jacques-Martin Lagarde

100th *Régiment d'Infanterie de Ligne* (2 battalions)
Colonel Joachim-Jerome Quiot*

2nd Brigade
Commander: *Géneral de Brigade* Jean-Pierre Maransin but probably commanded during the battle by *Colonel* Jean-André Praefke+

28th *Régiment d'Infanterie Légère* (3 battalions)
Colonel Jean-André Praefke+ (probably leading brigade)

103rd *Régiment d'Infanterie de Ligne* (3 battalions)
Colonel Jean-Gerard Bonnaire

1st and 4th Corps

Brigade Werlé

Commander: *GdB* François-Jean Werlé+

12th *Régiment d'Infanterie Légère* (3 battalions)
Colonel Louis-Etienne Dulong de Rosnay

55th *Régiment d'Infanterie de Ligne* (3 battalions)
Colonel Henri-Cesar-Auguste Schwiter*

58th *Régiment d'Infanterie de Ligne* (3 battalions)
Colonel Jean-Baptiste-Henri-Legrand*

Brigade Godinot

Commander: *GdB* Deo-Gratias-Nicolas Godinot

16th *Régiment d'Infanterie Légère* (3 battalions)
Colonel Annet Morio de l'Isle

51st *Régiment d'Infanterie de Ligne* (3 battalions)
Colonel Louis-Paul Baille

Reserve

Grenadiers Réunis (11 companies)
Commander: *Colonel* Pierre-Louis Vare

Commanding companies from the 45th, 63rd and 95th *Régiments de Ligne* and 4th *Régiment d'Infantrie de la Legion de la Vistule* (Polish)

Artillery

Commander: *GdB* Charles-Etienne-François de Ruty

1st and 4th Corps Artillery

Commander: *Colonel* François-Louis Bouchu

5th Corps Artillery

Commander: *Colonel* François Berge

Number and Calibre of Weapons

2 x 12-pdr. guns
9 x 8-pdr. guns
5 x 4-pdr. guns
7 x 6-inch howitzers
6 x 4-inch howitzers

PART II: STRENGTHS AND LOSSES

	Strength	Losses
CAVALRY		
Brigade Briche		
2nd *Régiment de Hussards*	305	73
10th *Régiment de Hussards*	262	32
21st *Régiment de Chasseurs*	256	25
Total	823	130

Brigade Bron		
4th *Régiment de Dragons*	406	70
20th *Régiment de Dragons*	266	25
26th *Régiment de Dragons*	421	21
Total	1093	116
Brigade Bouvier		
14th *Régiment de Dragons*	316	24
17th *Régiment de Dragons*	314	45
27th *Régiment de Dragons*	249	19
Total	879	88
Unbrigaded		
1st *Régiment Lanciers de la Vistule*	591	130
27th *Régiment de Chasseurs*	431	26
4th *Régiment de Chasseurs*	195	6
Total	1217	162

INFANTRY OF 5TH CORPS

1st Division

1st Brigade		
34th *Régt. de Ligne*	953	419
40th *Régt. de Ligne*	813	348
Total	1766	767
2nd Brigade		
64th *Régt. de Ligne*	1589	651
88th *Régt. de Ligne*	899	405
Total	2488	1056

2nd Division

1st Brigade		
21st *Régt. Légère*	788	255
100th *Régt. de Ligne*	738	267
Total	1526	522
2nd Brigade		
28th *Régt. Légère*	1367	496
103rd *Régt. de Ligne*	1290	287
Total	2657	783

INFANTRY OF 1ST AND 4TH CORPS

Brigade Werlé		
12th *Régt. Légère*	2164	769
55th *Régt. de Ligne*	1815	351
58th *Régt. de Ligne*	1642	328
Total	5621	1448
Brigade Godinot		
16th *Régt. Légère*	1673	381
51st Régt. de Ligne[1]	2251	3
Total	3924	384

Reserve

Grenadiers Réunis	1033	372

ARTILLERY

1st and 4th Corps Artillery[2]	625	-
5th Corps Artillery	608	95
Total	1233	95

Miscellaneous (staff, engineers, etc)Number unknown		13

RECAPITULATION

Arm	Strength	Losses
Cavalry	4,012	496
Infantry	19,015	5332
Artillery	1,233 with 16 guns and 13 howitzers	95
Miscellaneous and staff	Number unknown	13
Total	24,260	5,936[3]

Notes

1. The strongest regiment in Soult's army, the 51st *Ligne,* reported three casualties during the battle, which makes it quite probable it did not see action in the battle. I am indebted to Guy Dempsey for this observation.
2. According to Oman, no casualty returns appear to have been submitted for these units.
3. The historian Charles Oman, after reviewing these figures, based on French returns, concluded that they were far too low and, after making an analysis of officer casualties, came to the conclusion that Soult's loss was actually about 7,900. It is worthwhile noting that Edouard Lapène, a fairly careful commentator who fought at Albuera, calculated in his *Conquête d'Andalousie* that the French losses was about 7,000.

Sources

The main source for units, strength and organization of the French army is Charles Oman, *History of the Peninsula War*, vol 4, Appendix XVI which is based on French archival sources. Also useful were; John Gurwood, ed. *The Dispatches of Field Marshal the Duke of Wellington, 1799-1818* (London, 1834-1839), vol 5, 770, Soult to Berthier, 21 May 1811; British Library, Additional Mss 37425, f65, La Tour-Maubourg to Soult, 27 May 1811; and Edouard Lapène, *Conquête de l'Andalousie, Campagne de 1810 et 1811 dans le Midi de L'Espagne* (Paris, 1823). Finally, some information was found in Robert de Saint-Chamans, *Mémoires du Général Comte de Saint-Chamans* (Paris, 1896) and *Victoires et Conquêtes … des Français, de 1792 à 1815. Tome Vingtième* (Paris, 1820).

Information on the names of officers comes from Soult's dispatch and La Tour-Maubourg's dispatch noted above; Alfred Fierro, André Palluel-Guillard and Jean Tulard. *Histoire et Dictionnaire du Consulat et de L'Empire* (Paris, 1995); Georges Six, *Les généraux de la Revolution et de l'Empire* (Paris, 1948) and the fine series of articles on French units by Tony Broughton on the "Napoleon Series" website.

The number and calibers of French artillery at Albuera deserve special mention. Many commentators, including Soult himself, have stated that there were between 40 and 48 pieces of artillery in the French army. The most reliable source, and that which provided the information above, are two strength returns for the Army of the Midi dated 16 April and 1 June 1811, in the *Service Historique de l'Armée de Terre*, carton C[8], 356. It is worth noting that Lapene, a fairly careful and reliable commentator – and an artillery officer in Soult's army who almost certainly fought at Albuera – states in his *Conquête de l'Andalousie* that the army had about 30 pieces of artillery at Albuera manned primarily by units of horse artillery.

APPENDIX D

"WITH WHAT A STRENGTH AND MAJESTY THE BRITISH SOLDIER FIGHTS."

WILLIAM NAPIER'S DESCRIPTION OF THE ATTACK OF THE FUSILIER BRIGADE AT ALBUERA

William Napier (1785-1860) was commissioned in the British army in 1800 and served in the Peninsula with the 43rd Foot, rising to the rank of lieutenant-colonel by 1815. He retired from the army in 1819 and began writing a history of the Peninsular War, with the first volume appearing in 1829 and the sixth and final volume appearing in 1840. A gifted writer, Napier's description of the attack of the Fusilier Brigade at Albuera has become one of the most famous prose passages in the English language relating to a battle. Unfortunately, it is not accurate as Napier, largely working from published records, never visited the battlefield at Albuera and thus his mention of heights and cliffs which did not exist. He also has the two brigades of the 4th Division making separate attacks when, in reality, all components of the division moved foward together. His description, however, is a fine example of writing and is reproduced below for the interested reader.

The fourth division was composed of two brigades, the one of Portuguese under General Harvey, the other, commanded by Sir William Myers, consisted of the seventh and twenty-third regiments and was called the fusileer brigade. Harvey's Portuguese being immediately pushed in between Lumley's dragoons and the hill, were charged by some French cavalry, whom they beat off, and meanwhile General Cole led the fusileers up the contested height. At this time six guns were in the enemy's possession, the whole of Werlé's reserves were coming forward to reinforce the front column of the French, the remnant of Houghton's brigade could no longer maintain its ground, the field was heaped with carcasses, the lancers were riding furiously about the captured artillery on the upper parts of the hill, and behind all, Hamilton's Portuguese and Alten's Germans, withdrawing from the bridge, seemed to be in full retreat. Cole's fusileers, flanked by a battalion of the Lusitania legion under Colonel Hawkshawe, soon mounted the hill, drove off the lancers, recovered five of the captured guns and one color, and appeared on the right of Houghton's brigade precisely as Abercrombie passed it on the left.

Such a gallant line, issuing from the midst of the smoke, and rapidly separating itself from the confused and broken multitude, startled the enemy's heavy masses, which were increasing and pressing onwards as to an assured victory: they wavered, hesitated, and then vomiting forth a storm of fire, hastily endeavored to enlarge their front, while a fearful discharge of grape from all their artillery whistled through the British ranks. Myers was killed, Cole, the three Colonels, Ellis, Blakeney, and Hawkshawe, fell wounded, and the fusileer battalions, struck by the iron tempest, reeled and staggered like sinking ships. But suddenly and sternly recovering, they closed on their terrible enemies, and then was seen with what a strength and majesty the British soldier fights. In vain did Soult, by voice and gesture, animate his Frenchmen; in vain did the hardiest veterans, extricating themselves from the crowded columns, sacrifice their lives to gain time for the mass to open out on such a fair field; in vain did the mass itself bear up, and fiercely striving, fire indiscriminately upon friends and foes, while the horsemen hovering on the flank threatened to charge the advancing line. Nothing could stop that astonishing infantry. No sudden burst of undisciplined valor, no nervous enthusiasm weakened the stability of their order; their flashing eyes were bent on the dark columns in their front, their measured tread shook the ground, their dreadful volleys swept away the head of every formation, their deafening shout overpowered the dissonant cries that broke from all parts of the tumultuous crowd, as slowly and with a horrid carnage it was pushed by incessant vigor of the attack to the farthest edge of the height. There, the French reserve, mixing with the struggling multitude, endeavored to sustain the fight, but the effort only increased the irremediable confusion, the mighty mass gave way and like a loosened cliff went headlong down the steep. The rain flowed after in streams discolored with blood, and fifteen hundred unwounded men, the remnant of six thousand unconquerable British soldiers, stood triumphant on that fatal hill!

Source
William Napier, *History of the War in the Peninsula and in the South of France from the Year 1807 to the Year 1814*, Thomas and William Boone, 1833, vol 3, 545-547.

THE "SECOND BATTLE OF ALBUERA," 1831–1841

The "Second Battle of Albuera" was a series of controversies concerning the engagement that were waged in print for nearly a decade between William Beresford, his detractors and his proponents. It began in 1831 with the publication of the third volume of William Napier's *History of the War in the Peninsula,* which included an account of the battle. Napier, a former officer in the 43rd Foot who had a distinguished war record, was a gifted writer and in his third volume took Beresford to task for his leadership at Albuera, stating rather harshly that: "No general ever gained a great battle with so little increase of military reputation as Marshal Beresford".[1]

Beresford and Napier had already exchanged shots over the second volume of Napier's *History,* published in 1829, which had also contained criticisms of the marshal. In 1831, friends of Beresford had published *Strictures on Certain Passages of Lieutenant Colonel Napier's History of the Peninsular War which related to the Military Opinions and Conduct of General Lord Viscount Beresford.* Although this publication had no author, it was certainly the work of a person or persons close to Beresford and there is some suspicion that it was written by the marshal in conjunction with his former quartermaster-general, Benjamin D'Urban. Napier had responded with *A Reply to Various Opponents: Particularly to "Strictures on Colonel Napier's History of the War in the Peninsula,"* which was contained in the 2nd edition of his first volume published in 1832 and later reprinted as a pamphlet. The attack on Beresford contained in his third volume, however, really set things in motion, particularly as it concerned the Albuera campaign.

The response of Beresford's proponents (again, possibly the marshal and D'Urban) to this attack took the form of the 1832 publication, *Further Strictures on those Parts of Col. Napier's History of the Peninsular War which relate to the Military Opinions and Conduct of General Lord Viscount Beresford to which is added a Report on the Operations in the Alemtjo and Spanish Extramdura during the year of 1811 by M. General Sir Benjamin D'Urban.* The authors of *Further Strictures* attempted rather clumsily to refute, point by point, Napier's criticism of Beresford's conduct of the battle. In doing so they pointed out that, given his description of the ground, it was obvious that Napier had never visited Albuera. *Further Strictures* is a useful item for historians because it not only has a complete review of the battle in which the authors attempt to set out Beresford's case more clearly, but also D'Urban's

"Report on the Operation of the Right Wing of the Allied Army … During the Campaign of 1811." Somewhat strangely, the anonymous authors (one of them possibly Beresford) corrects and criticizes some of the statements made in D'Urban's "Report." In 1833 Napier responded with *Colonel Napier's Justification Of His Third Volume; Forming A Sequel To His Reply To Various Opponents* in which, without admitting his mistakes or even moderating his views of Beresford's generalship, he made some new criticisms of the marshal.

Unfortunately for Beresford, *Further Strictures* brought a new opponent into the lists. The publication had contained some criticism of Brigadier-General Robert Long, Beresford's cavalry commander in 1811, whom he had replaced at the beginning of the battle. Long had died by this time but his nephew, Charles Edward Long, took up his uncle's case and produced *A Reply to the Misrepresentations and Aspersions on the Military Reputation of the late Lieutenant-General R.B. Long Contained in a Work Entitled "Further Strictures on those parts of Col. Napier's History of the Peninsular War which relate to the Military Opinions and Conduct of General Lord Viscount Beresford,"* which was published in 1832. This is also a useful item for historians because it contains Long's journal of the 1811 campaign and some of his private correspondence written during it.

Although Beresford might have been better advised not to get into more print battles, in 1833 he replied, under his own name, with *A Letter to Charles Edward Long Esq. on the Extracts Recently Published from the Manuscript Journal and Private Correspondence of the late Lieut.-General R.B. Long.* Back came Long that same year with *A Letter to General Viscount Beresford in Reply to his Lordship's Letter to the Author relative to the Conduct of the Late Lieut.-General R.B. Long in the Campaign of 1811.*

Beresford was now fighting on two fronts but, undaunted, in 1834 he counterattacked with *A Refutation of Colonel Napier's Justification of His Third Volume* and *A Second Letter to Charles Edward Long Esq. on the Manuscript Journal and Private Correspondence of the late Lieut.-General R.B. Long.* For his part, Long waited until 1835 when he came out with *A Reply to Lord Beresford's Second Letter to the Author Relative to the Conduct of the late Lieut.-General R.B. Long then Commanding the Allied Cavalry.* Napier's response was longer in coming and took the form of *A Letter to General Lord Viscount Beresford. Being An Answer to his Lordship's Assumed Refutation of Colonel Napier's Justification of His Third Volume,* which appeared as a preface to volume 6 of the new edition of history, published in 1840. At this point, all three contenders, having mauled each other about as much as they could, broke off the battle.

Just as the Beresford-Long-Napier controversies died down, however, a new one flared up. It came in the form of an exchange in the pages of the *United Service*

Journal in 1840-1841 between Henry Hardinge, Beresford's deputy quartermaster-general, and Lowry Cole, commander of the 4th Division. In the third volume of his *History*, Napier had written that at Albuera Hardinge had "boldly ordered" Cole to attack with his 4th Division.[2] This was an error and, apparently, Cole talked to Hardinge about the matter and was given the impression that Hardinge would contact Napier and have it corrected in a subsequent printing. This correction was not made but, as Cole was out of Britain for many years afterward, he only discovered this in 1840.

In the October 1840 issue of the *United Service Journal*, letters written by Hardinge and Napier appeared on various aspects of the battle. Hardinge did not take the opportunity to correct the error and the result was a letter from Thomas Wade, who was Cole's aide-de-camp at the battle, which was published in the April 1841 issue of the *Journal*. Wade tried to make it clear that Hardinge did not order Cole to attack but merely suggested that the commander of the 4th Division attack. He included in his letter statements from not only Cole but other senior officers of the division, and even a note written by Hardinge to Cole a week or so after the battle which stated that Cole's "movement on the left flank of the enemy unquestionably saved the day, and decided the victory."[3]

Napier and Hardinge responded in the May 1841 issue of the *United Service Journal* and, while their lengthy letters touched on a lot of irrelevant points, Napier mildly acknowledged that he might have made a slight error while Hardinge – without really saying it in so many words – acknowledged that he did not order Cole to make the attack but merely suggested that Cole do so. In essence, the two finally agreed that Hardinge had proposed, but Cole had disposed.

The copious literature resulting from these controversies is long on unsubstantiated opinion and mild vituperation but does contain some useful primary sources. Those interested may obtain copies of the major publications of the controversies from Mark S. Thompson, 11 Friarsfield Close, Chapelgarth, Sunderland, SR3 2RZ, Britain.

Notes
1. William Napier, *History of the War in the Peninsula and in the South of France from the Year 1807 to the Year 1814*, (London: Thomas and William Boone, 1833, vol 3, 563.
2. William Napier, *History of the War in the Peninsula and in the South of France from the Year 1807 to the Year 1814*, (London: Thomas and William Boone, 1833, vol 3, 545.
3. *United Service Journal*, April 1841, 540, Hardinge to Cole, 24 May 1811.

ORDERS OF BATTLE, CRYSLER'S FARM, 11 NOVEMBER 1813

BRITISH AND CANADIAN FORCES

Commander: Lieutenant-Colonel Joseph W. Morrison, 89th Foot
Chief of Staff: Lieutenant-Colonel John Harvey

Main Force

49th Regiment of Foot	304 all ranks
89th Regiment of Foot	240 all ranks

Advance Guard

Commander: Lieutenant-Colonel Thomas Pearson

49th Foot, flank companies	78 all ranks
89th Foot, three companies	144 all ranks
Canadian Fencibles, 2 companies	108 all ranks

Light Troops

Commander: Major Frederick Heriot

Canadian Voltigeurs, 3 companies	150 all ranks
Provincial Light Dragoons	12 all ranks
Mohawk warriors	30

Artillery

Commander: Captain Henry Jackson, RA

Three 6-pdr guns and 63 gunners

Totals

Infantry	1064
Cavalry	12
Artillery	63
Mohawk warriors	30

Total British Forces	**1169 and 3 guns**

AMERICAN FORCES

Commanding Officer: Brigadier-General John P. Boyd

First Brigade

Commanding Officer: Colonel Isaac Coles

Twelfth Infantry Regiment	225
Thirteenth Infantry Regiment	225

Third Brigade
Commanding Officer: Brigadier-General Leonard Covington
    Ninth Infantry Regiment   300
    Sixteenth Infantry Regiment   225
    Twenty-Fifth Infantry Regiment   375

Fourth Brigade
Commanding Officer: Brigadier-General Robert Swartout
    Eleventh Infantry Regiment   300
    Fourteenth Infantry Regiment   125
    Twenty-First Infantry Regiment   425

Boat Guard
Commanding Officer: Lieutenant-Colonel Timothy Upham
    Detachments   600

Second Regiment of Dragoons   150
Commanding Officer: Major John Woodford

Artillery
Commanding Officer: Lieutenant Henry Craig
    100 gunners with 6 x 6-pdr. guns
    Totals
    Infantry   2800
    Cavalry   150
    Artillery   100

Total   **3050 with 6 x 6-pdr. guns**

Source
Donald E. Graves, **Field of Glory: The Battle of Crysler's Farm, 1813** (Toronto, 1999), 360-362.

ORDERS OF BATTLE, CHIPPAWA, 5 JULY 1814

BRITISH AND CANADIAN FORCES

Commanding Officer: Major-General Phineas Riall

Main Force

1st Foot	450
8th Foot	350
100th Foot	410
19th Light Dragoons, squadron	70
Royal Artillery	70 gunners with 2 x 24-pdr. guns, 3 x 6-pdr. guns
and 1 x 5.5-inch howitzer	

Pearson's Force

Commanding Officer: Lieutenant-Colonel Thomas Pearson

1st Foot light company	50
8th Foot, light company	50
103rd Foot, light company	50
2nd Lincoln Militia Regiment	200
Aboriginal Warriors	
Western nations	100
Grand River Nations	200

Totals

British Regulars

Cavalry	70
Infantry	1360
Artillery	70 with 6 pieces of artillery
Canadian militia	200
Aboriginal warriors	300

Total	**2000**

AMERICAN FORCES

Commanding Officer: Major-General Jacob Brown

First Brigade

Commanding Officer: Brigadier-General Winfield Scott

Ninth/Twenty-Second Infantry Regiment:	549
Eleventh Infantry Regiment:	416
Twenty-Fifth Infantry Regiment:	354

Second Brigade
Commanding Officer: Brigadier-General Eleazar Ripley
    Twenty-First Infantry   651
    Twenty-Third Infantry   341

Third Brigade
Commanding Officer: Brigadier-General Peter B. Porter
    5th Pennsylvania Regiment   540 (200 engaged)
    Aboriginal warriors   386

Artillery
Commanding Officer: Major Jacob Hindman
    est. 200 gunners with 1 x 12-pdr. gun, 4 x 6-pdr. guns and 2 x 5.5-inch howitzers

Totals
Regular Infantry   2311 of which 1399 were engaged
Militia   540 of which 200 were engaged
Warriors   386 of which est. 300 were engaged
Artillery   200 with 7 pieces of artillery

Total   **3437 of which 2099 were engaged**

Source
Donald E. Graves, *Redcoats and Grey Jackets: The Battle of Chippawa, 1814* (Toronto, 1994), 163-167.

ORDERS OF BATTLE, LUNDY'S LANE, 25 JULY 1814

BRITISH AND CANADIAN FORCES

Commanding Officer: Lieutenant-General Gordon Drummond
Second-in-Command: Major-General Phineas Riall

Pearson's Force
Commanding Officer: Lieutenant-Colonel Thomas Pearson

2nd or Light Brigade (est. 857 all ranks)
Commanding Officer: Lieutenant-Colonel Thomas Pearson

Provincial Light Dragoon	30
Glengarry Light Infantry	376
Incorporated Militia Battalion	336
Royal Artillery	20 with 2 x 6-pdr. guns and 1 x 5.5 inch howitzer

1st Militia Brigade (est. 300 all ranks)
Commanding Officer: Lieutenant-Colonel Love Parry
detachment, 1st Lincoln Regiment
detachment, 2nd Lincoln Regiment
detachment, 4th Lincoln Regiment
detachment, 5th Lincoln Regiment
detachment, 2nd York Regiment

Mohawk and other warriors	50

Morrison's Force (est. 761 all ranks)
Commanding Officer: Lieutenant-Colonel Joseph Morrison

1st Foot, 3 companies	171
8th Foot, 1 company	65
41st Foot, light company	60
89th Foot	425
Royal Artillery	40 with 2 x 24-pdr. guns
Royal Marine Artillery	Congreve rocket section
Force of aboriginal warriors	400-500

Scott's Force
Commanding Officer: Colonel Hercules Scott

1st Brigade

8th Foot, 5 companies	275
103rd Foot, 7 companies	635
104th Foot, 2 companies	120
Royal Artillery	40 with 3 x 6-pdr. guns

Reserve
Commanding Officer: Lieutenant-Colonel John Gordon

1st Foot, 7 companies	400

2nd Militia Brigade (est. 250 all ranks)
Commanding Officer: Lieutenant-Colonel Christopher Hamilton
    detachment, 1st Norfolk Regiment
    detachment, 2nd Norfolk Regiment
    detachment, 1st Essex Regiment
    detachment, 1st Middlesex Regiment
    detachment, Caldwell (Western) Rangers

Totals

British regulars	2226
Canadian regulars	852
Canadian militia	550
Total	**3638**

AMERICAN FORCES

Commanding Officer: Major-General Jacob Brown

First Brigade
Commanding Officer: Brigadier-General Winfield Scott

Ninth Infantry Regiment	200
Eleventh Infantry Regiment	200
Twenty-First Infantry Regiment	300
Twenty-Fifth Infantry Regiment	380

Second Brigade
Commanding Officer: Brigadier-General Eleazar W. Ripley

First Infantry Regiment	150
Twenty-First Infantry Regiment	432
Twenty-Third Infantry Regiment	300

Third Brigade
Commanding Officer: Brigadier-General Peter B. Porter

New York Militia Regiment	250
5th Pennsylvania Regiment	246
Canadian Volunteers	50

Artillery
Commanding Officer: Major Jacob Hindman
    200 gunners with 4 x 6-pdr. guns, 3 x 12-pdr. guns and 2 x 5.5 inch howitzers

Cavalry
Commanding Officer: Captain Samuel D. Harris

Company, U.S. Light Dragoons	35
Company, N.Y. Volunteer Dragoons	35

Totals

Infantry	2508
Cavalry	70
Artillery	200 with 9 pieces of artillery
Total	**2778**

Source
Donald E. Graves, *Where Right and Glory Lead! The Battle of Lundy's Lane, 1814* (Toronto, 1997).

NOTES

Abbreviations Used in the Notes

AO	Archives of Ontario, Toronto
BHC	Burton Historical Collection, Detroit Public Library
BM	British Museum, London
CBD	Ernest A. Cruikshank, ed., *Documents Relating to the Invasion of the Niagara Peninsula by the United States Army, Commanded by General Jacob Brown in July and August, 1814*. Niagara-on-the-Lake: Niagara Historical Society, 1920.
CHS	Connecticut Historical Society
CL	Clements Library
CO	Colonial Office
Dispatches	John Gurwood, ed. *The Dispatches of Field Marshal the Duke of Wellington, 1799-1811*. London: William Clowes, 13 vols, 1834-1839
Doc. Hist.	Ernest A. Cruikshank, ed. *Documentary History of the Campaigns on the Niagara in 1812-1814* (titles vary slightly). Welland: Tribune Press, 1896-1908
JSAHR	*Journal of the Society for Army Historical Research*
MDAH	Mississippi Department of Archives and History, Jackson
MG	Manuscript Group
NAB	National Archives of Britain, Kew
NLAC	National Library and Archives of Canada, Ottawa
NYSL	New York State Library, Albany
Reg Records	A.D.L. Cary and Stoupe McCance, *Regimental Records of the Royal Welch Fusiliers (late the 23rd Regiment of Foot), Vol. I, 1689-1889*, London, 1921
RG	Record Group
RWFM	Royal Welch Fusiliers Museum, Caernarfon
Supp. Dispatches	A.R. Wellington, ed. *Supplementary Dispatches, Correspondence and Memoranda of Field Marshal Arthur, Duke of Wellington, 1797-1815*. London: 14 vols, 1858-1872.
UCA	United Church Archives, Toronto
UCV	Upper Canada Village Archives, Morrisburg, Ontario
USJ	*United Services Journal*
USNA	United States National Archives, Washington
vol	volume
WO	War Office

Chapter 1: "Dreadful times are approaching"

Unless otherwise noted, this chapter is based on the following sources.

On the Pearson family of Somerset see records in the Somerset Record Office, and *(Almost) A Thousand Years of Thorne* (np, nd); Robert Dunning and William Page, *Victoria History of the County of Somerset* (1992); Joanna Martin, ed., *A Governess in the Age of Jane Austen: The Journals and Letters of Agnes Porter* (London, 1998), 90, 345; wills of the Reverend Thomas Horner Pearson and Thomas Pearson, Family Records Centre, London.

On the origins of the war with France and the course of that war to 1796: Arthur Bryant, *Years of Endurance, 1793-1802* (London, 1942); David Chandler, *The Campaigns of Napoleon* (New York, 1966); Edouard Detaille and Jules Richard, *L'Armée Française: An Illustrated History of the French Army 1790-1885* (New York, 1992); Michael Glover, *The Napoleonic Wars: An Illustrated History, 1792-1815* (New York, 1978); Christopher Hibbert, *George IV* (London, ,1976) and *George III: A Personal History* (London,1998).

On the British army and navy, 1783-1796, and the Duke of York and his reforms: Alfred Burne, *The Noble Duke of York: The Military Life of Frederick Duke of York and Albany* (London, 1949);

Michael Duffy, "The Caribbean Campaigns of the British Army, 1793-1801," in Alan Guy, ed., *The Road to Waterloo* (London, 1990); H. De Watteville, *The British Soldier: His Daily Life from Tudor to Modern Times* (London, 1954); G.J. Evelyn, "'I learned what one ought not to do'; The British Army in Holland, 1793-1795," in Alan Guy, ed., *The Road to Waterloo* (London, 1990); John Fortescue, *History of the British Army* (20 vols, New York, 1899-1930), vol 4, part 1; Richard Glover, *Peninsular Preparation: The Reform of the British Army 1795-1809* (Cambridge, 1963); Philip Haythornewaite, *The Armies of Wellington* (London, 1998); Richard Holmes, *Redcoat: The British Soldier in the Age of Horse and Musket* (London, 2001); John Houlding, *Fit for Service: The Training of the British Army, 1715-1795* (Oxford, 1981); Piers Mackesy, "Abercromby in Egypt: The Regeneration of the Army," in Alan Guy, ed., *The Road to Waterloo* (London, 1990); N.A.M. Roger, *The Wooden World: An Anatomy of the Georgian Navy* (London, 1986); James Lawrence, *The Iron Duke* (London, 1992); Glenn Steppler, "The British Army on the Eve of War," in Alan Guy, ed., *The Road to Waterloo* (London, 1990); and E.S. Turner, *Gallant Gentlemen: A Portrait of the British Officer, 1600-1956* (London, 1956).

On careers of individual officers, see: *Army Lists*, 1793-1797, personal entries in the *Dictionary of National Biography*; and Stewart Sutherland, *His Majesty's Gentlemen: A Directory of British Regular Army Officers of the War of 1812* (Toronto, 2000).

On the history of the Royal Welch Fusiliers, see: Rowland Broughton-Mainwaring, *Historical Record of the Royal Welch Fusiliers late The Twenty-Third Regiment or The Royal Welch Fusiliers* (London, 1889); Richard Cannon, compiler, *Historical Record of The Twenty-Third Regiment or The Royal Welsh Fusiliers* (London, 1850); A.D.L. Cary and Stouppe McCance, *Regimental Records of the Royal Welch Fusiliers (Late the 23rd Foot)* (2 vols, London, 1921); and Michael Glover, *That Astonishing Infantry: Three Hundred Years of the History of the Royal Welch Fusiliers (23rd Regiment of Foot), 1689-1989)* (London, 1989).

1. "Hey for the life of a soldier" comes from Thomas Cooke's opera "Frederick the Great" of 1814 and was popular during the Napoleonic period. George Bell, who served with the 34th Foot in the Peninsula records that it was sung at the outbreak of the Crimean War but terms it an "old song," see George Bell, *Soldier's Glory being 'Rough Notes of an Old Soldier'* (Tunbridge Wells, 1991), 194. The version reproduced here is from Lewis Winstock, *Songs and Music of the Redcoats* (London, 1970), 156.

2. *A Book of Common Prayer* (Oxford, 1762).
3. James Woodforde, *The Diary of a Country Parson, 1758-1802* (Oxford, 1978), 3 February 1768.
4. Woodforde, *Diary*, 54, 22 November 1768.
5. Woodforde, *Diary*, 295, 28 January 1787.
6. Woodforde, *Diary*, 68, 15 July 1770.
7. Woodforde, *Diary*, 171, 8 June 1781.
8. Woodforde, *Diary*, 192, 3 December 1782.
9. William Cowper, "The Yearly Distress," quoted in Woodforde, *Diary*, 289.
10. Woodforde, *Diary*, 355, 24 July 1789
11. Woodforde, *Diary*, 431, 26 January 1793.
12. Corporal Robert Brown, *The Campaign: A Poetical Essay* (London, 1797), quoted in Lawrence, *Iron Duke*, 37.
13. "The Military Nurse, or Modern Officer," a broadside ballad quoted in Turner, *Gallant Gentlemen*, 35.
14. Glover, *Peninsular Preparation*, 148.
15. Henry Bunbury, *Passages in the Great War with France* (1854, reprinted London, 1927), xv.
16. Major Henry Calvert, quoted in Bryant, *Years of Endurance*, 87.
17. Quoted in Turner, *Gallant Gentlemen*, 118-119.
18. Bunbury, *Passages*, xxi.
19. Philip Henry, Earl Stanhope, *Notes of Conversations with the Duke of Wellington* (London, 1889), 182.
20. Quoted in Turner, *Gallant Gentlemen*, 65.
21. Gardner's *Recollections*, 16, quoted in Bryant, *Years of Endurance*, 196.
22. Adjutant-General's Circular Letter to Generals, 16 May 1795, quoted in Glover, *Peninsular Preparation*, 121.
23. That evidence should be in the War Office 31 series or the commander-in-chief's papers, which contain letters of recommendations, but, unfortunately, several determined searches of this series in the National Archives of Britain have failed to find Thomas Pearson's letter of recommendation.
24. That this was the case seems to be inferred from a letter written by John Hill, who obtained a commission in the 23rd Foot in July 1796. Writing to his parents, Hill noted that a "commission may be bought in another Regiment besides those in the West Indies I should think at equally as cheap a rate," an indication that recent casualties in the army had created vacancies for apiring officers. See John Hill to parents, 1796 in the Hill correspondence, RWFM.
25. *General Regulations and Orders for the Army, 1811* (London, 1816), 31.

26. *General Regulations and Orders for the Army, 1811* (London, 1816), 31.
27. Thomas Simes, *The Military Guide for Young Officers* (London, 1772) quoted in Hew Strachan, *British Military Uniforms, 1768-1791* (London, 1975), 188.
28. Strachan, *British Military Uniforms*, 199, 216.
29. Bell, *Soldier's Glory*, 2.
30. *Advice to Officers of the British Army* (London, 1783), 75-76. This anonymous publication is generally attributed to the satirist, Francis Grose.
31. David Roberts, *Military Instructions; Including Each Particular Motion of the Manual and Platoon Exercises* (London, 1798), 21.
32. Henry Dundas, *Rules and Regulations for the Formation, Field-Exercise, and Movements of His Majesty's Forces* (London, 1808), 318.
33. *Reg Records*, vol 1, 318.
34. *Advice to Officers*, 75.
35. *Reg Records*, vol 1, 319-320.
36. Glover, *Astonishing Infantry*, 26.
37. Glover, *Astonishing Infantry*, 26.
38. Roger Buckley, ed., *The Napoleonic War Journal of Captain Thomas Henry Browne, 1807-1816* (London, 1987), 73.
39. *Reg Records*, vol 1, 157-158.
40. Turner, *Gallant Gentlemen*, 79.
41. *Advice to Officers*, 77.
42. *Advice to Officers*, 77.

Chapter 2: "The French have read a lesson today they will not soon forget."

Unless otherwise noted, this chapter is based on the following sources.

On the course of the war with France to 1802, see: Bryant, *Years of Endurance*; Chandler, *Campaigns of Napoleon*; and M. Glover, *The Napoleonic Wars*.

On the British army and its campaigns, 1797-1802, see: Burne, *Noble Duke of York*; Fortescue, *History of the British Army*, vol 4; Haythornewaite, *Armies of Wellington*; Piers Mackesy, "Abercromby in Egypt: The Regeneration of the Army," in Alan Guy, ed., *The Road to Waterloo* (London, 1990) and *British Victory in Egypt, 1801: The End of Napoleon's Conquest* (London, 1995).

On careers of individual officers, see: *Army Lists*, 1797-1802 and personal entries in the *Dictionary of National Biography*.

On the loading for Ostend, see NAB, Admiralty 36, Ship's Registers, vol 13304, 1798-1799.

On the history of the Royal Welch Fusiliers, see: Broughton-Mainwaring, *Historical Record of the Royal Welch Fusiliers*; Roger Buckley, ed. *The Napoleonic War Journal of Captain Thomas*

Henry Browne, 1807-1816 (London, 1987); Richard Cannon, compiler, *Historical Record of The Twenty-Third Regiment*; Cary and McCance, *Reg Records*; and Glover, *Astonishing Infantry*.

On Thomas Pearson, see biography of Thomas Pearson, *British Military Journal*, 1816 quoted in R.G. Harris, "Two Military Miniatures, *JSAHR*, vol 63 (1985), 101-103.

1. British ballad, current in the early 19th century, see Roy Palmer, ed., *The Rambling Soldier* (London, 1985), 171-172.
2. Paul Barras, quoted in Bryant, *Years of Endurance*, 220.
3. Bryant, *Years of Endurance*, 218.
4. Woodforde, *Diary*, 562, 1 April 1798.
5. Woodforde, *Diary*, 564, 23 April 1798.
6. Woodforde, *Diary*, 564, 24 April 1798.
7. Woodforde, *Diary*, 565-566, 27 April 1798.
8. Quoted in Bryant, *Years of Endurance*, 222.
9. *Reg Records*, vol. 1, 197.
10. Anonymous, *A Soldier's Journal* (London, 1770) quoted in Roy Palmer, ed., *The Rambling Soldier* (London, 1985), 142-143.
11. Quoted in Haythornethwaite, *Armies of Wellington*, 225.
12. Quoted in Glover, *The Napoleonic Wars*, 53.
13. Bryant, *Years of Endurance*, 250-251.
14. Inspection Report by Major-General Hew Dalrymple, 4 October 1798, quoted in *Reg Records*, vol 1, 198.in.
15. Mackesy, *British Victory*, 7.
16. Bunbury, *Passages*, 29.
17. Bunbury, *Passages*, 25.
18. Bunbury, *Passages*, 25-26.
19. John Beresford, ed., *The Diary of a Country Parson. Volume IV. 1793-1796* (Oxford, 1968), 209, 10 August 1799.
20. RWFM, Hill correspondence, Hill to parents, 5 September 1799.
21. Bunbury, *Passages*, 14.
22. William Surtees, *Twenty-Five Years in the Rifle Brigade* (1833, reprinted London, 1996), 10
23. Bunbury, *Passages*, 14.
24. Bunbury, *Passages*, 14.
25. RWFM, Hill correspondence, Hill to father, 5 September 1799.
26. Surtees, *Twenty-Five Years*, 15.
27. Hill letters, RWFM, Hill to father, 23 sep 1799.
28. Bunbury, *Passages*, 21.
29. Surtees, *Twenty-Five Years*, 24.
30. Surtees, *Twenty-Five Years*, 25.
31. Surtees, *Twenty-Five Years*, 26.
32. Surtees, *Twenty-Five Years*, 27.
33. RWFM, Hill correspondence, Lieutenant John Hill's account of the sinking.
34. *Reg Records*, vol 1, 200-201.

35. RWFM, Hill correspondence, Hill's notes on the offical account of the *Valk* disaster.
36. RWFM, Hill correspondence, Hill to mother, 10 August 1800.
37. RWFM, Hill correspondence, Hill to mother, 10 August, 1800.
38. Réné Nicolas Desgenettes, *Souvenirs de la fin du XVIII siècle et du commencement du XIXe, ou Mémoires de R.D.G.* (2 vols, Paris, 1835 & 1836), vol 2, 348.
39. Speech by Richard Sheridan, Leader of the Opposition, in parliament, 15 June 1808, quoted in Charles Oman, *A History of the Peninsular War* (7 vols, London, 1902-1930) vol 1, 222.
40. NLAC, MG 24, F70, Diary of Lt. Thomas Evans, 18 March 1800.
41. RWF Musuem, Hill correspondence, Hill to mother, 11 Jan 1801.
42. NLAC, MG 24, F70, Diary of Lt. Thomas Evans, 22 January 1801.
43. Mackesy, *British Victory*, 35-37.
44. J.F. Maurice, ed., *Diary of Sir John Moore* (2 vols, London, 1904), vol 2, 3-4.
45. NLAC, MG 24, F70, Diary of Lt. Thomas Evans, 22 January 1801.
46. NLAC, MG 24, F70, Diary of Lt. Thomas Evans, 8 March 1801.
47. NLAC, MG24, F70, Diary of Lt. Thomas Evans, 7 March 1801.
48. Unidentified witness quoted in David Daniell, *Cap of Honour. The Story of the Gloucestershire Regiment* (London, 1951), 75.
49. Daniell, *Gloucestershire Regiment*, 76.
50. Maurice, ed., *Diary of Sir John Moore*, vol 2, 3-4.
51. NLAC, MG 24, F70, Diary of Lt. Thomas Evans, 8 March 1801.
52. John Macdonald, "Sir Ralph Abercromby by a Contemporary," *Blackwood's Magazine*, Dec 1915, 843-844, quoted in Mackesy, *British Victory*, 74.
53. Miller quoted in Palmer, *Rambling Soldier*, 167.
54. Quoted in Mackesy, *British Victory*, 76.
55. Maurice, ed., *Diary of Sir John Moore*, vol 2, 9-10.
56. Daniell, *Gloucestershire Regiment*, 79, Paget to father.
57. RWFM, Hill correspondence, Statement of Services, c.1816.
58. Maurice, ed., *Diary of Moore*, 15.
59. Daniell, *Gloucestershire Regiment*, 82.
60. Maurice, ed., *Diary of Moore*, 16,.
61. AO, MU 2635, Extract of a letter from an Officer in the 30th Regiment, in Egypt, to his friend in Aberdeen, 1801.
62. NLAC, MG 24, F70, Diary of Lt. Thomas Evans, 21 March 1801.
63. Miller quoted in Palmer, *Rambling Soldier*, 170.
64. AO, MU 2635, Extract of a letter from an officer of the 30th Regiment, in Egypt, to his friend in Aberdeen, 1801.
65. R.M. Grazebrook, "The Wearing of Equipment, 1801," *JSAHR*, vol 25 (1946).
66. Bunbury, *Passages*, 101-102.
67. Circular Letter, 6 July 1802, in *Reg Records*, vol 1, 207.

Chapter 3: "God Bless the King and Damn the French."

Unless otherwise noted, this chapter is based on the following sources.

On the course of the war with France to 1808 and the tensions with America, see: Arthur Bryant, *Years of Victory,* (London, 1944); Chandler, *Campaigns of Napoleon*; and Glover, *The Napoleonic Wars*; and J.M. Hitsman, *The Incredible War of 1812: A Military History* (Toronto, 1999).

On the British army and its campaigns, 1802-1808: Burne, *Noble Duke of York*; Fortescue, *History of the British Army*, vols 5 and 6; and Haythornewaite, *Armies of Wellington*.

On careers of individual army and naval officers, see: *Army Lists*, 1801-1807; personal entries in the *Dictionary of National Biography*; and William O'Byrne, *A Naval Biographical Dictionary* (London, 1849).

On the history of the Royal Welch Fusiliers, see: Broughton-Mainwaring, *Historical Record of the Royal Welch Fusiliers*; Richard Cannon, compiler, *Historical Record of The Twenty-Third Regiment*; Currie, *Letters to a Vicarage*; Cary and McCance, *Reg Records*; and Glover, *That Astonishing Infantry*.

On Pearson, see biography, *British Military Journal*, 1816, quoted in Harris, "Two Military Miniatures."

1. "The Rambling Soldier," traditional in the early 19th century, see Roy Palmer, ed., *The Rambling Soldier* (London, 1985), 276-277.
2. RWFM, Hill correspondence, Hill to mother, 25 December 1801.
3. "Extracts from the Standing Orders in the Garrison of Gibraltar. Established by General H.R.H. the Duke of Kent, Governor, 1809," *JSAHR*, vol 2, 126-127.
4. "Extracts from the Standing Orders in the Garrison of Gibraltar, 1803," *JSAHR*, vol 2, 181.
5. "Extracts from the Standing Orders in the Garrison of Gibraltar, 1803," *JSAHR*, vol 2, 183.
6. NAB, WO 27, vol 87, Report of 23rd Royal

Welch Fusiliers ... reviewed ... at Gibraltar, 4 March 1803.

7. *Memoir of the Military Career of John Dayes* (London, 2004), 7.

8. Nursery rhyme assembled from two variants contained in Bryant, *Years of Victory*, 62, and Norman Longmate, *Island Fortress. The Defence of Great Britain 1603-1945* (London, 1991), 246.

9. Glover, *Napoleonic Wars*, 90.

10. RWFM, Hill correspondence, Hill to father, 8 September 1803.

11. AO, MU 2635, Military scrapbook, recruiting advertisement, n.d., c. 1805.

12. Handbill for the 81st Foot, c. 1793, in "Old Recruiting Posters," *JSAHR*, vol 1, 132.

13. Poster, Midlothian Light Dragoons, 1798, in "Old Recruiting Posters," *JSAHR*, vol 1, 119.

14. Poster, 14th Light Dragoons, 1803 to 1812, "Old Recruiting Posters," *JSAHR*, vol 1, 120.

15. Poster, Glengarry Light Infantry Fencibles, 1812, author's collection.

16. James Donaldson, *Recollections of an Eventful Life* (1825, reprinted Staplehurst, 2000), 85-86.

17. Lewis Winstock, *Songs and Music of the Redcoats*, 38-39.

18. Woodforde, *Diary*, 387, 20 November 1790.

19. John Shipp, *The Path of Glory*, (London, 1969), 3.

20. Woodforde, *Diary*, 522, 10 May 1796.

21. Woodforde, *Diary*, 522-523, 11 May 1796.

22. His Majesty's Warrant Concerning Necessaries, 14 January 1792 in *Standing Orders and Regulations for the Army in Ireland* (Dublin, 1794), 1.

23. Woodforde, *Diary*, 478, 12 January 1798.

24. Inspection Report by Brigadier-General Maitland, 28 October 1804, quoted in *Reg Records*, vol 1, 210.

25. Broadside ballad, "The Bellman and Little Boney," quoted in Bryant, *Years of Victory*, 73.

26. Glover, *Napoleonic Wars*, 104.

27. RWFM, Hill correspondence, Hill to mother, 11 September 1803.

28. RWFM, Hill correspondence, Hill to father, 2 September 1803.

29. Fortescue, *History of the British Army*, vol 6, 65.

30. Fortescue, *History of the British Army*, vol 6, 65-66.

31. E.32. Kirby, "The Youth who was to save our Flash," *Y Dddraig Goch*, (March 1979).

32. E.L. Kirby, "The Youth who was to save our Flash," *Y Dddraig Goch*, (March 1979).

33. *The Military Adventures of Johnny Newcome ... By An Officer* (1816, reprinted London, 1804), 11n.

34. E.L. Kirby, "The Youth who was to save our Flash," *Y Dddraig Goch*, (March 1979).

35. E.L. Kirby, "The Youth who was to save our Flash," *Y Dddraig Goch*, (March 1979).

36. Buckley, ed., *Journal of Captain Browne*, 50.

37. Fortescue, *History of the British Army*, vol 6, 69.

38. Quoted in Buckley, ed., *Journal of Captain Browne*, 56.

39. Buckley, ed., *Journal of Captain Browne*, 55.

40. Buckley, ed., *Journal of Captain Browne*, 62.

41. Buckley, ed., *Journal of Captain Browne*, 63.

42. Surtees, *Twenty-Five Years*, 72.

43. Surtees, *Twenty-Five Years*, 70.

44. Glover, *Napoleonic Wars*, 129.

45. Buckley, ed., *Journal of Captain Browne*, 67-68.

46. Buckley, ed., *Journal of Captain Browne*, 68.

47. Buckley, ed., *Journal of Captain Browne*, 68.

48. Buckley, ed., *Journal of Captain Browne*, 68.

49. Joseph Donaldson, *Recollections of the Eventful Life of a Soldier* (1853, reprinted London, 200), 51-53.

50. Buckley, ed., *Journal of Captain Browne*, 69.

51. Thomas Pakenham, ed., *Pakenham Letters. 1800-1815* (London, 1914), 38, Pakenham to mother, 5 February 1808.

52. Buckley, ed., *Journal of Captain Browne*, 73.

53. "The Tenth Regiment Song" from Lewis Winstock, *Songs and Music of the Redcoats*, 64-65.

54. Buckley, ed., *Journal of Captain Browne*, 74.

Chapter 4: "Fair complexions lit up by soft blue eyes."

Unless otherwise noted, this chapter is based on the following sources.

On the course of the war with France to 1810 and the trouble with America, see: Bryant, *Years of Victory*; Chandler, *Campaigns of Napoleon*; Hitsman, *Incredible War of 1812*; and Glover, *Napoleonic Wars*.

On the British army and its campaigns, 1808-1810, and the Martinique campaign of 1809, see: Richard Cannon, compiler, *Historical Records of the Seventh Regiment or the Royal Fusiliers* (London, 1847); Buckley, ed., *Journal of Captain Browne*; Fortescue, *History of the British Army*, vol 7; Haythornewaite, *Armies of Wellington*; and M.E.S. Laws, "The Royal Artillery at Martinique 1809," Journal of the Royal Artillery Institution, vol 78, no 1 (January 1950), 70-81.

On the careers of individual officers, see: *Army Lists*, 1808-1810 and personal entries in the *Dictionary of National Biography*.

On the history of Halifax, Thomas Raddall, *Halifax: Warden of the North* (New York, 1965), is the main source.

On the Coffin family, see H.E. Coffin, *A Memoir of John Coffin* (Reading, 1860).

On the history of the Royal Welch Fusiliers, see: Broughton-Mainwaring, *Historical Record of the Royal Welch Fusiliers*; Richard Cannon, compiler, *Historical Record of The Twenty-Third Regiment*; Cary and McCance, *Reg Records*; and Glover, *That Astonishing Infantry*.

On Pearson, see biography, *British Military Journal*, 1816 quoted in Harris, "Two Military Miniatures."

1. The second verse of "The girl I left behind me," a "loath-to-depart" dating from the Seven Years' War traditionally played when regiments left a station where they had long served. It is still played to this day in the British army.
2. *Nova Scotia Gazette*, 7 April 1808.
3. Raddall, *Halifax*, 140.
4. Raddall, *Halifax*, 103.
5. Raddall, *Halifax*, 132.
6. RWF, Hill correspondence, Hill to brother, 12 June 1808.
7. Buckley, ed., *Journal of Captain Browne*, 84.
8. Buckley, ed., *Journal of Captain Browne*, 91.
9. Buckley, ed., *Journal of Captain Browne*, 93.
10. Buckley, ed., *Journal of Captain Browne*, 93.
11. Neville Connel, "Hotel Keepers and Hotels in the Barbadoes," *Journal of the Barbados Museum and Historical Society* 32 (November 1970), quoted in Buckley, ed., *Journal of Captain Browne*, 335n.
12. Buckley, ed., *Journal of Captain Browne*, 94.
13. Cannon, *Historical Record of the Twenty-third Regiment*, 132.
14. Prevost to Maitland, quoted in *Reg Records*, vol 1, 223.
15. Broughton-Mainwaring, *Historical Record of the Royal Welch Fusiliers*, 122.
16. Richard Cannon, *Historical Records of the Seventh Regiment or the Royal Fusiliers* (London, 1847), 40-41, Order of the day, 3 February 1809.
17. AO, MU 2635, Military scrapbook, *London Gazette Extraordinary*, 12 April 1809, Pearson to Prevost, 11 February 1809.
18. Buckley, ed., *Journal of Captain Browne*, 107.
19. Buckley, ed., *Journal of Captain Browne*, 108,
20. *Reg Records*, vol 1, 224.
21. Buckley, ed., *Journal of Captain Browne*, 117-118.
22. C.B Norman, *Battle Honours of the British Army* (1911, reprinted London, 1971), 119.
23. *Nova Scotia Gazette*, 18 April 1809.
24. RWFM, Hill correspondence, Hill to mother, 30 April 1808.
25. *Nova Scotia Gazette*, 2 May 1809.
26. *Nova Scotia Gazette*, 2 May 1809.
27. *Nova Scotia Gazette*, 31 March 1809.
28. Buckley, ed, *Journal of Captain Browne*, 113.
29. NLAC, MG 24, A9, Diary of Anne Elinor Prevost, 3 May 1809.
30. W.M. Brown, "Recollections of Old Halifax," *Collections of the Nova Scotia Historical Society*, vol 13 (1908), 77.
31. T.B. Akins, "History of Halifax City," *Collections of the Nova Scotia Historical Society*, vol 8, (1892-1894), 162.
32. Brown, "Recollections," 78.
33. Brown, "Recollections," 78.
34. Brown, "Recollections," 82.
35. William Moorsom, *Letters from Nova Scotia* (London, 1830), 26.
36. Charles Leslie, *Military Journal of Colonel Leslie* (Aberdeen, 1887), 288.
37. Leslie, *Military Journal*, 286.
38. Leslie, *Military Journal*, 289.
39. Thomas Winslow to his sisters, 9 July 1809, in W.O. Raymond, *Winslow Papers* (Saint John, 1891), 624.
40. General John Coffin and his wife left Canada for Britain in 1817 and most of their children, either being in the service or having married into it, spent the remainder of their lives in the United Kingdom. For this reason, there is actually very little information in Canada today about this once-prominent New Brunswick family.
41. Donald E. Graves, ed., *Merry Hearts Make Light Days: The War of 1812 Journal of Lieutenant John LeCouteur, 104th Regiment of Foot* (Ottawa, 1994), 76.
42. Graves, ed., *Merry Hearts*, 76.
43. NLAC, MG 24, A9, Diary of Anne Elinor Prevost, 36.
44. *Nova Scotia Gazette*, 22 May 1809.
45. *Nova Scotia Gazette*, 12 September, 1809.
46. *Nova Scotia Gazette*, 5 September 1809.
47. *Nova Scotia Gazette*, "New Museum of Waxworks," 20 June 1809.
48. François Bourneuf, *Diary of a Frenchman* (Halifax, 1990), 38-39.
49. Brown, "Recollections," 83.
50. *Nova Scotia Gazette*, 6 June 1809.
51. NLAC, MG24, A9, Diary of Anne Elinor Prevost, 23.
52. NLAC, MG 24, A9, Diary of Anne Elinor Prevost, 28.
53. NAB, WO 27, vol 94, Inspection Return, 1/23rd Foot, 27 June 1809.

54. NAB, WO 27, vol 94, Inspection Return, 1/23rd Foot, 27 June 1809.
55. Buckley, ed., *Journal of Captain Browne*, 114.
56. Buckley, ed., *Journal of Captain Browne*, 115.
57. Buckley, ed., *Journal of Captain Browne*, 118.
58. Buckley, ed., *Journal of Captain Browne*, 119.
59. Buckley, ed, *Journal of Captain Browne*, 120-121.
60. William Dunlop, *Tiger Dunlop's Upper Canada* (Ottawa, 1967), 21.
61. Penelope Winslow to Edward Winslow, 30 October 1809, in W.O. Raymond, *Winslow Papers*, 640.
62. Buckley, ed., *Journal of Captain Browne*, 120.
63. Buckley, ed., *Journal of Captain Browne*, 120.
64. Buckley, ed., *Journal of Captain Browne*, 120.
65. NAB, WO 25, vol 747, Statement of Service of Major Thomas Pearson, 10 December 1810.
66. *Royal Gazette, or New Brunswick Advertizer*, 7 May 1810.
67. Buckley, ed., *Journal of Captain Browne*, 122.
68. *Royal Gazette, or New Brunswick Advertizer*, 2 July 1810.
69. NAB, WO 27, vol 88, Report of Inspection of 1/23rd Foot, Halifax, 11 August 1810.
70. Buckley, ed., *Journal of Captain Browne*, 122.
71. *Nova Scotia Gazette*, 17 October 1810.
72. Buckley, ed., *Journal of Captain Browne*, 122.

Chapter 5: "Johnny Newcomes"
Unless otherwise noted, this chapter is based on the following sources.

On the campaigns of 1810-1811 and the preparatory movements relating to the battle of Albuera, see: Antonio Burriel, ed., *Batalla del la Albuhera* (Cadiz, 1811); Benjamin D'Urban, *The Peninsular Journal, 1808-1817* (London, 1930, reprinted 1990); Charles Esdaile, *The Peninsular War: A New History* (London, 2002); Fortescue, *History of the British Army*, vol 7; David Gates, *The Spanish Ulcer: A History of the Peninsular War* (London, 1986); D.J. Goodspeed, *The British Campaigns in the Peninsula. 1808-1814* (Ottawa, 1958); Edouard Lapène, *Conquête de l'Andalousie, Campagne de 1810 et 1811 dans le Midi de L'Espagne* (Paris, 1823); Charles E. Long, *A Reply to the Misrepresentations and Aspersions on the Military Reputation of the late Lieutenant-General R.B. Long Contained in a Work Entitled "Further Strictures on those parts of Col. Napier's History of the Peninsular War which relate to the Military Opinions and Conduct of General Lord Viscount Beresford"* (London, 1832); T.H. McGuffie, *Peninsular Cavalry General, 1811-1813: The Correspondence of Lieutenant-General Robert Ballard Long* (London, 1951); Charles Oman, *A History of the Peninsular War. Vol IV. December 1810 to December 1811* (London, 1911,

reprinted 1996); Mark S. Thompson, *Fatal Hill: The Allied Campaign under Beresford in Southern Spain in 1811* (Chapelgarth, 2002); and Charles B. Vere, *Marches, Movements, and Operations of the 4th Division of the Allied Army in Spain and Portugal in the Years 1810, 1811 & 1812* (original 1812, reprinted 2003).

On the history of the Royal Welch Fusiliers during 1810-1811, see: Broughton-Mainwaring, *Historical Record of the Royal Welch Fusiliers;* Cary and McCance, *Reg Records;* and Glover, *Astonishing Infantry.*

On Pearson, see biography, *British Military Journal*, 1816 quoted in Harris, "Two Military Miniatures."

On the experience of campaigning in Portugal and Spain, see: Bell, *Soldier's Glory* (Tunbridge Wells, 1991); Robert Blakeney, *A Boy in the Peninsular War* (1899, reprinted 1989); Charles Boutflower, *The Journal of an Army Surgeon* (Staplehurst, 1997); John Cooper, *Rough Notes of Seven Campaigns* (1869, reprinted Staplehurst, 1996); James Donaldson, *Recollections of an Eventful Life* (1825, reprinted Staplehurst, 2000); William Grattan, *Adventures with the Connaught Rangers* (1902, reprinted London, 1989); Christopher Hibbert, ed., *A Soldier of the Seventy-First* (1819, reprinted London, 1975); Robert Knowles, *The War in the Peninsula* (1913, reprinted Staplehurst, 2004); Jonathan Leach, *Rough Sketches of the Life of an Old Soldier* (London, 1831); Leslie, *Military Journal;* Basil Liddell Hart, ed. *Letters of Private Wheeler* (London, 1951); Friedrich Lindau, *Erinnerungen eines Soldaten* (Hameln, 1846); Charles Madden, "The Diary of Charles Dudley Madden, Lieutenant, 4th Dragoons, Peninsular War, 1809-1811," *Journal of the Royal United Services Institute*, vol 58 (1914); W.H. Maxwell, *Peninsular Sketches* (2 vols, 1844, reprinted, London, 1998); McGuffie, ed., *Peninsular Cavalry General;* Ian Fletcher, ed., *For King and Country* (Staplehurst, 1995); *Military Adventures of Johnny Newcome;* Moyle Sherer, *Recollections of the Peninsula* (1824, reprinted Staplehurst, 1996); William Surtees, *Twenty-Five Years in the Rifle Brigade* (1833, reprinted London, 1996); William Swabey, "Diary of Lieutenant Swabey, R.H.A. in the Peninsula," *Journal of the Royal Artillery Institute*, vol 22 ( ), no. 4, 193; and William Tomkinson, *The Diary of a Cavalry Officer* (1894, reprinted Staplehurst, 1999).

1. Sung to the tune of the "Brags of Washington," this song dates from 1812 and was written to commemorate the battle of Salamanca fought in July of that year. See Roy Palmer, ed., *The Rambling Soldier* (London, 1985), 177-178.

2. Buckley, ed. *Journal of Captain Browne*, 123.
3. Buckley, ed. *Journal of Captain Browne*, 124.
4. *Johnny Newcome*, 54.
5. McGuffie, *Peninsula Cavalry General*, 59, Long to brother, 4 March 1811; Liddell Hart, *Letters of Private Wheeler*, 49, Letter to family, 13 March 1811.
6. Anonymous, "Santarem," in Maxwell, *Peninsular Sketches*, vol 2, 360.
7. Blakeney, *Boy in the Peninsular War*, 209.
8. Blakeney, *Boy in the Peninsular War*, 210.
9. *Johnny Newcome*, 36.
10. Thomas Henry Browne never returned to the 23rd Foot. When he had recovered from his illness, he was assigned to garrison duties in Lisbon until September 1812 when he was appointed to Wellington's staff, where he remained until 1814. By the time of his death in 1855, Browne had reached the rank of general and his journal of his service during the years 1807-1816, edited by Roger N. Buckley, has been published as *The Napoleonic War Journal of Captain Thomas Henry Browne, 1807-1816* (London, 1986).
11. Leslie, *Military Journal*, 99.
12. RWFM, Hill to parents, 21 November 1809.
13. *Johnny Newcome*, 14n.
14. Grattan, *Adventures with the Connaught Rangers*, 50.
15. Harrison to father, 27 October 1810, Harrison Letters, Royal Welch Fusiliers Museum.
16. Oman, *History of the Peninsular War*, vol 3, 445.
17. "A Most Extraordinary Creature," *Y Draig Goch* (Winter 1947), 5. The source was from a scrapbook that had "recently come to hand."
18. Harrison to father, 8 February 1811, Harrison letters, Royal Welch Fusiliers Museum.
19. Albany Institute, Prevost collection, Lieutenant Henry Prevost to John A. Prevost, 17 November 1810.
20. *Dispatches*, vol 6, 518, Wellington to Liverpool, 21 December 1811.
21. Boutflower, *Journal of an Army Surgeon*, 75.
22. *Supplementary Dispatches*, vol 7, 69, Liverpool to Wellington, 20 February 1811.
23. Unfortunately, Offley would be killed leading his battalion at the battle of Salamanca in 1812.
24. McGuffie, ed., *Peninsular Cavalry General*, Long to brother, 9 March 1811.
25. *Reg Records*, vol 1, 238, letter dated 17 March 1811 by an unidentified officer.
26. McGuffie, *Peninsular Cavalry General*, 63, Long to brother, 17 March 1811.
27. Hibbert, ed., *A Soldier of the Seventy-First*, 56.
28. Hibbert, ed., *A Soldier of the Seventy-First*, 56.
29. *Johnny Newcome*, 56n.
30. To put the Portuguese civilian casualties suffered in the French invasion of 1810 into perspective, they amounted to about 4% of a population estimated to be 1.8 million and this was only one of three French invasions of that long-suffering nation. It has also been estimated that one million Spanish citizens lost their lives in the six years, 1808-1814, that the Peninsula War lasted, or about 10% of that nation's population.
31. Donaldson, *Recollections*, 115n.
32. *Reg Records*, vol 1, 237, letter dated 17 March 1811, by an unidentified officer.
33. Cooper, *Rough Notes*, 53.
34. *Reg Records*, vol 1, 237, letter dated 17 March 1811 by an unidentified officer.
35. *Reg Records*, vol 1, 239, letter dated 17 March 1811 by an unidentified officer.
36. Cooper, *Rough Notes*, 53.
37. Glover, *Astonishing Infantry*, 48, letter of Lieutenant John Harrison.
38. *Dispatches*, vol 7, 515, Wellington to Beresford, 28 March 1811.
39. *Supplementary Dispatches*, vol 13, 614, Cole to Beresford, 16 April, 1811,. .
40. Sherer, *Recollections*, 59-60.
41. Leslie, *Military Journal*, 135. Leslie is describing Spanish troops in the Talavera campaign of 1809 but given the vicissitudes of the Spanish supply system, things had not improved that much by the spring of 1811.
42. Leslie, *Military Journal*, 135.
43. Leslie, *Military Journal*, 135.
44. Jean-Baptiste Jourdan, *Mémoires militaires du Maréchal Jourdan* (Paris, 1899), 167-168.
45. Wellington to Beresford, 23 April 1811, *Supplementary Dispatches*, vol 7, p. 490. The other two memorandum written by Wellington, to Beresford, Fletcher and Dickson on the siege of Badajoz, and that to the Spanish Officers Commanding Corps in Estremadura, are to be found on pages 494 and 495 respectively.
46. Boutflower, *Journal of an Army Surgeon*, 89.
47. Sherer, *Recollections*, 152.
48. Albany Institute, Prevost papers, John A. Prevost to Augustin Prevost, n.d. [June or July] 1811.
49. Boutflower, *Journal of an Army Surgeon*, 90.
50. Royal Engineers Museum, John Hancock, "Military Engineers in the Peninsular War," Ross to Dalrymple, 20 May 1811, Elvas.
51. Boutflower, *Journal of an Army Surgeon*, 91.
52. Oman, *History of the Peninsula War*, vol 4, 369.

53. *Supplementary Dispatches*, vol 7, 490, Wellington to Beresford, 23 April 1811.
54. Thompson, *Fatal Hill*, 100.
55. Maximilien Foy, *History of the War in the Peninsula under Napoleon*, (London, 1827), 214.
56. Guy Godlowski, "Le Maréchal Soult," *Souvenir Napoléonien*, No. 327, January 1983, 2, quoted in John Elting, *Swords Around a Throne* (New York, 1988), 151.
57. Charles Oman, *Wellington's Army*, (London, 1913), 121.
58. Thomas Pakenham, ed. *The Pakenham Letters. 1800-1815* (London, 1914), Pakenham to Longford, 15 April 1811.
59. Quoted in Thompson, *The Fatal Hill*, 102.
60. J. Emerson, "Recollections of the Late War," in Maxwell, *Sketches*, II, 236.
61. Charles Oman, "Albuera," *Journal of the Royal Artillery*, vol 36 (1909), no. 2, 54.
62. Charles Long, *A Reply to Lord Beresford's Second Letter* (London, 1835), 109.
63. Madden, "Diary," 516.
64. *Victoires et Conquêtes ... des Français, de 1792 a 1815* (20 vols, Paris, 1816-1823) vol 20, 236-237.
65. Burriel, ed., *Batalla de la Albuera*, Report of Burriel. This very useful monograph contains not only the Spanish official report on the battle compiled by *Teniente-Colonel* Antonio Burriel, Blake's chief of staff, but also the reports of the senior Spanish officers who fought in the battle.
66. Cooper, *Rough Notes*, 58.
67. *Batalla de la Albuera*, Account of Burriel.
68. Leslie, *Military Journal*, 218
69. Sherer, *Recollections*, 158.
70. *Batalla de la Albuera*, Account of Burriel.
71. Lindau, *Erinnerungen*, 35-36.
72. Lindau, *Erinnerungen*, 35-36.
73. Sherer, *Recollections*, 158.
74. Leslie, *Military Journal*, 218.

Chapter 6: "Oh, what a day was that."
Unless otherwise noted, my account of the battle of Albuera in Chapters 6 and 7 is based on the following sources: Beresford's dispatch to Wellington dated 18 May 1811, contained in *Dispatches*, vol 7, 588; Soult's dispatch to Berthier dated 21 May 1811 in *Dispatches*, vol 5, 770, La Tour-Maubourg to Soult, 27 May 1811, BM Add Mss 3742F, f65; and the following published works: Anonymous, *Strictures on Certain Passages of Lieutenant Colonel Napier's History of the Peninsular War which relate to the Military Opinions and Conduct of General Lord Viscount Beresford* (London, 1831) (hereafter *Strictures*); Anonymous, *Further Strictures on those Parts of Col. Napier's*

History of the Peninsular War which relate to the Military Opinions and Conduct of General Lord Viscount Beresford (London, 1832) (hereafter *Further Strictures*); Jose Arteche y Moro, *Guerra de la Independencia* (Madrid, 1896); William C. Beresford, *A Letter to Charles Edward Long Esq. on the Extracts Recently Published form the Manuscript Journal and Private Correspondence of the late Lieut.-General R.B. Long* (London, 1833); William C. Beresford, *A Second Letter to Charles Edward Long Esq. on the Manuscript Journal and Private Corespondence of the late Lieut.-General R.B. Long* (London, 1834); Antonio Burriel, *Battle of Albuera* (Cadiz, 1811); José Maria, Conde de Toreno, *Historia del Levantaminento, Guerra Y Revolucion de España* (Madrid, 1953); Benjamin D/Urban, *The Peninsular Journal, 1808-1817* (London, 1930, reprinted 1990); H. Everard, *History of Thos. Farrington's Regiment* (Worcester, 1891); Fortescue, *A History of the British Army. Vol. VIII 1811-1812*, 181-215; Edouard Lapène, *Conquête de l'Andalousie, Campagne de 1810 et 1811 dans le Midi de L'Espagne* (Paris, 1823); Charles E. Long: *A Reply to the Misrepresentations and Aspersions on the Military Reputation of the late Lieutenant-General R.B. Long Contained in a Work Entitled "Further Strictures on those parts of Col. Napier's History of the Peninsular War which relate to the Military Opinions and Conduct of General Lord Viscount Beresford"* (London, 1832); Charles E. Long, *A Letter to General Viscount Beresford in Reply to his Lordship's Letter to the Author relative to the Conduct of the Late Lieut.-General R.B. Long in the Campaign of 1811* (London, 1833); Charles Long, *A Reply to Lord Beresford's Second Letter to the Author Relative to the Conduct of the late Lieut.-General R.B. Long then Commanding the Allied Cavalry* (London, 1835); Charles Oman, *A History of the Peninsular War. Vol IV. December 1810 to December 1811* (London, 1911, reprinted 1996), 363-403; Andreas Schepeler's account by Charles Oman, ed., "Albuera Once More," in *The Army Quarterly*, vol 24, April, 1932, 337-342; Mark S. Thompson, *Fatal Hill. The Allied Campaign under Beresford in Southern Spain in 1811* (Chapelgarth, 2002); Charles B. Vere, *Marches, Movments, and Operations of the 4th Division of the Allied Army in Spain and Portugal in the Years 1810, 1811 & 1812* (original 1812, reprinted 2003); and *Victoires et Conquêtes ... des Français, de 1792 a 1815* (20 vols, Paris, 1816-1823) vol 20.

1. "*On va leur percer le flanc*," literally "We're going to jab 'em in the flank"), a favourite marching song of the infantry *fantassins* of the French army, was sung throughout the period and fits very well Soult's plan of attack at Albuera. "*Le petit tondu*" or "the little

shorn one" was Napoleon. A very literal translation would be:

> We're going to jab 'em in the flank,
> Ran-tan-plan, tire-lire lan,
> That will make us smile
> Ran-tan-plan, tire-lire lan,
> We're going to jab 'em in the flank,
> Ran-tan-plan, tire-lire lan,
> *Le petit tondu* will be happy
> Ran-tan-plan, tire-lire lan,
> As it will give him much pleasure,
> Ran-tan-plan, tire-lire lan,
> We're going to jab 'em in the flank,
> Ran-tan-plan, tire-lire lan,
> Because everything depends on it,
> Ran-tan-plan, tire-lire lan,
> We'll be the toast of the empire,
> Ran-tan-plan, tire-lire lan,
> We're going to jab 'em in the flank,
> Ran-tan-plan, tire-lire lan.

2. *Dispatches*, vol 5, 770, Soult to Berthier, 21 May 1811.
3. J.P. Groves, *The 66th Berkshire Regiment* (Reading, 1887), 51, letter of Lieutenant John Clarke.
4. BM, Additional Mss 37425 f65, La Tour-Maubourg to Soult, 27 May 1811.
5. Kajetan Wojciechowski, *Pamietniki Moje W Hiszpanii* (Warsaw, 1978), 70.
6. William Brooke, "A Prisoner of Albuera. The Journal of Major William Brooke from May 16th to September 28th, 1811," *Blackwood's Magazine*, October 1908, 427.
7. Lindau, *Erinnerungen*, 36.
8. Brooke, "Journal," 427.
9. Lapène, *Conquête*, 156.
10. "Battle of Albuera," *Minutes of the Proceedings of the Royal Artillery Institution*, vol 13 (1885), 126-127, letter of Lieutenant William Unger, 24 May 1811.
11. Lapène, *Conquête*, 156.
12. Lapène, *Conquête*, 151.
13. Lapène, *Conquête*, 152.
14. William Swabey, "Diary of Lieutenant Swabey, R.H.A. in the Peninsula," *Journal of the Royal Artillery Institute*, vol 22, 193.
15. There is some evidence that the allied army may have had more intelligence about Soult's attack plan than historians have previously believed. Lieutenant Augustus Wahrendorff of the 1st King's German Legion Battalion recorded in his diary that, on the evening "before the battle an enemy deserter came to our picquet whom we went to General Alten, who informed us of the entire plan of attack of his army, as it would be conducted the next day" – see Franz von Gottberg, *Geschichte des*

Hannoverischen Jäger-Bataillons Nr. 10. Vol. 1 (1803 bis 1866), (Berlin, 1913), 56. If this is so, this information either did not reach Beresford or it did and he did not act on it.
16. Andreas von Schepeler, "Albuera Once More," *The Army Quarterly*, vol 24, April, 1932, 337.
17. Schepeler, "Albuera Once More," 337-338.
18. And for those who wish to hear it, there is a scene in the film "Waterloo" when it is beat by young drummer boys as a French column moves to the attack.
19. Anonymous, *Further Strictures on those Parts of Col. Napier's HIstory of the Peninsular War* (London, 1832), Beresford, "Report of the Operations," 29.
20. McGuffie, ed., *Peninsular Cavalry General*, 106, Long to brother, 22 May 1811.
21. Cooper, *Rough Notes*, 58.
22. Charles Vere, *Marches, Movements and Operations, of the 4th Division* (n.d., reprinted London, 2003), 11-12.
23. Cooper, *Rough Notes*, 59.
24. William Napier, *Colonel Napier's Justification Of His Third Volume; Forming A Sequel To His Reply To Various Opponents* (London, 1833), 26.
25. José de Zayas was present at the battle of Cabezón (June 1808); Medina de Risoseco (July 1808); Bubierca (December 1808); Tarancón (December 1809); Medellin (March 1812); Alcabón (July 1809); Puente del Arzobispo (July 1809); Ocaña (November 1809); and smaller actions including the siege of Cadiz (March 1810-April 1811) and being tangentially involved in the battle of Barosa in March 1811. After Albuera in May 1811, Zayas fought at Niebla (June 1811) and Puzol (October 1811) before being captured at the surrender of Valencia in January 1812. Wounded three times in action. Zayas died in 1827 at the age of 55.
26. "The 'Die Hards' at Albuera," *The Times*, 25 February 1915, Ensign Benjamin Hobhouse to his father, 17 May 1811.
27. BM, La Tour-Maubourg to Soult, 27 May 1811.
28. Jean-Jacques Gassendi, *Aide-Mémoire, à l'usage des officiers d'artillerie de France* (2 vols, Paris, 1801), vol 2, 186.
29. George Guthrie, *Treatise on Gun Shot Wounds* (London, 1827), 3.
30. George Guthrie, *Commentaries on the Surgeries of the War in Portugal, Spain, France and the Netherlands* (Philadelphia, 1862), 25.
31. Schepeler, "Albuera Once More," 339.
32. Madden, "Diary," 517.
33. Lapène, *Conquête*, 156.

34. *Batalla de la Albuera*, Report of Zayas.
35. "Prepare to fire … aim … fire!" Spanish words of command from "*Reglamento práctico de instrucción de formaciones para recreadores históricos españoles*," based on the 1808 Spanish *Manual de Instrucción* for infantry.
36. *Batalla de la Albuera*, Report of Zayas.
37. *Further Strictures*, 157.
38. *Batalla de la Albuera*, Report of Burriel.
39. *Batalla de la Albuera*, Reports of Burriel and Miranda.
40. *Batalla de la Albuera*, Report of Zayas.
41. Schepeler, "Albuera Once More," 340.
42. G.C. Moore Smith, *The Life of John Colborne* (2 vols, London, 1903), vol 1, 160, Colborne to Yonge, 18 May 1811.
43. Sherer, *Recollections*, 158.
44. Sherer, *Recollections*, 158-159.
45. Groves, *The 66th Berkshire Regiment*, 52, letter of Lieutenant John Clarke.
46. "The 'Die Hards' at Albuera," *The Times*, 25 February 1915, Ensign Benjamin Hobhouse to his father, 17 May 1811.
47. Sherer, *Recollections*, 159.
48. William Stewart, *Outlines for A Plan for the General Reform of the British Land Forces* (1806), quoted in Arthur Bryant, *Jackets of Green* (London, 1972), 41.
49. *Regulations for the Rifle Corps* (1800) quoted in Bryant, *Green Jackets*, 25. On Stewart, see his entry in the *Dictionary of National Biography*.
50. Harry Smith, *Autobiography of Sir Harry Smith* (London, 1901), 118.
51. *Supplementary Dispatches*, vol 4, 94, Wellington to Torrens, 6 December 1812.
52. Smith, *Life of Colborne*, vol 1, 160, Colborne to Yonge, 18 May 1811.
53. Madden, "Diary," 517.
54. H. Julius Hartmann, "Beiträge zur Geschichte des Krieges auf der Pyrenäischen halbinself in den Jahren 1809 bis 1813, *Hannoverisches Militärisches Journal*, vol. 2 (1831), 111.
55. Brooke, "Journal," 427.
56. Guthrie, *Commentaries*, 26.
57. Brooke, "Journal," 427.
58. Schepeler, "Albuera Once More," 339.
59. *Further Strictures*, 31, D'Urban, "Operations."
60. "Libro con las noticieas mas particulares de los sitios qu ha sufrido Badajoz par las tropas Francesa, y del la conquista de los ingleses," in Cláudio Chaby, *Excerptos Historicos e Collecçao de Documentos Relativos a Guerra Denominada na Peninsula e as Anteriores de 1801, e do Roussilon e Cataluna* (Lisbon, 6 vols, 1863-1882), vol 3, 381.
61. BM, La Tour-Maubourg to Soult, 27 May 1811.
62. *Instruction Concernant Les Manoeuvres de la Cavalerie Légere* (Paris, 1799), 73.
63. My account of the organization and movement of the French cavalry is from *Instruction Concernant Les Manoeuvres de la Cavalerie Légere*.
64. Groves, *The 66th Berkshire Regiment*, 52-53, letter of Lieutenant Clarke.
65. BM, La Tour-Maubourg to Soult, 17 May 1811.
66. *Supplementary Dispatches*, vol 7, 588, Beresford to Wellington, 18 May 1811.
67. *Quebec Mercury*, 29 July 1811, letter from an officer of the Buffs, 20 May 1811. This is almost certainly Captain Gordon of the 3rd Foot.
68. *Cavalry Training. 1912* (War Office, London, 1912), 129.
69. *Cavalry Training. 1912*, 129.
70. *The Soldier's Companion or Martial Recorder*, quoted in Knight, *The Buffs*, 349.
71. C.R.B. Knight, *Historical Records of the Buffs … Part One. 1704-1814* (London, 1935), 351.
72. Brooke, "Journal," 428.
73. Russell Gurney, *History of the Northamptonshire Regiment* (Aldershot, 1935), 149.
74. Groves, *The 66th Berkshire Regiment*, 53, letter of Lieutenant Clarke.
75. "The Battle of Albuera," *JSAHR*, vol 1, 130, Lieutenant George Crompton to his mother, 18 May 1811.
76. Hugh Pearse, *History of the 31st Foot and 70th Foot subsequently … The East Surrey Regiment* (2 vols, London, 1916), vol 1, 122-123.
77. *Cumloden Papers* (Edinburgh, 1871), 88, Stewart to Beresford, 18 May 1811.
78. N. Ludlow Beamish, *History of the King's German Legion* (2 vols, 1832-1837, reprinted Dallington, 1997), vol 1, 385, Cleeves to Hartmann, 20 May 1811.
79. Beamish, *History of the King's German Legion*, vol 1, 385, Cleeves to Hartmann, 20 May 1811.
80. Schepeler, "Albuera Once More," 339.
81. Charles Vane, *Story of the Peninsular War* (New York, 1854), 308.
82. Vane, *Story of the Peninsular War*, 308.
83. Leslie, *Military Journal*, 221.
84. *United Service Journal*, No. 43 (June 1832), letter of Inglis.
85. Gurney, *Northamptonshire Regiment*, 149.
86. Brooke, "Journal," 428.
87. AO, MU 2635, Military scrapbook, letter

from an officer in the 2nd Light Infantry Battalion, King's German Legion, 27 May 1811.

88. AO, MU 2635, Military scrapbook, letter from an officer in the 2nd Light Infantry Battalion, King's German Legion, 27 May 1811.

89. *Batalla de la Albuera*, Report of Penne-Villemur.

90. William Napier, *History of the War in the Peninsula. Volume III* (2nd edition, London, 1833) Appendix IX, section 4, letter of William Light.

91. Madden, "Diary," 519.

92. Madden, "Diary," 518.

93. BM, La Tour-Maubourg to Soult, 27 May 1811.

94. *Dispatches*, vol 5, 770, Soult to Berthier, 21 May 1811.

95. Lapène, *Conquête*, 157-158.

96. Madden, "Diary," 517.

Chapter 7: "Fall in Fusileers!"

For the sources on which this chapter is based, see comments preceding the endnotes in Chapter 6.

1. Written in the mid-19th century, "The Jolly Die-Hards," a regimental song of the Middlesex Regiment, successor to the 57th Foot, celebrates that unit's gallantry during the battle of Albuera. See Lewis Winstock, *Songs and Music of the Redcoats* (London, 1970), 230-231.

2. "The 'Die Hards' at Albuera," *The Times*, 25 February 1915, Ensign Benjamin Hobhouse to his father, 17 May 1811.

3. Schepeler, "Albuera Once More," 339.

4. Lapène, *Conquête*, 159-160.

5. Schepeler, "Albuera Once More," 339.

6. *USJ*, 241, Inglis letter.

7. Leslie, *Military Journal*, 221.

8. Schepeler, "Albuera Once More," 340.

9. "The 'Die Hards' at Albuera," *The Times*, 25 February 1915, Ensign Benjamin Hobhouse to his father, 17 May 1811.

10. Sherer, *Recollections*, 159.

11. Sherer, *Recollections*, 159.

12. "The 'Die Hards' at Albuera," *The Times*, 25 February 1915, Ensign Benjamin Hobhouse to his father, 17 May 1811.

13. Leslie, *Military Journal*, 221-222.

14. Leslie, *Military Journal*, 222.

15. Sherer, *Recollections*, 160.

16. *Victoires et Conquêtes*, 241-242.

17. "The 'Die Hards' at Albuera," *The Times*, 25 February 1915, Ensign Benjamin Hobhouse to his father, 17 May 1811.

18. John Mitchell, *Thoughts on Tactics and Military Organization* (London, 1838), 160, quoted in Brent Nosworthy, *Battle Tactics of Napoleon and His Enemies*, (London, 1995), 209.

19. Francis Duncan, *History of the Royal Regiment of Artillery* (2 vols, London, 1872-1873), vol 2, 297.

20. *USJ*, April 1841, Inglis letter.

21. "The 'Die Hards' at Albuera," *The Times*, 25 February 1915, Ensign Benjamin Hobhouse to his father, 17 May 1811.

22. Leslie, *Military Journal*, 222-223.

23. Schepeler, "Albuera Once More," 340.

24. Stewart to Beresford, 18 May 1811, quoted in *Cumloden Papers* (Edinburgh, 1871), 89.

25. *Batalla de la Albuera*, Report of Zayas.

26. Charles Kingsford, *The Story of The Duke of Cambridge's Own (Middlesex) Regiment* (London, 1916), 73.

27. Leslie, *Military Journal*, 222.

28. H. Everard, *History of Thos. Farrington's Regiment … The 29th (Worcestershire) Foot* (Worcester, 1891), 323.

29. Leslie, *Military Journal*, 222.

30. Lapène, *Conquête*, 160-161.

31. Thomas Bugeaud, "Maxims, Advice and Instruction on the Art of War," originally written in 1815 and recently republished by Brent Nosworthy, ed., *Writings on the French Napoleonic Art of War* (Mount Pearl, 2003).

32. Lapène, *Conquête*, 161.

33. Robert de Saint-Chamans, *Mémoires du Général Comte de Saint-Chamans* (Paris, 1896), 193

34. Maximien Lamarque, *Mémoires et Souvenirs du Général Maximien Lamarque* (3 vols, Paris, 1835-1836), vol 2, 182.

35. Saint-Chamans, *Mémoires*, 35.

36. Gurwood, *Dispatches*, vol 5, 770, Soult to Berthier, 21 May 1811.

37. Lapène, *Conquête*, 161.

38. Fortescue, *History of the British Army*, vol 8, 201.

39. *Further Strictures*, 167.

40. *USJ*, October 1840, 247, Hardinge letter.

41. Vere, *Marches*, 12.

42. *USJ*, April 1841, 540, letter of Lowry Cole dated 19 March 1841.

43. *USJ*, April 1841, 540, letter of Lowry Cole dated 19 March 1841.

44. Maud Cole and Stephen Gwynn, *Memoirs of Sir Lowry Cole* (London, 1934), 73, Roverea's Journal.

45. *USJ*, April 1841, 540, letter of Cole, 19 March 1841.

46. *USJ*, April 1841, 540, letter of Cole, 19 March 1841.

47. Cooper, *Rough Notes*, 60.

48. RWFM, Harrison papers, Harrison to mother, 24 May 1811.
49. *USJ*, April 1841, 538, letter of Edward Blakeney.
50. Dundas, *Rules and Regulations for the Formation, Field-Exercise and Movements*, 73.
51. Cooper, *Rough Notes*, 63.
52. Vere, *Marches*, 15.
53. *USJ*, April 1841, 540, letter of Cole, 19 March 1841.
54. RWF Musuem, Harrison papers, Harrison to mother, 24 May 1811.
55. Lapène, *Conquête*, 163.
56. Cooper, *Rough Notes*, 60.
57. *USJ*, April 1841, 538, letter of Edward Blakeney.
58. William Mayne, *A Narrative of the Campaigns of the Loyal Lusitanian Legion* (London, 1812), 109.
59. *USJ*, April 1841, 538, letter of Edward Blakeney.
60. *Dispatches*, vol 5, 770, Soult to Berthier, 21 May 1811.
61. C.D. Hall, "Albuera and Vittoria: Letters from Lt. Col. J. Hill," *JSAHR*, 66 (1988), 194, Hill to mother, 22 May 1811.
62. RWFM, Harrison papers, Harrison to mother, 24 May 1811.
63. RWFM, Harrison papers, Harrison to mother, 24 May 1811.
64. BM, La Tour to Soult, 27 May 1811, quoted by permission of the British Library.
65. Hall, "Albuera and Victoria," Hill to mother, 22 May 1811.
66. RWFM, Harrison papers, Harrison to mother, 24 May 1811.
67. McGuffie, *Peninsular Cavalry General*, 106, Long to brother, 22 May 1811.
68. Madden, "Diary," 517.
69. Beresford to Wellington, 18 May 1811.
70. BM, La Tour to Soult, 27 May 1811, quoted by permission of the British Library.
71. *USJ*, April 1841, 538, letter of Edward Blakeney.
72. Cole and Gwynn, *Memoirs of Sir Lowry Cole*, 76, Cole to Enniskillen, 21 May 1811.
73. Cooper, *Rough Notes*, 61.
74. Cooper, *Rough Notes*, 60-61.
75. RWFM, Harrison papers, Harrison to mother, 24 May 1811.
76. *USJ*, April 1841, 538, letter of Edward Blakeney.
77. Account of the battle of Talavera, 1809, by General Chambray quoted in Paddy Griffith, *Forward into Battle* (London, 1990), 36.
78. Cole and Gwynn, *Memoirs of Sir Lowry Cole*, 73, Journal of Roverea.
79. Thompson, *Fatal Hill*, 140.
80. Cole and Gwynn, *Memoirs of Sir Lowry Cole*, 73, Journal of Roverea.
81. Madden, "Diary," 517.
82. Madden, "Diary," 516-517.
83. AO, MU 2635, letter from an officers of the 2nd Light Infantry Battalion, King's German Legion, 27 May 1811.
84. AO, MU 2635, letter from an officers of the 2nd Light Infantry Battalion, King's German Legion, 27 May 1811.
85. Lapène, *Conquête*, 159.
86. Gottberg, *Geschichte des Hannoverischen Jäger-Bataillons Nr. 10. Vol. 1 (1803 bis 1866)* (Berlin, 1813), 56, Diary of Major Wahrendorff of the 1st KGL Light Battalion.
87. William Beresford, *A Refutation of Colonel Napier's Justification of His Third Volume* (London, 1834), 238, letter of Alten.
88. Beresford, *Refutation of Colonel Napier's Justification of His Third Volume*, letter of Alten.
89. Lindau, *Erinnerungen*, 36.
90. As well as the 16th *Léger*, Godinot supposedly had the 51st *Ligne*, 2,251 all ranks, under his command. That unit, however, reported only two men killed and one wounded at Albuera, in stark contrast to the loss of the 16th *Léger* which reported 381 casualties of all types. This being the case, it seems quite likely that the 51st *Ligne* never saw action in the battle and therefore the criticisms of Godinot by some French historians – notably Lapène – that he could have done more on the French right flank, are unwarranted. I am grateful to Guy Dempsey for bringing this matter to my attention.
91. Schepeler, "Albuera Once More," 340.
92. Hall, "Albuera and Vittoria," 194, Hill to mother, 24 May 1811.
93. Vere, *Marches*, 15.
94. *Victoires et Conquêtes*, 242.
95. Schepeler, "Albuera Once More," 340.
96. Cole and Gwynn, *Memoirs of Sir Lowry Cole*, 74, Journal of Roverea.
97. Sherer, *Recollections*, 160.
98. "The 'Die Hards' at Albuera," *The Times*, 25 February 1915, Ensign Benjamin Hobhouse to his father, 17 May 1811.
99. Roberts, *Military Instructions*, 9.
100. "Anecdotes of Sir William Inglis," in Maxwell, *Sketches*, vol 2, 359.
101. "The 'Die Hards' at Albuera," *The Times*, 25 February 1915, Ensign Benjamin Hobhouse to his father, 17 May 1811.
102. In point of fact, both the Buffs and the French were right. The French claimed to have taken six Colours from the three bat-

talions of Colborne's brigade but what they actually seized were four complete sets of staffs and Colours from the 2/48th and 2/66th Foot but only the staffs, cords and some of the cloth from the Colours of the Buffs. In the French army of the period, the staff and the eagle that perched atop it were regarded as more important than the actual cloth Colour itself and for this reason, their possession of the staffs of the Buff's colours led them to believe that they took that regiment's Colours. For their part, the Buffs, having repossessed most of the cloth of their two Colours which, in the British army, are regarded as more important than the staffs, have caused them to claim that they retained the Colours they fought under at Albuera. On this subject, see Luis Sorando Muzas, "Trophies of Albuera (May 16, 1811)," *Napoleon-Series* website.

103. Lapène, *Conquête*, 165.
104. "The 'Die Hards' at Albuera," *The Times*, 25 February 1915, Ensign Benjamin Hobhouse to his father, 17 May 1811.
105. "The Learned Saddler," *London Times*, 26 August 1930, letter of Thomas Bennett.
106. Sherer, *Recollections*, 160.
107. Cole and Gwynn, *Memoirs of Sir Lowry Cole*, 74, Journal of Roverea.
108. Schepeler, "Albuera Once More," 341.
109. Lindau, *Erinnerungen*, 36.
110. AO, MU 2635, letter from an officers of the 2nd Light Infantry Battalion, King's German Legion, 27 May 1811.
111. "The 'Die Hards' at Albuera," *The Times*, 25 February 1915, Ensign Benjamin Hobhouse to his father, 17 May 1811.

Chapter 8: "The Royal Welch Fusiliers ... the very thing"
Unless otherwise noted, this chapter is based on the following sources: D'Urban, *Journal*; Esdaile, *The Peninsular War*; Fortescue, *A History of the British Army*, vol 8; McGuffie, *Peninsular Cavalry General*; Oman, *History of the Peninsular War*, vol 4; Thompson, *Fatal Hill*; Vere, *Marches, Movements, and Operations*.

On casualty statistics and casualty treatment at Albuera, see: Beresford's dispatch to Wellington dated 18 May 1811, *Dispatches*, vol 7, 588; Brooke, "Journal"; Guthrie, *Commentaries*; Leslie, *Military Journal*; Oman, *Peninsular War*, vol 4, appendices XV and XVI; and Mary Anne Wellington, *The Soldier's Daughter* (London, 1846). Oman carried out the most detailed analysis of the loss figures for both armies at Albuera of any historian who has written on the subject and his

figures have been followed here. On the fate of individual British and German officers, see John A. Hall, *A History of the Peninsular War. Volume VII. The Biographical Dictionary of British Officers Killed and Wounded, 1808-1814* (London, 1998).

On the history of the Royal Welch Fusiliers during 1810-1811, see: Broughton-Mainwaring, *Historical Record of the Royal Welch Fusiliers*; Cary and McCance, *Reg Records*; and Glover, *Astonishing Infantry*.

On Pearson, see biography, *British Military Journal*, 1816 quoted in Harris, "Two Military Miniatures."

On campaigning in the summer of 1811, see: Bell, *Soldier's Glory*; Blakeney, *A Boy in the Peninsular War*; Cooper, *Rough Notes of Seven Campaigns*; Knowles, *The War in the Peninsula*; Leslie, *Military Journal*; Basil Liddell Hart, ed. *Letters of Private Wheeler*; Madden, "Diary"; Maxwell, *Peninsular Sketches*; McGuffie, ed., *Peninsular Cavalry General*; Fletcher, ed., *For King and Country*; Sherer, *Recollections*; Swabey, "Diary; and Tomkinson, *The Diary of a Cavalry Officer*.

1. "The Soldier's Prayer" dates from the late 18th century and is attributed to Sergeant "Bauldy" Corson, see Roy Palmer, ed., *The Rambling Soldier* (London, 1885), ix.
2. McGuffie, *Cavalry General*, 106, Long to brother, 22 May 1811.
3. Cooper, *Rough Notes*, 61.
4. J. Emerson, "Recollections," in Maxwell, *Sketches*, vol 2, 234.
5. Schepeler, "Albuera Once More," 341.
6. Or so the commanding officer of the 3rd Foot reported. Fortunately, many of the casualties of the 3rd Foot were prisoners and so many escaped and returned to the ranks after this strength report was written and the unit's strength rose so rapidly that the Buffs received the nickname of the "Resurrection Men." See Guthrie, *Commentaries*, 38-39.
7. Cooper, *Rough Notes*, 66.
8. RWFM, Harrison correspondence, Harrison to mother, 24 May 1811.
9. Groves, *66th Berkshire Regiment*, 53, Letter of Lieutenant John Clarke.
10. Lindau, *Erinnungen*, 38.
11. Schepeler, "Albuera Once More," 341.
12. Cooper, *Rough Notes*, 66.
13. Sherer, *Recollections*, 163.
14. Schepeler, "Albuera Once More," 341.
15. J. Emerson, "Recollections of the Late War," in Maxwell, ed., *Peninsular Sketches*, 234.
16. J. Emerson, "Recollections of the Late War," in Maxwell, ed., *Peninsular Sketches*, 233-234.
17. Albany Institute, Prevost Papers, John A.

Prevost to August Prevost [no date but June or July] 1811,

18. Guthrie, *Commentaries*, 542.

19. Guthrie, *Commentaries*, 199-200.

20. Guthrie, *Commentaries*, 37.

21. "Reminiscences of a Light Dragoon," *United Service Journal*, November 1840, 362-363.

22. D'Urban, *Journal*, 217.

23. Brooke, "Journal," 429.

24. Madden, "Diary," 523.

25. Anonymous, *The Military Memoirs of an Infantry Officers* (Aberdeen, 1833), 163.

26. Boutflower, *Journal of a Surgeon*, 93-94.

27. RWFM, Harrison papers, Harrison to mother, 24 May 1811.

28. McGuffie, *Peninsular Cavalry General*, 118, Long to brother, 26 June 1811.

29. William Tomkinson, *The Diary of a Cavalry Officer* (1894, reprinted Staplehurst, 1999), 103.

30. John Mills, *For King and Country* (Staplehurst, 1995), 46, Mills to mother, 27 June 1811.

31. J. Emerson, "Peninsular Sketches," in Maxwell, *Sketches*, vol 2, 240.

32. Thompson, *Fatal Hill*, 156, Beresford to Wellington, 20 May 1811.

33. Thompson, *Fatal Hill*, 155, Wellington to Beresford, 19 May 1811.

34. Stanhope, *Notes of Conversations with the Duke of Wellington*, 90.

35. *Dispatches*, vol 7, 588, Beresford to Wellington, 18 May 1811.

36. *Gentleman's Magazine*, vol 81 (1811), 658.

37. Mills, *For King and Country*, 46, Mills to mother, 27 June 1811.

38. Fortescue, *History of the British Army*, vol 8, 189, Stewart to Castlereagh, 22 May 1811.

39. Thompson, *Fatal Hill*, Wellesley to Wellesley-Pole, 2 July 1811.

40. D'Urban, *Journal*, 233.

41. William Warre, *Letters from the Peninsula 1808-1812* (1909, reprinted Staplehurst, 1999), 121, Warre to father, 20 June 1811.

42. In later life, Beresford was forced to fight a second battle of Albuera against a number of detractors, the foremost being William Napier, who castigated him in print in the third volume of his history of the Peninsular War with the statement that "no general ever gained so great a battle with so little increase of military reputation as Marshal Beresford." This led to a pamphlet war between Beresford and Napier, and their supporters, during the 1830s but, in replying to Napier's criticisms, Beresford unfortunately incited a new controversy with the nephew of Brigadier-General Robert Long, which led to another exchange of pamphlets. See Appendix E.

43. Ernest Picard and Louis Tuetey, eds., *Correspondence inédite de Napoleon I*, vol 4 (1811), (Paris, 1913), 440, No. 5820, to Soult, 21 July 1811. On St. Helena, Napoleon blamed Soult for losing this battle by not pushing home his cavalry and cutting the allies to pieces, see Peter Hayman, *Soult: Napoleon's Maligned Marshal* (London, 1990), 163n.

44. Tompkinson, *Diary*, 108-109.

45. Cole and Gwynn, *Memoirs of Sir Lowry Cole*, 77, Hardinge to Cole, 24 May 1811.

46. Cannon, *Historical Records of the Seventh Regiment*, 63-64, Stewart to Beresford, 26 May 1811. On the commissioning of sergeants, see *Reg Records*, vol 1, 243-244. From the 1/23rd Foot, Sergeant David Scott was commissioned as an ensign in the 11th Foot.

47. Cannon, *Historical Record of the Seventh*, 64, Stewart to Beresford, 26 May 1811.

48. Despite his brevet promotion, it was Pearson's regimental seniority as a major which determined his duties in the Welch Fusiliers. The system of brevet promotions could lead to some strange anomalies such as officers with the regimental rank of captain serving as generals.

49. NAB, WO 17, vol 126, Monthly Returns of the 1/23 Foot for 25 May, 25 June, 25 Aug, 25 Sept and 25 Oct 1811.

50. Oman, *History*, vol 4, 420

51. *Maréchal* Soult, quoted in Oman, *History*, vol 4, 452.

52. Bell, *Soldier's Glory*, 9.

53. McGuffie, *Peninsular Cavalry General*, 202, Journal, 12 July 1811.

54. Cooper, *Rough Notes*, 80-81.

55. The best account of how a good regiment would have carried out its march routine in the Peninsula will be found in Charles Oman, *Wellington's Army*, 256-267.

56. Bell, *Soldier's Glory*, 60.

57. Sherer, *Recollections*, 42.

58. Cooper, *Rough Notes*, 66.

59. Cooper, *Rough Notes*, 66.

60. Cooper, *Rough Notes*, 66.

61. Cooper, *Rough Notes*, 66.

62. Robert Knowles, *The War in the Peninsula* (1913, reprinted Staplehurst, 2004), 34.

63. Cooper, *Rough Notes*, 67.

64. Paul Thiébault, *Mémoires du Général Baron Thiébault* (5 vols, Paris, 1913), vol 4, 513-514.

65. Thiébault, *Mémoires*, vol 4, 414.

66. Cooper, *Rough Notes*, 67.

67. Knowles, *War in the Peninsula*, 34.

68. Knowles, *War in the Peninsula*, 34-35.

69. Knowles, *War in the Peninsula*, 35.
70. Thiébault, *Mémoires*, vol 4, 516.
71. Thiébault, *Mémoires*, vol 4, 516. Souham had reached the rank of *général de brigade* when he became involved in Moreau's plot against Napoleon in 1804. He was arrested but later released although he was not given active military employment until 1807.
72. Thiébault, *Mémoires*, 524. Ironically, both Thiébault and Souham were criticized by Marmont for engaging in needless fighting, see Thiébault, vol iv, 528.
73. Knowles, *War in the Peninsula*, 35.
74. Leach, *Rough Sketches*, 235.
75. *Dispatches*, vol 8, 303, Wellington to Liverpool, 29 September 1811.
76. Cooper, *Rough Notes*, 69.
77. Broughton-Mainwaring, *Historical Record*, 128.
78. My account of the action at Aldea de Ponte differs somewhat from that provided by Wellington in his dispatch of 29 September 1811 which was followed by Fortescue (*British Army*, vol 9, 266-268) and Oman (*Peninsular War*, vol 4, 578-580). Wellington noted that the cavalry, which were stationed on the far side of the village, were forced through Aldea by the French but did not mention Pearson's light companies as defending the village itself. Thiébault, however, confirms that there were British infantry in the village before the first French attack commenced although he overestimates their strength. After Pearson was forced out of Aldea, Wellington ordered Pakenham to retake it, which he promptly did and then assumed a position to support Pearson, who moved back into Aldea. In the early evening Souham pushed Pearson out of the village before being pushed back, in turn, by Pakenham who, however, did not re-enter Aldea for reasons given in the text.
79. *Dispatches*, vol 8, 303, Wellesley to Liverpool, 29 September 1811.

Chapter 9: "As you were! As you were?"
Unless otherwise noted, this chapter is based on the following sources.

The official correspondence concerning Pearson's command and responsibilities on the St. Lawrence in 1812-1813 will be found in Record Group 8 I, British Military Records, of the National Library and Archives of Canada, particularly vols 89, 366, 387, 676-678, 681, 688, and 728-729.

On the background of the War of 1812 and its course, particularly in the St. Lawrence area, until May 1813, see: Ernest Cruikshank, *Documentary History of the Campaigns upon the Niagara Frontier in 1812-1814* (9 vols, Welland, 1896-1908), particularly vols 5, 6 and 7; Donald E. Graves, *Field of Glory: The Battle of Crysler's Farm, 1813* (Toronto, 1999); John Grodzinski, "The Vigilant Superintendence of the Whole District: The War of 1812 on the Upper St. Lawrence," MA Thesis, Royal Military College, Kingston 2002; Hitsman, *Incredible War*; Robert Malcomson, *Lords of the Lake: The Naval War on Lake Ontario* (Toronto, 1998).

On privateers in the War of 1812, see: George Coggeshall, *History of American Privateers and Letters of Marque* (New York, 1861); and Edgar Maclay, *A History of American Privateers* (London, 1900).

On the history of Prescott, its fortifications and its role in the war, see Robert Burns, *Fort Wellington: A Narrative and Structural History, 1812-1838* (Ottawa, 1979).

On Pearson's "reign of terror" among the troops in the garrison at Prescott, see NLAC, MG 19, A39, Clark Papers, Order Book, 1813-1814.

1. A broadside ballad dating to the American Revolutionary War, see Lewis Winstock, *Songs of the Redcoats* (London, 1885), 118.
2. RWFM, Harrison correspondence, Harrison to father, 5 November 1811.
3. Albany Institute, Prevost Papers, John A. Prevost to Augustin Prevost, 15 March 1812.
4. Guthrie, *Commentaries*, 458-459.
5. Sutherland, *His Majesty's Gentlemen*, 295.
6. Madison to Congress, 5 November 1811, quoted in Donald Hickey, *The War of 1812: A Forgotten Conflict* (Chicago, 1989), 22.
7. NLAC RG I, IV, vol 123, documents and affidavits concerning the capture of the schooner *Mary Ann* dated July and August 1812.
8. NLAC RG I, IV, vol 123, documents and affidavits concerning the capture of the schooner *Mary Ann* dated July and August 1812. Captain Isaac Bray and the *Buckskin* were taken by His Majesty's Frigate, *Statira*, on 8 August 1812. *Buckskin* was fitted out as a Canadian privateer, the *Fly*, and made a number of cruises in 1813, capturing or destroying 12 American vessels before being captured by the USS *Enprerise* in August, 1813, see C.H.J. Snider, *Under the Red Jack: Privateers of the Maritime Provinces of Canada in the War of 1812* (London, 1828), 232-236.
9. NLAC, RG8 I, vol 688a, 103, Baynes to Lethbridge, 10 July 1812.
10. AO, Miscellaneous Mss., Extract from *Literary Garland*, 7 June 1849.
11. NLAC, RG 8 I, vol 681, 323, Prevost to Brock, 19 October 1812.
12. Dunlop, *Tiger Dunlop*, 14.
13. "Artillero Viejo," "How to Fight Brother Jonathan," *Museum of Foreign Literature*,

Science and Art, vol 42 (1840), 211.

14. NLAC, RG8 I, vol 387, 10, Bruyeres to Prevost, 19 January 1813.

15. NLAC, RG 8 I, vol 388, 258, Nicolls to Prevost, 31 December 1814.

16. NLAC, RG 8 I, vol 695a, Pearson to Baynes, 2 December 1812.

17. Ross to Parish, 23 July 1813, in Harry Landon, "British Sympathizers in St. Lawrence County during the War of 1812," *New York History* (April 1954), 134.

18. Lydia Hayward, *Narrative of Mrs. Lydia Hayward* (Union Mills, 1846), 7

19. Hayward, *Narrative*, 7-8.

20. NLAC, RG8 I, vol 681, 35, Harvey to Baynes, 16 November 1813.

21. The use of intelligence by both sides during the War of 1812 could form the subject of a separate book.

22. NAB, WO 6, vol 133, 47, Castlereagh to York, 1808.

23. Le Couteur, *Merry Hearts*, 113.

24. Le Couteur, *Merry Hearts*, 113.

25. AO, Miscellaneous Mss., Extract from *Literary Garland*, 7 June 1849.

26. Le Couteur, *Merry Hearts*, 113.

27. *Montreal Gazette*, 10 November 1812.

28. Le Couteur, *Merry Hearts*, 109.

29. NAC, RG 9, IB1, vol 2, Pearson to Shaw, 19 January 1813.

30. NLAC, RG8 I, vol 678, 79, Pearson to De Rottenburg, 7 February, 1813.

31. AO, Miscellaneous Mss., Extract from *Literary Garland*, 7 June 1849.

32. AO, Miscellaneous Mss., Extract from *Literary Garland*, 7 June 1849.

33. AO, Miscellaneous Mss., Extract from *Literary Garland*, 7 June 1849.

34. AO, Miscellaneous Mss., Extract from *Literary Garland*, 7 June 1849.

35. AO, Miscellaneous Mss., Extract from *Literary Garland*, 7 June 1849.

36. AO, Miscellaneous Mss., Extract from *Literary Garland*, 7 June 1849.

37. NLAC, CO 42, vol 121, 117, Return of ordnance and stores captured at Ogdensburg, 22 February 1813.

38. *Doc. Hist.* vol 5, 78, Dearborn to Armstrong, 25 February, 1813.

39. AO, Miscellaneous Mss., Extract from *Literary Garland*, 7 June 1849.

40. William Boss, *The Stormont, Dundas and Glengarry Highlanders* (Ottawa, 1952), 218.

41. NLAC, RG8 I, vol 729, 50, Pearson to Freer, 29 March 1813.

42. Le Couteur, *Merry Hearts*, 103.

43. On the raising and early history of the Incorporated Militia Battalion of Upper Canada, see Ernest A. Cruikshank, "Record of the Service of Canadian Regiments in the War of 1812 – V. The Incorporated Militia," *Selected Papers of the Canadian Military Institute*, 6 (1894-1895), 9-23; and William Gray, *Soldiers of the King: The Upper Canadian Militia 1812-1815* (Boston Mills, 1995).

44. NLAC, MG 19, A39, Clark Papers, Order Book, Prescott, Garrison Order, 13 May 1813.

45. NLAC, MG 19, A39, Clark Papers, Order, Book, Garrison Order, 26 May 1813.

46. NLAC, MG 19, A39, Clark Papers, Order Book, Garrison Order, 29 May 1813.

47. NLAC, MG 19, A39, Clark Papers, Order Book, Garrison Order, 27 May 1813.

48. NLAC, MG 19, A39, Clark Papers, Order Book, Garrison Order, 5 July 1813.

49. NLAC, MG 19, A39, Clark Papers, Order Book, Garrison Order, 5 July 1813.

50. NLAC, MG 19, A39, Clark Papers, Order Book, Garrison Order, 27 July 1813.

51. NLAC, MG 19, A39, Clark Papers, Order Book, Garrison Order, 25 April 1813.

52. NLAC, MG 19, A39, Clark Papers, Order Book, various orders issued at Prescott between March and August 1813.

53. NLAC, MG 19, A39, Clark Papers, Garrison Order, 20 May 1813

Chapter 10: "The bravest men I have ever seen

Unless otherwise noted, this chapter is based on the following sources.

The official correspondence concerning Pearson's command and responsibilities on the St. Lawrence in 1813-1814 will be found in Record Group 8 I, British Military Records, of the National Library and Archives of Canada, particularly vols 16, 19, 553, 556, 655, 679, 681, 683, 688, 690 and 700.

On the background of the War of 1812 and its course, particularly in the St. Lawrence area, from June 1813 to May 1814, see: Cruikshank, *Documentary History*, particularly vols 7, 8 and 9; Graves, *Field of Glory*; Grodzinski, "The Vigilant Superintendence of the Whole District: The War of 1812 on the Upper St. Lawrence"; Hitsman, *The Incredible War of 1812*; and Malcomson, *Lords of the Lake*.

My account of the Crysler's Farm campaign and battle is based directly on my book *Field of Glory*.

On the record of the Welch Fusiliers in 1812-1814, see Glover, *Astonishing Infantry*.

On Pearson, see biography, *British Military Journal*, 1816 quoted in Harris, "Two Military Miniatures."

On Hill, see *Army Lists*, 1807-1814.

1. "The Bold Canadian," a period ballad from the War of 1812, see Morris Zaslow, *The De-*

fended Border (Toronto, 1964), 303-305.

2. Dunlop, *Tiger Dunlop*, 24.

3. *American State Papers, Military Affairs*, vol 1 (Washington, 1832), 384, Armstrong to Anderson, 26 July 1813.

4. NLAC, RG8 I, vol 679, 366, Pearson to Prevost, 9 August 1813.

5. NLAC, RG8 I, vol 679, 488, Pearson to Baynes, 25 August 1813.

6. NLAC, RG 8 I, vol 679, 574, Pearson to Baynes, 30 August 1813.

7. NLAC, RG 8 I, vol 679, 171, Pearson to Baynes, 12 October 1813.

8. AO, MU 1054, Ford Papers, A. Ford to D. Ford, 21 October 1813.

9. NLAC, RG5 A1, vol 26, 12127, Campbell to Halton, 27 February 1816.

10. NLAC, RG8 I, vol 704, 205, Pearson to Harvey, 12 April 1814.

11. Anonymous, "First Campaign of An A.D.C.," *Military and Naval Magazine*, No. 13, 256.

12. Winfield Scott, *Memoirs of Lieut.-General Scott* (2 vols, New York, 1864), vol 1, 107.

13. J. Smyth Carter, *History of Dundas* (Brockville, 1905), 171.

14. AO, MU 1032, Recollections of the Battle of Crysler's Farm by Colonel John Sewell.

15. John Boyd, *Documents and Facts Relating to Military Events* (Washington, 1816), Boyd to Armstrong, 29 April 1815.

16. UCV Archives, Ronald Way papers, Loucks narrative.

17. AO, MU 1032, Recollections of the Battle of Crysler's Farm by Colonel John Sewell.

18. AO, MS 537, Extract from a letter of Lieutenant-Colonel John Harvey, 12 November 1813.

19. AO, MU 1032, Recollections of the Battle of Crysler's Farm by Colonel John Sewell.

20. AO, MU 1032, Recollections of the Battle of Crysler's Farm by Colonel John Sewell.

21. AO, MU 1032, Recollections of the Battle of Crysler's Farm by Colonel John Sewell.

22. *Appleton's Encyclopedia of American Biography* (7 vols, New York, 1888), Walbach entry.

23. AO, MU 1032, Recollections of the Battle of Crysler's Farm by Colonel John Sewell.

24. AO, MS 537, Extract from a letter of Lieutenant-Colonel John Harvey, 12 November 1813.

25. NLAC, RG8 I, vol 681, Morrison to De Rottenburg, 12 November 1813.

26. For comments on their leaders by American officers who served in the 1813 St. Lawrence campaign, see Graves, *Field of Glory*, 286-290.

27. James Wilkinson, *Memoirs of My Own Times* (3 vols, Philadelphia, 1816, vol 3, 65n.

28. Dunlop, *Tiger Dunlop*, 26.

29. Dunlop, *Tiger Dunlop*, 25-26.

30. Dunlop, *Tiger Dunlop*, 27.

31. NLAC, MG 19, A39, Clark Papers, Order Book, Garrison Order, 6 February 1814.

32. Burns, *History of Fort Wellington*, 55.

33. NLAC, MG 19, A39, Clark Papers, Order Book, Garrison Order, 2 March 1814.

34. *NLAC, RG8 I, vol Prevost to Torrens, 31 July 1813.*

35. James, *Iron Duke*, 239.

36. NLAC, RG 8 I, vol 683, 8, Drummond to Prevost, 8 April 1814.

37. NLAC, RG 8 I, vol 556, 120, Freer to Pearson, 17 April 1814.

Chapter 11: "A fair trial of nerve and discipline"

Unless otherwise noted, this chapter is based on the following sources: Donald E. Graves, *Redcoats and Grey Jackets: The Battle of Chippawa, 1814* (Toronto, 1994) and *Where Right and Glory Lead! The Battle of Lundy's Lane, 1814* (Toronto, 1997); Hitsman, *Incredible War of 1812*; and Malcomson, *Lords of the Lake*.

1. "The British Bayoneteers," a song of the Napoleonic period sung to the tune of "The British Grenadiers." See Lewis Winstock, *Songs and Music of the Redcoats* (London, 1970), 110. The third line of the second verse has been altered here from "the French well know" to "the Yanks well know" as there is no doubt that this song, sung to one of the most popular tunes in the British army of the time, crossed the ocean and was suitably modified.

2. Le Couteur, *Merry Hearts*, 54.

3. NLAC, MG 24, L8, "Saberdache Bleu," vol 4, Mermet to Viger, 23 May 1814.

4. NLAC, MG 24, L8, "Saberdache Bleu," vol 4, Mermet to Viger, 23 May 1814.

5. PHS, Parker Papers, Armstrong to Brown, 10 June 1814.

6. CBD, 41, Chauncey to Brown, 25 June 1814.

7. C.F. Klinck and J.J. Talman, *The Journal of Major John Norton. 1816* (Toronto, 1970), 348.

8. These weapons, of a calibre not normally used for field artillery, were actually experimental guns, short in length and light in weight, cast in the reign of George II which had been sent to North America as part of the equipment for General John Burgoyne's expedition in 1777. They were still in the inventory of the RA in North America when war broke out in 1812 and saw some service. Unfortunately, like many hybrid, dual-purpose weapons, they fulfilled neither of their roles very well as they were too heavy to be good field pieces and too short to be good siege pieces.

9. *Doc. Hist.*, I, 38, Brown to Armstrong, 9 July 1814.

10. *Doc. Hist.*, I, 44, Scott to Brown, 14 July 1814.
11. Norton, *Journal*, 349.
12. Norton, *Journal*, 349.
13. Norton, *Journal*, 349.
14. *Doc. Hist.*, vol 2, 363, Porter to Stone, 26 May 1840.
15. *Doc. Hist.*, vol 2, 363, Porter to Stone, 26 May 1840.
16. *Doc. Hist.*, vol 2, 363, Porter to Stone, 26 May 1840.
17. UCA, Journal of the Reverend George Ferguson, 60.
18. Norton, *Journal*, 50.
19. Norton, *Journal*, 350.
20. Scott, *Memoirs*, vol 1, 128.
21. UCA, Ferguson, Journal, 60.
22. Mary Cates, "Benjamin Ropes' Autobiography," *Essex Institute Historical Collections*, 91 (1955).
23. *Doc. Hist.*, vol 1, 44, Scott to Adjutant-General, 12 July 1814.
24. MDAH, Edward Randolph autobiography.
25. UCA, Ferguson, Journal, 60.
26. AO, Niagara Historical Society Papers, Stevenson to Addison, July 1814,
27. CHS, Howard, "Letterbook", 110.
28. It might seem curious to the reader that formed bodies of troops could move through these woods without difficulty. The Niagara area, however, had been settled for more than three decades and the pioneers were prodigious woodcutters as it was not only their fuel in the winter but their main source of building materials. It was therefore not long before the undergrowth in these woods disappeared and they became considerably thinned out, permitting troops to move through them.
29. NYSL, Gardner Papers, Jesup to Brown, 12 July 1814.
30. NYSL, Gardner Papers, Jesup to Brown, 12 July 1814.
31. *Doc. Hist.*, vol 1, 46, .Scott to Adjutant General, 15 July 1814.
32. Norton, *Journal*, 350.
33. *Doc. Hist.*, vol 1, 38, Brown to Armstrong, 7 July 1814.
34. Norton, *Journal*, 350.
35. NLAC, RG 8 I, vol 694, 51, Riall to Drummond, 6 July 1814.
36. *Doc. Hist.*, vol 1, 35, Drummond to Prevost, 10 July 1814.
37. NLAC, RG8 I, vol 1222, 62, Prevost to Drummond, 12 July 1814.
38. NAB, WO 55, vol 1228, 338, Prevost to Glasgow, 26 August 1814.
39. CHS, Howard Letterbook, 112.
40. *Doc. Hist.*, vol 1, 38, Brown to Armstrong, 7 July 1814.
41. On encountering Pearson during the retreat, see Thaddeus Leavitt, *History of Leeds and Grenville* (Belleville, 1879), 70, John Kilborn, "Biographical Sketch."

Chapter 12: "Full blooded eaters of the pumpkin"

Unless otherwise noted, this chapter is based on my works *Where Right and Glory Lead!* and "William Drummond and the Battle of Fort Erie," *Canadian Military History* 1 (1992), 1-18; Hitsman, *Incredible War of 1812*; and Malcomson, *Lords of the Lake*.

On the course of the war in Europe in 1815 and the role of the Welch Fusiliers, see Michael Glover, *Astonishing Infantry* and *Napoleonic Wars*.

1. "The British Bayoneteers," the ever popular "British Grenadiers" with words sung during the Napoleonic Wars, see Lewis Winstock, *Songs and Music of the Redcoats* (London, 1970), 111.
2. NLAC, MG 19, A39, Clark Papers, file 3, Right Division Order Book, 1814.
3. BHC, Andrew Warffe diary.
4. NLAC, MG 19, A39, Clark Papers, file 3, Right Division Order Book, Brigade Order, 22 July 1814.
5. In *Where Right and Glory Lead!*, my study of the battle of Lundy's Lane published in 1997, I did not stress the fact that it was the veteran Thomas Pearson, not Drummond or Riall, who actually chose the fine defensive ground at Lundy's Lane which placed the British army in a good position when the battle began. That omission has now been corrected.
6. Although the British army suffered heavier casualties at Fort Erie on 15 August 1814 and at New Orleans on 8 January 1815, the total casualties suffered by both sides at Lundy's Lane make it the most sanguinary engagement of the War of 1812. The European reader, used to the heavy losses in Napoleonic engagements, should note that in North America, the distances were great and the armies very small.
7. John Linn, *Annals of Buffalo Valley* (Harrisburg, 1877), Brady to Vincent, 28 July 1814.
8. Norton, *Journal*, 357.
9. *Facts Relative to the Campaign on the Niagara* (Boston, 1815), Leavenworth Letter of 15 January 1815.
10. *Facts Relative to the Campaign on the Niagara*, Leavenworth Letter of 15 January 1815.
11. Norton, *Journal*, 35.
12. Dunlop, *Tiger Dunlop*, 40.

13. Norton, *Journal*, 357.
14. CL, War of 1812 Papers, Miller to wife, 28 July 1814.
15. David Douglass, "An Original Narrative of the Niagara Campaign of 1814," *Niagara Frontier* 46 (1964), 24.
16. CL, War of 1812 papers, Le Couteur to Robison, 27 July 1814.
17. Scott, *Memoirs*, vol 1, 343.
18. NLAC, MG 19, A39, Clark Papers, account of Lundy's Lane.
19. *American Watchman*, Letter dated 20 August 1814.
20. James Commins letters, "The War of 1812 on the Canadian Frontier," *JSAHR*, 18 (1939), 199-211.
21. DCL, Weekes Papers, Letter of John W. Weekes, 1 August 1814.
22. The British brass 6-pdr. gun captured at Lundy's Lane is currently on display at Fort McNair in Washington.
23. NLAC, RG8 I, vol 685, 56, Drummond to Prevost, 12 August 1814.
24. NLAC, RG8 I, vol 685, 56, Drummond to Prevost, 12 August 1814.
25. Norton, *Journal*, 362.
26. Dunlop, *Tiger Dunlop*, 40.
27. Dunlop, *Tiger Dunlop*, 42.
28. NAB, WO 55, vol 1860, Diary of Lt. Philpotts, RE, 14 August 1814.
29. NLAC, RG8 I, vol 686, 93, Arrangements for the Attack on Fort Erie, 14 August 1814.
30. Lecouteur, *Merry Hearts*, 193.
31. Norton, *Journal*, 363.
32. Merritt, *Journal*, 69.
33. LeCouteur, *Merry Hearts*, 193.
34. NLAC, RG 8 I, vol 685, 123, Drummond to Prevost, 21 August 1814.
35. *Doc. Hist.*, vol 1, 182, Drummond to Yeo, 18 August 1814.
36. *Doc. Hist.*, vol 2, 211, Brown to Monroe, 19 September 1814.
37. NLAC, CO 42, vol 128-2, 121, De Watteville to Drummond, 19 September 1814.
38. NLAC, RG8 I, vol 685, 216, Drummond to Prevost, 19 September 1814.
39. *Royal Gazette and New Brunswick Advertiser*, 19 November 1814.
40. *Royal Gazette and New Brunswick Advertiser*, 28 November 1814.
41. John Phillipart, *Royal Military Calendar* (London, 1816), vol 4, 341.
42. Glover, *Astonishing Infantry*, 57.

Epilogue: "The sodger's wealth is honour."

On the later career of Pearson and the circumstances of his family, see the wills of Reverend Thomas Horner Pearson and Thomas Pearson in the Family Record Centre in London, Pearson family records in the Somerset Record Office and O'Byrne, *Naval Biography*. On matters relating to the Welch Fusiliers, see Cary and McCance, *Reg Records* and Glover, *Astonishing Infantry*.

1. "The sodger's return," with words by Robbie Burns, was a favourite of Scots soldiers during the Napoleonic Wars, see Winstock, *Songs of the Redcoats*, 114-115.
2. *Reg Records*, vol 2, 6.
3. *Reg Records*, vol 2, on dates indicated.
4. Hibbert, *George IV*, 396-397.
5. Pearson to Major Ross, 3 August 1830, quoted in *Reg Records*, vol 2, 20-21.
6. Glover, *Astonishing Infantry*, 61.
7. Glover, *Astonishing Infantry*, 61-62.
8. Glover, *Astonishing Infantry*, 61-62.
9. *Bath Chronicle* on dates indicated.
10. Charles Dickens, *Pickwick Papers* (New York, 1944), 428-429.
11. *Bath Chronicle*, 21 April 1845.
12. Dunlop, *Tiger Dunlop*, 19
13. *USJ*, 1847, Pt II, 479.
14. NAB, WO 42, vol 37, 100, Application and certificate of Anne Pearson, 14 July 1847.
15. Over the years, the custom of keeping a goat, originated by the Welch Fusiliers, has spread throughout the English-speaking world. The Fusiliers' allied Canadian regiment, the *Royal 22e Régiment du Canada*, keeps a goat as do many other units in the Commonwealth. In the first decade of the 20th century, the Fusiliers presented a goat to the United States Marine Corps to commemorate the time the two corps fought alongside each other at the relief of Peking. The Marines kept their goat until they adopted a bulldog, an animal not much less intractable, as their symbol.

BIBLIOGRAPHY

PRIMARY SOURCES

Archival Sources

Albany Institute of Art and History, Albany
  Augustin Prevost Papers

Archives of Ontario, Toronto
  Sir John Harvey Papers
  Miscellaneous Manuscripts, Extract from
    Literary Garland, 7 June 1849.
  MS 537, Extract from a letter of Lieuten-
    ant-Colonel John Harvey, 12 Novem-
    ber 1813.
  MU 2635, Military Scrapbook
  MU 1054, Ford Papers
  MU 1032, Recollections of the Battle
    of Crysler's Farm by Colonel John
    Sewell.
  Niagara Historical Society Papers

British Museum, London
  Additional Mss 37425f65, La Tour-Mau-
    bourg to Soult, 27 May 1811.

Burton Historical Collection, Detroit Public
Library
  Andrew Warffe Diary.

Connecticut Historical Society, Hartford
  George Howard Letterbook

Clements Library, Ann Arbor
  War of 1812 Papers

Dartmouth College Library, Hanover
  John W. Weekes Papers

Family History Centre, London
  Wills of Thomas Horner Pearson and
    Thomas Pearson

Mississippi Department of Archives and
History, Jackson
  Autobiography of Edward Randolph

National Library and Archives of Canada,
Ottawa

Manuscript Group 11 (Colonial Of-
  fice 42), Original Correspondence,
  Canada
Manuscript Group 19, A39, Clark Papers,
Manuscript Group 24, L8, Viger Papers
Manuscript Group 24, A9, Diary of Anne
  Elinor Prevost
Manuscript Group 24, F70, Diary of Lt.
  Thomas Evans, 1800-1801
Record Group 1, Records of the Executive
  Council
Record Group 5, Records of the Civil
  Secretary's Office
Record Group 8 I, British Military and
  Naval Records
Record Group 9, Pre-Confederation Mili-
  tia Records

National Archives of Britain, Kew
  Admiralty 36, Ship's Registers
  War Office 6, Secretary of State, Out-
    Letters
  War Office 17, Monthly Returns of the
    Army
  War Office 25, Registers, Various
  War Office 27, Inspection Reports
  War Office 31, Commander-in-Chief's
    Papers
  War Office 42, Pension Records
  War Office 55, Ordnance Office, Out-
    Letters

New York State Library, Albany
  Charles K. Gardner Papers

Pennsylania Historical Society, Philadelphia
  Daniel Parker Papers

Royal Engineers Museum, Gillingham, Kent
  John Hancock, "Military Engineers in the
    Peninsular War," Ross to Dalrymple,
    20 May 1811, Elvas.

Royal Welch Fusiliers Museum, Gwynned, Wales
  Harrison papers
  Hill papers
Service Historique de l'Armée de Terre, Paris
  Carton C8, 356, Reports of the Army of the Midi, 16 April and 1 June 1811
Somerset Record Office, Yeovil
  Church records relating to the Pearson and Horner Families of Somerset
United Church Archives, Toronto
  Journal of George Ferguson
Upper Canada Village Archives, Morrisburg
  Ronald Way papers, Loucks narrative.

Newspapers and Periodicals
American Watchman, Wilmington, Delaware, 1814
Bath Chronicle, 1843-1847
Gentleman's Magazine, 1811
Montreal Gazette, 1812
Nova Scotia Gazette, 1808-1810
Quebec Mercury, 1811
Royal Gazette, or New Brunswick Advertizer, 1809-1810

Published Official Documents
American State Papers. Class V. Military Affairs. Washington: Gales and Seaton, 1832.
Boyd, John. *Documents and Facts Relating to Military Events*. Washington: n.p., 1816.
Burriel, Antonio, ed. *Batalla de la Albuhera (Ganada Sobre los Francese Mandados por Soult el dia 16 de mayo de 1811, por el Exercito Aliado Español, Ingles y Portugues)*. Cadiz: 1811.
Cruikshank, Ernest, ed. *Documentary History of the Campaigns upon the Niagara Frontier in 1812-1814*. Welland: Tribune Press, 9 vols, 1896-1908), particularly vols 5, 6 and 7.
———, ed. *Documents Relating to the Invasion of the Niagara Peninsula by the United States Army, Commanded by General Jacob Brown in July and August, 1814*. Niagara-on-the-Lake: Niagara Historical Society, 1920.
Facts Relative to the Campaign on the Ni-

agara. Boston: Patriot Office, 1815.
Gurwood, John, ed. *The Dispatches of Field Marshal the Duke of Wellington, 1799-1818*. London: William Clowes, 13 vols, 1834-1839.
Picard, Ernest and Louis Tuetey, eds. *Correspondence inédit de Napoléon Ier. Tome IV (1811)*. Paris: Henri Charles-Lavauzelle, 1913.
Wellington, A.R. ed. *Supplementary Dispatches, Correspondence and Memoranda of Field Marshal Arthur, Duke of Wellington, 1797-1815*. London: 14 vols, 1858-1872.

Period Miitary Regulations, Treatises and Technical Literature
Advice to Officers of the British Army. London: G. Kearsley, 1783. [attributed to Francis Grose].
Cavalry Training, 1912. London: War Office, 1912.
Dundas, Henry. *Rules and Regulations for the Formation, Field-Exercise, and Movements of His Majesty's Forces*. London: T. Egerton, 1808.
Gassendi, Jean-Jacques Basilien de. *Aide-Memoire, à l'usage des Officiers d'Artillerie de France*. Paris: Magimel, 2 vols, 1801.
General Regulations and Orders for the Army. London: T. Egerton, 1811.
Instruction Concernant Les Manoeuvres de la Cavalerie Légère. Paris: Magimel, 1799.
Nosworthy, Brent, ed. *Writings on the French Napoleonic Art of War. By Marshals Bugeaud & Ney, & Baron de Jomini*. Mount Pearl: Ad Signa, 2003.
Reglamento práctico de instrucción de formaciones para recreadores históricos españoles. Tomado del manual *de Instrucción de 1808*. Madrid: Voluntarios de Madrid, 2004.
Roberts, David. *Military Instructions; Including Each Particular Motion of the Manual and Platoon Exercises; Elucidated with very Minute Drawings by Mr. R.K. Porter*. London: T. Egerton, 1798.
Standing Orders and Regulations for the Army in Ireland. 1794, reprinted London: Frederick Muller, 1969.

Biographical Encyclopedias, Registers and Dictionaries

Dictionary of American Biography. New York: Scribner, 1958-1964, 22 vols.

Dictionary of Canadian Biography. Toronto: University of Toronto Press, 1976-1988, vols 5-9.

Dictionary of National Biography. London: Smith, Elder, 65 vols.

Fierro, Alfred, Andre Palluel-Guillard and Jean Tulard. *Histoire et Dictionnaire du Consulat et de L'Empire.* Paris: Robert Lafont, 1995.

Great Britain, War Office. *A List of all the Officers of the Army and Royal Marines on Full and half-pay,* London: War Office, 1793-1832.

Kirby, E.L. ed. *Officers of The Royal Welch Fusiliers (23rd Regiment of Foot) 16 March 1689 to 4 August 1814.* N.p., 1997.

O'Byrne, William, ed. *A Naval Biographical Dictionary: Comprising the Life and Services of Every Living Officer in Her Majesty's Navy.* London: J. Murray, 1846.

Phillipart, John. *Royal Military Calendar.* London: T. Egerton, 4 vols, 1816.

Six, Georges. *Les généraux de la Revolution et de l'Empire.* Paris: Bordas, 1948.

Sutherland, Stewart. *His Majesty's Gentlemen: A Directory of British Regular Army Officers of the War of 1812.* Toronto: Iser, 2000).

Wilson, James and John Fiske, eds. *Appleton's Encyclopedia of American Biography.* New York: Appleton, 7 vols, 1888.

Published Memoirs, Diaries, Journals, Correspondence and Albuera Controversy Literature

Anonymous, "Reminiscences of a Light Dragoon," *United Service Journal,* November 1840.

———. *Strictures on Certain Passages of Lieutenant Colonel Napier's History of the Peninsular War which relate to the Military Opinions and Conduct of General Lord Viscount Beresford.* 1831, reprinted Chapelgarth: M. Thompson Publishing, 1995.

———. *Further Strictures on those Parts of Col. Napier's History of the Peninsular War which relate to the Military Opinions and Conduct of General Lord Viscount Beresford.* 1832, reprinted Chapelgarth: M. Thompson Publishing, 1995.

———, "First Campaign of An A.D.C.," *Military and Naval Magazine of the United States,* vol 4, no. 13.

———. *The Military Memoirs of an Infantry Officer.* Aberdeen: author, 1833.

"Artillero Viejo," "How to Fight Brother Jonathan," *Museum of Foreign Literature, Science and Art,* vol 42 (1840).

"Battle of Albuera," *Minutes of the Proceedings of the Royal Artillery Institution,* vol 13 (1885), 126-127, [letter of Lieutenant William Unger, 24 May 1811].

Bell, George. *Soldier's Glory being 'Rough Notes of an Old Soldier'.* Tunbridge Wells: Spellmount, 1991.

Beresford, John, ed. *The Diary of a Country Parson. Volume IV. 1793-1796.* Oxford: University Press, 1968.

———, ed. *The Diary of a Country Parson, 1758-1802.* Oxford: University Press, 1978.

Beresford, William C. *Refutation of Napier's Justification of His Third Volume.* 1834, reprinted Chapelgarth: M. Thompson Publishing, 1993.

Blakeney, Edward. letter in *United Service Journal,* April 1841.

Blakeney, Robert. *A Boy in the Peninsular War.* London: 1899, reprinted Greenhill, 1989.

Bourneuf, François. *Diary of a Frenchman: François Bourneuf's Adventures from France to Acadia, 1787-1871.* Halifax: Nimbus, 1990.

Boutflower, Charles. *The Journal of an Army Surgeon.* Staplehurst: Spellmount, 1997.

Brooke, William, "A Prisoner of Albuera. The Journal of Major William Brooke from May 16th to September 28th, 1811," *Blackwood's Magazine,* October 1908.

Brown, W.M. "Recollections of Old Halifax," *Collections of the Nova Scotia Historical Society,* vol 13 (1908).

Buckley, Roger, ed. *The Napoleonic War Journal of Captain Thomas Henry Browne,*

1807-1816. London: Army Records Society, 1987.

Bunbury, Henry. *Passages in the Great War with France. 1799-1810*. London: 1854, reprinted Peter Davies, 1927.

Cates, Mary, ed., "Benjamin Ropes' Autobiography," *Essex Institute Historical Collections*, 91 (1955).

Chaby, Cláudio, *Excerptos Historicos e Collecçao de Documentos Relativos a Guerra Denominada na Peninsula e Anteriores de 1801, e do Roussilon e Cataluna*. Lisbon: Imprensa Nacional, 6 vols, 1863-1882.

Cobbold, Richard. *Mary Anne Wellington. The Soldier's Daughter, Wife, and Widow*. London: Henry Coulburn, 2 vols, 1846.

Cole, Lowry, letter in *United Service Journal*, April 1841.

Cole, Maud and Stephen Gwynn, eds. *Memoirs of Sir Lowry Cole*. London: Macmillan, 1934. [Contains extracts from Roverea's Journal].

Cooper, John. *Rough Notes of Seven Campaigns. 1809-1815*. 1869, reprinted Staplehurst: Spellmount, 1996.

Commins, James, "The War of 1812 on the Canadian Frontier. Letters written by Sgt. James Comins, 8th Foot," *JSAHR*, 18 (1939).

Cumloden Papers. Edinburgh: n.p., 1871.

Currie, Jenny, ed. *Letters to a Vicarage 1796-1815. The Letters of Lt. Col. JHB Hill*. Exeter: Oriel Press, 1988.

Dayes, Joseph. *Memoir of the Military Career of John Dayes*. London: Ken Trotman, 2004.

Desgenettes, René Nicolas. *Souvenirs de la fin du XVIII siécle et du commencement du XIXe, ou Mémoires de R.D.G.* Paris: Didot, 2 vols, 1835 & 1836.

"The 'Die Hards' at Albuera," *The Times*, 25 February 1915, Ensign Benjamin Hobhouse to his father, 17 May 1811.

Donaldson, James. *Recollections of an Eventful Life*. 1825, reprinted Spellmount, Staplehurst, 2000.

Douglass, David, "An Original Narrative of the Niagara Campaign of 1814," *Niagara Frontier* 46 (1964).

Dunlop, William. *Tiger Dunlop's Upper Canada*. Ottawa: Carleton University Press, 1967.

D'Urban, Benjamin. *The Peninsular Journal, 1808-1817*. 1930, reprinted London: Greenhill, 1990.

Fletcher, Ian, ed. *For King and Country: The Letters and Diaries of John, Mills, Coldstream Guards, 1811-1814*. Staplehurst: Spellmount, 1995.

Gottberg, Franz von. *Geschichte des Hannoverischen Jäger-Bataillons Nr. 10. Vol. 1 (1803 bis 1866). Teil I (1803-1866)*. Berlin: Ernst Mittler und Sohn, 1913 [diary of Major Augustus Wahrendorff of the 1st KGL Light Battalion, actually Lieutenant in 1811].

Grattan, William. *Adventures with the Connaught Rangers. 1800-1814*. London: 1902, reprinted Greenhill, London, 1989.

Graves, Donald E. *Merry Hearts Make Light Days: The War of 1812 Journal of Lieutenant John LeCouteur, 104th Regiment of Foot*. Ottawa: Carleton University Press, 1994.

Grazebrook, R.M., ed. "The Wearing of Equipment, 1801," *Journal of the Society for Army Historical Research*, vol 25 (1946).

Guthrie, George. *Treatise on Gun Shot Wounds*. London: Burgess and Hill, 1827.

———. *Commentaries on the Surgeries of the War in Portugal, Spain, France and the Netherlands*. Philadelphia: J.P. Lippincott, 1862.

Hall, C.D. "Albuera and Vittoria: Letters from Lt. Col. J. Hill," *Journal of the Society for Army Historical Research*, vol 66 (1988).

Hardinge, Henry, letter in *United Service Journal*, October 1840.

Hayward, Lydia. *Narrative of Mrs. Lydia Hayward*. Union Mills: n.p. 1846.

Hibbert, Christopher, ed. *A Soldier of the Seventy-First*. 1819, reprinted London, Squadron Signal, 1975.

Inglis, William, letter in *United Service Journal*, June 1832.

Jourdan, Jean-Baptiste. *Mémoires militaires du Maréchal Jourdan (Guerre d'Espagne). Publiés d'après le manuscrit original par le vicomte de Grouchy*. Paris: E. Flammarion, 1899.

Klinck, C.F. and J.J. Talman, eds. *The Journal of Major John Norton. 1816.* Toronto: Champlain Society, 1970.

Knowles, Robert. *The War in the Peninsula: Some Letters of a Lancashire Officer.* 1913, reprinted Staplehurst: Spellmount, 2004.

Lamarque, Maximien. *Mémoires et Souvenirs du Général Maximien Lamarque. Publies par sa Famille.* Paris: K. Fournier, 3 vols, 1835-1836.

Lapène, Edouard. *Conquête de l'Andalousie, Campagne de 1810 et 1811 dans le Midi de L'Espagne.* Paris: Anslein et Pochard, 1823.

Leach, Jonathan. *Rough Sketches of the Life of an Old Soldier: During a Service in the West Indies ….* London: Rees, Orem, Brown and Green, 1831.

"The Learned Saddler," *London Times*, 26 August 1930, [letter of Sergeant Thomas Bennett].

Leavitt, Thaddeus. *History of Leeds and Grenville.* 1879, reprinted Belleville: Mika 1972. [includes "Biographical Sketch" of John Kilborn].

Leslie, Charles. *Military Journal of Colonel Leslie, D.H., of Balquhain: Whiltst Serving with the 29th Regt. in the Peninsula, and the 60th Rifles in Canada.* Aberdeen: Aberdeen University Press, 1887.

Liddell Hart, Basil, ed. *Letters of Private Wheeler. 1809-1828.* London: Michael Joseph, 1951.

Lindau, Friedrich. *Erinnerungen eines Soldaten aus den Feldzügen der Koeniglichendestschen Legion.* Hameln: Helwing'sche Hofbuchhandlung, 1846.

Madden, Charles, "The Diary of Charles Dudley Madden, Lieutenant, 4th Dragoons, Peninsular War, 1809-1811," *Journal of the Royal United Services Institute*, vol 58 (1914).

Martin, Joanna, ed. *A Governess in the Age of Jane Austen: The Journals and Letters of Agnes Porter.* London: Hambledon Press, 1998.

Maurice, John F. ed. *The Diary of Sir John Moore.* London: E. Arnold, 2 vols, 1904.

Maxwell, W.H. *Peninsular Sketches by Actors on the Scene.* 1844-1845, reprinted London: Ken Trotman, 2 vols, 1898.

McGuffie, T.H., ed. *Peninsular Cavalry General, 1811-1813: The Correspondence of Lieutenant-General Robert Ballard Long.* London: Harrap, 1951.

Merritt, William H. *Journal of Events Principally on the Detroit and Niagara Frontiers during the War of 1812.* St. Catharines: Historical Society of British North America, 1863.

Military Adventures of Johnny Newcome, The. With an Account of His Campaign in the Peninsula and Pall Mall with Notes. By An Officer. 1816, reprinted London: Methuen, 1904.

Moore Smith, G.C. *The Life of John Colborne, Field-Marshal Lord Seaton.* New York: Dutton, 2 vols, 1903.

Moorsom, William S. *Letters from Nova Scotia: Comprising Sketches of a Young Country.* London: Coulburn and Bentley, 1830.

Napier, William. *Colonel Napier's Justification Of His Third Volume; Forming A Sequel To His Reply To Various Opponents.* London: Thomas & William Boone, 1833.

Oman, Charles, ed., "Albuera Once More," *The Army Quarterly*, vol 24, April, 1932. [*Mayor* Andreas von Schepeler].

Pakenham, Thomas, ed. *Pakenham Letters. 1800-1815.* London: n.p. 1914.

Raymond, W.O., ed. *Winslow Papers. A.D. 1776- 1828.* St. John: Sun Printing, 1891.

Saint-Chamans, Robert de. *Mémoires du Général Comte de Saint-Chamans.* Paris: Plon, 1896.

Scott, Winfield. *Memoirs of Lieut.-General Scott.* New York: Sheldon, 2 vols, 1864.

Sherer, Moyle. *Recollections of the Peninsula.* 1824, reprinted Staplehurst: Spellmount, 1996.

Shipp, John. *The Path of Glory: Being the Memoir of the Extaordinary Military Career of John Shipp Written by Himself.* London: Chatto and Windus, 1969.

Smith, Harry. *Autobiography of Harry Smith.* G.C. Moore-Smith, ed. London: John Murray, 2 vols, 1901.

Stanhope, Phillip Henry, Lord. *Notes of Conversations with the Duke of Wellington, 1831-1851.* New York: Da Capo, 1973.

Surtees, William. *Twenty-Five Years in the*

Rifle Brigade. 1833, reprinted London: Greenhill, 1996.

Swabey, William, "Diary of Lieutenant Swabey, R.H.A. in the Peninsula," *Journal of the Royal Artillery Institute*, vol 22 (1895), no. 4.

Thompson, Mark S. ed. *The Letters of Charles Edward Long and General Lord Viscount Beresford Concerning the Operations of Lieut.-General R.B. Long during the Campaign in Southern Spain in 1811.* Chapelgarth: M. Thompson Publishing, 1993. This volume includes the following titles which were earlier published separately:

> William Beresford. *A Letter to Charles Edward Long Esq. on the Extracts Recently Published from the Manuscript Journal and Private Correspondence of the late Lieut.-General R.B. Long.* London: John Murray, 1833.

> ———. *A Second Letter to Charles Edward Long Esq. on the Manuscript Journal and Private Correspondence of the late Lieut.-General R.B. Long.* London: John Murray, 1834.

> Long, Charles E. *A Reply to the Misrepresentations and Aspersions on the Military Reputation of the late Lieutenant-General R.B. Long Contained in a Work Entitled "Further Strictures on those parts of Col. Napier's History of the Peninsular War which relate to the Military Opinions and Conduct of General Lord Viscount Beresford".* London: James Ridgeway, 1832.

> ———. *A Letter to General Viscount Beresford in Reply to his Lordship's Letter to the Author relative to the Conduct of the Late Lieut.-General R.B. Long in the Campaign of 1811.* London: James Ridgeway, 1833.

> ———. *A Reply to Lord Beresford's Second Letter to the Author Relative to the Conduct of the late Lieut.-General R.B. Long then Commanding the Allied Cavalry.* London: 1835. London: James Ridgeway, 1835.

Thiébault, Paul. *Mémoires du Général Baron Thiébault.* Paris: Plon, 5 vols, 1896-1913.

Tomkinson, William. *The Diary of a Cavalry Officer.* 1894, Staplehurst: Spellmount, 1999.

Vere, Charles B. *Marches, Movements, and Operations of the 4th Division of the Allied Army in Spain and Portugal in the Years 1810, 1811 & 1812.* 1812, reprinted London: Ken Trotman, 2003.

Warre, William. *Letters from the Peninsual 1808-1812.* Staplehurst: Spellmount, 1999.

Wilkinson, James. *Memoirs of My Own Times.* Philadelphia: Abraham Small, 1816, 3 vols.

Wojciechowski, Kajetan. *Pamietniki Moje W Hiszpanii.* Warsaw: Instytut Wydawniczy, 1978.

SECONDARY SOURCES

Published Books

Anonymous. *(Almost) A Thousand Years of Thorne.* N.p., n.d.

Arteche y Moro, José. *Guerra de la Independencia: Historia Militar de España de 1808 a 1814.* Madrid: Del Depósito de la Guerra, 1896.

Beamish, N. Ludlow Beamish. *History of the King's German Legion.* 1831-1832, reprinted Dallington, Naval and Military Press, 2 vols, 1997.

Book of Common Prayer, The. Cambridge: John Archdeacon Printer, 1758.

Boss, William. *The Stormont, Dundas and Glengarry Highlanders.* Ottawa: Runge Press, 1952.

Broughton-Mainwaring, Rowland. *Historical Record of the Royal Welch Fusiliers, late the Twenty-Third Foot.* London: Hatchards, 1889.

Bryant, Arthur. *Years of Endurance, 1793-1802.* London: Collins, 1942.

———. *Years of Victory, 1802-1812.* London: Collins, 1944.

———. *Jackets of Green.* London: Collins, 1972.

Burne, Alfred. *The Noble Duke of York. The Military Life of Frederick Duke of York and Albany.* London: Staples Press, 1949.

Burns, Robert. *Fort Wellington: A Narrative*

and Structural History, 1812-1838. Ottawa: Parks Canada, 1979.

Cannon, Richard. Historical Records of the Seventh Regiment or The Royal Fusiliers. London: Parker, Furnivall and Parker, 1847.

———. Historical Record of the Twenty-Third Foot or The Royal Welsh Fusiliers ... London: Parker, Furnivall and Parker.

Carter Smyth, J. The Story of Dundas. Iroquois: Iroquois News Press, 1905.

Cary, A.D.L. and Stouppe McCance. Regimental Records of the Royal Welch Fusiliers (Late the 23rd Foot). London: Foster and Groom, 2 vols, 1921.

Chandler, David. The Campaigns of Napoleon. New York: Macmillan, 1966.

Coffin, Henry E. A Memoir of General John Coffin: Compiled from Various Sources by Henry Coffin. Reading: E.T. and F. Blackwell, 1860.

Coggeshall, George. History of American Privateers and Letters of Marque. New York: author, 1861.

Daniell, David. Cap of Honour: The Story of the Gloucestershire Regiment. London: Harrap, 1951.

Detaille, Edouard and Jules Richard, L'Armée Française: An Illustrated History of the French Army 1790-1885. New York: Waxtell and Hasenauer, 1992.

De Watteville, H. The British Soldier: His Daily Life from Tudor to Modern Times. London: J.M. Dent, 1954.

Dickens, Charles. Pickwick Papers. New York: Doubleday, 1944.

Duncan, Francis. History of the Royal Regiment of Artillery. London: John Murray, 2 vols, 1872-1873.

Dunning, Robert and William Page, eds. The Victoria History of the County of Somerset. 1906, reprinted Oxford: University Press, 1992.

Elting, John. Swords Around a Throne: Napoleon's Grande Armée. New York: Free Press, 1988.

Esdaile, Charles. The Peninsular War: A New History. London, Penguin, 2002.

Everard, H. History of Thos. Farrington's

Regiment ... The 29th (Worcestershire) Foot. Worcester: Littlebury, 1891.

Fortescue, John W. A History of the British Army. New York: Macmillan, 13 vols, 1899-1930, particularly vols 4 to 8.

Foy, Maximilien. History of the War in the Peninsula under Napoleon. London: Treuttel and Würtz, 2 vols, 1827.

Gates, David. The Spanish Ulcer: A History of the Peninsular War. London: Norton, 1986.

Glover, Michael. The Napoleonic Wars: An Illustrated History, 1792-1815. New York: Hippocrene, 1978.

———. That Astonishing Infantry: Three Hundred Years of the History of the Royal Welch Fusiliers (23rd Regiment of Foot), 1689-1989. London: Leo Cooper, 1989.

Glover, Richard. Peninsular Preparation: The Reform of the British Army 1795-1809. Cambridge: University Press, 1963.

Goodspeed, D.J. The British Campaigns in the Peninsula: 1808-1814. Ottawa: Department of National Defence, 1958.

Graves, Donald E. Redcoats and Grey Jackets: The Battle of Chippawa, 1814. Toronto: Dundurn, 1994.

———. Where Right and Glory Lead! The Battle of Lundy's Lane, 1814. Toronto: Robin Brass, 1997.

———. Field of Glory: The Battle of Crysler's Farm, 1813 (Toronto, 1999)

Gray, William. Soldiers of the King: The Upper Canadian Militia 1812-1815. Toronto: Boston Mills, 1995.

Griffith, Paddy. Forward into Battle. London: Crowood, 1990.

Groves, J.P. The 66th Berkshire Regiment. Reading: Joseph Bancroft, 1887.

Gurney, Russell. History of the Northamptonshire Regiment. 1742-1914. Aldershot: Gale and Polden, 1935.

Halliday, Andrew. The Present State of Portugal and of the Portuguese Army ... Edinburgh: Longman, Hurst, Rees, Orme & Browne, 1812.

Hayman, Peter. Soult: Napoleon's Maligned Marshal. London: Arms and Armour Press, 1990.

Haythornewaite, Phillip. The Armies of Wellington. London: Brockhampton Press, 1998.

Hibbert, Christopher. *George IV*. London: Penguin, 1976.

———. *George III. A Personal History*. London: Basic Books, 1998.

Hickey, Donald. *The War of 1812: A Forgotten Conflict*. Chicago: University of Illinois Press, 1989.

Hitsman, J.M. *The Incredible War of 1812: A Military History*. Toronto: Robin Brass, 1999.

Holmes, Richard. *Redcoat: The British Soldier in the Age of Horse and Musket*. London: Harper & Collins, 2001.

Houlding, John. *Fit for Service: The Training of the British Army, 1715-1795*. Oxford: University Press, 1981.

James, Lawrence. *Iron Duke: A Military Biography of Wellington*. London: Weidenfield and Nicholson, 1992.

Kingsford, Charles. *The Story of The Duke of Cambridge's Own (Middlesex) Regiment*. London: Country Life, 1916.

Knight, C.R.B. *Historical Records of the Buffs ... Volume I: 1704-1814*. London: The Medici Society, 1935.

Linn, John. *Annals of Buffalo Valley*. Harrisburg: Lane and Haupt, 1877.

Longmate, Norman. *Island Fortress. The Defence of Great Britain 1603-1945*. London: Hutchinson, 1991.

López, Juan Priego, ed. *Guerra de la Independenicia. 1808-1814. Volume VI, Campaña de 1811 (Primer Periodo)*. Madrid: Servicio Historico Militar, 1992.

Mackesy, Piers. *British Victory in Egypt, 1801: The End of Napoleon's Conquest*. London, Routledge, 1995.

Maclay, Edgar Stanton. *A History of American Privateers*. London: Sampson, Marston, 1900.

Malcomson, Robert. *Lords of the Lake: The Naval War on Lake Ontario*. Toronto: Robin Brass, 1998.

Mayne, William and Lillie, John Scott. *A Narrative of the Campaigns of the Loyal Lusitanian Legion*. London: T. Egerton, 1812.

Norman, C.B. *Battle Honours of the British Army*. 1911, reprinted London: David and Charles, 1971.

Nosworthy, Brent. *Battle Tactics of Napoleon and His Enemies*. London: Constable, 1995.

Oman, Charles. *A History of the Peninsular War*. Oxford: 1902-1930, 6 vols, reprinted 1995-1998.

———. *Wellington's Army*. 1913, reprinted London: Greenhill, 1993.

Palmer, Roy, ed. *The Rambling Soldier: Life in the Lower Ranks, 1750-1900, through Soldier's Songs and Writings*. London: Penguin, 1977.

Pearse, Hugh. *History of the 31st Foot and 70th Foot subsequently ... The East Surrey Regiment. Volume I: 1702-1914*. London: Spottiswoode and Ballantine, 2 vols, 1916.

Raddall, Thomas. *Halifax: Warden of the North*. New York: Doubleday, 1965.

Rodger, N.A.M. *The Wooden World: An Anatomy of the Georgian Navy*. London, Collins, 1986.

Snider, C.H.J. *Under the Red Jack: Privateers of the Maritime Provinces of Canada in the War of 1812*. London: Martin Hopkinso, 1928.

Strachan, Hew. *British Military Uniforms, 1768-1791*. London: Arms and Armour, 1975.

Thompson, Mark S. *Fatal Hill: The Allied Campaign under Beresford in Southern Spain in 1811*. Chapelgarth: M. Thompson Publication, 2002.

Toreno, José Maria, Conde de. *Historia del Levantaminento, Guerra y Revolucion de España*. Madrid: Ediciones Atlas, 1953.

Turner, E.S. *Gallant Gentlemen: A Portrait of the British Officer, 1600-1956*. London: Michael Joseph, 1956.

Vane, Charles W. *Story of the Peninsular War*. New York, Harper, 1854.

Victoires et Conquêtes ... des Français, de 1792 à 1815. Tome Vingtième. Paris: Pancoucke, 1820. Paris.

Winstock, Lewis. *Songs and Music of the Redcoats*. London: Leo Cooper, 1970.

Zaslow, Morris, ed. *The Defended Border: Upper Canada and the War of 1812*. Toronto: University of Toronto Press, 1964.

Published Articles, Unpublished Theses and Internet Sources

Akins, T.B. "History of Halifax City," *Collections of the Nova Scotia Historical Society*, vol 8, (1892-1894).

Cruikshank, Ernest A., "Record of the Service of Canadian Regiments in the War of 1812 – V. The Incorporated Militia," *Selected Papers of the Canadian Military Institute*, vol 6 (1894-1895).

Duffy, Michael, "The Carribean Campaigns of the British Army, 1793-1801," in Alan Guy, ed., *The Road to Waterloo*. London: National Army Museum, 1990.

Evelyn, G.J., "'I learned what one ought not to do'; The British Army in Holland, 1793-1795," in Alan Guy, ed., *The Road to Waterloo*. London: National Army Museum, 1990.

"The Medals of Colonel Sir Henry Walton Ellis, KCB," *Y Ddraig Goch*, March 1934, 36-38.

"Memorial of Colonel Ellis," *Y Ddraig Goch*, March 1938, 83.

Gascoigne, F.R. ed., "Extracts from the Standing Orders of the Garrison of Gibraltar, 1803," *Journal of the Society for Army Historical Research*, vol 2 (1923), 86, 181.

Graves, Donald E, "William Drummond and the Battle of Fort Erie," *Canadian Military History*, vol 1 (1992).

Grodzinski, John. "The Vigilant Superintendence of the Whole District: The War of 1812 on the Upper St. Lawrence," MA Thesis, Royal Military College, 2002.

Harris, Joan, "Worcester Honours a Brave Soldier: A Military Family, 1760-1860," n.p., 2003.

Harris, R.G., "Two Military Miniatures,"
Journal of the Society for Army Historical Research, vol 63 (1985), 99-102.

Hartmann, H. Julius, "Beiträge zur Geschichte des Krieges auf der Pyrenäischen halbinself in den Jahren 1809 bis 1813," *Hannoverisches Militarisches Journal*, vol. 2 (1831).

Kirby, E.L., "The Puzzle of a Bundle of Love Letters and an MGSM, *Y Ddraich Goch*, April 1978.

———, "Silver and Plates of 1st Bn The Royal Welch Fusiliers with Descriptions and Historical Notes," typescript, 1983.

———, "The Youth Who Was to Save our Flash," *Y Ddraig Goch*, March 1979.

Landon, Harry, "British Sympathizers in St. Lawrence County during the War of 1812," *New York History* (April 1954).

Mackesy, Piers, "Abercromby in Egypt: The Regeneration of the Army," in Alan Guy, ed., *The Road to Waterloo*. London: National Army Museum, 1990.

"Military Posters," *Journal of the Society for Army Historical Research*, vol 1 (1922), 178.

"A Most Extraordinary Creature," *Y Ddraig Goch*, Winter 1947.

Oman, Charles, "Albuera," *Journal of the Royal Artillery*, vol 36 (1909), no. 2.

"Recruiting Posters," *Journal of the Society for Army Historical Research*, vol 1, 119-121, 131-133.

"The Royal Welch Martinique Eagle," *Y Ddraig Goch*, Winter 1958

Sorando, Luis, "Trophies of Albuera (May 16, 1811)," *Napoleon Series* website.

Steppler, Glenn, "The British Army on the Eve of War," in Alan Guy, ed., *The Road to Waterloo*. London: National Army Museum, 1990.

INDEX OF PERSONS, EVENTS,
MILITARY AND NAVAL UNITS

The author and the publishers
gratefully acknowledge the assistance
given by The Royal Welch Fusiliers
in the production of *Fix Bayonets!*

The Royal Welch Fusiliers Museum is situated in historic
Caernarfon Castle in Gwynedd, North Wales. On display are
artefacts relating to Thomas Pearson and his comrades during
the Great War with France, 1793-1815, including the keys to
Corunna, period uniforms, armament and equipment, portraits
of Pearson and his contemporaries, and their medals.

For further information about the Royal Welch Fusiliers
Museum and about the history of one of the most distinguished
regiments in the British army, visit the Fusiliers' website at
<http://www.rwfmuseum.org.uk>.

FORGOTTEN SOLDIERS: THE WAR OF 1812 IN THE NORTH

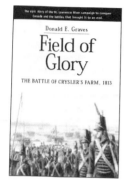

Field of Glory: The Battle of Crysler's Farm, 1813

The epic story of the American campaign to conquer Canada in 1813 and the battles at Châteauguay and Crysler's Farm that brought it to an end.

"Graves, Canada's leading expert on the subject, is a first-rate battlefield historian." *Maclean's.*

"This is history at its best: exciting, entertaining and readable." *Quill & Quire.*

448 pages • 6 x 9 inches • about 100 pictures and maps • paperback

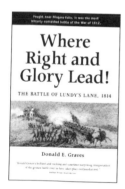

Where Right and Glory Lead! The Battle of Lundy's Lane, 1814

Fought near Niagara Falls, it was the most bitterly contested battle of the War of 1812 and has remained one of the most controversial.

"*Where Right and Glory Lead* is how military history should be written – deeply and carefully researched, salted with common sense, and put into a prose that stands you in a firing line that is fraying thinner by the minute." John Elting, author of *Amateurs to Arms.*

352 pages • 6 x 9 inches • about 60 pictures and maps • paperback

Coming soon, the third and final volume of this classic trilogy, which will cover the final battles in the northern theatre – Fort Erie, Plattsburgh and smaller engagements.